herapy Through Faërie

Anna Cholewa-Purgał

Therapy Through Faërie
Therapeutic Properties of Fantasy Literature by the Inklings and by U. K. Le Guin

PETER LANG
EDITION

Bibliographic Information published by the Deutsche Nationalbibliothek
The Deutsche Nationalbibliothek lists this publication in
the Deutsche Nationalbibliografie; detailed bibliographic
data is available in the internet at http://dnb.d-nb.de.

Cover illustration by courtesy of the author.

Library of Congress Cataloging-in-Publication Data
Names: Cholewa-Purgał, Anna, 1978- author.
Title: Therapy through Faerie : therapeutic properties of fantasy literature
   by the Inklings and by U. K. Le Guin / Anna Cholewa- Purgał.
Description: Frankfurt am Main ; New York : Peter Lang, 2016. | Series:
   Transatlantic studies in British and North American culture ; volume 17 |
   Includes bibliographical references.
Identifiers: LCCN 2016002149 | ISBN 9783631673812
Subjects: LCSH: Inklings (Group of writers) | Tolkien, J. R. R. (John Ronald
   Reuel), 1892-1973--Criticism and interpretation. | Lewis, C. S. (Clive
   Staples), 1898-1963--Criticism and interpretation. | Le Guin, Ursula K.,
   1929---Criticism and interpretation. | Fantasy fiction, English--History
   and criticism. | Fantasy fiction, American--History and criticism. |
   Bibliotherapy. | Literature--Psychology.
Classification: LCC PR478.I54 C46 2016 | DDC 823/.087660909--dc23 LC record
available at https://lccn.loc.gov/2016002149

ISBN 978-3-631-67381-2 (Print)
E-ISBN 978-3-653-06642-5 (E-PDF)
E-ISBN 978-3-631-70248-2 (EPUB)
E-ISBN 978-3-631-70249-9 (MOBI)
DOI 10.3726/b10742

© Peter Lang GmbH
Internationaler Verlag der Wissenschaften
Frankfurt am Main 2017
All rights reserved.
Peter Lang Edition is an Imprint of Peter Lang GmbH.

Peter Lang – Frankfurt am Main · Bern · Bruxelles · New York ·
Oxford · Warszawa · Wien

This publication has been peer reviewed.

www.peterlang.com

Natura sanat, medicus curat morbos
(Nature heals; the physician treats illnesses)
(Hippocrates, 460–377 BC)

To my Children: Robert and Nadia, and my Mother: Maria;
in memory of my deceased Grandparents, Father and Uncles, and
my Great-grandparents who perished in the massacre of Poles in Volhynia

Contents

Foreword

It has long been my desire to address the issue of an assumed therapeutic potential of fantasy literature, particularly that embedded in the fantasy works and thought of the Inklings and of the American writer Ursula Kroeber Le Guin, with regard to the notion of high fantasy, which I link here with J. R. R. Tolkien's concept of Faërie. I use the term 'high fantasy', which had been introduced by Alexander Lloyd in 1971[1] and subsequently elaborated by Kenneth J. Zahorski, Robert H. Boyer and some other critics[2], identifying it after John Clute as 'fantasies set in otherworlds, specifically secondary worlds, and which deal with matters affecting the destiny of those worlds.'[3] To this prerequisite of essential otherworldliness of secondary realms I wish to add, however, another crucial mark that helps distinguish high fantasy from its 'lower' type(s), and which is to me a 'high style', or a typically Inklingesque quality that results from the writers' medieval and Renaissance fascinations, from their particular preoccupation with myth, language and meaning, as well as from a distinctive 'moral imagination' of their otherworlds, an aspect which Philip Zaleski and Carol Zaleski recognize as 'moral realism' in which the fantastic stories are grounded,[4] that is an 'instinct for sacred things' recovered from the 'moralistic sentimentality' which had 'deadened it', and with which it must not be confused.[5]

---

1   Lloyd Alexander,'High Fantasy and Heroic Romance', 1971, as quoted by Brian Stableford, *The A to Z Fantasy Literature*, *The A to Z Guide Series, No. 46* (Plymouth, UK: The Scarecrow Press, 2009), p. 198.

2   Zahorski and Boyer exclude from high fantasy genre some immersive fantasies, such as animal fantasy, humorous fantasy, 'myth fantasy' (of the recycled type), fairy tales, Gothic fantasy, sword and sorcery, and science fantasy. As Stableford observes, 'the term [high fantasy] never thrived partly because it was difficult to establish dividing lines between high fantasy and some of these other subgenres, and partly because of the difficulty of accommodating portal fantasies to the scheme.' *The A to Z Fantasy Literature*, p. 198. In my understanding of high fantasy, portal fantasies, exemplified by C. S. Lewis's *Chronicles of Narnia*, belong to the genre.

3   John Clute, 'High fantasy', [in:] *The Encyclopedia of Fantasy*, John Clute and John Grant, eds. (London: Orbit, 1997), p. 406.

4   Philip Zaleski and Carol Zaleski, *The Fellowship: The Literary Lives of the Inklings: J. R. R. Tolkien, C. S. Lewis, Owen Barfield, Charles Williams* (New York: Farrar, Straus and Giroux, 2015), p. 13.

5   The Zaleskis, ibid., p. 390.

I developed the idea of attempting to view the fantasy works of the Inklings and of Le Guin, whom I consider classicists of the genre, from a point of view of (biblio)therapy while studying music therapy, whose immense non-verbal therapeutic power, although unique, also draws on the strength of the premises otherwise shared with literature, such as artistic imagination, free vicarious visualization and identification, a numinous potential and a cathartic effect. Since despite considerable scholarship on art therapy, music therapy and bibliotherapy, not much seems to have been written about therapeutic properties of fantasy fiction, I have attempted to undertake the challenge and argue for a therapeutic dimension of the genre, ill-qualified and inept though I am.

Bearing in mind the Inklings' considerable reluctance towards psychologizing interpretations of literature, and their mistrust of psychotherapy, and psychoanalysis in particular, I am aware of the fact that when viewing their fiction in therapeutic terms I may be suggesting an unlicensed interpretation, taking the liberty of transgressing the boundaries of fairyland which the Inklings had guarded so carefully, and enforcing not only a sophomoric but also an illegitimate reading of some of their major works. In one of his articles published in 1960 in the Cambridge *Broadsheet*, C. S. Lewis castigates that trend in literary criticism which approaches a literary text 'as a substitute for religion or philosophy or psychotherapy', exposing it as a vice of immature undergraduate scholarship.[6] In another essay, however, Lewis points to the unique quality of 'great literature', that is to 'an enlargement of our being' – an extension of man's being that is possible upon entering the literary realities invented by other people, which he compares to breaking free from a suffocating prison of one's own individual world.[7] The vicarious experience of immersing oneself in the realities of literary works, especially fantasy fiction, is to Lewis a prerequisite for self-development: 'the man who is contented to be only himself, and therefore less a self, is in prison.'[8] Thus, far from approaching literature in terms of an ersatz religious, philosophical or psychotherapeutic cure, Lewis seems to emphasize its liberating, healing, and personality-broadening potential, which might perhaps be understood in therapeutic terms:

> Literary experience heals the wound, without undermining the privilege, of individuality. There are mass emotions which heal the wound; but they destroy the privilege. In them

---

6   C. S. Lewis, 'Undergraduate Criticism', [in:] *Broadsheet* (Cambridge) 8, no. 17, March 9, 1960, quoted by Walter Hooper in C. S. Lewis, *The Collected Letters of C. S. Lewis*, Walter Hooper, ed. (New York: HarperCollins, 2004), vol. 3, p. 1230.

7   Lewis, 'An Experiment' [in:] *An Experiment in Criticism* (Cambridge, UK: Cambridge University Press, 1961, 2004), pp. 104–129, 105.

8   Ibid, p. 105.

our separate selves are pooled and we sink back into subindividuality. But in reading great literature I become a thousand men and yet remain myself. Like the night sky in the Greek poem, I see with a myriad eyes, but it is still I who see. Here, as in worship, in love, in moral action, in knowing, I transcend myself; and am never more myself than when I do.[9]

A contemporary example of 'great literature' is to Lewis Tolkien's *The Fellowship of the Ring*, which, interestingly enough, Lewis praises in his 1954 review in apparently psychological terms, emphasizing the epic being remarkably 'disinfected from the taint of an author's merely individual psychology', and remaining strikingly 'relevant to the actual human situation yet so free from allegory.'[10] This is one of the central tenets of my thesis, namely the fact that high fantasy of the Inklings and of Le Guin contains therapeutic properties by virtue of its universal relevance to 'the actual human situation', including, and, in fact, addressing directly a psychological and spiritual crisis, identified by Victor Frankl in its most severe form as an 'existential vacuum', 'mass neurosis', and 'learned meaninglessness', or 'a private and personal form of nihilism',[11] which finds its expression and treatment in secondary worlds, where it is approached from a fresh perspective, 'disinfected from the taint of an author's merely individual psychology', and from the mood of negation, trivialization and resigned acceptance.[12]

Lewis's emphasis laid on the transcendental dimension of literary experience, owing to which the reader's self is not inhibited but enriched and fortified with a multitude of other people's perceptions, plights and needs, as rendered by writers, can perhaps be linked with Victor Frankl's constitutive concept of 'the self-transcendence of human existence', whose motivation is the 'will to meaning':

> The true meaning of life is to be discovered in the world rather than within man or his own psyche, as though it were a closed system. (...) 'The self-transcendence of human existence' (...) denotes the fact that being human always points, and is directed, to something or someone, other than oneself -- be it a meaning to fulfill or another human being to encounter. The more one forgets himself -- by giving himself to a cause to serve or another person to love -- the more human he is and the more he actualizes himself. What is called self-actualization is not an attainable aim at all, for the simple reason that the

---

9   Ibid., p. 105.
10 Dust-jacket endorsement, as quoted by the Zaleskis, p. 423.
11 Victor Frankl, 'Logotherapy in a Nutshell' [in:] *Man's Search for Meaning* (New York: Pocket Books, 1959, 1984), pp. 117–159, 152.
12 Lewis, quoted by the Zaleskis, dust-jacket endorsement, p. 423.

more one would strive for it, the more he would miss it. In other words, self-actualization is possible only as a side-effect of self-transcendence.[13]

Employing the language of psychology and philosophy rather than that of literary criticism, Frankl seems to corroborate the same tenet, arguing that self-transcendence paradoxically strengthens and solidifies man's own individuality, and empowers rather than stems from self-actualization.

Far from attributing to high fantasy fiction a clinical effect that may replace psychotherapy, or a religious significance that can stand in for a system of faith, I intend to argue that the peculiar qualities of the genre, which rest on its essential imaginative otherworldliness, and on the central position of an immanent Logos that informs high fantasy worlds of the Inklings and of Le Guin, incapacitate some therapeutic properties of high fantasy, which I link with Victor Frankl's logotherapy or 'therapy through meaning'.[14] A similar aspect of the teleological nature of fantasy genre is what Brian Attebury seems to have identified when observing that 'fantasy does impose many restrictions on the powers of the imagination, but in return it offers the possibility of generating not merely a meaning but an awareness of and a pattern for meaningfulness. This we call wonder.'[15]

Wonder, enchantment, meaningfulness, and the other unique qualities of Faërie indicated by Tolkien in his seminal essay 'On Fairy-Stories', which include: Fantasy, Recovery, Escape (breaking free from the prison of suffocating reality), Consolation and Eucatastrophe, amount to the interdisciplinary nature of this book, which

---

13 Frankl, *Man's Search for Meaning*, pp. 152 and 177.
    Self-actualization is one of the key concepts of Abraham Maslow's psychology. Maslow, however, holds that man's self-actualization is only possible once the basic needs, such as food and drink, are provided (Maslow, 'Comments on Dr Frankl's Paper' [in:] *Journal of Humanistic Psychology*, VI (1966), pp. 107–112). Drawing on his concentration camp experience, Frankl disagrees with Maslow's theory, arguing that self-actualization is only possible as a secondary effect of self-transcendence, that is opening oneself to the needs and perspective of another human being (Frankl, 'Postscript 1984: The Case for a Tragic Optimism' [in:] *Man's Search for Meaning*, pp. 161–179).

14 The 'will to meaning' is Victor Frankl's central tenet, which he identifies as man's primary desire, as discussed in Chapter Three of this book. I use the term 'immanent Logos' as a meaningful pattern of universe captured in words, inherent to the works and thought of the Inklings and of Le Guin, and it is not to be confused with the 'immanent logos' (*logos endiathetos*), a term proposed by the Stoics and regarding man's reason present in him; cf. the *Greek Philosophical Terms: A Historical Lexicon*, Francis E. Peters, ed. (New York: New York University Press, 1967), pp. 110 and 164.

15 Brain Attebury, 'Fantasy as Mode, Genre, Formula' [in:] David M. Sandner, *Fantastic Literature: A Critical Reader* (Westport, Connecticut: Praeger, 2004), pp. 293–309, 309.

argues for a therapeutic ethos of high fantasy genre, as reflected in the works and thought of the Inklings and of Le Guin, the latter of whom might, from this perspective, be viewed as the Inklings' literary heiress of the next generation.

Seeking to establish the grounds for the assumed therapeutic properties of high fantasy, ill-qualified though I am, I have ventured into the fields of literary studies, psychotherapy, art therapy and philosophy, along the paths of man's universal search for self-identity and meaning, and largely against the mainstream of postmodern thought, identified by some thinkers as predominantly groundless and nihilistic.[16] This book has also grown out of an attempt to consider the issue of the continuing and increasing popularity of the very broadly understood fantastic mode in contemporary literature with all its multifarious instances, ranging from modern fairy-stories and speculative fiction to magic realism. Hoping to join those arguing for a revalorization of the position of the Inklings in the canon of literature(s) in English, and to emphasize their role in reviving Faërie in contemporary literature, I view their fantasy oeuvre, miscellaneous yet founded upon a common Christian foundation, in the light of logotherapy, and I focus on a logotherapeutic potential of the works of the Inklings and of Le Guin, the latter's fantasy fiction being a non-Christian, Taoist affirmation of an unconditional meaning of human life, based on an ethos of moral imagination, mythopoeia (myth-making), preoccupation with language and meaning (*Logos*), synergy of arts, and cathartic consolation.

The application of Victor Frankl's philosophy and psychotherapeutic thought to the generic qualities of the Inklings' and Le Guin's fantasy fiction may allow, as I would like to demonstrate, for approaching high fantasy genre from another perspective, and for gaining a fuller view of the writers' legacy. Reading fantasy fiction and non-fiction by the Inklings and by Le Guin from the standpoint of Frankl's logotherapy might offer a new insight into their works and into the genre as such. The reader of this book may be disappointed, though, to find here little literary analysis of high fantasy works and much reference to the non-fiction of the Inklings and of Le Guin, as well as to various theories that have been employed in order to argue for a therapeutic potential of Faërie. My only excuse is that this book sets out to present some therapeutic properties of high fantasy

---

16   The nihilistic mainstream of contemporary theory is recognized, for instance, by Ashley Woodward in his study *Nihilism in Postmodernity: Lyotard, Baudrillard, Vattimo* (Aurora: The Davies Group Publishers, 2009), which I discuss in Chapter Three. Similarly, Stuart Sim writes of 'the groundless relativism of much postmodern thought' when referring to Gianni Vattimo's philosophy in his *Routledge Companion to Postmodernism*, Stuart Sim, ed. (London: Routledge, 2001), p. 343.

as a genre, which calls for a theoretical background, but, subsequently, also for another volume that would provide detailed analysis of the corresponding elements found in the writers' fantasy oeuvre.

When outlining some crucial properties of high fantasy, which I attempt to identify in terms of literary therapy, I have distinguished several dimensions of its therapeutic potential: the powers of narrative itself, interartistic nature of fantasy fiction, and, most importantly, the peculiar characteristics of Faërie, as distinguished by Tolkien, which are capable of acting as a 'prophylactic against loss' and a means of recovering an awareness of meaningful patterns through an experience of suffering and sacrifice, with its eucatastrophic, and, as I view it, cathartic effect.[17]

In Chapter One I briefly introduce the Inklings, suggesting that their current marginal position in the history of English literature, as allocated by some of its leading historians, should perhaps be reconsidered, were the fantastic recognized as a prevailing mode of 20th century literature, as Tom Shippey claims.[18] I also establish here some other rudiments ruling my thesis: namely, the concept of high fantasy fiction or Faërie, the realm of fairy-stories and myth, after J. R. R. Tolkien's specification; and I try to trace some literary kinship between the works of the Inklings and those of Ursula K. Le Guin, thus justifying the inclusion of her (non-Christian) fantasy fiction in the scope of this analysis. I refer to the notion of the Inklings, and focus on the intellectual exchange, interaction and literary inspirations within the group.

Chapter Two presents the Inklings in the context of the literary scene of their day, that is the heyday of modernism, and early postmodernism, and their attitude to the mainstream literature and literary criticism of the period. I argue that the specialty and an important contribution of the Inklings, a largely anti-modernist and anti-postmodernist group, is their Christian fantasy fiction and non-fiction. Moreover, I suggest that the Inklings' collective legacy deserves academic attention and evaluation today, and perhaps makes a case for canonical reconsideration in the light of the contemporary massive revival of the fantastic mode, represented by several subsequent generations of writers of different cultures and beliefs, including Ursula K. Le Guin (born in 1929).

Postmodernity and postmodern thought with its inherent dilemmas, centred, as Ashley Woodward claims, upon the connecting thread of neonihilism, provide

---

17 J. R. R. Tolkien, 'On Fairy-Stories' [in:] *The Monsters and the Critics and Other Essays* (London: HarperCollins Publishers, 1997), pp. 109–161, 146.

18 Tom Shippey, *J. R. R. Tolkien. Author of the Century* (London: HarperCollins Publishers, 2000), p. vii.

context for a reflection regarding the contemporary severe crisis of meaning and man's search for sense, presented in Chapter Three.[19] Since this book deals with therapeutic properties of literature, I refer here to the philosophical and psychological predicament of postmodern man, and to a widely felt need for some (psycho)therapy, and hence I introduce Frankl's logotherapy, one of postwar schools of philosophy and psychotherapy, which seems to address the nihilistic reality of today's Western culture. By showing the anti-nihilistic, logocentric and foundational premises of logotherapy, I attempt to suggest some applicability of its tenets to the generic ethos of high fantasy fiction, as discussed in Chapter Four.

Devaluation of life and meaning emerges from Chapter Three as one of the gravest interrelated deficiencies of the postmodern condition, whose meeting place is language, and narrative in particular. In Chapter Four I examine some natural psychotherapeutic properties of narrative itself, viewed as the main means of communication and sense-making, and proceed to the narrative of literature as a potential space where those inherent elements of healing and meaning may bud. I wish to argue that a very special literary genre is high fantasy (affiliated in this book with Tolkien's Faërie), for it most naturally bridges *Logos* with art, and seems to correspond to logotherapy in its profoundly anti-nihilistic foundations, as endorsed by the Inklings and by Le Guin. Having referred to narrative therapy, I discuss bibliotherapy with reference to the philosophy of a literary work of art, as propounded by Roman Ingarden, and the psychology of art introduced by Lev Vygotsky, whose theories I attempt to employ arguing for a therapeutic power of literary narrative, and of high fantasy works in particular.

Chapter Five is an artistic interlude that attempts to approach Faërie as a peculiar art which corresponds to art therapy and psychotherapy, including Hanscarl Leuner's Guided Affected Imagery method, so as to corroborate certain psychotherapeutic properties of high fantasy fiction resulting from its interartistic rather than purely literary nature, with the general presumption that art *per se* is therapeutic. Following another assumption that fantasy is a particularly synaesthetic genre, which naturally incorporates elements of music, visual arts and verbal language, I provide some examples of literary ekphrasis and two painting techniques: sfumato and chiaroscuro, whose literary effects might be traced in the fantasy works of the Inklings and of Le Guin, suggesting that the genre's considerable intermediality and multimodality may also have some therapeutic potency.

---

19 Ashley Woodward *Nihilism in Postmodernity: Lyotard, Baudrillard, Vattimo* (Aurora: The Davies Group Publishers, 2009), p. 1.

Since this book addresses psychotherapeutic properties of the fantasy works written by the Inklings and by U. K. Le Guin, in Chapter Six I finally approach fantasy genre as endorsed by the Inklings and by Le Guin, trying to identify its key therapeutic properties resting on their literary qualities only. First, using the analogy of the ancient Greek theory of ethos that governed the theory of music, I argue that the theory of ethos may be relevant to literary studies as well, and that some genres, specifically high fantasy, have their distinct ethos, against the postmodern all-debunking tendencies towards fuzzy genrelessness and moral meaninglessness. Fantasy ethos is, I propose, another essential reservoir of psychotherapeutic properties of the genre, next to its intrinsic potential of narrative and interartistic healing. Secondly, it is Faërie's affinity to myth and its embedment in what I recognize as 'moral imagination' that seems to display even more therapeutic qualities inherent to the genre.

Chapter Seven focuses on the issue of catharsis, which, as I seek to demonstrate, is another, perhaps most important, therapeutic quality of fantasy literature, rooted in Aristotle's concept of catharsis, as mentioned in his *Poetics,* and implied, as it were, by Tolkien's notion of Consolation and Eucatastrophe. In this chapter I therefore focus on the singular, perhaps most directly therapeutic, property of high fantasy fiction, as defined by Tolkien in his essay 'On Fairy-Stories', and reflected in the fantasy works of himself, and also, in some other ways, of Lewis, and of Le Guin. This property is a cathartic effect of Faërie, which, although not named so by Tolkien, seems to characterize the last unique quality of Faërie indicated by Tolkien, that is Consolation, whose twin concept is the Tolkienian Eucatastrophe. Consolation accomplished through a joyous (cathartic, as I argue), Eucatastrophe appears to crown the therapeutic ethos of the genre.

Conclusions gathered in Coda reiterate some of the main points made in this book, suggesting that high fantasy fiction as conceived and created by the Inklings and by U. K. Le Guin might be approached in terms of *therapia pauperum,* or a vicarious therapy freely available to any reader or listener, without the assistance of a therapist; the food for thought that may cathartically turn harmful emotions into a formative experience of the Aeschylean *pathei mathos* (learning through suffering). Although neither the Inklings nor Le Guin supported any application of clinical psychotherapy, and were critical and wary of Freud's psychoanalysis in particular, I hope to prove that their works are capable of mediating a quasi-bibliotherapeutic effect in a non-clinical environment, with the postmodern reader entering the reality of high fantasy fiction based on a logocentric pattern of universe, which seems to make the warp and woof of the genre. The reader is encouraged to discover a meaning of a given situation and of life itself by a vicarious confrontation with rather than eschewal of the most difficult human experience, which lies at the core of high fantasy narrative, (and which Frankl calls the triad of:) pain, guilt and death.[20] High fantasy fiction seems to offer an alternative to the postmodernist neo-nihilistic crisis of meaning and of narrative, performing a kind of logotherapeutic function informed by the moral imagination of mythopoeia (myth-making), and by mythopathy (therapy through myth).

Last but not least, I would like to express my sincere gratitude to a number of scholars without whose support and encouragement I would not have completed this book. I wish to thank Professor Andrzej Wicher, of the University of Łódź, Poland, for his invaluable guidance, scholarly expertise, patience and inspiration, without which this book, originally a doctoral dissertation, would never have been written. My sincere thanks go also to the first readers of the manuscript, Professor Bartłomiej Błaszkiewicz, of the University of Warsaw, Poland, and Professor Bogusław Bierwiaczonek, of the Jan Długosz University of Częstochowa, Poland, whose constructive criticism has improved the quality of this work. I also owe a debt of gratitude to Barbara Kobusińska, PhD, of the University of Wrocław, Institute of Psychology, and Wrocław University of Music, Music Therapy Department, for her encouragement and advice which she offered me back in 2005, when a vague idea of formulating the main thesis of this book had just occurred to me.

Moreover, I feel greatly indebted to Professor Marek Wilczyński, of the University of Gdańsk, Poland, without whose kind support and approval this book would not have been published, and to the staff of the Peter Lang Publishing House, represented in Warsaw by Mr Łukasz Gałecki, and to Ms Andrea Kolb, the Production Manager, and her team, who patiently guided me through the publication procedures.

Finally, I sincerely apologize for all the mistakes and deficiencies that the reader may come across when reading this book, which are entirely my responsibility.

Anna Cholewa-Purgał, Częstochowa, 2016

---

20 Frankl, *Man's Search for Meaning*, p. 139.

Chapter One

The Inklings, Ursula Kroeber Le Guin, and Faërie

The Inklings

When discussing the European literature of the 20th century's interwar period and the post-war decades of the '50s and the '60s, a vast majority of literary historians and critics omit to mention the writings of the Inklings or give them scant attention, the group remaining marginal and often 'dangling' undealt with. For instance, some of the world's leading anthologies of English literature: *The Norton Anthology of English Literature*, (S. Greenblatt et all, eds., 9th ed., 2012), *The Oxford Anthology of English Literature*, (F. Kermode et all, eds., 1973), and *The Longman Anthology of British Literature*, (D. Damrosch et all., eds., 4th ed., 2009), do not seem to mention the Inklings, J. R. R. Tolkien, or C. S. Lewis at all. *Encyclopaedia Britannica*, 15th edition, does include an entry on the Inklings, however, from among the Inklings it features only Tolkien and Lewis under individual entries, leaving out the names of the other Inklings completely. The exclusion of the Inklings from among the literary luminaries of that period, which is a frequent case, or, at best, poor coverage of their works in the histories of English literature appears obvious and justifiable on the grounds of the Inklings' peripheral position to what had arisen to become the modernist and later postmodernist mainstreams, and due to the writers' considerable opposition to both academically acclaimed trends.[1]

---

1 To provide a few more examples: Andrew Sanders's *The Short Oxford History of English Literature* of 2004 (Oxford University Press) only cites Tolkien's name once, remarking that *The Lord of the Rings* was ranked by the readers as the most important work of 20th century's literature in English, beating Joyce's *Ulysses* that came the fourth (p. 661). Similarly, *A Brief History of English Literature* by John Peck and Martin Coyle of 2002 (Palgrave Macmillan) quotes Tolkien's name only once, too, together with the publication year of *The Hobbit* (p. 326). *The History of English Literature* by Michael Alexander (Palgrave Macmillan, 2000, 3rd edn. of 2013) does mention the Inklings three times: first under a heading 'Non-modernism: The Twenties and Thirties' (p. 362), then with the names of C. S. Lewis, J. R. R. Tolkien, and Charles Williams (p. 376), and finally, when contrasting J. K. Rowling's fantasy fiction with that of the Inklings: 'JKR has Good warring with Evil in a series of encounters. This is like a medieval Christian romance,

Another reason for that intended or unintended negligence is probably the frequent pigeonholing of the Inklings as writers of popular fiction, or second-rate novelists (and some of them also poets and playwrights) of little academic merit. Nonetheless, the Inklings' chronological compatibility with the early 20th century English, Irish and American modernist poets and writers, who were born and died at roughly the same time as the Inklings, as well as the Inklings' unquestionable contribution to literature, sometimes denigrated as the 'unbecoming' category of 'children's lit', 'popular fiction', or 'genre fiction', may call for some kind of classification or at least confrontation with the 'canonical' literati of their time.[2]

In this book I approach the Inklings as a group of writers centred upon but not limited to their most renowned representatives, C. S. Lewis and J. R. R. Tolkien, and assume that their literary works, diverse and sometimes even jettisoned by the other members of the circle, do share some important common ground and themes, which seem to have crystalized against the backdrop of postmodernism, and that, however different stylistically, rhetorically and aesthetically in their rendition, those universals of the Inklings result from like mind-sets and essentially similar philosophy of life and art. Tolkien's and Lewis's sweeping (and mostly posthumous) popularity has by no means been paralleled by the fame of the Inklings, a group that gathered the two giants and some other interesting writers and friends, who still remain relatively unknown. The scope of analysis in this work includes also the fantasy oeuvre of Ursula Kroeber Le Guin, an American writer who could be regarded as a high fantasy writer of the next generation,

---

though the cosmology is less abstractly Christian, more humanly embodied, than that of the Inklings.' (pp. 433–434). Alexander's judgement deeming the fantasy fiction of the Inklings as 'more abstractly Christian' and 'less humanly embodied' than that of Rowling might appear controversial, yet I do not discuss it within the scope of this book. More about the Inklings' attitude to modernism can be read in Chapter Two of this book.

2 The major representatives of modernism in the English-language literature lived in the same period as the Inklings, in Europe, for instance: James Joyce (1882–1941), Virginia Wolf (1882–1941), D. H. Lawrence (1885–1930), W. H. Auden (1907–1973), and the American expatriates: T. S. Eliot (1888–1965) and Ezra Pound (1885–1972); and in the US: William Faulkner (1897–1962), and the Lost Generation writers: Ernest Hemingway (1899–1961), Francis Scott Fitzgerald (1896–1940), John Dos Passos (1896–1970) and Waldo Peirce (1884–1970). Their temporal congruence may not be disregarded, suffice to mention the dates of birth and death of the most prolific Inklings: C. S. Lewis (1898–1963), J. R. R. Tolkien (1892–1973), Owen Barfield (1898–1997), and Charles Williams (1886–1945).

by virtue of her literary interests and tastes which are also centred upon myth and fantasy, and due to the symbolic time of her birth (she was born in 1929, the year when Tolkien's last child, his only daughter, Priscilla, was born).[3]

As for the inclusion of Le Guin's name and works in the leading anthologies of American literature, it must be noted that she has received a separate entry in the *Norton Anthology of American Literature, vol. E: American Literature since 1945*, with two of her short stories featured: 'Schrödinger's Cat' and 'She Un-names Them', and she has co-edited (with Brian Attebury) *The Norton Book of Science Fiction: North American Science Fiction: 1960–1990*, which includes her short story 'The New Atlantis'.[4] *The Cambridge Companion to American Novelists* of 2013, edited by Timothy Parrish, does not reference Le Guin's name at all, not even in the index, though.[5] It is noteworthy, though, that Le Guin's literary legacy has been recognized by the National Book Foundation of the USA, who presented the writer with the lifetime achievement award, which is the Medal for Distinguished Contribution to American Letters, in November 2014.

Le Guin is still writing, and, certainly, dust needs to settle on the writings of writers before any judgment can be made and their potential impact on the development of literature and, generally, culture, can be recognized, so that, if only due, 'praise shall still find room/even in the eyes of all posterity'.[6] The dust on the Inklings' works, despite the passage of time, has not apparently settled well enough yet, for, unlike their contemporaries, such as the Bloomsbury Group of England or

---

3   An important difference, however, is that while the Inklings were essentially Christian writers, Le Guin is a 'congenital non-Christian', fond of Taoism: 'I'm an inconsistent Taoist and a consistent non-Christian,' she declares in *The Language of the Night. Essays on Fantasy and Science Fiction,* Susan Wood, ed. (New York: Berkley Books, 1982), pp. 55 and 4.

4   *Norton Anthology of American Literature, vol. E: American Literature since 1945,* Nina Baym, Robert S. Levine, gen. eds. (New York: W. W. Norton and Company, 2011), 8th edn. *The Norton Book of Science Fiction: North American Science Fiction: 1960–1990,* U. K. Le Guin, Brian Attebury, eds. (New York: W. W. Norton & Company, 1993).

5   *The Cambridge Companion to American Novelists,* Timothy Parrish, ed. (Cambridge: Cambridge University Press, 2013).

6   In Sonnet 55, addressed to the Fair Youth, William Shakespeare says,
(…) 'Gainst death and all-oblivious enmity
Shall you pace forth; your praise shall still find room
Even in the eyes of all posterity
That wear this world out to the ending doom.
So, till the judgment that yourself arise,
You live in this, and dwell in lover's eyes.'

the Lost Generation of America, the Inklings tend to remain a non-existent group in the bulk of the most recent histories of English literature covering the 20th century, both as writers of fiction (and minor poetry and, in some cases, drama, which is usually forgotten), and, surprisingly enough, as literary critics.[7] Similarly, little seems to have changed in the paucity and cautiousness of literary criticism on the Inklings that would focus on their stance towards the mainstream literature of the period and their rapport with the 'classical' or 'canonical' writers and poets of their time since the 1978 George Allen and Unwin publication compiled by Humphrey Carpenter (1946–2005) – the Inklings' first historian and biographer.[8] As Carpenter himself put it in the *Preface* to the first edition of *The Inklings* in 1978, he 'merely told their story' and 'deliberately avoided making any general judgement of these men's [literary] achievements', for he thought 'it [was] too early to do so.'[9] In 1978, thirty-three years after Williams's death, fifteen after Lewis's, but only five years after Tolkien's and Warnie Lewis's, when the 'first and last Inkling', that is Owen Barfield (1898–1997), was still alive and active, and so were some other Inklings, (suffice it to mention Lord David Cecil, Nevill Coghill, and Robert 'Humphrey' Havard), and when postmodernism was entering its heyday, there was certainly a risk of forming premature judgements as to any long-lasting influence of the Inklings on the course of literary history.

Carpenter's disclaimer, however, appears in all the successive editions of the book, that is of 1981 and the posthumous of 2006, and seems to have set the standard for most of the subsequent publications devoted to the Inklings, whose authors usually concentrate on providing both encyclopaedic and anecdotal information on the writers, their thought, companionship, interaction and writings, (which makes a most compelling and essential reading,) but are likely to omit or glide over the problem what the Inklings' legacy as a literary phenomenon represents against the literary background of the past century, (that is roughly the 'litscape' of the two strong currents of modernism and early postmodernism), and what their role in the history of English literature from the perspective of the next century might be.

---

7   The Inklings are predominantly known for their novels and stories, less for their (abundant) non-fiction, and less still for their poetry. Most of the Inklings were also remarkable critics of literature, especially engaged in medieval and Renaissance studies, Lewis's and Williams's interests reaching further into the 17th and 18th c. literature).

8   Humphrey Carpenter, *The Inklings: C. S. Lewis, J. R. R. Tolkien, Charles Williams and Their Friends. A Group of Writers Whose Literary Fantasies Still Fire the Imagination of All Those Who Seek a Truth Beyond Reality* (London: George Allen and Unwin, 1978. Later editions: HarperCollins Publishers, 1981, 2006).

9   Ibid., p. x.

Justice must be done to the authors who discuss this issue in their books on the Inklings, however briefly. The position of the Inklings on the literary scene when modernism and later early postmodernism patronized their luminaries is what Carpenter alludes to in his publications (*The Inklings* and *J. R. R. Tolkien – A Biography*), and what Colin Duriez mentions in his works (*The Inklings Handbook* and *Tolkien and C. S. Lewis: The Gift of Friendship*), highlighting a rift between the Oxford writers and the champions of the new literary and aesthetic trends of the day, including Eliot, Auden, and the Cambridge scholars.[10] Neither Carpenter nor Duriez, however, seem to argue that the Inklings ought to be given more attention and recognition in the studies of literary history as a group parallel and equal to, although different from, the acclaimed modernists. It is only very recently that some scholars have openly recognized the import of the Inklings' contribution to the contemporary history of literature. Such opinions are voiced, for instance, in the two publications of 2015: Philip Zaleski and Carol Zaleski's *The Fellowship: The Literary Lives of the Inklings: J. R. R. Tolkien, C. S. Lewis, Owen Barfield, Charles Williams*, and Grevel Lindop's *Charles Williams: the Third Inkling*, the latter focused predominantly on Williams's life and legacy. It is the work of Philip Zaleski and Carol Zaleski that appears to have fulfilled only very recently Carpenter's prediction that the literary legacy of the Inklings will be critically viewed from a more detached vantage point, offering a long-overdue 'first complete rendering of the Inklings' lives and works.'[11]

In her study, *The Company They Keep: C. S. Lewis and J. R. R. Tolkien as Writers in Community*, Diana Glyer contests Carpenter's statement that the Inklings were not a proper group of writers and that they did not significantly influence one another, arguing that this group of Oxford writers, although recruited from various personalities, styles and literary tastes, would not have produced their unique legacy had it not been for their several-decade long interaction, inspiration and collaboration, which had an impact on all of the Inklings to some extent.[12] Referring to

---

10 Colin Duriez and David Porter, *The Inklings Handbook: The Lives, Thought and Writings of C. S. Lewis, J. R. R. Tolkien, Charles Williams, Owen Barfield, and Their Friends* (London: Azure, 2001).
Colin Duriez, *Tolkien and C. S. Lewis: The Gift of Friendship* (London: Hiddenspring, 2003).

11 Philip Zaleski and Carol Zaleski, *The Fellowship: The Literary Lives of the Inklings: J. R. R. Tolkien, C. S. Lewis, Owen Barfield, Charles Williams* (New York: Farrar, Straus and Giroux, 2015).

12 Diana Pavlac Glyer, *The Company They Keep: C. S. Lewis and J. R. R. Tolkien as Writers in Community* (Kent: Kent State University Press, 2007).

the question whether the Inklings could be called a literary movement, Carpenter compares the search for evidence that might prove it to a pursuit of a 'fox that isn't there', (quoting Lewis's phrase used elsewhere), and concludes that the Inklings were merely a group of friends, who shall neither be named 'the Oxford Christians' nor the writers who shared 'a common Inklings attitude'.[13] 'It must be remembered that the word "influence", he remarks, 'so beloved of literary investigators, makes little sense when talking about [the Inklings'] association with each other.'[14]

Taking issue with Carpenter, Glyer juxtaposes the Inklings with some other circles of writers, namely the Bloomsbury Group, the Transcendentalists, the Brideshead Generation, and the Lost Generation, claiming that the way the 'the Oxonians' worked and shared a *Weltanschauung* as a literary group, despite their unpretentiousness, informality and considerable differences among the members, was similar to that of those historically and critically better-established formations.[15] Similarly, Philip Zaleski and Carol Zaleski refer to the Inklings as a 'curious band' and an 'erudite club' who, despite their 'donnish dreaminess', which was charming in its own right, were more than mere 'dabblers in ink', and more than 'a loose association of rumpled intellectuals'.[16] What united the Inklings, the Zaleskis maintain, was their fascination with language and meaning, as well as their myth-loving and myth-making Christian worldview: the Inklings were 'philologists and philomyths: lovers of *logos* (the ordering power of words) and *mythos* (the regenerative power of story), with a nostalgia for things medieval and archaic and a distrust of technological innovation that never decayed into the merely antiquarian.'[17] Interestingly, although the Zaleskis never mention Frankl's logotherapy in their study of the Inklings, they identity the central position of '*logos*' as a unique quality of the Inklings' frame of mind.

---

13 Carpenter, *The Inklings*, pp. 159–160.

14 Carpenter, ibid., p. 160.

15 Ibid., p. xvii. The term 'Oxonians' does not technically embrace all the Inklings, as not all of them were Oxford graduates or dons, the 'non-Oxonians' including Warnie Hamilton Lewis, Charles Walter Stansby Williams and Commander Jim Dundas-Grant ('D–G'). All the Inklings, however, were connected with Oxford and with the University, at least for some time, which may somehow validate the term.
The Brideshead Generation, which may be less renowned than the other groups, according to Humphrey Carpenter, included Evelyn Waugh and his Oxford acquaintances: Graham Greene, Nancy Mitford, Cyril Connolly, John Betjeman and Randolph Churchill (H. Carpenter, *The Brideshead Generation: Evelyn Waugh and His Friends*; London: Houghton Mifflin, 1990).

16 The Zaleskis, *The Fellowship*, p. 3.

17 The Zaleskis, ibid., p. 4.

Lewis himself described the Inklings to Charles Williams (before Williams's joining the group) as an 'informal club' whose membership 'qualifications (as they [had] formally evolved) [were] a tendency to write, and Christianity.'[18] John Wain, a poet, novelist and critic associated with the Angry Young Men movement, and a former student of C. S. Lewis at Oxford, saw the Inklings as 'a circle of instigators, almost incendiaries, meeting to urge one another on in the task of redirecting the whole current of contemporary art and life.'[19] The Zaleskis wittingly introduce the term '*Inkling authenticus*', a distinctive 'genus' characterized by 'intellectual vivacity, love of myth, conservative politics, memories of war, and a passion for beef, beer, and verbal battle', to which one ought to add Christian faith, fascination with myth, and what David Cecil, one of the Inklings, defines as 'a feeling for literature, which united, in an unusual way, scholarship and imagination.'[20] Cecil himself calls the Inklings 'Oxford's magic circle'.[21]

The collective spirit and active cross-interaction of the Inklings, each of whom, nonetheless, remained a unique individual, is what the Zaleskis seem to emphasize, adding that there was not so much an Oxford school of the Inklings, as an '*ethos*' of the Inklings, which rested on their shared 'neo-Christian' fantasy, as the Cambridge opponents of the Inklings named it.[22] Besides, the Zaleskis remark, the Inklings were friends who shaped one another 'in myriad ways, obvious and subtle, and not always detectable to the principals involved.'[23] Some of those evident ways of interaction were their shared projects: Tolkien and Lewis planned to 'co-author a book on *Language and Human Nature*, intended to exorcise the influence of I. A. Richards and his colleagues at Cambridge', and decided to write 'excursionary "Thriller[s]"': Tolkien about time travel, and Lewis about space travel.'[24] Tolkien never completed his tale, producing only the beginning of *The Lost Road*, yet encouraged Lewis to pursue their project, which resulted in the publication of Lewis's *Out of the Silent Planet* (1938), the first part of his

---

18 Lewis, *Collected Letters*, vol. 2, p. 180.
19 John Wain, *Sprightly Running: Part of an Autobiography* (New York: St. Martin's, 1962), p. 181.
20 The Zaleskis, *The Fellowship*, p. 198. David Cecil, 'Oxford's Magic Circle', [in:] *Books and Bookmen 24*, no. 4 (January 1979), p. 10, quoted by the Zaleskis, p. 198.
21 Cecil, ibid., p. 10.
22 The Zaleskis, *The Fellowship*, p. 334. The phrase 'neo-Christians' was coined mockingly for the Inklings by William Empson, a Cambridge Leavisite critic, poet, and writer, as quoted by the Zaleskis, p. 334.
23 The Zaleskis, *The Fellowship*, p. 509.
24 The Zaleskis, ibid., pp. 509 and 240.

Space Trilogy. Without Lewis's unfailing support, Tolkien's *The Lord of the Rings* might never have been published.

Tracing further the most conspicuous forms of interaction and cross-influence among the Inklings, it must be noted that Tolkien and Lewis acknowledged the impact of Barfield's *Poetic Diction* on their thought and work, and that Lewis wrote *That Hideous Strength*, the last part of his Space Trilogy, in the Williamsesque mode, published in the year of Williams's sudden death.[25] In addition, Lewis and Williams intended to produce two literary collaborations, neither executed: a short Christian Dictionary, and 'a book of animal stories from the Bible, told by the animals concerned.'[26]

Critics remain divided, though, as to the degree and consequences of literary interaction and mutual influence among the Inklings. Gareth Knight notes that 'we have to be careful not to attribute influence where none existed;' 'Inklings or not, Tolkien would probably have gone on to do what he did anyway, as a man writing from great depths within himself.'[27] At the same time, however, Knight identifies a common *Weltanschauung* that the Inklings shared, which was 'more like a world look (…) than a doctrine', and which a few centuries ago 'might well have been *The Matter of the Inklings*,' which the Zaleskis, in turn, associate with the notion of 'Inklingsiana'.[28] Tolkien himself refers wittingly to 'the matter of the Inklings' in a few lines that parody the epic quality of *Beowulf*, in which he introduces the group beginning with Lewis, whom he names Hloðuig (Hlothwig, the Anglo-Saxon source of Lewis's surname):

> Hwaet! we Inklina on aerdagum searopancolra snyttru gehierdon.
> þara wæs Hloðuig sum, hæleða dyrost,
> brad ond beorhtword, cuþe he...[29]

Carpenter provides the following translation of that passage:

'Lo! We have heard in old days of the wisdom of the cunning-minded Inklings; how those wise ones sat together in their deliberations, skilfully reciting

---

25 The Zaleskis, ibid., p. 509.

26 The Zaleskis, ibid., p. 509. The last words are Lewis's from his introduction to the *Essays Presented to Charles Williams*, C. S. Lewis, ed. (London: Geoffrey Cumberlege, Oxford University Press, 1947), p. xii.

27 Gareth Knight, *The Magical World of the Inklings* (Cheltenham: Skylight Press, 1990, 2nd ed., 2010), p. 4.

28 Knight, ibid., p. 9. The Zaleskis, *The Fellowship*, p. 196.

29 Carpenter, *The Inklings*, p. 176.

learning and song-craft, earnestly meditating. That was true joy! One of them was Hlothwig, dearest of men, broad and bright of word; he knew...'[30]

Acknowledging Lewis's vital position among the Inklings, Carpenter does not seem, none the less, to view the writers' legacy as a fruit of their interaction and mutual interests, and observes that 'any attempt to search out important links between the work of these people' who are today called the Inklings might, to borrow Lewis's phrase, resemble 'chasing after a fox that isn't there.'[31] Should there be any fox to hunt, Carpenter argues, it shall be Lewis, the *spiritus movens* of the Oxford group of friends, thanks to whom that diverse company was kept together: '[Lewis] himself is the fox', Carpenter concludes.[32]

Following in Carpenter's footsteps, some other critics tend to emphasize the discrepancies between the Inklings rather than a coherent unity of their minds, arguing that it is problematic whether the Inklings constituted a single entity. For instance, William Ready asserts that 'the differences between [Tolkien, Lewis, and Williams] are far more important than the appearance of their likeness', and that 'trio they were not.'[33] In his *Imaginary Worlds*, Lin Carter observes that 'whatever criticism the Inklings offered, Tolkien paid no attention,' for 'the Inklings were not able to influence the writing of *The Lord of the Rings* in any way.'[34] 'Though [the Inklings] no doubt discussed it and commented upon it, they did not, apparently, have any appreciable influence on the trilogy as it took shape. Everyone concerned seems quite adamant on this point,' Carter concludes.[35] Carpenter likewise notes that, in his opinion, 'Tolkien and Lewis owed almost nothing to the other Inklings and would have written everything they wrote had they never heard of the group.'[36] When it comes to Tolkien and Williams, 'Tolkien and Williams had no real influence on each other's work,' John D. Rateliff remarks, corroborating Carpenter's view.[37] Candice Frederick and Sam McBride make a similar statement, contending that 'one would never be tempted to suggest that the Inklings' reading and critiquing could be appropriately labelled

---

30 Ibid., pp. 176–177.
31 Carpenter, *The Inklings*, p. 154.
32 Ibid., p. 171.
33 William Bernard Ready, *Understanding Tolkien and The Lord Of The Rings* (London: Warner Paperback Library, 1973), pp. 37–38.
34 Lin Carter, *Imaginary Worlds* (London: Ballantine Books, 1973), pp. 112–113.
35 Ibid., p. 118.
36 Carpenter, *The Inklings*, p. 160.
37 John D. Rateliff, *The History of the Hobbit* (New York: Houghton Mifflin Harcourt, 2007), p. 51.

"collaboration".[38] Mark Hillegas adds that 'each [Inkling] writer is excellent in his own fashion, unique in style and technique'.[39]

Arguing for a sense of unity deeply ingrained in the thought and beliefs of the Inklings, I must admit that the afore-mentioned observations are based on the words of the Inklings themselves. Lewis stated that, except for the authors of the Norse mythology, Anglo-Saxon literature, and the Bible, 'no one ever influenced Tolkien – you might as well try to influence a bandersnatch'.[40] According to Tolkien, Lewis once said to him, 'it's no use trying to influence you. You're uninfluenceable!'[41] Tolkien, on the other hand, said of Lewis that he was 'too impressionable'.[42] Moreover, it is a well-known fact that Tolkien was intensely reserved about Williams, who, according to him, 'dabbled in the occult'[43] and was in a way a 'witch doctor'[44]. 'I was and remain wholly unsympathetic to Williams mind,' Tolkien notes.[45] '(…) We liked one another and enjoyed talking (mostly in jest), but we had nothing to say to one another at deeper (or higher) levels. (…) I find his work wholly alien, and sometimes very distasteful, occasionally ridiculous'.[46] The sharpness of this remark is somehow moderated by Tolkien's explanation that follows: 'This is perfectly true as a general statement, but is not intended as criticism of Williams; rather it is an exhibition of my own limits of sympathy'.[47]

Thus, although Williams's fantasy 'was not the sort of myth making that seemed to have any "truth" to Tolkien,' interestingly enough, as Carpenter observers,

---

38 Candice Frederick and Sam McBride, *Women Among the Inklings: Gender, C. S. Lewis, J. R. R. Tolkien, and Charles Williams. Contributions in Women's Studies* (Santa Barbara: Praeger, 2001), p. 150.

39 Mark Hillegas, 'Introduction' to *Shadows of the Imagination: The Fantasies of C. S. Lewis, J. R. R. Tolkien, and Charles Williams,* Mark Hillegas, ed. (Carbondale: Southern Illinois University Press, 1969), p. xii.

40 *Letters of C. S. Lewis,* W. H. Lewis, ed. (London: Mariner Books, 2003), p. 481. The word 'bandersnatch', coined by Lewis Carroll, was borrowed by C. S. Lewis from Carroll's 1872 novel *Through the Looking Glass* and from Carroll's 1874 poem 'The Hunting of the Snark'.

41 Charlotte and Denis Plimmer, 'The Man Who Understands Hobbits', an interview with J. R. R. Tolkien, [in:] *Daily Telegraph Magazine,* 22 March 1968, pp. 31–35, 31.

42 Colin Duriez, *Tolkien and C. S. Lewis: The Gift of Friendship* (New York: Hiddenspring, 2003), p. 116.

43 Duriez, ibid., p. 119.

44 Carpenter, *The Inklings,* p. 121.

45 Tolkien, *The Letters of J. R. R. Tolkien,* p. 361.

46 Tolkien, ibid., pp. 361–362.

47 Ibid., p. 362.

'Tolkien listened with full attention when Williams read the [Arthurian *Taliessin*] poems aloud to the Inklings; and if Williams's ideas did not appeal [to him], then the man himself (he found) was undeniably charming.'[48] The evidence of some kind of attention (if not recognition) that Tolkien gave Williams could perhaps be found in the poem written during the war by the former and dedicated to the latter, in which Tolkien admits:

> Our dear Charles Williams many guises shows;
> The novelist comes first. I find his prose
> Obscure at times. Not easily it flows;
> Too often are his lights held up in brackets.
> Yet error, should he spot it, he'll attack its
> Sources and head, exposing ramps and rackets,
> The tortuous byways of the wicked heart
> And intellect corrupt. Yea, many a dart
> He crosses with the fiery ones! The art
> Of minor fiends and major he reveals –
> When Charles is on his trail the devil squeals,
> For cloven feet have vulnerable heels.
>
> But heavenly footsteps, too, can Williams trace,
> And after Dante, plunging, soaring, race
> Up to the threshold of Eternal Grace.
> (…) Tolkien, please!
> What's biting you? Dog in the Manger's fleas?
> Let others hear, although you have no mind,
> Or have not seen that Lewis has divined
> And has expounded what you dully find
> Obscure. See here, some thirty lines you've squandered.
> You came to praise our Charles, but now you've wandered.
> Much else he wrote that has not yet been pondered.'
>
> (…) So, heed me not! I swear
> When you with tattered papers take the chair
> And read (for hours maybe), I would be there.
> And ever when in state you sit again
> And to your car imperial give rein,
> I'll trundle, grumbling, squeaking, in the train
> Of the great rolling wheels of Charles' Wain.'[49]

---

48 Carpenter, *The Inklings*, p. 123.

49 Carpenter, *The Inklings*, pp. 123–126. Charles' Wain (also known as the Big Dipper, Arthur's Plough or Great Bear) is a group of seven bright stars in the constellation Ursa Major, which rotates around the North Star. The name 'Charles' Wain' probably

None the less, despite the apparently friendly warmth spreading through the poem, Tolkien wrote elsewhere about Williams, 'I do not think we influenced one another at all! Too "set" and too different.'[50] Although Tolkien denied it himself, there might have been some little influence exerted indirectly by Williams on Tolkien's works, connected perhaps to the bulk of the Arthurian and medieval lore, and the Bible.[51] Some critics argue that Tolkien's attempted and unfinished novel of 1945–46 *The Notion Club Papers* (interrupted by Williams's death in 1945) was influenced by Williams.[52] It is also worth noting that Tolkien's seminal essay 'On Fairy-Stories' was first published in a collection of *Essays Presented to Charles Williams*, prepared by the Inklings and their circle for Williams on the occasion of his prospective leaving Oxford, and printed upon his sudden death in 1945.[53] Tolkien, a Catholic, and Williams, an Anglican who had belonged for a few years to the semi-secret occult Fellowship of the Rosy Cross, though radically different in their approach to Christianity, were both men of strong faith who had chosen it very consciously: Tolkien following the footsteps of his beloved 'martyr' mother, Mabel Tolkien, a Catholic convert among Anglicans; and Williams, a high Anglican who had left the esoteric society of black magic and

---

comes from the Middle English *charleswen*, Charles' (Charlemagne's) wain, which had most likely originated from the Old English *carleswægn*, churl's wain: carl, *churl* (from Old Norse karl) and *wægn*, *wain*. The *Anglo-Saxon Manual of Astronomy* uses the term reads that 'Arhetonhatte an tungol on norðdæle, se hæfðseofonsteorran, & is for ðioþrumnamange-hatanseptemtrio, þonehataðlæwedemeoncarles-wæn.' cf. *The Online Etymology Dictionary*, Douglas Harper, ed. (2001–2016) http://www.etymonline.com/index.php?term=Charles%27s%20Wain, accessed 23 April 2016.

50 *The Letters of J. R. R. Tolkien*, p. 209.

51 Williams wrote 3 volumes of Arthurian poetry: *Taliessin through Logres* (1938), *The Region of the Summer Stars* (1944) (London: Oxford University Press, 1954), as well as *The Figure of Arthur* as part of the unfinished *Arthurian Torso* (with C. S. Lewis's commentary, London: Oxford University Press, 1948.) He also wrote several theological works on Christianity, marked by dense mysticism, e.g.: *He Came Down from Heaven* (London: Heinemann, 1938), and *The Descent of the Dove: A Short History of the Holy Spirit in the Church* (London: Longmans, Green, 1939).

52 Bruce Charlton, 'Tolkien's The Notion Club Papers', http://notionclubpapers.blogspot.com/2012/12/was-tolkien-jealous-of-charles-williams.html, accessed 23 April 2016.

53 The contents of the *Essays Presented to Charles Williams* were: Preface by C. S. Lewis; and the essays: Dorothy Sayers: '"... And Telling you a Story": A Note on *The Divine Comedy*'; J. R. R. Tolkien: 'On Fairy-Stories'; C. S. Lewis: 'On Stories'; Arthur Owen Barfield: 'Poetic Diction and Legal Fiction'; Gervase Mathew: 'Marriage and *Amour Courtois* in Late-Fourteenth-Century England'; and W. H. Lewis: 'The Galleys of France'.

alchemy, yet retained the secret knowledge and a profound awareness of evil.[54] 'No one can possibly do more than to decide what to believe', says one of Williams's characters, expressing most probably the writer's own, and perhaps also Tolkien's, conviction.[55]

Some critics suggest that Williams was actually 'a literary sparring partner for J. R. R. Tolkien', an opinion which may sound dubious, considering the writers' very different literary interests, backgrounds, styles, tastes and preferred genres (Williams thought of himself first and foremostly as a poet).[56] Others argue that Tolkien grew jealous of Lewis's friendship and fascination with Williams, a view challenged by some readers and biographers of the Inklings who interpret it as an attitude of reservedness towards Williams adopted by Tolkien only after Williams's death upon Tolkien's reading some of the first biographies of the late Inkling,

---

54 As Grevel Lindop argues, correcting the information provided for instance by Carpenter (*The Inklings*, p. 89), Williams was not initiated to the famous Order of the Golden Dawn, to which W. B. Yeats, Evelyn Underhill, and some leading occultists of the day, such as Aleister Crowley and A. E. Waite, had belonged. Williams corresponded with Yeats and some other members, though, with regard to *The Oxford Book of English Mystical Verse*, published in 1917, as an OUP employee whose job was to obtain the permission of the authors to reprint their work. According to Lindop, upon Waite's invitation Williams joined instead Waite's newly-established secret *Fellowship of the Rosy Cross* in 1917, soon after his wedding to Florence Conway; cf. Lindop, *Charles Williams: The Third Inkling* (Oxford: Oxford University Press, 2015), pp. 56–57. Lindop admits, however, that Williams might have joined the Order of the Golden Dawn later on as well, which is Anne Ridler's opinion, thus he might have clandestinely commenced parallel membership (Lindop, pp. 65–66). It is not clear when Williams left the order(s), yet he kept some of the paraphernalia (his ritual sword and robes) in his office desk till his sudden death in 1945 (Lindop, p. 423).

Tolkien's mother Mabel Tolkien, nee Suffield, converted to the Catholic Church in 1900, which caused her parents' and her late husband's family's outrage, and threw Mabel and her little sons into poverty. She died of tuberculosis in 1904, leaving John Ronald Reuel and his younger brother Hilary in the custody of Fr. Francis Morgan of the Birmingham Oratory. Nine years after his mother's death J. R. R. Tolkien wrote: 'My own dear mother was a martyr indeed, and it was not to everybody that God grants so easy a way to His great gifts as He did to Hilary and myself, giving us a mother who killed herself with labour and trouble to ensure us keeping the faith.' Cf. Joseph Pearce, *Tolkien: Man and Myth* (San Francisco: Ignatius Press, 1998), p. 50.

55 Charles Williams, *War in Heaven* (Grand Rapids, Michigan: William B. Eerdmans, 1930, 1949), p. 113.

56 Gavin Ashenden, *Charles Williams: Alchemy and Integration* (Cleveland: The Kent State University Press, 2007), p. 4.

which revealed Williams's pre-Inkling involvement in the occult and his weird master-disciple relationships with women.[57] The true picture of Tolkien's rapport with Williams is, according to Duriez, that at the time of their Inklings gatherings 'Tolkien got a lot out of his friendship with Williams, and deeply appreciated his attentive listening to the episodes of *The Lord of the Rings* as they were written.'[58] It must be noted that not only Tolkien, but also most of the other Inklings could not make sense of Williams's poetry, which he considered his foremost achievement, and that only Lewis was enthusiastic about it, even though he admitted it was rather obscure.[59]

There is definitely some of Williams's impact, (especially with regard to his Theology of Romantic Love and Co-inherence, as well as the occult elements of the esoteric societies,) felt in Lewis's works, especially in his science fiction dystopian novel of 1945 *That Hideous Strength: A Modern Fairy-Tale for Grown-Ups*, disapprovingly nicknamed by Tolkien 'That Hideous Book.'[60] The beginning of Lewis's and Williams's acquaintance in 1936 was marked by their mutual admiration and praise of the novels: *The Place of the Lion* (written by Williams and received enthusiastically by Lewis), and *The Allegorical Love Poem* (later renamed as *The Allegory of Love: A Study in Medieval Tradition*, written by Lewis and acclaimed by Williams as 'practically the only [book], since Dante, that shows the slightest understanding of what this very peculiar identity of love and religion means.')[61] Moreover, some critics venture a theory that Williams's *Place of the Lion* had provided Lewis with an idea of his leonine Christ figure of Aslan to rule

---

57 Cf. Charlton, 'Tolkien's *The Notion Club Papers*'. Williams had a platonic love affair with Phyllis Jones, a librarian at Oxford University Press in London, and acted as a kind of spiritual guide in master-disciple relationships for many young women, for instance Lois Lang Sims ('Lalage').

58 Duriez, *J. R. R. Tolkien: The Making of a Legend* (Oxford: Lion Hudson, 2012), p. 184.

59 Ibid., p. 108.

60 *That Hideous Strength* is the last part of Lewis's space trilogy, prequelled by *Out of the Silent Planet* (1938) and *Perelandra* (1943). Elwin Ransom, an important character uniting the parts of the trilogy, is a philologist and a university professor, modelled partly on Lewis himself (Ransom is a declared bachelor), partly on Tolkien (in Old English *elwin* means 'elf friend', and Ransom, as Elwin Ransom explains in *Perelandra*, Chapter 11, is a contraction of the Old English 'Ranolf's son'), and, in *That Hideous Strength*, also on Williams (Ransom is here a visionary prophet-like figure). Tolkien found some of Ransom's opinions similar to his own but 'Lewisified' (cf. Carpenter, *J. R. R. Tolkien: A Biography*, p. 173).

61 Carpenter, *The Inklings*, pp. 99–100.

the Narnian heptalogy.[62] It is also noteworthy that Williams dedicated his *The Forgiveness of Sins* of 1941, (a singular study of forgiveness in Shakespeare, in theology, and in the reality of the Second World War), to the Inklings.[63]

As far as Tolkien and Lewis's friendship and mutual impact are concerned, there seems to exist abundant evidence testifying to both, even though the latter, that is their bilateral influence, has been questioned by the two Inklings themselves, as mentioned before in this chapter. In one of his letters Lewis observes, for instance, that '[he doesn't] think Tolkien influenced [him], and [he is] certain, [he] didn't influence Tolkien.'[64] It is also well-known that Tolkien approved neither of Lewis's *Chronicles of Narnia* nor of his Christian apologetics, as Tolkien despised a thinly-disguised allegory just as much as he mistrusted amateur theology.[65]

Some further examples of the Inklings' mutual criticism include their comments on Tolkien's work: some of them, with Hugo Dyson in the lead, jocularly responded to Tolkien's descriptions of Elves and the storyline of the 'New Hobbit', which was to become eventually the matter of *The Lord of the Rings*, demanding more variety and a radical change of subject ('Oh, God! Not another Elf!').[66] As Warnie Lewis put it in his dairy, Dyson even exercised 'most unfairly' his veto against 'the New Hobbit', so whenever he turned up at the meetings, Tolkien 'had to stop' reading the new bits of the work in progress.[67]

Another example of sound criticism among the Inklings is the 'Great War' between Lewis and Barfield, which they had fought prior to the former's conversion (in the years 1925–1930), and at the Inklings' meetings they would still engage themselves in intellectual battles and vivid polemics.[68] Referring to the 'Great War' of incessant philosophical debate and polemics between himself and Lewis, Owen Barfield remarked: 'What am I supposed to have taught him? He continues to deny everything I say.'[69] Also Humphrey, or doctor Havard, a member

---

62 Brenton Dickieson, 'The Place of the Lion in C. S. Lewis' Fiction', https://apilgriminnarnia.com/2013/10/02/lion/, accessed 4 July 2016.

63 Cf. Carpenter, *The Inklings*, p. 153.

64 Warren Hamilton Lewis, *Brothers and Friends: The Diaries of Major Warren Hamilton Lewis*, Clyde S. Kilby, Marjorie Lamp Mead, eds. (New York: HarperCollins, 1982), p. 76.

65 Carpenter, *The Inklings*, pp. 223, 224, and 238.

66 Andrew Norman Wilson, *C. S. Lewis: A Biography* (London: Collins, 1990), p. 58.

67 Carpenter, *The Inklings*, pp. 212–213.

68 Lionel Adey, *C. S. Lewis's 'Great War' with Owen Barfield* (London: Ink Books, 2000), p. 15.

69 Owen Barfield, *Poetic Diction: A Study in Meaning* (London: Wesleyan Paperback, 1984), p. 150.

and an astute observer of the Inklings, notes, 'I don't think any of us were much affected by the criticism or altered what had been written. (…) We really had no corporate existence. In my view we were simply a group of C. S. Lewis's wide circle of friends who lived near enough to him to meet together fairly regularly.'[70]

As Glyer observes, the Inklings and most of the scholars who study them 'seem unanimous in their insistence that the Inklings were nothing more than an informal association of friends,' yet she argues that, despite numerous denials, the Inklings' long-standing interaction, interconnectedness and friendship were undoubtedly influential and fruitful, and to a lesser or greater extent, 'made the Inklings change one another.'[71] The 'third' and 'oddest Inkling', that is Charles Williams, expressed perhaps the same truth about the Inklings when addressing the importance of friendship in *The Place of the Lion*:

> Much was possible to a man in solitude, but some things were possible only to a man in companionship, and of these the most important was balance. No mind was so good that it did not need another mind to counter and equal it, and to save it from conceit and bigotry and folly.[72]

Returning to Glyer's thesis that the Inklings deserve the same merit as the well-known and universally recognized groups of writers, one may wonder why it is so that the Bloomsbury Group or the Lost Generation are the famous literary groups of the same half of the 20th century, a part of the literary canon, while the Inklings are not. Is this so because of scant literary merit the Inklings deserve in comparison to the other groups, which were not very formal, either, or because the Inklings' works failed the test of time and that of academics? Or does the fact that the Inklings have reputedly failed to be entered into the canon of literature result from their preoccupation with myth and fantasy, often denigrated as either popular fiction or children's literature; or maybe from the remarkable (Christian) spirituality of their works; or, last but not least, from a rather uneasy rapport between the Inklings and the avant-garde of modernism and, later on, of postmodernism, who have triumphed in the annals of literatures in English? This book does not aspire to fill in the apparent gap existing in the continuity of

---

70 Carpenter, *The Inklings*, p. 161.

71 Glyer, *The Company They Keep*, p. 45.

72 Carpenter, *The Inklings*, p. 117. The phrase 'the oddest Inkling' has been attributed to Williams by a critic and scholar Sørina Higgins on her website https://theoddestinkling.wordpress.com/ (accessed 23 April 2016), while the epithet 'the third Inkling' is Grevel Lindop's suggestion and a title of his recent book on Williams (*Charles Williams: The Third Inkling*, Oxford University Press, 2015).

20th century literary history in English, as it takes far greater minds to revise it, yet it attempts to call attention to the Inklings as a group confronted with the great writers and poets of their day, suggesting that a canonical revalorization might be needed, so that the Inklings may receive more universal scholarly attention and recognition. It must not, of course, be opening the open door, but it ought to consolidate the facts concerning the literary output of the Inklings and their contribution to the history of literature and culture from a perspective of the second decade of the 21st century.

Tom Shippey's scholarship offers succour here, as the critic addresses directly the issue of the role played by the Inklings in the history of the past century's literature in English. One of the leading experts on Tolkien, Shippey approaches the Inklings as the writers who were instrumental in turning fantasy from the minor into the major literary genre, and argues that 'the dominant literary mode of the [20th] century has been the fantastic' – a claim which may appear surprising today; which 'would not have seemed even remotely conceivable at the start of the 20th century'; and which is still 'bound to encounter fierce resistance' in future.[73] 'However, when the time comes to look back at the century,' Shippey remarks,

> It seems very likely that future literary historians, detached from the squabbles of our present, will see as its most representative and distinct works books like J. R. R. Tolkien's *The Lord of the Rings*, and also George Orwell's *Nineteen Eighty-Four* and *Animal Farm*, William Golding's *Lord of the Flies* and *The Inheritors*, Kurt Vonnegut's *Slaughterhouse-Five* and *Cat's Cradle*, Ursula Le Guin's *The Left Hand of Darkness* and *The Dispossessed*, Thomas Pynchon's *The Crying of Lot-49* and *Gravity's Rainbow*. The list could readily be extended, back to the late nineteenth century with H. G. Wells's *The Island of Dr Moreau* and *The War of the Worlds*, and up to writers currently active like Stephen R. Donaldson and George R. R. Martin. It could take in authors as different, not to say opposed, as Kingsley and Marin Amis, Anthony Burgess, Stephen King, Terry Pratchett, Don DeLillo, and Julian Barnes.[74]

What Shippey suggests is that 'the fantastic' informed the literature of the past century and apparently continues to unite the otherwise incongruous contemporary fiction, because 'even authors deeply committed to the realist novel have often found themselves unable to resist the gravitational pull of the fantastic as a literary mode.'[75] Should that interpretation be universally acknowledged by academia, one may consider the Inklings' contribution to the phenomenon of re-establishing

---

73 Shippey, *J. R. R. Tolkien. Author of the Century* (London: HarperCollins Publishers, 2000), p. vii.

74 Shippey, ibid., pp. vii–viii.

75 Ibid., p. viii.

fantasy not merely as a genre of popular fiction but as the primary mode of literature. Certainly, their approach to fantasy differed appreciably from that of most of the other writers listed above by Shippey. Firstly, each Inkling developed their own idiosyncratic vision of fantasy as a genre and literary mode, which they disputed and argued about; and, secondly, their visions, even if somehow uniform on the basis of their Christian, more or less Georgian (that is traditional) and neoromantic foundations, stand in sharp contrast to the fantastic mode rendered, for instance, by George Orwell, William Golding, Kurt Vonnegut, Thomas Pynchon, Terry Pratchett, Kingsley and Marin Amis, Anthony Burgess, Stephen King, Don DeLillo and Julian Barnes, to name but a few. It seems hardly possible to group the Inklings together with postmodernists, political writers, or parodists, to name but a few categories. When juxtaposed with the other representatives of the fantastic mode in literature, the Inklings might be viewed as classicists or purists (especially Tolkien) of 'the fantastic', (the 'fantastic' being understood in its broadest sense, wider than Tzvetan Todorov's), and can be viewed as a group who largely sparked the mythopoeic Christian revival in contemporary culture.[76]

After Shippey's bold statement of 2000 indicating the significance of the Inklings' legacy to the history of 20th century's literature and culture, the Zaleskis' study of 2015 is one of the works that seeks to explore the theme of the long-overdue reassessment of the Inklings' contribution. The Zaleskis note that:

History would record, however modest [the Inklings'] pretensions, that their ideas did not remain half-formed nor their inkblots mere dabblings. Their polyvalent talents – amount

---

76 In his famous work *The Fantastic: A Structural Approach to a Genre* (Ithaca, New York: Cornell University Press, 1970, 1975, trans. by Richard Howard), Todorov defines his notion of 'the fantastic' as a moment of the reader's hesitation and suspense, when the literal meaning of the text does not conform to the laws of immediate reality: "'I nearly reached the point of believing": that is the formula which sums up the spirit of the fantastic. Either total faith [which marks the literary mode Todorov identifies as 'the uncanny', when the strangeness is scientifically explained'] or total incredulity [which he labels 'the marvellous mode' of the supernatural, which is accepted but not accounted for] would lead us beyond the fantastic. It is hesitation which sustains [the life of the fantastic].'(p. 31). By contrast, Tolkien's understanding of Fantasy and its fantastic mode is radically different, for he rules out the element of lasting hesitation as a mark of ill-made Fantasy: genuine Faërie is the realm whose 'arresting strangeness' is accepted by the reader according to the logical and rational laws of the otherworld (the 'Sub-Creation'), and no 'willing suspension of disbelief' is required ('On Fairy-Stories', p. 132). 'The moment disbelief arises, the spell is broken; the magic, or rather art, has failed.' (p. 132). Thus, Tolkien's concept of Faërie seems to correspond to Todorov's notion of 'the marvellous' rather than 'the fantastic'.

to genius in some cases – won out. (…) The group had altered, in large or small measure, the course of imaginative literature (fantasy, allegory, mythopoeic tales), Christian
theology and philosophy, comparative mythology, and the scholarly study of the *Beowulf*
author, of Dante, Spenser, Milton, courtly love, fairy tale, and epic.[77]

When comparing the Inklings to the Bloomsbury Group, the Zaleskis observe that
although, unlike Bloomsbury, the Inklings had not launched 'those giddy and often glorious assaults upon convention that have found a secure place in the twentieth century's literary canon', they 'have made serious inroads into that canon.'[78]
While Bloomsbury 'now seems part of history', the Zaleskis argue, it is the Inklings,
none the less, who 'continue to shape significant aspects of modern religion and
worldwide culture.'[79] The claim that the impact of the Inklings' legacy is first felt in
'modern religion' as such, and then in 'worldwide culture', including literature, may
come as a surprise, for it is usually the realms of fantasy fiction and literary criticism that are considered the major fields of the Inklingian impact, the lay theology
of Lewis and of Williams, despite its ingenious and inspirational freshness, being
often deemed marginal and amateurish. The Zaleskis' professional and personal
interest in religion, especially Christianity, and in contemporary spiritual writing,
accounts, none the less, for that assertion, and for evaluating the Inklings' impact
first in spiritual terms, and then in purely artistic, and thus also literary, categories.

Indeed, the apologetic fiction, non-fiction, and BBC talks of Lewis, which followed his conversion to theism and then to Christianity; the idiosyncratic Romantic theology of Williams's fiction and non-fiction, based on the principles
of Co-inherence, Exchange and Substitution, which he had derived largely from
St. Paul's epistles; as well as the non-apologetic and not explicitly manifested yet
fundamentally inherent Catholic fabric of Tolkien's mythopoeia and non-fiction,
revealed especially in his essay 'On Fairy-Stories', testify to the considerable religious import of the Inklings' oeuvre, precious to Christians but also to any people
pursuing paths of spiritual development and interested in mysticism, as reflected
in the esoteric inspirations of Williams and Barfield.[80] In my book, notwithstanding, I attempt to approach the legacy of the Inklings in terms of its logocentric
and therapeutic purport, which must not be mistaken for spiritual guidance they
had not claimed, and which is of universal appeal, regardless of the reader's beliefs

---

77 The Zaleskis, *The Fellowship*, pp. 3–4.
78 The Zaleskis, ibid., p. 9.
79 Ibid., p. 10.
80 Barfield endorsed Anthroposophy, a religious philosophy and spiritual science, which
   is discussed, for instance, by the Zaleskis in chapter five, 'Words Have a Soul', in their
   The Fellowship: The Literary Lives of the Inklings, pp. 99–122.

and views. The very fact that I argue for an applicability of logotherapy to the ethos of the Inklings' high fantasy genre outside of any religious system (Victor Frankl, an Austrian Jew, was not a Christian), and that I identify an extension of the Inklings' ethos in the fantasy works of Le Guin, (who is a Taoist and a 'congenital non-Christian'), is because the Inklings' re-humanized fantasy, oriented toward a search for meaning, just like Le Guin's, and just like Frankl's thought, is addressed to everyone.[81] The unique essence of the fantasy works of the Inklings, and also of Ursula K. Le Guin, who has arguably somehow or other continued the tradition of the English 'high fantasy' genre in the US, bridging the Anglo-American realm, is considered further on, and particularly in Chapter Six.

Ursula K. Le Guin and the Inklings

An important assumption of this book which calls for an explanation is that there exists some literary affinity between the fantasy works of Tolkien and Le Guin, despite significant differences resulting, for instance, from their radically dissimilar cultural and historical backgrounds, from Le Guin's interest in non-Christian philosophical systems of Taoism and Buddhism, and from her involvement in feminism.[82] Le Guin came across Tolkien's *The Lord of the Rings* in the mid-1950s, and was 'instantly transfixed':

> Middle-earth has been one of the great kingdoms of this world to me, [she says], and I have gone back to it, as often as to *War and Peace*, I suppose. I was grateful that I was in my twenties when I first read Tolkien and had gone far enough towards finding my

---

81 Le Guin calls herself a 'congenital non-Christian' in her essay 'Dreams Must Explain Themselves' [in:] *Language of the Night. Essays on Fantasy and Science Fiction*, Susan Wood, ed. (New York: Berkley Books, 1979), p. 55.

82 Le Guin admits an influence of Taoism and Buddhism (especially Zen) on her fiction in various places, for instance in an interview 'First Contact: A Talk with U. K. Le Guin', by Ligaya Mishan, *New Yorker*, July 24, 2009; http://www.newyorker.com/online/blogs/bookclub/2009/07/first-contact-a-talk-with-ursula-k-le-guin.html, accessed 23 April 2016. Le Guin has translated Lao Tzu's work *Tao Te Ching – Lao Tzu's Tao Te Ching. A Book about the Way and the Power of the Way* (Boston: Shambhala, 1998). Lao Tzu was an ancient Chinese philosopher, a founder of the philosophical and religious system of Taoism. Le Guin's feminism, best seen in her science fiction novels (where she tends to opt for a gender-free world) and some of her essays, is addressed, for instance, in Margarete Keulen's book *Radical Imagination: Feminist Conceptions of the Future in Ursula Le Guin, Marge Piercy and Sally Miller Gearhart* (Frankfurt am Mein: Peter Lang, 1991).

own voice and way as a writer that I could learn from him (endlessly) without being overwhelmed, overinfluenced by him.[83]

In another place Le Guin expands on the influence which Tolkien's fiction has exerted upon her writing:

I wonder what would have happened if I had been born in 1939 instead of 1929, and had first read Tolkien in my teens, instead of my twenties. That achievement might have overwhelmed me. I am glad I had some sense of my own direction before I read Tolkien.[84]

By the time I read Tolkien, though I had not yet written anything of merit, I was old enough, and had worked long and hard enough at my craft, to be set in my ways: to know my own way. Even the sweep and force of that incredible imagination could not dislodge me from my own little rut and carry me, like Gollum, scuttling and whimpering along behind. So far as *writing* is concerned, I mean. When it comes to *reading*, there's a different matter. I open the book, the great wind blows, the Quest begins, I follow… (…) I reread a great deal, but have lost count only with Dickens, Tolstoy, and Tolkien.[85]

Moreover, Le Guin's essay 'The Child and the Shadow' (1974), written a year after Tolkien's death, provides Le Guin's own definition of fantasy, which seems akin to Tolkien's conception of Faërie, and largely draws on his approach to the genre, as exemplified by his fantasy works frequently cited by Le Guin. Despite its Jungian references connected to the concept of the self and the shadow in fantasy, Le Guin's text somehow corresponds to Tolkien's classical essay propounding his notion of Faërie, that is 'On Fairy-Stories' (1939), a likeness that is examined below and in some other chapters of this book.[86]

---

83 Leonard S. Marcus, *The Wand in the Word: Conversations with Writers of Fantasy* (New York: Candlewick, 2006), p. 96. There is apparently no evidence suggesting an influence exerted by the other Inklings on Le Guin, however in her book *To Live or To Love: The Hero's Goal in the Science Fiction of Ursula K. Le Guin and C. S. Lewis*, Alexandra McGee examines the science fiction of Le Guin, representing to some extent, as McGee claims, a Buddhist spirituality that can be juxtaposed with Lewis's Christian message of his science fiction (Amazon Digital Services, 2012, kindle edition).

84 Le Guin, 'A Citizen of Mondath', [in:] *Language of the Night*, p. 16.

85 Le Guin, 'The Staring Eye', [in:] *Language of the Night*, pp. 162–163.

86 The essay is discussed in more detail in Chapter Six of this book. Although there are many Jungian interpretations of Tolkien's fantasy works (pointing to his use of archetypal symbols and the collective unconscious, and their impact on the readers' subconscious), Tolkien himself had never encouraged any psychological or psychologizing reading of his tales.

Interestingly, it also appears that Le Guin and Tolkien share to some extent the same source of reference, which is Lord Dunsany's fantasy fiction, acknowledged by Le Guin as an influence, and probably never named by Tolkien as such, yet traced by some critics in Tolkien's works.[87] John D. Rateliff argues that Tolkien once presented Clyde S. Kilby with a copy of Dunsany's *The Book of Wonder* (1912) as a kind of preparation for Kilby's aiding Tolkien in compiling *The Silmarillion* in the 1960s; and that Tolkien's poem 'The Mewlips', included in *The Adventures of Tom Bombadil,* might be a recasting of Dunsany's story 'Hoard of the Gibbelins' (a part of *The Book of Wonder*).[88] Tolkien 'never referred to Dunsany publicly', Shippey says, yet he probably alluded to Dunsany's' tale of the rival idols Chu-Bu and Sheemish in one of his letters of 1972.[89] Lyon Sprague de Camp remarks, however, that Tolkien commented disparagingly on Dunsany's 'Distressing Tale of Thangobrind', also collected in *The Book of Wonder*.[90] Shippey notes that by 1937 Tolkien 'had read widely enough in literary fantasies of Lord Dunsany to feel competent to judge his nomenclature unfavourably in his letters', which does not perhaps come as a surprise if one considers Tolkien's particular passion and care for philology, and his friendly but critical remarks exchanged, for instance, with Lewis, suggesting frequently some philological correction.[91]

Le Guin, in turn, refers to Dunsany as an important influence:

Dunsany's influence was wholly benign, and I never tried much to imitate him, in my prolific and derivative adolescent scribblings. I must have known already that this sort of thing is inimitable. He was not a model to me, but a liberator, a guide.[92]

From the age of nine, I was writing fantasy, and I never wrote anything else. It wasn't in the least anybody else's fantasy. I read whatever imaginative fiction I could get hold of

---

87 Edward Plunkett, 18th Baron of Dunsany (1878–1957) was an Irish writer, playwright and poet, most famous for his fantasy works, among which *The Book of Wonder* of 1912 (a collection of stories) and his novel *The King of Elfland's Daughter* of 1924 are probably the most notable.

88 Rateliff, *The History of the Hobbit,* p. 30.

89 Shippey, 'Literary Influences: Nineteenth and Twentieth Century' [in:] *J. R. R. Tolkien Encyclopaedia: Scholarship and Critical Assessment*, p. 375.

90 Lyon Sprague de Camp, *Literary Swordsmen and Sorcerers: The Makers of Heroic Fantasy* (Sauk City: Arkham House, 1976), p. 243.

91 *The Letters of J. R. R. Tolkien*, p. 26. Shippey, 'Literary Influences', p. 375. Tolkien advised Lewis on some philological matters, for instance with regard to the latter's first science fiction novel *Out of the Silent Planet* of 1939 (cf. *Letters*, p. 36).

92 Le Guin, 'A Citizen of Mondath', p. 16.

then – *Astounding Stories*, and this and that: Dunsany was the master, the man with the keys to the gates of horn and ivory, so far as I knew. (…) [But] I never tried to write like Dunsany, nor even like *Astounding*, once I was older than twelve. I had somewhere to go and, as I saw it, I had to get there by myself.[93]

What Tolkien acknowledges is his debt to George MacDonald (1824–1905), a Scottish writer, poet, and Christian minister, often called 'the grandfather of the Inklings', who had inspired Tolkien, C. S. Lewis, and Charles Williams, (and also Lewis Carroll, Edith Nesbit, W. H. Auden and G. K. Chesterton, among others).[94] In her essay on Charles Williams, Kerryl Lynne Henderson actually calls MacDonald 'a kind of 19th century proto-Inkling', acknowledging the Inklings' great indebtedness to his legacy.[95] C. S. Lewis, on whom MacDonald's writings and theological thought had made a huge impact, said of MacDonald in a Preface to the anthology of MacDonald's works, 'I have never concealed the fact that I regarded him as my master; indeed I fancy I have never written a book in which I did not quote from him.'[96] In the same Preface Lewis also refers to his first reading of MacDonald's *Phantastes*, which shaped his creative thinking: 'what it actually did to me [Lewis confesses] was to convert, even to baptize… my imagination.'[97] MacDonald's preoccupation with Christianity and fairy-stories had made its imprint on Tolkien as well, for he admits that MacDonald achieved 'stories of power and beauty when he succeeded, as in *The Golden Key* (which he called a fairy-tale); and even when he partly failed, as in *Lilith* (which he called a romance).'[98]

Another contemporary influence, which descended from MacDonald's legacy and is reflected in the Inklings' works and philosophy, was that of Gilbert Keith

---

93 Le Guin, 'The Staring Eye', pp. 162–163. *Astounding Stories* is an American science fiction magazine, the longest running continuously published magazine of the genre (since 1930).

94 Cf. Tolkien, *Letters*, Letter no. 31, 'On Fairy-Stories', p. 125; also Gisela Kreglinger, 'MacDonald, George (1824–1905), [in:] *J. R. R. Tolkien Encyclopedia: Scholarship and Critical Assessment*, p. 399; also Donald T. Williams's *Mere Humanity: G. K. Chesterton, C. S. Lewis, and J. R. R. Tolkien on the Human Condition* (Nashville: B&H Books, 2006).

95 Kerryl Lynne Henderson, '"It is Love that I am Seeking": Charles Williams and *The Silver Stair*', [in:] *Charles Williams: A Celebration*, Brian Horne, ed. (London: Gracewing, 1995), pp. 131–152, 131.

96 C. S. Lewis, *Preface* to *George MacDonald - An Anthology. 365 Readings*, C. S. Lewis, ed. (London: HarperCollins, 2009), p. 20.

97 Lewis, ibid., p. 18.

98 Tolkien, 'On Fairy-Stories', p. 125.

Chesterton's (1874–1936).[99] Tolkien refers to Chesterton's works and ideas many times in his essay 'On Fairy-Stories', for instance to Chestertonian Fantasy or 'Mooreeffoc' (coffee-room read backwards), and to Chesterton's understanding of children's mentality.[100] As far as Chesterton's impact on Tolkien is concerned, it might be relevant to mention Alison Milbank's study *Chesterton and Tolkien as Theologians*, in which she argues that Tolkien was 'a Catholic writer steeped in Chestertonian ideas and sharing his literary-theological poetics', regarded by Milbank as redemptive, by virtue of its cathartic and consoling power rising from the writers' deeply Augustinian fictional worlds.[101] Although Milbank refers to both writers as 'theologians', (a name which, when given himself, Tolkien would most probably have dismissed as preposterous, for he disliked and distrusted amateur theology, including Lewis's), she makes interesting observations about a shared foundation of Chesterton's and Tolkien's works that lies in a dynamic Catholic theology of creation and incarnation, and that has contributed much to the contemporary revival of Christian imagination.[102]

In his book *Literary Converts. Spiritual Inspiration in an Age of Unbelief*, Joseph Pearce also focuses on the Christian basis of Tolkien's, Chesterton's, and also Lewis's writings, discussing their lives and works, in the light of their or their family's conversion to Christianity, which, to Pearce, had informed the writers' oeuvre.[103] David Langford draws another parallel, marking several stylistic and textual similarities between Chesterton's fantasy *The Ball and the Cross* and Lewis's *That Hideous Strength*, noting his preference for Chesterton's ending of the novel (Lewis's *deus-ex-machina* fire from heaven was most probably inspired by Charles Williams's style, disliked by Tolkien).[104]

---

99 Gilbert Keith Chesterton (1874–1936) was an English writer, poet, dramatist, lay theologian, literary and art critic.

100 Tolkien, 'On Fairy-Stories', pp. 146 and 136.

101 Alison Milbank, *Chesterton and Tolkien as Theologians. The Fantasy of the Real* (Bloomsbury T&T Clark, 2009), p. 41.

102 Milbank, ibid., p. 45.

103 In the book Joseph Pearce presents a number of other English writers cum Christian converts of the late 19th c., and early 20th c., namely: Oscar Wilde, Evelyn Waugh, Malcolm Muggeridge, Graham Greene, George Bernard Shaw, H. G. Wells, Hilaire Belloc, Dorothy Sayers, and T. S. Eliot.

104 David Langford, 'Digging Up the Future: On G. K. Chesterton' [in:] *Up Through an Empty House of Stairs. Reviews and Essays 1980–2002* (Rockville: Wildside Press, 2003), p. 48. *That Hideous Strength* had influenced, for instance, George Orwell, who wrote its review in 1945: 'The Scientist Takes Over', [in:] *Manchester Evening News*, 16 August 1945; reprinted in *The Complete Works of George Orwell*, Peter Davison,

Returning to some of Le Guin's literary inspirations, which might be akin to those of Tolkien's and the other Inklings', it is worthwhile to observe that, although Le Guin does not mention McDonald or Chesterton among the writers who have influenced her, there is some evidence of her familiarity with and, perhaps, also interest in those writers' legacy. The first proof could be the fact that Le Guin has written an introduction to a 2011 Puffin Classics edition of George MacDonald's famous story *The Princess and the Goblin*, (which was one of Tolkien's childhood favourites); another that there exist some similarities between MacDonald's Curdie books and Le Guin's Earthsea series.[105] As for Chesterton, some critics find affinity between his and Le Guin's approach to fantasy and children: Katharine Kimbriel suggests, for instance, that in her essay 'Why Are Americans Afraid of Dragons' 'Le Guin understood Chesterton's comment about children and dragons', saying that 'children do not need fairy tales to tell them that dragons exist – they already know that. Fairy tales tell children that dragons can be killed.'[106] David Langford, in turn, implies that Le Guin uses a Chestertonian technique of holding all improbabilities together by 'careful touches of realistic observation' and 'love of paradox', for example in order to build the climactic confrontation in the science fiction novel *The Eye of the Heron*.[107] Furthermore, in her essay 'Science Fiction and Mrs Brown', Le Guin, according to Langford, shares Chesterton's conviction that real, commonplace people are needed if fantasy worlds are to work, because 'without the transmuting touch of ordinary homeliness they are mere cardboard.'[108] That seems to have been also Tolkien's, Lewis's, and, generally speaking, the Inklings' conviction, who valued the simplicity and humbleness of ordinary life above all. In the light of a greater or lesser indebtedness of the Inklings' and of Le Guin's works to George MacDonald and G. K. Chesterton, it might appear that a re-discovery of MacDonald's and Chesterton's fantasies is long overdue.

When attempting to view Le Guin in the context of MacDonald's, Chesterton's, and the Inklings' fantasy legacy, one must not fail to note many differences,

---

ed., vol. XVII, 1998, no. 2720 (first half), pp. 250–251, whose echoes could be traced in his *Nineteen Eighty-Four*.

105   Cordelia Sherman, 'The Princess and the Wizard: The Fantasy Worlds of Ursula K. Le Guin and George MacDonald' [in:] *Children's Literature Association Quarterly*, Volume 12, Number 1, Spring 1987; pp. 24–28 | 10.1353/chq.0.0163.

106   Katharine Kimbriel, 'Fantasy is the Language of the Night', 5 December 2012, http://bookviewcafe.com /blog/2012/12/05/fantasy-is-the-language-of-the-night-on-ursu-la-k-le-guin/, accessed 25 April 2016.

107   Langford, 'Digging Up the Future: On G. K. Chesterton', p. 50.

108   Ibid., p. 50.

resulting first of all from her inherently non-Christian upbringing and life. 'I was raised as irreligious as a jackrabbit', Le Guin declares; and in another place admits, 'I'm an atheist', always distancing herself from explicitly Christian references made by the Inklings, especially by Lewis in his fantasy allegories and lay-theologian apologetics.[109] Of Tolkien's works she says, 'evil beings [in Tolkien's fiction] are only a metaphor for the evil in our lives; he never casts people into the outer darkness as Lewis [or Williams, one might add,] enjoyed doing.'[110] Although critical of Lewis's Christian 'hot-gospelling' that pervaded his works after his conversion of 1929, Le Guin, none the less, seems to share Lewis's approach to writing fantasy, in that it starts with a compelling image conjured up in the writer's imagination. Lewis explains the origins of his Narnian heptalogy as follows:

> Everything began with images; a faun carrying an umbrella, a queen on a sledge, a magnificent lion. At first there wasn't even anything Christian about them; that element pushed itself in of its own accord.[111]

And so does Le Guin, referring to her fantasy fiction:

> A person is seen, seen at a certain distance, usually in a landscape. The place is there, the person is there. I didn't invent him; I didn't make her up: she or he is there. And my business is to get there too.[112]

Thus, as Elizabeth Cummins explains, 'writing a novel for Le Guin begins with an image of place and person. Place and person are somehow related; when Le Guin sees one, she also sees the other.'[113]

Sharing her visual sensitivity as a source of writing with Lewis, Le Guin follows also Tolkien in his preoccupation with words and meaning (Tolkien does not commence writing with working on images but on words that invite story telling), although Tolkien's philological expertise and passion is out of her league. A superb philologist and myth-maker, Tolkien 'had been inside language', as Lewis observed

---

109   Maya Jaggi, 'The Magician' with fragments of an interview with Le Guin,'[in:] *The Guardian*, Saturday, 17 December 2005; accessed 25 April 2016, http://www.theguardian.com/books/2005/dec/17/booksforchildrenandteenagers.shopping.

110   Ibid. 'Hot gospelling' is a term used first probably by Dame Helen Gardner in an obituary she wrote upon Lewis's death, as quoted by Colin Duriez in *The Gift of Friendship*, p. 148.

111   C. S. Lewis, 'Sometimes Fairy Stories May Say Best What's To Be Said', [in:] *Of Other Worlds. Essays and Stories,* (London: Geoffrey Bles, 1986), p. 36.

112   Le Guin, 'Science Fiction and Mrs Brown', [in:] *The Language of the Night*, p. 110.

113   Elizabeth Cummins, *Understanding Ursula K. Le Guin* (Columbia: University of South Carolina Press, 1993), p. 5.

of him.[114] Le Guin also seems to have been delving into the depths of language, so that the power of her protagonists, especially in her Earthsea hexalogy, rests in their mastery of words, which have the power of making and unmaking; binding and unbinding.[115] To know the true name of a person, a living thing or an object in Earthsea (not merely their use name) is to have complete control over them, to be a master or mistress of their life and death; hence a voluntary revealing of one's true name is an act of absolute trust. 'Naming has been the essence of the art-magic as practised in Earthsea', Le Guin admits.[116] Language is of central importance to the Earthsea mythos and, according to Le Guin, to poetry and fantasy fiction in particular. She argues that:

> A writer is a person who cares what words mean, what they say, how they say it. Writers know words are their way towards truth and freedom, and so they use them with care, with thought, with fear, with delight. By using words well they strengthen their souls. Story-tellers and poets spend their lives learning that skill and art of using words well. And their words make the souls of their readers stronger, brighter, deeper.[117]

Language is the tool of writerly (sub)creation and an instrument of (literary) art, which not only demands a responsible use but also artistic excellence and a virtuoso performance, for it conveys meaning that verbally creates the fabric of a literary work.[118] Although her language is simple, Le Guin takes great care of how she uses it, so that, according to Susan Wood, Le Guin's writing is like 'casting word-spells'.[119] Le Guin herself observes that:

> The artist deals with what cannot be said in words. The artist whose medium is fiction does this in words. The novelist says in words what cannot be said in words. Words can be used thus paradoxically because they have, along with a semiotic usage, a symbolic or metaphoric usage. (They also have a sound - a fact the linguistic positivists take no interest in. A sentence or paragraph is like a chord or harmonic sequence in music: its

---

114 Carpenter, *J. R. R. Tolkien: A Biography* (London: Houghton Mifflin Company, 2000), p. 144.

115 The power of words appears in the very first fantasy story written by Le Guin and published in 1964, 'The Word of Unbinding', which later developed into *A Wizard of Earthsea* and the subsequent parts of the Earthsea hexalogy.

116 Le Guin, 'Dreams Must Explain Themselves', [in:] *The Language of the Night*, p. 42.

117 Le Guin, quoted by Cummins, *Understanding Ursula K. Le Guin*, p. 48.

118 Sub-Creation is the term used by Tolkien in 'On Fairy-Stories', pp. 139–140.

119 Susan Wood, 'Introduction' to *The Language of the Night*, p. 8. The last phrase comes from Le Guin's essay 'Why Are Americans Afraid of Dragons?' [in:] *The Language of the Night*, p. 35.

meaning may be more clearly understood by the attentive ear, even though it is read in silence, than by the attentive intellect).[120]

Interestingly, Le Guin points at the interartistic nature of language, involving its musical quality and internal harmony, which to her appears superior to its purely intellectual content. The affinity between language and mental pictures conjured up by verbal metaphors and symbols, as well as between language and music, is of vital importance to literary art, and particularly to poetry and fantasy fiction, as addressed in some detail in Chapter Four of this book, especially with regard to Roman Ingarden's theory of a literary work of art.

Returning to the creative and artistic power of language, revealed in a singular fashion in fantasy literature, one must refer to Tolkien, a humble virtuoso of language and a passionate philologist, who suggests that Fantasy is a 'sub-creative art which plays strange tricks with the world and all that is in it, combining nouns and redistributing adjectives', and that 'it was in fairy-stories that [he] first divined the potency of words'.[121] 'In such "fantasy", as it is called,' he remarks, 'new form is made; Faërie begins; Man becomes a sub-creator,' for the primary creator of everything that exists is, as he believes, the divine Maker, whose creative genius inspires man to little acts of sub-creation, an endless ripple sent by the Almighty's matchless artistry.[122] Thus, 'to ask what is the origin of stories (however qualified) is to ask what is the origin of language and of the mind', Tolkien asserts.[123]

Furthermore, Tolkien argues that 'Escape is one of the main functions of fairy-stories', yet warns against the common misinterpretation and misuse of the term, which often causes confusion:

I do not accept the tone of scorn and pity with which 'escape' is now so often used: a tone for which the uses of the word outside literary criticism give no warrant at all. In what the misusers of Escape are fond of calling Real Life, Escape is evidently as a rule very practical, and may even be heroic. (…) [However], [w]hy should a man be scorned, if, finding himself in prison, he tries to get out and go home? Or if, when he cannot do so, he thinks and talks about other topics than jailers and prison-walls? The world outside has not become less real because the prisoner cannot see it. In using Escape in this way the critics have chosen the wrong word, and, what is more, they are confusing, not always by sincere error, the Escape of the Prisoner with the Flight of the Deserter. Just so a Party-spokesman

---

120   Le Guin, Introduction to *The Left Hand of Darkness* (New York: Ace Books, 1987), p. 4.

121   Tolkien, 'On Fairy-Stories', pp. 143 and 147.

122   Ibid., p. 122.

123   Ibid., p. 119.

might have labelled departure from the misery of the Führer's or any other Reich and even criticism of it as treachery.[124]

Similarly to the Inklings, Le Guin does not miscast fantasy as escapist or second-rate, or merely 'children's lit', but regards it as a 'natural language of the spiritual journey and the struggles of good and evil in the soul', which may help readers 'arrive, in a peculiar way, at the truth' about themselves and the world:

> Fantasy is true; it isn't factual, but it is true. Children know that. Adults know it too, and that is precisely why many of them are afraid of fantasy. They know that its truth challenges, even threatens, all that is false, all that is phony, unnecessary, and trivial in the life they have let themselves be forced into living. They are afraid of dragons because they are afraid of freedom. (…) It is by such statements as, 'Once upon a time there was a dragon', or 'In a hole in the ground there lived a hobbit' – it is by such beautiful non-facts that we fantastic human beings arrive, in our peculiar fashion, at the truth.[125]

Tolkien, who 'had been into the dragons' lair', also writes about children and dragons in his seminal essay 'On Fairy-Stories':[126]

> [Being a child] I never imagined that the dragon was of the same order as [for instance] the horse. (…) The dragon had the trade-mark *Of Faërie* written plain upon him. In whatever world he had his being it was an Otherworld. Fantasy, the making or glimpsing of Other-worlds, was the heart of the desire of Faërie. I desired dragons with a profound desire.[127]

As for children and fairy-stories, Tolkien continues, that rather unfortunate and simplistic association 'is an accident of our domestic history':

> Fairy-stories have in the modern lettered world been relegated to the nursery, as shabby or old-fashioned furniture is relegated to the playroom, primarily because adults do not want it, and do not mind if it is misused. (…) In my opinion fairy-stories should not be specially associated with children. They are associated with them: naturally, because children are human and fairy-stories are a natural human taste (though not necessarily a universal one); accidentally, because fairy-stories are a large part of the literary lumber that in latter-day Europe has been stuffed away in attics; unnaturally, because of erroneous sentiment about children, a sentiment that seems to increase with the decline in children.[128]

'If fairy-story as a kind is worth reading at all', Tolkien argues, then 'it is worthy to be written for and read by adults.'[129] Adults should 'read fairy-stories as a

---

124 Ibid., p. 148.
125 Le Guin, 'Why Are Americans Afraid of Dragons?' pp. 34–35.
126 Carpenter, *J. R. R. Tolkien: A Biography*, p. 144.
127 Tolkien, 'On Fairy-Stories' [in:] *The Monsters and the Critics and Other Essays*, p. 135.
128 Tolkien, ibid., pp. 130 and 136.
129 Tolkien, ibid., p. 137.

natural branch of literature – neither playing at being children, nor pretending to be choosing for children, nor being boys [or girls] who would not grow up.'[130] 'The value of fairy-stories is thus not, in my opinion, to be found by considering children in particular', Tolkien concludes.[131]

Worth noting is, nevertheless, the fact that Tolkien's first readers were his children, and that *The Hobbit,* his first published book set in Arda, was published by George Allen and Unwin thanks to a favourable review of Stanley Unwin's ten-year-old son, Rayner (1925–2000), who subsequently participated in preparing *The Lord of the Rings* for publication.[132] Tolkien's approach to the books of Faërie seems to reiterate George MacDonald's opinion, who wrote 'not for children, but for the child-like, whether they be of five, or fifty, or seventy-five.'[133]

Although C. S. Lewis does not avail himself of Tolkien's nomenclature and uses the term 'the Fantastic or Mythical' instead of Faërie, his message is essentially like Tolkien's (and MacDonald's):

> The Fantastic or Mythical is a Mode available at all ages for some readers; for others, at none. At all ages, if it is well used by the author and meets the right reader, it has the same power: to generalise while remaining concrete, to present in palpable form not concepts or even experiences but whole classes of experience, and to throw off irrelevancies. But at its best it can do more; it can give us experiences we have never had and thus, instead of 'commenting on life', can add to it. I am speaking, of course, about the thing itself, not my own attempts at it.[134]

Addressing the relationship between fairy-stories and children, Lewis admits,

> When I was ten, I read fairy tales in secret and would have been ashamed if I had been found doing so. Now that I am fifty, I read them openly. When I became a man I put away childish things, including the fear of childishness and the desire to be very grown up.[135]

Furthermore, referring to *The Lord of the Rings,* called sometimes 'a fairy story for adults' or 'an epic fairy tale', Lewis expands on the problem of children's and adults' stories and comments on Tolkien's own remarks:[136]

---

130   Tolkien, ibid., p. 138.
131   Tolkien, ibid., p. 131.
132   Cf. Tolkien's *Letters,* e.g., nos. 125 and 140.
133   Tolkien, 'On Fairy-Stories', p. 129. George MacDonald, *The Gifts of the Child Christ and Other Stories and Fairy Tales,* Glenn Edward Sadler, ed. (Grand Rapids: Wm. B. Eerdmans Publishing Company, 1996), p. 25.
134   Lewis, 'Sometimes Fairy Stories May Say Best What's To Be Said', p. 37.
135   Lewis, 'On Three Ways of Writing for Children', [in:] *Of Other Worlds,* p. 25.
136   John D. Davenport, for instance, regards *The Lord of the Rings* as 'an epic fairy tale' in his 'Happy Endings and Religious Hope: The Lord of the Rings as an Epic Fairy

You will notice that I have throughout spoken of Fairy Tales, not 'children's stories'. Professor J. R. R. Tolkien in *The Lord of the Rings* has shown that the connection between fairy tales and children is not nearly so close as publishers and educationalists think. Many children don't like them and many adults do. The truth is, as he says, that they are now associated with children because they are out of fashion with adults; have in fact retired to the nursery as old furniture used to retire there, not because the children had begun to like it but because their elders had ceased to like it. (…) I never wrote down to anyone; and whether the opinion condemns or acquits my own work, it certainly is my opinion that a book worth reading only in childhood is not worth reading even then.[137]

Understanding the realm of Faërie in a manner similar to Tolkien's and Lewis's, Le Guin, a mother of three, adds, 'sure, it's simple, writing for kids; just as simple as bringing them up.'[138] And she reiterates mockingly how some critics and writers conceive of writing a book that is meant for children:

All you do is take all the sex out, and use little short words, and little dumb ideas, and don't be too scary, and be sure there's a happy ending. Right? [No, not at all]. (…) Kids will devour vast amounts of garbage (…) but they are not like adults: they have not yet learned to eat plastic.[139]

Children can be quicker at recognizing the value of fairy tales, Le Guin suggests, yet the stories should not be written for them exclusively.[140] 'Fairy-stories banished in this way, cut off from a full adult art,' Tolkien warns, 'would in the end be ruined; indeed in so far as they have been so banished, they have been ruined', just like a 'beautiful table, a good picture, or a useful machine (such as a microscope) would be defaced or broken if it were left long unregarded in a schoolroom.'[141]

Le Guin's understanding of fantasy genre, which appears akin to Tolkien's vision of Faërie, is what can perhaps justify placing her in the line of his and the Inklings' literary successors. Born in Berkeley, California, in 1929, when Tolkien and Lewis were in their thirties, Le Guin could chronologically be placed as an heiress to Tolkien's (and the Inklings') legacy. Interestingly, her paternal ancestors, like Tolkien's, had come from Germany (from the German village of Kroebern,

---

Tale' [in:] *The Lord of the Rings and Philosophy: One Book to Rule Them All*, Gregory Bassham, and Eric Bronson, eds. (Chicago: Open Court, 2003), pp. 204–218.

137 Lewis, 'Sometimes Fairy Stories May Say Best What's To Be Said', p. 36.
138 Le Guin, 'Dreams Must Explain Themselves', [in:] *The Language of the Night*, p. 44.
139 Le Guin, ibid., p. 44.
140 Le Guin, ibid., p. 45.
141 Tolkien, 'On Fairy-Stories', p. 131.

hence her maiden name Kroeber).[142] The youngest child of Theodora Kracaw-Kroeber (1897–1979, a psychologist and anthropologist, who in her sixties wrote two books about the last surviving native Indian of the Californian Yahi tribe, Ishi) and Alfred Kroeber (1876–1960, a cultural anthropologist, who studied the tribe's history), Le Guin had majored in French and Italian Renaissance literature, and in 1952 won a Fulbright scholarship to complete a doctoral thesis on the works of a Walloon poet Jean Lemaire de Belges (c. 1473–c. 1525), leaving for Paris and London.[143]

However, Le Guin abandoned the prospects of academic career having married a fellow Fulbright student and given birth successively to three children, while assisting her French husband, Charles, a historian, in earning his doctoral degree. What might make Le Guin somehow affiliated with the Inklings is their shared interest in myth (the Norse lore in the case of Tolkien, Lewis, and Le Guin, and the native American Indian and Chinese heritage for Le Guin), as well as in medieval and early Renaissance literature. When it comes to Norse myths, so important to Tolkien's and Lewis's mind-sets, their influence can also be traced in some of Le Guin's works, especially in her first novel, *Rocannon's World* (1966), where she mingles science fiction with fantasy genre, and reiterates the story of Freya, the Norse goddess, and her Brisingamen necklace, drawing on Padraic Colum's *Children of Odin* (1920) and on the Eddas (Icelandic works of Norse mythology: *The Poetic Edda* and *Prose Edda*).[144]

Faërie

In this book I approach fantasy genre as the realm of Faërie, following Tolkien's understanding and specification thereof, according to which Faërie is the 'realm of fairy-story', 'a perilous land [in which there] are pitfalls for the unwary and dungeons for the overbold.'[145] It is the 'land full of wonder, but not of information',

---

142 Her maternal ancestors, named Kracaw or Kraków, had probably come from Kraków and were Polish, as Elizabeth Cummins suggests in her *Understanding Ursula K. Le Guin*, p. 15.

143 Cummins, ibid., p. 4. Theodora Krakaw-Kroeber was first married to Clifton Brown, and after his death to Alfred Kroeber. Theodora's two books about Ishi are: *Ishi in Two Worlds: A Biography of the Last Wild Indian in North America* (1961); *Ishi, Last of His Tribe* (1964).

144 Cf. Le Guin's introduction to the 1977 edition of *Rocannon's World* (New York: Ace Books, 1977).

145 Tolkien, 'On Fairy-Stories', p. 109. Tolkien seems to have introduced the term Faërie meaning the 'supernatural kingdom, or Elfland', borrowed from the Old French word

marked by 'richness and strangeness'; 'wide and deep and high and filled with many things: all manner of beasts and birds are found there; shoreless seas and stars uncounted; beauty that is an enchantment, and an ever-present peril; both joy and sorrow as sharp as swords.'[146]

Moreover, as Tolkien observes:

> Faërie cannot be caught in a net of words; for it is one of its qualities to be indescribable, though not imperceptible. (…) Faërie itself may perhaps most nearly be translated by Magic – but it is magic of a peculiar mood and power, at the furthest pole from the vulgar devices of the laborious, scientific, magician. There is one proviso: if there is any satire present in the tale, one thing must not be made fun of, the magic itself. That must in that story be taken seriously, neither laughed at nor explained away. (…) A fairy-story is one which touches on or uses Faërie, whatever its own main purpose may be: satire, adventure, morality, fantasy (…) but its borders are inevitably dubious. (…) It is at any rate essential to a genuine fairy-story, as distinct from the employment of this form for lesser or debased purposes, that it should be presented as 'true'.[147]

'The magic of Faërie is not an end in itself', Tolkien explains, as 'its virtue is in its operations: among these are the satisfaction of certain primordial human desires'; namely: 'to survey the depths of space and time' and 'to hold communion with other living things'.[148] As to the latter, it is one of the essential assets of the stories 'out of or about the past', as contrasted with modern fiction of sterile urban artificiality. 'The notion that motor-cars are more "alive" than, say, centaurs or dragons is curious', Tolkien remarks; and 'that they are more "real" than, say, horses, is pathetically absurd. How real, how startlingly alive is a factory chimney compared with an elm tree: poor obsolete thing, insubstantial dream of an escapist!'[149]

Tolkien defines Fantasy as a 'natural human activity', a creative faculty 'founded upon the hard recognition that things are so in the world as it appears under the sun; on a recognition of fact, but not a slavery to it.'[150] When abused, Fantasy is superseded by Morbid Delusion.[151] Fantasy 'aspires to Enchantment, or the elvish-craft', and when fantasy is successful, it approaches Enchantment most nearly of all

---

'fairie', as used around 1300, cf. *Online Etymology Dictionary*, Douglas Harper, ed., 2001–2016, http://www.etymonline.com/index.php?term=faerie, accessed 23 April 2016.

146 Tolkien, 'On Fairy-Stories', p. 114. The qualities of Faërie that I interpret as therapeutic are discussed in more detail in Chapter Six of this book.

147 Tolkien, ibid., pp. 114 and 116.

148 Ibid., p. 116.

149 Ibid., p. 149.

150 Ibid., p. 144.

151 Ibid., p. 144.

forms of human art.[152] Yet, 'Fantasy is a rational not an irrational activity,' Tolkien claims, not to be confounded with mental disorders, delusion or hallucination.[153] 'Uncorrupted [Fantasy] does not seek delusion, nor bewitchment and domination; it seeks shared enrichment, partners in making and delight, not slaves.'[154]

Hence, from the pure order of fairy-stories, which dwell in Faërie and rest upon Fantasy, Tolkien rules out 'any story that uses the machinery of Dream, the dreaming of actual human sleep, to explain the apparent occurrence of its marvels' (for instance Lewis Carroll's *Alice* stories); any story that explains the enchantment away by means of a 'preposterous and incredible' scientific device, such as a time machine (for instance H. G. Wells's *Time Machine*); beast-fables, where 'the animal form is only a mas upon a human face, a device of the satirist or the preacher' (e.g., G. Chaucer's *The Nun's Priests' Tale*); and last but not least, stories that have 'any allegorical *significatio*.'[155] Due to Tolkien's reservedness towards the use of scientific and dream machinery, and also because of a narrow scope of this book, which strives to focus on fantasy at its purest, according to Tolkien's discernment, Lewis's and Le Guin's science fiction works, although a vital part of their literary output, are not included in the study.

As far as science fiction is concerned, Tolkien warns that when written by 'prophets who foretell (and many often seem to yearn for) a world like one big glass-roofed railway-station', 'who will use this freedom [of imagination] mainly, it would appear, in order to play with mechanical toys in the soon-cloying game of moving at high speed,' then the genre may become 'the most escapist form of all literature.'[156] Just like fantasy, science fiction can 'be carried to excess', 'can be ill-done' and 'put to evil uses', and 'may even delude the minds out of which it came; but of what human thing in this fallen world is that not true?' Tolkien enquires rhetorically.[157] It needs to be remembered, though, that Tolkien himself

---

152 Ibid., p. 143.
153 Ibid., p. 139.
154 Ibid., p. 143.
155 Tolkien, ibid., pp. 116–118. Tolkien's dislike of allegory is well-known. He allowed 'applicability', though, which he understood as follows: 'I cordially dislike allegory in all its manifestations, and always have done so since I grew old and wary enough to detect its presence. I much prefer history – true or feigned– with its varied applicability to the thought and experience of readers. I think that many confuse applicability with allegory, but the one resides in the freedom of the reader, and the other in the purposed domination of the author'; 'Foreword to the Second Edition' of *The Lord of the Rings* (London: HarperCollins, 1996), p. xvi.
156 Tolkien, 'On Fairy-Stories', pp. 150–151.
157 Tolkien, ibid., p. 144.

commenced writing a 'time journey' tale in 1936, which was to accompany Lewis's 'space journey' novel (later titled *Out of the Silent Planet*, the first part of
Lewis's science fiction trilogy, published in 1938), so that there would have been
two 'excursionary thrillers' as the two Inklings had hoped – the work that Tolkien, unfortunately, never completed.[158]

Elizabeth Cummins, one of Le Guin's biographers and critics, seems to expand on the difference between fantasy and science fiction, which might shed
some light on Tolkien's reservations towards the latter:

> The worlds of science fiction and fantasy literature offer readers a chance to stretch their
> minds by experiencing an alternate world and then a chance to return to consensus real-
> ity with a changed perspective. (…) Science fiction and fantasy belong at opposite ends
> of the spectrum because they differ in how they derive their alternate worlds from con-
> sensus reality. Science fiction's alternate world is derived by supposing a radical difference
> from some organized body of scientific knowledge, including both the 'hard' sciences
> (such as physics, chemistry, or geology), and the 'soft' sciences (such as anthropology,
> psychology, or history). The radical difference may be the existence of the colossal sen-
> tient computer, a time machine, a culture without war, or a human race in which each
> individual can function sexually [androgynously] as either male or female. Once this
> difference is posited, however, the work rigorously uses science – both the body of knowl-
> edge and the method of inquiry – to make the world seem possible.

Cummins's commentary on the differences and affinities between fantasy and
science fiction may help to account for Tolkien's preference of the former, which
he associates with Faërie. Cummins seems to view fantasy in a Tolkienesque way,
adopted also by Le Guin, as a genre whose 'alternate world is derived by supposing a radical difference from a rational foundation of all knowledge,' which
does not mean negating rational thinking, as its standards are very rigorous in
genuine fantasy (otherwise it would never succeed), but by supposing the existence of otherworldly elements or forces which suffuse the daily activities of the
imaginary world.[159] 'The radical difference may be [Faërie] characters, such as
hobbits, [elves, dwarves, goblins], talking animals, [talking trees], ancient and
wise dragons, or magic-workers such as sorcerers and wizards,' embedded in the
depths of space and time, in some pre-industrial age.[160] Thus, 'compared to the
world of consensus reality, science fiction creates a world that might be possible,'

---

158 Tolkien, *Letters*, letter 24, p. 38. Elements of time travel are used by Tolkien in his
     unfinished story *The Lost Road*, edited by Christopher Tolkien and published in *The
     Lost Road and Other Writings* in 1987.
159 Cummins, *Understanding Ursula K. Le Guin*, p. 7.
160 Cummins, ibid., p. 8.

Cummins concludes, expressing probably also Le Guin's view; 'whereas fantasy creates an alternate world that is possible.'[161] Still, as Susan Wood remarks, 'science fiction and fantasy [may] overlap so closely as to render any effort at exclusive definition useless.'[162]

Le Guin argues that 'science fiction is the mythology of the modern world', and observes that:

> All fiction is metaphor. Science fiction is metaphor. What sets it apart from older forms of fiction seems to be its use of new metaphors, drawn from certain great dominants of our contemporary life - science, all the sciences, and technology, and the relativistic and the historical outlook, among them. Space travel is one of these metaphors; so is an alternative society, an alternative biology; the future is another. The future, in fiction, is a metaphor. A metaphor for what? If I could have said it non-metaphorically, I would not have written all these words and [these science fiction] novels.[163]

This reminds of Lewis's remark concerning fantasy tales and claiming that 'sometimes fairy stories may say best what's to be said', by virtues of their timeless, archetypal, universal and moral nature.[164]

Although her fantasy works differ considerably from those of the Inklings', Le Guin could perhaps be viewed as a writer who approaches fantasy genre in a way similar to the Inklings; namely, she regards fantasy as the highest and most ambitious form of man's art, whose otherworldliness, in order to be convincing, is founded upon sounder realism than that of any realistic novel, and which is meant to tell the truth about people and the world, without mockery, parody, abuse, and commodification of the fantastic.[165] Fantasy is about reality, especially its psychological or even spiritual aspect, although it may not be the consensus reality, she seems to suggest.[166]

Following Shippey's reading of the past century's literary history with his almost panoptic approach to the fantastic, one may only wonder whether fantasy or the fantastic is the contemporary literature's weakness or strength. Since this

161   Cummins, ibid., p. 8.
162   Wood, 'Introduction' to Le Guin's 'A Citizen of Mondath', [in:] *The Language of the Night*, p. 11.
163   Le Guin, Introduction to *The Left Hand of Darkness*, p. 5.
164   This is a title of Lewis's essay, included in his book *Of Other Worlds*, quoted in this chapter.
165   Le Guin's approach to fantasy is presented in more detail in the following chapters of this book.
166   Le Guin, 'Why Are Americans Afraid of Dragons?' [in:] *The Language of the Night*, p. 30.

book deals with therapeutic properties of the Inklings' fantasy works, it does not seek to delve into the issue, which needs to be resolved by literary historians, and my primary starting assumption developed in the following chapters is that the role which the group played in the history of English literature is vital as an alternative to the postmodernist mainstream culture of neo-nihilism. In the following chapters I would like to challenge the marginal position of the Inklings in the history of literature, and to show the uniqueness of their fiction and scholarship as an instance of a potentially therapeutic medium.

Another reason that may create an opportunity for a revision of the past century's literary history is the recent Inklings' anniversaries. Thirty-eight years after Carpenter's first edition of *The Inklings* (1978), the first publication dealing with the group, it could be interesting to re-view their legacy, especially because of some anniversaries that have fallen or fall on recently, encouraging retrospection and revaluation. Anniversaries usually provide context and pretext for reflections, conclusions and evaluation of the past, which in the case of the Inklings perhaps justifies an attempt at a revalorisation of their position in the history of English-language literature. The important Inklings dates include, for instance: the hundred and twenty-fifth anniversary of Tolkien's birth to be celebrated in January 2017; the forty-fifth anniversary of Tolkien's death that falls on in 2018; the hundred and twentieth anniversary of C. S. Lewis's birth and Owen Barfield's birth, both due in 2018; and the fiftieth anniversary of Lewis's death, celebrated in 2013 (when he was honoured with a memorial in Poet's Corner at Westminster Abbey); the hundred and thirtieth anniversary of Charles Williams's birth, which falls on this year (2016), and the seventieth anniversary of his death that seems to have passed largely unnoticed in 2015; as well as the twentieth anniversary of Barfield's death due next year. 2017 marks also the seventieth anniversary of the first Inklings publication, which was *Essays Presented to Charles Williams, with a Memoir by C. S. Lewis*, released by Oxford University Press in 1947, including contributions by: J. R. R. Tolkien (the first printing of his ground-breaking study 'On Fairy-Stories'), C. S. Lewis (Preface and essay 'On Stories'), Barfield ('Poetic Diction and Legal Diction'), Gervase Mathew ('Marriage and Amour Courtois in Late-Fourteenth-Century England'), Warnie Lewis ('The Galleys of France'), as well as Dorothy Sayers ('"… And Telling you a Story": A Note on The Divine Comedy').[167] As for Le Guin's anniversaries, in 2018 falls the fiftieth anniversary of the first publication of *A Wizard of Earthsea* (1968), the novel opening her Earthsea series.

---

167 Cf. footnote 73 in this chapter.

There is, certainly, a plethora of works addressing Tolkien's and Lewis's achievements respectively, and fairly many studies discussing their friendship, a fusion of minds and imaginations, and their mutual interaction, but probably much less on the Inklings considered collectively as a group that consisted not only of the two giants but also of the 'lesser Inklings'.[168] Fewer still are there attempts to recognize and evaluate the role the Inklings played in the development of the English literary and cultural history, providing one assumes they did play a role other than escapist old-timers and fusty professors entertaining their romantic minds and toying with fantasy, unable to go with the flow of modernism.[169] Some centres study the works of the Inklings together with the legacy of Chesterton, George Macdonald and Dorothy L. Sayers; the first two of whom had certainly been the source of inspiration for at least some of the Inklings (indubitably for Tolkien and Lewis), and Sayers was a friend of Lewis and, as Suzanne Bray suggests, a 'disciple' of Williams, but

---

168   The term 'the lesser Inklings' is often used by readers and critics with regard to the lesser-known Inklings that is those excluding Tolkien and Lewis, and sometimes also setting aside Williams and Barfield. In an entry on the Inklings in *J. R. R. Tolkien Encyclopaedia: Scholarship and Critical Assessment*, edited by Michael D. C. Drout, Colin Duriez specifies the term as follows: 'There are major and lesser Inklings, defined in terms of attendance or nonattendance at the literary gatherings, and by their literary influence or light they shed on Lewis, Tolkien, Williams, Barfield, or more than one of the four.' (New York: Routledge, 2007), p. 297.

169   Some other publications featuring the Inklings after Carpenter's work and not mentioned above (some of which focus only on the 'greater Inklings', that is on Tolkien and Lewis) are:
Myth and Magic: Art According to the Inklings, Eduardo Segura and Thomas Honegger, eds. (Zollikofen: Walking Tree Publishers, 2007), which expands on the Inklings' understanding of myth, art and Sub-creation;
Charles Williams and His Contemporaries, Suzanne Bray and Richard Sturch, eds. (Newcastle upon Tyne: Cambridge Scholars Publishing, 2009), featuring Williams, Tolkien, Lewis, but also Dorothy Sayers and Barfield;
Karlson, Henry, *Thinking with the Inklings: A Contemplative Engagement with the Oxford Fellowship* (North Charleston: Book Surge Llc, 2010) – deals with the Christian thought of the Inklings and its implications;
Poe, Harry L., James R., *The Inklings of Oxford* (Aston: Zondervan, 2009) – an illustrated Oxford guide following the Inklings' places in Oxford;
C. S. Lewis and Friends: Faith and the Power of Imagination, David Hein, Edward Henderson, eds. (London: SPCK, 2011) - a collection of essays on Lewis, Tolkien, Williams, and Lewis's non-Inkling friends: Dorothy L. Sayers, Austin Farrer, and Rose Macaulay.

never a member of the all-male club, who met weekly to enjoy the 'cut and parry of prolonged, fierce and masculine argument.'[170]

What were the Inklings, then? 'Properly speaking, the Inklings was neither a club nor a literary society, though it partook of the nature of both,' wrote Warren Lewis, C. S. Lewis's brother and an Inkling himself; for 'there were no rules, officers, agendas, or formal elections.'[171] It was 'an undetermined and unelected circle of friends who gathered about C. S. L.,' the linchpin of the Inklings, and met in his rooms in Magdalen, and whose 'habit was to read aloud compositions of various kinds (and lengths!)', said Tolkien himself.[172] The name 'Inklings' had been used before by an undergraduate society founded at Oxford by Tangye-Lean, an undergraduate at University College, who had also invited the dons, (including C. S. Lewis and Tolkien).[173] Whether the name had been suggested by Lewis or invented by Tangye-Lean is not clear, yet after the society had dissolved, the word was adopted by Lewis for his circle of friends as a jest, as Tolkien observes, 'because it was a pleasantly ingenious pun in its way, suggesting people with vague or half-formed intimations and ideas plus those who dabble in ink.'[174]

A group of kindred spirits and like-minded individuals, though not without differences of opinion, the Inklings were 'linked through friendship with Lewis but also through a common interest in mythology from a Christian viewpoint [and] gathered simply in order to have a scintillating conversation' in smoked-filled rooms at Lewis's quarters at Magdalen on Thursday evenings or at *The Eagle and the Baby* private back room on Tuesdays.[175] The Inklings were all Lewis's friends, 'the Lewis séance', as Tolkien once said, or, 'a drinking gang spirited by C. S. Lewis' and, if it comes to drinking, by his brother, the diarist of the Inklings,

---

170 Colin Duriez, and David Porter, *The Inklings Handbook*, p. 13. Suzanne Bray, 'Dorothy L. Sayers: Disciple and Interpreter of Charles Williams' [in:] *Charles Williams and His Contemporaries*, Suzanne Bray and Richard Sturch, eds. (Newcastle upon Tyne: Cambridge Scholars Publishing, 2009), pp. 96–116.

171 B. Edwards, *C. S. Lewis: Apologist, philosopher, and theologian* (New York: Praeger, 2007), p. 279.

172 *Letters of J. R. R. Tolkien*, letter no. 298, p. 416.

173 Tolkien, ibid., p. 416.

174 Ibid., p. 416. Tolkien also quotes an example of another short-lived undergraduate society he remembered from his early days at Oxford when he was a student, whose name was Discus, implying 'a roundtable conference' and the verb 'discuss', as it was a discussion club. (ibid., p. 416).

175 Simon Blaxland de Lange, 'Obituary for Owen Barfield,' http://davidlavery.net/barfield/barfield_resources/death.html, accessed 25 April 2016.

Major Warner H. Lewis or 'Warnie'.[176] C. S. Lewis 'had a passion for hearing things read aloud, a power of memory for things received in that way, and also a facility in extempore criticism, none of which were shared (especially not the last) in anything like the same degree by his friends,' Tolkien adds.[177]

A group of Oxford dons and their friends, characterized by 'pipe-and-flannels geniality', 'male-only membership', 'diversity of professions', and 'love of argument', the Inklings gathered approximately from 1933 to 1949, centred around Clive Staples Lewis ('Jack') (1898–1963), and included John Ronald Reuel Tolkien ('Tollers') (1892–1973), Owen Barfield (1898–1997), Hugo Dyson (1896–1975), Nevill Coghill (1899–1980), Lord David Cecil (1902–1986), Charles Williams (1886–1945), Warren Hamilton Lewis ('Warnie'; 1895–1973), Robert Havard ('Humphrey', Lewis's physician and friend; 1901–1985), and, occasionally, a few other guests, including Tolkien's youngest son Christopher (born in 1924).[178] Lewis and Tolkien began working at Oxford accidentally in the same year, 1925, and they met first probably in 1926. At Oxford they made acquaintances with the other members-to-be: Barfield, Coghill, Dyson and Cecil, who were all college fellows, attracted by Lewis's polemical artistry and personal charisma of his unpretentious jovial simplicity, and by Tolkien's philological expertise. During the war, they were joined by Williams – a London evacuee, an Oxford University Press editor, a self-made literary devotee, critic, poet, playwright and writer, invited to the meetings by Lewis. They gathered weekly at Lewis's quarters in Magdalen College or at '*The Bird and the Baby*' (*The Eagle and Child*) pub, reading and discussing drafts of their works over a pint of beer, a cup of tea and some plain food.

A minor group as they were, the Inklings made a lasting impact on the development of contemporary literature and culture, especially the fantasy and mythopoeia genre, as well as on literary studies, especially those handling the Old English, Middle English and Renaissance periods, and although their literary output could hardly be more different from that of the modernists and early postmodernists, its seminality and continuing popularity with both scholars and popular readers cannot be overestimated and may call for a canonical revalorization.[179] The next

---

176 Carpenter, *The Inklings*, p. 171.
177 Tolkien, *Letters*, p. 416.
178 The Zaleskis, *The Fellowship*, p. 462.
179 Lewis, Barfield and Williams also wrote essays on Romantic literature. One of Lewis's favourite Romantic poet was Percy Bysshe Shelley, cf. C. S. Lewis's essay 'Dryden, Shelley, and Mr. Eliot' [in:] *Rehabilitations and Other Essays* (Oxford: Oxford University Press, 1939), pp. 3–34.

chapter shows in more detail the relationship between the Inklings and modernist celebrities of their day in the wake of the First, and then the Second World War – the events that shook the foundations of Western culture and further problematized man's universal search for meaning.

Chapter Two
Difficult relationships: Inklingsiana and the mainstream of modernism

The Inklings and modernism

It is impossible to approach the legacy of the Inklings, that is the body of the writings by the Inklings and about the Inklings, which I associate here with the term 'Inklingsiana', nor argue for its therapeutic dimension without a reference to their times, which coincided with the heyday of modernism and the beginnings of postmodernism in culture, and specifically in literature.[1]

A general term 'applied retrospectively to the wide range of experimental and avant-garde trends in the literature and other arts of the early 20th century', modernism is characterized chiefly by 'a rejection of 19th century traditions and of their consensus between author and reader', by a departure from the continuity of chronological development in fiction, and an introduction of multiple points of view, especially by means of experimental narrative techniques, such as interior monologue and stream of consciousness; and in poetry by a repudiation of traditional metres and logical exposition of thought in favour of free verse and collages of fragmentary images, all these marks frequently expressing 'a sense of urban cultural dislocation, along with an awareness of new anthropological and psychological theories'.[2] Modernist writing was mostly cosmopolitan, and often disturbed the reader with its complex new forms and styles. It usually denied religious faith as a pillar of the old establishment, which had finally tumbled after the First World War, and whose 'centre [did] not hold' anymore.[3] Christianity became anathema among most modernist writers, with Yeats's more complex relationship to religion, and the notable exception of T. S. Eliot, whose conversion to

---

1 I have also addressed this problem in my paper 'A few Inklings on the Inklings and (post)modernism', [in:] *Wielowymiarowość i Perspektywy Nauki za Progiem XXI w.* [Multidimensionality and Perspectives of Academic Research beyond the 21st century], E. Widawska, K. Kowal, eds. (Częstochowa: Jan Długosz University of Czestochowa Press, 2012), pp. 79–94.

2 *Oxford Dictionary of Literary Terms*, Chris Baldick, ed. (Oxford: Oxford University Press, 2008), pp. 213–214.

3 'Things fall apart; the centre cannot hold;/Mere anarchy is loosed upon the world,' says W. B. Yeats in his poem 'The Second Coming' of 1919.

Anglo-Catholicism, the highest of Anglican modes, met with sarcastic mockery and outrage among the other modernists, for instance, the Bloomsbury Group, as testified by Virginia Woolf in one of her letters of early 1928:

> I have had a most shameful and distressing interview with dear Tom Eliot, who may be called dead to us all from this day forward. He has become an Anglo-Catholic believer in God and immortality, and goes to church. I was shocked. A corpse would seem to me more credible than he is. I mean, there's something obscene in a living person sitting by the fire and believing in God.[4]

Postmodernism, in turn, according to Jean-François Lyotard's succinct definition, in general means 'incredulity toward metanarratives', and, according to *Encyclopedia Britannica*, in philosophy it refers to 'a new, radical form of skepticism that emerged in the last half of the 20th century', which questions the possibility of applying 'any rational, objective framework for discussing intellectual problems', and undermines 'the validity of any kind of human investigation of the world by showing that such an investigation itself would need to be investigated.'[5] In literature, architecture, music and arts, as *The Compact Oxford English Dictionary* explains, postmodernism refers to 'a late 20th-century style (…) which represents a departure from modernism and is characterized by the self-conscious use of earlier styles and conventions, a mixing of different artistic styles and media, and a general distrust of theories.'[6] Postmodernism implies various forms of meta-physical, epistemological and ethical relativism, (although some postmodernists vehemently reject the relativist label), and questions the notions of objective knowledge, objective reality, and absolute values, which can all vary, since

---

4   Virginia Woolf's letter to her sister, Vanessa, of 11 February 1928, *A Change of Perspective: Letters of Virginia Woolf*, III, 1923–1928, Nigel Nicolson, ed. (London: The Hogarth Press, 1977, 1994), pp. 457–458.

5   Jean-François Lyotard, *The Postmodern Condition: A Report on Knowledge*, transl. G. Bennington and B. Massumi, (Minneapolis: University of Minnesota Press, 1984), p. 29. *Encyclopaedia Britannica*, 'Post-modernism', http://www.britannica.com/EB-checked/topic/547424/skepticism/281058/Postmodernism, 2013, accessed 23 April 2016.

6   http://oxforddictionaries.com/definition/english/postmodernism?view=uk, accessed 25 April 2016. Umberto Eco, for instance, likens 'the postmodern attitude' to 'that of a man who loves a very cultivated woman and knows he cannot say to her, *I love you madly*, because he knows that she knows (and that she knows that he knows) that these words have already been written by Barbara Cartland,' qtd. in *Derrida and Negative Theology*, Harold G. Coward and Toby Foshay, eds. (Albany: State University of New York Press, 1992), p. 276.

they rely on and are constructed by discourses - unreliable entities as such.[7] Fredric Jameson contrasts postmodernism with modernism, noting that while 'in modernism some residual zones of "nature" or "being" of the old, the older, the archaic, still subsist, so that culture can still do something to that nature and work at transforming that "referent"; in postmodernism (...) the modernization process is complete and nature is gone for good.'[8]

The above-quoted definitions by no means exhaust the wealth of interpretations of the term 'postmodernism', which has been subject to intense debates. Most often, however, it refers to the three following concepts:

(1) to 'the non-realist and non-traditional literature and art of the post-World-War-Two period';

(2) to 'literature and art which takes certain modernist characteristics to an extreme stage', a view propounded in John Barth's 'The Literature of Exhaustion' [1967, 1984];

(3) and to 'a more general human condition in the "late-capitalist" world of the post 1950s' in which the myths by which we once legitimized knowledge and practice – Christianity, Science, Democracy, Communism, Progress, no longer have the unquestioning support necessary to sustain the projects which were undertaken in their name, resulting in a radical decentring of our cultural sphere.'[9] Thus, as Christopher Keep suggests, 'it is not simply that the postmodernism does not believe in "truth", so much that it understands truth and meaning as historically constructed and thus seeks to expose the mechanisms by which this production is hidden and "naturalized".'[10] Interestingly, as some critics suggest, postmodernism has already died, and 'ambiguity has been done to death', too, so that 'the next big thing is clarity', or some kind of 'natural classicism' or authenticity.[11] Were that speculation true about the trends in contemporary literature and philosophy, the legacy of

---

7   http://www.britannica.com/EBchecked/topic/1077292/postmodernism/282559/Postmodernism-and-relativism, accessed 25 April 2016.

8   Fredric Jameson, *Postmodernism, or, The Cultural Logic of Late Capitalism* (Durham, NC: Duke University Press, 1990), p. x.

9   Christopher Keep, Tim McLaughlin, Robin Parmar, 'Postmodernity and the Postmodern novel', http://www2.iath.virginia.edu/elab/hfl0256.html, accessed 23 April 2016.

10 Keep, McLaughlin, and Parmar, ibid.

11 Edward Docx, 'Postmodernism is dead', *Prospect Magazine*, July 20, 2011; http://www.prospectmagazine. co.uk/magazine/postmodernism-is-dead-va-exhibition-age-of-authenticism, accessed 23 April 2016.

the Inklings, of Le Guin, and of Victor Frankl would certainly count among the works representing 'natural classicism' and 'authenticity', whose vision of life and meaning, although made of difficult truths, is clear, and stands in sharp contrast to the postmodern tendencies identified by Fredrick Jameson as 'antifoundationalism', which 'eschews all foundations altogether', and 'non-essentialism', which has lost 'the last shred of essence'.[12]

'An internally conflicted and contradictory' term, which, nonetheless, as Jameson admits, 'cannot *not* be used', postmodernism may not be understood without reference to postmodernity.[13] Some thinkers consider postmodernity as a new distinct period in the history of culture and society, (a view represented, for instance, by Jean-Francois Lyotard, Jean Baudrillard, and Fredric Jameson), whereas others as an extended stage of modernity – its 'late', 'liquid' or 'network' phase (to name but a few scholars: Anthony Giddens, Zygmunt Bauman, and Manuel Castells with their interpretations quoted respectively).[14] Barely mentioned here, the concept of postmodernity is discussed in more detail in Chapter Two of this book, where I attempt to approach it in terms of neo-nihilism.

The bulk of the Inklings' lives coincided after the Edwardian and Georgian beginnings with the heyday of modernism, and the Inklings' deaths, stretching over the post-war period from Williams's in 1945 to Barfield's in 1997, occurred during what has hitherto been umbrella-termed as postmodernity, with postmodernism as its characteristic trend. Lewis and Tolkien, who died in 1963 and 1973, respectively, saw the beginnings and an early stage of development of that cultural era, unaware of its name, yet apprehensive of its further growth and implications.[15] In confrontation with modernism, the Inklings felt estranged and remote from its mainstream, and from most of their Oxford colleagues, making their Inklings' circle a quiet 'island of resistance' and a little stronghold of opposition, reflected in their approach to literature, language, academic studies, literary criticism and writing.[16] Most critics and literary historians agree that the

12 Fredrick Jameson, *Postmodernism, or the Cultural Logic of Late Capitalism* (Durham: Duke University Press, 1991), p. xii.

13 Jameson, ibid., p. xxii.

14 Anthony Giddens, *Modernity and Self-Identity: Self and Society in the Late Modern Age* (Cambridge: Polity, 1991); Bauman, *Liquid Modernity: Living in an Age of Uncertainty* (Cambridge: Polity, 2000); Manuel Castells, *The Rise of the Network Society, The Information Age: Economy, Society and Culture* (Oxford: Blackwell, 2000).

15 Duriez, *J. R. R. Tolkien and C. S. Lewis: The Gift of Friendship* (Boston: Paulist Press, 2003), p. 113.

16 Duriez, ibid., p. 102.

Inklings did not endorse the underlying aesthetics of modernism that happened to have set the time frame for their first attempts to 'dabble in ink', and that they were largely at odds with the progressive modernist spirit.[17]

It was perhaps even a badge of honour for the Inklings to be denigrated and marginalized by the panjandrums of the English faculty at Oxford and Cambridge in their day and ever since, and to be held in disregard for the very sake of not being T. S. Eliot, D. H. Lawrence, or James Joyce. Robert Havard 'Humphrey', an Inkling, comments on the uneasy interaction between Lewis and non-Inkling dons in the following way:

> [Lewis] was unhappy at his Oxford College. At dinner there I sensed the occasional whiff of hostility from some of his colleagues. The academic mind is a master of the politely barbed shaft. The college was pervaded by an abrasive anti-Christian humanism at that time, which gave Lewis a good deal of painful opposition.[18]

Humphrey Carpenter describes Lewis's and his college fellows' mutual rapport likewise:

> The widespread antipathy of many senior members of the University to [Lewis and his Christian fantasy] books such as *The Screwtape Letters* had not been modified by Lewis's openly contemptuous attitude towards much of the academic work done in Oxford.[19]

Despite Tolkien's efforts this resulted in the Oxford electors' failing twice to honour Lewis with a vacant Chair in English Literature, and in Lewis's eventual decision to move to Cambridge University in 1954.[20] Dame Helen Gardner (1908–1986), an Oxford tutor and the first woman to hold the chair of Merton Professor of English literature in the University of Oxford, and influential scholar on John Donne, John Milton and T. S. Eliot, wrote the following in Lewis's

---

17 Tolkien, *Letters*, p. 36.

18 Robert Havard, 'Philia. Jack at ease' [in:] *C. S. Lewis at the Breakfast Table, and Other Reminiscences*, James T. Como, ed. (London: Harcourt Publishers, 1992), p. 226. The University of Oxford is still today a centre of anti-Christian and anti-religious thinking, as represented, for instance, by Richard Dawkins, who in his bestselling 2006 book *The God Delusion* compares religious upbringing to child abuse; and Philip Pullman, a graduate of Oxford and fantasy writer, who has also written a blasphemous book on Jesus Christ (published in 2010).

19 Carpenter, *The Inklings*, p. 228.

20 Lewis was elected a fellow of Magdalen College, Oxford, on May 20, 1925, where he served as tutor in English Language and Literature for 29 years until leaving for Magdalene College, Cambridge, in 1954; cf. http://www.cslewis.org/resource/chronocsl/, accessed 24 April 2016.

obituary, accounting for the reluctance of the majority of non-Inkling Oxford dons towards Lewis:

> In the early 1940's, when I returned to Oxford as a tutor, Lewis was by far the most impressive and exciting person in the Faculty of English. He had behind him a major work of literary history; he filled the largest lecture-room available for his lectures; and the Socratic Club, which he founded and over which he presided, for the free discussion of religious and philosophic questions, was one of the most flourishing and influential of undergraduate societies. In spite of this, when the Merton Professorship of English Literature fell vacant in 1946, the electors passed him over and recalled his old tutor, F. P. Wilson, from London to fill the chair. In doing so they probably had the support of many, if not a majority, of the Faculty; for by this time a suspicion had arisen that Lewis was so committed to what he himself called 'hot-gospelling' that he would have had little time for the needs of what had become a very large undergraduate school... (...) There were a good many people in Oxford who disliked Christian apologetics per se, there were others who were uneasy at Lewis's particular kind of apologetic, disliking both its method and its manner.[21]

The other Inklings, including Tolkien and Williams, (the latter of whom did not hold a degree, and was eventually awarded an honorary Master of Arts degree in 1943, two years before his death, and was a self-educated man and an odd Christian), most likely felt at times at Oxford the same attitude of thinly-disguised mockery bordering on disdain, which, even if not generated by other academics' dislike of the Christian message of the Inklings' works, must have grown from their scholarly contempt for the Inklings' dedication to fantasy and 'fairytale-ness'.[22]

This is what Ursula K. Le Guin writes about the cold reception of Tolkien's *opus magnum*, that is *The Lord of the Rings*, by academia, influenced by such critical works as William Epson's *Seven Types of Ambiguity* of 1930:

> It is no matter of wonder that so many people are bored by, or detest, *The Lord of the Rings*. (...) Judged by any of the Seven Types of Ambiguity that haunt the groves of Academe, it is totally inadequate. For those who seek allegory, it must be maddening. (It must be an allegory! Of course, Frodo is Christ! – or is Gollum Christ?) For those whose grasp on reality is so tenuous that they crave ever-increasing doses of 'realism' in their reading, it offers nothing – unless, perhaps, a shortcut to the loony bin. And there are many subtler reasons for disliking it; for instance the peculiar rhythm of the book (...) – the rocking-horse gait, [which] may not suit a jet-age adult. (...) [These] are the

---

21 Duriez, *The Gift of Friendship*, p. 148.
22 Williams's diploma of an honorary Master of Arts degree awarded by Oxford University is displayed at the Marion E. Wade Center of Wheaton College, Illinois, the USA; http://www.wheaton.edu/wadecenter, accessed 23 April 2016.

same arguments which Tolkien completely exploded, thereby freeing *Beowulf* forever from the dead hands of the pedants, in his brilliant 1934 article, 'The Monsters and the Critics' – an article which anyone who sees Tolkien as a Sweet Old Dear, by the way, would do well to read.[23]

As far as Charles Williams's writing is concerned, his idiosyncratic lay theology and cockney-like background were completely at odds with what was expected of university tutors; nevertheless, during the war Tolkien and Lewis arranged for Williams to lecture and take tutorial pupils at Oxford, which he started on January 29, 1940, and did with considerable success, although the students were baffled by Williams's singular manner of lecturing and the subjects he discussed, for instance chastity in Milton's masque *Comus*.[24] Another Inkling, Hugo Dyson, joked about that extraordinary lecture and its impact on the student community saying that Williams was 'in danger of becoming a thoroughgoing "chastitute".'[25] Commenting on the same episode, Lewis concluded:

> Simply as criticism it was superb because here was a man who really cared with every fibre of his being about 'the sage and serious doctrine of virginity' which it would never occur to the ordinary modern critic to take seriously. But it was more important still as a sermon. It was a beautiful sight to see a whole roomful of modern young men and women sitting in that absolute silence which cannot be faked, very puzzled but spellbound ... That beautiful carved room had probably not witnessed anything so important since some of the great mediaeval or Reformation lectures. I have at last, if only for once, seen a university doing what it was founded to do: teaching wisdom.[26]

Interestingly, when on one occasion in 1943 there happened to be concurrent lectures held by Tolkien and Williams, all the undergraduates except for one who was obliged to take notes for the rest filled Williams's auditorium (he was to lecture on Hamlet); so 'Tolkien was left to lecture on Anglo-Saxon to a solitary student. Unperturbed, Tolkien had a drink with Williams afterwards.'[27]

Although Williams's (and the other Inklings') adherence to the Christian doctrine was generally not in vogue at the crest of the modernist wave, Williams took interest in the literature of the day, especially in T. S. Eliot's works (possibly

---

23 Le Guin, 'The Staring Eye' [in:] *The Language of the Night*, pp. 163–164. The *Seven Types of Ambiguity*, published in 1930, was a successful book of William Empson, a Cambridge opponent of the Inklings.

24 E. L. Mascall, 'Charles Williams as I Knew Him', [in:] *Charles Williams: A Celebration*, Brian Horne, ed. (London: Gracewing, 1995), p. 2.

25 Duriez, *J. R. R. Tolkien: The Making of a Legend* (Oxford: Lion Hudson, 2012), p. 183.

26 Carpenter, *The Inklings*, p. 119.

27 Duriez, *J. R. R. Tolkien: The Making of a Legend*, p. 183.

due to the latter's conversion), which Tolkien ignored and which Lewis (when it came to Eliot's poetry in particular) disliked.[28] Lindop goes as far as to call Williams 'the only left-wing Inkling', whose poetry, 'beside that of Eliot and Yeats' is 'a late, densely symbolist flowering of modernism in English.'[29] Lindop argues that Williams's work bridges Edwardian poetry with the modernist revolution, only to usher in the arrival of postmodern trends during Williams's last years at Oxford, and, thus, it provides 'the missing centrepiece from the story of twentieth-century British literature':

> At the start of his career [Williams] was associating with Edwardian poets Alice Meynell and Robert Bridges; later his closest friends included not only C. S. Lewis and Tolkien but T. S. Eliot and Dylan Thomas; he was an inspiration to young poets of the World War II generation like Sidney Keyes, Drummond Allison and John Heath-Stubbs; and he drank in the Oxford pubs with Kingsley Amis and Philip Larkin.[30]

That openness towards both tradition and radically new trends can hardly be ascribed to Lewis, Tolkien, Barfield, and many other Inklings. In his *The Pilgrim's Regress*, for instance, Lewis refers disparagingly to modernist literature as to 'the poetry of the Silly Twenties', 'the swamp-literature of the Dirty Twenties', and 'the gibberish-literature of the Lunatic Twenties'; criticizing that 'darkest *Zeitgeistheim*' or Spirit of the Age.[31] Lewis regarded modernist poems in general as 'very nonsensical, but with a flavour of dirt all through', and indicated the connection between modernism and 'dirt' in one of his essays:

> The 'Dirty Twenties' of our own century produced poems which succeeded in communicating moods of boredom and nausea that have only an infinitesimal place in the life of a corrected and full-grown man. That they were poems, the fact of communication and the means by which it was effected, are, I take, sufficient proof… If it truly reflected the personality of the poets, then the poets differed from the mass, if at all, only by defect.[32]

---

28 Carpenter, *The Inklings*, p. 49.

29 Lindop, *Charles Williams: The Third Inkling* (Oxford: Oxford University Press, 2015), p. viii.

30 Lindop, 'Charles Williams: The Third Inkling', http://grevel.co.uk/poetry/charles-williams-third-inkling/, accessed 25 April 2016.

31 Lewis, *The Pilgrim's Regress*, rev. ed. (London: Geoffrey Bles, 1933/1946), pp. 50, 52, and 54.

32 Lewis, and Eustace Mandeville Wetenhall Tillyard, *The Personal Heresy – A Controversy* (Chicago: Concordia University Press, 2008), chapter 5, p. 88. Originally printed by the Oxford University Press in 1939, the book contains 6 essays, three by Lewis and three by Tillyard, in which each critic argues his point: Lewis opposes the 'personal heresy' critical approach, and disagrees with Tillyard's view that poetry is foremostly an

In *The Pilgrim's Regress* Lewis presents Eliot, the main representative of modernist verse, critically through the character of Mr. Neo-Angular:

> What I am attacking in Neo-Angular [Lewis explains] is a set of people who seem to me to be trying to make of Christianity itself one more highbrow, Chelsea, bourgeois-baiting fad. T. S. Eliot is the single man who sums up the thing I am fighting against.[33]

Thus, although after their conversions Eliot and Lewis were both considered as fellow defenders of Christianity, sometimes grouped together in the 1920s and 30s as literary converts, Lewis did not share Eliot's approach to religion, which was, according to him, 'High and Dry', and 'not merely 'sectarian in its Anglo-Catholicism but also emotionally barren and counter-romantic'; unlike, perhaps, Williams's Romantic theology of Christianity.[34] Lewis's reluctance towards Eliot, which largely melted away towards the end of Lewis's life, especially after his wife's death, when Eliot published Lewis's study of bereavement *A Grief Observed* (1960), may show Lewis at his worst, when he wages a regular war with a radically different view on poetry, whose living embodiment was a poet that had won, unlike Lewis, considerable fame and critical acclaim.

After his conversion to Christianity (1927), Eliot found much in common with Williams, and, as some critics argue, had been influenced by Williams, who encouraged Eliot to read Christian mysticism, such as Julian of Norwich's, as reflected in Eliot's poem *Little Gidding* (1942), addressing similar themes to those that had appeared in Williams's study *The Forgiveness of Sins* of the same year.[35] As Barbara Newman argues, 'the [spiritual] friendship between Eliot and Williams was a close one that can be documented through letters, book reviews, and memoirs.'[36] But, regrettably, 'Williams himself, a consistently underrated writer, seldom earns more than a footnote from Eliot's scholars.'[37] Tom Howard likewise regrets that

---

expression of the poet's personality, and that poems are studied to discover the poet's personality and experience; while Tillyard defends that approach to poetry, claiming also that the poet is a cut above ordinary people.

33 Roger Lancelyn Green and Walter Hooper, *C. S. Lewis: A Biography* (London: Collins, 1974), p. 130.

34 Carpenter, *The Inklings*, p. 49. Cf. Charles Williams's *Outline of Romantic Theology* (Berkeley: Apocryphile Press, 2005), in which he claims that romantic love between people offers glimpses of perfection and helps experience God.

35 Barbara Newman, 'Eliot's Affirmative Way: Julian of Norwich, Charles Williams, and Little Gidding' [in:] *Modern Philology*, Vol. 108, No. 3 (February 2011) (Chicago: University of Chicago Press), pp. 427–446, p. 428.

36 Newman, ibid., p. 428.

37 Newman, ibid., pp. 429–430.

'Williams's name is [still] strictly a name for insiders'.[38] When viewing Williams's interaction with Eliot, Barbara Newman names William 'an Anglo-Catholic modernist', a statement that seems to be corroborated by Lindop in his recent work on Williams, yet a judgement not universally acknowledged.[39]

Apart from his literary friendship with Eliot, Williams had largely influenced non-modernist writers and poets, for instance Dorothy L. Sayers, (whom he encouraged to read *The Divine Comedy* in Italian and to translate it into English), and Wystan Hugh Auden, (who reportedly re-read Williams's theological book *The Descent of the Dove* every year).[40]

This is what Williams wrote wittily, but not superciliously, in his review of Eliot's *The Waste Land*, an acclaimed masterpiece of modernist poetry:

> Whatever his more difficult poems mean, his simpler nearly always mean Hell pure and simple. But not in any prejudiced or invented mode. Mr. Eliot's poetic experience of life would seem to be Hell varied by intense poetry. It is also, largely, our experience. It is also, generally, our experience of Mr. Eliot's poetry. But Hell, like heaven, has many mansions. If Mr. Eliot has gone to prepare a place for us, it is only courteous to attend, so far as we can, to the particular kind of place he has prepared.[41]

Despite their friendship and mutual admiration, Williams clashed swords with Eliot a few times, for instance over Milton, whom Williams (and Lewis) highly respected and defended, and whom Eliot (and Ezra Pound) did not.[42]

Lewis, Tolkien and Williams, and probably the other Inklings as well, were greatly upset by the new school of criticism which had come from Cambridge University after 1928, with I. A. Richards and F. R. Leavis in the lead, and which

---

38 Thomas Howard, 'What About Charles Williams?' [in:] *Touchstone*, Vol. 17, issue 10 (Chicago, 2004), pp. 30–36; p. 33.

39 Lindop, *Charles Williams: The Third Inkling*, 2015. Barbara Newman, 'Eliot's Affirmative Way', p. 430. Newman enumerates many common denominators between Williams and Eliot: they belonged to the same parish in London (St. Silas), which as the first church in England since Reformation had performed its own mystery plays; both contributed to a revival of religious verse drama; four of Williams's books were published (and three commissioned) by Eliot's Faber and Faber. A critic who calls Williams's writings anti-modernist is, for instance, Lydia R. Browning, cf. her 'Charles Williams's Anti-Modernist *Descent into Hell*' [in:] *Mythlore*, Vol. 31, No. 1–2., 2012, pp. 5–19.

40 Alice Mary Hadfield, *Charles Williams: An Exploration of His Life and Work* (Oxford: Oxford University Press, 1983), p. 141.

41 Charles Williams, *Poetry at Present* (Oxford: Clarendon, 1930), p. 166.

42 Newman, 'Eliot's Affirmative Way', p. 433. It should be noted that Tolkien did not respect Milton's works, either, but for different reasons than Eliot and Pound. To Tolkien, Milton's Puritan interpretation of the Bible was very much an anti-Catholic heresy.

promoted a 'self-conscious dissociation from the literary, philosophical and political assumptions of the previous century' to the detriment of Anglo-Saxon literature and several giants such as Shakespeare, Milton or P. B. Shelley.[43] Milton in particular became the target of that criticism, for, as Eliot declared, Milton's style 'had damaged the structure of the English language and his theology was "repellent".[44] Therefore, Tolkien and Lewis struggled to implement a reformed syllabus at Oxford, which would focus on the literature of the previous centuries at the expense of contemporary literature.

Lewis, whose literary taste was eclectic, read much of the moderns' oeuvre, including the works of the Georgian poets: Rupert Brooke, John Elroy Flecker, Walter de la Mare, and John Masefield; as well as of his compatriot Yeats, counting them among the 'best moderns'; and enjoyed reading E. M. Forster's fiction, Edith Sitwell's poetry, W. H. Auden's alliterative verse, but disliked, for instance, Virginia Woolf's writing.[45] As Jonathan Fruoco argues:

> Lewis remained all his life a Georgian, both in his approach to criticism and to poetry, and eventually found himself living on an island whose shores were progressively eaten away by the ocean. Far from giving up, he tried for many decades to turn the tide in attacking Eliot, who symbolised everything he disliked in Modernism. Lewis discovered Eliot's poetry as soon as he read *Prufrock and Other Observations* (published in 1917) and immediately considered Eliot's use of language and his lack of structure as a deliberate attack upon traditional English poetry.[46]

Lewis believed in the unexhausted possibilities of 'metrical poetry on sane subjects', and blamed modernist poetry for introducing the state of 'decay' and corruption to English poetry and its language; a view shared, for instance, by Owen Barfield in his *Poetic Diction: A Study in Meaning* (1928).[47] As Carpenter observers,

---

43 Heather O'Donoghue, *From Asgard to Valhalla: the Remarkable History of the North Myths* (London: I. B. Tauris, 2008), pp. 163–64.

44 Jonathan Fruoco, 'C. S. Lewis and T. S. Eliot – Questions of Identity' [in:] *Persona and Paradox: Issues of Identity for C. S. Lewis, His Friends and Associates,* Suzanne Bray, William Gray, eds. (Newcastle upon Tyne: Cambridge Scholars Publishing, 2012), pp. 81–92, p. 84.

45 Carpenter, *The Inklings,* pp. 118 and 158. Fruoco, 'C. S. Lewis and T. S. Eliot', p. 85.

46 Fruoco, ibid., p. 85. Lewis's early ambition was poetry and his dream seemed to have come true when he had a volume of poetry published in 1918 (*Spirits in Bondage*). It attracted scarcely any attention, though, to Lewis's considerable disappointment; cf. Carpenter, *The Inklings,* p. 12.

47 Lewis, *The Collected Letters of C. S. Lewis,* Volume 1: Family Letters 1905–1931, Walter Hooper, ed. (San Francisco: HarperCollins, 2004), p. 492.

Lewis read much more widely than Tolkien among modern writers, and disliked much of what he saw. His projected crusade against T. S. Eliot in 1926 was the opening shot in what was to be years of snipping at that poet. He did come to have a guarded respect for Eliot's criticism, but he continued to attack his verse. At an Inklings in 1947 he declared one of Eliot's poems to be 'bilge', and in 1954, writing to Katherine Farrer, he defined his dislike of Eliot's image of evening 'like a patient etherized upon a table' [in Eliot's 'The Love Song of J. Alfred Prufrock'].[48]

Expanding on Eliot's use of metaphors and similes in 'Prufrock', especially Eliot's likening an evening to a 'patient etherised upon a table', Lewis observes:

> I have heard Mr Eliot's comparison of evening to a patient on an operating table praised, nay gloated over, not as a striking picture of sensibility in decay, but because it was so 'pleasantly unpleasant'. (…) That elementary rectitude of human response, at which we are so ready to fling the unkind epithets of 'stock', 'crude', 'bourgeois', and 'conventional', so far from being 'given' is a delicate balance of trained habits, laboriously acquired and easily lost on the maintenance of which depend both our virtues and our pleasures and even, perhaps, the survival of our species.[49]

This may perhaps show Lewis at this worst, when he combats his opponent resorting to hyperbole, yet this results from Lewis's determination to expose the aesthetic, artistic and spiritual perils which he believed the new experimental poetry of modernism had championed, as represented by lionized Eliot. In his letter to Paul Elmer More of 1935, Lewis evaluates Eliot's position of a poet and literary critic in the following way, objecting to the phenomenon of 'Eliotolatry':

> There may be many reasons why you [Paul More] do not share my dislike of Eliot, but I hardly know why you should be surprised at it. On p. 154 of the article on Joyce you yourself refer to him as a 'great genius expending itself on the propagation of irresponsibility'. To me the great genius is not apparent: The other thing is. Surely it is natural that I should regard Eliot's work as a very great evil. He is the very spearhead of that attack on πέρας [i. e. proper limitations] which you deplore. His constant profession of humanism and his claim to be a 'classicist' may not be consciously insincere, but they are erroneous. (…) His intention only God knows. I must be content to judge his work by its fruits, and I contend that no man is fortified against chaos by reading the *Waste Land*, but that most men are by it infected with chaos.[50]

---

48 Carpenter, *The Inklings*, p. 158.
49 Lewis, *The Collected Letters*, vol. 2, p. 1030. In the poem Eliot writes: 'LET us go then, you and I, /When the evening is spread out against the sky. /Like a patient etherized upon a table.'
50 Lewis, ibid., vol. 2, p. 163.

Christopher Ricks calls that piece of Lewis's criticism 'a scarred tissue of prejudicial incitements and excitements', built upon chaotic and 'madly unmisgiving rhetoric', as contrasted with Eliot's 'lucidly fraught' style.[51]

Eliot's lack of response encouraged Lewis to continue his campaign against modernist poetry. In 1939 Lewis wrote *Rehabilitations*, a volume of essays defending his literary and linguistic values. In 1926 Lewis, together with another Inkling, Nevill Coghill, and two other friends, Franck Hardie and Henry Yorke, worked 'in 'conspiracy' writing a parody of Eliot's verse, planning to submit it for publication to *The Criterion*, edited by Eliot, using the made-up names of a brother and sister Rollo and Bridget Considine. The prank, eventually abandoned, had been inspired by the love of 'pure fun' (in Hardie's and Coghill's case), 'the love of mischief' in Yorke's, and by 'burning indignation' in Lewis's, despite his own great sense of humour.[52] Lewis's attitude to Eliot's poetry is perhaps best summarized in a letter Lewis wrote to Dorothy Sayers in October 1942:

> Oh Eliot! How can a man who is neither a knave nor a fool write so like both? Well, he can't complain that I haven't done my best to put him right – hardly ever write a book without showing him one of his errors. And still he doesn't mend. I call it ungrateful.[53]

Giving vent to his dislike of modernism in literature, Lewis, who was unable to do things by halves, plunged himself into an anti-modernist campaign so as to disband what he considered a common modernist misconception, namely 'a very elementary confusion between poetry that represents disintegration and disintegrated poetry.'[54] To illustrate the difference Lewis argued that while 'the *Inferno* is not infernal poetry, the *Waste Land* is.'[55]

---

51 Christopher Ricks, *T. S. Eliot and Prejudice* (London: Faber and Faber, 1994), pp. 197–198.
52 Carpenter, *The Inklings*, p. 21.
53 Carpenter, ibid., p. 533.
54 Lewis, *The Collected Letters*, p. 163.
55 Lewis, ibid., pp. 163–164. Eliot famously declared that he was 'an Anglo-Catholic in religion, a classicist in literature, and a royalist in politics' (in *For Lancelot Andrewes: Essays on Style and Order*, London: Faber and Gwyer, 1929, p. 59). It is noteworthy that Eliot's poetry was not altogether enthusiastically received in America. William Carlos Williams (1883–1963), for instance, although connected to the movement of modernism and imagism, regarded Eliot's verse, especially *The Waste Land*, 'as a disaster to American poetry.' 'Eliot had turned his back on the possibility of reviving my world,' William Carlos Williams complained; and [since Eliot] was 'an accomplished craftsman, better skilled in some ways than I could ever hope to be, I had to watch him

Paradoxically, Eliot's masterpiece, the *Waste Land* (1922), a document of ultimate dissolution and impotence, which, as Lewis observes, may deeply disturb the unfortified reader with its bleak picture of spiritual chaos, seems to play a(n) (auto)therapeutic role, expressed in the poet's confession: 'These fragments I have shored against my own ruins' (line 431).[56] The landscape of the post-war sterility and desolation was to Eliot a reflection of modern barrenness and spiritual debris, and his own plight of living a life devoid of meaning, whose shattered splinters lay in 'a heap of broken images, where the sun beats' (line 22).[57] Depicting the chaos, dryness and emptiness of the contemporary moral landscape was to Eliot therapeutic, and perhaps it marked his first step towards a personal search for meaning, and spiritual survival, achieved along with psychological recovery and crowned with his religious conversion and baptism into the Church of England in 1927.

Lewis's own conversion to Christianity, also to the Church of England, came later, in 1933, very much thanks to the impact of his Inkling friends. As I wish to argue, Lewis's fiction, just like the works of the other Inklings, can also be viewed in terms of therapy, yet its essence appears to be very different from Eliot's. First of all, the therapeutic effect of Lewis's works is perhaps less autotherapeutic than Eliot's, and more focused on the reader, (perhaps with at least one exception, namely Lewis's reflections *A Grief Observed*, written after his wife's death of cancer, and published by Eliot); secondly, and more importantly, rather than examining the parched and fragmented landscape of meaninglessness, Lewis paints a logocentric world, in which emptiness is an absence of meaning that is to be sought and to be discovered in every, even most difficult and hopeless, situation. While Eliot's *Waste Land* is a contemplation of the shattered images and the ruins, which helps to take stock of one's position, Lewis's fantasy fiction, and the Inklingsiana as such, is more a picture of a recovered image of a meaningful, although at times also bitterly painful, reality. Philip Zaleski and Carol Zaleski seem to have captured aptly that unique characteristic of Lewis's mind, shared with the other Inklings:

> [The Inklings] were twentieth-century Romantics who championed imagination as the royal road to insight and the 'medieval mode' as an answer to modern confusion and anomie; yet they were for the most part Romantics without rebellion, fantasists who prized reason, for whom Faërie was a habitat for the virtues and literature a sanctuary

---

carry my world off with him, the fool, to the enemy.' *Autobiography* (New York: New Directions, 1967), p. 174.

56 Eliot, *The Waste Land* (New York: Classic Books International, 2010), p. 16.

57 Ibid., p. 1.

for faith. (…) They were at work on a shared project, to reclaim for contemporary life what Lewis called the 'discarded image' of a universe created, ordered, and shot through with meaning.[58]

Disintegration, meaninglessness, degradation of language, corruption of poetic diction, and devaluation of art and moral principles was what Lewis and the other Inklings sought to oppose, Lewis being perhaps the most radical and devoted antagonist. 'Lewis's work was all of a piece: as literary scholar, fantasist, and apologist, he was ever on a path of rehabilitation and recovery,' the Zaleskis argue, stressing what might be named a reconstructing and consolidating quality of his and other Inklings' work, which I view in therapeutic terms.[59] 'The Inklings came together because they shared a longing to reclaim the goodness, beauty, and cultural continuity that had been so violently disrupted,' the Zaleskis assert, accounting for the radically different stand of the Inklings as compared to that of modernists:

> Far from breaking with tradition, [the Inklings] understood the Great War and its aftermath in the light of tradition, believing, as did their literary and spiritual ancestors, that ours is a fallen world yet not a forsaken one. It was a belief that set them at odds with many of their contemporaries, but kept them in the broad current of the English literary heritage. (…) The Inklings were comrades, who had been touched by war, who viewed life through the lens of war, yet who looked for hope and found it, in fellowship, where so many other modern writers and intellectuals saw only broken narratives, disfigurement, and despair.[60]

Paradoxically again, Eliot's motives were similar to Lewis's in that he strove to cope with the post-war spiritual crisis and his own mental breakdown (resulting largely from marital problems and overwork), although he chose a completely different aesthetics and stylistics, and instead of conducting a 'holistic therapy' that would draw on sound foundations as the Inklings resolved to do, Eliot immersed the readers in modern sterility, fragmentation and void, perhaps with a view to inoculating them against the corrupting effect of sprawling nothingness. Thus, despite some similarities resulting from the fact that both Lewis and Eliot had come from outside Britain (Ireland and the US, respectively), and both became religious converts and lay defenders of the Christian faith, admitted to the Church of England in the inter-war period, their intellectual and artistic relationship was a 'highly

---

58 The Zaleskis, *The Fellowship*, p. 510.
59 The Zaleskis, ibid., p. 511.
60 The Zaleskis, ibid., p. 9.

uneasy one' and drew on tension and mutual criticism, particularly on Lewis's part, and improved only in his last years.[61]

Lewis's ardent criticism of Eliot's works and his 'noble rage' against Eliot's modernism gradually waned after 1945, that is after Charles Williams's, their mutual friend's, unexpected death, although Lewis never came to embrace either Eliot's poetry or his prose.[62] In 1945 Lewis requested Eliot to contribute to the volume that had been dedicated to Williams by the Inklings (*Essays Presented to Charles Williams*), planned as a farewell gift to Williams on his prospective leaving Oxford, and then edited as a posthumous tribute. Compiling the volume, Lewis wrote to Eliot: 'a critique of Charles's own poetry or an account of the man from your hand would be of very great value'; Eliot, however, did not submit any paper on time, and the book appeared without his contribution in 1947.[63] It must be noted, though, that Eliot, an experienced publisher at Faber and Faber, advised Lewis on some publishing matters prior to the publication.[64] In 1959 Lewis and Eliot collaborated on the revision of the Psalter and even 'sealed their friendship when they dined together with their wives Joy and Valerie' - 'an event, which [according to Carpenter,] the pre-war Lewis would have declared to be in every respect impossible.'[65] Significantly, Lewis's *A Grief Observed*, which addresses the problem of death, pain, despair and faith, written after Lewis's wife's death from bone cancer (1960) and signed with a pseudonym N. W. Clerk, was published by Eliot's Faber and Faber. Although Lewis did not wish to reveal his identity when submitting the manuscript, (his authorship was disclosed only after his death in the subsequent editions), Eliot 'immediately recognised Lewis's style' and found the book particularly moving, publishing it in 1961.[66]

When it comes to Tolkien's stance towards the modernist movement in literature, he seemed barely interested in the literature of the day, which he generally disliked as much as Lewis did. Carpenter argues that:

> Though Tolkien lived in the twentieth century he could scarcely be called a modern writer. Certainly some comparatively recent authors made their mark on him: men such as William Morris, Andrew Lang, George MacDonald, Rider Haggard, Kenneth

---

61 Bart Jan Spruyt, 'One of the enemy: C. S. Lewis on the very great evil of T. S. Eliot's work,' [in:] *De Edmund Burke Stichting* (The Hague, 2004), accessed 16 December, 2015, www.burkestichting.nl/nl/stichting/isioxford.html.

62 Fruoco, 'C. S. Lewis and T. S. Eliot', p. 87.

63 Fruoco, ibid., p. 88.

64 Fruoco, ibid., p. 88.

65 Fruoco, ibid., p. 91; Carpenter, *The Inklings*, p. 246.

66 Fruoco, ibid., p. 92.

Grahame and John Buchan. There are also, perhaps, certain 'Georgian' characteristics about him. But his roots were buried deep in early literature, and the major names in twentieth-century writing meant little or nothing to him. He read very little modern fiction, and took no serious notice of it.[67]

It is an unquestionable fact that Tolkien was not generally interested in modern literature, but it is a striking statement that, as Patchen Mortimer claims in his paper 'Tolkien and Modernism', Tolkien was a 'modernist writer', unless, as Mortimer argues, one understands modernism as a complex multi-faceted phenomenon; or 'a collection of [sometimes contradictory] movements'.[68] There is a 'tendency to consider Tolkien's works as escapist and romantic; the work of a man removed from his own time', Mortimer explains; yet, that common belief is, as he views is, 'an appalling oversight' because 'Tolkien's project was as grand and avant-garde as that of Wagner, or the Futurists, and his works are as suffused with the spirit of the age as any by Eliot, Joyce, or Hemingway'.[69] Therefore, Mortimer proposes,

> It is vital that Tolkien's work be regarded not as isolated or anachronistic, but as part of the literary current. By turns a soldier, linguist, and mythographer, Tolkien was a writer fully in touch with his era, and his work reveals modernist attributes – and even ambitions of modernist scope – that deserve to be explored.[70]

Among these modernist attributes and characteristics Mortimer places, for instance, Tolkien's preoccupation with the problem of war, overwhelming technology, urban and mechanical sterility, and a sense of displacement in the new reality.[71] Instead of spreading the modernist malady, though, Tolkien chose to address contemporary issues through the lens of the (often pre-industrial) past, such as in *The Lord of the Ring, Hobbit* or *Silmarillion*); from a perspective distanced in time (and sometimes space), which allowed a more comprehensive and objective overview of the immediate reality. As Tolkien put it himself, he chose Faërie, whose attributes are Fantasy, Escape (not to be confused with escapism), Recovery, and Consolation, which are all conducive to the reader's enrichment and refreshment, as they provide new insights into the real-world quandaries.[72] Mortimer seems to suggest that Tolkien, just like Lewis and the

---

67 Carpenter, *The Inklings*, pp. 157–158.
68 Patchen Mortimer, 'Tolkien and Modernism', [in:] *Tolkien Studies 2005: An Annual Scholarly Review*, vol. 2, Douglas A. Anderson, Michael D. C. Drout, Verlyn Flieger, eds. (Morgantown: West Virginia University Press, 2005), pp. 113–129, 113.
69 Mortimer, ibid., p. 113.
70 Mortimer, ibid., p. 113.
71 Mortimer, ibid., p. 115.
72 Tolkien, 'On Fairy-Stories', pp. 143–154.

other Inklings, while dealing with modern problems does not abandon the disillusioned reader in the waste land, but through the experience of enchantment in the Logos-based realm of Faërie seems to equip them with ways of dealing with the immediate reality. 'In the final analysis,' Mortimer concludes, 'one might say that Tolkien is engaged in a delicate balancing act – mourning the past while facing the future, and transcribing the modern age with tools of the past.'[73]

As far as Ursula K. Le Guin's approach to modernism is concerned, (whom I view as a writer that largely shares the Inklings' understanding of fantasy and myth), she protests against denigrating meaning-based high fantasy, grounded in the Inklings' contribution to the literary legacy of the day, often considered by critics as mere 'genre fiction' and placed far behind the classical works of modernism by the 'ivied or ivory towers' of English departments; and she opposes the genre fiction versus literature division:[74]

> A lot of literature is happening outside the sacred groves of modernist realism. But still the opposition of literature and genre is maintained; and as long as it is, false categorical value judgment will cling to it, with the false dichotomy of virtuous pleasure and guilty pleasure.[75]

To Le Guin 'literature is the extant body of written art', to which 'all novels belong'; therefore, 'the value judgment concealed in distinguishing one novel as literature [for instance Joyce's or Woolf's] and another as genre [for example Tolkien's, Lewis's, Williams's, or her own] vanishes with the distinction.'[76] Le Guin's personal desire is to be considered an American novelist and poet, and not just a genre writer of fantasy and science fiction, which is the way she is usually pigeonholed by mainstream critics who somehow rule out fantasy and science fiction from the genre of novel proper.[77] In his book, *Ursula K. Le Guin Beyond Genre*, Mike Cadden argues that Le Guin's work represents a perilous but excellently performed frequent crossing over from genre to genre (from fiction to her recent poetry, from fiction to non-fiction, from fantasy to science fiction, from science fiction to literary criticism, from fantasy to realism, 'there and back again'), which reflects Le Guin's various interests and, paradoxically, her preoccupation with maintaining

---

73 Tolkien, ibid., p. 126.
74 Le Guin, 'Le Guin's Hypothesis', June 18, 2012, http://bookviewcafe.com/blog/2012/06/18/le-guin-s-hypothesis/; accessed 23 April 2016.
75 Le Guin, ibid.
76 Le Guin, 'Le Guin's Hypothesis'.
77 As I have observed in Chapter One, an example could be *The Cambridge Companion to American Novelists* (2013), edited by Timothy Parrish, which neither mentions nor indexes Le Guin's name.

'continuity rather than separation'[78] Le Guin 'has made that crossing, seemingly unscathed, many times now', Cadden notes, disregarding generic boundaries, as 'she speeds by in a vehicle that is at once spaceship, stroller, family wagon, and dragon'[79] 'She's a writer more interested in matters of degree than kind, which is why she rails against the dividing lines critics, bookstores, and libraries impose on the literary world'[80] Perhaps more dust needs to settle on her work until she is recognized by Academia not only as an author of children's and young adults' fantasy and science fiction (the genres endorsed by the Inklings but not limited to any particular age group), but also as an American novelist who has authored excellent imaginative and speculative fiction, as well as poetry and essays, and whose most recent novel is an interesting generic hybrid, *Lavinia* (2008).[81] A notable milestone in the history of critical evaluation of Le Guin's writing is certainly the Medal for Distinguished Contribution to American Letters, which she received in November 2014 from the National Book Awards Foundation in appreciation of her life achievement. In this book, which focuses on high fantasy fiction, I approach Le Guin's legacy with regard to this part of her oeuvre only, tracing the parallels between her understanding of fantasy and the thought of the Inklings, in the context of Faërie's therapeutic qualities.

Returning to the Inklings viewed as a group, one might ask what their rapport with modernism was, and whether there was anything that could be summarized as a common Inkling attitude towards the mainstream literature of the day. Were the Inklings a group of die-hards that shunned novelty and progress at university, in literature, and in life? 'Whatever the Inklings may have been during their most clubbable years, today they constitute a major literary force, a movement of sorts', the Zaleskis maintain, 'and what prevented the Inklings from being considered as a formal school or movement, the way modernists were, was very much their humility'[82] 'As symbol, inspiration, guide, and rallying cry, the Inklings grow more influential each year', the Zaleskis note.[83] 'This acclamation has led to much grinding of teeth, not least because the Inklings

---

78 Mike Cadden, *Ursula K. Le Guin Beyond Genre* (New York: Routledge, 2005), pp. xii-xiii. The phrase 'there and back again' is a quote borrowed from the tile of Tolkien's children's story *The Hobbit, or There and Back Again.*
79 Cadden, ibid., p. xii.
80 Cadden, ibid., p. xii.
81 Tolkien did not write science fiction, but supported Lewis in his writing of the Space Trilogy, especially *Out of the Silent Planet*, as discussed in Chapter One of this book.
82 The Zaleskis, *The Fellowship*, pp. 508–509.
83 Ibid., p. 509.

never achieved the formal brilliance of the greatest of their contemporaries, such as Joyce, Woolf, Nabokov, Borges, or Eliot.[84]

The true novelty which the Inklings championed, safeguarding tradition at the same time, was a mythopoeic awakening, perhaps more powerful and challenging than that of modernists, inasmuch as the Inklings set myth-making rather than myth-recycling standards. Another landmark of the Inklings' legacy, as the Zaleskis observe, was 'a Christian awakening', which, instrumental to the thought of the Inklings, was a spiritual experience shared by some modernists as well, primarily by T. S. Eliot, yet that was an experience which proved an exception rather than a rule among the other representatives of the movement, suffice it to mention Ezra Pound, James Joyce, Virginia Woolf, D. H. Lawrence, or E. M. Forster, who all rejected religion as such, and Christianity in particular.[85] The mentor of modernists, Pound observes that 'there is no need to pretend that everyone [for instance the Inklings] subscribes to a bastard faith [that is Christianity,] designed for the purpose of making good Roman citizens slaves, and which is thoroughly different from that preached in Palestine. In this sense Christ is thoroughly dead.'[86]

In a sense, modernity of the 1920s was nothing new, for 'modernity is a qualitative, not a chronological category,' which had manifested itself many times, for instance with the 'God is dead' slogan, before the advent of the 20th century.[87] Nevertheless, the modernity of the interwar period, or at least its futurist movement, heralded an outright rejection of tradition and an uprooting of values on an unprecedented scale. The modernist stress on the unlimited experimentation, radicalism, and primitivism, as well as its fascination with science and technology, with transgressing boundaries and desacralizing reality, meant that modernist writers dismissed intelligible plots, characterization in novels, and abolished grand narratives, promoting in their stead texts that would defy conventions and challenge critical interpretation. In Pound's words, modernism was about annihilating

---

84 The Zaleskis, ibid., p. 509.
85 The Zaleskis, ibid., p. 510. E. M. Forster's relationship with modernism was vexed, yet he rejected Christian faith as well.
86 Ezra Pound, Letter to Harriet Monroe, 20 January 1914, *The Selected Letters of Ezra Pound, 1907–1941*, D. D. Paige, ed. (New York: New Directions, 1950, 1971), p. 30.
87 Theodor W. Adorno, *Minima Moralia. Reflections from Damaged Life* (London: Verso, 2005), p. 218. 'God is dead' is a famous statement made by Fredrich Nietzsche in his *Die fröhliche Wissenschaft* (*The Gay Science*) of 1882 and *Also sprach Zarathustra* (*Thus Spoke Zarathustra*) (1885–1891).

tradition so as to 'make it new.'[88] That categorical imperative involved all: the content, form, style, aesthetics, language, meaning, and the underlying idea of the text, leading over time to a profound sense of new nihilism that has come to permeate contemporary culture and literature.[89] The fusion of the mass consumerist and high elitist forms of modernism, which had occurred by the mid-20th c., cushioned the original revolutionary impact of the trend and to some extent gave rise to what became known as postmodernism, the subsequent period in the history of culture and thought, viewed by some critics and scholars as a distinct entity and by others as a merely chronological extension of modernism.[90]

Postmodernism, whose birth and early growth the Oxford writers witnessed rather unknowingly yet with much concern, started after the Second World War around 1945 or the 50s in the Western culture (it first entered the *Oxford English Dictionary* in 1949), and reinforced the denial of an objective truth and a refusal to recognize a universal sense or pattern. The postmodernist preoccupation with neo-Nietzschean nothingness arose in the atmosphere of 'broad skepticism, subjectivism, as well as metaphysical, epistemological and ethical relativism', 'a general suspicion of reason and an acute sensitivity to the role of ideology in asserting and maintaining political and economic power.'[91] Václav Havel describes the postmodern world as one based on science, in which, paradoxically, 'everything is possible and almost nothing is certain.'[92] Josh McDowell and Bob Hostetler offer a similar definition of postmodernism naming it 'a worldview characterized by the belief that truth does not exist in any objective sense but is created rather than discovered'; 'created by the specific culture and existing

---

88 Ezra Pound, *Poetry and Prose*, 11 vols. (London: Garland, 1991), IV, C603, p. 102. Pound writes, 'the artist is always beginning. Any work of art which is not a beginning, an invention, a discovery is of little worth. The very name *Troubadour* means a 'finder'; 'one who discovers.'

89 Cf. Jean Baudrillard, *On Nihilism* (chapter XVIII) [in:] *Simulacra and Simulation*, transl. S. F. Glaser (Ann Arbor: Michigan University Press, 1994); and Ashley Woodward, *Nihilism in Postmodernity: Lyotard, Baudrillard, Vattimo* (Denver: The Davies Group Publishers, 2009).

90 Perry Anderson, *The Origins of Postmodernity* (London: Verso, 1998), p. 12.

91 *Encyclopædia Britannica*, http://www.britannica.com/EBchecked/topic/1077292/postmodernism; accessed 25 April 2016.

92 Václav Havel, 'The Need for Transcendence in the Postmodern World', 4 July 1994, [in:] *The Futurist*, July-August 1995, pp. 46–49; http://www.hrad.cz/president/Havel/speeches/index_CHU.html, accessed 20 December 2015.

only in that culture, therefore, any system or statement that tries to communicate truth is a power play, an effort to dominate other cultures.'[93]

The prevailing climate of postmodernism in the West, that is one of demise, ultimate deconstruction and existential vacuum, has intensified the severity of the modernist symptoms of defragmentation and meaninglessness that developed in the aftermath of the First World War and worsened after the Second, as manifested in the philosophical works of Baudrillard, Lyotard, Vattimo, and Lacan, to name but a few. However, postmodernism has taken the modernist rejection of rules, standards and principles to the extreme, for, unlike modernism, it has rejected everything, offering virtually nothing instead.[94] 'It seems sometimes that the postmodern mind is a critique caught at the moment of its ultimate triumph: a critique that finds it ever more difficult to go on being critical just because it has destroyed everything it used to be critical about,' Zygmunt Bauman observes.[95]

And yet much criticism, whether explicit or implicit, has survived in literature – the criticism of or concern with the postmodernist and postmodern neonihilism and its dismal picture of existence, which is not demonized but shown as reductionist and distorted. There is a yearning for long-abandoned and compromised wholesome systems that could make an alternative to the contemporary mainstream philosophy of moral relativism and liquidity, and that might affirm purposefulness and meaningfulness of life, of morality, culture, language, and any human action. It is not merely an expression of an incorrigible romantic *Sehnsucht* but of firm reassurance that there is a pattern in the seemingly unpatterned universe, and sense that never devalues.[96] This kind of opposition to the philosophy of modernism and early postmodernism seems to constitute much of the essence

---

93 Josh McDowell and Bob Hostetler, *The New Tolerance* (Carol Stream IL: Tyndale House, 1998), p. 208.

94 Zygmunt Bauman, *Intimations of Postmodernity* (London: Routledge, 1991), p. vii.

95 Bauman, ibid., p. vii.

96 The German word *Sehnsucht* means 'longing, yearning, or craving for', http://www.collinsdictionary. com/dictionary/german-english/sehnsucht. It gained a particular significance in the works of C. S. Lewis, who viewed it as an inconsolable longing in the human heart for something that escapes definition. In the afterword to the third edition of his *The Pilgrim's Regress* Lewis mentions the source of *Sehnsucht*: 'that unnameable something, desire for which pierces us like a rapier at the smell of bonfire, the sound of wild ducks flying overhead, the title of *The Well at the World's End* [William Morris's fantasy novel of 1896], the opening lines of 'Kubla Khan', the morning cobwebs in late summer, or the noise of falling waves.' (London: Geoffrey Bles, 1992), p. 201.

of the Inklings' oeuvre and thought, for in their mature works they unwaveringly represent values and principles alien to the spirit of modernism and postmodernism, that is those striving towards spiritual and moral integrity, coherence, meaningfulness, and hope. However, the Inklings can hardly be called tradition-alists, either, due to their innovative approach to literature, especially the peculiar synthesis of fantasy and Christianity that defines their works, as borrowed mostly from medieval lore, and their mythopoeic fiction, which exemplifies myth-making rather than, common among many writers, including prominent modernists, myth-recycling or myth-rewriting. That logo-centric, consistently Christian, and thus unfashionable and unabashedly unmodern pattern of their thought and writing is perhaps what has made them a group of practically negligible writers in the history of English literature, as some of its major anthologies and study guides mentioned in the first chapter of this book seem to suggest.[97]

The Inklings and their place in the literary history of the past century

In the heyday of modernism and then at the onset of the post-modernist era, when the most prolific Inklings (Lewis, Tolkien, Williams, and Barfield) wrote their works, the thought, academic teaching and fiction of the Oxford writers, with their distinct blend of Christianity, myth, and Faërie, was certainly marginal and cast adrift beyond the mainstream. Yet, over time their quasi neo-medieval (and neo-romantic) frame of mind has come to signify a landmark in the history of literature and scholarship. Their works have excited considerable academic interest, especially posthumously, despite numerous controversies over their academic value, still courted by some critics today, but it is Tolkien who was voted the most important author of the past century in the UK, beating the canonical modernists and postmodernists, and receiving attention from many scholars (some of whom found Tolkien's victory outrageous) and non-academics alike.[98] An example of considerable reluctance towards Tolkien's fiction and, consequently, towards the Inklings' legacy, can be a declaration of Germaine Greer, an Australian critic, who admits:

> Ever since I arrived at Cambridge as a student in 1964 and encountered a tribe of full-grown women wearing puffed sleeves, clutching teddies and babbling excitedly about

---

97 Cf. footnote 1 in Chapter One of this book.

98 Tolkien was voted the author of the century in three independent polls, which met with considerable disbelief and hostility on the part of some critics, cf. om Shippey, *J. R. R. Tolkien: Author of the Century* (London: Mariner Books, 2001), p. 8.

the doings of hobbits, it has been my nightmare that Tolkien would turn out to be the most influential writer of the twentieth century. The bad dream has materialised. The books that come in Tolkien's train are more or less what you would expect; flight from reality is their dominating characteristic.[99]

It appears to be an expression of unjustified prejudice provoked by a sophomoric reaction of some readers rather than a result of a critical study of Tolkien's work. Tolkien profoundly detested the cloy, ill logic and escapism of fake Fantasy, and ruled it out from the realm of Faërie both in his essay 'On Fairy-Stories' and in his own fantasy works. So did the other Inklings and Le Guin, as I try to demonstrate in this book. *The Hobbit*, *The Lord of the Rings*, *The Chronicles of Narnia*, and the Earthsea series, to name but a few titles, can hardly be called immature or escapist fantasy, even though it is enjoyed also by children, inasmuch as instead of flying from reality these stories of Faërie show reality from a different and fresher, and larger, perspective, sometimes more wittingly and playfully, sometimes more painfully, but often more clearly and accurately than non-fantasy fiction, especially with regard to human psychological and spiritual life.

This view, espoused by the Inklings and by Le Guin, does not appear popular among some scholars, represented by Professor Harold Bloom, one of the most eminent American literary critics and 'a gatekeeper of the Western literary canon', who expresses his considerable aesthetic reservations as to the import of Tolkien's work and Tolkien's position in the history of English literature, approaching *The Lord of the Rings* as an early product of the short-lived hippie movement.[100] 'I suspect that *The Lord of the Rings* is fated to become only an intricate period piece, while *The Hobbit* may well survive as children's literature', Bloom declares as an editor of *J. R. R. Tolkien*, a volume of criticism.[101] 'Its style is quaint, pseudobiblical, overly melodramatic, and its personages are so much cardboard', he concludes, '[b]ut then I am aware that my standards are literary-critical, and many now find them archaic in our age of pop culture.'[102] It is interesting to note that

99   W: The Waterston's Magazine, Winter/Spring 1997, qtd. by Shippey in his foreword to *J. R. R. Tolkien: Author of the Century*, p. xxii.

100 Chris Mooney, 'Kicking the Hobbit', November 5, 2001, *The American Prospect*, http://prospect.org/article /kicking-hobbit, accessed 26 April 2016. In 1994 Bloom published *The Western Canon: The Books and School of the Ages* (New York: Harcourt Brace).

101 Harold Bloom, Introduction to *J. R. R. Tolkien* (New York: Bloom's Literary Criticism, 2008), p. 2.

102 Bloom, Editor's Note to *J. R. R. Tolkien's The Lord of the Rings* (New York: Bloom's Literary Criticism, 2008), p. vii.

Bloom calls his own standards 'archaic' and 'literary-critical', while suggesting that Tolkien's epic is only successful because of the low pop-culture standards it meets, and because of its pseudobiblical and melodramatic appeal. Hardly anything could be farther from the truth if one considers Tolkien's exceptionally high standards of language, matter, and style, and also his ambition to reconstruct the missing mythology of England, rather than to provide a piece of ephemeral entertainment for the masses, however modest and ordinary life Tolkien lived. Bloom agrees with Roger Sale, another critic, observing that:

> [*The Lord of the Rings*] purports to be a quest but is actually a descent into hell. Whether a visionary descent into hell can be rendered persuasively in language that is acutely self-conscious, even arch, seems to me a hard question. I am fond of *The Hobbit*, which is rarely pretentious, but *The Lord of the Rings* seems to me inflated, over-written, tendentious and moralistic in the extreme. Is it not a giant Period Piece? … I am not able to understand how a skilled and mature reader can absorb about fifteen hundred pages of this quaint stuff…. Sometimes, reading Tolkien, I am reminded of the Book of Mormon. Tolkien met a need, particularly in the early days of the Counter-culture, in the later 1960s. Whether he is an author for the coming century seems to me open to some doubt.[103]

Michael Moorcock, a famous fantasy and science fiction writer, who has also contributed a paper on Tolkien to Bloom's volume concerning *The Lord of the Rings*, mockingly points to a 'therapeutic' dimension of Tolkien's epic, reading it in terms of an enlarged soothing Pooh-like story, which features a 'willy nilly silly old bear' kind of protagonist, that is Frodo, who has, just like A. A. Milne's fluffy hero, 'a very little brain', all cast in a nursery-room like language and tone:

> The sort of prose most identified with 'high' fantasy is the prose of the nursery-room. It is a lullaby; it is meant to soothe and console. It is mouth-music. It is frequently enjoyed not for its tensions but for its lack of tensions. It coddles, it makes friends with you; it tells you comforting lies. It is soft.[104]

In short, Moorcock claims, *The Lord of the Rings* is an 'epic Pooh.'[105] This seems to stand in marked contrast to Bloom's statement that Tolkien's work exemplifies a 'descent into hell', regardless of what criteria of judgement are to be applied. Anyhow, if one fails to identify the imaginative, linguistic, and moral depth of Tolkien's otherworld, (indeed, populated not only by humans, but also by elves, hobbits, dwarves, dragons, and talking trees), with its underlying tensions and

---

103 Bloom, Introduction to *J. R. R. Tolkien's The Lord of the Rings*, p. 1.
104 Michael Moorcock, 'Epic Pooh', [in:] *J. R. R. Tolkien's The Lord of the Rings*, Harold Bloom, ed., pp. 3–18, 4.
105 Ibid, p. 3.

havoc wrought by the corrupting power of evil, and misses the final eucatastrophe or a happy ending which comes almost painfully, as it costs much suffering, sacrifice, and brings along a radical change, then one may well dub *Beowulf* or *Sir Gain and the Green Knight* (some of Tolkien's favourite texts) children's 'lullabies' meant to 'soothe and console' at bedtime, full of ridiculous creatures (ogres, water-hags, trolls, giants, elves, and dragons) that picture a blissful 'Merry England' utopia. In this book, over the following chapters, especially the sixth and seventh, I suggest a therapeutic reading of Tolkien's and other Inklings', as well as Le Guin's, high fantasy fiction in very different categories from Moorcock's 'epic Pooh' pastoral.

Considering the apparently anti-fantasy attitude professed by some of today's critics, who view the lore of the Inklings in terms of antiquated neo-Christian nursery lullabies, it comes as no surprise that fantasy fiction did not bring the Inklings much recognition in their day, and that for much of their lifetime the Inklings remained relatively unknown outside their closest circle of friends, fellows and students. Tolkien's sweeping popularity grew after the publication of *The Lord of the Rings* in 1954–1955, when he was in his sixties. Lewis became famous first in the wartime thanks to his BBC Christian talks (1941–44), and massively, as a writer, only after the publication of the Narnian heptalogy (1949–1954), yet died nearly forgotten on 22 November 1963, his quiet departure being eclipsed by the news of J. F. Kennedy's assassination and of Aldous Huxley's death, which all happened on the same day. The third most prolific Inkling, Charles Williams, died suddenly in 1945 and lingers in the shadow of Tolkien and Lewis, remaining scarcely a familiar name, despite his sizeable legacy. Similarly, few recognize the name of Owen Barfield, often hailed the first and last Inkling, as he was Lewis's old friend and lived the longest of them all – the author of a unique study of myth that made the Inklings' informal artistic manifesto (*Poetic Diction*, 1928). Little as it is known, *Poetic Diction* inspired the Inklings and other generations of writers, and, as Howard Nemerov, US Poet Laureate admitted, it had been 'valued not only as a secret book, but nearly as a sacred one among the poets and teachers of [his] acquaintance.'[106]

Barfield, whose literary recognition in Europe seems to be slowly dawning, received some acclaim in America, but only in his late sixties, when he was invited by Stanley Hopper to lecture at Drew University in New Jersey and was accosted as a celebrity - 'an honour which he [had] never been accorded in his own land (to its eternal shame)', as his biographer, Simon Blaxland-de Lange

---

106   Howard Nemerov, Foreword to *Poetic Diction* (Middletown: Wesleyan University Press, 1978), pp. 1–10, 3.

observes.'[107] Towards the end of his long life, in the United States Barfield won many admirers and even became for a time 'something of a cult', probably in the wake of the adulation for Tolkien, Barfield being 'somewhat too indigestible for cult-mania'.[108] The self-effacing Barfield, still retaining the stutter he had developed in his adolescence, treasured the recognition he had earned in the New World very much.[109] Blaxland-de Lange calls Barfield 'a man who had written many books which most people never read (even those who might be expected to have done so)', a label that seems to fit Williams as well. However, instead of growing bitter, Barfield emanated serenity and humility, and with his great sense of humour propounded his own law of book reading: 'those who read it don't need it, and those who need it don't read it.'[110] Blaxland-de Lange argues that 'it is safe to say that this was a man whose greatness will be recognized more fully and richly after his death than it was while he was alive', a presumption that has proved true in the case of a great many posthumously rehabilitated writers.[111]

Considering Barfield's contribution to the formation of the Inklings' mind-set and their shared artistic creed, if it had existed, that is one based on the mythopoeic fusion of imagination, faith and reason, one must not overlook the fact that it was Barfield who led Lewis to accept the fact that imagination could be a tool of intellectual research and a vital auxiliary to rational discernment, the truth which Tolkien had acclaimed early and Lewis embraced only in the wake of the 'Great War' he fought with Barfield in the 1920s.[112] 'Barfield tower[ed] above us all... the wisest and best of my unofficial teachers', confessed Lewis, who dedicated to Barfield his first scholarly book, *The Allegory of Love* (1936), and to Barfield's adopted daughter Lucy – his first Narnian chronicle, *The Lion, the Witch and the Wardrobe* (1949).[113]

---

107 Simon Blaxland-de Lange, *Obituary for Owen Barfield;* accessed 25 April 2016; http:// davidlavery.net/barfield/barfield_resources/death.html. Blaxland de Lange has also written Barfield's biography *Owen Barfield: Romanticism Come of Age: A Biography* (Forest Row: Temple Lodge, 2006), whose title reiterates Barfield's collection of essays *Romanticism Comes of Age: Essays on the Creative Imagination* (London: Barfield Press UK, 2012).

108 Blaxland-de Lange, *Obituary for Owen Barfield.*

109 Blaxland-de Lange, ibid.

110 Blaxland-de Lange, ibid.

111 Blaxland-de Lange, ibid.

112 Carpenter, *The Inklings*, p. 98.

113 Quoted on the front cover of Blaxland-de Lange's *Owen Barfield: Romanticism Come of Age: A Biography. The Lion, the Witch and the Wardrobe* was written and published as the first part of the *Chronicles of Narnia*, although is recommended to be read as

In spite of the Inklings' quiet and unpretentious demeanour and humble lives, rather different from those of the leading modernists, their fiction partakes of the vitality of masterpieces and holds an invigorating power which has catalysed the development of contemporary fantasy culture. Without Tolkien's *The Lord of the Rings, The Silmarillion, The Hobbit,* and other stories and essays, and without Lewis's *The Chronicles of Narnia,* his Space Trilogy, Christian fiction and non-fiction, the new genre of high fantasy, fairy tale for grown-ups, and modern myth would probably not have gained ground nor become an iconic expression of a fantasy renaissance that has marked the end of the bimilennial culture. Furthermore, without the work of the Inklings, including the little known novels, plays and Arthurian poetry of Williams, and Barfield's works on the spiritual development of human consciousness, the ancient and neo-medieval mind-set that promotes a union of faith and fantasy, intellect and imagination, reason and emotion, which is a natural mythopoeic faculty, (a synthesis that could be called the 'association of sensibility', an inversion of T. S. Eliot's concept,) might not have been reframed.[114]

'Fantasy remains a human right,' Tolkien says; 'we make in our measure and in our derivative mode, because we are made: and not only made, but made in the image and likeness of a Maker.'[115] Nevertheless, despite the fact that Fantasy contains a splinter of the divine creativity and the highest form of art, like any human thing it can be misused and ill-done, twisting the minds of people and becoming a sheer commodity; '[Fantasy] can be carried to excess' and 'put to evil uses,' Tolkien observes, so that it may result in perversion, trash or kitsch.[116] Le Guin states alike that, when ground by 'the mills of capitalism,' 'fantasy becomes a commodity, an industry;' a pulp.[117] When it 'invents nothing but [merely] imitates and trivialises', it ceases to be art, which Tolkien labels the 'elvish craft' and

---

the second part of the heptalogy in the reading chronological order, after *The Magician's Nephew,* which was completed by Lewis as a penultimate book of Narnia. *The Lion, the Witch and the Wardrobe* tells a story of four evacuee children from London: the Pevensie siblings: Peter, Susan, Edmund and Lucy, who are staying at Professor Digory Kirke's house in the country in 1940.

114 The term 'association of sensibility' is antonymous to T. S. Eliot's notion of the 'dissociation of sensibility', that is a separation of thought and feeling, which he believed had occurred in literature after the period of 'Metaphysical Poetry' of the early 17th c. (T. S. Eliot, 'The Metaphysical Poets', 1921).

115 Tolkien, 'On Fairy- Stories', p. 145.

116 Tolkien, ibid., p. 144.

117 Le Guin, 'Foreword' to *The Tales of Earthsea* (London: Orion, 2003), p. xiv.

the act of 'sub-creation', that is the human faculty of making, which dimly reflects the genius of 'a Maker'.[118] Wary of the contemporary danger of corrupting fantasy, Le Guin warns that:

> Commodified fantasy, [which is sheerly imitative and reductionist], proceeds by depriving the old stories of their intellectual and ethical complexity, turning their action to violence, their actors to dolls, and their truth-telling to sentimental platitude. Heroes brandish their swords, lasers, wands, as mechanically as combine harvesters, reaping profits. Profoundly disturbing moral choices are sanitized, made cute, made safe. The passionately conceived ideas of the great story-tellers are copied, stereotyped, reduced to toys, molded in bright-colored plastic, advertised, sold, broken, junked, replaceable, and changeable.[119]

Fantasy as propounded by the Inklings, (now often dubbed as 'high' not just due to its otherworldly settings, but also in contrast to its trite copies), that is the intellectually demanding and inherently moral, though not moralizing, imaginative fiction, which 'catches the glimpse of otherworld', has been carefully defined and characterized in detail by Tolkien in his essay 'On Fairy-Stories', on which Le Guin partly draws in her own non-fiction on fantasy. 'High fantasy' mythopoeia might not have entered the post-modern culture without the Inklings' collective effort, to some extent continued across the Atlantic by Le Guin. Hence, the following questions arise, waiting for an answer that time trial and critical scholarship may provide:

Is the thought and output of the Inklings, especially of Tolkien, Lewis, Barfield, and Williams, a negligible periphery or one of the 'peripheral' centres of the 20th century's fragmented literary landscape? Can the Inklings be counted as 'modernist writers', once a more comprehensive understanding of the term is adopted? Is their literary legacy an instance of hobbyist low-brow writing [for children or young adults] assembled by otherwise respectable conservative Oxford scholars and affiliates, or a legacy that deserves universal academic recognition as a phenomenon in the history of 20th c. literature? Was the fiction of the Inklings a contradictory response to the technological and moral revolution after the First World War and a part of modernism, as the movement developed various, often conflicting forms, or was it a separate, detached faction – an Oxford splinter group? Do the Inklings belong to the second generation of modernists (1930s–ca. 1945), critical of the mainstream movement, yet following the modernist fascination with myth and its archetypal logic that may impose a pattern on the increasingly defragmented reality? Were the Inklings Christian

---

118 Le Guin, ibid., p. xiv. Tolkien, *On Fairy-Stories*, p. 124.
119 Le Guin, ibid., p. xiv.

writers of Oxford, whose 'fairytaleness' had a *sui generis* quality? And finally, were the Inklings, in a way, neo-romantics, who drew on fantasy, ancient myth and medieval romance and thus anticipated the anti-postmodernist movement that seeks the revival of imagination and spirituality against the cult of science and consumerist narrative? Can their fiction be viewed as an instance of a minor neoromantic or neo-Christian revival in the British literature? And, finally, can their unique legacy be approached in terms of fantasy bibliotherapy and logo-therapy? It is impossible to do justice to all these questions within the scope of this book, as that requires more thorough research and a much sharper and learned mind, yet a few aspects of the position of the Inklings against the background of modernism and early postmodernism considered below may shed some light on the problems posed above.

The Inklings definitely saw themselves at odds with their time and its progressive literature, and would frequently emphasize their incompatibility with the movement of the day. Joy Davidman-Gresham, Lewis's prospective wife, described the Inklings as 'a few scattered survivors' of the Old Western Culture, which was centred upon Christianity; the men who 'loved being a minority, even a lost-cause minority', like '*Athanasius contra mundum*' or 'Don Quixote against the windmills'; determined to swim against the tide, outnumbered but undaunted.[120] The Inklings' lonely crusade against modernism, led by their arguably most outspoken and active member, Lewis, (Tolkien remaining more elusive in style, form and content), sought to revive the 'Old Western Culture', as Lewis called it himself in his inaugural lecture at Cambridge.[121] By contrast with the pre-Christian and Christian stages of human civilization, he named modernity the 'post-Christian period' and identified it as an age of the machine and of a new mentality – the 'machine mentality', which engenders the abuse of power and possession, and urges man to dominate and suppress nature.[122]

---

120 Duriez, *J. R. R. Tolkien and C. S. Lewis: The Gift of Friendship*, p. 150. '*Athanasius contra mundum*' (Athanasius against the world) is a phrase related to Saint Athanasius of Alexandria (ca.296–373), the twentieth bishop of Alexandria and one of the fours eastern doctors of the Roman Catholic Church. Athanasius opposed the Arian heresy and was involved in a theological and political struggle against the emperors Constantine the Great and Constantius II.

121 Lewis, *De description temporum*, an inaugural lecture, Cambridge University, 25 November 1954. Duriez, *The Gift of Friendship*, p. 153.

122 Duriez, ibid., p. 153. Harry Blamires, Lewis's former student and a noted British Christian thinker, born in 1916, has written several books on Christianity in postmodernity,

To Lewis and Tolkien the new technocracy and the machine attitude were yet another form of black magic and abused art, and Tolkien understood it as an inversion of the elvish craft, a genuine art driven by the pure altruistic desire to create beauty and harmony, outlined in his lecture-cum-essay 'On Fairy-Stories'. At the heart of the elvish craft lies Enchantment, Tolkien says, and 'the desire for a living, realised sub-creative art, which (however much it may outwardly resemble it) is inwardly wholly different from the greed for self-centred power which is the mark of the mere Magician.'[123] When uncorrupted, the elvish craft 'does not seek delusion, nor bewitchment or domination; it seeks shared enrichment, partners in making and delight, not slaves.'[124] The modernist and post-modernist cult of materialism and the machine aims, however, (often covertly) at enslavement, manipulation and surveillance rather than freedom or spiritual development. The elvish craft nobilitates and elevates human nature; the modern reification of machines, gadgets and objects degrades man and subjugates humanity to the mechanical world.

If the Inklings might be called neo-romantics, as they were in love with myth, enchantment and fantasy, and felt estranged from the modern technological craze, they would not have suffered being accused of daydreaming, sentimentality or irrationality.[125] On the contrary, logical and reasonable thinking was their high priority. The Inklings' literary legacy, particularly that of Tolkien, Lewis, Barfield, and Williams, varied and heterogeneous though it was, resulted from the union of minds and imaginations, and a fusion of reason and faith, as the writers believed that the path to Faërie and myth leads through rational cognition. Tolkien accounts for this seemingly paradoxical relationship between fantasy and reason in the following way:

> Fantasy is a natural human activity. It certainly does not destroy or even insult Reason, and it does not either blunt the appetite for, nor obscure the perception of, scientific verity. On the contrary. The keener and the clearer is the reason, the better fantasy will it make. If men were ever in a state in which they did not want to know or could not perceive truth (facts or evidence), then Fantasy would languish until they were cured.[126]

Le Guin argues in the same vein that fantasy narrative is not antirational, for rather than escaping from reality it intensifies and 'heightens' it:

---

some of them influenced by Lewis's thought, e.g., *The Christian Mind* (1996) and *The Post-Christian Mind* (2004).
123 Tolkien, 'On Fairy-Stories', p. 143.
124 Tolkien, ibid., p. 143.
125 Cf. R. J. Reilly, *Romantic Religion: A Study of Barfield, Lewis, Williams, and Tolkien* (Athens, GA: University of Georgia Press, 1972, 2006).
126 Tolkien, 'On Fairy-Stories', p. 144.

Fantasy, seen as art, not a spontaneous play (…) [offers] a different approach to reality, an alternative technique for apprehending and coping with existence. It is not antirational, but pararational; not realistic, but surrealistic, superrealistic, a heightening of reality.[127]

Those who have not managed to grasp the meaning of this axiom have accused the Inklings, Le Guin, and other high fantasy writers (that is those following the Tolkienian approach to the genre) of writing escapist fiction and cowering from reality into some absurd otherworldliness. This otherworldliness, however, favoured so much by the Inklings, was to them a means of bringing people closer to reality by demonstrating the timelessness of universal human traumas and offering a distance from the oppressive immediate actuality; a means of showing not only genuine beauty and spiritual love, but also intense suffering, guilt and death, that is the triad of human pain (referred to in more detail in Chapter Four), which enhances rather than eradicates meaningfulness of life. And, above all, the fantastic mode of dealing with reality in the Inklings' (and also in Le Guin's) works, attempts to point towards a renewal of hope based on simple eternal truths and humility, as well as towards a confirmation of a sense of existence, which some modernist and postmodernist works have compromised. In a word, there is, as it seems, a therapeutic aspect of their fantasy legacy, presented and discussed in the following chapters of this book.

Duriez places this shared antipathy to the ideology of the modern world at the very core of Tolkien and Lewis's friendship, yet hastens to remark that, despite their general dislike of new machinery and various state-of-the-art developments, the two Inklings:

Were not opposed to dentists, buses, draft beer and other features of the 20th century, but to what they viewed as the underlying mentality of modernism. They were not against science or scientists, but the cult of science found in modernism, and its tendency to monopolize knowledge, denying alternative approaches to knowledge, through the arts, religion and ordinary human wisdom. [They] felt that this mentality was a malaise that posed a serious threat to humanity.[128]

What the Inklings abhorred was the cult of science and the artificial urban jungle of a cosmopolitan city or industrialized countryside, which they viewed as a prison for man and a major threat to the freedom of thought. Hence comes their mythopoeic 'fabling' – writing fantasy and 'sub-creating' otherworldliness in order to offer liberty to the prisoners of modern civilization, but not to recruit

---

127   Le Guin, 'From Efland to Poughkeepsie', [in:] *The Language of the Night*, pp. 73–86, p. 74.
128   Tolkien, 'On Fairy-Stories', p. 154.

deserters escaping from reality.[129] The Inklings were obviously not against development itself, the one that is now called 'sustainable', and they did not express visceral hatred towards modernity, but rather feared the corrupting influence of power-and-profit-hungry scientists and dictators.

Another common denominator of Tolkien, Lewis and the other Inklings was a peculiar pre-modern Christian perception, based largely on a medieval insight into nature and humanity, and the medieval cosmology with its imaginative model of reality, showing the world as black and white, in the 'chiaroscuro' convention, if one borrows the light and darkness visualization from fine arts (as illustrated in Chapter Five of this book). That was a logical corollary of the Inklings' Christian thought, resisted, for instance, by Le Guin, who prefers a balanced complementariness of good and evil and a more 'sfumato-like', that is misty and mingled, imagery, in which the relationship between good and evil appears more complex and the discernment of good seems to depend on the existence of evil.[130]

The pre-modern mind-set, drawing a sharp line of demarcation between good and evil, was what the Inklings tried to 'smuggle' into the minds of modern readers as an alternative to and liberation from the self-imposed incarceration of relativism. The Inklings strove to create a chance of liberating the readers minds from the confines of sheer technology and materialism, and of reanimating people's starved imagination by showing them a glimpse of the world outside the prison walls of their oppressive routine; yet by no means did they advise desertion from reality.[131] On the contrary, the Inklings sought to make the secondary worlds recast the reality more vividly and lead the readers from the modernist and post-modernist nothingness to meaning, from the world of starved imagination to its haven; and so did and still does Le Guin, with a number of other writers, unanimous with the Inklings in this respect.[132]

The Inklings' road to meaning led very much along the mythopoeic paths of their underlying philosophy, which was a Christian way.[133] It split into multiple tracks, though: Tolkien was a conservative Roman Catholic, distinctly uneasy about

---

129 Tolkien, ibid., p. 147.
130 This discrepancy between the Inklings' Christian mind-set and Le Guin's non-Christian approach, as illustrated in visual terms by the chiaroscuro and sfumato dichotomy, is discussed in more detail in Chapter Five.
131 Tolkien, 'On Fairy-Stories', p. 139.
132 Duriez, *The Gift of Friendship*, p. 134. Tolkien, 'On Fairy-Stories', p. 146.
133 Mythopoeia means myth-making, as it comes from the Greek word *mythopoiein* (to make a myth) composed of *mythos* (myth) and *poiein* (to make), cf. *An Intermediate Greek–English Lexicon,* Henry George Liddell and Robert Scott, eds. (Oxford:

Williams's esotericism and its influence on Lewis. Christianity makes the bedrock of Tolkien's fiction, yet it is never explicit, remaining subtly and meticulously, and, perhaps, somehow elusively, interwoven into its very depth. Nonetheless, Christianity received prominent treatment in Tolkien's non-fiction, for instance in his 'On Fairy-Stories' essay, where Tolkien argues that: 'a piercing glimpse of joy, and heart's desire, that for a moment passes outside the frame, rends indeed the very web of story, and lets a gleam come through', may be 'a far-off gleam or echo of *Evangelium* in the real world.'[134] Although detached from Lewis's radical apology for Christianity, Tolkien himself propounds a radical interpretation of Faërie, reading it as a derivative of the Gospels – the four Biblical stories which have 'embrace[d] the essence of fairy-stories':[135]

> I would venture to say [Tolkien admits], that approaching the Christian Story from this direction, it has long been my feeling (a joyous feeling) that God redeemed the corrupt making-creatures, men, in a way fitting to this aspect, as to others, of their strange nature. The Gospels contain a fairy-story, or a story of a larger kind which embraces all the essence of fairy-stories. They contain many marvels – peculiarly artistic, beautiful, and moving: 'mythical' in their perfect, self-contained significance; and among the marvels is the greatest and most complete conceivable eucatastrophe [happy resolution]. But this story has entered History and the primary world; the desire and aspiration of sub-creation has been raised to the fulfilment of Creation. The Birth of Christ is the eucatastrophe of Man's history. The Resurrection is the eucatastrophe of the story of the Incarnation. This story begins and ends in joy. It has pre-eminently the 'inner consistency of reality'. There is no tale ever told that men have accepted as true on its own merits. For the Art of it has the supremely convincing tone of Primary Art, that is, of Creation. To reject it leads either to sadness or to wrath. (…) The Evangelium has not abrogated legends; it has hallowed them, especially the 'happy ending'.[136]

Drawing a parallel between the Christian *Evangelium* and the realm of fairy-stories, Tolkien seems to explain that, since the Gospels are not escapist, though marvellous, Faërie is not escapist, either; and just like the Gospels Faërie paves the way for hope through a trauma of suffering, doubt, and fear, only to reward sacrifice, faithfulness and humbleness with an unexpected joyous ending. And, above all, just like the Gospels, Faërie strives to show meaning and hope against what seems to have eradicated them for good. The importance of that interpretation of fairy-stories, including the key role of Tolkien's concept of Eucatastrophe,

---

Clarendon Press, 1889). 'Mythopoeia' is also a title of one of Tolkien's poems, quoted further on in this book.

134   Tolkien, 'On Fairy-Stories', pp. 154–155.
135   Tolkien, ibid., p. 155.
136   Tolkien, ibid., pp. 155–156.

to what may constitute psychotherapeutic properties of fantasy literature is discussed in Chapter Seven of this book.

Tracing the Christian paths of the Inklings further on, one must not fail to distinguish Lewis's religious formation. Born and baptized in the Church of Ireland, Lewis became an atheist in his youth, and after his conversion in 1931 (in which his passionate reading of books, as well as Dyson's, Tolkien's, Barfield's, and R. E. Havard's influence had played a vital role), he became an Anglican, 'a very ordinary layman of the Church of England, not especially "high", nor especially "low", nor especially anything else', and an ardent Christian apologist, consistently and unflaggingly accomplishing his 'hot-gospelling' mission.[137] Apart from Lewis's lay theology put forward in his Christian books, all his post-conversion fictional works bear an indelible mark of Christianity, often left as an allegory, pastiche or variation on Christian themes. Some critics identify a few quasi-Catholic elements of Lewis's faith, such as his practice of making confessions, believing in Purgatory, praying for the dead, and opposing liberalism among Anglican clergy; whereas others emphasize various non-Catholic elements of his religious belief, for instance his scepticism towards saluting Virgin Mary, angels and the saints, as well as his doubtful attitude to the doctrine of transubstantiation.[138] In his reading Lewis was versatile, as he acknowledged writers of various Christian denominations, for instance 'Roman Catholics such as Dante, Patmore, and Chesterton, non-Conformists like Bunyan, Milton, or George MacDonald, and Anglican writers from Hooker, Lancelot Andrewes, William Law, Jeremy Taylor and Dr Johnson to his own friends like Charles Williams, Dorothy L. Sayers and Austin Farrer.'[139]

Charles Williams, in turn, was a high Anglican, and, according to Theodore Maynard, an Anglo-Catholic who, due to his former initiation to the esoteric Fellowship of the Rosy Cross, and probably also to the occult Order of the Gold Dawn, 'established for himself a philosophical point of contact between Paganism and the Christian faith'.[140] Although Williams left the occult societies after a few years, their rites of alchemy, astrology, tarot divination and geomancy

---

137 Lewis, *Mere Christianity* (Glasgow: Fount Paperback, Collins, 1984), p. 4. R. E. Havard, Lewis's and Tolkien's doctor, was received into the Catholic Church in 1931.

138 Suzanne Bray, 'C. S. Lewis as an Anglican', [in:] *Persona and Paradox: Issues of Identity for C. S. Lewis, his Friends and Associates*, Suzanne Bray, William Gray, eds. (Cambridge: Cambridge Scholars Publishing, 2012), pp. 19–36; p. 22.

139 Bray, 'C. S. Lewis as an Anglican', p. 26.

140 Kerryl Lynne Henderson, '"It is Love that I am Seeking"': Charles Williams and *The Silver Stair*', [in:] *Charles Williams: A Celebration*, Brian Horne, ed. (London: Gracewing, 1995), pp. 131–152, 132.

had made a lasting impact on his mind and imagination. Williams developed his own Christian 'Romantic Theology' of Substituted Love, Exchange and Co-inherence, and a very conscious personal faith rationalized against his previous rather profound experience of occultism and kabbalah (he had been accused of Satanism by some critics – a judgement renounced later on upon closer examination of Williams's works by Theodore Maynard).[141] Williams also wrote several Christian theological books which continue to captivate and puzzle readers. Wystan Hugh Auden, for instance, reputedly reread Williams's *The Descent of the Dove* (1939) every year, which he considered to be Williams's masterpiece, and to which he wrote an introduction (1956 edition).[142] Its influence on Auden's poetry can be seen for example in Auden's *New Year Letter* (1940).[143]

When analysing the Christian ways of the Inklings one must also mention Owen Barfield's growth in faith. Born and raised in an agnostic family, Barfield became a member of the Church of England only in his late forties (around 1946), retaining, none the less, most of the Anthroposophical beliefs of Rudolf Steiner's, which were close to occult science, and which, to Barfield, did not constitute a religion but rather a form of knowledge based on the premise that poetry could create knowledge and that imagination is a means to truth.[144] As Blaxland-de Lange observes:

> The core experience of Barfield's life was supported and greatly enriched by his studies of the work of Rudolf Steiner, and became transformed by Barfield's brilliant mind into a faculty of perception capable of gaining insight into not only the history of words and

---

141 Henderson, ibid., p. 132.
142 Carpenter, *The Inklings*, p. 188, footnote 1.
143 It was also to a large extent thanks to Charles Williams that Auden developed an interest in Søren Kierkegaard's philosophy (at Oxford University Press Williams was the editor of the first English publication of Kierkegaard's works, translated from Danish by academics: Alexander Dru, David F. Swenson, Douglas V. Steere, and Walter Lowrie).
144 Formulated by Rudolf Steiner (1861–1925), an Austrian philosopher, scientist, and artist, anthroposophy is a 'philosophy based on the premise that the human intellect has the ability to contact spiritual worlds', and that there exists 'a spiritual world comprehensible to pure thought but fully accessible only to the faculties of knowledge latent in all humans.' Steiner believed in reincarnation, as he 'regarded human beings as having originally participated in the spiritual processes of the world through a dreamlike consciousness.' He founded the Anthroposophical Society in 1912; cf. *Encyclopaedia Britannica*, http://www.britannica.com/EBchecked/topic/27550/anthroposophy, accessed 25 April 2016.

the origins of language, but also the evolution of human consciousness which, as he saw it, is the key to the whole mystery of human evolution.[145]

Barfield's basic treatise on this theme, *Poetic Diction* (1928) was acclaimed by the Inklings, as well as by T. S. Eliot among others; and its germinal ideas on the evolution of consciousness were brought to clearer expression in what many critics would regard as Barfield's masterpiece: the book *Saving the Appearances: A Study in Idolatry* (1957).

To Lewis, Barfield's friend from their undergraduate days, Steiner's philosophy, which Barfield had encountered probably around 1928, was 'hideously shocking'; yet thanks to the Great War that Barfield and Lewis fought as a corollary of the former's enthusiasm for Anthroposophy, Lewis eventually came to recognize the importance of imagination and faith as a complementary balance to intellect and reason, (which brought him closer to Christianity), so that, as Barfield concluded, as a result of the Great War Lewis 'taught [Barfield] how to think, and [Barfield] taught Lewis what to think.'[146] Lewis never adopted Anthroposophy, and Barfield pursued it as a way of interpreting literature, especially high Romanticism, with its emphasis on poetic imagination (Coleridge's thought in particular), and wrote several books on Anthroposophy, eventually to become 'a convinced Christian.'[147]

This is how Lewis views Barfield's contribution to his own philosophical and religious formation:

---

145 Blaxland-de Lange, *Owen Barfield Funeral Address*, December 18, 1997, http://davidlavery.net/barfield/barfield_resources/death.html, accessed 25 April 2016. Lewis, Tolkien and definitely most, if not all, of the Inklings, except Barfield, rejected reincarnation, a belief which is acknowledged by Anthroposophy.

146 Carpenter, *The Inklings*, pp. 36–37. The last quote is cited by James S. Cutsinger, Owen Barfield's American correspondent and acquaintance, who consulted with Barfield his work on Coleridge; cf., 'C. S. Lewis as Apologist and Mystic', Lecture delivered for the Narnia Clubs of New York, December 1998; http://cutsinger.net/pdf/lewis _as_apologist_and_mystic.pdf, p. 1; accessed 23 April 2016. Lewis and Barfield were matches for each other in their 'Great War', that is the heated polemics regarding Barfield's belief in Anthroposophy. Lewis was Barfield's 'chief intellectual sparring-partner', as Blaxland-de Lange says in Owen Barfield Funeral Address, and Barfield was not so much Lewis's alter ego as his 'anti-self'', as Lewis stated himself in *Surprised by Joy*, pp. 199–200.

147 An interview with Owen Barfield by Lyle W. Dorsett; Kent, England, July 19–20, 1984; The Marion E. Wade Center Oral History Collection (call no.: OH/SR-3). With regard to Romantic literature Barfield wrote, e.g., a book on Romanticism: *Romanticism Comes of Age* (1944), and on Coleridge: *What Coleridge Thought* (1971).

Barfield never made me an Anthroposophist, but his counterattacks destroyed forever two elements in my own thought. In the first place he made short work of what I have called my 'chronological snobbery', the uncritical acceptance of the intellectual climate common to our own age and the assumption that whatever has gone out of date is on that account discredited. (…) In the second place, Barfield convinced me that the positions we had hitherto held left no room for any satisfactory theory of knowledge. We had been, in the technical sense of the term, 'realists'; that is, we accepted as rock-bottom reality the universe revealed by the senses. But at the same time we continued to make, for certain phenomena of consciousness, all the claims that really went with a theistic or idealistic view. We maintained that abstract thought (if obedient to logical rules) gave indisputable truth, that our moral judgment was 'valid', and our aesthetic experience not merely pleasing but 'valuable'. (…) Barfield convinced me that it was inconsistent. If thought were a purely subjective event, these claims for it would have to be abandoned. (…) I was therefore compelled to give up realism. (…) I must admit that mind was no late-come epiphenomenon; that the whole universe was, in the last resort, mental; that our logic was participation in a cosmic Logos.[148]

A belief in a cosmic Word and Meaning, that is some unconditional Logos, is what all the Inklings seem to have shared and derived from Christianity, and it is what Le Guin adheres to and distils from Eastern philosophy, all of these writers drawing on a symbiotic relationship between imagination and reason. A possible connection between fantasy Logos of these writers and Victor Frankl's philosophical and psychotherapeutic concept of logotherapy (therapy through meaning), an affinity that constitutes an important element of the purported therapeutic properties of high fantasy, is addressed in Chapter Six.

Recapitulating the Christian theme of the Inklings' mind-set, one ought to note that the ethics of Christian philosophy, which the Inklings attempted to endorse both in their lives and their writings, framed by their distinctly rational scholarly intellect, produced some of the most convincing Christian fiction and non-fiction of the past century; the works that aim to display the logic of the faith scrutinized through the splendour and misery of human existence, human mind, human fantasy, and human (sub)creation. The Christian perspective on pain, death, and suffering had been shaped by the Inklings' personal experience of the First World War: Tolkien and Lewis fought as soldiers and witnessed the death of their closest friends during the War; (moreover, in 1960 Lewis grieved bitterly over his wife's, Joy Davidman's, death, who passed away at the age of 45 only a few years after their marriage); Barfield served in the Royal Engineers and although

---

148   Lewis, *Surprised by Joy: The Shape of My Early Life* (London: Harcourt, 1966), pp. 208–209. In 1929, at the time of his conversion, Lewis felt like 'the most dejected and reluctant convert in all England', (*Surprised by Joy*, p. 266).

he did not fight, he was equally horrified by the war, the experience that largely caused his marked stutter; Hugo Dyson was severely wounded at Passchendaele; Williams had not been enlisted due to his poor eyesight and a neurological disorder of shaking hands, but two of his close friends joined the army and were killed, in his place, as he felt, which shook Williams to the core and perhaps instigated his own idea of Christian Substituted Love, Exchange and Co-inherence, a vital part of his Romantic Theology (inspired also by Dante's concept of love).[149]

The harrowing experience of the war did not twist or disarm their faith, as it, for instance, did impair the outlook of the American Lost Generation, but, contrariwise, it led to an even greater affirmation of religion, and, indirectly, to conversion: Lewis's to Anglicanism over the years 1929–1931; Havard's to Catholicism in 1931, and Barfield's to Anglicanism in 1946. Indeed, the Christianity of the Inklings had many names and faces, but constituted one of their characteristic qualities, although it had cost them much of their academic and literary reputation. The Inklings (Lewis and Williams in particular) seem to have paid a price for declaring their religious faith openly and consistently in their works, being denigrated and scorned by most of the critics: a photograph of Lewis's, for instance, once adorned the cover of *Time* (the issue of 8 September, 1947) with a heading: 'Oxford's C. S. Lewis, His Heresy: Christianity', and an article inside the issue entitled 'Don V. Devil', in which Lewis was classified as a member of a growing club of 'heretic' intellectuals, together with T. S. Eliot, W. H. Auden, Dorothy L. Sayers, and Graham Greene. Tolkien, Williams, and the other Inklings were not mentioned probably because they were virtually unknown at the time to a wider public.

Considering the miscellaneous interpretations of Christianity that the Inklings endorsed, it may prove objectionable to refer to them as to the Oxford 'Christian writers'; yet Christianity remains a common landmark of their fictional and theological works and a common denominator of their complete *Weltanschauung*.[150] Robert James Reilly sees the Inklings Christianity as an essentially romantic religion which the Inklings embraced in 'a deliberate and conscious attempt to revive certain well-known doctrines and attitudes of romanticism and to justify these doctrines and attitudes by showing that they have not merely literary but religious validity.'[151] 'Lewis, Williams, and Tolkien in various ways affirm that the

149 Cf. Carpenter, *The Inklings*, pp. 255–259. Williams's doctrine was based on St. Paul's recommendation: 'bear you one another's burdens, and so fulfill the law of Christ.' (Galatians 6:2). Cf. Charles Williams, *Outline of Romantic Theology* (London: Apocryphile Press, 2005).
150 Duriez, *The Gift of Friendship*, p. 57.
151 Reilly, *Romantic Religion: A Study of Barfield, Lewis, Williams and Tolkien*, p. 8.

experiences which we generally call romantic – *Sehnsucht*, sexual love, Faërie – are also, or can be, religious experiences,' Reilly remarks.[152]

Even if they somehow revived Romanticism, as Reilly seems to argue placing the Inklings in line with what he has distinguished as a minor British Romantic revival, represented also by George MacDonald (1824–1902) and Gilbert Keith Chesterton (1874–1936), the Oxford writers were neither epigones of the past nor mere imitators. Inspired by MacDonald and Chesterton as they were, (especially Tolkien and Lewis), the Inklings drew heavily on the olden lore of literature and mythology, however rather than replicating or archiving it in a neo-medieval or neo-romantic style, they created a new mythology itself.

Attempting to draw another comparison between the Inklings and high modernists, one might observe that while the modernist writers tended to embrace the new reality by means of a familiar framework of existing myths (for instance, T. S. Eliot casts his *Waste Land* in the mould of ancient vegetation rites and the Fisher King myth; and Joyce uses Odysseus's story to shape *Ulysses*), thus pursuing their quest for a pattern by applying a kind of mythological frame narrative, the Inklings (and Tolkien in particular) created mythology anew. In other words, while modernists replicated the matrix of familiar myths in the new reality, the Inklings set to creating myths, to mythopoeia; and if the Inklings followed any existing frame narrative, more or less closely, then it was the fairy-story of the gospels, which they found to be true. When viewed from this perspective, the literary legacy of the Inklings might appear more innovative and ingenious than that of the avant-garde modernists.

What motivated Tolkien to begin and complete his painstaking work on *The Lord of the Rings* and *The Silmarillion* was the desire to create a missing mythology for England, to make myth, which engendered also Lewis's Narnia and his Space Trilogy, even if it was not as conscious an intention and not as clearly and explicitly articulated as Tolkien's. Was that 'romantic bent' of the Inklings merely a consequence of their Edwardian childhood experience and the period's 'fin de siècle' inclination towards the psychic, the psychological, the mystical, the medieval, the spiritual, and the apotheosis of Art? The following opinion of Marjorie Hope Nicolson regarding Lewis's oeuvre may well refer to Tolkien's and Williams's mythopoeic works:

> The earlier writers have created new worlds from legend, from mythology, from fairy tale. Lewis has created myth itself, myth woven of desire and aspirations deep-seated in some,

---

152   Reilly, ibid., p. 5.

at least, of human race. As I journey with him into worlds at once familiar and strange, I experience (...) 'a sensation not of following an adventure but enacting a myth.'[153]

The Inklings made their myths and made their other worlds, blending some pagan heroic elements with Christianity, in the quasi Old English mode, combined also with medieval chivalry, but did not merely create worlds from legends and stories, as most of the Romantic poets and writers did. They attempted to create legends and myths themselves. By setting a new tradition of mythopoeia, the Inklings endeavoured to introduce high fantasy and modern myths to literature addressed to adults, the Faërie for the grown-ups, at the heart of which lay an 'inherent morality'–'a strong moral element' discerning good from evil, the divide denigrated by the modernist post-Christian vogue and trivialized by the commodified fantasy that appeared in the wake of Tolkien's feat.[154]

That the Inklings were disinclined to the spirit of technocratic modernity and scientism, and that they defended tradition, understood both as moral standards and literary conventions, was hardly surprising and original. Except for Williams, a native Londoner born to the working class family, the blueprint of the Inklings' imagination drew on the pastoral pre-industrial landscapes of England and, in Lewis's case, Ulster, and embodied (after Lewis's conversion) specifically Christian thought. Little wonder, then, that Ezra Pound's modernist manifesto of 'making it new', which meant modifying or overriding the existing modes of representation and driving them towards the abstract and the introspective, was received with attention but also some revulsion by the Oxford fellows. It was perhaps only Lewis, the 'voracious and eclectic reader' of both high and low-brow literature, for whom 'the word unreadable had no meaning', who studied the works of modernists with interest and due diligence.[155] It was also Lewis, none the less, who concluded that 'instead of pursuing the new, it's better to stick to the tradition.'[156]

The Inkling who appears most modernist in his singular approach to writing, poetics and fiction, was probably Williams, an enigmatic, idiosyncratic, self-made literary wizard, 'an odd charismatic man', prolific writer and poet, still remaining rather controversial, whose stunning poetry was acknowledged by T. S. Eliot and W. H. Auden, whose plays influenced some of Eliot's dramas, and

---

153 Marjorie Hope Nicolson, *Voyages to the Moon* (London: Macmillan, 1948, 1st ed.), p. 45. The quote is Elwin Ransom's phrase from Lewis's *Out of the Silent Planet*, cf. Nicolson, ibid., p. 45.
154 Tolkien, 'On Fairy-Stories', p. 118.
155 Duriez, *The Gift of Friendship*, p. 35.
156 Duriez, ibid., p. 40.

whose novels, especially *The Place of the Lion*, greatly impressed C. S. Lewis.[157] Yet, even Williams, despite his quirk mottled imagery that combines Christian theology with parapsychology and esoteric beliefs, an eerie ambience and unconventional stylistics championing hybrids of genres cast in a queer style, wrote Christian fantasy, religious drama and theologizing treatises, which drew on the past tradition of mysticism and Christian ethics. If there was any tangible link between some of the English or American-English modernists and the Inklings, of a different nature than mere space-time compatibility, then it was probably Williams's forging, especially when it comes to his influence on Eliot and Auden.

Harry Blamires, Lewis's former student, an Anglican theologian and literary critic, observes that the Inklings, particularly Williams, contributed much to what he has named a minor Christian Renaissance in Britain, which fell on in the 1930s and was spurred by an institution of the Canterbury drama festival in 1928.[158] T. S. Eliot's and Williams's Christian plays were first staged at Canterbury in the 1930s, followed by Dorothy L. Sayers's works. That decade saw more Christian themes brought up also by Graham Greene, Evelyn Waugh, Lewis (*The Pilgrim's Regress*, 1933), Christopher Fry, Helen Waddell, and others, leading up to Auden's *New Year Letter* of 1940, inspired by Williams's *The Descent of the Dove* (1939). Tolkien's 'fabling' or his 'secret vice', that is writing fantasy, the genre upon which he 'lavished such incredible pains' and which was to most of the other dons 'a trifling by definition', was 'very shocking', even though it did not contain any explicit or implied religious themes.[159] Christianity is not explicitly apparent in the works of Barfield, ('the first and last Inkling'), either, whose emphasis on meaning and the profound sense of the earliest mythical language derived from Logos results, however partially, from his religious beliefs.[160] The other part of Barfield's scholarly formation had been shaped by the

---

157 Alan Jacobs, *The Narnian: The Life and Imagination of C. S. Lewis* (London: Harper-Collins, 2005), p. 196. Duriez, *The Gift of Friendship*, p. 67.

158 Harry Blamires, *A Short History of English Literature* (Oxford: Oxford University Press, 1984, 2nd ed.), qtd. in Duriez, *The Gift of Friendship*, pp. 73–74. Blamires has also written *A History of Literary Criticism* (1991).

159 Duriez, *The Gift of Friendship*, p. 142; W. H. Auden's review of Tolkien's *The Lord of the Rings*, cf. http://tolkiengateway.net, accessed 23 April 2016.

160 Barfield, *Poetic Diction*, 1928. Barfield is said to have been the first Inkling, as he was Lewis's oldest Oxford friend and his best country-walking companion, Lewis being the rock foundation of the group. Barfield was also the last Inkling, as he outlived the others (he died in 1997); cf. Georg Bernhard Tennyson, 'Owen Barfield: First and Last Inkling', [in:] *The World and I*, April 1990, pp. 540–555.

writer's rational and sceptical upbringing, which he retained. As Blaxland- de Lange wrote in Barfield's obituary in 1997:

> Barfield had in a certain sense devoted a large part of his life to laying bare the dogmas and reductionist assumptions underlying what he often referred to as the 'materialistic paradigm', the conviction – or more usually the blind belief – that matter is some sort of primal cause, that mind arose from a mindless universe and that man, and his evolution, is a highly complex cosmic accident. Not that, unlike many non-believers in scientific materialism, he approached these things from the standpoint of religious belief. On the contrary, he always looked back gratefully to the mood of sceptical agnosticism in which he was brought up by his parents, and retained this approach throughout his life. Some – especially those who knew him less well –- would argue that he threw this mood of sceptical inquiry to the winds when he joined the Anthroposophical Society. (…) Suffice it to say that he did not see it that way.[161]

Barfield's book *Saving the Appearances: A Study in Idolatry* was placed under the auspices of HarperCollins Publishers on Philip Zaleski's 1999 list of the hundred best spiritual books of the past century.[162] Interestingly enough, on the same list were featured Lewis's *The Chronicles of Narnia* and *Mere Christianity*, Tolkien's *The Lord of the Rings*, Viktor Frankl's *Man's Search for Meaning* (discussed in Chapter Four of this book), John Henry Newman's *Meditations and Devotions*, Evelyn Underhill's *Mysticism,* and among the top ten - Gilbert Keith Chesterton's *Orthodoxy,* and (influenced by Williams) T. S. Eliot's *The Four Quarters*.[163] That spiritual aspect of the Inklings' legacy, which Tolkien associates not only with Christianity but also with Faërie's 'strong moral element' and 'inherent morality', and which Le Guin identifies with the 'intellectual and ethical complexity' of the old great fantasy stories, regardless of religion and culture, is, as I seek to argue, an important quality that allows for linking high fantasy ethos with Frankl's therapy through meaning, as presented in Chapters Three and Four.[164]

---

161 Blaxland- de Lange, *Obituary for Owen Barfield.*

162 'The 100 Best Spiritual Books of the Century: A List', accessed 20 December 2015, http://www.faith. com/library/articlesfaith/articles/f_lib_books_home_bestlist.html.

163 Ibid. T. S. Eliot reputedly wrote about Barfield's *Saving the Appearances* that it was 'one of the few books which made [him] proud to be director of the firm which published them.' [Source of the quote unknown]. As to Lewis's first Christian books, according to George Stade and Karen Karbeiner they are 'preachy'; but the Narnia series is far less so, because although it 'replicates a children's Bible' in a way, [and] represents God as a mythical figure' (the leonine Christ), it 'also emphasizes humans' freedom of choice,' thus producing 'a mix of childhood innocence and a moral message.' *The Encyclopaedia of British Writers* (London: Infobase, 2009), p. 299.

164 Tolkien, 'On Fairy-Stories', p. 118. Le Guin, 'Foreword' to *The Tales of Earthsea,* p. xiv.

As for the Christian dimension of the Inklings' thought and writing, it is suggested that the resurgence of Christian themes in the 1930s in England, to which they largely contributed, was a noticeable, yet 'not a conscious movement like the Enlightenment,' as the authors of the *Encyclopaedia of British Writers* argue.[165] Can thus the Inklings be named Christian writers of the period immediately preceding, coinciding with and succeeding the Second World War? Can they be called modernists, if one considers their interest in myth-making, or maybe 'anti-reductionist' writers, for whom spirituality and imagination were superior to materialism and scientism, and who yearned for the long-lost union of imagination and reason? Their *Sehnsucht* seems to have found its rest in Christianity, much against the tide of modernism and early postmodernism, but the last word assessing their position in the history of literature of the past century has probably not been said yet.

It ought to be remarked, furthermore, that Tolkien's and Lewis's reluctance to the modernist trends revealed itself also in their academic work and turned the Oxford's School of English of the 30s and 40s into a lonely island of counter-modernist teaching. At the time it shared many affinities with the 19th c. outlook, which differed considerably from that of Cambridge, the universities of the Continent, and of America. It was the historical and comparative model of philological and literary research that prevailed at Oxford and that found its epitome in Tolkien's studies – the contradiction of the Cambridge progressive school of 'practical criticism', as represented by I. A. Richards (1893–1979) and his followers who co-founded New Criticism, chiefly F. R. Leavis (1895–1978) and his disciples, the 'Leavisites'.[166] In contrast with the modernity-oriented Cambridge model of reading literature, Tolkien and Lewis propounded jointly a new reformed curriculum of language and literature (The Oxford Final Honours English School Curriculum), which focused on the old periods, particularly on the mediaeval lore, and sought to unite the literary and linguistic scholarship in their effort to rehabilitate the past, disregarding literature after the Romantics. As a result, the Anglo-Saxon and Middle English studies were made more attractive to the Oxford undergraduates, at the expense of the Victorian literature, whose study was virtually forsaken. Delighted at his and Tolkien's success, Lewis commented on their victory triumphantly, saying that they had 'forced [the reform] upon the junto after hard fighting.'[167] To Tolkien, as a matter of fact, English studies could

---

165   *The Encyclopaedia of British Writers*, George Stade and Karen Karbiener, eds. (London: Infobase, 2009), p. 299.

166   Carpenter, *The Inklings*, pp. 63–64.

167   Carpenter, ibid., p. 55.

well end with Chaucer, but the other Inklings, including Lewis, were also fond of the subsequent periods, especially Renaissance and Romanticism (Lewis adored, for instance, Shelley's poetry, and Dyson excelled at Shakespearean studies).[168]

Little wonder, then, that Lewis continually fired guns at the Cambridge School of English Literature, as it downplayed the pre-Shakespearean periods and promoted contemporary writings instead. Lewis questioned also the critical stand of some Cambridge dons, notably Eustace Mandeville Wetenhall Tillyard (1889–1962), who approached literary works on the basis of the authors' biographical information and their psychological makeup, a theory jettisoned by Lewis as a 'personal heresy'.[169] The Lewisian interest in the inherent nature of literature might have put him in a sense in step with the subsequent founders of New Criticism, for instance with Frank Raymond Leavis. Lewis, nevertheless, did not share Leavis's elitist approach to literature, as he himself keenly read both high and low-brow texts. Nor did he sympathize with Leavis's campaign for analytical and evaluative criticism, having dedicated his life to wide reading and continuous learning.

Therefore, on the grounds of its espousal of modernism, the Cambridge School of Literature contrasted sharply with that of Oxford, if one regards Tolkien's and Lewis's stance, of course, which was not shared by many other non-Inkling dons. Ironically, it was, however, the University of Cambridge that in 1954 offered Lewis a chair in English Medieval and Renaissance Literature, the post which had been available twice at Oxford (the Merton Professorship of English Literature), yet had never been proposed to Lewis, in spite of Tolkien's best endeavours. The reason was Lewis's Christian apologetic campaign and his incurable 'hot- gospelling', following his conversion in 1931 – the most inappropriate and ludicrous activity in which an Oxford don could ever have engaged himself, and thus repellent for the Oxford electors, whose vast majority strongly resented Lewis's overtly Christian storytelling and rhetoric.[170] Williams, a non-academic Inkling, was also shunned by the Oxford university establishment, and the honorary master's degree was bestowed upon him mostly thanks to Lewis's intercession. Barfield's works, with the early but essential *Poetic Diction,* did not earn him academic recognition, either, and he failed to be appointed as Lewis's successor (much to the latter's regret) at Magdalen College in the mid-1950s, turning instead to professional soliciting practice and lecturing in America. None the less, lack of understanding and recognition at

---

168   Cf. Emma B. Hawkins's paper on Tolkien and Chaucer: 'Eagles with Attitude: Chaucer and Tolkien', [in:] *Seven: An Anglo-American Literary Review,* Volume 23 (Chicago: Marion E. Wade Center of Wheaton College Publishers, 2006).

169   Duriez, *The Gift of Friendship,* p. 67.

170   Duriez, ibid., p. 69.

home (which hurt especially Williams and Barfield) did not embitter the Inklings; on the contrary it fed their spiritual *Sehnsucht*, and eventually turned it into greater modesty and loving warmth.[171] Nor did the rather unexpected and belated fame of Lewis and Tolkien change their humbleness, who, surprised by their sudden popularity, remained unaffected till their last days.

In conclusion, while swimming against the tide of modernism and postmodernism, the Inklings attempted to redefine 'classical tradition'.[172] Their literary creed posed a challenge not only to the new progressive movement that abolished conventions, but also to the established pre-modernist literary establishment, despite many affinities, inasmuch as their fiction characteristically employed an existing yet hardly recognized genre of Christian fantasy, that is a blend of Christianity and myth (or its offshoot – Faërie), rooted in the Old English and Middle English lore, as rejuvenated in the 19th century by MacDonald and Chesterton.

Not only did the Inklings rewrite and reinterpret Norse mythology and Christian themes, but also they created their own mythologies and pioneered modern mythopoeia, or myth-making, together with an alternative approach to myth and fantasy, different from that of the other writers and poets of the period.[173] The 'mythic method' applied by the modernist *avant garde*, as T. S. Eliot named it in his essays on *Ulysses*, meant to Joyce and other modernists employing myth as a tool for 'controlling, (…) ordering, [and] giving a shape and a significance to the immense panorama of futility and anarchy which [was the then] history', and, generally, as a tool for 'manipulating a continuous parallel between contemporaneity and antiquity'.[174] Thus, by trying to view the modern world through the prism of

---

171 Blaxland-de Lange, 'Funeral Address for Owen Barfield', http://davidlavery.net/barfield/barfield_resources/death.html, accessed 23 April 2016.
172 The Inklings focused on what had belonged to the perhaps neglected tradition at the beginning of the 20th c., that is largely Christian fantasy literature, rooted in the Old English and Middle English lore and pagan myths. Their concept of tradition differed from that of T. S. Eliot, as expressed in his essay *Tradition and the Individual Talent* (1919), in many ways, for instance in their understanding of the literary cannon and in their tastes (Eliot generally disregarded medieval literature, Shakespeare, and the Romantics, favouring the Metaphysical Poets, John Webster and John Dryden instead). Moreover, Eliot viewed tradition mostly in terms of poetry as a poet, whereas among the Inklings only Lewis and Williams were poets, still much more famous for their prose.
173 C. Moorman, *Arthurian Triptych: Mythic Materials in Charles Williams, C. S. Lewis and T. S. Eliot*, University of California Press, Berkeley 1960, p. 5.
174 T. S. Eliot, 'Ulysses, Order and Myth,' [in:] *The Dial*, November 1923, pp. 480–483, 482.

myth, modernists tried to seek a pattern in chaos, but also, in a way, to demytholo-
gize contemporaneity, a tendency reinforced by postmodernists, so as to show the
void resulting from the absence or impenetrability of a logical structure and sense.

The Inklings, on the contrary, attempted to make new mythology for modernity in order to show the universality of sense and values, identified by them with
Christian imponderables, and thus to confirm the startling logic of the world,
whose apt expression was the Gospel. The essential union of imagination and intellect produced the Inklings' firm faith, *fides et ratio*, and found its medium in a
mythopoeic language, closest to the original metaphorical Logos and the texture of
Evangelium.[175] The unity of thought and language, thinking and feeling, facthood
and fantasy, could perhaps make the Inklings' mythopoeia an example of Eliot's
desired 'association of sensibility', (although Eliot himself saw its model realization
in the works of the Metaphysical Poets, which the Inklings did not hold in equally
high esteem, much as they shared the Christian foundation of their works).[176]

As for myth, the Inklings considered it as a common palimpsest of everlast-
ing truths, or in Owen Barfield's words, 'a true child of Meaning, begotten upon
Imagination'.[177] To their minds, myth was a powerful tool of reconstructing
meaning directly at its very source, in the primordial, genuinely metaphorical
language of ancient days. Fascinated with Norse, Germanic, and Celtic mythology, the Oxford writers made an attempt at creating their own mythos, and coupled their myth-making with a distinctly Christian Logos, thus merging the two
major sources of European culture in their works. As they planted their myths in
a more or less visible but thoroughly Christian soil (with some idiosyncrasies of
particular members of the group), the Inklings achieved a remarkable effect of
novelty, rekindling the ancient spirit and recasting its paradigms. The worlds of
Middle-earth, Arda, Narnia, and Perelandra unfold their mythologies and reveal
a pattern that approaches meaning and a sense of joy through imagination, in the
Barfieldian way, for it is the spiritual road to truth and Logos from the dawn of
time journeyed by their minds, which determines the Inklings' collective vision
and artistic pursuit.

---

175   *Fides et Ratio* (faith and reason) is also the title of John Paul II's Encyclical Letter on
      the Relationship between Faith and Reason, 14 September, 1998.
176   Eliot, 'The Metaphysical Poets', 1921. In the essay Eliot introduces the term 'dissocia-
      tion of sensibility', which, as he argues, ensued in the history of English poetry after
      the Metaphysical Poets.
177   Barfield, *Poetic Diction: A Study in Meaning* (London: Wesleyan Paperback, London
      1973, 3rd ed.), p. 93.

One could conclude that not only was the mind-set of the Inklings mytho-poeic, but also 'mythopathic', to use a word coined by Tolkien, meaning: preoc-cupied with myths, receptive to myths, receiving nourishment, understanding, and therapy from myth; and not to be confused with the word 'mythopathologi-cal', which may imply a deviation or addiction, in the fashion of 'mythoholic', that is addicted to myth (which, in the case of the Inklings does not anyhow seem to appear derogative).[178] Thus, the term 'mythopathy' may function in the posi-tive context of therapy, denoting 'therapy through myth', like some other terms, such as 'electropathy' (the treatment of an illness with electricity), 'hydropathy' or 'hydropathology' (using water to treat illnesses), or 'motorpathy' (treatment through the use of gymnastics).[179]

On 19 September 1931, during a long walk and conversation with Dyson and Lewis that contributed to Lewis's conversion to Christianity, Tolkien said, 'if God is mythopoeic, man must become mythopathic'.[180] Lewis commented on that mythopoeic genius of God as reflected in man's (sub)creative attempts at myth-making in the following way: 'God is none the less God by being Man; so the Myth remains Myth even if it becomes Fact.'[181]

Indubitably, the Inklings catalysed fantasy resurgence in English literature, and, in particular, helped rejuvenate a theologizing myth that carries an unambigu-ous moral message – implicit as it remains in Tolkien's works, or often allegorized and explicit as in Lewis's and Williams's legacy. The Inklings' quaint mythopoeia, whose roots dwell in the mediaeval culture with more remote echoes resounding in the Renaissance and Romantic period, was a novelty to both modernism and tradition – to the former inasmuch as the writers opposed the major modernist

---

178 The word 'mythopathic' seems to stem from the Greek *mythos* (myth, story, thought) and *pathos*, the latter meaning here, (as in 'empathic', which comes from the Greek *empatheia*),'feeling in a specified way', rather than 'suffering or grief'. Interestingly, even the Greek word 'pathologia' meant originally a 'study of the passions'; therefore 'mythopathology' might not imply any disorder, the Greek term for a study of dis-ease being *pathologike*; cf. *Online Etymology Dictionary*, Douglas Harper, ed., 2014, http://www.etymonline.com/index.php?allowed _in_frame=0&search=empathy&s earchmode=none, accessed 23 April 2016. Carpenter quotes Tolkien using the word 'mythopathic' in his *The Inklings*, p. 45.

179 *Robertson's Words for a Modern Age: A Dictionary of English Vocabulary Words De-rived Primarily from Latin and Greek Word Families, Presented Individually and in Family Units;* http://wordinfo.info/.

180 Carpenter, *The Inklings*, p. 45. That occasion is also connected with the creation of Tolkien's poem 'Mythopoeia', which is discussed in Chapter Six of this book.

181 Lewis, *Miracles* (London: HarperOne, 2009), p. 161, footnote 1.

tenets, and to the latter in their singular approach to literary convention. Instead of uprooting and felling the tree of universal wisdom and knowledge in the modernist mode, the Oxford dons strove to rediscover its roots and prove their strength, whereby to indicate some hope and sense to the wobbling post-war self in the mechanical world of uncertainty and relativism. The Inklings' originality resulted from representing tradition as a fusion of the mythical and the mystical, a synergy of fantasy and faith, with intellect. It seems that their valiant, if not, as some critics hold, a completely successful effort, deserves academic recognition and an entry in the annals of literary historians of the 20th c., but perhaps still leaves judgement to posterity.

A consequence of their non-modernist outlook and their peculiar literary tastes (which some of the critics found 'very shocking'), the liminal position of the Inklings as a group in the history of the 20th c. literature perhaps testifies to their 'quite remarkable – and still insufficiently recognized achievement'.[182] The quaint epithet Blaxland-de Lange has assigned to Barfield when he called him 'the Knight of the Word', may indeed serve as a kenning implying the nature of all the Inklings, not only of Barfield but also Tolkien, the first-rate philologist who 'had been inside language' and for whom 'language was the real thing', and of Lewis, whose *Studies in Words* of 1960 focus on the history of words and warn against the alarming modern phenomena of what he named verbicide and verbiage, that is 'murdering words' and using words 'as a promise to pay that will never be kept'.[183]

Will the Inklings 'grow in stature' as a group? The question may well be replaced with the following: will the contemporary thought return to its mythopoeic, poetic roots and meaningful spirituality? Or, will the fantastic mode be recognized, as Shippey claims, to be the leitmotif of the contemporary fiction?[184] The Inklings' interest in the human consciousness and the poetic nature of human thinking must not be confused with some New Age movement, which they were not. Even Williams, a former member of the occult Golden Dawn Order and Rosicrucianism, and Barfield, an enthusiastic anthroposophist, explored those esoteric domains as a mythical introduction to Christianity. What the Inklings cherished at Oxford and elsewhere was 'the synthesis of intellectual inquiry and romantic love', which led

---

182 Blaxland-de Lange, 'Owen Barfield Funeral Address'.
183 'Owen Barfield Funeral Address'. Lewis said of Tolkien that 'he had been inside language', as quoted in Carpenter's, *J. R. R. Tolkien: A Biography*, p. 144. Lewis, *Studies in Words* (Cambridge: Cambridge University Press, 1960), p. 7. Lewis's reflections on language, verbicide and verbiage are discussed in more detail in Chapter Six of this book.
184 Shippey, *J. R. R. Tolkien. Author of the Century*, p. vii.

them to the 'rediscovery of meaning through myth.'[185] The Inklings drew on faith, reason and myth as the treasure of language and, above all, as the source of meaning – the meaning that is timeless and unconditional and that firmly opposes the infirm (neo-)nihilistic discourse of the modern and postmodern ages.

Should the Inklings deserve nobilitation in the history of literature, the chivalric name of the 'knights of the word' (or of Logos, as Lewis named it) might aptly capture their mythical, neo-medieval and neo-romantic frame of mind, embedded in Christianity.[186] Their humble discourse of meaning, produced by the fusion of imagination, faith, and reason, seems to challenge the postmodern philosophy of nothingness and senselessness, which is briefly sketched in the following chapter as a background to the contemporary need for (logo)therapy.

185 Blaxland-de Lange,' Owen Barfield Funeral Address'. *The Rediscovery of Meaning* is one of Barfield's books, (London, Barfield Press, 2006, 2nd ed.)
186 Lewis, *Surprised by Joy*, p. 209.

Chapter Three
From neo-nihilism to logotherapy

Is there a need for therapy in the (post)modern world, the world which the Inklings were so much concerned with, and whose perils they had forecast and addressed in their work? Which philosophy might run along the lines of the main
stream of postmodern culture, if that major current were possible to identity and
if the lines were not too erratic to follow? If there is one underlying philosophy in
contemporary Western thought, is it therapeutic or perhaps therapeutogenic; that
is, does it offer some help and relief, or rather spread the blight, creating a need
for some therapy? Which school of (psycho)therapy appears most relevant to the
needs of the postmodern man? This chapter attempts to address these questions,
trying to point to the existing (existential) predicament of today's world, and to
its more or less conscious search for some remedy, which, regardless of clinical practice, could be universally available to everyone by means of therapeutic
narrative in arts, including literature.[1] The chapter serves as a rough sketch introducing the issue of logotherapy, a philosophical and psychotherapeutic concept that emerged after the Second World War, in the light of which I attempt to
identify in the subsequent chapters a therapeutic potential of high fantasy fiction
locked in the legacy of the Inklings and of Ursula K. Le Guin.

Postmodernity and its nihilistic aporia

Victor Frankl's logotherapy emerged very much in response to postmodernity,
the latter being, according to Zygmunt Bauman, 'modernity conscious of its true
nature – modernity for itself.'[2] Another Polish thinker, Karol Wojtyła, or Saint
John Paul II, interprets the nature of postmodernity as follows:

> Our age has been termed by some thinkers the age of 'postmodernity' (…), [which]
> has remained somewhat ambiguous, both because judgement on what is called 'post-
> modern' is sometimes positive and sometimes negative, and because there is as yet no
> consensus on the delicate question of the demarcation of the different historical periods.

---

1 I have attempted to address this problem also in my paper 'Neo-nihilism and the
   Self-industry of Logotherapy' [in:] *The Self-Industry. Therapy and Fiction*, Jarosław
   Szurman, Agnieszka Woźniakowska, Krzysztof Kowalczyk-Twarowski, eds. (Katowice:
   University of Silesia Press, 2015), pp. 205–227.
2 Zygmunt Bauman, *Intimations of Postmodernity* (London: Routledge, 1992), p. 187.

One thing however is certain: the currents of thought which claim to be postmodern merit appropriate attention. According to some of them, the time of certainties is irrevocably past, and the human being must now learn to live in a horizon of total absence of meaning, where everything is provisional and ephemeral. In their destructive critique of every certitude, several authors have failed to make crucial distinctions and have called into question the certitudes of faith.

This nihilism has been justified in a sense by the terrible experience of evil which has marked our age. Such a dramatic experience has ensured the collapse of rationalist optimism, which viewed history as the triumphant progress of reason, the source of all happiness and freedom; and now, at the end of this century, one of our greatest threats is the temptation to despair.[3]

A diffuse phenomenon as it is, postmodernity has proved unpropitious to those who attempt to define it, and its vagueness and elusiveness are hardly a wonder. Umberto Eco observes that postmodernity has a tendency to become 'increasingly retroactive'; so that, he concludes, 'the postmodern category will [in the end] include Homer.'[4] It is 'no longer a quip', though; 'it has already happened', Reiner Friedrich remarks, quoting Paul de Man, who interprets the act of Helen's weaving a robe and depicting on it 'the many struggles the Achaeans and Trojans endured for her sake at the hands of the war-god' as an instance conducive to considering the Homeric epic as a self-referential postmodern text.[5] 'Such retroactive designation, combined with the widespread indiscriminate use of the postmodern category, threatens', as Friedrich observes, 'to render it altogether vacuous, or nonsensical à la Lyotard', who argues that 'a work can become modern only if it is first postmodern. Postmodernism thus understood is not modernism at its end but in the nascent state, and this state is constant.'[6]

Reflecting upon the paradoxical nature of what has come to be called postmodernity, Bauman observes in turn that 'postmodernity means many different

3   John Paul II, *Fides et Ratio* [Faith and Reason], *Encyclical Letter*, Chapter VII, 1998, http://www.vatican.va/holy_father/john_paul_ii/encyclicals/documents/hf_jp-ii_ enc_15101998_fides-et-ratio_en.html, accessed 23 April 2016.
4   Umberto Eco, Postscript to *The name of the Rose* (London: Harvest Books, 1994), pp. 65–66.
5   Rainer Friedrich, 'The Enlightenment Gone Mad. The Dismal Discourse of Postmodernism's Grand Narratives' [in:] *Arion: Journal of Humanities and the Classics at Boston University* (Boston, MA, 2012), Arion 19–3, winter 2012; pp. 31–47, 31. The quote comes from *Iliad* (3.125–128).
6   Friedrich, 'The Enlightenment Gone Mad', p. 31; Jean-Francois Lyotard, Appendix to *The Postmodern Condition: A Report On Knowledge*, trans. G. Bennington and B. Massumi, [in:] *Theory and History of Literature*, vol. 10 (Minneapolis 1984), p. 79.

things to many different people,' and, generally, 'it means licence to do whatever one may fancy and advice not to take anything you or the others do too seriously. It means the speed with which things change and the pace with which moods succeed each other so that they have no time to ossify into things.'[7] But above all, Bauman argues, postmodernity is:

> A state of mind marked (…) by its all-deriding, all-eroding, all-dissolving destructiveness. It seems sometimes that postmodern mind is a critique caught at the moment of its ultimate triumph: a critique that finds it ever more difficult to go on being critical just because it has destroyed everything it used to be critical about; with it, off went the very urgency of being critical. There is nothing left to be opposed to. The world and the life in the world have become themselves nothing but an unstoppable and obsessive self-criticism – or so it seems.[8]

Postmodern theory and criticism have virtually invalidated themselves, as there seems to be nothing left any more that might still beg criticism, everything having already been debunked, perhaps with the exception of debunking itself. This mind-boggling ubiquitous destructiveness and negation of the very essence of negation appear as landmarks of the late (post)modern era. 'The critical theory confronts an object that seems to offer no more resistance; an object that has softened, melted and liquidized to the point that the sharp edge of critique goes through with nothing to stop it,' Bauman notes.[9] Impossibility of opposition and of resistance, as well as futility, relativeness, meaninglessness, and melancholia are some of the distinctive characteristics of postmodernity identified by its critics. Jean Baudrillard, for instance, observes that today's 'melancholia is the inherent quality of the mode of the disappearance of meaning,' and this disappearance is only possible in a system that is 'nihilistic, in the sense that it has the power to pour everything, including what denies it, into indifference.'[10]

Nothingness under the name of neo-nihilism, that is nihilism of the post-Nietzschean era, may thus brand the mainstream culture and thought of postmodernity, otherwise perhaps too paradoxical, self-contradictory, discontinuous, fuzzy and nebulous to be viewed as a kind of entity. 'While a contentious and problematic tradition, the discourse of nihilism provides a philosophical framework for thinking through the problem of meaning in the contemporary world

---

7   Bauman, *Intimations of Postmodernity*, p. vii.
8   Bauman, ibid., pp. vii-vi.
9   Bauman, ibid., p. ix.
10 Jean Baudrillard, Simulacra *and Simulations*. XVIII: 'On Nihilism'; trans. Sheila Faria Glaser (Ann Arbor: University of Michigan Press, 1994), pp. 162–163.

that otherwise stands in danger of remaining too amorphous to analyze, Ashley Woodward likewise suggests.[11]

What emerges from the thought of such diverse thinkers as those quote-above, including Bauman, John Paul II, Baudrillard, and Woodward, (the list being merely a sample, readily extendable to embrace a great number of other philosophers as well), is, therefore, a nihilistic and all-dismantling nature of postmodernity, which, arguably, provides an answer to one of the basic questions I have formulated at the beginning of this chapter. Now, what distinguishes postmodernity from modernity, (modernity understood as the period which had started with the Enlightenment), is, Bauman continues, the 'universal dismantling of power-supported structures,' for 'no new and improved order has emerged (...) from beneath the debris of the old and unwanted one,' and no new order is ever meant to arise.[12] Bauman acknowledges one difference between the culture of modernity and that of postmodernity, the latter being 'a rightful issue and a legatee of the former': unlike modernity, postmodernity 'does not seek to substitute one truth for another,' as it 'splits the truth, the standards and the ideal into already deconstructed and about to be deconstructed.'[13] The vacated spaces remain empty and are not to be filled. 'The postmodern mind seems to condemn everything, propose nothing,' Bauman adds.[14] 'Demolition is the only job the postmodern mind seems to be good at. Destruction is the only construction it recognizes. Demolition of coercive constraints and mental blocks is for it the ultimate purpose and the end of emancipatory effort,' he concludes.[15]

The postmodern deconstruction work, according to Woodward, continues in various areas, whose overarching concerns involve: the critique of reason (rejection of the foundational character of reason); the critique of the subject (refutation of the knowing subject as a self-conscious being of a stable identity); anti-humanism (opposition to philosophical humanism, whose standard for knowledge is human being; Jean-François Lyotard, for instance, in the place vacated by God, and by man, puts the Great Zero, the dead God, 'an empty centre' and an absence of meaning); the end of history (denial of a unilinear, logically progressing, teleological philosophy of history, which had defined the thought of modernity and the ideas of various prominent thinkers, for instance Hegel, and Marx); the collapse

---

11 Ashley Woodward, *Nihilism in Postmodernity* (Aurora: The Davies Group Publishers, 2009), p. 1.
12 Bauman, *Intimations of Postmodernity*, p. ix.
13 Bauman, ibid., p. ix.
14 Bauman, ibid., p. ix.
15 Bauman, ibid., p. ix.

of Western master narratives and metanarratives (totalizing and universally acknowledged narrative paradigms such as historiographical narratives, the idea of progress, and national histories), and their segmentation into myriads of 'localised stories told from different perspectives and by different cultures,' (to Lyotard, the negation of grand metanarratives makes the essence of postmodernity: 'Simplifying to the extreme,' he says, 'I define the postmodern as incredulity toward metanarratives'); and, last but not last, the principle of difference (enhancement of difference, which is not to be subordinated to a prior identity that in modernity used to draw on a unity of assimilated differences).[16]

Demolition, deconstruction, dismantling and fragmentation originate from and lead again to the ideology of meaninglessness and nothingness. Distinguished in the 19th century by Nietzsche as an increasingly important trend, nihilism, which over the 20th century evolved into what might be called neo-nihilism, can thus perhaps be recognized as a leitmotif of postmodernity, a uniting thread running through its patches, debris, dump sites, and not-to-be-filled vacancies, and as the underlying philosophy of the era. 'The vision of postmodernity that emerges from the works of Lyotard, Baudrillard, and Gianni Vattimo,' the three important theorists of the era, Woodward argues, 'is one of a world in which nihilism persists as a problem to be critically confronted, despite an abandonment of the hope for its definitive overcoming.'[17] Nihilism is apparently not to be criticized or opposed, for there is nothing left to be criticized or resisted any more; yet, according to Woodward, its pervasive nature requires attention and recognition, as the current crisis of meaning and erosion of all values that used to give orientation and sense to human life seem to have scored their final triumph.[18]

The discourse of the postmodern, Woodward continues, needs to be considered 'in relation to that of nihilism', for nihilism can serve as a guiding thread through the miscellaneous streaks of Continental philosophy, including the thought of the grandfathers of postmodernism: Nietzsche, Heidegger, Spengler, and other German thinkers, as well as the tenets of existentialism, structuralism, post-structuralism, contemporary Italian philosophy (Vattimo's weak thought,

---

16 Ashley Woodward, *Nihilism in Postmodernity* (Aurora: The Davies Group Publishers, 2009), pp. 16–19. Lyotard's concept of the Great Zero comes from his *Libidinal Economy* (Bloomington: Indiana University Press, 1993), pp. 1–13; and Lyotard's idea of the collapse of metanarratives is presented, for instance, in his study *The Postmodern Condition: A Report on Knowledge* (Minneapolis: University of Minnesota Press, 1984), p. 20.
17 Woodward, *Nihilism in Postmodernity*, p. 167.
18 Woodward, ibid., p. 1.

il pensiero debole, in particular,) and to some extent also Marxism, Hegelian dialectics, psychoanalysis, hermeneutics and Critical Theory.[19] Woodward speculates that 'the often hazy concept of the postmodern may be given sharper focus by examining it through the lens of nihilism.'[20]

Postmodernity is nihilistic, Woodward observes, for it 'undermines the normative framework of modernity', and 'leaves us without the resources for constructing a new formative framework', for it abolishes the power of reason and is the product of postmodernity, which questions the foundations of modernity.[21] There are some contradictory theories, though, which locate the sources of nihilism not in the postmodern denunciation of reason, but precisely in the hegemony of reason introduced by the philosophy of the Enlightenment, which denied a constructive role of un-rational sources of knowledge, and which, taken to extreme, has apparently devalued itself in the aura of a deep-seated distrust of reason.[22] 'As a result of the crisis of rationalism what has appeared finally is nihilism,' argues John Paul II, who endorses a contemporary anti-nihilistic philosophy, be it Christian or not, and promotes a necessary balance between the rational and the un-rational, and the importance of human spiritual dimension.[23] 'Faith and reason are like two wings on which the human spirit rises to the contemplation of truth', he writes, for 'there is a profound and indissoluble unity between the knowledge of reason and the knowledge of faith;' faith understood in its broadest philosophical sense as a belief or trust in another person or thing.[24] This echoes the tenets of some medieval philosophers, for instance Thomas Aquinas, who holds that 'faith has no fear of reason, but seeks it out and has trust in it;' and who draws in turn Anselm of Canterbury's famous maxims: '*credo ut intelligam*' (I believe so that I may understand), '*intellego ut credam*' (I think so that I may believe), and '*fides quaerens intellectum*' (faith seeking understanding).[25] Focusing on the significance of faith, John Paul II notes that:

---

19 Woodward, ibid., p. 3.
20 Woodward, ibid., p. 6.
21 Woodward, ibid., p. 12.
22 Cf. Woodward, ibid., p. 12.
23 John Paul II, *Fides et Ratio,* Chapter IV.
24 John Paul II, ibid., Introduction and Chapter III.
25 Thomas Aquinas (1225–1274), *Summa Theologiae* [Theological Compendium], I, 1, 8 ad. 2. Anselm of Canterbury (1033–1109), *Proslogion,* 1. Anselm holds that faith precedes reason, but reason can expand upon faith, which reiterates St. Augustine of Hippo's (354–430) thought; cf. C. Hollister and C. Warren, *Medieval Europe: A Short History* (New York: John Wiley & Sons, 1982), p. 302.

There are in the life of a human being many more truths which are simply believed than truths which are acquired by way of personal verification. Who, for instance, could assess critically the countless scientific findings upon which modern life is based? Who could personally examine the flow of information which comes day after day from all parts of the world and which is generally accepted as true? Who in the end could forge anew the paths of experience and thought which have yielded the treasures of human wisdom and religion? This means that the human being—the one who seeks the truth—is also the one who lives by belief.[26]

John Paul II lays emphasis on the essential connection between reason and faith, remarking that 'the parrhesia of faith must be matched by the boldness of reason,' and quoting St. Augustine: 'to believe is nothing other than to think with assent... Believers are also thinkers: in believing, they think and in thinking, they believe... If faith does not think, it is nothing.'[27] To sum up the Augustinian point, paradoxically, faith without rational thinking turns into nothingness.

John Paul II's firm belief in the necessity of the union and complementariness of faith and reason stands in sharp contrast to the message of the contemporary mass culture and philosophy, expressed, for instance, in the billboard slogan displayed in the UK and Spain, reading: 'Do you still believe? Or have you started thinking yet?'[28] Nihilism undermines the power of both, faith and reason, and tries to invalidate their symbiotic status. 'A philosophy which no longer asks the question of the meaning of life,' John Paul II remarks, 'would be in grave danger of reducing reason to merely accessory functions, with no real passion for the search for truth.'[29] Commenting on the perils of nihilism, he also notes that:

In the nihilist interpretation, life is no more than an occasion for sensations and experiences in which the ephemeral has pride of place. Nihilism is at the root of the widespread mentality which claims that a definitive commitment should no longer be made, because everything is fleeting and provisional.[30]

What conditions human existence is, John Paul II argues, a foundation of meaning, the sole condition for responding to man's universal desire for truth and cognition. Therefore, he suggests, it is vital now 'to move from phenomenon to foundation, a step as necessary as it is urgent. We cannot stop short at experience alone; even if experience does reveal the human being's interiority and spirituality, speculative

26 John Paul II, *Fides et Ratio*, Chapter III.
27 John Paul II, *Fides et Ratio*, Chapter IV. Saint Augustine, *De Praedestinatione Sanctorum* [On the Predestination of the Saints], 429, 2, 5: PL 44, 963.
28 Cf. https://www.youtube.com/watch?v=G_T_EYM9Pn8, accessed 23 April 2016.
29 John Paul II, *Fides et Ratio*, Chapter IV.
30 John Paul II, ibid., Chapter IV.

thinking must penetrate to the spiritual core and the ground from which it rises.[31] Man has always needed foundations, even though some postmodern men have obliterated them, for in postmodernity, just like in all the ages before,

> There arise (…) the fundamental questions which pervade human life: Who am I? Where have I come from and where am I going? Why is there evil? What is there after this life? These are the questions which we find in the sacred writings of Israel, as also in the Veda and the Avesta; we find them in the writings of Confucius and Lao-Tze, and in the preaching of Tirthankara and Buddha; they appear in the poetry of Homer and in the tragedies of Euripides and Sophocles, as they do in the philosophical writings of Plato and Aristotle. They are questions which have their common source in the quest for meaning which has always compelled the human heart. In fact, the answer given to these questions decides the direction which people seek to give to their lives.[32]

Should someone frown at my choice of quoting some passages from John Paul II's (Karol Wojtyła's) thought in this book, they ought to bear in mind the fact that he was, apart from being a Pope, thus the head of the Catholic Church, also a philosopher, or, as Simon F. Nolan says, 'a philosopher Pope,' and a 'profoundly philosophical Pope,' whose poetry, plays and other writings produced before and during his priesthood 'are all highly philosophically flavoured,' and addressed to all readers, regardless of their worldview and beliefs.[33] 'What [Wojtyła] did and said,' Nolan observes, 'was informed by his philosophical outlook; and, in turn, his philosophical outlook was very much informed by his life experience.'[34] As a philosopher, formed in the Artistotelian-Thomistic tradition and Max Scheler's phenomenology, based on the conviction that the world is intelligible and has unconditional meaning, John Paul II, whose philosophical formation had to confront the ideology and reality of Nazism and Communism, propounds the essential dignity of human nature and man's desire to search for truth.[35] Influenced by Scheler's

---

31 John Paul II, ibid., Chapter III.
32 John Paul II, ibid., Chapter I.
33 Simon F. Nolan, 'The Philosopher Pope: Pope John Paul II and the Human Person', www.carmelites.ie/PDF/PhilosopherPope.pdf, accessed December 3, 2015.
34 Nolan, ibid.
35 Nolan, ibid. Wojtyła's first encounter with philosophy took place during WW2, when he studied in a clandestine seminary in Nazi-occupied Poland. After his ordination to the priesthood, Wojtyła wrote two doctoral theses in philosophy: the first (in Latin) in 1946 concerning the mystical philosophy of St. John of the Cross, whose English translation is *The Problem of Faith in the Works of St. John of the Cross*, and the other (in Polish) in 1953, regarding the thought of Max Scheler, whose translation reads *An Evaluation of the Possibility of Constructing a Christian Ethics on the Basis of the System of Max Scheler*. From 1954 to 1978 Wojtyła taught advanced courses on philosophical

thought, John Paul II espouses philosophical realism, according to which what is evil and cruel in the world is in a sense an 'unreality', for it results from a distortion of the real, a denial of the truth of man's dignity and of the goodness of creation; thus, the artificiality and abnormality of the 'reality' of these anti-human depersonalizing totalitarian ideologies consist in an absence of the good.[36] Even though he later grew critical of some aspects of Scheler's phenomenology, mainly the over-idealization of the moral act, and skepticism about the ability of the human being to get at the truth of things, till the end of his life Wojtyła had remained a 'philosophical realist who saw moral acts as real, involving real choices between right and wrong;' for whom 'moral choices were character forming' and were never merely a matter of personal preferences.[37]

Among the 'foundational' and anti-nihilistic philosophers of modernity one can also mention John Henry Newman, Vladimir S. Soloviev, Petr Chaadaev, Antonio Rosmini, Pavel A. Florensky, Edith Stein (St. Teresa Benedicta of the Cross), Vladimir N. Lossky and, in the postmodern era, next to John Paul II, Jacques Maritain, Étienne Gilson, or Victor Frankl, whose philosophical enquiry was all enriched by (not necessarily religious) faith. Referring to that stream in philosophy, which radically opposes nihilism and seeks foundations, Woodward labels it in the neo-nihilistic manner, as sentimentalism driven by a' nostalgic desire to hold fast to foundations,' which, in the present post-Nietzschean era, 'is untenable.'[38]

What, therefore, is nihilism, the leading philosophy of late modernity opposed by some thinkers, and why may its transformation into neo-nihilism be understood as a landmark of postmodernity? Woodward defines nihilism as 'a concept that suggests that certain philosophical positions or beliefs about the world negate so much that is of value in life that the desirability of living is called into question'; a

---

ethics, sexual ethics, and history of philosophy at the Catholic University of Lublin, Poland, and wrote more books on philosophy and humanism, for instance *Love and Responsibility* (1960), *The Acting Person* (1969), considered by some as his philosophical *magnum opus*, and *Memory and Identity* (2005), apart from his 14 encyclicals and a great number of other writings. In 1983 John Paul II began an innovative biennial series of summer humanities seminars at Castel Gandolfo, gathering scholars of various faiths and denominations for a serious exchange of ideas. Some of the leading intellectuals who attended the seminars were: Hans-Georg Gadamer, Charles Taylor, Emmanuel Lévinas, Paul Ricoeur, Gerhard Ebeling, and Johannes Metz.

36 Nolan, 'The Philosopher Pope', p. 6.

37 Nolan, ibid., p. 7.

38 Woodward, *Nihilism in Postmodernity*, p. 115.

concept that 'indicates a (dis)connection between abstract philosophical ideas and the practical desire and necessity of living a meaningful life.'[39] In its broadest sense, nihilism refers to a 'negative attitude to life' (*nihil* means 'nothing,') or to 'any doctrine that denies the existence of something,' and can be traced back at least to the philosophy of ancient Greece.[40] The modern roots of nihilism dwell, however, in Nietzsche's theory, which sprang from the waning of Hegelian philosophy, and ran through Feuerbach, Kierkegaard, Stirner and Schopenhauer, followed by its 20th century reworkings and reverberations, such as the thought of Heidegger, existentialists (mostly Marcel, Jaspers, Sartre, Camus), and the German thinkers: Jünger and Löwith.[41] Friedrich Nietzsche (1844–1900) and many subsequent philosophers used the term to mark the decline of Western civilization and a difficulty or impossibility of living a meaningful line in the aftermath of that decline.[42] 'What I relate is the history of the next two centuries,' said Nietzsche in 1887; 'I describe what is coming, what can no longer come differently: the advent of nihilism.'[43]

Indeed, Nietzsche's prediction seems to have proved correct. The pervasive feeling of devaluation and meaninglessness of life was heightened by the atrocities of the past century's world wars, especially by the Holocaust, Stalin's genocides, and many other crimes against humanity. According to Baudrillard, contemporary nihilism:

> No longer wears the dark, Wagnerian, Spenglerian, fuliginous colours of the end of the century. It no longer comes from a Weltanschauung of decadence nor from a metaphysical radicality born out of death of God and of all the consequences that must be taken from this death. Today's nihilism is one of transparency, and it is in some sense more radical, more crucial than in its prior and historical forms, because this transparency, this irresolution is indissolubly that of the system, and that of all the theory that still pretends to analyse it.[44]

---

39 Woodward, ibid., p. 8.
40 Woodward, ibid., p. 7.
41 Keiji Nishitani, *The Self-Overcoming of Nihilism*, trans. Graham Parkes with Setsuko Aihara (Albany: State University of New York Press, 1990), p. xx.
42 Woodward, *Nihilism in Postmodernity*, p. 1. The first philosophical use of the term 'nihilism' is attributed to Friedrich Heinrich Jacobi, who in his 'Open Letter to Fichte' of 1799 accused Fichte of nihilism in his idealist philosophy; cf. Woodward, *Nihilism in Postmodernity*, p. 7.
43 Friedrich Nietzsche, *Will to Power*, trans. Walter Kaufmann and R. J. Hollingdale; W. Kaufamann, eds. (New York: Vintage, 1968), *Preface*, par. 2–3.
44 Baudrillard, *Simulacra and Simulation*, p. 159.

Lyotard develops a term 'neo-nihilism', which I have borrowed and used in this book, referring to a form of Nietzschean theory transformed through the theoretical frames of Freudian psychoanalysis, post-Marxist politics, semiotics and structuralism.[45] Thus, one might say, neo-nihilism appears to be the ostentatious (dis)ease of postmodernity – its dissolution and, at the same time, its leaven; its debunker but also its denominator, its artisan and its annihilator, which is in charge of both constituting and demolishing postmodernity.

Among various typologies of nihilism, such as, for instance, epistemological, moral, political and existential, it is the existential nihilism, or a negation of the value of life, which seems to best characterize the postmodern standing of nihilism. Woodward distinguishes two dimensions of existential nihilism, or two 'poles to which nihilism tends' and through which existential meaning is negated: the reductive and the abyssal. 'Reductive nihilism', he explains, involves a negation of meaning by means of some kind of reduction, which is frequently connected with 'philosophical reductionism, whereby phenomena are construed as "nothing but".[46] Many theorists derive nihilism from reductionism because, as Woodward notes, 'what gets left out of the reduction is precisely what makes life existentially valuable.'[47] 'Abyssal nihilism', in turn, refers to the 'inability to choose existential values', as there is 'no coherent ground of normative framework for assessing knowledge claims, deciding moral values, or taking politically efficacious action'; just like Kierkegaard's and Nietzsche's experience of reaching the abyss, or 'plunging into a bottomless pit.'[48] This type of nihilism, Woodward notes, declares the 'non-existence of anything that could ground meaning in a secure foundation', all the traditional values having been delegitimized, whereby 'abyssal nihilism' negates the value of existence.[49]

Studying the theories of Lyotard, Baudrillard and Vattimo, Woodward attempts to view neo-nihilism holistically and critically, or so it seems, as he admits that the problem can neither be actively overcome nor effectively tackled, much as it compels a response and careful examination.[50] Simon Critchley, in

---

45 Jean-François Lyotard, 'Notes on the Return and Kapital', trans. Roger McKeon, [in:] *Semiotexte 3.1.* (1978), pp. 44–53, and 48.
46 Woodward, *Nihilism in Postmodernity*, p. 11.
47 Woodward, ibid., p. 11.
48 Woodward, ibid., p. 11. An analysis of the metaphor of the abyss can be found in David K. Coe's *Angst and the Abyss: The Hermeneutics of Nothingness* (New York: Oxford University Press, 1985).
49 Woodward, *Nihilism in Postmodernity*, p. 12.
50 Woodward, ibid., p. 8.

turn, distinguishes five ways of responding to the problem of today's nihilism, which are:

1. overcoming the problem through a return to religion or (pre-modern) metaphysics;
2. rejecting it as a pseudo-problem resulting from an apparently fallacious view of history;
3. accepting meaninglessness as *status quo* by means of passive nihilism;
4. overcoming nihilism by promoting the self-destructiveness of nihilism till it overcomes itself – a form of active nihilism;
5. overcoming the desire to overcome nihilism.[51]

Each response is sketched briefly below, but I focus on the first approach to nihilism, as it provides the ground for logotherapy, Victor Frankl's philosophical concept and his school of psychotherapy, which is the subject of this chapter introduced as a psychotherapeutic basis for the Inklings' and Le Guin's peculiar 'mythopathy' (that is therapy through myth).

Following the tradition of Nietzsche and his successors, both Critchley and Woodward deem the first stance towards nihilism unsustainable, as exemplified by Saint John Paul II's approach, which they see as a 'nostalgic' call for the contemporary philosophy to abandon nihilism and reach back into 'some premodern form of metaphysical philosophy.'[52] To all the philosophers inspired by Nietzsche's thought, this approach to nihilism evades a critical encounter with the intellectual legacy of modernity and denies its validity; and, moreover, preserves and reinstitutes 'religious nihilism, with its faith in transcendent categories of valuation, and consequent devaluation of life.'[53] It is interesting that a (foundational) philosophy that promotes an unconditional meaningfulness and value of life, as well as dignity of a human being, according to Vattimo and other neo-Nietzschean thinkers, devalues life and is strongly 'reductive, violent', and nihilistic.[54] The aporia of nihilism is that nihilists, who preach that nihilism should be overcome by a passive attitude to nihilism, accuse anti-nihilists of being nihilistic, because to nihilists any foundation rejects non-foundational

51 Simon Critchley, *Very Little... Almost Nothing: Death, Philosophy, Literature* (London: Routledge, 1997), 'Preamble'; cf. Woodward, *Nihilism in Postmodernity*, p. 169.
52 Woodward, *Nihilism in Postmodernity*, p. 170.
53 Woodward, ibid., p. 170.
54 Gianni Vattimo, 'Hermeneutics and Democracy', [in:] *Philosophy and Social Criticism* 23.4 (1997), pp. 1–7, 5.

thought, and is hence violently nihilistic, which, as nihilists argue, is an untenable position.

As Vattimo, a nihilistic philosopher, claims, foundational thought, which is, by necessity, metaphysical, 'devalues a range of interpretations', and 'delegitimizes these aspects of life that bring along change, growth, mortality and variety.'[55] Metaphysics, according to Heidegger, draws on a conception of a strong Being that serves as a foundation for all beings and as an ontological framework, (not to be confused with the notion of eternal truths, which Heidegger rejects); therefore, a foundational thought entails a return to metaphysics, Vattimo explains.[56] This metaphysical 'foundationalism', Vattimo argues, 'imposes authority in the form of a foundation', whereby it 'limits the free play of dialogue and interpretation, and silences the voices questioning the foundation'; hence its 'violence and restrictiveness'.[57] The 'grand thing' about nihilism, as it seems, is that it propounds nothing and criticizes nothing. Consequently, Vattimo positively reassesses nihilism; and 'what other critics name "nihilism" (devaluation of the richness of existence), he, [paradoxically] calls "metaphysics."'[58]

It seems that much of the contemporary Western thought, exemplified by Vattimo's *il pensiero debole* (the weak thought), advocates 'accomplished nihilism', that is ontological and epistemological anti-foundationalism, which compromises metaphysics and any other attempt at reestablishing a foundational system, and overcomes 'the violence of metaphysical thinking', so that 'nothing is left of being as such.'[59] Postmodernity is the era of a 'weak thought' and 'weak being', Vattimo claims, for there is very little of Being and beings left now, and the notions of truth and foundation for thought are decomposed in the process similar to 'chemical decomposition', which, to Vattimo, represents the workings of philosophy as 'chemistry'.[60] Does this imply that the accomplished deconstruction and

55 Woodward, *Nihilism in Postmodernity*, p. 170.
56 Martin Heidegger, *Sein und Zeit* [Being and Time], (1927), trans. Joan Stambaugh (Albany: State University of New York Press, 1996), p. 229.
57 Vattimo, 'Hermeneutics and Democracy', p. 5.
58 Woodward, *Nihilism in Postmodernity*, p. 112.
59 Vattimo, 'Nietzsche and Heidegger', trans. Thomas Harrison, [in:] *Stanford Italian Review* 6. 1–2, 1986, pp. 19–30, 28.
60 This is Vattimo's interpretation of Nietzsche's idea of deconstructing metaphysics to base feelings and motivations, introduced in Nietzsche's *Human. All-Too-human*, par. 638, pp. 266–267. Vattimo, *The End of Modernity: Nihilism and Hermeneutics in Post-Modern Culture*, trans. John R. Snyder (Baltimore: John Hopkins University Press, 1988), p. 169.

decomposition of all values and foundations have obviated the human need for a meaningful existence? Certainly not, but, according to the thinkers inspired by Nietzsche, no foundational thought may resist nihilism, as all foundations have already tumbled; on the contrary, a foundational thought, as Vattimo maintains, being 'nihilistic', can strengthen the sense of senselessness and nothingness.[61]

The second approach to nihilism, which flatly rejects its existence by virtue of a fallacious interpretation of history, is, according to Critchley and Woodward, erroneous, as it questions the correctness of the philosophy of history and refuses to acknowledge the gravity of the problem.[62] Critchley observes that this view appears in fact metaphysical, as it rejects 'the cultural and historical conditionedness of thought', and promotes 'faith in positive science and transcendent "rationality", which is to replace "historical" thinking.'[63]

The third response to nihilism, as identified by Critchley, is passive nihilism, a term borrowed from Nietzsche's differentiation into passive and active nihilism.[64] This alternative reaction to nihilism involves 'accepting the meaninglessness of life, whether as a perennial condition of absurdity, or as the result of the prevailing historical and cultural conditions underlying contemporary Western society.'[65] It is, therefore, a defeatist attitude that succumbs to nihilism and does not offer any alternative whatsoever. Most post-Nietzschean thinkers, including Baudrillard, Lyotard and Vattimo, do not approve of passive nihilism. Nor do they endorse active nihilism, though, which is the fourth response analyzed by Critchley, for it strives to radically overcome nihilism by taking it to its end till it destroys itself, so that a non-nihilistic utopia might be built.[66] Most postmodernist theorists consider this idea to be mistaken and combative, arguing that an attempt to overcome nihilism preserves and reinforces nihilism and may never succeed, for, as Heidegger illustrates it, 'no one can jump over [their] own shadow.'[67] The human self is so much embedded in nihilism, they claim, that the

---

61 Vattimo, *The End of Modernity*, p. 170.
62 Woodward, *Nihilism in Postmodernity*, p. 171.
63 Woodward, ibid., p. 170. Critchley, *Very Little...Almost Nothing*, p. 10.
64 Woodward, ibid., p. 171. Cf. Nietzsche, *KSA* 12:9 [35] *Kritische Studienausgabein 15 Bänden: Sämtliche Werke*, (KSA), G. Colli and M. Montinari, eds. (Berlin: De Gruyter, 1980).
65 Woodward, *Nihilism in Postmodernity*, p. 171.
66 Critchley, *Very Little... Almost Nothing*, p. 11.
67 Woodward, *Nihilism in Postmodernity*, p. 172. Heidegger, *An Introduction to Metaphysics*, trans. Ralph Manheim (New Haven, London: Yale University Press, 1959), p. 199.

more it struggles to be liberated from it, the more it plunges into it.[68] What is needed, Critchley suggests, is a subtler response to nihilism reflected in the fifth approach, which entails 'overcoming the desire to overcome nihilism.'[69] 'It does not stipulate that nihilism must not be resisted,' Woodward explains, but that an 'imaginative resistance' ought to be developed 'in new ways,' whose variations can be found, for instance, in the writings of Lyotard, Baudrillard, and Vattimo, especially in Vattimo's 'weak thought', which attempts neither to promote nor to overcome nihilism.[70]

Swimming against the tide of nihilistic postmodernity – the foundational and logocentric thought of logotherapy

Since this book does not aspire to explore the pressing problem of postmodernity in relation to neo-nihilism, but merely hints at their notions as a background and a starting point for the discussion of logotherapy, the first part of this chapter at best scratches the surface of the problem and suggests few of its corollaries. What I attempt to present below is now a more practical consideration of people's responses to the contemporary culture of neo-nihilism, which seems to provide an answer to another question I have formulated at the beginning of the chapter, that is the issue of a universal need for therapy in postmodernity. It comes as no surprise that neo-nihilism, with its oppressive sense of nothingness and anti(foundational), hence all-permissive, thought, and its promotion of 'fashionable nonsense,' can hardly offer a solution to the existential impasse, unless, as Woodward proposes after Vattimo, one chooses neither to espouse nor to resist nihilism, and to linger instead in the permanently suspended, yet apparently efficient torpidity.[71]

The following question comes to mind: if accomplished nihilism is 'positive,' as Vattimo suggests, and if it is an achievement and a remedy not to desire to oppose nihilism any more, as many postmodern thinkers claim, (since 'positive nihilism,'

---

68 Woodward, *Nihilism in Postmodernity*, p. 172.
69 Woodward, *Nihilism in Postmodernity*, p. 172.
70 Woodward, ibid., p. 172.
71 *Fashionable Nonsense: Postmodern Intellectuals' Abuse of Science* or *Intellectual Impostures* (1997, 1998; American and British edition, respectively,) is the title of a famous controversial book by Alan Sokal and Jean Bricmont (*Impostures Intellectuelles*, written originally in French). The book argues that some leading postmodern and postmodernist thinkers (such as J. Lacan, J. Kristeva, J. Baudrillard, or G. Deleuze) have incorrectly used scientific terms, thus producing intentional nonsense or 'learned meaninglessness'.

to Vattimo, is 'the sole opportunity for social emancipation in the current situation'), why, then, is the acclaimed nothingness and meaninglessness still bothering people?[72] Why are the rates of existential neurosis, depression and, finally, suicide, still staggering in postmodernity, the age whose ideology largely endorses neo-nihilism?[73] Why cannot so many people endure the 'accomplished nihilism' of relativeness and futility, feeling that something is missing?

These questions are rhetorical. The neo-nihilistic ideology has not aborted man's natural craving for meaning and purpose that inform life. 'Today, life is fast. It vaporizes morals, [Baudrillard says]. Futility suits the postmodern, for words as well as things. But that doesn't keep us from asking questions: how to live, and why? You're not done living because you chalk it up to artifice.'[74] John Paul II observes likewise that life 'can never be grounded upon doubt, uncertainty or deceit; such an existence would be threatened constantly by fear and anxiety. One may define the human being, therefore, as the one who seeks the truth.'[75] And once that truth has been found, one lives it and applies it to their life, which can thus become meaningful. 'As far as we can discern, the sole purpose of human existence is to kindle a light of meaning in the darkness of mere being', Carl Gustav Jung says.[76] In the culture of the postmodern nihilism, this appears a daunting if not a foolhardy task, though, for meaning has almost been eradicated from its language. 'There is a subject nowadays which is taboo in the way that sexuality was once taboo; which is to talk about life as if it had any meaning', Nicholas Mosley writes in one of his novels.[77] Yet, if life has no sense and no purpose, 'why is there something rather than nothing?' one may ask.[78]

Since neo-nihilism negates the value and sense of existence, little wonder that suicide is still so popular. The statistics indicate that in the United States

---

72 Vattimo, *Nihilism and Emancipation: Ethics, Politics, and Law*, trans. William McCuaig, Santiago Zabala, ed. (New York: Columbia University Press, 2004), p. 87.

73 Suffice it to mention the names of some celebrity suicides, such as Ernest Hemingway, Sylvia Plath, Gilles Deleuze, James Robert Baker (a writer), Kurt Cobain (a musician), Michael Dorris (a novelist and a scholar), Sam Gillespie (a philosopher), or Jerzy Kosiński (a novelist).

74 Jean Baudrillard, *Postmodern Fables*, trans. Georges Van Den Abbeele (Minneapolis: University of Minnesota Press, 1997), p. vii.

75 John Paul II, *Fides et Ratio*, Chapter III.

76 Carl Jung, *Memories, Dreams, Reflections*; trans. Aniela Jaffé (New York: Random House, 1965), p. 326.

77 Nicholas Mosley, *Natalie Natalia* (London: Delkey Archive Press, 1996), p. 125.

78 This is a famous, radically metaphysical question, discussed for instance by G. W. Leibniz in his essay 'On the Ultimate Origination of Things', 1697.

of America alone, on average, someone attempts suicide every 40 seconds, and someone dies of suicide every 16 minutes, and 88 people die by suicide each day; moreover, suicide is the third leading cause of death for young people aged 15–24; and the second leading cause of death for 25–34 year olds, and also for college students.[79] The World Health Organization concludes that globally a death by suicide occurs every 40 seconds, and that 'in the last 45 years [or so] suicide rates have increased by 60% worldwide.'[80] Interestingly, it is often the states of the highest standard of life in the US, as well as wealthy countries of the other continents, (for instance Finland, Belgium, Switzerland, and Japan), which score a high suicide rate, caused mostly by an oppressive feeling of emptiness and existential absurdity.[81] Indeed, affluent postmodernity appears to be 'an age of improved means to deteriorated ends;' whose 'essential malady' of nihilism produces 'the desire to escape', not only from the 'self-made misery', from the acute consciousness of 'both the ugliness of our works, and of their evil', but also, most dramatically, from life.[82]

Victor Frankl (1905–1997), an Austrian doctor and philosopher who can hardly be called a theorist, as his thought resulted both from his experience of the Holocaust and his clinical practice of a neurologist, psychiatrist and psychotherapist, observes that the feeling of meaninglessness, which has been increasing and spreading rapidly in the postmodernity, symptomizes the 'existential vacuum', or, in other words, a 'mass neurosis.'[83] This existential neurosis results from and reveals itself through the 'mass neurotic triad': 'depression, aggression, and addiction', and the majority of patients today, Frankl observes, 'no longer complain of inferiority feelings or sexual frustrations as they did in the age of Freud and Adler', but they seek counseling from psychiatrists and psychotherapists 'because of the feeling of futility: the problem that brings them crowding into our clinics and offices now is the existential frustration, their existential vacuum.'[84]

---

79 Cf. http://www.suicide.org/suicide-statistics.html, accessed 23 April 2016.
80 Ibid., and http://www.who.int/mental_health/prevention/suicide/suicideprevent/en/, accessed 23 April 2016.
81 Ibid., and http://fathersforlife.org/health/who_suicide_rates.htm, accessed 23 April, 2016.
82 The quoted phrases come from Tolkien's essay 'On Fairy-Stories', in which he warns of the perils of the inter-war modernity (p. 151).
83 Frankl, *The Unheard Cry for Meaning* (New York: Washington Square Press, 1978, 1997), p. 25.
84 Frankl, ibid., p. 23.

What constitutes the essence of humanness and 'man's primary concern,' Frankl argues, is man's 'will to meaning,' rather than Freud's 'will to pleasure,' or Adler's 'will to power' (whose variation is the 'will to money'); and the 'will to meaning' is not merely a 'secondary rationalization of instinctual drives,' but the 'true manifestation of humanness,' and the most fundamental desire to find meaning and purpose of life.[85] There are three tenets of logotherapy, Frankl explains, and these are: the freedom of will, the will to meaning, and the meaning of life.[86] While the first and the last notion are unconditional invariables in logotherapy, the second concept, that is the will to meaning, is permutable and can be perturbed, which results in 'existential frustration,' or the 'frustration of man's striving to find a concrete meaning in personal existence.'[87] Existential frustration can in turn lead to 'noögenic neurosis,' another term coined by Frankl, which to him is not psychogenic, that is not identical to 'traditional' neurosis, but rather noögenic' – the one that originates in man's 'noölogical' dimension.[88] 'The noölogical dimension,' Frankl explains, 'goes beyond the psychological dimension, and thus is "higher"; yet being "higher" means only that it is more inclusive, encompassing the lower dimension;' therefore this type of neurosis is more profound and elusive, and more difficult to treat, as it reflects people's inner emptiness and frustration at their inability to find a meaning of life.[89]

To Frankl, human existence is not only a composite of biological and psychological mechanisms, 'conditioning processes and conditioning reflexes;' nor is man merely a being 'whose basic concern is to satisfy drives and gratify instincts;' rather 'a being in search of meaning – a search whose futility seems to

---

85 Frankl, *Man's Search for Meaning* (Boston: Beacon Press, 2006, 1st ed. 1946), p. 121.
86 Frankl, *The Will to Meaning: From Psychotherapy to Logotherapy. Foundations and Applications of Logotherapy* (Cleveland: The World Publishing Company, 1969), p. 68.
87 Frankl, *Man's Search for Meaning*, p. 123.
88 Frankl, ibid., p. 123. *Noos* or *nous* (νοῦς, νοός), in Greek 'mind' or 'intellect', is the faculty of critical existential thinking, considered as the first component of spiritual intelligence; 'in philosophy, it is the faculty of intellectual apprehension and of intuitive thought; in a narrower sense, it applies to the apprehension of eternal intelligible substances and first principles, and is identified with the highest or divine intellect'; cf. *Encyclopaedia Britannica*, http://www.britannica.com/EBchecked/topic/420882/nous, accessed 23 April 2016.
The term 'spiritual intelligence' comes from Howard Gardner's *Frames Of Mind: The Theory Of Multiple Intelligences* (New York: Basic Books, 1993).
89 Frankl, *The Unheard Cry for Meaning*, p. 22.

account for many of the ills of our age,' which often lead to suicidal thoughts.[90] Nowadays, Frankl remarks,

Suicides happen in the midst of affluent societies and in the midst of welfare states, (…) for too long we have been dreaming a dream from which we are now waking up: the dream that if we have just improved the socioeconomic situation of people, everything will be okay, people will become happy. The truth is that as the struggle for survival has subsided, the question has emerged: survival for what? Ever more people today have the means to live, but no meaning to live for.[91]

This, Frankl claims, is the effect of nihilism, or 'learned meaninglessness', that is frequently espoused not only by thinkers, but, unfortunately, also by therapists.[92] 'Meaning orientation', he concludes, 'plays a decisive role in the prevention of suicide.'[93]

What Frankl offers as an alternative to the contemporary neo-nihilism is logotherapy (*logos* in Greek stands for word, reason, also sense), that is 'therapy through meaning', the third Viennese school of psychotherapy (after Freud's psychoanalysis and Adler's individual psychology), which bridges therapy and philosophy in a unique foundational thought and practice. Its purpose, Frankl declares, is to help people seek the 'hidden logos of existence,' which must be personally found by everyone in order to make their life meaningful under any conditions, especially in the face of the tragic triad of pain, guilt, and death, which constitutes an intrinsic part of human existence.

A survivor of four concentration camps (Theresienstadt, Auschwitz, as well as Kaufering and Türkheim – two camps associated with Dachau), where he spent three years (1942–45) as a Jewish prisoner, and where his parents, brother, and wife in her pregnancy perished, Frankl claims that 'the meaning of life always changes, but it never ceases to be,' and that a human being 'is responsible and must actualize the potential meaning of [their] life.'[94] In spite, or, perhaps, precisely because of his personal experience of the Holocaust, one of the severest traumas conceivable, Frankl developed logotherapy, according to which meaning is available and can be discovered under any conditions, even the most extreme ones, and its sources are always to be found in at least one of the three potentials: 1) 'a deed to do (that is some work to create), 2) a person to encounter

---

90 Frankl, ibid., p. 17.
91 Frankl, ibid., p. 21.
92 Frankl borrows the 'learned meaninglessness' phrase from George A. Sargent, quoted in *Man's Search for Meaning*, p. 177.
93 Frankl, *Man's Search for Meaning*, p. 167.
94 Frankl, ibid., p. 133.

(to love and to be loved), 3) an attitude one can always adopt when fate and suffering are unavoidable.'[95]

Of this trichotomy of creative, experiential and attitudinal values that compose the meaning of life, the noblest and most difficult to choose, as he says, is the last option, which Frankl witnessed and learned personally in the extermination camps, for this is the stand everyone may take when being deprived of everything else, yet still exercising their own freedom to adopt an attitude towards inescapable suffering.[96] It was the last potential, which, when realized, enabled many prisoners of the concentration camps to discover meaning of their unthinkable suffering and imminent death. 'It is true that if there was anything to uphold man in such extreme situation as Auschwitz and Dachau,' Frankl notes, 'it was the awareness that life has a meaning to be fulfilled, albeit in the future. But meaning and purpose were only a necessary condition of survival, not a sufficient condition. Millions had to die in spite of their vision of meaning and purpose. Their belief could not save their lives, but it did enable them to meet death with heads held high.'[97] 'Everything can be taken from a man [or a woman] but one thing,' Frankl adds: 'the last of human freedoms to choose one's attitude in any given set of circumstances, to choose one's own way.'[98]

Synopsized by the editors of *The American Journal of Psychotherapy* as an 'unconditional faith in an unconditional meaning,' and 'perhaps the most significant thinking since Freud and Adler,' logotherapy does not prescribe a ready-made meaning, yet helps people launch a search for it, because 'this meaning is unique and specific, and must be fulfilled by every individual alone.'[99] Frankl makes it clear that 'logotherapy does not dispense and distribute prescriptions,' for 'meaning must be found but cannot be given.'[100] Therefore, 'what is demanded of man is not, as some existential philosophers teach, to endure the meaninglessness of life, but rather to bear his [or her] incapacity to grasp its unconditional meaningfulness in rational terms. Logos is deeper than logic.'[101] Meaning, one might conclude, needs both – the rational and the un-rational to be discovered

---

95   Frankl, *The Unheard Cry for Meaning*, p. 41.
96   Frankl, *Man's Search for Meaning*, p. 121.
97   Frankl, *The Unheard Cry for Meaning*, p. 34.
98   Frankl, *Man's Search for Meaning*, p. 49.
99   Frankl, ibid., p. 121. The opening two phrases are parts of a review of Frankl's *The Doctor and the Soul*, published in the *American Journal of Psychiatry*, as quoted by Frankl.
100   Frankl, *The Will to Meaning*, p. 69.
101   Frankl, *Man's Search for Meaning*, p. 141.

and fulfilled. Logotherapy equally draws on faith, (understood as an un-rational belief in the meaningfulness of existence), and on a purely empirical ground and scientific reasoning, for 'logotherapy is not moralistic but simply empirical,' Frankl remarks.[102] That Aristotelian-Thomistic premise resounds also in the Inklings' thought, as expressed, for instance, by Owen Barfield: 'reason, when it's laced with feeling, becomes imagination. ... Or can become Imagination;' and imagination – a possible avenue to truth.'[103]

That embedment of thought in both reason and faith seems to convey precisely the same message as that of Saint John Paul II, expressed synthetically in the title of his *Fides et Ratio* encyclical, quoted above in this chapter, even though Frankl was never a Christian and never linked his psychotherapy to any religion. Frankl's school of thought is addressed to all people, regardless of their views, beliefs and religious or non-religious convictions; quite similarly to John Paul II's universal message to humanity, addressed to 'all who are searching', which calls for a return to foundations and resistance towards neo-nihilism. 'Logotherapy is neither teaching nor preaching,' Frankl notes, and its concept of unconditional meaning 'is not necessarily theistic,' though it does not exclude the possibility for the person who shares it to be religious and to espouse a belief in some ultimate meaning.[104] None the less, there is no arbitrary meaning logotherapy advocates, as everyone needs to find it on their own; hence, as Elizabeth S. Lukas says, 'throughout the history of psychotherapy there has never been a school as undogmatic as logotherapy.'[105]

Of course, medical and philosophical ministry is neither pastoral ministry nor spiritual guidance, and no logotherapist claims to have the answers to people's existential questions, nor do they impose any *Weltanschauung* or values on the patients.[106] True, logotherapists are convinced that there is always a meaning for a person to fulfill, Frankl admits, 'but they do not pretend to know what the meaning is;' they may only help people search for it.[107] Responding to the question of his personal religiousness, Frankl states in the interview of 1997:

---

102   Frankl, *The Unheard Cry for Meaning*, p. 40. *The Will to Meaning*, p. 69.
103   An interview with Owen Barfield by Lyle W. Dorsett; Kent, England, July 19–20, 1984. The Marion E. Wade Center Oral History Collection (Call no.: OH/SR–3). The possible affinity between logotherapy and the Inklings' literary legacy is shown in the following chapters of this book.
104   Frankl, *The Unheard Cry for Meaning*, p. 63.
105   Frankl, *Man's Search for Meaning*, p. 178.
106   Frankl, *The Will to Meaning*, p. 67.
107   Frankl, ibid., p. 67.

I'm writing as a psychologist, I'm writing as a psychiatrist, I'm writing as a man of the medical faculty. (…) And that made the message more powerful because if you were identifiably religious, immediately people would say, 'Oh well, he's that religious psychologist. Take the book away!'(…) I don't shy away, I don't feel debased or humiliated if someone suspects that I'm a religious person for myself.… If you call 'religious' a man who believes in what I call a Supermeaning, a meaning so comprehensive that you can no longer grasp it, get hold of it in rational intellectual terminology, then one should feel free to call me religious, really. And actually, I have come to define religion as an expression, a manifestation, of not only man's will to meaning, but of man's longing for an ultimate meaning, that is to say a meaning that is so comprehensive that it is no longer comprehensible… But it becomes a matter of believing rather than thinking, of faith rather than intellect. The positing of a supermeaning that evades mere rational grasp is one of the main tenets of logotherapy, after all. And a religious person may identify Supermeaning as something paralleling a Superbeing, and this Superbeing we would call God.[108]

There seems to be a common denominator between Frankl's philosophy and John Paul II's thought, which is not necessarily theistic or religious; namely, the solid foundation of unconditional meaning and man's need for transcendence, for reaching toward other beings. John Paul II views man as a transcendent being, making a gift of himself or herself, and, likewise, Frankl remarks that:

Existence is dependent on self-transcendence; on the direction 'what for' and 'whom for' one lives; at pointing to something or someone other than oneself; to a meaning to fulfill or another human being to encounter, a cause to serve or a person to love. Only to the extent that someone is living out this self-transcendence of human existence is he truly human or does he become his true self. Man must focus outward.[109]

Even though he does not directly espouse logotherapy, John Paul II, as a philosopher, also emphasizes man's search for meaning and the urgent need to seek foundations and to overcome today's reductive and abyssal nihilism. He argues that:

The need for a foundation for personal and communal life becomes all the more pressing at a time when we are faced with the patent inadequacy of perspectives in which the ephemeral is affirmed as a value and the possibility of discovering the real meaning of life is cast into doubt. This is why many people stumble through life to the very edge of the abyss without knowing where they are going.[110]

---

108 'Victor Frankl at Ninety' – an interview with Frankl conducted by Matthew Scully, 1995, accessed 12 December, 2015, http://www.firstthings.com/article/2008/08/004-viktor-frankl-at-ninety-an-interview-18.

109 Frankl, *The Unheard Cry for Meaning*, pp. 34–35. John Paul II, *The Theology of the Body* (Boston, MA: Pauline Books and Media, 1997), p. 56.

110 John Paul II, *Fides et Ratio*, Chapter VI.

Frankl's logotherapy addresses also the problem of the fleeting nature of time and human life, which, when approached from a nihilistic perspective of triviality and purposelessness of existence, often frustrates people's will to meaning. However, as Frankl argues, 'transitoriness of our existence in no way makes it meaningless, but it does constitute our responsibleness; for everything hinges upon our realizing the essentially transitory possibilities.'[111] If there are no more possibilities ahead, as was, for instance, the case for most of the Holocaust victims, there are always realities of the past, Frankl explains: 'not only the reality of work done and of love loved, but of sufferings bravely suffered.'[112] This is so, Frankl continues, because, when confronted with inescapable suffering or with imminent death, man can always draw on the rich resources of their past, 'for in the past nothing is irretrievably lost but everything irrevocably stored; [in the past] nothing can be undone, and nothing can be done away with;' therefore, it seems that *having been* is the surest kind of being.'[113] Studying the collective existential neurosis of postmodernity, Frankl observes that 'usually, to be sure, man considers only the stubble fields of transitoriness and overlooks the full granaries of the past, wherein they had salvaged once and for all their deeds, their joys and their sufferings.'[114]

To conclude, in all his books Frankl takes a clear stand against neo-nihilism, against its passive and active forms, as well as against a resignation from attempts to overcome it. The nihilistic thought must be overcome, he claims, if the mass neurosis of today is to be effectively challenged, for 'the existential vacuum, which is the mass neurosis of the present time, can be described as a private and personal form of nihilism; and nihilism can be defined as the contention that being has no meaning.'[115] Consequently, Frankl warns of the corrupting influence of nihilism:

If contemporary psychotherapy does not keep itself free from the impact and influence of the contemporary trends of a nihilistic philosophy, it represents [yet another] symptom of the mass neurosis rather than its possible cure. The neurotic fatalism is fostered and strengthened by a psychotherapy which denies that man is free. To be sure, a human being is a finite thing, and his [or her] freedom is restricted. It is not freedom from conditions, but it is freedom to take stand toward the conditions.[116]

Frankl takes issue with the European existentialists: he disagrees, for instance, with Albert Camus' philosophy of the absurd, and with Jean-Paul Sartre's idea that man

---

111   Frankl, *Man's Search for Meaning*, p. 143.
112   Frankl, ibid., p. 143.
113   Frankl, ibid., p. 143–144.
114   Frankl, ibid., p. 144.
115   Frankl, ibid., p. 153.
116   Frankl, ibid., p. 153.

ought to accept the ultimate meaninglessness of life: what we must accept instead, Frankl argues, is our 'incapacity to recognize the ultimate meaning within rational or logical terms'.[117] Logotherapy, which bears some affinity to existential analysis, as it also deals with the nature of existence, is, however, unlike existentialism, 'neither pessimistic nor antireligious;' on the contrary, Frankl's philosophy 'faces fully the ubiquity of suffering and the forces of evil, [yet] takes a surprisingly hopeful view of man's capacity to transcend his [or her] predicament and discover an adequate guiding truth.'[118] Frankl's original term for logotherapy was the German *Existenzanalyse*, but when its translation was later mixed in English publications with Ludwig Biswanger's *Daseinanalyse*, (whose concepts result from an application of Heideggerian philosophy to psychiatry, as Frankl remarks), in order to avoid ambiguity Frankl resigned from the 'existential analysis' term, which is not to be confused with existentialist analysis, either.[119]

Logotherapy is called the third Viennese school of therapy, after Freud's psychoanalysis and Adler's psychotherapy (the latter having affinities with what came to be known as the cognitive behavioural therapy); and Frankl consciously draws on that Viennese tradition. A student of Freud and of Adler, Frankl does not undermine their legacy, and, although critical of psychoanalysis, he admits that, 'after all, [in some respects] psychoanalysis is, and will remain forever, the indispensable foundation of every psychotherapy, including any future schools.'[120] Although he acknowledges Freud's genius and his groundbreaking findings, Frankl disagrees, none the less, with Freud's nihilistic approach, arguing that 'even a genius cannot completely resist his Zeitgeist, the spirit of his time;' hence, in the aftermath of the mechanistic ideology of the 19th century, Freud simply 'forgot the upper stories', the realm beyond man's sexuality and mere psyche.[121] To express both his indebtedness to and difference from Freud, Frankl invokes an analogy of a 'dwarf who, standing on the shoulders of a giant, sees a bit farther than the giant himself.'[122]

What Frankl advises is 'rehumanization' not only of psychiatry and psychotherapy, but also of philosophy, which ought to be wary and critical of nihilism, and ought not to follow the postmodern pan-reductionism (the ubiquitous

---

117   Frankl, ibid., p. 41.
118   Gordon W. Allport, *Preface* to Victor E. Frankl's *Man's Search for Meaning*, pp. 12–13.
119   Frankl, *The Will to Meaning*, p. 5.
120   Frankl, ibid., p. 10.
121   'Victor Frankl at Ninety', an interview; http://www.firstthings.com/article/1995/04/004-viktor-frankl-at-ninety-an-interview, accessed 23 April 2016.
122   Frankl, *The Will to Meaning*, p. 10.

'nothing-but-ness' approach), pan-determinism (the view that man may not take any stand toward any conditions), and 'sub-humanism' – the three 'masks of nihilism today.'[123] The Freudian debunking and unmasking of man's unconscious drives and motives, a crucial finding though it is, has to stop at some point when it reaches the authentic, Frankl asserts.[124] Logotherapy by no means nullifies or invalidates the Freudian and Adlerian schools of thought, he remarks, but rather reinterprets and reevaluates them by rehumanizing their findings; namely, having included their dimensions, it reaches further and deeper, to the noölogical, meaning-oriented essence of humanness, which seems to have been overlooked in the other two schools of Viennese therapy.[125] Frankl explains:

> As a professor in two fields, neurology and psychiatry, I am fully aware of the extent to which man is subject to biological, psychological and sociological conditions; but in addition to being a professor in two fields, I am a survivor of four camps – concentration camps, that is – and as such I also bear witness to the unexpected extent to which man is capable of denying and braving even the worst conditions conceivable.[126]

Such extremities prove, according to Frankl, that man's orientation towards meaning overarches in many cases (depending on the person) the biological and psychological needs, so that human beings may rise above themselves by adopting an attitude to suffering, when it is inescapable, turning it into a valuable experience of personal growth. Frankl disagrees with the Freudian axiom expressed by Bertold Brecht in his *Threepenny Opera*, 'food comes first; then morals,' and describes the reality of the concentration camps: while some inmates followed their base instincts, losing the remnants of their humanity, there were also many others who gave away their last piece of bread, who supported firmly the weakest, or who organized religious activities, risking in each case a cruel, usually protracted death.[127] 'He who has a why to live for can bear almost any how,' Frankl concludes.[128]

In his critique of nihilism, Frankl goes so far as to express his conviction that 'the gas chambers of Auschwitz, Treblinka, and Majdanek were ultimately prepared not in some ministry or other in Berlin, but rather at the desks and in

---

123 Frankl, *Man's Search for Meaning*, p. 178.
124 Frankl, *The Unheard Cry for Meaning*, p. 114.
125 Frankl, ibid., p. 114.
126 Frankl, *Man's Search for Meaning*, p. 153.
127 Frankl, *The Doctor and the Soul* (New York: Second Vintage Books Edition, 1986), p. 38.
128 Frankl, *The Will to Meaning*, p. 4.

the lecture halls of nihilistic scientists and philosophers.'[129] To Frankl this is an example of what the anti-foundational culture of meaninglessness and relativity may produce, debunking all values, and revealing the destructive power of anti-human nihilism, which can very easily be turned against humanity, yet which cannot obliterate meaning: 'man is that being who invented the gas chambers of Auschwitz; however, he [and she] is also that being who entered those chambers upright, with the Lord's Prayer or the Shema Yisrael on [their] lips,' said a 90-year-old Frankl in 1995.[130] As Matthew Scully puts it, 'Frankl reminded modern psychology of one detail it had overlooked, the patient's soul,' that is of man's supreme noölogical dimension.[131] In conclusion, Frankl seems to argue, the trauma of concentration camps and gas chambers, generated by the Nazi on the grounds of nihilistic relativism, meaninglessness and 'subhumanization,' testifies, paradoxically, to the opposite philosophy of life, strongly defending the universal foundation of meaning.

The same thought dwells in John Paul II's writings, for he says that 'the great totalitarian evils of modernity, that is the ideologies of Nazism and Communism, had their roots in a distorted and disordered kind of philosophizing,' established on the grounds of nihilism; yet, despite their most fatal and tragic consequences to humanity, they did not manage to undermine transcendental values nor made the world unintelligible.[132] 'The twentieth century was the "theatre" in which particular historical and ideological processes were played out, leading toward a great "eruption" of evil,' John Paul II observes, 'but it also provided a setting for their defeat.'[133] The common denominator between Frankl's and John Paul II's thoughts is also Max Scheler's philosophy: Frankl declares that 'logotherapy is the result of an application of Max Scheler's concepts to psychotherapy;' and John Paul II's philosophical legacy attempts to reconcile the Aristotelian-Thomistic foundation with Scheler's phenomenological philosophy of consciousness.[134]

Another affinity between Frankl's and John Paul II's philosophy is that Frankl's appeal for a rehumanization of philosophy and all sciences and for an orientation towards man's search for meaning and man's will to meaning resembles what

---

129 Frankl, *The Doctor and the Soul*, p. 42.
130 'Victor Frankl at Ninety', an interview.
131 Ibid.
132 Nolan, 'The Philosopher Pope', p. 5.
133 John Paul II, *Memory and Identity: Conversations at the Dawn of a Millennium* (New York: Rizzoli, 2005), p. 3.
134 Frankl, *The Will to Meaning*, p. 10. Karol Wojtyła, *Osoba i czyn* [The Acting Person], 1969, (English edition: London: Springer, 1979).

John Paul II, speaking as a philosopher, calls a 'sapiential' element of philosophy, which is now being lost. To John Paul II, the ills of postmodernity reflect the crisis of humanism and an urgent need to rehumanize philosophy, so that it abandons its 'false modesty' and resumes its vocation, that is assistance in man's search for truth and meaning:

> Philosophy needs first of all to recover its sapiential dimension as a search for the ultimate and overarching meaning of life. This first requirement is in fact most helpful in stimulating philosophy to conform to its proper nature. In doing so, it will be not only the decisive critical factor which determines the foundations and limits of the different fields of scientific learning, but will also take its place as the ultimate framework of the unity of human knowledge and action, leading them to converge towards a final goal and meaning. This sapiential dimension is all the more necessary today, because the immense expansion of humanity's technical capability demands a renewed and sharpened sense of ultimate values. If this technology is not ordered to something greater than a merely utilitarian end, then it could soon prove inhuman and even become potential destroyer of the human race.[135]

Stanislaus Swamikannu comments on that stand of John Paul II observing that 'against the postmodern nihilistic view, John Paul II pits a set of absolute values based upon the radical question of truth about personal existence, about being, and about God'; and thus 'reaffirms the truth of faith and the faith in truth as a foundation for personal and communal life.'[136] Although John Paul II acknowledges the importance of contemporary philosophy saying that 'the currents of thought that claim to be postmodern merit appropriate attention', he argues that postmodernity is not nihilistic.[137] Moreover, John Paul II uses the ancient Greek concept of *orthós logos* (in Latin *recta ratio*) to refer to 'the right reason', which is right when aided by faith (a belief in sense and meaning):

> Once reason successfully intuits and formulates the first universal principles of being and correctly draws from them conclusions which are coherent both logically and ethically, then it may be called right reason or, as the ancients called it, *orthós logos, recta ratio*.[138]

Although Frankl's thought does not draw on Christianity, his philosophical and psychotherapeutic stance appears similar to John Paul II's critique of the philosophy of nothingness. When referring to the majority of post-Nietzschean

---

135 John Paul II, *Fides et Ratio*, Chapter VII.
136 Stanislaus Swamikannu, '*Fides et Ratio* and Metaphysics', [in:] *Faith and Reason Today: Fides Et Ratio in a Post-modern Era*, Varghese Manimala, ed. (Washington: Council for Research in Values & Philosophy 2008), pp. 51–63, p. 53.
137 *Fides et Ratio*, Chapter VII. Cf. Swamikannu, '*Fides et Ratio* and Metaphysics', p. 56.
138 *Fides et Ratio*, Introduction.

thinkers of postmodernity, who flatly reject the viability of any foundational thought, Frankl enquires, 'how can a person who refuses to listen a priori to the unheard cry for meaning [which to Frankl is the voice of postmodernity], come to grips with the mass neurosis of today?'[139] If therapists and philosophers no longer acknowledge the necessity of foundations and purposefulness, how can they holistically view postmodernity and its ills, and how can they continue assisting people in understanding themselves, their lives, and in seeking wisdom, which is the goal of philosophy?[140] Referring to some contemporary philosophers, John Paul II remarks likewise that 'at times (…) those whose vocation it is to give cultural expression to their thinking no longer look to truth, preferring quick success to the toil of patient enquiry into what makes life worth living. With its enduring appeal to the search for truth, philosophy has the great responsibility of forming thought and culture; and now it must strive resolutely to recover its original vocation.'[141] Similarly, what Frankl calls the 'unheard cry for meaning' is usually identified in the mainstream philosophy of postmodernity as a nostalgic and ridiculous sentiment for long-invalid foundations, or as a religious phobia, metaphysical horror (fear of the possible terrifying truths behind existence), or *horror vacui* (fear of the existential void and nothingness).[142]

A special focus of logotherapy is the search for 'the logos of pathos', for the meaning of suffering, which is a universal human dilemma postmodernity has tried to devalue, and which can be a valuable formation experience when faced proudly.[143] Because of its rather unpopular tenets, which include the long-compromised notions of the unconditionality of meaning and the nobilitating experience of suffering, when it is unavoidable (a triad of pain, guilt or death), logotherapy has engendered both enthusiasm, as its effectiveness as a school of psychotherapy seems unquestionable, and criticism, for some philosophers have

---

139 Frankl, *The Unheard Cry for Meaning*, p. 17.

140 *Philosophia* in Greek means 'love of knowledge, pursuit of wisdom; systematic investigation', and wisdom tends to involve being able to respond and counsel. Cf. *Online Etymology Dictionary*, Douglas Harper, ed. http://www.etymonline.com/index.php?term=philosophy, accessed 25 April 2016.

141 John Paul II, *Fides et Ratio*, Chapter VI.

142 'Metaphysical Horror' is a book by Leszek Kołakowski (Chicago: University of Chicago Press, 2001).

143 'The logos of pathos' understood as 'the meaning of suffering' is Frankl's phrase used, for instance, in his *The Will to Meaning*, p. 28.

accused Frankl of authoritarianism and religiousness.[144] Frankl retorts that a doctor who cares the most for the well-being and recovery of their patients and recommends treatment they have developed and used personally in the most extreme conditions, must not be reproached for authoritarianism; and, likewise, religion cannot be discarded only because it is 'as an expression of man's longing for meaning' and because it seeks an ultimate meaning far beyond therapy.[145] Quite certainly, logotherapy has contributed to flouting the postmodern taboo of talking about meaning as something meaningful, swimming against the tide of the neo-nihilistic mainstream.

Derrida's critique of logocentrism

It is perhaps worthwhile to juxtapose logotherapy with logocentrism, especially with the interpretation of the latter offered by Jacque Derrida (1930–2004) from his deconstructionist stand. There are two dictionary meanings of logocentrism: it is a 'a philosophy holding that all forms of thought are based on an external point of reference which is held to exist and given a certain degree of authority'; and 'a philosophy that privileges speech over writing as a form of communication because the former is closer to an originating transcendental source.'[146] The first definition seems to point towards a universal 'logos', which is epistemologically superior and dwells in a system that can only be known through logocentric metaphysics. The second approach focuses on the relationship between speech and writing in language, and promotes speech (that is the sound of a word which is coupled with its meaning) as the representation of the logos that reflects an original irreducible object and is the site of metaphysical significance.

Derrida takes issue with the Western philosophical tradition, which he identifies as logocentric and hence metaphysical, arguing that it rests on binary oppositions that draw on 'a violent hierarchy', where 'one of the two terms governs the other'.[147] This, according to Derrida, can be referred to as the 'metaphysics

144 Clinical effects of logotherapy are presented, for instance, in the study of T. E. Zuehlke and J. T. Watkins, 'Psychotherapy with Terminally Ill Patients' [in:] *Psychotherapy, Therapy, Research, and Practice 14* (4)1977, pp. 403–410. One of the critics of logotherapy is Rollo May, cf. his *Existential Psychology* (New York: Random House, 1961).

145 'Victor Frankl at Ninety', an interview.

146 Cf. *Merriam-Webster Dictionary*, http://www.merriam-webster.com/dictionary/logocentrism, accessed 23 April 2016. The term 'logocentrism' was coined in the 1920s by the German chemist, philosopher and psychologist Ludwig Klages.

147 Jacques Derrida, *Positions* (Chicago: University of Chicago Press, 1992), p. 41.

of presence' or 'metaphysics' for short, because it favours the first part of the dichotomies, such as presence over absence, good over evil, the positive over the
negative, the pure over the impure, and so forth, marginalizing the contingent
and the complicated, which are considered, in his view, not as alternatives that
determine the difference but as mere aberrations.[148] Thus, Derrida claims, metaphysical thought represented by all metaphysicians (that is logocentric philosophers), from Plato to Rousseau, from Descartes to Husserl, introduces hierarchies
and orders of subordination in the various dualisms it encounters.[149] Derrida's
deconstruction is the 'event' or 'moment' at which a binary opposition seems to
contradict itself and undermine its own authority; it is a theory which does not
attempt to synthesize the dichotomies but rather to mark their difference, unde-
cidability, as well as their eternal interplay.[150] While logocentrism acknowledges
the existence of a realm of 'truth' and a reality prior to and independent of linguistic signs, deconstruction, therefore, views meaning, whether transcendental
or linguistic, as a dependent variable resulting from the play of differences and
contrasts – a play which is 'limitless', 'infinite' and 'indefinite'.[151]

Frankl's philosophical thought, from Derrida's perspective appears as metaphysical and logocentric (in the first sense of logocentrism quoted above), for it
is centred upon some unconditional logos, which is always to be discovered, and
whose meaning is always prioritized over the feeling of emptiness, nothingness,
and relativity. Logotherapy strives to construct sense of every life situation and
existential dilemma in a meaningful way, its rock foundation being the existence
of some non-arbitrary meaning available to every person at any moment of their
life; whereas Derrida's deconstruction, being anti-logocentric and nihilistic, suggests that meanings, metaphysical constructs and hierarchical oppositions are
never stable and enduring, since they rely on ultimately arbitrary signifiers.

If one attempted to place Frankl's logotherapy within Critchley's scheme of
contemporary responses to nihilism, cited above in this chapter, it would probably come as a variation of the first attitude, that is one based on metaphysics or
on religion, discredited by Critchley, Derrida, and the majority of postmodern

---

148   Derrida, *Limited Inc.* trans. Jeffrey Mehlman, Samuel Weber; Gerald Graff, ed. (Ev-
      anston: Northwestern University Press, 1998), p. 236.
149   Derrida, *Limited Inc*, p. 236.
150   Derrida, *Positions*, pp. 41–43. Derrida coined the term *différance*, which refers to both
      a difference and an act of deferring, so as to characterize the way in which meaning is
      created through the play of differences between words; cf. *Encyclopaedia Britannica*,
      accessed 23 April 2016, http://www.britannica.com/topic/deconstruction#toc222928.
151   *Encyclopaedia Britannica*, ibid.

philosophers as unsustainable. Logotherapy, however, is not religious, as it draws on strictly empirical, experiential and scientific foundation proposed by a doctor who reminds, however, of the supreme spiritual dimension – a system some postmodern thinkers regard as unthinkable. Logotherapy appears as one of many anti-nihilistic alternatives questioning the mainstream theory of postmodernity, and a thought applicable not only to psychotherapy and philosophy, but also to other areas of human activity that constitute the potential media of quotidian therapy, such as arts and literature. 'Every therapy must in some way, no matter how restricted, also be logotherapy,' remarks Magda Arnold, concluding that helping people to seek meaning of particular situations and their lives is the prerequisite for aid.[152] In the light of Derrida's deconstruction, it is actually Frankl's thought that pertains to the marginalized and discarded element of 'metaphysical' philosophy, overwhelmed and denigrated by the mainstream school of neo-nihilism, and that binary opposition calls for detailed study and analysis, which is beyond the scope of this book.

Logocentric therapy through narrative

Returning to logotherapy, one ought to mark its obvious connection with narrative. To many psychotherapists, for instance John McLeod, the basic vehicle of therapy is narrative, which 'bridges the culture and the self.'[153] McLeod argues that 'all therapies are narrative therapies. Psychotherapy can only function in terms of telling and re-telling stories, yet there is no "narrative therapy" [as such], (...) no one way of doing this. Psychotherapy can be viewed as a culturally sanctioned form of healing that reflects the values and needs' of the contemporary post-industrial world; 'a cultural form' that 'has undergone transition from religious to scientific modes of intervention', and whose popularity has thrived precisely since the beginning of the postmodern period, roughly the second half of the 20th c.[154]

Interestingly, McLeod, not being connected with Frankl's school of psychotherapy, seems to agree with Frankl's orientation towards meaning as a core of therapy, as he observes that 'narrative, even when tragic and seemingly without hope, can help reclaim some of the more affirming chapters in the person's life, and find ways of seeing the awful things that have happened as episodes in a

---

152 Magda B. Arnold and John Gasson, *The Human Person* (New York: Ronald Press, 1954), p. 618.
153 John McLeod, *Narrative and Psychotherapy* (London: Sage Publications, 2006), p. 2.
154 McLeod, ibid., p. 2.

"bigger" life story that has meaning and purpose.[155] McLeod argues that meaning is what can be sought and discovered through narrative processes, by telling, editing and re-writing one's own story, which has become especially important in the 'postmodern era of growing alienation and fragmentation', and in its culture of 'the continual consumption of nonessential and quickly obsolete items and experiences.'[156] Hence, as Philip Cushman remarks, 'psychotherapy is one of the professions responsible for healing the post-war self', that is in charge of counselling people and guiding them towards a meaning and purpose of their particular lives.[157] 'Unfortunately', Cushman adds, 'many psychotherapy theories attempt to treat the postmodern self by reinforcing the very qualities of the self that have initially caused the problem', thus leaving a massive void and offering no help.[158]

The word narrative comes from the Latin *narrare* ('to tell, relate, recount, explain', literally 'to make acquainted with'), and *gnarus* ('knowing'); therefore 'to narrate' means 'to make known by telling.'[159] As Victor Turner, a cultural anthropologist, observes, narrative is a 'term for a reflexive activity which seems to know [about] antecedent events, and about the meaning of these events.'[160] He notes also that there seems to be an implication of meaning embedded in the nature of narrative, and this brings narrative perhaps even closer to the therapy through meaning, which employs narrative. Another affinity between therapy through meaning (or logotherapy) and narrative is the notion of Logos, which embraces both 'word' and 'meaning.'[161] Meaning, which is the goal of logotherapy, cannot be construed outside words, ideas and events, which constitute narrative. This narrative of meaning may be professionally therapeutic, advised or inspired by clinical practitioners, and then the therapy will involve specialist medical treatment, or it may come from non-professionals, telling stories or helping others

---

155   McLeod, *Narrative and Psychotherapy*, p. x.

156   McLeod, ibid., p. 3.

157   McLeod, ibid., p. 4.

158   Philip Cushman, 'Why the self is empty: towards a historically-situated psychology', [in:] *American Psychologist 45* (1990), pp. 599–611, 601.

159   *Online Etymology Dictionary*, Douglas Harper, ed. http://www.etymonline.com, accessed 24 April 2016.

160   Victor Turner, *From Ritual to Theatre: The Human Seriousness of Play* (New York: PAJ Publications, 1982), pp. 86–87.

161   I capitalize the word 'Logos' after C. S. Lewis, who, in his *Surprised by Joy* (p. 209) refers to Barfield and writes that 'our logic was participation in a cosmic Logos.' Thus, I signal a connection which I intend to make between the thought of the Inklings (and of Le Guin) and that of logotherapy, which does not capitalize the word.

tell their stories in order to help those seeking meaning understand themselves, their thoughts, actions, and the narrative of their lives.

Thus, outside psychotherapy and philosophy, which are examples of professional disciplines able to pass on some advice and guidance on people's life situations, therapy can also work in its quotidian mode, among ordinary people in the narratives they make and exchange, as an ancient 'culturally sanctioned' form of aiding and healing. That mode of therapy is reflected in its meaning: in Greek therapy (*therapeia*; Latin: *therapia*) refers to a 'service rendered by one to another; medical service of curing or healing; and household service, a body of attendants, servants and domestics;' so it does not originally refer only to specialist medical treatment, but also to assistance and help rendered simply 'by one to another'.[162] A distinct space of such quotidian therapy or '*therapia pauperum*' (available to everyone, outside the professional clinical practice,) is the narrative of literature, the natural habitat of language and Logos, and hence, as it appears, of therapy.[163] Bibliotherapy, that is therapy through reading and writing literature, has been known since antiquity; for instance, the inscription above library doors in ancient Greece read that the library was a 'healing place for the soul'.[164] This mode of literary *therapia pauperum* is universally available, inexpensive and not limited to a group of professionals.

Moreover, it is not only therapy through narrative that can be universal; so are its 'patients', the recipients of therapy. The tales of psychotherapy, as Irvin Yalom, a psychiatrist, psychotherapist and writer, observes, 'are everyman, everywoman stories,' for 'patienthood is ubiquitous; [and] the assumption of the label is largely arbitrary and often dependent more on cultural, educational, and economic factors than on the severity of pathology'.[165] Both the patients and the therapists, the tellers and the listeners, the writers and the readers, the narrators and the narratees need therapy, and for its sake they may often swap places in the collective realm of narrative; for, as Yalom notes, both these groups must equally confront 'the givens

---

162   *The Greek Lexicon*, http://www.studylight.org/lex/grk/view.cgi?number=2322; accessed 25 April 2016.

163   The Latin term '*therapia pauperum*' coined by me is modelled on the '*Biblia pauperum*' concept, and means therapy that is available to everyone in a domestic, non-clinical environment, and irrespective of medical or psychotherapeutic treatment.

164   Amie. K. Sullivan, Harold R. Strang, 'Bibliotherapy in the classroom: Using literature to promote the development of emotional intelligence' [in:] *Childhood Education*, 79. 2 (2002), pp. 74–80, 76.

165   Irvin D. Yalom, *Love's Executioner and Other Tales of Psychotherapy* (London: Penguin Books, 1991), p. 14.

143

of existence' and the peril of existential vacuum.'[166] Hence, he concludes, 'the professional posture of disinterested objectivity, so necessary to scientific method, is [in the narrative of therapy] inappropriate.'[167] Bibliotherapy, one may conclude, can serve both the narrative maker and its recipient.

Logotherapy through various narratives of bibliotherapy appears viable and worthwhile because literature has a considerable therapeutic potential and may have a therapeutic content due to its narrative means that can lead to a therapeutic end, if it is dedicated to the search for meaning and relates closely to a person's problem. This is what many psychologists and psychotherapists practicing bibliotherapy have confirmed, and what Frankl also mentions, making a disclaimer that, unlike 'so many contemporary writers dabbling in the field of psychiatry and psychotherapy', he by no means wishes 'to become a psychiatrist dabbling in the field of [post]modern literature.'[168] Frankl observes that a considerable 'part of contemporary literature is a symptom of feelings of meaninglessness and emptiness, a sense of futility and absurdity, and frustrated will to meaning,' and remarks that as long as literature reflects its authors' sense of nonsense and absurdity, it remains 'just another symptom of the mass neurosis today.'[169] Identification of the symptoms of the problem, essential though it is for diagnosis, needs, however, as Frankl argues, to be followed by therapy: 'writers who themselves have gone through the hell of despair over the apparent meaninglessness of life can offer their suffering' in order to support other people, and can 'help the reader who is plagued by the same condition with overcoming it.'[170] Of course, Frankl continues, 'the writer should be granted freedom of opinion and expression, but freedom is not the last word, it is not the whole story; freedom threatens to degenerate into arbitrariness unless it is balanced by responsibleness.'[171] And, finally, Frankl refers to literature as a feasible medium of logotherapy:

> The least service the writer could render the reader would be to evoke a sense of solidarity. In this case, the symptom would be the therapy. However, if modern literature is to carry out this therapeutic assignment – in other words, if it is to actualize its therapeutic potential – it has to refrain from turning nihilism into cynicism. As justified as the writer might be in sharing his [or her] own sense of futility with the reader, it is irresponsible cynically to preach the absurdity of existence. If the writer is not capable of

---

166   Yalom, ibid., p. 14.
167   Yalom, ibid., p. 14.
168   Frankl, *The Unheard Cry for Meaning*, p. 86.
169   Frankl, ibid., p. 90.
170   Frankl, ibid., p. 90.
171   Frankl, ibid., p. 92.

immunizing the reader against despair, he [or she] should at least refrain from inoculating them with despair.[172]

Thus, as Frankl seems to argue, when freed from the confines of 'fashionable nonsense' and from the impact of the postmodern mass culture of ultimate meaninglessness and cynicism, literature may empower the self-industry of logotherapy, when the reader interacts with a narrative that encourages him or her to seek a meaning of their particular life situation rather than overwhelming them with a prevailing sense of emptiness and nothingness.[173] And this, Frankl claims, must not be a utopian, escapist or naïve narrative, as therapy can only succeed by helping a person grasp the value of suffering, when it is inescapable, connected with the human experience of pain, guilt, and death.[174] Perhaps the foundation of logotherapy offers an alternative to the 'liquid times' of postmodernity – 'the age of uncertainty', whose instability and consumerism do not seem to leave space for an ethic of meaning.[175] 'Challenging the meaning of life is the truest expression of the state of being human,' Frankl remarks, and this can be done by anyone in any conditions.[176] As many readers of his books have agreed, 'logotherapy is psychotherapy for the man in the street; for all of us,' and its literary extension, perhaps one of many, is, as I would like to argue, high fantasy fiction as conceived by the Inklings and by Le Guin, which I view in terms of *therapia pauperum*, or a therapy 'for the man in the street; for all of us.'[177]

Mediated by means of narrative, logotherapy (or therapy through meaning) is perhaps in a sense the first and earliest form of therapy that humankind has developed, because narrative, not necessarily verbalized but also expressed by body language, dance, rhythm, music, or visual arts, constitutes the most basic and most natural medium of expression and communication. Viewed in this light, narrative defines therapy; hence, as McLeod observes, 'there are no new therapies,' for each school and technique that has emerged over the centuries draws on constructing,

---

172 Frankl, ibid., p. 91.

173 *Fashionable nonsense: Postmodern Intellectuals' Abuse of Science* is the title of a book by Alan Sokal and Jean Bricmont (American edition of 1997), as mentioned above in this chapter.

174 Frankl, *The Unheard Cry for Meaning*, p. 95.

175 The quoted phrases come from Bauman's book: *Liquid Times: Living in an Age of Uncertainty*.

176 Frankl, *Man's Search for Meaning*, p. 65.

177 Reviewers from Oxford, UK; Princeton, NJ, USA; and North Carolina, USA; reviews accessed 29 May 2015 from http://www.amazon.com/Doctor-Soul-Psychotherapy-Logotherapy/dp/0394743172.

reconstructing, editing, retelling, and rewriting narratives.[178] In the culture of postmodernity, when man's existential dimension is generally downplayed and often frustrated, therapy, according to Frankl, needs to return to the foundation of meaning, which, when discovered personally, may subsequently enhance the person's psychotherapy and physiotherapy, and allow a holistic approach to the person, including their noölogical dimension. The existential neurosis that continues in the first decades of the new millennium, voiced in the prolonged but largely 'unheard cry for meaning,' seems to ensure the relevance of logotherapy as an alternative anti-nihilistic thought. Maybe Jerry Mandel's prediction made in the 1970s, when he speculated that 'logotherapy [might] have more to say to the 21 c. America than it has already said to the 20th c. America,' will prove correct, and maybe it will come true not only in America.[179]

Regardless of other possible applications of logotherapy, in this book it is seen as a school of psychotherapy and philosophy which, when transposed onto the ground of fantasy literature, particularly that of the Inklings and of Le Guin, seems to correlate with its intrinsic therapeutic properties. The next chapter addresses in greater detail the issue of (logo)therapeutic properties of narrative as such, which, as I argue in Chapter Six, find one of their fullest realizations in high fantasy narrative, the realm of Faërie, as represented by the Inklings, and by Le Guin, even though those writers do not make any reference to Frankl's philosophy in their works, and, most probably were not familiar with his thought.

---

178 McLeod, *Narrative and Psychotherapy*, 'Preface'.
179 Jerry Mandel, an unpublished paper, quoted in *The Unheard Cry for Meaning*, p. 24.

Chapter Four
(Logo)therapy through narrative

How can therapy, and, more precisely, Frankl's logotherapy, be carried out through narrative? This chapter is meant as an introduction to an analysis of therapeutic properties of high fantasy narrative exemplified by the works of the Inklings and of U. K. Le Guin, which, as I would like to argue, lend themselves to a (logo) therapeutic use within a universal context of *therapia pauperum*, available to all readers and listeners outside the clinical context, and based on its two inherently therapeutic pillars: fantasy and narrative. Before examining how art therapy may work in the realm of Faërie, which is the subject matter of Chapter Five, then how logotherapy might apply to high fantasy, as discussed in Chapter Six, and, finally, what cathartic potential Tolkien's concept of Eucatastrophe may reveal, as considered in Chapter Seven, I address now some fundamental properties of Faërie that appear therapeutic and result from its narrative nature, a quality fantasy stories share with other literary works of art, and from its singular reliance on visual and musical arts, which do not only construct a narrative world, but mediate its otherworldliness and 'arresting strangeness'.[1]

Narrative therapy

In its broadest senses narrative encompasses 1.'something that is narrated, a story or an account; 2. the art or practice of narration, and 3. the representation in art of an event or story; also an example of such a representation.'[2] According to a narrower definition, narrative is 'a spoken or written account of connected events; a story', or 'the narrated part or parts of a literary work, as distinct from dialogue',

---

1   The phrase 'arresting strangeness', which is an attribute of Fantasy, pertaining to Faërie, is Tolkien's ('On Fairy-Stories', p. 139).

2   *The Merriam-Webster Dictionary*, http://www.merriam-webster.com/dictionary/narrative, accessed 23 April 2016. I have referred to the problem of narrative therapy and some elements of art therapy in fantasy fiction in my paper 'Framing ekphrasis in fantasy narrative: chiaroscuro and sfumato in the works of J. R. R. Tolkien and U. K. Le Guin' [in:] *Image, Imagery, Imagination in Contemporary English Studies,* Bożena Cetnarowska, Olga Glebova, eds. (Częstochowa: Jan Długosz University Press, 2012), pp. 48–77.

thus a representation bound with verbal language.[3] When approached as a strictly literary term, narrative designates 'a telling of some true or fictitious event or connected sequence of events, recounted by a narrator to a narratee (although there may be more than one of each),' which ought to be distinguished from 'descriptions of qualities, states, or situations, and also from dramatic enactments of events.'[4]

Narrative relies on story-making and, when understood in its broadest sense quoted above, it may be delivered through pictures, music, dance, gestures, words, or other narrative vehicles, all serving as basic modes of man's self-expression, perception of the world and communication with other people and living things, and as basic instruments of coming to grips with selfhood and otherness. Narrative appears therefore to be a principal way of existing in the world, that is experiencing, knowing, and communicating with oneself and the other, which becomes possible through a kind of 'story-telling', however miscellaneous forms and media, verbalized or not, the 'story' and the 'telling' may assume.

Regardless of the variety of narrative vehicles, or maybe precisely owing to their wealth, narrative is a universal human phenomenon and a peculiar faculty. 'Each of us is a biography, a story; each of us is a singular narrative, which is constructed, continually, unconsciously, by, through, and in us – through our perceptions, our feelings, our thoughts, our actions; and not least, our discourse, our spoken narrations,' remarks Oliver Sacks, a clinical neurologist.[5] 'We are narratives and we live by and through narrative,' he concludes.[6] Imagination and reason, the distinct human attributes and abilities, many not function without the paradigm of narrative. Odo Marquard, a contemporary German philosopher, speaks of 'the anthropological necessity to structure our lives by telling stories,' and, having converted the famous sentence of Pompeius 'navigare necesse est', asserts that 'narrare necesse est'.[7]

---

3   *The New Oxford Dictionary of English*, Judy Pearsall, ed. (Oxford: Oxford University Press, 1998), p. 1231.
4   Chris Baldick, *Oxford Dictionary of Literary Terms* (Oxford: Oxford University Press, 2008), p. 219.
5   Oliver Sacks, *The Man who Mistook his Wife for a Hat* (London: Duckworth, 1985), p. 105.
6   Ibid., p. 105.
7   Plutarch (50–125 AD), a Greek historian and biographer, who later became a Roman citizen, in his *Life of Pompey* attributes the famous sentence *navigare necesse est; vivere non est necesse* (it is necessary to sail; it is not necessary to live) to Pompey the Great (Gnaeus Pompeius Magnus, 106–48 BC), an outstanding Roman political and military leader, who in 56BC commanded the sailors during a storm to set sail and bring food from Africa to Rome.

Recognized as an 'instrument for making meaning' and for creating and maintaining one's identity, narrative forms the core of contemporary narrative philosophy.[8] One of its British representatives, Alasdair MacIntyre defines man as an 'essentially story-telling animal', claiming that what constructs our lives is stories, and that they had existed well before we were born, and continue well after we die.[9] We are rooted in the narrative of our culture, therefore, 'we are never more (and sometimes less) than the co-authors of our own narratives', MacIntyre observes.[10] Expanding upon this point, John McLeod, who represents the 'narrative turn' in psychology and psychotherapy, notes that 'the task of being a person in a culture involves creating a satisfactory-enough alignment between individual experience and the story of which I find myself a part', for narrative is the 'centre of gravity of the self' that contributes to and draws from the common universe of human nature and experience.[11]

From the linguistic point of view, according to Mikhail Bakhtin, the great semiotician and philosopher of language, discourse, that is a classifiable instance of language use, whose special kind is narrative, (which Bakhtin analyzes with reference to written and spoken communication organized into speech genres), is made from speech utterances, each of which is 'a special kind of creative activity embodying a specific sense of experience', and each of which 'refutes, affirms, supplements, and relies upon the others, presupposes them to be known, and somehow takes them into account.'[12] 'Therefore,' Bakhtin remarks, 'each kind of utterance is filled with various kinds of responsive reactions to other utterances of the given sphere of speech communication.'[13] No one speaks in the void, and no one creates narrative which might have been unheard of. 'No one breaks the eternal silence of the universe,' Bakhtin asserts, because all our words, the products of language, which is the most powerful semiotic tool, are 'filled with, and

---

8   Jerome Bruner, *Acts of Meaning* (Cambridge, MA: Harvard University Press, 1990), p. 97. Bruner (1915–2016) was a pioneer of cognitive educational psychology.
9   Alasdair MacIntyre, *After Virtue: A Study in Moral Theory* (London: Duckworth, 1981), p. 216.
10 Ibid., p. 213.
11 John McLeod, *Narrative and Psychotherapy* (London: Sage Publications, 2006), p. 27. Daniel Dennett, a philosopher connected with cognitive science, has published a paper entitled 'The Self as a Centre of Narrative Gravity' [in:] *Self and Consciousness: Multiple Perspectives*, F. Kessel, P. Cole and D. Johnson, eds. (Hillsdale, NJ: Erlbaum, 1992), pp. 275–288.
12 Mikhail Bakhtin, *Speech Genres and Other Late Essays*, trans. Vern W. McGee, (Austin: University of Texas Press, 1986), p. 91.
13 Ibid., p. 92.

are echoes of and responses to, others' words, so that 'our utterances are dialogic responses to earlier utterances.'[14]

In the Bakhtinian theory of language and discourse human imagination is dialogic, and all utterances, or units of communication in discourse, rely on intertextuality and polyphonic heteroglossia, that is on the interconnectedness of all texts in a culture and on the multitude of voices uttering their texts (in an oral or written form), best exemplified in novels.[15] Bakhtin argues that:

> A word (or in general any sign) is interindividual, [for] everything that is said, expressed, is located outside the 'soul' of the speaker and does not belong only to him [or her]. The word cannot be assigned to a single speaker. The author (speaker) has his own inalienable right to the word, but the listener has his rights, and those whose voices are heard in the word before the author comes upon it also have their rights (after all, there are no words that belong to no one).[16]

Echoes of the Bakhtinian interpretation of discourse and speech reverberate in the contemporary narrative philosophy, according to which not only human discourse and culture but also existence is defined by the mode of narrative, whose common universal elements everyone needs to discover, select, appropriate and match with their lives, and which everybody needs to (re)construct in order to communicate and make sense of anything. 'To become a logic of narrative, [the plot of any story] has to turn toward recognized cultural configurations, toward the schematism of narrative constituted by the plot-types handed down by tradition,' remarks Paul Ricoeur, a French philosopher of hermeneutic phenomenology, reiterating Bakhtin's view.[17] 'Only in this way, in finding a suitable narrative paradigm, can our lives become intelligible to us,' Ricoeur concludes.[18] Everyone needs to find an intelligible meaning of their own life, yet the meaning-making medium, that is narrative, appears, as Bakhtin remarks, essentially 'interindividual.'[19] One of the most natural and universal narrative paradigms, which helps discover meaning, is, one may add, fantasy narrative, for it is rooted in myth and folklore, some of the earliest forms of human thought

---

14 Ibid., p. 69.
15 Bakhtin, *The Dialogic Imagination: Four Essays*, trans. Caryl Emerson and Michael Holquist; Michael Holquist ed. (Austin and London: University of Texas Press, 1981), (written in Russian in the 1930s).
16 Bakhtin, *Speech Genres and Other Late Essays*. pp. 121–122.
17 Paul Ricoeur, *Time and Narrative* (*Temps et Récit*), trans. Kathleen McLaughlin and David Pellauer, (Chicago: University of Chicago Press, 1985), p. 43.
18 Ricoeur, ibid., p. 43.
19 Cf. footnote 15 above.

and communication, which have informed human discourse since the beginning of time, regardless of place and culture.

According to the psychological approach to narrative, the person is a constant narrator and a narratee, and hence, as Kenneth Gergen points out, everyone can be approached as a 'living text' inhabiting what Theodore Sarbin calls a 'storied world'.[20] Jerome Bruner defines the self likewise as a 'perpetually rewritten story',[21] and Charles Taylor argues in the same vein that 'a basic condition of making sense of ourselves is that we grasp our lives in a narrative', and see our lives as an 'unfolding story'.[22] This story is composed of 'consistent narrative themes', which contribute to constructing human metanarratives, and which are of great import, Haim Omer and Carlo Strenger observe.[23]

Moreover, seen as man's natural habitat and an inherent mode of experience and self-expression, narrative, according to many scholars and scientists, has considerable healing properties. C. Jeffrey Terrell and William Lyddon posit that 'by underscoring the storied nature of the human condition, narrative provides an integrative and contextually sensitive framework for psychotherapeutic theory and practice'.[24] Lisa Capps and Elinor Ochs, in turn, note that 'people create and maintain social, cognitive and emotional order in their lives by their narrative construction;' and that 'all human beings are guided by the stories they construct'.[25] Elaine Chaika remarks likewise that 'continuity of self is maintained and created by constructing a narrative of one's life'.[26]

These few selected assumptions have not merely been inspired by the neo-Freudian cult of story-telling in the wake of psychoanalysis, which rediscovered and rested on talking, listening and 'narrativizing' lives as a means of therapy.

20 Kenneth J. Gergen, *The Saturated Self: Dilemmas of Identity in Contemporary Life* (New York: Basic Books, 1991); p. 55. Theodore Sarbin, ed. *Narrative Psychology: The Storied Nature of Human Conduct* (Santa Barbara: Praeger Publishers, 1986), p. 13.

21 Jerome Bruner, *Making Stories: Law, Literature, Life* (New York: Farrar, Straus and Giroux, 2002), p. 33.

22 Charles Taylor, *Sources of the Self: The Making of Modern Identity* (Cambridge, Mass.: Harvard University Press, 1989), p. 47.

23 Haim Omer and Strenger Carlo, 'The Pluralist Revolution: From the One True Meaning to an Infinity of Constructed Ones', [in:] *Psychotherapy* no. 29, 1992, pp. 253–261, 257.

24 C. Jeffrey Terrell, and William Lyddon,'Narrative and Psychotherapy' [in:] *Journal of Constructivist Psychology*, Vol. 9, Issue 1, (London: Routledge, 1996), p. 27.

25 Lisa Capps and Elinor Ochs, *Constructing Panic: The Discourse of Agoraphobia* (Cambridge, Mass.: Harvard University Press, 1995), pp. 18 and 75.

26 Elaine Chaika, *Linguistics, Pragmatics and Psychotherapy* (London: Whurr Publishers, 2000), p. 147.

Instead, they seem to reflect a truth acknowledged by many scholars and practitioners of anthropology, philosophy, sociology, psychology, ethnology, religious studies, literary studies, political theory, psychotherapy, art and music therapy and the like, postulating that the concept of selfhood and a meaning of life hinges on narrative. Obviously, the idea that human life constitutes a (well or badly constructed, meaningful or apparently meaningless) story is by no means novel, as it can be encountered in various ancient and modern texts, suffice it to mention the famous sentence of Macbeth's ('[Life] is a tale/Told by an idiot, full of sound and fury,/Signifying nothing'); yet the tenet that narrative is a starting point and the main tool of therapy and its ultimate goal, as I wish to argue in this chapter, may not be so evident.[27]

A contemporary Icelandic philosopher Stefán Snaevarr argues that human beings are story-telling beings, and coins a term *Homo quixotienses*, or narrative selves, that is beings who construct their identity on the basis of narratives (like Cervantes's Don Quixote, preposterous though Quixote's choice and handling of the narrative is), as contrasted with *Homo roquentinenses*, the beings whose existence lacks any logic or sense (derived from the name of Antoine Roquentin, the protagonist of Jean-Paul Sartre's novel *Nausea*, who lived a life which apparently did not form any narrative unity).[28] Reflecting upon the role of narrative in life, Sartre writes in his novel that:

> For the most trivial event to become an adventure, all you have to do is start telling about it. This is what deceives people: a man is always a teller of stories, he lives surrounded by his stories and the stories of others, he sees everything which happens to him through these stories; and he tries to live his life as if it were a story he was telling. But you have to choose: live or tell…While you live, nothing happens…but when you tell about life, everything changes.[29]

---

27 Devastated by remorse and awareness of his wasted life, in the oft-quoted phrase Macbeth compares life to a fool's story; William Shakespeare, *Macbeth*. Act 5, Scene 5.

28 Stefán Snaevarr, 'Don Quixote and the Narrative Self' [in:] *Philosophy Now*, Rick Lewis, ed., issue no. 60, 2007, pp. 19–27, p. 21. Snaevarr derives the latter term from the name of Antoine Roquentin, the protagonist of Jean-Paul Sartre's novel *Nausea*, who lived a life which apparently did not form any narrative unity.

29 Jean-Paul Sartre, *Nausea*, trans. Robert Baldick (London: Penguin Books, 1965), p. 41. [*La Nausée*, 1938]. The difference between 'living' and 'telling', marked by Sartre, resembles the ancient concept of choice that was to be made between *vita active* (practical life) and *vita contemplative* (philosophical life), preferably by maintaining an equilibrium of the two states of life.

Even though Sartre seems to suggest, somewhat ironically, that, when applied to life, narrative turns it into some colourful picaresque and adventure story, and detaches us from reality (for when telling our life story we feel like story-tellers addressing an audience rather than the protagonists struggling with life and its problems in private, away from the limelight), he admits that narrative provides man's natural environment. There is no ready-made narrative to follow and no inherent essence to draw upon; therefore one may attempt to forge their own values and meanings individually in the absurd world, Sartre's existential phenomenology proclaims, emphasizing man's freedom and the precedence of existence over essence.[30]

The view of the 'narrativity' or 'narrativism' of human existence, which rests on the conviction that life is a story and that selfhood emerges from the palimpsest of various existing narratives, has been counteracted not only by Sartre's suspicious stance towards narrative representation of existence, but generally by a strong nihilistic opposition of 'anti-narrativism,' endorsed, for instance, by Galen Strawson, who rejects the importance of personal memory, and considers 'narrativizing' life as irrelevant to man's self-constitution.[31] Since the problem of narrative *per se* is beyond the scope of this book, in which I focus on therapeutic properties of fantasy narrative, the stand of postmodernist 'anti-narrativists' is not presented here in detail.

Regardless of the philosophical argument whether narrative determines and represents the essence and template of human existence or not, it seems an incontestable fact that narrative is an omnipresent form of human perception, a medium of interaction with reality, and 'an instrument of mind in the construction of reality,' as Jerome Bruner notes.[32] Narrative lays ground for psychotherapy, McLeod argues, for 'underneath the theoretical overlay and scientific gloss, psychotherapy

---

30 Cf. Sartre, *Existentialism and Humanism*, trans. Philip Mairet, (London: Methuen, 1973); *Being and Nothingness: An Essay on Phenomenological Ontology*, trans. Hazel E. Barnes, (London: Methuen, 1958).

31 Galen Strawson, 'Against Narrativity' [in:] *Ratio* XVII, Dec. 2004, pp. 430--52. Lyotard, for instance, dismisses the role of meta-narratives (he writes about the postmodern incredulity towards meta-narratives) and of grand-narratives (huge-scale philosophies underlying human existence), yet sees the importance of micronarratives adapted by people in the postmodern conditions; cf. *The Postmodern Condition: A Report on Knowledge*, trans. Geoffrey Bennington and Brian Massumi (Minneapolis: University of Minnesota Press, 1984).

32 Jerome Bruner, 'The Narrative Construction of Reality' [in:] *Critical Inquiry*, 18:1, 1–21, 1991, p. 6.

is a kind of conversation, a type of meeting space, and a form of social drama. In a traditional or pre-modern culture, the encounter between the 'petitioner' and a priest, healer, or shaman, can be seen as an event through which a personal story becomes re-aligned with and assimilated into the story of the community.[33]

McLeod stresses also the importance of the moral aspect of therapy, which seems to echo Victor Frankl's emphasis on the essentially meaningful orientation of a therapeutic narrative: through psychotherapy, McLeod observes, 'the person is "re-moralized", accepted back into the moral order of the culture. (…) The result is that psychotherapy offers a particular type of narrative reconstruction, one that is embedded in the (largely American) cultural milieu of late twentieth-century industrial society.[34] As Victor Frankl points out, the post-modern nihilistic cultural milieu of the West, which questions all the foundations of culture and society, severely impairs the success of psychotherapy.[35] This is what McLeod and MacIntyre call the contemporary 'denial of morality', resulting from 'the lack, in most Western societies, of a cohesive set of religious beliefs or other traditions, within which moral argument can take place, and from the 'trivialization of the moral debate that still exists through "soundbites" and other types of distorted or sensationalized media coverage of moral issues.[36] Of course, 'therapists are meant to be morally neutral' and not judgmental, McLeod explains, but it appears that the foundation of psychotherapy may not be 'value-free', insofar as the purpose of therapy, he concludes, is to 'enable [the person] to arrive at his or her own moral judgments.[37]

What emerges from the claims of narrative psychology is thus a strong link identified not only between narrative and therapy, but also between therapy and meaning, and, henceforward, between meaning and the quality which the Zaleskis call 'moral realism.[38] Without the moral foundation of meaning, psychotherapy proves at best a palliative rather than a cure; in the light of which therapy through meaning (logotherapy), as conveyed by narrative, appears to offer an adequate remedy. Fighting nihilism with nihilism, like fire with fire, or, as Woodward puts it, 'overcoming the desire to overcome nihilism' may not provide an effective

---

33 McLeod, *Narrative and Psychotherapy*, p. 17.
34 McLeod, ibid., p. 17.
35 Frankl, *The Unheard Cry for Meaning*, p. 91.
36 McLeod, *Narrative and Psychotherapy*. p. 20. MacIntyre, *After Virtue: A Study in Moral Theory*, p. 48.
37 McLeod, ibid., p. 20.
38 The Zaleskis, *The Fellowship*, p. 13.

measure against the postmodern acute crisis of meaning and the universal existential neurosis.[39]

Similarly to Frankl, McLeod seems to hint at the discrepancy between the very idea of psychotherapy and the ideology underlying much of the postmodern thought, which promotes the discourse of radical relativism and neo-nihilism: 'there is a gap between what the mental health industry promises,' McLeod notes, 'and what it can deliver,' and '[it] becomes more and more visible;' this is so because 'for the most part, the telling of the story does not function to reintegrate the person into a somehow bigger, shared narrative that binds together the members of a culture.'[40] The mainstream stories of postmodernity are 'permeated by reflexivity and irony,' and oriented on debunking and undermining any values or foundations.[41] 'Mythic stories are no longer mutual experiences where the audiences can "join in",' McLeod adds, for the 'contemporary mythic stories are relayed by CNN and viewed by millions; and the story is told less by the word than by the image.'[42]

The rapidly devaluing logos, (that is, as Frankl interprets it, the meaning, and the word), the domination of commercial iconosphere over logosphere, and the global deconstruction of narratives do not seem to enhance therapy, though the need for therapy seems to be steadily, if not rapidly, increasing.[43] Cushman explains this postmodern aporia as follows: 'the patient is diagnosed as empty and fragmented, usually without addressing the sociohistorical predicament that caused the emptiness and fragmentation. Thus, through the activity of helping, psychology's discourse and practices perpetuate the causes of the very problems it is trying to treat.'[44]

Another cause of this paradox is the fact that psychology, as Bruner argues, focuses too much on the 'paradigmatic knowing', that is the 'scientific modes of thought, representing the world through abstract propositional knowledge', abandoning largely the 'narrative knowing', essential to therapy, which is, by contrast, 'organized through the stories that people recount about their experiences.'[45]

---

39 Woodward, *Nihilism in Postmodernity*, p. 169.
40 McLeod, ibid., p. 21.
41 McLeod, ibid., p. 25.
42 McLeod, ibid., p. 25.
43 Frankl, *Man's Search for Meaning*, p. 95.
44 Philip Cushman, 'Why the self is empty: toward a historically-situated psychology', [in:] *American Psychologist, 45*, 1990, pp. 599–611, 600.
45 Jerome Bruner, 'The narrative construction of reality' [in:] *Critical Inquiry, 18*, pp. 1–21; cf. McLeod, *Narrative and Psychotherapy*, p. 28.

Narrative knowing, dismissed by the mainstream psychology as 'irrational, vague, irrelevant and somehow illegitimate', is, none the less, an inherent part of therapy, catalyzing catharsis and helping to find a meaning of life.[46] 'Scientific thinking', McLeod continues, is 'abstract, impersonal, free of social context, logical and predictive. (…) [It] seems to work well for designing engine blocks and other technological wonders. But does it work so well when applied to human affairs? What happens when we think scientifically about ourselves, our relationships, the societies we have created?' he asks rhetorically.[47]

The answer can be linked with extreme reductionism, or 'pan-reductionism', and sub-humanism', if one borrows Frankl's terms defining some of the most devastating corollaries of the postmodern nihilism that impoverish the truth about man.[48] There is more to the biological, psychological and sociological conditions man is subject to, Frankl argues, because there is the moral and spiritual dimension above them: spiritual 'logos is deeper than [the] logic [of science]'.[49] 'Personal and cultural realities', McLeod points out, are 'constructed through narrative and storytelling' rather than scientific knowledge; and thus, narrative and storytelling provide the master key to the world of human experience, and an indispensable tool for therapy.[50] Joseph de Rivera and Janice Lindsay-Hartz, clinical psychologists, argue that the nature of emotion, which is inextricably connected with humanness, is 'intrinsically "storied", because 'stories are used to "emplot" emotions', and passions are not only stored but, above all, 'storied'.[51] 'The story acts to "emplot" emotions', McLeod remarks likewise, 'often leading from a partial distancing from disturbing feelings into and through a more comprehensive re-experiencing of them'.[52]

How does narrative thinking, which 'emplots emotions', differ from scientific or paradigmatic thinking? The former, based on stories, is, as McLeod explains,

---

46 McLeod, *Narrative and Psychotherapy*, p. 28.
47 McLeod, ibid., p. 30.
48 Cf. Frankl, *Man's Search for Meaning*, pp. 140–142.
49 Frankl, ibid., p. 153.
50 McLeod, *Narrative and Psychotherapy*, p. 31.
51 Joseph de Rivera, 'The Structure and Dynamics of Emotion', [in:] *Approaches to Understanding Lives. Perspectives in Personality*, Vol. 3. Part A. A. J. Stewart, J. M. Healy, Jr. and D. Ozer, eds. (London: Jessica Kinsley, 1990), pp. 191–212, 198. Janice Lindsay-Hartz, Joseph de Rivera, M. F. Mascolo, 'Differentiating Shame and Guilt and their Effects on Motivation' [in:] *Self-Conscious Emotions:The Psychology of Shame, Guilt, Embarrassment and Pride*, J. P. Tangnay and K. W. Fischer, eds. (New York: Guilford Press, 1995), pp. 274–300, 280.
52 McLeod, *Narrative and Psychotherapy*, p. 76.

'a form of thinking and communication that recounts some concrete event that has already happened. A story is contextualized in a social world known to teller and audience; [and, unlike sciences,] stories convey intention and feeling. (...) A story is a basic building-block of human communication.'[53] Jerome Bruner adds that the core features of storytelling make it the basic tool of conveying meaning, and the framework for therapy.[54] These core features of storytelling, according to him, include: 'sequentiality' (the structured form of a sequence of events, implying a sense of 'nextness' rooted in temporality); 'accounting for departures from the ordinary' (stories are often told to manage or explain diversions from the expectable or 'canonical' norms), 'communicating subjectivity' (or, as Edward Bruner terms is, 'subjectification', that is 'giving an entry not only into a "landscape of action" but also into a "landscape of consciousness" of the teller or the protagonists); and ambiguity (the meaning of the story is to be discovered in an active process by the reader or listener).[55]

Referring to the sequentiality of narrative, Edward Bruner observes that 'narrative emphasizes order and sequence, [and that] stories give meaning to the present and enable us to see that present as part of a set of relationships involving a constituted past and a future.'[56] Moreover, the sequentiality of narrative might help 'recast chaotic experiences into causal sequences, thereby helping the person gain an understanding of how and why something happened,' McLeod notes.[57] The convention of storytelling, he adds, is that the events that are recounted took place at a particular time and place; none the less, they may have actually happened, or may be imaginary, or may be a combination of the imaginary and the real.[58] Putting events into a story form is, as McLeod suggests, 'an effective method of sorting out and making sense of what happened.'[59]

Jerome Bruner stresses the importance of the second factor featured above, that is the 'extraordinary' element of narrative, which, obviously, does not necessarily entail partaking in fantasy, (however, as I would like to argue further in this book, high fantasy genre in particular endorses this aspect of narrative), but

53 McLeod, ibid., p. 31.
54 J. Bruner, 'The Narrative Construction of Reality', p. 10.
55 McLeod, *Narrative and Psychotherapy*, pp. 33–36.
56 Edward Bruner, 'Ethnography as Narrative' [in:] *The Anthropology of Experience*, W. Turner and E. M. Bruner eds. (Chicago: University of Illinois Press, 1986), pp. 139–155, 153.
57 McLeod, *Narrative and Psychotherapy*, p. 37.
58 McLeod, ibid., p. 35.
59 McLeod, ibid., p. 38.

may consist in 'violating some implicit cultural norm, and hence calling for an explanation', whereby the moral standards are enhanced.[60] 'Accounting for departures from the ordinary', Bruner argues, is an essential mechanism of stories, which first introduces and finally resolves dilemmas and tensions, inasmuch as:

> A part of the meaning of any story arises from the tension created between the exceptional events that are being recounted, and the ordinary routines that have been breached. A story, then, relies on, and hints at, an implicit set of social and cultural rules, and each story that is told reinforces this shared set of rules. But the story itself is a means of problem-solving, of reconciling the tension between the exceptional and the expected.[61]

When discussing stories and narrative from a psychotherapeutic viewpoint, McLeod clarifies his understanding of the two key terms: 'narrative is [to him] a therapeutic discourse as a whole', whereas 'stories are accounts of specific incidents'.[62] 'The therapeutic narrative', he suggests, represents, therefore, 'an attempt to "narrativize" a problematic experience through the production of a series of stories, [which can be] connected by linking passages and therapists interventions.'[63] Narrative is therapeutic, McLeod states, because of its emotion-evoking potential, and also thought-provoking impact.[64] This first quality is what science, generally speaking, lacks. Stories, by contrast, move people, inasmuch as all narrative events, whether they involve reading a novel, watching a film, listening to someone recount an episode in their life, or being exposed to yet another form of narrative, may result in arousing feelings that the 'recipient' of the story had not been aware of before.[65] 'From an experiential perspective, the audience for such a story will engage in the meaning of the story by allowing the themes or images of the narrative to resonate with appropriate areas of inner feeling', McLeod notes.[66]

This emotional or 'affective side of narrative', as McLeod calls it, is crucial to therapy, because 'feelings and emotions are central to the personal meaning of stories and to the place that stories have in the sense of self of a person', which is being discovered in the process of creating 'an on-going self-narrative.'[67] Donald

60 J. Bruner, 'The Narrative Construction of Reality', p. 11.
61 Bruner, ibid., p. 13.
62 McLeod, *Narrative and Psychotherapy*, p. 51.
63 McLeod, ibid., p. 51.
64 McLeod, ibid., p. 43.
65 McLeod, ibid., p. 43.
66 McLeod, ibid., p. 43.
67 McLeod, ibid., p. 44.

Polkinghorne argues likewise, saying that 'the person's concept of self can be best understood as comprising a self-narrative that tells the story of the whole of a life, [and] this self-narrative gives coherence to the multiplicity of episodes, events and relationships experienced in the course of a life to date, including the prospective anticipation of its ending.'[68] A frustrated, fragmented, discontinued, or deconstructed 'self-narrative' of a person, so common nowadays, is what usually seems to necessitate therapy, which, in turn, as Chaika suggests, allows for a reinterpretation of people's life stories and provides ways of 're-authoring or co-authoring the narratives of their lives'.[69]

Moreover, Polkinghorne and McLeod observe that in the 'rich cultural stock of narrative plots', these are fairy tales and religious stories that take the central place, as they are based on myth; and myth, as Polkinghorne suggests, 'is a story having the power to provide life with meaning.'[70] McLeod also notes that 'fairy stories and myths help people bring more sense and meaning to their own personal narrative.'[71] According to him and a group of contemporary psychotherapists, narrative *per se* is therapeutic, and the core of its 'storied essence' is myth, for myth 'reflects the fundamental moral and existential issues faced in a culture.'[72] As they distinguish the importance of providing meaning to one's life, and suggest doing so by means of the narrative of myth, these statements seem to refer to logotherapy and mythopathy (although the two terms are not mentioned), the concepts that I consider instrumental in identifying a therapeutic nature of Faërie.

Returning to the contrast between scientific knowing of the present and narrative knowing of the past, one might add that the renewed interest in the latter, as evinced by McLeod, Jerome Bruner, Edward Bruner, and many other thinkers and practitioners of psychotherapy, sounds as a reiteration of Frankl's statement stipulating that, however important, science itself does not suffice to produce successful therapy, because what is also needed is the person's rather unscientific 'capacity to transcend [their] predicament and discover an adequate guiding truth,' a logos which dwells beyond the realm of empiricism, rooted in the narrative of some, perhaps not strictly rational, tradition and foundation.[73] This may provide an explanation why Frankl, for instance, introduces his idea

---

68   Donald E. Polkinghorne, 'Narrative Knowing and the Self-Concept' [in:] *Journal of Narrative and Life History*, 1, 1991, pp. 135–153, 145.
69   Chaika, *Linguistics, Pragmatics and Psychotherapy*, p. 146.
70   Polkinghorne, 'Narrative Knowing and the Self-Concept', p. 145.
71   McLeod, *Narrative and Psychotherapy*, p. 126.
72   McLeod, ibid., p. 44.
73   Gordon W. Allport, Preface to Frankl's *Man's Search for Meaning*, pp. 12–13.

of logotherapy in *Man's Search for Meaning*, his most famous book on psycho-therapy, by means of a narrative recounting his concentration camp experience, rather than by a purely scientific account of his school of therapy. Another echo of Frankl's preoccupation with meaning as the core of therapy is McLeod's tenet that 'at the heart of psychotherapy is the *retrieval* of meaning, the reflective dis-covery and assimilation of the meanings implicit in the stories told [or heard or read] by a person.'[74] Even though there is no direct link between Frankl's school of psychotherapy and the late postmodern turn to narrative in psychotherapy, the assumptions and foundations of both streams seem to share an affinity.[75]

Stories used to construct the world of knowledge, experience, and identity, McLeod notes, yet the values and morality conveyed by the Bible and other reli-gious texts, as well as by fairy tales, myths and legends, all consisting of various stories, have been undermined in modernity, for the significance of stories as such has been considerably diminished.[76] 'In the modern world, characterized by urbanized industrial societies,' McLeod explains, 'it is only scientific knowl-edge that can claim to be true, and can therefore serve as the basis for reasonable action. The growth of science and technology over the last 200 years has been associated with a gradual loss in legitimacy of stories as a way of communicating truths about the world, to be replaced by a belief in the validity of scientific pro-cedures as means of arriving at reliable and accurate knowledge.'[77] Little wonder,

---

74 McLeod, *Narrative and Psychotherapy*, p. 53. Italics preserved as in the original.
75 Victor Frankl's publications on psychotherapy might have anticipated and inspired the narrative turn in psychology, psychotherapy and philosophy, as their chronology and similar precepts tend to suggest. Some of the key texts marking the development of the narrative approach to therapy include: In philosophy: Wiggins, J. B. ed. *Religion as Story*, 1975; McIntyre, A., *After Virtue: A Study in Moral Theory*, 1981; Polinghorne, D. F., *Narrative Knowing and the Human Sciences*, 1988. In psychology: McAdams, D. P., *Power, Intimacy, and the Life Story: Personological Inquiries into Identity*, 1985; Bruner, J. S. *Actual Minds, Possible Worlds*, 1986; Sarbin, T. R. ed. *Narrative Psychology: The Storied Nature of Human Conduct*; 1986; Mishler, E. G., *Research Interviewing: Context and Narrative*, 1986; Kleinman, A. *The Illness Narratives: Suffering, Healing and the Human Condition*, 1988; Birren, J. E., et al. eds. *Aging and Biography: Explorations in Adult Development*, 1996.
In psychotherapy: Schafer, R., *Narration in the Psychoanalytic Dialogue*, 1980; Spence, D. P., *Narrative Truth and Historical Truth: Meaning and Interpretation in Psychoa-nalysis*, 1982; White, M., and D. Epston. *Narrative Means to Therapeutic Ends*, 1990; McLeod, J. *Narrative and Psychotherapy*, 2006.
76 McLeod, *Narrative and Psychotherapy*, p. 28.
77 McLeod, ibid., p. 29.

then, that in order 'to participate in a scientific world we have all had to learn to think and communicate scientifically; we have needed to be socialized into the realm of abstract propositional knowledge,' regarding those once universal master narratives as obsolete.[78] Many psychologists and psychoanalysts, for instance: Eric Berne, Bruno Bettelheim, Rinsley, and Bergmann, have written extensively on the universal and therapeutic power of fairy tales, approaching it from the points of view of various schools of psychotherapy and providing numerous cases of people unconsciously selecting the fairy story that best makes sense of their life situation and problem, identifying with the characters and finding a relief in the course of that vicarious experience.[79]

The rehabilitation of myth and fairy tales, and also the distinctly Christian overtones of their fiction, is, as I would like to argue, the Inklings' notable contribution to the postmodern culture, aimed at laying the groundwork for restoring some grand foundational narratives, against the erosive impact of the neo-nihilistic void. So is Le Guin's fantasy legacy, which draws on Taoism and a specific literary anthropology. The balance which the Inklings and Le Guin strive to strike between what Bruner calls the paradigmatic and the narrative knowing, or between reason and imagination, (and perhaps also reason and faith), is also, in the light of today's theory and practice of narrative psychotherapy, what might contribute to the therapeutic properties of the Inklings' fiction. Moreover, this unique equilibrium might sound like a distant echo of T. S. Eliot's concept of the 'association of sensibility', as contrasted with the phenomenon of the 'dissociation of sensibility', prevalent in modernity.[80]

Viewing the development of contemporary psychotherapy, McLeod speaks of an increasingly common tendency among specialists to 'reinvent therapy' these days, that is to promote an approach 'based on an appreciation of the centrality of narrative in human communication and society', and on a rediscovery of the importance of moral values and an underlying sense of life.[81] This 'reinvention' of the essence of therapy can perhaps be viewed in parallel to the rehabilitation

---

78 McLeod, ibid., p. 29.
79 Eric Berne, *What Do You Say after You Say Hello?* (New York: Corgi, 1975); Bruno Bettelheim, *The Uses of Enchantment: The Meaning and Importance of Fairy Tales* (London: Vintage, 1989); C. Cath and J. Cath, 'On the Other Side of Oz: Psychoanalytic Aspects of Fairy Tales' [in:] *The Psychoanalytic Study of the Child*, 33, 1978, pp. 621–639; D. Rinsley and E. Bergmann, 'Enchantment and Alchemy: the Story of Rumplestiltskin' [in:] *Bulletin of Menninger Clinic*, 47, 1983, pp. 1–13.
80 Eliot, *The Metaphysical Poets*, 1921.
81 McLeod, *Narrative and Psychotherapy*, p. 138.

and revalorization of myth and fairy tales, and a renaissance of high fantasy literature as such, which, as I would like to argue, had been largely instigated by the Inklings, and which has been continued in a (rather different) way by Le Guin and some other writers. It may not be a coincidence that the modern and the postmodern mainstream skepticism toward morality, their debunking of values, and deconstruction of master narratives and of logocentric thought, have produced, at least to some extent, the counter-effect of a return to the most traditional narratives and moral 'metaphysical' systems in both literature and therapy. This may, of course, appear as a crude simplification, demonizing the philosophies of modernity and postmodernity, undermining the canonical works of postmodernism, and prioritizing the simple over the complicated; yet such a tendency becomes observable and more pronounced.

As MacIntyre argues, since we try to make sense of both our lives as a whole, and of its particular situations, we 'are all engaged in a *quest* for narrative unity, attempting to create and maintain a coherence in the stories we tell about our lives.'[82] The choice of the medieval concept of the quest, as used by MacIntyre, is certainly not accidental, for it also reaches back into the traditional modes of thought, and, in literature, into the myths and fairy stories in particular. In order 'to engage meaningfully in the life issues facing us in these times,' McLeod concludes, 'psychotherapy and counseling must seek ways of contributing to the re-establishment, somehow, of a "sacred balance".'[83] This 'sacred balance' between reason and imagination, or reason and faith (not necessarily understood in a religious context), or the scientific and the sacred, seems to provide another affinity between that orientation of modern psychotherapy and Frankl's system, as well as John Paul II's philosophy, as discussed in Chapter Three of this book.

McLeod refers in the above-quoted statement to Peter Reason's thesis that 'a secular science is inadequate for our times', and that there is a 'pressing need to re-sacralize our experience of ourselves and our world', because 'a sacred human inquiry based on love, beauty, wisdom and engagement is one of the highest virtues and possibilities of human consciousness.'[84] This ancient approach to man and to the world, Reason claims, ought to be re-introduced nowadays in order to rehabilitate the sense of humanness and man's place in the world, and in order to stop the 'gross desacralization of this planet, of the universe and of our own

---

82 MacIntyre, *After Virtue: A Study in Moral Theory*, p. 219.
83 McLeod, *Narrative and Psychotherapy*, p. 157.
84 Peter Reason, 'Reflections on Sacred Experience and Sacred Science' [in:] *Journal of Management Inquiry*, 2(3), 1993; pp. 273–283, 275.

souls', in which 'humankind has been involved for the last three hundred years.'[85] In that progressing 'desacralization' and deprecation of most that used to be considered sacred, Reason notes, the sense of the sacred has nearly been lost, and the 'spiritual dimension of human inquiry' has virtually been abandoned.[86] The scientific myth of reductionism, materialism and nihilism has set the stage for the secular, disenchanted world of (post)modernity, in which, Reason observes, lies not only the origin of ecological violence, but also the source of the violence against human nature, which has been debased and travestied.[87]

It seems to be good news, therefore, that in the contemporary psychotherapy, as McLeod remarks, there appears a tendency to rehumanize its theory and practice by returning to narrative knowing, and by restoring a balance between scientific and narrative thinking, which promises to stop the hegemony of the scientific approach, and, consequently, to move towards some long-abandoned foundations and unconditional meaning, which Frankl associates with the noölogical, that is spiritual, dimension of man. Remaining largely independent of Frankl's legacy, McLeod seems to reiterate Frankl's thesis, noting that:

> Psychotherapy of today is increasingly reflecting the contemporary awareness that the good life cannot be construed within a moral vacuum. Morality, banished from the early 'psychotherapy' of the Emmanuel movement and other 19th-century religious groups, is edging back into therapy discourse. In recent years, there appears to have been a greater readiness to acknowledge the moral dimension of psychotherapy.[88]

Bibliotherapy as a form of narrative therapy

This 'moral dimension of psychotherapy', which seems to lie at the very basis of therapy, emerges from what McLeod recognizes as a 'moral landscape of narrative' with its capacity to convey 'a sense of a moral order', which can be restored and affirmed.[89] McLeod argues that:

> *Any* therapy that takes stories seriously will necessarily open up a space for moral discourse. Stories are structured around an 'evaluation' of what has happened. A story is

---

85 Reason, 'Reflections on Sacred Experience and Sacred Science', p. 276.
86 Reason, ibid., p. 276.
87 Reason, ibid., p. 278.
88 McLeod, *Narrative and Psychotherapy*, p. 22. Cf. Jeff Sugarman, and Jack Martin, 'The Moral Dimension: A Conceptualization and Empirical Demonstration of the Moral Nature of Psychotherapeutic Conversations' [in:] *The Counseling Psychologist*, 23, 1995; pp. 324–347.
89 McLeod, *Narrative and Psychotherapy*, p. 46.

not merely a chronicle of events. A story is an account of events set against a landscape of moral values. Narrative therapy involves the rediscovery of the 'moral'.[90]

Narration and re-narration of the central dilemmas and issues of a person's life help to reflect upon those problems at length so as to develop a fresh insight, and, consequently, construct 'a new story that is more intelligible and purposeful' – a 'unitary and coherent life-story', McLeod states, emphasizing the orientation toward meaning as the ultimate goal of therapy, which again corresponds to Frankl's thought.[91]

Following McLeod's reflections on the relationship between psychotherapy and narrative, one shall not overlook an affinity which McLeod identifies between the psychotherapeutic narrative and another, 'distinctly modern narrative form', that is the novel, which brings his understanding of psychotherapy close to bibliotherapy.[92] 'Like novels', he argues, 'therapy stories are often concerned with the attempts of a singular hero/self to find meaning and fulfillment in the face of restrictive social conditions.'[93] Moreover, novels and therapy stories are often 'constructed around a linear time-frame, making connections between past and present within the span of an individual life.'[94] Both novels and therapy sessions, McLeod continues, 'are like little cultural modules that can be purchased and slotted into a life for some period of time, then discarded; and, finally, the novelist, like the therapist, is in the position of a privileged narrator, enjoying an omniscient "God's eye" view of events.'[95] Of course, this is not to claim that neither a non-linear type of narrative, a typical (post)modernist quality, which often introduces (an) unreliable narrator(s), nor even lack of narrative proper, such as in non-narrative poetry, which represents a state of mind or an emotional state, or in drama, where stories are enacted rather than told, may not have therapeutic properties. In this chapter I try to argue after narrative psychologists and therapists that narrative is a particularly useful tool of literary therapy, yet by no means the only one, suffice it to mention a variety of major therapeutic methods related to the other genres, such as drama therapy, psychodrama, playback theatre, and, last but not least, poetry therapy.[96]

---

90 McLeod, ibid., p. 153. Italics as in the original.
91 McLeod, ibid., p. 57.
92 McLeod, ibid., p. 23.
93 McLeod, ibid., p. 23.
94 McLeod, ibid., p. 23.
95 McLeod, ibid., p. 23.
96 Cf. for instance: Jacob Gershoni, *Psychodrama in the 21ˢᵗ Century: Clinical and Educational Applications* (New York: Springer, 2003); Jack J. Leedy, ed., *Poetry the Healer:*

In their book on bibliotherapy and children, Irena Borecka and Sylwia Wontorowska-Roter present bibliotherapy as an auxiliary to psychotherapy, akin to pedagogical therapy, (which they view as a branch of corrective pedagogy designed for the children with special needs), on the strength of their common goals: both bibliotherapy and pedagogical therapy avail themselves of psychotherapeutic techniques attempting to 'help the person discover values and, thereby achieve personal growth, love themselves and other people, be willing and able to respect the work of other people, enjoy living in the world, and feel happy.'[97] It seems that bibliotherapy may also benefit mentally healthy people, both children and adults, as it can foster their intellectual and emotional development, and serve, outside a clinical therapeutic framework, as *therapia pauperum*, the concept I have introduced in this book with regard to (logo)therapy through (high fantasy) literature. Because of the 'storied' nature of human experience and feeling, and the structure of human life that resembles a book with its episodes and chapters, however erratic and rambling its narrative may be, bibliotherapy appears as a universal tool of therapy, and, even more importantly, self-therapy. Fantasy literature, as defined by Tolkien and his understanding of Faërie, is, as I wish to demonstrate, a genre of special bibliotherapeutic valour, which is presented in the following chapters.

Borecka and Wontorowska-Roter recognize the validity, universality and benevolence of a self-conducted bibliotherapy, that is one undertaken without the assistance of a therapist, and distinguish its five stages:

First, the person reads, listens to or watches specifically selected therapeutic texts (stories, poems or theatre plays, their fragments, alternative texts, as well as film or theatre adaptions of the texts). Secondly, the person identifies themselves with the characters and emotions with which the text or visual adaptation is imbued, and through a vicarious experience is either calmed down or emotionally activated. Thirdly, the person undergoing bibliotherapy experiences catharsis, when reading the text or afterwards, which brings relief and a release of burdensome tensions and other psychic blockages. This results in the fourth phase, namely in allowing the person an insight into themselves and recognition of their problems, which is the starting point of personal work

---

Mending the Troubled Mind (New York: Vanguard, 1985); or Rosemary S. McGee, *Poetic Justice – Writing for Health and Emotional Freedom: Creating a Therapeutic Writing Programme for Chronically Ailing Poor* (Ann Arbor: ProQuest LLC, 2009).

97 Irena Borecka, Sylwia Wontorowska-Roter, *Biblioterapia w edukacji dziecka niepełnosprawnego intelektualnie* [Bibliotherapy in the Education of a Mentally Disabled Child], trans. mine (Wałbrzych: Unus, 2003), p. 49.

or work aided by a therapist. The last stage of the bibliotherapeutic process is a change instigated in the attitude or the behaviour of the person.[98]

When coupled with logotherapy, bibliotherapy may allow the person an insight into and recognition of their own problems, and encourage to discover a sense of their plight, if it is inescapable and cannot be helped, so as to turn it into a meaningful, albeit difficult or painful, experience. However, despite the findings of various research studies concerning the application and effects of bibliotherapy, the issue how reading can help people seems to have received relatively little attention, especially in the medical world.[99]

Speaking of narrative therapy in general terms, that is including bibliotherapy but not being limited to it, McLeod states that therapy, as a 'part of Western indigenous psychology', has always addressed people's 'problems in living' through a 'combination of listening, re-framing, catharsis, interpretation and behaviour change.'[100] When referring to bibliotherapy, McLeod defines it as 'a narrative-informed activity that has often been used within therapy, or as an alternative to face-to-face psychotherapy', which draws on 'self-help books', recommended by the majority of psychologists.[101] Interestingly, Benjamin M. Ogles et al. have compared the effectiveness of bibliotherapy based on four 'self-help books' with the outcome of conventional face-to-face psychotherapy for a group of people struggling with the problem of divorce and separation, and found out that 'the levels of improvement on measures of depression and other symptoms before and after "treatment" were very similar.'[102] L. Jonathan Cohen's study, for instance, has revealed that some people benefit from therapeutic reading 'by entering into the story or stories recounted in the book,' and by recognizing themselves in the characters, for the vicarious experience lets them feel relieved, 'validated, comforted and more hopeful as a result.'[103] This was true of all the patients who took part in his study, and could probably be said about many more people, facing to a lesser or greater extent some emotional or existential frustration or

---

98   Borecka, and Wontorowska-Roter, ibid., p. 49, trans. mine.

99   McLeod, *Narrative and Psychotherapy*, p. 80.

100   McLeod, ibid., p. 25.

101   McLeod, ibid., p. 80.

102   Benjamin M. Ogles, Michael J. Lambert, Derik E. Craig, 'Comparison of Self-help Books for Coping with Loss: Expectations and Attributions' [in:] *Journal of Counseling Psychology*, 38, 1991, pp. 387–393.

103   L. Jonathan Cohen, 'Phenomenology of Therapeutic Reading with Implications for Research and Practice of Bibliotherapy' [in:] *The Arts in Psychotherapy*, 21 (1), 1994; pp. 37–44.

neurosis, and somehow partaking in the 'neurotic personality of our time', as Karen Horney (1885–1952) dubbed it back in 1937 – the time when the Inklings had already been meeting as an informal group, when Tolkien had his 'Beowulf: The Monsters and the Critics' and the *Hobbit* published, and when he conceived of the 'New Hobbit' story, the Lord-of-the Rings-to-be, and Lewis of his *Out of the Silent Planet* science fiction novel; when Barfield had also several works published, including his *Poetic Diction: A Study in Meaning*, and when a large part of Williams's works had been written.[104] Conscious or unconscious, the most active Inklings seem to have enhanced bibliotherapy through writing and sharing their works with their Oxford friends, against the increasing 'noölogical' crisis of meaninglessness and existential neurosis of the period (as Frankl might have said).[105] As I attempt to suggest in this book, their narrative, meaning-centred and myth-oriented as it is, could be interpreted as therapeutic narrative, corresponding to such psychotherapeutic schools as narrative therapy, logotherapy, bibliotherapy, and, in a way, art therapy (empowered by the interartistic nature of the Inklings' mythopoeia, as discussed in Chapter Five).

As far as Ursula K. Le Guin is concerned, she actually makes a reference to bibliotherapy, which appears to be her self-therapy method, and even though she does not use the term explicitly, she seems to provide her own definition of bibliotherapy:

> We read book to find out who we are. What other people, real or imaginary, do and think and feel – or have done and thought and felt; or might do and think and fell – is an essential guide to our understanding of what we ourselves are and may become.(…) The story – from 'Rumpelstiltskin' to *War and Peace* – is one of the basic tools invented by the mind of man, for the purpose of gaining understanding. There have been great societies that did not use the wheel, but there have been no societies that did not tell stories.[106]

In another essay Le Guin adds:

> The book is what is real. You read it; you and it form a relationship, perhaps a trivial one, perhaps a deep and lasting one. As you read it word by word and page by page, you participate in its creation, just as a cellist playing a Bach suite participates, note by note, in the creation, the coming-to-be, the existence, of the music. And, as you read and reread,

---

104   Karen Horney, *The Neurotic Personality of Our Time* (New York: Norton, 1937).

105   Interestingly, Owen Barfield's two books address the problem of meaning, which may trigger associations with Frankl's logotherapy (although Barfield concentrates on the meaning of words rather than life). These are: *Poetic Diction: A Study in Meaning* (1928), and *The Rediscovery of Meaning, and Other Essays* (1984).

106   Le Guin, 'Prophets and Mirrors: Science Fiction as a Way of Seeing' [in:] *The Living Light 7* (3), 1970, p. 24.

the book of course participates in the creation of you, your thoughts and feelings, the size and temper of your soul.[107]

Focusing on fantasy literature, and high fantasy genre in particular, as an instance of 'self-help books', I attempt to characterize some elements of this 'therapeutic reading' mechanism in the following chapters, referring beforehand to another interpretation of the therapeutic potential of narrative, now viewed in broader terms, not just as a literary narrative, but as a narrative of arts, expressed verbally. In their notes on bibliotherapy both Borecka and McLeod, as well as a great many other critics and therapists, conceive of narrative in that broad sense, incorporating verbal texts as well as verbal-based visualizations, for instance drawings inspired by a story that has been read or heard, or music composed on the same basis. McLeod defines narrative as 'a story-based account of happenings, containing within it other forms of communication in addition to stories'.[108] I wish to argue that the syncretic nature of fantasy fiction, engaging visual arts and music in a unique manner, and thus producing what Tolkien names 'the most potent Art' of 'Sub-creation', or 'an elvish art',[109] might provide an auxiliary service to Faërie's primarily bibliotherapeutic and, more precisely, logotherapeutic potential. Fantasy contains 'images of things', Tolkien notes, emphasizing what appears to be an ekphrastic nature of the genre, perhaps more importantly ekphrastic than in the case of non-fantasy genres, for the 'arresting strangeness' of secondary (other)worlds in fantasy fiction rests entirely on the verbal skill of the writer and their image-making and sound-making imaginative artistry.[110] 'That the images are of things not in the primary world (if that indeed is possible) is a virtue not a vice', Tolkien claims: 'Fantasy (in this sense) is (…) not a lower but a higher form of Art. Indeed the most nearly pure form, and so (when achieved) the most potent.'[111]

In the subsequent part of this chapter I attempt to consider the question whether the synthesis of arts accomplished in Faërie, as understood by Tolkien and achieved in various ways in the works of the Inklings and of Le Guin, may have a therapeutic effect in its own right. I do not refer here to the works of visual arts and music inspired by high fantasy fiction of the Inklings and of Le Guin, which have been created and performed by various artists, but to mental pictures

---

107 Le Guin, 'The Book is What is Real' [in:] *The Language of the Night*, pp. 117–118.
108 McLeod, *Narrative and Psychotherapy*, p. 31.
109 Tolkien, 'On Fairy-Stories', pp. 139–140.
110 Tolkien, ibid., p. 139.
111 Tolkien, ibid., p. 139.

and sounds the genre (sub-)creates in the readers' or listeners' imagination. Tolkien remarks that:

> The mental power of image-making is one thing, or aspect; and it should appropriately be called Imagination. The perception of the image, the grasp of its implications, and the control, which are necessary to a successful expression, may vary in vividness and strength: but this is a difference of degree in Imagination, not a difference in kind. The achievement of the expression, which gives (or seems to give) 'the inner consistency of reality' [which commands or induces Secondary Belief] is indeed another thing, or aspect, needing another name: Art, the operative link between Imagination and the final result, Sub-creation.'[112]

The word that 'shall embrace both the Sub-creative Art in itself and a quality of strangeness and wonder in the Expression, derived from the Image: a quality essential to fairy-story' and one of the signposts of Faërie is, according to Tolkien, 'Fantasy'.[113] Tolkien points at the sub-creative potency of Fantasy, which results from the (divine) Fantasy of a Maker of universe, and which has interartistic nature, embedded in language and in images, which originate from the likeness of man to the image of the Creator, however that is to be conceived. A question may arise whether the 'Sub-creative Art' of Fantasy, which includes visual and musical arts revealed through 'a quality of strangeness and wonder in the Expression', can be a therapeutic means in its own right, that is as a peculiar fantastic form of art therapy.[114]

Sub-creative art therapy through Fantasy. Roman Ingarden's theory of a literary work of art

Assuming that narrative *per se* is therapeutic, one may wonder whether its plasticity and musicality that are inscribed into its verbal mode, for instance in fantasy narrative, have any share in its therapeutic nature. May a combination of arts enhance their natural therapeutic potential, which makes the basis for art therapy? 'Art therapy is a form of psychotherapy that uses art media as its primary mode of communication,' the British Association of Art Therapists explains.[115] Once the notion of art is extended to verbal and musical phenomena, art therapy includes also bibliotherapy (including narrative therapy, poetry therapy and drama therapy), and music therapy, both serving as important auxiliaries of psychotherapy.

---

112 Tolkien, ibid., pp. 138–139.
113 Tolkien, ibid., p. 139.
114 Tolkien, ibid., p. 139.
115 http://www.baat.org/About-Art-Therapy, accessed 23 April 2016.

Below I attempt to address the problem of what I name the interartistic or poly-artistic nature of narrative, viewing bibliotherapy in a broader context of its embedment in other arts, that is visual arts and music. The interartistic character of fantasy narrative, in which the verbal mixes with the visual and the auditory, is what Tolkien seems to refer to in his seminal essay 'On Fairy-Stories', where he defines the genre and challenges numerous misconceptions regarding Faërie.[116] Tolkien views fantasy narrative as the highest form of art, and refers to the wealth of non-verbal matter inherent to fantasy art that constitutes Faërie:[117]

'Faërie cannot be caught in a net of words; for it is one of its qualities to be indescribable, though not imperceptible,' he observes.[118] 'A Secondary World [of Fantasy], commanding Secondary Belief (…) will probably demand a special skill, a kind of elvish craft. Few attempt such difficult tasks. But when they are attempted and in any degree accomplished, then we have a rare achievement of Art: indeed narrative art, story-making in its primary and most potent mode. In human art fantasy is a thing best left to words, to true literature. In painting, for instance, the visible presentation of the fantastic image is technically too easy; the hand tends to outrun the mind, even to overthrow it.'[119] As Tolkien argues, the drawn or painted image does not have the same power as the imagined one, projected in words, the latter being open to an unlimited number of interpretations, visualizations and animations. The same could be said about music: when actually heard it is powerful, yet when imagined, it appears even more so, for then it expresses an individual's personal (sub-)creative interpretation of its verbal description.

The unique quality of verbal narrative is thus that it 'paints' and 'sings' by means of words without imposing one particular visualized or musicalized performance,

---

116 Tolkien, 'On Fairy-Stories', pp. 109–161.
117 Carpenter, *J. R. R. Tolkien: A Biography*, p. 133. Tolkien's argument that language is superior to visual arts, as it renders more complex reality and does so in a fuller, subtler and more creative way, appears also, for instance, in George Eliot's *Middlemarch* (1871–2), when Will Ladislaw, addressing his German friend and painter, Adolf Naumann, claims: 'Your painting and Plastik are poor stuff after all. They perturb and dull conceptions instead of raising them. Language is a finer medium. (…) Language gives a fuller image, which is all the better for being vague. After all, the true seeing is within; and painting stares at you with an insistent imperfection.' (London: Penguin Books, 1994), chpt. 19, p. 186). Similarly, E. Chaika, a psychologist, argues that 'language is the greatest human resource for representing and structuring events in our lives, as well as for letting others know who we are, or who we want to be.' (*Linguistics, Pragmatics and Psychotherapy: A Guide for Therapists*, p. 146).
118 Tolkien, 'On Fairy-Stories', pp. 114.
119 Ibid., p. 140.

so that the concretization of such visual and musical descriptions depends on each individual reader. This characteristic seems to be akin to Roman Ingarden's concept of 'the spots of indeterminacy', which he identifies in the third stratum of a literary work of art.[120] In his elaborate study *Das Literarische Kunstwerk, (O dziele literackim; The Literary Work of Art*), Ingarden (1893–1970), a Polish phenomenologist, ontologist and aesthetician, proposes and examines a scheme of four heterogeneous strata of a literary work of art:

1. 'word sounds and phonetic formations';
2. 'meaning units' (conveyed by individual words, as well as phrases, sentences, and paragraphs);
3. 'manifold schematised aspects' (visual, auditory, and other sensory aspects, whereby the setting and characters of literary narrative can be 'quasi-sensorially' apprehended);
4. 'represented objectivities' (such as objects, events, states of affairs, intellectual and emotional states, represented in the literary work of art and forming its characters, plot, and their development).[121]

According to Ingarden, a work of literature is a work of (literary) art, 'an aesthetic object', in some ways similar to works of visual arts and of music, with some essential differences concerning, for instance, their medium, concrete material, stratified structure, composition, and temporal extension.[122] As viewed by Ingarden, a literary work of art is a multi-stratum product of 'polyphonic harmony', forming an 'organic unity', with its assonances and dissonances in each stratum, much like a work of polyphonic music.[123] Ingarden defines a literary work of art as an 'intersubjective purely intentional object', whose meaning stratum 'has the source of its existence in the author's creative acts but at the same time has a certain physical ontic foundation,' and which 'deals primarily with

---

120 Roman Ingarden, *The Literary Work of Art*, trans. George G. Grabowicz (Evanston: Northwestern University Press, 1973), p. 30. The work was written probably in 1926, published in German in 1931, and in English for the first time in 1973. Ingarden had been a student of Edmund Husserl, a phenomenologist, in Göttingen, and developed his philosophy of realistic phenomenology as opposed to Husserl's transcendental idealism. Ingarden had also studied mathematics and philosophy at the University of Lvóv in Poland; cf. Amie Thomasson, 'Roman Ingarden' [in:] Stanford Encyclopedia of Philosophy, http://plato.stanford.edu/entries/ingarden/, accessed 26 April 2016.
121 Ingarden, ibid., p. 30.
122 Ingarden, ibid., p. 341.
123 Ingarden, ibid., p. 341.

psychic and spiritual reality.'[124] In that light, although Ingarden does not name it, a psychotherapeutic potential of a literary work of art may appear ontologically justifiable, avoiding at the same time the risk of what Ingarden refutes as a 'psychologistic tendency', that is psychologising, or approaching it only in terms of its psychological content and its impact on the reader.[125]

It is within the third stratum of 'manifold schematized aspects' that Ingarden distinguishes 'spots of indeterminacy', which do not determine how exactly a given objectivity represented in the literary work of art is to be concretized by the reader, for instance what exactly a described image or sound is like. The literary 'spots of indeterminacy' appear akin to the somehow indeterminate nature of a music work as noted on a sheet, for it is usually not rigorously determined by musical terms in a score of music how fast or how loudly a given piece ought to be performed, for the verbal terms provide only approximate suggestions referring to the tempo, volume, and expression, so that their realization depends on the person's interpretation. The same quality of indeterminacy, according to Ingarden, applies to a work of literature and to its descriptions of images and sounds, of which there can be as many visualisations and musicalizations as there are readers or listeners. Rather than aiming at a homogeneity of interpretation, this quality of a literary work of art produces an amazing wealth of interpretations, each reflecting the person's individual imaginative perception and creativity. 'It is impossible for the reader to actualize with complete precision the same aspects that the author wanted to designate through the structure of the work,' Ingarden observes.[126]

One may wonder what role the 'spots of indeterminacy' play in a literary work art and what their significance is. To Ingarden, 'spots of indeterminacy' constitute an essential element of the 'manifold schematized aspects', 'whose removal would transform a literary work of art into a mere written work', 'a dry treatise or chitchat on paper'; in other words, it would deprive a literary work of its artistic merit and turn it into a non-artistic and hence non-literary text, however difficult the very notion of a text's artistic literariness is to define.[127] According to Ingarden, owing to the 'spots of indeterminacy', a literary work of art, 'though now no longer containing fully determinate aesthetic qualities and having instead

---

124 George G. Grabowicz, 'Translator's Introduction' [in:] Ingarden, *The Literary Work of Art*, pp. xlv–lxx, p. lvii. Ingarden, *The Literary Work of Art*, p. 272.
125 Cf. ibid., p. 275.
126 Ingarden, *The Literary Work of Art*, p. 265.
127 Ibid., pp. 287 and 277.

172

only loci which in given instances are filled out by specific kinds of values, is still a determinate structure, pertaining to, and only to, works of art.'[128]

What emerges from Ingarden's philosophy of literature is that the 'spots of indeterminacy' are some of the indispensable qualities that decide on the artistic nature of a literary work. I intend to suggest that this artistic value of a literary work, enabled largely by its indeterminate nature of visualizations and musicalizations embedded into a determinate manifold structure of the literary work, can be a part of its therapeutic potential, just as music or art therapy is. I develop this aspect of a therapeutic potential of a literary work of art, viewed in this book with regard to Faërie only, in Chapter Five.

Images and sounds described by the author are 'held in readiness' as 'sensory data' to be concretized differently by each reader in the process of 'imaginational modification' rather than of genuine perception, as the reader cannot see or hear the exact concretization that the author has conceived of.[129] The only genre that is naturally 'predisposed to such "realization"' or 'concretization' is, Ingarden notes, drama, for 'the mode of the realization of dramatic works is theatrical performance.'[130] In his essay 'On Fairy-Stories' Tolkien points to drama likewise, remarking that 'drama is naturally hostile to Fantasy', precisely for the same reason that Ingarden provides: imaginative and individual concretization of the worlds described in the literary work of art, which Tolkien in his essay considers with regard to fairy-stories only and associates with Fantasy, 'hardly ever succeeds in Drama, when that is presented as it should be, visibly and audibly acted.'[131] 'It is a misfortune that Drama, an art fundamentally distinct from Literature, should so commonly be considered together with it, or as a branch of it,' Tolkien concludes.[132] 'For this precise reason – that the characters, and even the scenes, are in Drama not imagined but actually beheld – Drama is, even though it uses a similar material (words, verse, plot), an art fundamentally different from narrative art.'[133]

When examining the process of concretizing verbal descriptions of visual and auditory phenomena, as embedded into a literary work of art, Ingarden argues that sensory data is 'imaginatively actualized' in a 'pulsating mode of experiencing',

---

128   Grabowicz, 'Translator's Introduction', pp. xlv–lxx, p. lviii, based on Ingarden's 'Szkice z filozofii literatury' [Essays of the Philosophy of Literature], p. 186.

129   Ingarden, ibid., pp. 268–269.

130   Ibid., p. 271.

131   Tolkien, 'On Fairy-Stories', p. 140.

132   Ibid., p. 140.

133   Tolkien, ibid., p. 142.

that is not as a continuum but as a 'jumpy' sequence, in which an image or sound appears in a flash, to be followed by another:[134]

> Every aspect of this kind is almost like a momentary photographic flash – suddenly illuminated and just as suddenly extinguished. If a new aspect emerges, it is not a continuation, a directly successive phase of the same aspect continuum, but something disconnected from the preceding aspect. [...] Perhaps because of this sudden illumination and extinction, this jerky succession, the individual 'flash pictures' [...] have great illuminating power and, simultaneously, the great power of revealing the objects that appear in them.[135]

Interpreting the concretization of those visual 'aspects' of a literary work of art that are 'held in readiness' to be imagined by every reader differently as an alternating process of 'illumination' and 'extinction', Ingarden provides an example of Thomas Mann's narrative technique in *The Magic Mountain*, in which the reader, when reading that the protagonist is walking from his room along a corridor, down the staircase, into the dining hall, may concretize those objects and places sequentially.[136] To Ingarden, the 'aspects held in readiness' belong to the 'spots of indeterminacy' and are there for the reader to be conretized, and although they do not exhaust the essence of the literary work of art, they constitute an 'essential feature of literary expressionism', as they 'do reinforce the momentariness of the world thus represented and incarnate it in a characteristic *imprint*.'[137] The 'characteristic imprint' mentioned by Ingarden relates to 'the nature of the predominant aspects in a given work', and I narrow it here to the genre of high fantasy, whose otherworldliness seems to necessitate a heightened 'expressionism', so that the 'manifold schematized aspects' of the sub-created places, objects, and characters, can be concretized by the reader.[138] The sensorial indeterminacy of what Ingarden calls the 'manifold schematized aspects' of literary works of art, (which appears particularly challenging in fantasy fiction, whose otherworlds, or, as Tolkien refers to them, Secondary or Sub-created worlds, are to be imagined by the reader), is the element that I view as potentially therapeutic, for it engages the reader/listener of the literary narrative in an artistic activity and production, which can perhaps be an indirect form of art therapy inherent to the overall phenomenon of bibliotherapy.

---

134   Ingarden, *The Literary Work of Art*, pp. 269–270.
135   Ibid., p. 283.
136   Ibid., p. 283.
137   Ingarden, ibid., pp. 283–284. Italics are Ingarden's.
138   Ingarden, ibid., p. 284.

Tolkien's definition of Art, an essential element of the literary works that stem from Faërie and dwell in Secondary Worlds, appears syncretic, as it represents integrated arts, which, being embedded in language, open up a vista on an virtually indeterminate number of possible artistic concretizations:

> Art is the human process that produces by the way (it is not its only or ultimate object) Secondary Belief (…) The more potent and elvish craft I will, for a lack of less debatable word, call Enchantment. Enchantment produces a Secondary World into which both designer and spectator can enter, to the satisfaction of their senses while they are inside; but in its purity it is artistic in desire and purpose. To the elvish craft, Enchantment, Fantasy aspires, and when it is successful of all forms of human art most nearly approaches.[139]

The interartistic and synaesthetic nature of fantasy narrative, especially fairy-stories, emerges, perhaps even more clearly, also from C. S. Lewis's *Of Other Worlds* essays, where he remarks:

> A 'children's story' is the best art-form for something you have to say: just as a composer might write a Dead March not because there was a public funeral in view but because certain musical ideas that had occurred to him [or her] went best into that form.(…) Within the species of 'children's story' the sub-species which happened to suit me is the fantasy or (in a loose sense of that word) the fairy tale.[140]

Mental pictures that instigate writing are particularly important to Lewis, and he finds fairy tales most suitable for that type of picture-language translation or transposition:

> [With my Narnia stories] everything began with images; a faun carrying an umbrella, a queen on a sledge, a magnificent lion. (…) Then came the Form. As these images sorted themselves into events (i.e., became a story) they seemed to demand no love interest and no close psychology. But the Form which excludes these things is the fairy tale. And the moment I thought of that I fell in love with the Form itself: its brevity, its severe restraints on description, its flexible traditionalism, its inflexible hostility to all analysis, digression, reflections and 'gas'. I was now enamoured of it. Its very limitations of vocabulary became an attraction; as the hardness of the stone pleases the sculptor or the difficulty of the sonnet delights the sonneteer. (…) I wrote fairy tales because [this form of art], the Fairy Tale, seemed the ideal Form for the stuff I had to say.[141]

139   Tolkien, 'On Fairy-Stories', pp. 142–143.
140   Lewis, 'On Three Ways of Writing for Children' [in:] *Of Other Worlds – Essays and Stories*, pp. 22–34, p. 23.
141   Lewis, 'Sometimes Fairy Stories May Say Best What's To Be Said' [in:] *Of Other Worlds – Essays and Stories*, pp. 35–38, pp. 36–37.

Lewis emphasizes the importance of his visual imagination to his fantasy writing (especially with regard to the seven Narnia books and his three science fiction novels) also in his one-page essay 'It All Began with a Picture':

> One thing I am sure of. All my seven Narnia books, and my three science fiction books, began with seeing pictures in my head. At first they were not a story, just pictures. The *Lion* all began with a picture of a Faun carrying an umbrella and parcels in a snowy wood. This picture had been in my mind since I was about sixteen. Then one day, when I was about forty, I said to myself: 'let's try to make a story about it.' At first I had very little idea how the story would go. But then suddenly Aslan came bounding into it. I think I had been having a good many dreams of lions about that time. (…) In a sense, I know very little about how this story was born. This is, I don't know where the pictures came from.[142]

What is more, Lewis mentions some synaesthetic impressions he has when writing fantasy narrative, which involve the visual and the olfactory:

> In a certain sense, I have never exactly 'made' a story. Within me the process is much more like bird-watching than like either talking or building. I see pictures. Some of these pictures have a common flavour, almost a common smell, which groups them together. Keep quiet and watch and they will begin joining themselves up. If you were very lucky (I have never been as lucky as all that) a whole set might join themselves so consistently that there you had a complete story: without doing anything yourself. But more often (in my experience always) there are gaps. Then at last you have to do some deliberate inventing (…). It is the only [way of writing stories] I know: images always come first.[143]

Ursula Kroeber Le Guin explains the process of writing fantasy narrative, as exemplified by her Earthsea hexalogy, in a way similar to Lewis's in that her otherworlds begin as mental pictures:[144]

> I'm not an engineer, but an explorer. I discovered Earthsea. (…) The [Earthsea] story is essentially a voyage, a pattern in the form of a long spiral. I began to see the places where the young wizard [Ged] would go. Eventually I drew a map. Now that I knew where everything was, now was the time for cartography. Of course, a great deal of it only appeared above water, as it were, in drawing the map.(…) People often ask how I think of names in fantasies, and again I have to answer that I find them, that I hear them.[145]

---

142 Lewis, 'It All Began with a Picture' [in:] *Of Other Worlds – Essays and Stories*, p. 42.
143 Lewis, 'On Three Ways of Writing for Children', p. 32.
144 Susan Wood, 'Introduction' to Le Guin's book of essays *The Language of the Night*, p. 2.
145 Le Guin, 'Dreams Must Explain Themselves', *The Language of the Night*, pp. 37–46, pp. 40–42.

Le Guin also acknowledges the non-verbal-arts-mediating capacity of fantasy narrative, which allows to translate both the visual and the unconscious into words:

With the universality proper to art, written fantasy translates into verbal images and coherent narrative forms the intuitions and perceptions of the unconscious mind – body language, dream stuff, primary process thinking. This idiom, for all its intense privacy, is one we all seem to share, whether we speak English or Urdu, whether we're five or eighty-five.[146]

Le Guin's statement about the relationship between fantasy, reality, and art resembles what Freud seems to have once expressed, saying that 'there is a path that leads back from phantasy to reality – the path, that is, of art.'[147] Le Guin's and Lewis's reflections on fantasy and its affiliation to dreams may also resound of Freud's postulate that art can be likened to dreams, but, of course, here the similarity ends, as neither the two fantasy writers in question nor Tolkien could be identified with psychoanalysis.[148] Freud observes that:

We experience a dream predominantly in visual images; feelings may be present, too, and thoughts interwoven in it as well; the other senses might also experience something, but nonetheless it is predominantly a question of images. Part of the difficulty of giving an account of dreams is due to our having to translate these images into words. 'I could draw it,' a dreamer often says to us, 'but I don't know how to say it.'[149]

---

146 Le Guin, 'Introduction', *The Language of the Night*, p. 1.
147 Sigmund Freud, 'Civilisation and Its Discontents' (1930) [in:] *The Standard Edition Of The Complete Psychological Works of Sigmund Freud - The Future of an Illusion, Civilization and its Discontents, and Other Works*, trans. James Strachey (London: Hogarth Press, 1961), p. 423. It must be noted, though, that Freud views art as a product of an effective sublimation of human sexual and aggressive urges that are sourced in the Id, and channeled by the Ego, as directed by the Super ego. Sublimation is, to Freud, one of man's original defence mechanisms. Art, according to Freud, results from the sublimated wish to play with one's own excrements, and painting, for instance, is to him an expression of a potentially sublimated desire to smear one's own faeces. ('Civilisation and Its Discontents', pp. 79–82).
148 Le Guin's fiction, though, appears, as she declares, quite unconsciously akin to Carl Jung's psychology, especially to his concept of archetypes, of the collective unconscious, and of the shadow and the self (cf. Le Guin, 'The Child and the Shadow' [in:] *The Language of the Night*, pp. 49–61).
149 Freud, *The Standard Edition Of The Complete Psychological Works of Sigmund Freud*, p. 90.

In one of passages quoted above Le Guin uses precisely the same word: 'translation', referring to the same mode of transition from visual to verbal imagery that Freud suggests; and in another essay she adds that that 'dreams must explain themselves', and must be rendered into word-symbols so as to reach our consciousness.[150] Le Guin also argues that 'we like to think we live in daylight, but half the world is always dark; and fantasy, like poetry [and dreams], speaks the language of the night.'[151] Commenting on the experience of reading fantasy literature, she remarks: '[It is] new; a revelation; a vision; a more or less powerful or haunting dream. A view in, not out. A space-voyage through somebody else's psychic abysses.'[152]

Tolkien elaborates on the kinship between dreams and fantasy narrative, excluding, however, from among fairy tales those that 'use the machinery of Dream, the dreaming of actual human sleep, to explain the apparent occurrence of its marvels; and declares that 'at the least, even if the reported dream was in other respects itself a fairy-story, [he] would condemn the whole as gravely defective: like a good picture in a disfiguring frame.'[153] Having made that provision, Tolkien admits that:

> It is true that Dream is not unconnected with Faërie. In dreams strange powers of the mind may be unlocked. In some of them a man may for a space wield the power of Faërie, that power which, even as it conceives the story, causes it to take living form and colour before the eyes. A real dream may indeed sometimes be a fairy-story of almost elvish ease and skill – while it is being dreamed. But if a waking writer tells you that his [or her] tale is only a thing imagined in [their] sleep, [they] cheat deliberately the primal desire at the heart of Faërie: the realization, independent of conceiving mind, of imagined wonder.[154]

Tessa Dalley, an art therapist, points, in turn, towards some therapeutic properties of dreamwork, which she also associates with art, as they both allow for a 'pictorial expression of inner experience' and are 'processes of spontaneous imagery, released from the unconscious, using the mechanism of repression, projection, identification, sublimation, and condensation, which are fundamental in the

---

150   Le Guin, 'Dreams Must Explain Themselves' [in:] *The Language of the Night*, pp. 37–46.
151   Le Guin, 'Fantasy, Like Poetry, Speaks the Language of the Night' [in:] *The Language of the Night*, p. 1.
152   Le Guin, 'The View In' [in:] *The Language of the Night*, pp. 17–18.
153   Tolkien, 'On Fairy-Stories', p. 116.
154   Tolkien, ibid., p. 116.

therapeutic method.'[155] Margaret Naumburg, a pioneer of American art therapy, explains likewise how dreams and pictures may enhance therapy: 'Objectified picturization acts as an immediate symbolic communication which frequently circumvents the difficulties of speech', that is, one may add, following Le Guin, of translating visual images into word images, which is the essence and the genuine art of fantasy narrative.'[156] 'Another advantage inherent in the making of unconscious pictured projections [Naumburg observes] is that such symbolic images more easily escape repression by what Freud called the mind's "censor" than do verbal expressions, which are more familiar to the patient.'[157] The interartistic properties of fantasy narrative of the Inklings and of Le Guin, and its dream-like quality as one aspect of its therapeutic potential are discussed in the next chapter, which makes a prelude to discussing the other generic attributes of fantasy literature that pertain to logotherapy.

Returning to the main theme of this chapter, that is logotherapy through narrative as such, one may wonder whether the fact that fantasy narrative, as emerges from the reflections of Tolkien's, Lewis's and Le Guin's, has a singularly synaesthetic nature, like poetry, may contribute anyhow to its therapeutic power, and whether there is any relationship between synaesthesia and therapy. The first theory of therapeutic properties of synaesthesia was probably developed around 530 BC by Pythagoras (ca. 570–ca. 490 BC), who considered synaesthesia as an ideal perception, 'the greatest philosophical gift and spiritual achievement,[which] ultimately reconciles the illusory quotidian world with the authentic world of universal, enduring, abstract concepts.'[158] To Pythagoras, synaesthetic synergy of arts and sciences (especially of music, visual arts, astronomy and mathematics, all believed to be based on the same system of numerical proportions manifested in numbers, visual angles, shapes and sounds) is a gateway to an absolute spiritual experience, to the music of spheres that includes but overarches the music of man; a means of reaching towards universal meaning and order.[159] Pythagoras' theory of the Harmony of the Spheres followed the

---

155   Tessa Dalley, *Art as Therapy: An Introduction to the Use of Arts as a Therapeutic Technique* (New York: Routledge, 1984), p. xvi.

156   Margaret Naumburg, *Dynamically Oriented Art Therapy: Its Principles and Practice* (Chicago: Magnolia Street Pub, 1987), p. 2.

157   Ibid., p. 2.

158   Qtd. in William Moritz, 'Abstract Film and Color Music,' http://www.awn.com/animationworld/lifetime-animation-glamorous-dr-william-moritz, accessed 23 April 2016.

159   Cf. Pliny the Elder, *Naturalis Historia* [Natural History], pp. 277–278.

vision of macrocosm, whose internal music and order are reflected in the world's and man's microcosm, in which all numbers 'have their own personality,' and generate specific tones and colours.[160]

An overlapping and interconnectedness of music, other arts and sciences is what Boethius (ca. 480–ca. 524) emphasizes after Pythagoras in his works.[161] Boethius perceives the harmony of man in terms of *musica humana*, the internal music of the human body, and in its artistic counterpart, *musica instrumentalis*, the instrumental music performed by people, both 'worldly' types of music pertaining to *musica mundana*, the inaudible but fundamental and all-engrossing music of universe, the harmony of the spheres.[162] According to Boethius, the embedment of all sensory perceptions in music results from the fact that 'music is so naturally united with us that we cannot be free from it even if we so desired.'[163] The 'ordered' music of universe, of the natural world, and of the human body creates psychosomatic responses of unity, order and relaxation.[164] Disorderly music with irregular beat, shrill sounds, and unresolved dissonances, disturbs the internal bodily mechanism not only of people but also of animals, and may cause malady or violent behaviour.[165] Pythagoras, Aristotle, and some other ancient scholars studied the correspondences of musical intervals and shades of grey, and the correlation between colour and sound.[166] The Pythagorean theory of music appears also in Plato's *Republic*, where Plato associates colour explicitly with music and represents universe as a model of eight concentric spheres, each having its distinct colour and a musical note, and contributing to the Harmony of the Spheres.[167] The order of the hemispheres and the order of the colours on their rims reflect the balance and the harmony of universe.

---

160 John Gage, *Colour and Culture: Practice and Meaning from Antiquity to Abstraction* (London: Thames & Hudson, 1993), p. 35.

161 Anicius Manlius Severinus Boëthius: *De Consolation Philosophiae* [The Consolation of Philosophy], *De Topicis Differentiis* [Different Topics in Dialectics], *De Arithmetica* [The Arithmetic], and, in particular, *De Institutione Musica* [The Institution of Music].

162 Boethius, *De Institutione Musica*.

163 Boethius, as quoted by Anthony Storr in his *Music and the Mind* (New York: Ballantine Books, 1992), p. 1.

164 Robert W. Lundin, *An Objective Psychology of Music* (Malabar: Robert E. Krieger Publishing Company, 1985).

165 Anthony Storr, *Music and the Mind* (New York: The Free Press, 1992).

166 Gage, *Colour and Culture*, p. 37. R. Ferwerda and P. Struycken, *Aristoteles Over Kleuren* [Aristotle on Colours] (Budel: Damon, 2001).

167 Plato, *The Republic*, The Myth of Er', 10.612 E– 617. A.

My supposition on which this chapter rests is that a synaesthetic narrative of combined arts that informs a literary work of art, and a literary work of fantasy, (or as Tolkien calls it, of Faërie), in particular, may potentially enhance rather than weaken the therapeutic properties of art *per se*, which seem indisputable. A narrative that borrows from visual arts and music, and which draws on verbal language and its meaning, may contain therapeutic properties and may be capable of offering logotherapy, the therapy through meaning, based on both a meaningful and moral foundation of verbal narrative, which, according to Victor Frankl, can be profoundly therapeutic, and on the therapeutic nature of a work of art, which appears therapeutic as well. Frankl's theory of logotherapy has been introduced in Chapter Three as an instance of a foundation philosophy of a meaningful life both as a micro and macro-narrative, that is the one in which each situation and event, as well as man's existence itself, are endowed with a sense that needs to be discovered. How the narrative of art, including literature, may perform a (logo)therapeutic function is what follows now in this chapter. Arthur Robbins comments on the interartistic nature of therapy in similar terms to Ingarden's understanding of a literary work of art, concluding that:

> The therapeutic process is an ongoing struggle to discover true inner representations and symbols and give them form in terms of developing richer, more congruent living realities. Together, patient and artist create a matrix in which verbal and nonverbal communications come alive as both parties are touched by common experience. This complicated mode of interaction takes on a form similar to a symphony or work of art; where multiple levels of consciousness and meaning exist simultaneously.[168]

I intend now to trace some therapeutic properties of art, specifically of the narrative art, drawing on Lev Vygotsky's contribution to the psychology of art.

A psychology of art by Lev Vygotsky

It could be surprising that a philosophy of a Soviet psychologist with a Marxist background can still be of interest and value to the psychologists and theoreticians today; yet, as Michael Cole remarks, Vygotsky's ideas of the 'centrality of culture and history to human psychological functioning' are still of relevance, and Vygotsky's theory offers 'both a classical and fresh insight into the apparent gap in psychology, namely the psychological theory of art, whose shortcomings he had been struggling with, and which do not seem to have been overcome

---

168   Arthur Robbins, *The Artist as a Therapist* (New York: Human Sciences Press, 1987), p. 7.

by his scientific successors' ever since.'[169] According to Cole, Vygotsky (1896–1934) and his colleagues had 'formulated a meta-psychology that encompassed the phylogeny, cultural history ontogeny and moment to moment dynamics of human psychological functioning as a lifelong process of becoming;' an accomplishment whose synthetic and fundamental import to the human thought of the 20th and 21st centuries should not be forgotten.[170] What Cole wrote in the 1970s, forty years after Vygotsky's death, when Vygotsky was hailed 'the Mozart of psychology,' and when there was a 'Vygotsky boom' in the West, appears relevant also today, as the numerous publications on Vygotsky's theory seem to confirm.[171]

In his study *The Psychology of Art* of 1925, Vygotsky polemicizes with Wilhelm von Humboldt's approach, which defines art as perception and follows the theory of art rooted in antiquity and pronouncing art as the 'perception of wisdom', whose main tasks are teaching and instruction.[172] Vygotsky's major point is that art is not merely perception but a powerful mechanism activating emotions, imagination and rational thinking, whose psychological effect conditions man's individual and social well-being. The psychological power of art, which Vygotsky views holistically with regard to visual arts, music, and literature, is, as he claims, of enormous import and benevolence to both artists (creators) and art audience (viewers, listeners, and readers), and provides a basis for art therapy (the term which Vygotsky does not use, yet whose theoretical foundation he seems to provide), a part of which is bibliotherapy.[173] In his study of the psychology of art Vygotsky argues that 'art systematizes a very special sphere in the

---

169   Michael Cole, 'Reading Vygotsky': Preface to *The Edited Collection of Vygotsky's Writings*, Robert Rieber and David Robinson, eds. (San Diego: University of California Press, 2005), p. 6. Cf. also *The Cambridge Companion to Vygotsky*, Harry Daniels, Michael Cole, and James V. Wertsch, eds. (Cambridge: Cambridge University Press, 2007).

170   Cole, 'Reading Vygotsky', p. 8.

171   For instance, Bettina Dahl, 'A Synthesis of Piaget and Vygotsky?' [in:] *Philosophy Of Mathematics Education Journal 17*, 2003, http://www.ex.ac.uk/~PErnest/pome17/contents.htm; Carl Ratner, 'Vygotsky's Conception of Child's Psychology', 2004, [in:] *Essential Vygotsky*, Robert Rieger, ed., pp. 401–413; Ricardo Schütz, *Vygotsky and Language Acquisition*, 2004, http://www.english.sk.com.br/sk-vygot.html/; all accessed 12 May 2016.

172   Lev Vygotsky, *The Psychology of Art*, trans. Marie J. Hall (New York: The MIT Press, 1972), p. 74. (The original book Психология искусства was written in Russian in 1925).

173   Vygotsky, ibid., p. 52.

182

psyche of social man – his [or her] emotions.'[174] Contradicting the school of the Russian formalists on the one hand, and the theories of positivistic sociologizing and psychologizing on the other, Vygotsky constructs his theory of art, which attempts to combine the tenet of an autonomous form of art with the conviction of its pivotal social and psychological role. It is precisely in the space between Russian formalism (which rejected any psychological background or impact of a work of art, especially of literature), and positivistic psychologizing (which concentrated mostly on the psychology of the artist and of the art receptor, questioning the autonomy of a work of art), where Vygotsky lays the foundations for a pioneer theory of psychological semantics of a form of art.[175]

Referring to the Marxist philosophy, officially introduced to Russia after the October Revolution of 1917, Vygotsky emphasizes the social function of art and its universal role in society, and defines art as 'the social technique of emotion, a tool of society which brings the most intimate and personal aspects of our being into the circle of social life.'[176] Nevertheless, he remains wary of the difference between art and ideology, as well as between social psychology and individual psychology:

> It is of paramount importance to understand what distinguishes psychology from ideology. We can now understand the distinct role assigned to art as a special ideological form dealing with a totally distinct and peculiar aspect of the human psyche. And, if we are to understand this particular characteristic of art and to know what exactly distinguishes it and its action from all other ideological forms, we cannot but resort to psychological analysis. (…) Everything within us is social, but this does not imply that all the properties of the psyche of an individual are inherent in all the other members of this group as well. Only a certain part of the individual psychology can be regarded as belonging to a given group, and this portion of individual psychology and its collective manifestations is studied by collective psychology when it looks into the psychology of the army, the church, and so on.[177]

Vygotsky suggests focusing on the psychology of a work of art itself, following the methodology introduced by Richard Müller-Freienfels, a philosopher and

---

174 Vygotsky, ibid., p. 54. The phrase the 'Mozart of psychology' comes from Stephen Toulmin's review of Vygotsky's *Mind in Society*, the *New York Review of Books*, cf. Michael Cole, 'Reading Vygotsky', p. 7.

175 Cf. Stanisław Balbus, 'Vygotsky and his Theory of Culture: Psychology, Language and Art', introduction to *Psychologia sztuki* [The Psychology of Art], trans. mine (Krakow: Wydawnictwo Literackie, 1980), p. 12.

176 Vygotsky, *The Psychology of Art*, p. 339.

177 Vygotsky, ibid., p. 54.

an early psychologist of art, who distinguishes three branches of theoretical psychology of art: 'the study of perception, the study of emotions, and the study of imagination and fantasy,' of which the first branch is of tertiary importance, for, as Vygotsky explains, 'the response to art begins with sensory [aesthetic] perception, but does not end with it.'[178] Thus, 'the psychology of art must begin not with a chapter on elementary aesthetic experiences, but with the other two problem areas – emotion and imagination.'[179] 'Indeed, all psychological systems which attempt to explain art,' Vygotsky adds, 'are nothing but various combinations of the theories of imagination and emotion;' however, these two concepts create a major difficulty for psychologists, for 'in psychology there are no areas more obscure than these two.'[180] This problem results from the fact that one of the characteristics of emotions is their certain 'indefiniteness,' Vygotsky observes, which is precisely the quality that differentiates emotion from sensation, and which makes the analysis of the relationship between emotional facts and imagination problematic.[181]

To Vygotsky, emotion, which is an inherent part of art, constitutes an output of psychic energy, 'an expenditure of psychic force,' which is directly proportional to the psychological power of art: 'the greater the expenditure of nervous energy, the more intense is the effect produced by the work of art.'[182] 'Art is indissolubly associated with a complex play of emotions', and it does not entail 'pure perception, but requires the highest psychic activity,' Vygotsky notes.[183] Moreover, he continues, art often violates the principle of the 'economy of strength,' according to which things ought to be expressed in the most economical and direct way, 'at least insofar as its immediate effect is concerned, and [instead] obeys an opposite principle in the construction of artistic forms.'[184] This is so, Vygotsky argues, because 'art is an explosive and sudden expenditure of strength, of psychic forces, and a discharge of energy.'[185]'A work of art perceived coldly and prosaically, or processed and treated to be perceived in this way, saves much more energy and force than if it were perceived with the full effect of its artistic

---

178 Vygotsky, *The Psychology of Art*, p. 63. Richard Müller-Freienfels, *The Psychology of Art* (Cleveland: Cleveland Museum of Art, 1940).
179 Vygotsky, ibid., pp. 63 and 277.
180 Vygotsky, ibid., p. 277.
181 Ibid., p. 278.
182 Ibid., p. 285.
183 Ibid., p. 286.
184 Ibid., p. 285.
185 Ibid., p. 338.

form in mind.'[186] Therefore, he concludes, 'our aesthetic response, above all, is a response that annihilates our nervous energy; it is an explosion, not a penny-pinching economy.'[187]

However, Vygotsky remarks, although art is 'an explosive discharge of psychic energy', or maybe precisely because of that, it 'does introduce order and harmony into the "psychic household" of our feelings.'[188] And this mechanism allows for its therapeutic impact, one may add. The dynamics produced as a result of the conflict between the content and the form of the work of art, (in which, as Vygotsky argues, agreeing in this respect with the Russian formalists, the former, that is the content, is always overcome by the latter, that is the form), as well as the tension caused by the collision and cathartic purification of contradictory emotions evoked by the work of art, ultimately create peace and bring relief.[189]

When analyzing literary genres, Vygotsky observes that 'the law of aesthetic response' is the same for the beast fable, (to which Vygotsky devotes much time and attention in his study, focusing mostly on Ivan Krylov's fables,) as for the tragedy (here Vygotsky studies Shakespeare's *Hamlet*): namely, 'it comprises an affect that develops in two opposite directions but reaches annihilation at its point of termination.'[190] This is the dynamic and benevolent process that Vygotsky calls, after Aristotle and many other thinkers, catharsis.[191] Vygotsky points out that:

> While [art] generates in us opposing affects, it delays (on account of the antithetic principle) the motor expression of emotions and, by making opposite impulses collide, it destroys the affect of content and form, and initiates an explosive discharge of nervous energy. Catharsis of the aesthetic response is the transformation of affects, the explosive response which culminates in the discharge of emotions.[192]

In conclusion, Vygotsky ascertains that 'contradiction is the essential feature of artistic form and material,' and that 'the essential part of aesthetic response is the manifestation of the affective contradiction,' which he designates by the term catharsis; discussed in more detail with regard to fantasy narrative in Chapter Seven of this book.[193]

---

186 Vygotsky, Ibid., p. 338.
187 Ibid., p. 285.
188 Ibid., p. 338.
189 Ibid., p. 340.
190 Ibid., p. 300.
191 Ibid., p. 300.
192 Ibid., p. 300.
193 Ibid., p. 301.

Even though, as has been mentioned, Vygotsky does not use the notion of 'therapy', he explicitly concentrates on the powerful psychological and purifying impact of art, whether it is visual, auditory, verbal, or of mixed modes, and ascribes this effect to the cathartic power of art. According to Vygotsky, catharsis results from the strain between the material, object, and form, and, as he argues, 'the artist always overcomes content with form.'[194] This is another point of affinity with the Russian formalists, which accounts for the effect of catharsis, as propounded by Vygotsky, on the grounds of a purely formal analysis of a work of art. Chapter Seven of this book ventures to view catharsis as one of the key mechanisms of bibliotherapy, and of high fantasy in particular, with regard to Tolkien's concept of Eucatastrophe, which, none the less touches upon a broader perspective than Vygotsky's, reaching beyond the narrative's form itself.

Expanding on the formal basis of catharsis in a work of art, Vygotsky argues, echoing Russian formalists, that art is an interaction and a struggle founded on the principle of flow and dynamics, resulting from a subordination of some factors to others, and, specifically, from the overcoming of the content by the form. 'Without this subordination, there can be no art,' Vygotsky claims, because 'form is the result of the constructive subordination of certain factors to others, rather than of their fusion into one.'[195] This view might appear somewhat reductionist, as it does not regard the cathartic impact of what the content contributes to the psychological impact of work of art, and also because it emphasizes subordination rather than a possibility of an ultimate synthesis of form, content, and other factors, which, at least in the case of fantasy narrative as advocated and practised by Tolkien, Lewis and Le Guin, seems vital. Genre, however, contributes to the cathartic effect of a literary work of art, and of fantasy fiction in particular. As has been mentioned before, Lewis, for instance, says that 'sometimes fairy stories may say best what's to be said', concluding that he 'wrote fairy tales because [this form of art], the Fairy Tale, seemed the ideal Form for the stuff [he] had to say.'[196]

Even though Vygotsky stresses the formal source of catharsis, he does not disregard the emotional power of a work of art, observing that 'the purpose of a work of literature [and of art, in general], is to cause specific emotions that cannot be directly expressed in action,' and adds that 'it is the delay in the external manifestation which is the distinguishing characteristic of an artistic emotion and the reason for its extraordinary power.'[197] This 'delay in the external manifestation of

194   Ibid., p. 300.
195   Vygotsky, ibid., p. 303.
196   Lewis, 'Sometimes Fairy Stories May Say Best What's To Be Said', pp. 36–37.
197   Vygotsky, ibid., p. 296.

affect that takes place in art' results from mixed feelings evoked by art, Vygotsky claims, from the 'affective contradiction' of feelings and conflicting emotions, which all lead to the 'short-circuiting and destruction of these emotions, [and that is] the true effect of a work of art.'[198] This appears to correspond to the effect of catharsis, as introduced by Aristotle with regard to the Greek tragedy; the effect which Vygotsky recognizes as the core of the psychological impact of art. 'Despite the certain indefiniteness of its content, and despite our failure to explain the meaning of catharsis in the Aristotelian sense,' Vygotsky remarks,

There is no other term in psychology which so completely expresses the central fact of aesthetic reaction, according to which painful and unpleasant affects are discharged and transformed into their opposites. Aesthetic reaction as such is nothing but catharsis, that is, a complex transformation of feelings. Though little is known at present about the process of catharsis, we do know, however, that the discharge of nervous energy (which is the essence of any emotion) takes place in a direction which opposes the conventional one, and that art therefore becomes a most powerful means for important and appropriate discharges of nervous energy. The basis for this process reveals itself in the contradiction which inheres in the structure of any work of art.[199]

To Vygotsky, catharsis is a transformation of the feelings of horror, fear, and pity into the opposite ones, that is of beauty, peace and joy, and their subsequent resolution, a concept borrowed from Aristotle's study of the Greek tragedy.[200] As mentioned above, in his theory of the psychology of art Vygotsky embraces all aspects of artistic creation, including not only literature but also visual arts and music, and, likewise, identifies catharsis as a major effect of all these types of art. In visual arts and in music, Vygotsky argues, catharsis is achieved by a clash between the content and the form of a work of art, or between the content and the material, – a duality whose elements seem to contradict one another.[201] He observes that 'the impression of horror or fear must find its resolution and purification in an element of Dionysian enthusiasm; horror is represented not for its own sake but as an impulse to be overcome, and this distracting element must signify overcoming and catharsis simultaneously.'[202]

Considering the cathartic power of music, Vygotsky remarks that, in comparison to visual arts:

---

198   Ibid., p. 297.
199   Vygotsky, ibid., p. 299.
200   Ibid., p. 335.
201   Ibid., p. 310.
202   Ibid., p. 310.

The effect of music reveals itself much more subtly, by means of hidden shocks, stresses, and deformations of our constitution; it may reveal itself unexpectedly, and in an extraordinary way. First, music incites, excites, and irritates in an indeterminate fashion not connected with any concrete reaction, motion, or action. This is proof that its effect is cathartic, that is, it clears our psyche, reveals and calls to life tremendous energies which were previously inhibited and restrained. This, however is a consequence of art, not its action. Secondly, music has coercive power. Tolstoy suggests that music should be an affair of state. He believes that music is a public affair.[203]

Sharing Tolstoy's opinion and illustrating it with an analysis of Ludwig van Beethoven's *Kreutzer Sonata*, Vygotsky concludes that 'music acts like an earthquake as it throws open unknown and hidden strata. Although music does not generate any direct actions, its fundamental effect, the direction it imparts to psychic catharsis, is essential for the kind of forces it will release, what it will release, and what it will push into the background.'[204]

In his observations of how art affects our bodies, Vygotsky follows Charles Scott Sherrington's interpretation of the nervous system, according to which it works like:

> [...] a funnel with its narrow part turned toward action, and the wider part toward the world. The world pours into man, through the wide opening of the funnel, thousands of calls, desires, stimuli, etc. enter, but only an infinitesimal part of them is realized and flows out through the narrowing opening. It is obvious that the unrealized part of life, which has not gone through the narrow opening of our behavior, must be somehow utilized and lived. The organism is in equilibrium with its environment where balance must be maintained, just as it becomes necessary to open a valve in a kettle in which steam pressure exceeds the strength of the vessel.[205]

Thus, there must be a mechanism that brings relief and 'utilizes' the unrealized emotions, calls and stimuli, and, to Vygotsky, it is art that serves as a 'psychological means for striking a balance with the environment at critical points of our behavior', and it does so by means of catharsis.[206] Vygotsky argues that the central 'action of art [which testifies to its meaning and its moral dimension] is catharsis', whereby

---

203   Ibid., p. 341.
204   Ibid., p. 342.
205   Vygotsky, ibid., p. 337. Sir Charles Scott Sherrington (1857–1952) was a famous English neurophysiologist, histologist, bacteriologist and pathologist, awarded the Novel Prize in Physiology and Medicine in 1932 (together with Edgar Adrian).
206   Vygotsky, ibid. p. 337.

art 'pushes into this purifying flame the most intimate and important experiences, emotions, and feelings of the soul.'[207]

Emphasizing his preoccupation with the cathartic power of art, Vygotsky actually puts an equality sign between art and catharsis, with a proviso:

> If we consider art to be catharsis, it is perfectly clear that it cannot arise where there is nothing but live and vivid feeling. A sincere feeling taken *per se* cannot create art. It lacks more than technique or mastery, because a feeling expressed by a technique will never generate a lyric poem or a musical composition. To do this we require the creative act of overcoming the feeling, resolving it, conquering it. Only when this act has been performed – then and only then is art born. This is why the perception of art requires creativity: it is not enough to experience sincerely the feeling, or feelings, of the author; it is not enough to understand the structure of the work of art; one must also creatively overcome one's own feelings, and find one's own catharsis; only then will the effect of art be complete.[208]

Vygotsky seems to claim that catharsis results from the creative processing of feelings, from reworking emotions, which must involve a rational activity; from a union of emotion and reason. His statement that 'art is based upon the union of feeling and imagination' might thus, as I discern, be completed by adding: 'the union of feeling and imagination' that is 'aided by reason, without which the process of creation cannot be called art.'[209] Only a cooperation of imagination, which propels emotions, with reason, which casts and transforms emotions into a form of art, may succeed in creating art that offers a cathartic opportunity.

J. R. R. Tolkien, who comes from a totally different culture and background, yet who belongs to Vygotsky's generation, (Vygotsky was four years younger than Tolkien and two years older than C. S. Lewis), seems to understand Fantasy, with regard to the narrative art of literature, in a similar way, that is the product of both imagination and reason, and a great, if not the greatest, artistic form, as discussed in Chapter Two of this book:

> Fantasy is a natural human activity. It certainly does not destroy or even insult Reason; and it does not either blunt the appetite for, nor obscure the perception of, scientific verity. On the contrary. The keener and the clearer is the reason, the better fantasy will it make. If men were ever in a state in which they did not want to know or could not perceive truth (facts or evidence), then Fantasy would languish until they were cured. Fantasy will perish, and become Morbid Delusion. For creative Fantasy is founded upon

---

207   Ibid., p. 338.
208   Ibid., p. 311.
209   Ibid., p. 313.

the hard recognition that things are so in the world as it appears under the sun; on a recognition of fact, but not a slavery to it.'[210]

Accounting for the relationship between imagination and fantasy, Tolkien observes that 'the mental power of image-making is one thing, or aspect; and it should appropriately be called Imagination.'[211] Art, he says, is 'the operative link between Imagination and the final result, Sub-creation', that is the work of art, the product of human creativity, which may at best clumsily reflect the creative genius of the Maker.'[212] In Tolkien's understanding, Faërie, considered as a peculiar genre of narrative art, represents a secondary world, based on the primary world, which is always transformed or 'processed' through reason and artistic imagination, and its Fantasy, he is careful to point out, 'is not a lower but a higher form of Art, indeed the most nearly pure form, and so (when achieved) the most potent.'[213]

To clarify his understanding of the relationship between emotion and reason in the process of creating art, Vygotsky, in turn, attempts to distinguish 'artistic emotion' from 'ordinary emotions', positing that 'the enigmatic difference that exists between artistic feeling and ordinary feeling may be explained as follows: artistic feeling is the same as the other, but it is released by extremely intensified activity of the imagination. The contrasting elements of which any aesthetic response is composed are thus joined into a unit.'[214] Moreover, Vygotsky quotes Émile Hennequin's interpretation of this problem, suggesting that the 'difference between aesthetic and real emotion [lies] in the fact that aesthetic emotion does not immediately express itself in action; however, if repeated over and over again, these emotions can become the basis for an individual's behavior; thus, an individual can be affected by the kind of literature he [or she] reads.'[215] This might suggest that art, including literature, may have a delayed but actual effect on people's thoughts and actions, and in some cases it may probably be benevolent, which again touches upon the essence of bibliotherapy.[216]

Elaborating on the relationship between emotion and imagination, Vygotsky also claims that 'an emotion is serviced by imagination and expressed in a series

---

210 Tolkien, 'On Fairy-Stories', p. 144, quoted also in Chapter Two of this book.
211 Tolkien, ibid., p. 144.
212 Ibid., p. 139.
213 Ibid., p. 139.
214 Vygotsky, The Psychology of Art, p. 295.
215 Vygotsky, ibid., p. 340. Émile Hennequin (1858–1888) was a French writer who sought to create a scientific theory of artistic production (a theory which he named 'aesthopsychology') in his Scientific Criticism of 1888.
216 Vygotsky, ibid., p. 340.

of fantastic ideas, concepts, and images that represent its second expression,' and adds that an emotion is always real, as it is really felt, even if based on irrational stimuli, such as, for instance, the feeling of fear evoked by a sight of a coat hanging on a hook in the dark, when it is mistaken for a suspicious stranger.[217] 'All our fantastic experiences,' he concludes, 'take place on a completely real emotional basis'; hence 'emotion and imagination are not two separate processes; on the contrary, they are the same process: we can regard a fantasy as the central expression of an emotional reaction.'[218] This 'fantasy', however, is not the product or expression of an emotional reaction only; it matures in a process of rationalizing the emotion. Hence, the purpose of art is certainly not to 'infect people with certain emotions', for then 'art would have a dull and ungrateful task if its only purpose were to infect one or many persons with feelings. If this were so, its significance would be very small, because there would be only a quantitative expansion and no qualitative expansion beyond an individual's feeling.'[219] Instead, Vygotsky claims, 'art arises originally as a powerful tool in the struggle for existence', and 'the idea of reducing its role to a communication of feeling with no power or control over that feeling, is inadmissible.'[220] The biological and psychological function of art, Vygotsky concludes, is to help us 'discharge the unused energy and give it free rein in order to reestablish our equilibrium with the rest of the world.'[221] Art is 'an indispensable discharge of nervous energy and a complex method of finding an equilibrium between our organism and the environment in critical instances of our behaviour', Vygotsky argues.[222]

Vygotsky also comments on the transforming power of art, illustrating it with an example from the Gospel:

> The miracle of art reminds us much more of another miracle in the Gospel, the transformation of water into wine. Indeed, art's true nature is that of transubstantiation, something that transcends ordinary feelings; for the fear, pain, or excitement caused by art includes something above and beyond its normal, conventional content. This 'something' overcomes feelings of fear and pain, changes water into wine, and thus fulfills the most important purpose of art.[223]

---

217 Vygotsky, ibid., p. 292.
218 Ibid., p. 293.
219 Ibid., p. 332.
220 Ibid., p. 334.
221 Ibid., p. 334.
222 Ibid., p. 338.
223 Ibid., p. 333.

By means of that simile Vygotsky seems to point again towards catharsis in art, which transforms the feelings of fear and pity into an experience of relief and peace, (to Tolkien this is the effect of Eucatastrophe, 'the Consolation of the Happy Ending', which produces a tenuous yet hopeful joy, the only joy that is possible, as he believes, in this world); just like water turns miraculously into wine, that is into something it does not contain.[224] This quality of art is also what characterizes fantasy narrative in literature – it is not explicitly therapeutic and does not include any elements of deliberate 'therapy placement' strategy, for it is not instrumental or commercial; yet, in an encounter with the reader or listener, when received and accepted with faith and open mind, without mockery or, as Tolkien says, a forced 'suspension of disbelief', it may turn into a therapeutic tool.[225]

Should there be a common denominator between Vygotsky's view on the psychology of art and Frankl's proposition of logotherapy through narrative, it is probably the concept of meaningfulness and purposefulness to which both an artistic experience and a therapeutic experience may lead: the psychological and spiritual equilibrium that Vygotsky sees as the ultimate effect of art is what Frankl refers to as the result of searching for a sense of every life situation and of life itself, and when discovering it one may achieve a harmony between their psychosomatic and spiritual needs. It is true that literature and other arts, which Frankl only briefly mentions as some possible media of logotherapy, focusing on people's life narratives instead, is what preoccupies Vygotsky, who deals in his work with art exclusively. However, Vygotsky's observations that concern the psychological properties of art, including literature, may perhaps bridge Frankl's psychotherapeutic system with the field of high fantasy narrative, a part of literary art, which is the focus of this book. Ingarden's theory of a literary work of art seems, in turn, to emphasize its immersion in other arts, and its peculiar indeterminate nature of ekphrastic descriptions, which leaves much space for the reader's or listener's imagination and creative concretization of sounds and

---

224   Tolkien, 'On Fairy-Stories', pp. 153–155.
225   A 'willing suspension of disbelief' is a concept introduced by S. T. Coleridge in his *Biographia Literaria of* 1817, Chapter XIV, where Coleridge observes that 'supernatural persons and characters' and other 'shadows of imagination' should 'procure a human interest', a 'semblance of truth', and thus 'a willing suspension of disbelief' – a 'poetic faith'. Tolkien disagrees with that attitude, arguing that, 'if the story-maker proves a successful sub-creator, he [or she] makes a Secondary World which [the reader's] mind can enter; [and] inside it, what he [or she] relates is "true": it accords with the laws of that world. [The reader] therefore believes it, while they are, as it were, inside;' 'On Fairy-Stories', p. 132.

pictures, as neither music nor visual arts can be adequately verbalized. I attempt to discuss art therapy, as somehow mediated through a literary work of art, and a literary work of Faërie, in particular, in the following chapter.

Neither Ingarden nor Vygotsky uses the term 'therapy', yet what emerges from their interpretations of a work of art, including a work of literature, or, as Ingarden names it, 'a literary work of art', seems to be provide fertile ground a therapeutic reading of narrative, and, specifically, high fantasy fiction. While Ingarden identifies and examines the synchronization of different strata of a literary work, which needs the reader's creative effort to have its 'places of indeterminacy' concretized, Vygotsky highlights the cathartic potential of a literary work, which I associate with therapy, and examine in Chapter Seven of this book. In the cathartic process of discharging psychic energy, Vygotsky says, artistic emotions are reworked by artists and in their final 'rethought' form they become imbued in a work of art, and, consequently, are set as a task for art audience to be received and reworked by each individual on their own.[226] Vygotsky notes that:

> Artistic emotions are not collected by the psyche as if they were a handful of seeds thrown into a bag. They require a process of germination and growth, and a psychologist may be able to discover the auxiliary and secondary needs of this process. Art is a central emotion; one that releases itself in the cerebral cortex. The emotions caused by art are [however] intelligent emotions [that is those that are processed through thinking]. Instead of manifesting themselves in the form of fist-shaking or fits, they are usually released in images of fantasy.[227]

None the less, it should be borne in mind, Vygotsky seems to insist, that art must not be limited to its emotional aspect, which is indubitably of great import, just as perception of art is, because it cannot alone create a work of art: 'art's end is not its emotional content', he admits, adding that, obviously, 'to entertain our feelings is not the final purpose of an artistic design or plot'.[228] Hence, 'the most important part in music is that which we cannot hear; in sculpture, that which we cannot see or touch'.[229] This is what Keats also seems to have said in his 'Ode on a Grecian Urn' in the well-known sentence: 'Heard melodies are sweet, but those unheard are sweeter'. This is also perhaps what Ingarden identifies with the 'spots of indeterminacy', which are unique properties of a literary work of art,

---

226 Vygotsky, *The Psychology of Art*, p. 296.
227 Vygotsky, ibid., p. 296.
228 Vygotsky, ibid., p. 83.
229 Ibid., p. 83.

and, in an even heightened form, as I wish to argue, of a literary work of Faërie, due to its otherworldliness.

If the essence of an art dwells not in what that art appears to be in an act of perception, but rather in what it creates after emotions are rethought, then, as Vygotsky seems to observe, the power of literature considered as an art does not consist in its verbal dimension itself, (important though it is), but in the non-verbal, or maybe non-verbalizable effect it exerts on the reader's psyche, which might create an experience not to be rendered in words. This quality which literature seems to share with other arts, making the materials they draw on (for instance sound, words, shapes, and colours) a means to an end rather than an end in itself, may also testify to the interartistic nature of literature – not only of poetry (especially its lyric type) but also fantasy fiction, which has much in common with both poetry and audiovisual arts, as argued in Chapter Five of this book.

According to Vygotsky, 'psychological investigation reveals that art is the supreme centre of biological and social individual processes in society,' and 'that it is a method for finding an equilibrium between man and his world, in the most critical and important stages of his life. This view, of course, completely refutes the approach according to which art is an ornament,' he concludes.[230] Similarly, making another cross-reference to Tolkien and his understanding of fantasy narrative as 'one of the highest forms of Art', one might add that fairy tales rejoice in simplicity and exclude the cloying embellishments of the 'dainty and diminutive' type, 'the flower-and-butterfly minuteness', as well as 'the flower-fairies and fluttering spirits with antennae'.[231]

The psychological dimension of a literary work of art is what seems to correlate in Ingarden's theory to 'metaphysical qualities' within the fourth stratum of 'represented objectivities'.[232] 'Metaphysical qualities' are 'essences', for example 'the sublime, the tragic, the dreadful, the shocking, the inexplicable, the demonic, the holy, the sinful, the sorrowful, (…) as well as the grotesque, the charming, the light, the peaceful, etc.', which, according to Ingarden, 'are not "properties" of objects in the usual sense of the term, nor are they, in general, "features" of some psychic state, but instead they are usually revealed, in complex and often very disparate *situations* or *events*, as an atmosphere which, hovering over the men and the things contained in these situations, penetrates and illuminates everything with its light'.[233] As Ingarden argues, the purpose of a work of literature is

---

230 Vygotsky, ibid., p. 345.
231 Tolkien, 'On Fairy-Stories', p. 111.
232 Ingarden, *The Literary Work of Art*, p. 290.
233 Ibid., pp. 290–291.

precisely to reveal those 'metaphysical qualities', rather than a logical truth, which, nevertheless is an essential element of the work's ontological constitution.[234] In- garden goes even further, claiming that revealing the 'metaphysical essences' is the role of art *per se*, and a literary work may only become a literary work of art when it reveals these 'metaphysical qualities'.[235] In Chapter Six I discuss the 'metaphysical qualities' of Faërie with regard to what I argue constitutes the ethos of high fantasy, or the tales from the 'Perilous Realm', as stipulated by Tolkien, who distinguishes the following landmarks or essences of the genre: Fantasy, Recovery, Escape from Deathlessness, Consolation of the Happy Ending, and 'a fleeting glimpse of Joy, beyond the walls of the world, poignant as grief', which is achieved through Eucatastrophe.[236]

Before I proceed to a discussion of how art therapy may work in Faërie, espe- cially in the works of the Inklings and of Le Guin, I refer briefly to some other critical observations highlighting the interartistic nature of a literary work. Ken- neth Rexroth, an American poet (1905–1982), in his essay 'The Art of Litera- ture' remarks that 'literature has an obvious kinship with the other arts', and that 'the cross-fertilization' of literature, visual arts and music has always been taking place.[237] He explains the close affinity between literature and music as follows:

> [Just like music, literature also] takes time to read or listen to, and it usually presents events or the development of ideas or the succession of images or all these together in time. The craft of literature, indeed, can be said to be in part the manipulation of a struc- ture in time, and so the simplest element of marking time, rhythm, is therefore of basic importance in both poetry and prose.[238]

Moreover, in his reflections upon the art of literature and literature as art, Rexroth emphasizes the importance of myth and fantasy tales, arguing that they had laid the foundations for both literature and its art, and that they enhance the reality rather than detract from it:

> Myths, legends, and folktales lie at the beginning of literature, and their plots, situations, and allegorical (metaphorical narrative) judgments of life represent a constant source of literary inspiration that never fails. This is so because mankind is constant (…), so the themes of literature have at once an infinite variety and an abiding constancy. They can be

---

234 Ibid., p. 291.
235 Ingarden, ibid., p. 351.
236 Tolkien, 'On Fairy-Stories', pp. 138 and 153.
237 Kenneth Rexroth, 'The Art of Literature' [in:] *Encyclopaedia Britannica* (15th Edition, 1974), reprinted in *World outside the Window: Selected Essays of Kenneth Rexroth* (New York: New Directions, 1987), pp. 275–302, p. 299.
238 Rexroth, ibid., p. 277.

taken from myth, from history, or from contemporary occurrence, or they can be pure invention (but even if they are invented, they are nonetheless constructed from the constant materials of real experience, no matter how fantastic the invention).[239]

Rexroth also notes that, when not approached in a purely utilitarian and commercial fashion, 'literature may be an art, but writing is a craft, and a craft must be learned', just like painting, sculpting, or playing a musical instrument, which again shows another aspect of likeness between literature and non-verbal arts.[240]

The kinship of literature with arts emerges also from psychological and therapeutic studies. For instance, Daniel Ellis Berlyne, a psychologist with a special interest in aesthetics, defines art as 'harmony in disorder, or unity in diversity'; Tessa Dalley, an art therapist, refers to it as to 'the harnessed mess'; and they both add that the essence of the peculiar condition of 'consonance in dissonance', which lies at the heart of art, is that it offers a scope for an imaginative aesthetic creativity, whereby people may achieve 'both conscious and unconscious expression', and which 'can be used as a valuable agent for therapeutic change.'[241] Of course, Dalley remarks, 'there is no automatic fusion between art and therapy, in that the latter is a natural consequence of the former', for there are specific conditions under which art becomes therapeutic.[242] Some conditions that a literary work of art needs to meet to be recognized as one of Faërie, and thus, as I would like to argue, as one that is inherently therapeutic, are presented in Chapter Six and Seven.

The problem of the theory of artistic narrative has barely been hinted at in this chapter, and would require volumes and a far greater mind to be properly addressed. It has been mentioned, though, in the context of a relationship between therapy and art, whose narrative, according to McLeod, Vygotsky, and many other scholars, may offer a considerable cathartic potential. Following the theme of this chapter, the next part is a little 'artistic intermezzo', which illustrates several samples of how the interartistic and synaesthetic quality of the fantasy narrative in the works by the Inklings and by Le Guin can have a therapeutic effect, whose nature is explained in detail in Chapters Six and Seven of this book.

---

239   Rexroth, ibid., p. 283.
240   Rexroth, ibid., p. 285.
241   Daniel Ellis Berlyne, *Conflict, Arousal, and Curiosity* (New York: McGraw Hill, 1960), p. 120). Dalley, *Art as Therapy*, Introduction, p. xviii.
242   Dalley, ibid., p. xviii.

Chapter Five
Art therapy through Faërie according to the Inklings and to U. K. Le Guin – an artistic intermezzo

In this chapter, which makes a little 'artistic intermezzo', I would like to argue that a portion of therapeutic effects of high fantasy results from its kinship with other arts and from the nature of art therapy, which appears interwoven with bibliotherapy in the (otherworldly) realm of Faërie in a singular way. An inherent element of visual and musical arts generically ingrained in fantasy, just as much as in poetry and myth, might provide, as this chapter aims to suggest, a literary environment for art therapy, enhancing therapeutic properties of fantasy literature as an art *per se*.

Art therapy obviously combines art and psychotherapy, and 'ideally each is enhanced by its coupling with the other'.[1] 'Art involves the creation of aesthetically stimulating representations of reality', whereas 'psychotherapy entails the treatment of psychologically disturbed individuals', John Birtchnell, an art therapist, explains.[2] At face value these contrasting disciplines have little in common; however, as Birtchnell matter-off-factly observes, 'both are concerned with emotional issues and the practitioners of each need to be sensitive and intuitive'.[3] The combination of art and therapy is likely to evoke cathartic reactions that may make way for treatment and healing, greatly facilitating clinical medicine procedures. In his book *Catharsis: On the Healing Power of Nature and Art*, Andrzej Szczeklik (1938–2012), a cardiologist and a writer, points to the common roots of art and medicine, arguing that visual and musical arts, as well as 'the art of words', used to assist mankind in finding man's place in universe and in divining the harmony of spheres, which was to resound in the human mind and body.[4] 'The sense of analogy between the structure and rhythm of universe and the rhythms of human

---

1 John Birtchnell, 'Art Therapy as a Form of Psychotherapy' [in:] *Art as Therapy: An Introduction to the Use of Art as a Therapeutic Technique*, Tessa Dalley, ed. (London: Tavistock, 1984), pp. 30–45, 30.

2 Birtchnell, ibid., p. 30.

3 Birtchnell, ibid., p. 31.

4 Szczeklik, *Katharsis. O uzdrowicielskiej mocy natury i sztuki*, [*Catharsis: On the Healing Power of Nature and Art.*; trans. mine], (Kraków: Wydawnictwo Znak, 2003), p. 17.

body, between the macrocosm and the microcosm, has always inspired both philosophers and physicians,' Szczeklik notes.[5] 'Man used to harmonize with universe, and an illness was a sign of disharmony, a dissonance with the world and universe,' he adds, referring to the ancient theory represented by the Boethian tenet of *harmonia divina, harmonia mundana, harmonia humana* and *harmonia instrumentalis*, as mentioned in Chapter Four of this book.[6] The motions of the celestial bodies and the revolution and rotation of the planets around the Sun is reflected, Szczeklik argues, in the blood circulation system, and is, likewise, immersed in music and perfect harmony, which, although never heard by us, lies at the very basis of the existence of universe, animals and human beings.[7] Indeed, rarely do we hear the rhythm of our hearts or the swoosh of our blood, but if we do, it is usually in times of crisis, signaling some psychic or somatic turbulence or illness, the internal harmony having been violated.[8]

The element of art in art therapy corresponds perhaps to the resources of nature, with its self-healing capacity, present in medical treatment and superior to medical science, inasmuch as musical and visual arts operate on the primordial, non-verbal, sensory and spontaneous basis, conducting therapy in an intuitive rather than prescriptive way. This Hippocratic belief in *vis medicatrix naturae*, the healing power of nature, heralds yet again the effect of catharsis, whose role has been highlighted in the previous chapter as a major tenet of Vygotsky's psychology of art, including the psychology of literature, and is examined in Chapter Seven as a crucial element of therapy through Faërie with regard to the works of the Inklings and of Le Guin. To the ancient Pythagoreans, catharsis of the soul and of the body was 'man's loftiest aim'; and, according to Aristotle, 'Pythagoreans used medicine to purge the body [*catharsis peri to soma* – the Latin *purgatio*], and music to purify the souls [*catharsis peri to psyche* – the Latin *purificatio*]', in accordance with the theory of ethos, which is discussed in Chapter Six of this book.[9] Novalis, a German poet and philosopher of the early Romantic period, goes so far as to say that 'every disease is a musical problem, and every treatment

---

5   Szczeklik, ibid., p. 17.
6   Szczeklik, ibid., p. 17, trans. mine.
7   Szczeklik, ibid., p. 74.
8   Szczeklik, ibid., p. 74.
9   Enrico Fubini, *Historia estetyki muzycznej* [The History of Musical Aesthetics; trans. mine], trans. Z. Skowron, (Kraków: Wydawnictwo Musica Jagiellonica, 1997), p. 31. Artistotle's words quoted after Władysław Tatarkiewicz, *Estetyka starożytna* [The Ancient Aesthetics; trans. mine], (Wrocław: Zakład Narodowy im. Ossolińskich, 1960), p. 94; cf. Szczeklik, *Catharsis*, p. 81.

is a musical solution.'[10] Music, which in the Greek culture inherently overlapped with other arts: dance, song, and poetry united symbiotically in *choreia*, was thus a sister of medicine.[11]

A valuable auxiliary to clinical therapy, 'art activity provides a concrete rather than verbal medium through which a person can achieve both conscious and unconscious expression, and can be used as an important agent for therapeutic change', Tessa Dalley observes.[12] That non-verbal mode of communication, preceding the use of spoken or written language, draws on the recognition of the fact that man's most fundamental feelings and thoughts, derived from the unconscious, tend to reach expression first in images rather than words, Dalley remarks.[13] According to Margaret Naumburg, art therapy rests on the knowledge that 'every individual, whether trained or untrained in art, has a latent capacity to project their inner conflicts into visual form; as the individuals picture such inner experiences, they often become more verbally articulate.'[14] Thus, an image seems to stimulate and drive words; and, unsurprisingly, so does music. The plasticity and musicality of literature, especially of fantasy fiction, are, of course, mediated verbally, and hence, work indirectly as a secondary effect to bibliotherapy, yet they might foster the therapeutic power of the genre. Even though the plasticity and musicality of fantasy literature emerge from words rather than pictures or sounds, they do create pictures and sounds in the minds of the readers and listeners, thus engaging art in bibliotherapy, as they liberate the artistic re-creations or, to use Ingarden's term, concretizations of the pictures and sounds described by language from any rigid frames and the limitations of the primary world, so that their realization depends entirely on the individual person's imaginative ability to visualize images and design sounds.

It would be naïve, none the less, to assume that art is synonymous with therapy, and that any artistic activity has necessarily some healing properties; for this would erroneously imply an automatic fusion between art and therapy, and a relationship in which the latter is simply the consequence of the former. Still, there is a considerable therapeutic potential residing in art, due to its non-verbal expressiveness, primordial and spontaneous nature, and its immediate availability

---

10 Novalis (Georg Philipp Friedrich Freiherr von Hardenberg), qtd. in Oliver Sack's *A Leg to Stand On* (New York: Touchstone, 1998), p. 99; cf. Szczeklik, *Catharsis*, p. 88.

11 Szczeklik, *Catharsis*, p. 76.

12 Dalley, 'Introduction' to *Art as Therapy: An Introduction to the Use of Art as a Therapeutic Technique*, p. xi.

13 Dalley, ibid., p. xii.

14 Naumburg, *Dynamically Oriented Art Therapy: Its Principles and Practice*, p. 103.

at the very least; therefore some artistic elements embedded in literature might partake of and contribute to literature's therapeutic properties. Should literature be approached as an art, as the ancient Greek tradition saw it, promoting the idea of the symbiotic relationship of music, dance, image and words blended in *choreia*, (which was also a form of *therapeia)*, the power of words painting images, words playing music and dancing dances could perhaps create an environment for an imaginative art therapy. The Greek term *poiēsis* (Latin: *poesis*), which later developed in English into poesy, and finally, poetry, can be translated as a 'creation or production' (in Greek *poiein* is to create, produce), and originally refers to any form of creation, in this case any artistic mode.[15] Another Greek word *techne* (art, craft, skill) likewise refers to art, including literature, but does not name it distinctively; and its derivative, *logotechnia* (*techne* combined with *logos* – word, meaning,) denotes literature and 'contains the notion of art of [verbal] expression', resting on 'the contribution of oral transmission originating principally from the folksong.'[16]

When approaching literature as a form of art, one must not fail to do justice to the connections which the literary narrative may have with therapy, resulting from literature's inherent affinity to visual and musical arts, disregarding for a moment the therapeutic effects produced by its very logos. Verbal communication in therapy tends to be most valued in the clinical practice; yet non-verbal expression through imagery, symbols and sounds concretised by the reader or listener in their mind may also trigger some indirect therapy and must not be discarded. 'The ambiguity of art in general places it at a tangent, detached from the mainstream of communication, as people have little confidence in understanding its meaning or message', Dalley remarks; nevertheless, it is of great import to therapy.[17] Fairy stories, which belong to the realm of Faërie, and are marked by Fantasy and mythopoeia, represent the genre that is, like poetry, probably the closest to art, owing to its singularly imaginative, creative and expressive power, called by Tolkien an art indeed, (the highest form of art, to be precise, 'indeed the most nearly pure form, and so, when achieved, the most potent'.[18] Therefore,

---

15 *Online Etymology Dictionary*, Douglas Harper, ed. http://www.etymonline.com/Etym, accessed 23 April 2016. '*Ut pictura poesis*', the famous Latin sentence, quoted by Horace in his *Ars Poetica*, also emphasises a kinship between literature and other arts: 'as is painting, so is poetry': poetry, that is imaginative writing, is like painting.

16 Kōnstantinos Dēmaras, *A History of Modern Greek Literature* (New York: SUNY Press, 1972), p. ix.

17 Dalley, 'Introduction' to *Art as Therapy*, p. xiv.

18 Tolkien, 'On Fairy-Stories', p. 115, quoted in Chapter Four as well.

they seem to play an essential role in bibliotherapy as a special vehicle of fantasy narrative related to art therapy. Discussed below are two sample forms of interartistically therapeutic properties of fantasy literature: ekphrasis, and the techniques of sfumato and chiaroscuro, which dwell in visual arts but pertain to literature, and thus betray its belonging therein, as analyzed on the basis of the works of Tolkien and Le Guin.

Ekphrasis in fantasy literature

An interesting case of artistic cross-narrative, that is the narrative that creatively engages its various verbal and non-verbal modes of expression, and thus endorses synaesthetic experience, is ekphrasis (in Greek: ἔκφρασις means description; the Latin counterpart in rhetoric being *descriptio*).[19] Chris Baldick's *Oxford Dictionary of Literary Terms* defines it as 'a verbal description of, or meditation upon, a non-verbal work of art, real or imagined, usually a painting or sculpture.'[20] Ekphrasis can be a description of a work belonging to visual arts or music, the latter being perhaps rarer in literature; and the non-verbal subject matter that inspires the writer may exist as a work of art or music, providing a firm point of reference, or may bud in the writer's imagination as a yet unrealized project. Ekphrasis appears as a compound discourse, which is both expository, (as it describes and explains a work of art, dance or music) and narrative, (for it often provides a verbal account of events illustrated by picture, movement or music, expressed by verbs of motion and action). Not only does ekphrasis provide a special example of an interconnectedness of various verbal and non-verbal modes of communication, but it also seems to partake in the Bakhtinian 'interindividuality' of signs and language.[21] This is so because ekphrastic descriptions often bridge the works of different authors and draw on the content that has already been expressed by another person, which is the case when ekphrasis refers to someone else's work of art. Thus, the content which is 'located outside the "soul" of the speaker', as Bakhtin says, becomes the interindividual subject matter of ekphrasis, having been borrowed as an inspiration by an author of the ekphrastic work.[22]

19 'Ekphrasis' [in:] *The Westminster Dictionary of New Testament and Early Christian Literature*, David Edward Aune, ed. (Louisville, KY: Westminster John Knox Press, 2003), pp. 143–144.
20 Chris Baldick, *Oxford Dictionary of Literary Terms*, p. 104.
21 Bakhtin, *Speech Genres and Other Late Essays*, pp. 121–122, cf. Chapter Four.
22 Bakhtin, ibid., p. 122.

It ought to be emphasized that, although ekphrasis is primarily identified as a verbal description of a work of art, in its extended meaning it also embraces a visual or a musical description of a literary text, the latter type of ekphrasis being as ancient as the former. An early example of visual ekphrasis can be the group of paintings on the Pompeian walls, representing the scenes from Homer's *Odyssey* and Vergil's *Aeneid*. There is no other universally acknowledged name for this type of visual ekphrasis, although some critics have introduced the term 'reverse ekphrasis' or *eidetikos ekphrasis* ('eidetic ekphrasis') (in Greek: description pertaining to images), with regard to visual illustrations of literary texts.[23] Examples of ekphrastic music, in turn, include such famous pieces of programme music as Pyotr Tchaikovsky's symphonic poems *The Tempest, Hamlet*, and *Romeo and Julia* (illustrating Shakespeare's masterpieces) or Tchaikovsky's ballets, e.g. *The Swan Lake* and *The Sleeping Beauty* (inspired by folk tales), to name but a few.

A specifically literary form of ekphrasis featuring a non-existing work of art, which is imagined by a character in a text is what Frederick de Armas refers to as 'Ur-ekphrasis' or 'a description of the creation of an art object in the character's mind'.[24] In the case of Ur-ekphrasis, De Armas claims, 'the imagination [of the character] has as one of its functions to foreground the imaginative qualities of the text itself'.[25] Multiple instances of Ur-ekphrasis in literature include Robert Browning's dramatic monologue 'My Last Duchess' (based on a painting of the Duchess, possibly Lucrezia de Medici, by a fictional artist and monk 'Frà Pandolf', and a sculpture of Neptune by a fictional artist Claus of Innsbruck); Charlotte Brontë's novel *Vilette*, (whose fragment describes a portrait of Cleopatra exhibited in a museum in Vilette aka Brussels); Oscar Wilde's only novel *The Picture of Dorian Gray* (describing the portrait of the protagonist painted by his friend, Basil Hallward); and Tolkien's allegorical story 'Leaf by Niggle', (telling a

---

23 In Greek *idos* means 'form or image'. Cf. Patrick Hunt, 2005 'Ekphrasis or Not? Ovid in Pieter Bruegel the Elder's *Landscape with the Fall of Icarus*', 2005, accessed 2 May 2016, http://traumwerk.stanford.edu/philolog/2005/11/ekphrasis_ovid_in_pieter_bruegel. html. Interestingly, there exists 'eidetic psychotherapy', 'a method of psychotherapy that makes systematic use of the natural images of consciousness in the identification and resolution of psychological disturbance.' That image or idetic (eidetic) is a 'self-organizing nucleus within the psyche', and has 'a visual core that is either the memory of an actual event in the past or an image from the unconscious,' to which 'profound meaning is attached'; cf. *A Dictionary of Psychotherapy*, Sue Walrond-Skinner ed. (London: Routledge, 2014), pp. 111–112.

24 Frederick De Armas, *Ekphrasis in the Age of Cervantes* (Lewisburg: Bucknell University Press, 2005), p. 241.

25 De Armas, *Ekphrasis*, p. 242.

story about Niggle, a painter who works on the canvas of his life, representing a tree with beautiful leaves, which he never manages to finish).[26]

Ekphrasis defines a multitude of literary works from antiquity to late postmodernity, and, according to Peter Wagner, its notion extends also to non-literary texts, such as critical assessments, reviews, or history of art accounts, for, in its broadest sense, ekphrasis designates 'any set-piece of vivid description generally', thus laying foundations for inter-art scholarship.[27] This universal understanding and application of ekphrasis results from the fundamental role of images and imagination, which, as the ancient writer Pseudo-Longinus observes in his treatise 'On the Sublime', constitute 'mental representations applied to every idea of the mind, in whatever form it presents itself, which gives birth to speech.'[28] If human thoughts and ideas correspond so closely to images, as Pseudo-Longinus suggests, and thence inspire verbal expression, then the indispensable role of ekphrasis in its broadest sense appears obvious. Pseudo-Longinus also remarks that 'an image has one purpose with the orators and another with the poets, and the design of the poetical image is enthrallment, of the rhetorical – vivid description. Both, however, seek to stir passions and emotions.'[29] Ekphrasis can therefore serve as a rhetorical device and a mere description, as well as an expressive and suggestive medium of translating images into words.

Scholars have coined various terms referring to interartistic relationships and the effects of synthesis and synaesthesia, for instance: 'word painting', 'the sculpted word', 'literary pictorialism', 'picturacy', 'a concert of paintings' or 'sonic texts'.[30] Picturacy, a term coined by James Heffernan, is 'the capacity to interpret

---

26 The correct form of the Italian name would be 'Pandolfo'. In the text of 'My Last Duchess' the Duke comments on the painting of his late wife: 'I said Frà Pandolf by design.'
27 Peter Wagner, ed. *Icons – Texts – Iconotexts: Essays on Ekphrasis and Intermediary* (New York: de Gruyter, 1996), p. 14.
28 Pseudo-Longinus, 'Perihupsos' ['On the Sublime'], trans. W. Rhys Roberts (Cambridge: Cambridge University Press, 2011), chapter XV, p. 8.
29 Pseudo-Longinus, ibid., p. 8.
30 Cf. Jean H. Hagstrum, *The Sister Arts: The Tradition of Literary Pictorialism and English Poetry from Dryden to Gray* (Chicago: University of Chicago Press, 1987); Siglind Bruhn, 'A Concert of Paintings: Musical Ekphrasis in the Twentieth Century' [in:] *Poetics Today* 22:3, 2001, pp. 551–605; Siglind Bruhn, ed. *Sonic Transformations of Literary Texts: From Program Music to Musical Ekphrasis* [in:] *Interplay: Music in Interdisciplinary Dialogue*, vol. 6. (Hillsdale, NY: Pendragon Press, 2008); Grant F. Scott, *The Sculpted Word: Keats, Ekphrasis, and the Visual Arts* (Hanover, NH: University Press of New England, 1994); James A. W. Heffernan, *Cultivating Picturacy. Visual Art and Verbal Interventions* (Waco: Baylor University Press, 2006); Stanley Sadie, ed. *Word*

pictures', which, as Heffernan argues, 'must be cultivated and deserves a name', just as much as literacy does, for 'learning to decode the language of pictures resembles the process of learning to read', he concludes.[31] In the same vein, one might perhaps introduce the notion of 'musicacy', or an ability to understand and interpret music, based on the knowledge of its rhetoric and language.

Both 'picturacy' and 'musicacy' seem to correspond to Ingarden's notion of the 'spots of indeterminacy', within which the reader employs picturacy and musicacy to concretize verbal descriptions of non-verbal arts, as discussed in Chapter Four, and, obviously, neither picturacy nor musicacy would operate without ekphrasis. A popular micro-genre that forms an image of a non-verbal work in the mind of the reader, ekphrasis is 'an intersection of the verbal and the visual' (or the aural), whose aim is 'not only to provide astute details of a work, but to share the emotional experience and content with someone who has never encountered the work in question.'[32] Ekphrasis is thus not merely a descriptive but frequently a narrative rhetorical device. It is 'an art that describes art', Ryan Welsh observes, and an art that narrates art; a fulfillment of the Horatian '*ut pictura poesis*' principle, which emphasizes a close relationship and equality of *poesis* (understood as imaginative writing) and painting; a form of Plato's mimesis (imitation or representation of nature) and diegesis (narration or report), and the meeting space of the visual (or aural) and the linguistic.[33] 'Painting is silent poetry; and poetry is painting that speaks (with the gift of speech),' remarks Simonides of Ceos, capturing the ekphrastic nature of art and language.[34]

The first masterpiece of ekphrasis known in the Western literature is Homer's description of Achilles' shield being forged by Hephaestus, provided in the eighteenth book of the *Iliad* (lines 478–608), which established the enduring tradition of ekphrastic writing. A *locus classicus* of ekphrasis, this seminal description received its 20th century rendition in W. H. Auden's poem 'The Shield of Achilles',

---

Painting. The New Grove Dictionary of Music and Musicians, 2nd ed., vol. 27 (Macmillan 2001).

31 James A. W. Heffernan, *Cultivating Picturacy,* a book jacket.

32 Ryan Welsh, 'Ekphrasis' [in:] *Theories of Media: Keywords Glossary,* University of Chicago 2007, accessed 23 April 2016, http://humanities.uchicago.edu/faculty/mitchell/glossary2004/ekphrasis.htm.

33 Welsh, 'Ekphrasis'. Plato introduces the notions of mimesis and diegesis, used also by Aristotle, in his *Ion* and in *The Republic* (Books II, III, and X).

34 Words attributed to Simonides by Plutarch, quoted in Plutarch's *Glory of Athens* [in:] *Lyra Graeca* [Greek Lyric], vol. 2. (London: Heinemann, 1952), p. 259.

which differs radically from Homer's treatment of ekphrasis. Modern ekphrastic poetry, especially that written after 1800, has departed from the ancient tradition of focusing on elaborate descriptions, aiming instead at a deeper insight into the well-known works of art by not merely describing but rather reinterpreting, inhabiting, contemplating and addressing them from a fresher perspective.

The triumph of pictures in today's iconosphere, that is man's entire visual environment, has established a reality infused with images, which verbal language attempts to mediate and translate into words, and this has necessitated picturacy, whose role today proves as vital as that of literacy.[35] Richard Macksey observes that ekphrastic writing 'celebrates the power of the silent image, even as it tries to circumscribe that power with the authority of the word,' defied, undermined and deconstructed though that authority has been in the age of postmodernity.[36] In so doing, ekphrasis sets to overcome an inherent conflict between the word and image (or between the word and music that evokes mental images), thus staging 'a battle for mastery between the image and the word,' Heffernan notes.[37]

In this book ekphrasis is considered with regard to literature only, as framed by imaginative narrative, where ekphrasis makes a frequent 'excursus within the larger traditional genres, whether in verse or prose.'[38] It is, therefore, Macksey argues, an important 'appendix or digression that contains further exposition of some point or topic.'[39] Since it expands on a point or topic being discussed by the poet or writer referring to an object of art, ekphrasis endorses plasticity of imagination, interartistic perception and expression, as well as a cross-narrative synaesthesia. Bridging the non-verbal and the verbal, it mediates and helps integrate human narrative into one discourse. In the age that has emerged from the 'pictorial turn', the significance of ekphrasis seems even greater, as it provides a tool for perceiving and experiencing the contemporary culture. The 'pictorial or iconic turn', according to Mitchell, does not merely amount to a 'restoration of a naïve mimesis, copy or correspondence theories of representation,' but affects contemporary narrative with its, often symbolic, 'imagist' power, whereby signs

---

35 Heffernan, *Cultivating Picturacy*, p. 8. Iconosphere [in Polish ikonosfera] is the term coined by Mieczysław Porębski (1921–2012), a Polish art historian and critic, in his book *Ikonosfera* (Warsaw: PIW, 1972).

36 Richard Macksey, 'Review of James Heffernan's *Museum of Words*, [in:] *Comparative Literature Issue*, vol. 10, no. 4, pp. 1010–1015, 1010.

37 Heffernan, *Museum of Words: The Poetics of Ekphrasis from Homer to* Ashbery (Chicago and London: University of Chicago Press, 1993), p. xi.

38 Macksey, 'Review of James Heffernan's *Museum of Words*, p. 1010.

39 Macksey, ibid., p. 1012.

may capture the evanescent, and mediate the inexpressible.[40] On the one hand, the shortcomings of language disable it from doing justice to a work of visual arts or music; yet on the other, language painting enables far more visual or auditory concretisations than an artifact.

Polemicizing with Mitchell, who does not clarify a distinction between literature and painting, and remarks that any image is 'linguistic in its inner workings', Stefan Beyst applies the division into mediated and unmediated mimesis accounting for the nature of literature and plastic arts respectively, and notes that the world which is disclosed by temporal and non-temporal arts is essentially the same, the only difference dwelling in the way this world is reached: 'whereas painting and music have only one entrance gate, literature has many.'[41] Beyst classifies visual arts in the same line as music, as opposed to literature, unlike Ingarden, for instance, who argues that a concretization of music, as noted on a sheet, depends to a great extent on the musician's interpretation, and offers some liberty as well, just like literature, which painting does not.

From among the three arts: painting, music, and literature, it is literature, none the less, according to both Beyst and Ingarden, which activates the person's (the reader's or listener's) imagination the most when concretizing descriptive signs. Tolkien also emphasizes the superiority of literature over visual arts with regard to its imaginative power and creative impact on the recipient, observing that 'in human art Fantasy is a thing best left to words, to true literature. In painting, for instance, the visible presentation of the fantastic image is technically too easy; the hand tends to outrun the mind, even to overthrow it. Silliness or morbidity are frequent results.'[42] Interestingly, however, Tolkien, a skilled illustrator, created his own illustrations for many of his fairy stories and epics, including numerous maps of Arda, pictures presenting borderlands of Fairy Land (Faërie), and plentiful illustrations of characters, places and objects featured in *The Hobbit*, *The Silmarillion* and *The Lord of the Rings*.[43] Still, he believed that language is a far better tool of demonstrating and preserving the Enchantment of Faërie, despite the genre's hardly describable nature, than visual arts, as the job of visualizing

40 Mitchell, *Picture Theory*, p. 16; cf. Stefan Beyst: 'W. J. T. Mitchell and the Image: The Discovery of the Imagetext', a review of Mitchell's Iconology: *Images, Text, Ideology*, and of his *Picture Theory. Essays on Verbal and Visual Representation*, http://d-sites. net/english/mitchell.htm, July 2010; accessed 2r April 2016.

41 Mitchell, *Iconology: Image, Text, Ideology*, p. 71. Beyst, 'W. J. T. Mitchell and the Image.'

42 Tolkien, 'On Fairy-Stories', p. 140.

43 Cf. over 100 'Images by J. R. R. Tolkien' at Tolkien Gateway, http://tolkiengateway.net/ wiki/Category:Images_by_ J. R. R._Tolkien, accessed 23 April 2016.

the Secondary Worlds as initially imagined by the writer depends on the reader and informs the uniqueness of Faërie, whose intangible realm nears tangibility in the reader's mind.

Exploring the nature of literary and visual arts, Beyst speaks of 'images that are directly perceptible', as rendered by visual arts, (an instance of unmediated mimesis), and 'images that are conjured up by words', or created in verbal language, (mediated mimesis), and discerns the 'spatiotemporal properties of image-conjuring signs (in spoken as well as written texts)' from the 'spatiotemporal properties of the images', which belong to the unmediated world.[44] That literature 'conjures up' images, not only mental but also visual ones, is obvious and indisputable, Beyst asserts, and it is testified, for instance, by 'the fact that we are mostly disappointed when we see the screen version of a novel.'[45] Literature differs from painting, he continues, in that the former mediates visual and mental images, whereas the latter represents them directly.[46] While dance, theatre performance, film and opera provide ready-made moving images, and instrumental music can well evoke them, as these are all temporal arts, painting and sculpting do not, as they produce single freezes or polyptychs.[47] In its rendition of ekphrasis, literature is also 'always seriously handicapped' due to the 'discrete nature of verbal language', Beyst observes; however, it is capable of conjuring up images for all the senses (even the interoceptive ones,) Beyst asserts; whereas paintings and sculptures 'can only show visual appearances, and music only aural ones.'[48]

Ekphrastic writing mediates and verbalizes visual and mental images, which, as Macksey argues, are not of merely instrumental or ornamental value, but which may serve as a synecdoche, 'embedding the world which ekphrastic passages represent.'[49] That figurative and emblematic role of ekphrasis, as constituted by Homer's precedent, can be a pivot supporting a literary work, foreshadowing and encapsulating its essence, and representing a perception of the world underlying that work. The shield of Achilles in Homer's rendition embodies art as well as the poet's conception of the world captured within the shield's nine layers, and so do many other ekphrastic passages in literature, which, following suit, complement and illustrate a given narrative with images that help convey its message. It

---

44 Beyst, 'W. J. T. Mitchell and the Image'.
45 Beyst, ibid.
46 Beyst, ibid.
47 Cf. Beyst, ibid.
48 Beyst, ibid.
49 Macksey, 'Review of James Heffernan's *Museum of Words*', p. 1010.

seems that, depending on the scope of ekphrasis in a text, literary ekphrasis may work as a symbolic 'cameo', a collection of concatenated 'cameos' or as an entire 'canvass' of emblematic representation, into which a given narrative is inscribed. Hence, one could perhaps venture to say that ekphrasis can sometimes serve as a peculiar case of interartistic 'conceit', defining and capturing the whole idea of a literary work, numerous instances of which might be identified among the ekphrastic works mentioned above, suffice it to mention Keats's ode, in which the Grecian urn epitomizes the beauty, truth, stillness, expressiveness and immortality of art. The last part of this chapter focuses on the elements of light and dark featured in the ekphrastic narratives of Tolkien and of Le Guin, suggesting that their artistic representations may serve as metaphors, visually and symbolically enhancing the philosophies which define the described otherworlds of Faërie.

Returning to the relationship between ekphrasis and literature, it is important to observe that, by virtue of its kinship to non-verbal arts, which provide a source of inspiration and oftentimes a subject matter for literature, all imaginative literature, recognized by Horace, Simonides, and many other thinkers as *poesis*, appears intrinsically ekphrastic and synaesthetic.[50] Even if a literary work does not explicitly draw on an existing work of visual art or music, its imagery inescapably contains ekphrasis (description) of a world – the primary, 'off-the-peg' reality, or a secondary one, usually called fantastic, as perceived, in the former case, or conceived, in the latter case, by the writer. Hence, it seems that ekphrasis is present, to a greater or lesser extent, in all genres of imaginative (and also non-fictional) literature, as they all partake in and contribute to literature's pictoriality and, in a way, also to its musicality. These two terms: pictoriality and musicality, proposed here as mediators of the interartistic and ekphrastic nature of literature, may need clarification, and are therefore discussed below.

Pictoriality is understood here as a literary quality of being pictorial, that is of suggesting or conveying visual images. Since this book addresses the genre of high fantasy fiction rooted in Faërie, (as variously endorsed by the Inklings and by Le Guin), the source of its mythopoeic pictoriality lies in primordial mythological iconoscape, which has been reflected in folk tales and literary fantasy narrative.[51] The pictoriality of literature results from the obvious fact that verbal language

---

50 Horace, *Ars Poetica*. According to Plutarch, Simonides was the first thinker to compare painting with poetry (*ut pictura poesis*), cf. *De Gloria Atheniensium* 3.346f.

51 'Iconoscape' is a term introduced by Professor W. J. T. Mitchell in his lecture 'Iconoscape: Method, Madness, and Montage', a part of a work in progress, delivered at the Institute of Fine Arts, New York, and accessed on 22 July 2016 at https://vimeo.com/161061426.

itself is largely pictorial, and that the plasticity of language may find its expression in a creative iconographic imagery. When used in its original context of the theory of visual culture, pictoriality refers to 'the consolidated depictive aspectivity of configuration, and one of the aspectively interdetermined successions that constitute visual culture, especially in the context of the iconographic succession.'[52] Pictoriality rests on ekphrasis, inasmuch as it is 'recursively consolidated as depiction', and has its 'occasionality, particularity, singularity, and intentionality in replication, as well as its conventionality and communicability.'[53] Whitney Davies notes that 'pictoriality germinates in an event of seeing-as; an autonomic happening in vision. It is an unpredictable occurrence, but not inexplicable or ungovernable: there are many ways to provoke seeing-as, and to guide it.'[54] Literature can be precisely the medium of depiction and description, as it encourages and guides the process of visualisation and 'seeing-as', despite it being autonomic and largely unpredictable. This is possible thanks to the unique attribute of a literary work of art that Ingarden calls 'spots of indeterminacy', in which the 'undetermined successions that constitute visual culture', as quoted above, which are visually indeterminable within the boundaries of verbal language, assume specific shapes and shades as they become concretized in the imaginative mind of the reader. Moreover, literary narrative allows for a replication of that 'happening in vision', and for its 'recursive consolidation', to borrow Davies's terms.[55]

In addition, 'pictoriality seems to be one-off: it happens anew with every look; and it is context-specific' and reader or beholder-specific, too.'[56] Although Davies discusses pictoriality with reference to visual culture and visual arts, he acknowledges its relevance to language and literature, remarking that 'the occasionality of pictoriality has a relevant parallel in natural language, that is in speech, and, to a lesser extent, in writing, even if it is only a partial one;' for the pictoriality of visual arts is its very essence, while the pictoriality of literature may constitute one of its secondary, yet by no means negligible qualities.[57] Among literary genres poetry appears most pictorial, and, as Mitchell observes, 'we tend to think [...] that to compare poetry with painting is to make a metaphor, while to differentiate

---

52 Whitney Davies, *A General Theory of Visual Culture* (Princeton: Princeton University Press, 2011), p. 155.
53 Davies, ibid., p. 155.
54 Davies, ibid., p. 156.
55 Cf. Davies, ibid., p. 156.
56 Davies, ibid., p. 156.
57 Davies, ibid., p. 156.

poetry from painting is to state a literal truth.'[58] The ekphrastic nature of poetry, the genre of remarkable figurativeness and plasticity, remains unchallenged, but can perhaps be attributed to some other genres as well. Beyst, for instance, argues that, apart from poetry, also novels provide a natural generic environment for ekphrasis in literature.[59]

As for musicality, in this book it denotes a literary attribute of being connected to music, which is not merely revealed by a melodiousness of language and the rhythm of its prosody, but also, perhaps more importantly, by suggesting and referring to sound patterns and other musical phenomena, thus intimating quasi-musical compositions that offer to be concretised by the reader. Literature-inspired music that may sound in the reader's mind is 'intimate' and 'inner', and its realisation depends on both the level of musicality of a given literary text, and on an individual reader's own musicality, which ought to be both receptive and creative.

An interesting aspect of literary musicality might be derived from Peter Kivy's theory of literature being a performance art. Kivy argues that the musicality of literature stems from the basic fact that literature, just like music, is a performative art, and this does not only regard drama and poetry (whose musicality and performative nature are usually acknowledged), but also novels.[60] According to Kivy, fictional narrative corresponds to a musical score: the literary text, he argues, is not a 'token of the literary work', but, like a musical score, it is a 'character in a notation for generating instances of the work.'[61] Discussing Kivy's theory, Anthony Gritten expands on the affinity between music and literature in the following way:

> Tokens of the musical work are performances, and tokens of the novel are readings, construed as datable events. Silent readings of the novel are analogous to performances of musical works 'in the head' by score readers. Performances of literary works 'in the head' can be seen as expressive 'soundings' that, as in the case of 'soundings' of musical works by score readers, embody an interpretation of the overall sense of the work.'[62]

Literature's musicality may thus partly result from the performative nature of the process of reading a text, which, to Kivy, resembles reading a score; yet, as this

---

58 Mitchell, *Iconology: Image, Text, Ideology* (Chicago: University of Chicago Press, 1986), p. 49.
59 Beyst, 'W. J. T. Mitchell and the Image'.
60 Peter Kivy, *The Performance of Reading: An Essay in the Philosophy of Literature* (Malden, MA: Blackwell, 2006), p. 12.
61 Kivy, ibid., p. 12.
62 Anthony Gritten, 'Literary Music: Writing Music in Contemporary Fiction' [in:] *Journal of Aesthetics and Art Criticism*, Vol. 66, 2008, pp. 99–102, 100.

book seeks to argue, it predominantly resides in the 'music-making' capacity of literature. The musical dimension that may accompany the verbal 'performance', all construed in the mind of the reader, could perhaps enrich the literary perception with an abstract affective quality of music. Kivy points to a therapeutic effect of musical experience *per se*, which does not completely lose its power when interwoven into literary narrative:

> Listening to absolute music is, among other things, the experience of going from our world, with all of its trials, tribulations, and ambiguities, to another world, a world of pure sonic structure, that, because it need not be interpreted as a representation or description of our world, but can be appreciated on its own terms alone, gives us the sense of liberation that I have found appropriate to analogize with the pleasurable experience we get in the process of going from a state of intense pain to its cessation.[63]

As Kivy seems to argue, it is not only programme music, (which illustrates certain events or themes), but also absolute music, (which is not guided by any other-than-sonic material, and, hence, arguably more demanding, imaginative and affective), that offers 'liberty' and may help one come to terms with a difficult experience.[64] This is actually the basis for music therapy, known since the beginning of man's civilisation. Music expressed by means of words that are to be 'performed' in the 'performance of reading' is also to be imagined and 'performed' in the mind of the reader. The musical element of verbal narrative may thus add up to the therapeutic effect of the narrative itself. As Claude Levi-Strauss argues, 'since music is the only language with the contradictory attributes of being intelligible and untranslatable, the musical creator is a being comparable to the gods, and music itself the supreme mystery of the science of man.'[65] Musical themes in a literary work of art, although verbalized, hint at the untranslatability of music and at is divine provenience, viewed by Boethius in terms of *musica mundana, musica humana* and *musica instrumentalis,* and point to the genius of its creation, which is one of the greatest mysteries of mankind, fully unleashing man's artistic imagination and touching upon the element of divinity itself. The potential of music, implanted also into a literary work of art, and, specifically, fantasy narrative, as highlighted in this book, finds its own uses in music therapy and, perhaps also in bibliotherapy.

Pictoriality and musicality of fantasy narrative are addressed in some detail in the following sections of this chapter, whose thesis is that this genre combines

---

63 Qtd. in Stephen Benson, *Literary Music: Writing Music in Contemporary Fiction* (Aldershot: Ashgate Publish ing Limited, 2006), p. 123.
64 Kivy, *The Performance of Reading,* p. 20.
65 Qtd. in Anthony Storr's *Music and the Mind,* p. ix.

interartistic qualities of poetry and story that spring from myths and their kin, and has a peculiar image-conjuring and sound-making ability, and a 'power of making the visions [and sounds] of "fantasy" immediately effective by the will', the properties which lie at the heart of genuine Faërie.[66] 'All things may be fore-thought in music or foreshown in vision from afar,' Tolkien adds in *The Silmaril-lion*, pointing, as it seems, at the importance of musicality and pictoriality of high fantasy, discussed in more detail further on in this chapter.

Finally, a key question arises whether ekphrasis is anyhow related to therapy, for it is the latter that is the subject matter of this book. In her study *Art Therapy: Research and Evidence-based Practice*, Andrea Gilroy defines ekphrasis as 'a ver-bal recreation of a visual artwork or a verbal evocation of something seen for others who cannot see it', which 'involves a translation from one language to another, from the visual to the verbal' and which 'enables the discovery, articu-lation and intellectual understanding of meaning.'[67] Gilroy refers to ekphrasis as 'artwriting' and mentions its role in art therapy in the context of co-creating artworks by clients in the process of a therapeutic session.[68] According to Gilroy, ekphrasis or 'artwriting' helps the clients to 'interrogate' artworks, and their in-terrogation depends on their individual approach, life situation, time, and place, and corresponds to the needs of every single person.[69] Thanks to 'artwriting', 'new ways of looking [at] and seeing' art emerge, for the client is granted liberty of imagining the described work during the 'pre-iconographic narrative' stage of art therapy and can actively participate in 'the necessary value-free identification of what an artwork actually is.'[70] That identification may aid an identification of the client's emotions and needs, which is the core of therapy, and which is used, for instance, in Hanscarl Leuner's Guided Affective Imagery therapy (GAI), also known as catathymic-imagery psychotherapy, akin to psychoanalytic methods of therapy, especially to Bleuler's depth psychology.

Leuner defines catathymic imagery, a term introduced first by Ernst Maier, as 'inner visions which occur in accordance with and are related to affect and

---

66 Beyst, 'W. J. T. Mitchell and the Image.' The last quoted phrase comes from Tolkien's essay 'On Fairy-Stories', p. 152.
67 Andrea Gilroy, *Art Therapy: Research and Evidence-based Practice* (London: Sage Pub-lications, 2006), p. 94.
68 Gilroy, ibid., pp. 94–95.
69 Ibid., p. 95.
70 Gilroy, ibid., p. 94.

emotions.[71] The method, called by William Swartley the 'Initiated Symbol Projection', involves the client's 'fantasy production', that is producing free imaginings prompted by the therapist, who asks the client to visualise and describe subsequently (during one or several sessions) 'ten standard imaginary situations', interpreted by the therapist symbolically, which include:[72]

1. a meadow;
2. a path leading from the meadow to a mountain, which is to be climbed, and a landscape view from the mountain top;
3. a brook that flows on the meadow, which the client needs to follow uphill to find its source, or downstream, according to their preference;
4. a house that appears near the meadow or somewhere in the countryside, and the exterior and interior of the house;
5. a close relative;
6. being lost in the countryside and meeting a driver that offers a lift (a situation for females); or seeing a rose bush in a garden and picking roses (for men);
7. a lion and the place where it appears;
8. a name of the same sex as the patient and a person who could bear that name;
9. taking a concealed position at a distance from a dark forest or a cave and watching what/who emerges from the darkness;
10. a swamp in the meadow and a figure that arises from its murky waters.[73]

Leuner's GAI draws on 'subconscious motivation, the significance of symbols, resistance, and the therapeutic importance of the mobilization of affect', and employs the methods of 'mobile projection' and 'associated imagery'.[74] The therapeutic effect of GAI, according to Leuner, results from the fact that 'guiding and transformation of imagery [can] lead to desirable changes in both affect and attitudes toward life situations.'[75] A substantial attribute of GAI seems to be also its reliance on the patient's visualisations, which are often depicted graphically, so that the therapy depends less on 'the patient's ability accurately to verbalize [their] attitudes than [in] conventional methods.'[76]

---

71 Hanscarl Leuner, 'Guided Affected Imagery': Abbreviation of a lecture given at the New Jersey Neuropsychiatric Institute, Princeton, N. J., May 16, 1966. Reprinted from *American Journal of Psychotherapy*, vol. XXIII, No. 1, pp. 4–22, January 1969, p. 4.
72 Swartley considers ISP as a diagnostic tool, while Leuner stresses GAI's therapeutic potential; Leuner, p. 11.
73 Leuner, ibid., pp. 6–10.
74 Ibid., p. 24.
75 Ibid., p. 24.
76 Leuner, ibid., p. 24.

What is, therefore, connection between ekphrasis and therapy in the light of Leuner's Guided Affected Imagery? Although Leuner does not use the term 'ekphrasis' but instead 'fantasy production' of images guided by the therapist, his technique of psychotherapy relies on ekphrasis, that is a description of images produced by the patient/client, those images being the patient's own visions rather than existing works of art. Additionally, Leuner remarks that the patient's visions can be and often are visualised by them as drawings, sketches, paintings or maps.[77] Moreover, the images that are to be conretised by the patient/client involve archetypal themes, events and figures, which are particularly powerful in fairy stories and high fantasy (a meadow, a path, a mountain, a landscape viewed from a mountain top, a brook, a source, a house, a stranger, a rose bush, a close relative, a lion, a cave or a dark forest, etc.), and which have significant implications for a psychoanalytic interpretation and for Jungian psychology, to name but two. Although neither the Inklings nor Le Guin identify themselves with any school of psychotherapy (except for the Jungian archetypes, especially that of the shadow and the other, traceable in Le Guin's Earthsea world, as discussed further on in this chapter), it is hardly possible not to associate the imagery of the Inklings' and Le Guin's fantsaty worlds with the ten images proposed by Leuner's GAI therapy. The realm of Faërie represented in Tolkien's Arda and Middle-earth, Lewis's Narnia, and Le Guin's Earthsea, abounds in ekphrastic images of meadows, paths, mountains, summits, houses that emerge in the countryside, encountered strangers, caves, murky forests and waters, as well as eerie creatures that emerge from them. Interestingly, the lion figure happens to play a central role in Lewis's Narnia, although, obviously, it had not been inspired by any psychoanalytic theory, which Lewis firmly shunned, as discussed in Chapter Six, but it might have been inspired by Platonic archetypes and by Charles Williams's *The Place of the Lion* (1931), which Lewis admired much as Williams admired Lewis's *The Allegory of Love* (1936), and by the Christian vision of God drawing on several leonine qualities, thanks to which Aslan stands for a leonine Christ.[78]

Of course, in high fantasy it is not the reader who creates their own otherworldly places, figures and events, but the writer, who encourages the reader to concretize those visions as pre-conceived by the writer, for fantasy narrative provides guidance and signposts leading the reader or listener into the realm of Faërie, so that, owing to Ingarden's 'places of indeterminacy', it is ultimately

---

77 Leuner, ibid., p. 10.
78 The situation when Lewis intended to praise Williams's novel, and Williams intended to congratulate Lewis on his new critical study is mentioned in some detail in Chapter One of this book. Aslan as a leonine Christ is mentioned further on in this chapter.

the reader's individual interpretation that concretizes the writer's ekphrastic descriptions, turning them in their mind into specific visions. Therefore, the reader might be called a sub-creator of the writer's artwork, the writer being its creator; or, to follow Tolkien's religious approach, if the writer himself or herself is a sub-creator, the Maker being the primary Creator of everything, presenting man with His creative genius to the degree that man is able to receive, then the reader appears to be the tertiary creator, or 'secondary' sub-creator. Were a group of readers concerned with the same high fantasy story requested to draw a picture or map of their visions, their productions would certainly be different. They would definitely differ as well in the case of visualising a piece of non-fantasy fiction, yet the creative imagination and independence of the readers would probably be activated to a lesser degree.

Moreover, even though Leuner's GAI does not make use of the term 'art therapy', it seems to entail its very mechanism, which Gilroy calls 'artwriting' and other critics 'word painting'[79], with the only difference that in GAI the patient produces and describes a vision of places, figures, and situations, as suggested by Leuner, which does not necessarily result in creating an artwork, (although the patient may graphically represent their mental images on paper, canvas or another material), while in art therapy the patient, assisted by a professional trained in both therapy and art, creates an artwork of their own, which may be described and discussed as well, although greater emphasis is laid on visual arts considered as the main vehicle of art therapy, insofar as the verbal dimension is far less important here than the non-verbal expressivity of visual arts. In literary ekphrasis, in turn, which I attempt to view in a therapeutic light, there is a cooperation between the writer, who produces ekphrastic descriptions, and the reader, who, guided by the writer, produces their own concretizations of what Ingarden names 'schematized aspects' a literary work of art, responding to the challenge posed by the 'spots of indeterminacy', whose concretizations might also be represented graphically by the reader. Ekphrasis ceases to operate when the visual dimension completely ousts verbally conveyed imagery, which happens, for instance, in drama or film.

The following sections attempt to address the problem of what can be therapeutic about literary ekphrasis, as well as about Faërie's pictoriality and musicality, as rendered in the works of the Inklings and of Le Guin.

---

79 Cf. footnote 30 in this chapter.

Ekphrasis and interartistic mediation according to the Inklings and to U. K. Le Guin

Whether ancient or contemporary, folk or literary, fantasy tales enhance ekphrasis, as they describe the imagined 'covert works of art', that is the visions which may not exist in reality, yet which are the writers' or the story tellers' poetic pictures of the world and reality framed in a narrative. 'Faërie cannot be caught in a net of words; for it is one of its qualities to be indescribable, though not imperceptible,' Tolkien notes, calling fantasy 'an elvish craft' and emphasizing a special affinity between fantasy literature and visual arts, as they both frequently attempt to render the 'indescribable, though not imperceptible.'[80] The same refers to music, one may add, for it also builds on the realm of otherworldliness, imagined by a composer, and may all the more sound 'indescribable though not imperceptible'.

C. S. Lewis says that his Narnia fantasy tales originated from a few pictures and dreams that he had borne in mind, which somehow forced him to translate them into verbal language.[81] 'It all began with a picture,' he admits; 'all my seven Narnian books, and my three science fiction books, began with seeing pictures in my head. At first they were not a story, just pictures.'[82] Le Guin likewise remarks that fantasy genre facilitates a process of 'translation', as it transcribes dreams and other mental pictures into words, which seems to represent another interesting case of ekphrasis:

> Written fantasy translates into verbal images and coherent narrative forms the intuitions and perceptions of the unconscious mind – body language, dream stuff, primary process thinking. This idiom, for all its intense privacy, is one we all seem to share, whether we speak English or Urdu, whether we're five or eighty-five. The witch, the dragon, the hero; the night journey, the helpful animal, the hidden treasure… we all know them; we recognize them (because, if Jung is right, they represent profound and essential modes of thought). Modern fantasy attempts to translate them into modern words.[83]

It seems, therefore, that fantasy fiction is a peculiar realm of human narrative that corresponds verbally to the unconscious and the imagined, just as arts do, yet the

---

80 Tolkien, 'On Fairy-Stories', p. 114. I have addressed the theme of ekphrasis in fantasy literature also in the paper 'Framing ekphrasis in fantasy narrative: chiaroscuro and sfumato in the works of J. R. R. Tolkien and U. K. Le Guin', [in:] *Image, Imagery, Imagination in Contemporary English Studies*, pp. 48–77.

81 Lewis, 'It All Began with a Picture' [in:] *Of Other Worlds*, p. 42.

82 Lewis, ibid., p. 42.

83 Le Guin, *The Language of the Night: Essays on Fantasy and Science Fiction*. ed. Susan Wood, (New York: Berkley Books, 1982), pp. 1–2.

manner of that correspondence or translation differs: literature leaves space for individual re-imagining of the rendered pictures, whereas visual arts impose a ready-made rendition. Ruminating upon the relationship between fantasy literature and visual arts and their role in the process of mediating Fantasy, the process which Le Guin names 'translation', Tolkien emphasizes the superiority of literature over pictorial arts, 'good in themselves' though the latter are, and explains that visual arts 'impose only one visible form' of realization.[84] 'Literature works from mind to mind and is thus more progenitive', he claims, adding that 'if a story says "he climbed a hill and saw a river in the valley below", the illustrator [of the book] may catch, or nearly catch, [their] own vision of such a scene; but every hearer of the words will have [their] own picture, and it will be made out of all the hills and rivers and dales [they have] ever seen, but specially out of The Hill, The River, The Valley which were for [them] the first embodiment of the word.'[85]

Lewis remarks in a similar vein that 'nothing can be more disastrous than the view that the cinema can and should replace popular written fiction', because for an 'untrained mind [this fiction] is its only access to the imaginative world. There is death in the camera', Lewis concludes.[86] These comments seem to confirm Beyst's suggestion quoted above that while visual arts offer a single gateway to our imaginative powers, literature, pictorial though it also is, provides many; and hence high fantasy, which is profoundly ekphrastic, corresponds somehow to Leuner's Guided Affective Imagery therapy.[87]

The same could probably be said about music in fantasy literature, for instance Tolkien's interpretation of the creation of universe through the music of the Ainur in *The Silmarillion*, or Lewis's creation of Narnia rendered entirely by means of Aslan's song. As long as this music is described, it leaves room for the reader's musical imagination; but when it is performed, for instance in a film or stage adaptation of the book, it imposes again its one audible version, which might differ greatly from what each reader of the story has imagined and heard in their mind and heart. Professional musical practice seems to work likewise: a composed score on the paper opens up many entrance gates to the world of the composer, and leaves much space for the performer's interpretation, depending on their expressivity, ability, technical skill, emotional maturity, sensitivity and imaginative powers. It may enchant or dismay.

---

84 Tolkien, 'On Fairy-Stories', 159, note E.
85 Tolkien, ibid., p. 159, note E.
86 Lewis, 'On Stories', p. 17.
87 Beyst, 'W. J. T. Mitchell and the Image'; cf. footnote 48 in this chapter.

To Lewis, both literature and music can serve as 'good images of what we really desire'; but if we mistake them for the thing itself, 'they turn into dumb idols, breaking the hearts of their worshippers.'[88] Lewis regards books as potential 'carriers' or mediators of art, along with works of music, arguing that they may constitute art and may convey a sense of moving beauty and truth, touching upon the fulfillment of human desires; yet, they are not beauty and truth themselves:

> The books or the music in which we thought the beauty was located will betray us if we trust to them; it was not in them, it only came through them, and what came through them was longing. (…) For they are not the thing itself; they are only the scent of a flower we have not found, the echo of a tune we have not heard, news from a country we have never yet visited.[89]

This statement resembles Tolkien's conviction that human art, which he calls 'Sub-creation', is merely a far-off echo and a faint gleam of the music and light that we all come from and yearn for; a splinter of the all-comprising artistry of 'a Maker.'[90]

Following the ancient belief in the harmonious music of universe meant to reverberate in the world and in the human minds and bodies, and thus to maintain their inner harmony, Lewis presents ekphrastically the creation of Narnia, one of his fantastic secondary worlds, drawing on its musicality:[91]

> In the darkness (…) a voice had begun to sing. There were no words. (…) Then two wonders happened at the same moment. One was that the voice was suddenly joined by other voices; more voices than you could possibly count. They were in harmony with it, but far higher up the scale; cold, tingling, silvery voices. The second wonder was that the blackness overhead, all at once, was blazing with stars. (…) One moment there had been nothing but darkness; next moment a thousand, thousand points of light leaped out – single

---

88 Lewis, *The Weight of Glory* (London: HarperCollins, 2001), p. 74.
89 Lewis, ibid., p. 24.
90 Tolkien, 'On Fairy-Stories', p. 126.
91 Despite some similarities, it should be remembered that Tolkien did not have much appraisal of the Lewisian Narnian Chronicles, as noted in Chapter Two of this book, which was due to Lewis's keenness on allegory, and his blending of mythical (Greek, Roman, Arthurian, Norse) and Christian characters into one world. In his biography of C. S. Lewis, Andrew Norman Wilson writes, 'Tolkien hated *The Lion, the Witch and the Wardrobe*. He regarded it as scrappily put together, and not in his sense a 'sub-creation'; that is, a coherently made imaginative world. Moreover it was an allegory, a literary form which he never enjoyed.' (New York, London: W. W. Norton and Company, 1990, 2002), p. 222.

stars, constellations and planets. (…) The new stars and the new voices began at exactly the same time.[92]

So does Tolkien in *The Silmarillion*, interpreting the creation of Arda, the Earth, in terms of making divine music, which is the source of harmony and understanding, and runs parallel with Lewis's musical description of the creation of Narnia:

(…) Eru, the One, who in Arda is called Ilúvatar (…) made first the Ainur, the Holy Ones, that were the offspring of his thought (…), and he spoke to them, propounding to them themes of music; and they sang before him, and he was glad. But for a long while they sang only each alone, or but few together, while the rest hearkened. (…) Yet ever as they listened they came to deeper understanding, and increased in unison and harmony. (…) And it came to pass that Ilúvatar called together all the Ainur and declared to them a mighty theme, unfolding to them things greater and more wonderful that he had yet revealed. Then Ilúvatar said to them: 'Of the theme that I have declared to you, I will now that ye make in harmony together a Great Music. And since I have kindled you with the Flame Imperishable, ye shall show forth your powers in adorning this theme. (…) But I will sit and hearken, and be glad that through you great beauty has been wakened into song.' Then the voices of the Ainur, like unto harps and lutes, and pipes and trumpets, and viols and organs, and like unto countless choirs singing with words, began to fashion the theme of Ilúvatar to a great music; and a sound arose of endless interchanging melodies woven in harmony that passed beyond hearing into the depths and into the heights.'[93]

Interestingly, it is the musical discord introduced by Melkor, the greatest of the Ainur, which marks the first appearance of evil to the world, as Melkor attempts to compete with Ilúvatar by creating his own theme, and desires power and glory for himself. Moreover, Tolkien seems to endorse the synaesthetic union of arts in his mythology, as music can actually be seen at the inception of Arda. Addressing the Ainur, Ilúvatar says: 'Behold your music!', and shows to them 'a vision, giving them a sight where before was only hearing.'[94]

In the Boethian way, Tolkien's rendering of music in *The Silmarillion*, Ainulindalë, reaches the depth of being, marks the beginning of time and lays foundations of universe:

Then Ilúvatar said to them: 'Of the theme that I have declared to you, I will now that ye make in harmony together a Great Music. And since I have kindled you with the Flame Imperishable, ye shall show forth your powers in adorning this theme, each with his

---

92 Lewis, *The Magician's Nephew* (London: HarperCollins 1955, 2002), p. 93.
93 Tolkien, *The Silmarillion* (New York: Ballantine Books, 1977, 2001), Christopher Tolkien, ed., pp. 3–4.
94 Tolkien, ibid., p. 6.

own thoughts and devices, if he will. But I will sit and hearken, and be glad that through you great beauty has been wakened into song.

Then the voices of the Ainur, like unto harps and lutes, and pipes and trumpets, and viols and organs, and like unto countless choirs singing with words, began to fashion the theme of Ilúvatar to a great music; and a sound arose of endless interchanging melodies woven in harmony that passed beyond hearing into the depths and into the heights, and the places of the dwelling of Ilúvatar were filled to overflowing, and the music and the echo of the music went out into the Void, and it was not void. Never since have the Ainur made any music like to this music, though it has been said that a greater still shall be made before Ilúvatar by the choirs of the Ainur and the Children of Ilúvatar after the end of days.[95]

The echo of the Great Music of the Ainur, preserved in universe as the Boethian *musica mundana,* although forgotten and unrecognized, lives in Tolkien's Arda in the music of the sea:

It is said by the Eldar that in water there lives yet the echo of the Music of the Ainur more than in any substance that is in this Earth; and many of the Children of Ilúvatar hearken still unsated to the voices of the Sea, and yet know not for what they listen.[96]

The particle of this great cosmic music, as Szczeklik argues, is forever contained also in the blood circulation system, whose swoosh harmonises with the music of spheres, although it is hardly ever heard.[97]

Due to the convergence of arts and music in fantasy, all of them springing forth equally freely from imagination, it seems that in few other genres is ekphrasis more powerful and indispensable than in fantasy literature, whose generic credibility rests on its ekphrastic skill. Should ekphrasis in fantasy stories fail, the genre is ill-made, ruined and mocked. Mimicry and parody may never succeed in rendering an 'otherworld' whose internal structure and logic, though apparently different from our immediate reality, merit recognition and serious consideration, and are, in a sense 'true'.[98] Tolkien considers fantasy as man's 'Sub-creation', the most artistic and refined of literary genres, similar to the sub-creation that painters, composers and other artists accomplish when creating worlds that are rooted in the 'consensus' or immediate reality, yet, at the same time, express their longing for the 'Mystical towards the Supernatural', for the 'Magical towards Nature', and for a 'Mirror of scorn and pity towards Man'.[99]

---

95 Ibid., pp. 3–4.
96 Ibid., p. 8.
97 Cf. the beginning of this chapter.
98 Tolkien, 'On Fairy-Stories', p. 117.
99 Tolkien, ibid., p. 125.

A fantasy story-maker proves a successful 'sub-creator' only if what is related and described in the story is 'true' inside that imagined world, Tolkien explains, which seems to rely to a great extent on the ekphrastic ability of the writer's fantasy, as it defines the story's mimetic, diegetic and interpretive levels.

If fantasy distorts or caricatures reality, it fails and becomes buffoonery, kitsch or 'morbid delusion', because then it betrays and disembodies the essence of Faërie, which, as Tolkien claims, consists in its 'arresting strangeness' and enchantment, in the 'realization, independent of the conceiving mind, of imagined wonder'; in its otherworldliness that is not an escape or a flight of a deserter, but a refuge of a prisoner longing for freedom and truth.[100] Only a lucid and sober mind can succeed at imagining true Faërie, Tolkien argues, for 'Fantasy is a natural human activity, [which] certainly does not destroy or even insult reason; and it does not either blunt the appetite for, nor obscure the perception of, scientific verity; on the contrary: the keener and the clearer is the reason, the better fantasy will it make.'[101] Lewis remarks likewise that 'the logic of a fairy-tale is as strict as that of a realistic novel, though different.'[102]

How does ekphrasis work in the paradoxically realistic and rational narrative of fantasy literature? The following section attempts to address these questions with reference to Tolkien's 'Leaf by Niggle' tale, which epitomizes ekphrasis and pictoriality in fantasy literature.

Ekphrasis in Tolkien's 'Leaf by Niggle'

Written around 1938–39, 'Leaf by Niggle' is an interesting case of a fantasy narrative informed by ekphrasis and pictoriality. The title of this perhaps lesser-known text of Tolkien's is at the same time the title of a little work of art central to the story and imagined by Tolkien. It is a piece of canvas representing a leaf painted by Niggle, the protagonist, who is 'a silly little man, worthless, of no use to Society at all,' as Councillor Tompkins and most of his townsmen think.[103] Niggle 'was the sort of painter who can paint leaves better than trees;' 'not a very successful [painter] partly because he had many other things to do. Most of these things he thought were a nuisance; but he did them fairly well'[104]. Niggle 'used to

---

100   Tolkien, ibid., pp. 148 and 144.
101   Tolkien, ibid., p. 144.
102   Lewis, 'On Stories', p. 13.
103   Tolkien, 'Leaf by Niggle', in *Tales from the Perilous Realm* (London: HarperCollins, 2002), p. 141.
104   Tolkien, ibid., p. 121.

spend a long time on a single leaf, trying to catch its shape and its sheen, and the glistening of dewdrops on its edges. Yet he wanted to paint a whole tree, with all of its leaves, in the same style, and all of them different.[105] This particular picture, which 'bothered him':

> Had begun with a leaf caught in the wind, and it became a tree; and the tree grew, sending out innumerable branches, and thrusting out the most fantastic roots. Strange birds came and settled upon the twigs and had to be attended to. Then all around the Tree, and behind it, through the gaps in the leaves and boughs, a country began to open out; and there were glimpses of a forest marching over the land, and of mountains tipped with snow.[106]

Niggle's work that he wished to complete despite many other commitments, 'actually seemed to him wholly unsatisfactory, yet very lovely, the only really beautiful picture in the world.'[107] Due to many calls from visitors, and especially from his only neighbour, the needy and grumpy Parish, (whose visits and requests Niggle regards as 'interruptions'), Niggle never succeeds in completing his work.[108] A single leaf is the only surviving part of a huge painting Niggle has worked upon, because after Niggle's inevitable departure, as announced by a strict Inspector, the huge unfinished canvas which contains the work of his life is utilized to patch the leaky roof of Parish's house. A tiny piece of the painting featuring a single leaf is salvaged by Atkins, a schoolmaster, 'nobody of importance', and probably the only person among the local society who seems to appreciate or value art, who finds the picture beautiful and displays it in the town's museum.[109] This little painting named 'Leaf by Niggle' hangs there until the museum burns down, leaving seemingly nothing of Niggle the painter's niggling work.

After the strict Inspector orders Niggle to set out on a 'long wretched journey', as Niggle refers to it, the Driver takes Niggle to his carriage and leaves him at a railway station just in time to board a train, which arrives at a 'large dim railway station', where a Porter takes exhausted Niggle to a Workhouse Infirmary, which is 'more like a prison than a hospital.'[110] Niggle works there very hard digging, doing some carpentry and painting, yet he is not allowed to continue working on his tree, being forced instead to do a mundane job of painting 'bare boards all one plain colour.'[111] After his strength gives way, 'a Medical Board' or 'a Court of Inquiry'

---

105   Tolkien, ibid., pp. 121–122.
106   Tolkien, ibid., p. 122.
107   Tolkien, ibid., p. 123.
108   Tolkien, ibid., p. 123.
109   Tolkien, ibid., p. 124.
110   Tolkien, ibid., pp. 124 and 130.
111   Ibid., p. 130.

decide on assigning Niggle a 'Gentle Treatment' and send him by train to another place, where Niggle finds his bicycle and discovers a turf and a sweep of grass that look strangely familiar. There, to his astonishment and delight, he meets his Tree, now real, complete and awesome, featured in another ekphrastic passage:[112]

> A great green shadow came between his and the sun. Niggle looked up, and fell off his bicycle. Before him stood the Tree, his Tree, finished. If you could say that of a Tree that was alive, its leaves opening, its branches growing and bending in the wind that Niggle had so often felt or guessed, and had so often failed to catch. He gazed at the Tree, and slowly lifted his arms and opened them wide. 'It's a gift,' he said. He was referring to his art, and also to the result; but he was using the word quite literally. He went on looking at the Tree. All the leaves he had ever laboured at were there, as he had imagined them rather than as he had made them; and there were others that had only budded in his mind, and many that might have budded, if only he had had time.... Some of the most beautiful [of leaves] were seen to have been produced in collaboration with Mr. Parish.[113]

'The Tree [is] finished, though not finished with – just the other way about to what it used to be,' says Niggle, and, together with Parish, who arrives soon after, they work in the place, making a beautiful garden and a small house.[114] The area around the magnificent Tree comes to be called 'Niggle's Country', and most of it is 'Niggle's Picture', with 'Parish's Garden' within. When the Great Tree is in full blossom, shining like a flame and busy with various birds, Niggle leaves for the Mountains, and, guided by a shepherd, sets forth to explore the borders of his Picture, 'walking always uphill' and 'learning about sheep and high pastures.'[115]

Ekphrasis seems to be a vital element of the story, as the narrative centres first upon the process of creating that imaginary painting, upon its description and meaning to Niggle, and later on, upon its perfect realization as a real Tree, the Forest and the Mountains, which Niggle is in the end allowed to see. The things which he had faintly imagined and at which he had only glimpsed in his fleeting vision of the painting, as they would appear on or beyond its edges, have now proved to be real in the other land. The Great Tree, with its unique foliage, the Forest, and the Mountains behind are alive and perfect, in the way which Niggle had not even been able to conceive. Even a cursory glance at 'Leaf by Niggle' reveals the consistently ekphrastic texture of the story. As this chapter seeks to argue, ekphrasis defines this tale, for, in some sense, ekphrasis is the starting point, the kernel and the resolution of 'Leaf by Niggle'; its driving force and at the same

---

112   Ibid., p. 135.
113   Ibid., p. 136.
114   Ibid., p. 137.
115   Ibid., p. 141.

time its coda. The description of Niggle's painting, first imagined, then painstakingly sketched and left unfinished, and, finally and unexpectedly, encountered live as a complete perfect realization of Niggle's artistic vision, seems to function as both a mimetic and a diegetic device, and as a 'conceit' of the story.

Firstly, ekphrasis seems to play here a mimetic role, for it repeatedly shows a work of art by providing a description of a painting that finally reaches completion and becomes a live picture as 'Niggle's Picture' land. Secondly, ekphrasis appears as a diegetic device, as its recurrence and final appearance as a live landscape shapes the storyline and unites both parts of the narrative – Niggle's life before he sets out on the 'troublesome journey', and afterwards.[116] Ekphrasis provides also a coda to the story, when Niggle, having marvelled at the beauty of his Tree and other trees in the Forest, crosses the very borders of his Picture, fascinated by the distant snowy Mountains. The extension of the Picture, or its continuation beyond the borders, welcomes another description of the mountainous country, which the reader is invited to imagine.

Not only does ekphrasis define the Tolkienian fantasy in 'Leaf by Niggle', but it also empowers its allegory, which is a rare exception among his works, considering Tolkien's congenital reluctance towards allegory. In an oft-quoted letter to Milton Waldman, a publisher, Tolkien notes, 'I dislike Allegory - the conscious and intentional allegory'; and in the Foreword to the second edition of *The Lord of the Rings*, he adds:[117]

> I cordially dislike allegory in all its manifestations, and always have done so since I grew old and wary enough to detect its presence. I much prefer history, true or feigned, with its varied applicability to the thought and experience of readers. (…) I think that many confuse 'applicability' with 'allegory'; but the one resides in the freedom of the reader, and the other in the purposed domination of the author.[118]

What Tolkien might approve of in Faërie is 'applicability', the concept he uses himself, some elusive type of 'allegoricality', rather than an obvious allegory. This does not seem to be the case in the 'Leaf by Niggle' story, though, because in a draft of a letter to Peter Hastings, the manager of the Newman Bookshop in Oxford, Tolkien remarks: 'I tried to show allegorically how [Sub-creation] might come to be taken up into Creation in some plane in my "purgatorial" story 'Leaf by Niggle'.[119]

---

116 Tolkien, 'Leaf by Niggle', p. 124.
117 Tolkien, *Letters of J. R. R. Tolkien*, p. 145.
118 Tolkien, 'Foreword to the Second Edition' of *The Lord of the Rings* (London: HarperCollins, 1996), p. xvi.
119 Tolkien, *Letters*, p. 195.

Therefore, Tolkien apparently deems some kind of allegory acceptable, that is allegory which does not impose an obvious, one-to-one mapping, and which could serve a justifiable intention, such as helping to account for an important tenet a writer wishes to expose. Even though in 1962 Tolkien wrote to his aunt, Jane Neave, that 'Leaf by Niggle' 'is not really or properly an "allegory" so much as "mythical", for Niggle is meant to be a real mixed-quality *person* [italics Tolkien's] and not an "allegory" of any single vice or virtue', in the story Tolkien seems to have resorted to using allegory so as to elucidate his artistic and religious understanding of man's creative efforts, which he calls Sub-creation.[120] To Tolkien any act of human creativity is powered by the Maker, the Creator of all, whose inconceivable genius can at best be reflected as a splinter of light shining through man's mind and heart, captured in various morally benign products of human creativity.[121]

Ekphrasis in 'Leaf by Niggle' espouses allegory or, at least, a symbolic applicability. Tom Shippey argues that this story, an 'extended allegory', corresponds to *Everyman*, a canonical morality play, and also bears some semblance to Dante's masterpiece, *The Divine Comedy*, especially to its middle part, *Purgatory*.[122] Accordingly, Niggle might stand for Everyman, who is forced to set on a long and troublesome journey, suggesting death, an idea 'wholly distasteful to him', and is summoned to give 'rekenynge' of his life.[123] Like Everyman, Niggle is neither ready nor willing to go. According to Shippey, Tolkien 'bifurcates' the character of Death, showing Him as both the Inspector and the Driver, 'tall [figures], dressed all in black', who arrive unexpectedly and communicate what must not suffer delay.[124] It seems that this Christian and, indeed, Catholic, reading of the story, which recognizes the purgatorial theme of Niggle's toil in the Workhouse, would not be complete without ekphrasis, as it provides the heavenly resolution following Niggle's penance and purification. His heaven begins in his painting, 'Niggle's Picture', now finished and perfect, revealing more than he had ever imagined, and allowing a blissful contemplation of what he had merely caught a glimpse of as a painter.

This profound understanding of images and essences, merely foreshadowed in the earthly experience and completed in their radiant fullness in some other reality is what emerges as well from Lewis's *The Last Battle*, when after the demise of Narnia, the protagonists encounter mountains, meadows and rivers that appear

---

120   Tolkien, ibid., p. 321.
121   Tolkien, 'On Fairy-Stories', p. 144.
122   Shippey, *J. R. R. Tolkien: Author of the Century*, pp. 267 and 277.
123   The phrase 'wholly distasteful to him' is Tolkien's; 'Leaf by Niggle', p. 124.
124   Tolkien's, 'Leaf by Niggle', p. 125. Shippey, *J. R. R. Tolkien*, p. 274.

strangely familiar, yet are more intensive and powerful, like the sun that is a magnified image of a ray.

> 'If you ask me,' said Edmund, 'it's like somewhere in the Narnian world. Look at those mountains ahead - and the big ice-mountains beyond them. Surely they're rather like the mountains we used to see from Narnia, the ones up the Westward beyond the Waterfall?'
> 'Yes, so they are,' said Peter. 'Only these are bigger.'

> (...) 'And they they're not like,' said Lucy. 'They're different. They have more colours on them and they look further away than I remembered and they're more ... more ... oh, I don't know ...'

> 'More like the real thing,' said the Lord Digory softly. (...) [The old Narnia] had a beginning and an end. It was only a shadow or a copy of the real Narnia which has always been here and always will be here: just as our wold, England and all, is only a shadow or copy of something in Aslan's real world. You need not mourn over Narnia, Lucy. All of the old Narnia that mattered, all the dear creatures, have been drawn into the real Narnia through the Door. And of course, it is different; as different as a real thing is from a shadow or as waking life is from a dream.'[125]

Digory concludes that 'it's all in Plato, all in Plato,' implying Plato's allegory of the cave and theory of the Forms or Ideas, according to which the material world of the immediate reality that can be sensorially perceived is not the one that represents the highest and ultimate kind of reality, for the 'consensus reality' resembles a prison merely shadowing the true ideas that one remains unaware of before being liberated from the prison walls of shadows into the illuminated world of ideas themselves.[126] Similarly, through his analogy of the sun Plato suggests that true reality cannot be viewed by means of senses, as it needs the mind to be glimpsed at. The sun with its natural light is to Plato an analogy of goodness, the essential illumination that preconditions any knowledge and cognition: 'As goodness stands in the intelligible realm to intelligence and the things we know, so in the visible realm the sun stands to sight and the things we see.'[127] More about the significance of light and good in the context of Faërie, represented by the Inklings, is said in the following section concerning sfumato and chiaroscuro.

Platonic themes, such as the Socratic way to reality (followed, for instance, by Professor Digory Kirke), a 'gadfly' that awakens others from an intellectual and spiritual slumber, (e.g., Lucy Pevensie), liberation from the cave (e.g. Rilian's),

---

125   Lewis, *The Last Battle*, pp. 158–160.
126   Plato, *The Republic*, Robin Waterfield, ed., trans. Robin Waterfield (Oxford: Oxford University Press, 1993), 514a–520a.
127   Plato, ibid., 508c.

and knowledge that blinds (e.g., Uncle Andrew's), interweave with Christianity in Lewis's Narnia, and, as John Mark N. Reynolds claims, 'the Narnia books, like all the great Platonic dialogues, tell myths in order to show readers an image of their own soul.'[128] 'To lose what I owe to Plato and Aristotle would be like an amputation of a limb', admits Lewis himself.[129]

Now, a question arises if the Platonic philosophy employed in high fiction can add to the genre's assumed therapeutic potential. Plato's metaphor of the prisoners enslaved in a cave, who only know the shadows of reality, believing them to be essences of things themselves, seems to reverberate in Tolkien's vision of a man who desires to escape from the suffocating prison of material reality and illusion in order to reach beyond its confines, to win freedom, to gain an insight into the intangible and indescribable, to seek a genuine reality and meaning of universal things that last, to '[divine] the potency of the words, and the wonder of the things, such as stone, and wood, and iron; tree and grass; house and fire; bread and wine';[130] to see sunlight, or at least its splinter, rather than its shadow.

Epicurus calls philosophy 'the Medicine of the Mind', and Henry David Thoreau argues that 'the be a philosopher is (....) to solve some of the problems of life not theoretically, but practically.'[131] Interestingly, in his book *Plato, Not Prozac!: Applying Eternal Wisdom to Everyday Problems*, Louis Marinoff suggests that philosophical counselling may function on a similar basis to psychotherapy, offering practical solutions to various predicaments, a controversial view criticized by many, yet, containing perhaps a useful element of a therapeutic applicability of philosophy, for instance Platonism.[132]

---

128 John Mark N. Reynolds, 'Narnia, Plato, and C. S. Lewis on the Hope of Heaven', March 28, 2013, http://www.patheos.com/blogs/philosophicalfragments/2013/03/28/narnia-plato-and-c-s-lewis-on-the-hope-of-heaven/, accessed 23 April 2016. Cf. H. Dennis Fisher, 'C. S. Lewis, Platonism and Aslan's Country: Symbols of Heaven in *The Chronicles of Narnia*' [in:] *Inklings Forever, vol. VII, A Collection of Essays Presented at the Seventh Frances White Ewbank Colloquium on C. S. Lewis and Friends*, Taylor University, 2010, Upland, Indiana, https://library.taylor.edu/dotAsset/bc583632–9dc1–47fe-9edf-6f42bf8d64ee.pdf, accessed 23 April 2016.

129 Qtd. in William Luther White's *The Image of Man in C. S. Lewis* (Eugene, OR: Wipf and Stock, 1969, 2008), p. 32.

130 Tolkien, 'On Fairy-Stories', p. 147.

131 Qtd. by Lou Marinoff in *Plato, Not Prozac!: Applying Eternal Wisdom to Everyday Problems* (New York: HarperCollins, 1999), p. 3.

132 Cf. Shlomit C. Schuster, 'Marinoff's Therapy: A Critique of His Books on Philosophical Practice', 2004, http://npcassoc.org/docs/ijpp/SchusterMarinoff.pdf, accessed 20 July 2016.

Returning to Tolkien's 'Leaf by Niggle', a central ekphrastic story text analyzed in this section, and to the significance of the image of the completed Tree, which crowns and divines the joy of its heavenly coda, one might argue after Shippey that the tale 'ends as a comedy, even a "divine comedy", on more levels than one'.[133] Not only can it be read as an allegory of human life and afterlife, the Tree representing man's craving for and pursuit of beauty and truth, but also as Tolkien's 'autobiographical allegory'.[134] As Tolkien says himself, it is 'part apologia, part confession'.[135] Therefore, 'Leaf by Niggle' symbolizes the niggling work of Tolkien's, striving to complete his Middle-earth mythology; and Niggle stands for Tolkien 'the niggler', labouring painstakingly on details and struggling with various interruptions when writing his *opus magnum*, *The Lord of the Rings*, which Tolkien actually calls his 'internal tree'.[136] Shippey argues that Tolkien 'bifurcates' himself in that 'personal apologia', betraying frustration of a writer and academic who cannot finish the work of his life due to family and professional commitments: Niggle represents Tolkien the fantasy writer, and Parish stands for Tolkien the scholar.[137] Niggle and Parish are first at odds only to become reconciled in the other world, where they furnish 'Niggle's Parish' with a little house and a garden.

The 'autobiographical allegory' of Tolkien's casts him in the role of the niggling artist and writer, expressed, as Shippey remarks, 'for all his protestations, in the form of strict or "just" allegory'.[138] So does yet another reading of the story, which extends the character of Tolkien 'the niggler' to artists of various fields, experiencing first the mystery of Sub-creation, then failing to complete their imaginative *opera magna*, and finally cherishing the joy of the ultimate realization of their works, as perfected by the Maker.

In conclusion, 'Leaf by Niggle' is an interesting case of a fairy story which, thanks to ekphrasis, offers a range of possible interpretations. The 'Ur-ekphrastic' structure of the text seems to weave the 'conceit' of the story, based on the concept of Sub-creation, shapes the fairy tale on both descriptive and narrative levels, and enhances its allegorical readings. Whether 'Leaf by Niggle' represents an ekphrastic allegory or an allegorical ekphrasis, and whether one follows the Christian, autobiographical or 'sub-creative' interpretation of Tolkien's story, one treads on the ekphrastic ground, for Niggle's Tree seems to have entwined the tale, beckoning

133 Shippey, *J. R. R. Tolkien: Author of the Century*, p. 277.
134 Shippey, ibid., p. 267.
135 Tolkien, *Letters*, p. 55.
136 Tolkien, ibid., p. 143.
137 Shippey, *J. R. R. Tolkien: Author of the Century*, p. 265.
138 Shippey, ibid., p. 267.

the reader to transgress the immediate reality, enter 'Niggle's Picture', and, advancing towards the misty mountains, view the new horizons of man's old challenges, the essence of the thing itself, find meaning, and hope beyond hope.

Finally, one may wonder whether ekphrasis in fantasy literature can be therapeutic. It seems so, because it naturally engages imagination, helps to recreate art, conveying beauty and sense through its *logos*, and offers a vicarious experience that can be cathartic. Tolkien's ekphrasis in 'Leaf by Niggle' communicates a '*contra spem spero*' message: our human endeavours, if benevolent and pure, are never wasted, even if they remain unrealised and perish with our mortality; they enter eternity with us and somehow intercede for us, and may find their perfect completion when time ceases to exist. The tree, a symbol of life and vitality, stands for any work of the human mind and any work of creation that often informs a human life with meaning. As Tolkien suggests, failing to complete it does not mean a failure, for it might find its perfect completion and genuine form or idea beyond the borders of this world. Linking the theme of an *opus magnum* from Tolkien's 'Leaf by Niggle' with Frankl's triad of what constitutes meaning of life, one approaches the first potential: 'a deed to do (that is some work to create),' (which is Niggle's painting), but also, arguably, the other two sources of meaning: 'a person to encounter (to love and to be loved)', who, paradoxically, turns out to be Parish, and 'an attitude one can always adopt when fate and suffering are unavoidable,' when Niggle fails to complete his painting and when he realizes he will never do.[139] Tolkien seems to imply that the meaning of an unfinished or lost work, when centred upon beauty and truth, is never wasted, and it ennobles its sub-creator, informing their relationship with other people and their attitude to life and death. Although their life may end in grief, there is a eucatastrophe beyond it, piercing their heart with sudden joy upon revealing their magnificent work or deed now completed and perfect, in an otherworldly realm.

Sfumato and chiaroscuro techniques in the fantasy works of Tolkien, Lewis, and Le Guin

To Lewis, there was music first, and it gave birth to the light, the sun and stars in Narnia, as quoted above; and, likewise, to Tolkien, Ilúvatar's music created the Earth for his Children, that is Elves and Men, 'in the Deeps of Time and in the midst of the innumerable stars.'[140] Sounds and pictures blend in fantasy and

---

139   Cf. Chapter Three of this book. Frankl, *The Unheard Cry for Meaning*, p. 41.
140   Lewis, *The Magician's Nephew*, p. 93. Tolkien, *The Silmarillion*, p. 7. I have first introduced this theme in a paper 'Sfumato and Chiaroscuro or the Symbolic Interplay

channel creative powers which human 'sub-creators' may use. In this section of the chapter addressing interartistic properties of fantasy narrative the focus falls on the uses of light and dark in some selected works of Tolkien, Lewis, and Le Guin, and on their therapeutic potential.

In his analysis of textual images, Stefan Beyst speaks of image-constituting and object-constituting signs, remarking that both 'a contour and a hazy stain can produce the same effect', namely an impression of a spatial object; thus, 'the image-constituting signs [for instance a contour or a stain] differ from object-constituting signs in the real world only like different fonts differ from each other, while they are read as the same letters nevertheless.'[141] Over the following pages I would like to examine and compare the primary ekphrastic elements of fantasy narrative in some of Tolkien's, Lewis's and Le Guin's works, that is the visual outline of their word painting composed of an interplay of light and dark, which frames the imagery of their stories. Referring to the pictorial concepts of a contour and a stain, this section attempts to demonstrate how differently ekphrasis can be realized shaping the essence of otherworldliness, and to what different visual, symbolic and, perhaps, therapeutic effects. Before embarking upon the effects of the ekphrastic representation of light and dark in Faërie it is worthwhile to present briefly the use and symbolism of that visual antithesis in arts and in human thought.

Light and dark have been inspiring human thought and feeling from time immemorial as the most universal and elementary powers, measuring earthly existence and indicating the rhythm of life on earth. Since they provide the most immediate human environment and condition its visual reception, light and dark have long become an archetypal point of reference in virtually all cultures and religions. As the diurnal and nocturnal counterparts, they have come to signify the contrasting powers of life and death, vitality and inertia, order and chaos, wisdom and ignorance, truth and deceit, the divine and the beastly, the angelic and the demonic, and other miscellaneous shades of the benevolence and malevolence spectrum. By and large, they have grown to be quintessential symbols of good and evil. Together with an array of related concepts, mainly the sources of light, such as the sun, the moon, the candle, the lantern, the torch, the dawn, and the shapes of the dark, that is the night, dusk, underground or the shadow, they epitomize the lucidity of light and the mystery of murk, respectively. A pivot of religion and philosophy, the relationship of good and evil has found its symbolic

---

of Light and Shade in the Fantasy Works of J. R. R. Tolkien and U. K. Le Guin', [in:] *PASE Papers 2007: Studies in Culture and Literature*, vol. 2, Wojciech Kalaga, Marzena Kubisz, and Jacek Mydla, eds. (Katowice, University of Silesia Press, 2007), pp. 64–79.

141 Beyst, 'W. J. T. Mitchell and the Image: The Discovery of the Image-text.'

depiction in all traditions and systems, visualised as the light and dark antagonism. This duality of light and dark symbolizes the interactive coexistence of contradictory binaries, and as an archetype of culture and religion it has always been present in arts, myths, fairy tales and other forms of literature. Read in the context of good and evil, the universal symbolism of light and shade seems to be a part of common consciousness, reflected also in modern fantasy tales, and rooted deeply in virtually all systems of human thought, a few of which are briefed below.

In the Judeo-Christian and Islamic theology, light has an unequivocal symbolism, as it represents God and His grace, the only true and fundamental wisdom, which in Buddhism is called Enlightenment. The Bible clearly says that God is the embodiment of Light (Psalm 27:1), 'a light of the nations' (Isaiah 42:6), and 'the true light that enlightens every man coming into the world,' (John 1:9). Jesus says, 'I am the light of the world; he who follows me will not walk in darkness, but will have the light of life,' (John 8:12); and further on, 'I have come as light into the world, that whosoever believes in me may not remain in darkness.' (John 12:46). The Catholic creed declares faith in Jesus Christ, who is 'God from God, Light from Light, true God from true God.' The Bible separates light from darkness completely, making a sharp division between good and evil, which are irreconcilable. St. Paul teaches the first Christians: 'Do not be mismated with unbelievers. For what partnership have righteousness and iniquity? Or what fellowship has light with darkness?' (2 Corinthians 11:14). 'God is light and in him is no darkness at all,' concludes St. John (1:5).

Qur'an, the holy book of Islam, is divided into chapters called Suras, one of which, bearing number 24, is titled 'The Light' (An-Nur). According to the teaching of Islam, light is also an exclusive attribute of almighty God.

> God is the Light of the heavens and the earth. The parable of His light is as if there were a niche and within it a lamp: The lamp enclosed in glass: The glass as it were a brilliant star: Lit from a blessed tree. (…) Light upon Light! God doth guide whom He will to His light. And as for the unbelievers, they are as shadows upon a sea obscured.[142]

In Buddhism the most important task for man is to achieve a spiritual awakening and a perfect awareness of the true nature of universe by means of a lucid mind. The black colour represents primordial darkness, in which dwells an imperceptible sound beyond the hearing capacity of any physical being. The act of creation of universe was manifested through the gradual slowing down of inaudible vibrations. Their frequency became perceptible, darkness became light, the shadows

---

142   *The Light Verse: Qur'ānic Text and Sūfī Interpretation*, trans. by Gerhard Böwering, *Oriens*, vol. 36 (2001), pp. 113–144, verses 24–35, 39–40, p. 114.

turned into colours, the colours produced sound, and sound created form. In Buddhist symbolism white signifies learning, knowledge, purity and longevity, whereas black stands for hatred and killing.[143]

The symbolism of light is also of remarkable import to the tradition of Hinduism, as reflected in the ancient four-day Festival of Light called Divali, illuminating the triumph of truth over untruth and of death over immortality. Light brightens up people's homes and hearts, and is believed to shed life and hope, thus announcing the victory of good over evil. According to Hinduism, light empowers people to commit themselves to good deeds and brings them closer to divinity.

Another popular philosophy of the East that draws on the light and dark antinomy, yet differs considerably from the Christian perspective, is Taoism. This is so because, while marking a division between light and dark, Taoism does not interpret this relationship as a conflict of two forces, which irrevocably leads to a victory of the mightier party, that is the good. Unlike the above-mentioned religions, Taoism approaches the black and white archetype as a duality of arbitrary values, existing symbiotically as two indispensable complements. The fundamental principle of this system is a belief in Tao, omnipresent and omnipotent life energy of a two-fold nature, manifested in the yin-yang binary. The inherent duality of Tao reveals itself through the interdependence of the male and female, light and dark, active and passive, motion and stillness. Taoism teaches that neither side surpasses the other, as they make equal aspects of the whole; therefore the interpretation of good and bad varies over time and among different groups of people. Taoism emphasises the significance of equilibrium in universe and in the human spirit, essentially composed of contrasting powers coexisting with each other and sharing an element of each other's nature.

A younger system of religion is Manichaeism, a dualistic system propounded by Mani in Persia. The most prominent principle of Manichaean theology is dualism based on two primary natures of light and darkness. The realm of light represents peace, while the realm of darkness signifies chaos and a constant conflict. The Manichaean cosmogony views the universe as a mixture of light and dark, created by the Living Spirit, that is an emanation of light, and views the world as a temporary result of an assault of darkness upon light. It stipulates a perfect equality of the two powers and denies the omnipotent quality of the good. This principle, also called the absolute duality, differentiates Manichaeism from many other religious systems. The Manichean binary of light and dark results in a

---

143 Jules Renard, *The Handy Buddhism Book* (Mumbai: Jaico Publishing House, 2005), p. 12.

fierce war between equal powers of good and evil, whose battlefield is mankind. Manichaeism teaches that 'good and evil have existed both co-eternally and independently in the form of finite deities. Neither has yet destroyed the other, and this accounts for the mixture of good and evil in our world.'[144]

In the light of the above it appears that Abrahamic religions, that is, most importantly, Judaism, Christianity and Islam, as well as Dharmic religions, represented by Hinduism, Buddhism, Jainism, and Sikhism, unequivocally interpret light as symbol of a superior benevolent power and view the dark as an embodiment of evil and chaos. Taoist philosophies, mostly Taoism and Confucianism, construe the archetype of light and dark as a paradigm of a balanced dichotomy, which makes the warp and waft of universe. Manichaeism, in turn, develops a vision of a full-scale war between two equal powers of good and evil, whose resolution may ultimately bring a triumph of light. Some related Gnostic beliefs also recognize the duality of good and evil, but instead of following the Manichean radical model of equality, they advocate a 'weak' or mitigated dichotomy, according to which evil is the inferior power.

However different the interpretation of the light and dark archetype appears in various religious systems, their symbolic antagonism of good and evil seems universal. The problem of evil has been a great challenge especially to theism, for the existence and omnipresence of evil might appear contradictory to God's benevolence and His creative omnipotence. In response to the question of evil, Christianity offers theodicy, that is a special branch of theology and philosophy which attempts to reconcile the assumed benevolence of God with the existence of evil and suffering in the world. Theodicean dissertations attempt to account for the universal problem of the origin and the role of evil. Some non-Christian theories deny God's almighty power or His benevolence, thus viewing evil as an independent element equal in nature to good. Most Christian theodicies teach that evil in the world does not contradict God's benevolence.[145] Leibnitz refers to the free will of man and the original sin to explain the roots of evil. St. Augustine (354–430), the Bishop of Hippo, and later Boethius (480–524), a Roman philosopher, developed a theory called the absence theodicy, which stipulates that there is no evil as an independent power equal to good.[146] There is only an absence of

---

144   Steven Runciman, *The Medieval Manichee: A Study of the Christian Dualist Heresy* (Cambridge: Cambridge University Press, 1982), p. 53.

145   Cf. W. Gary Crampton, *A Biblical Theodicy* (Addison: Trinity Foundation, 1999).

146   St. Augustine's philosophy exerted an important influence on Tolkien's and C. S. Lewis's thought, as reflected, for instance, in the latter's essay 'The Abolition of Man', and his novels *The Great Divorce* and *Till We Have Faces: A Myth Retold*; cf. Thomas

good. According to this tenet, God is not the source of evil, but solely of good, which, of course, does not make evil an illusory threat. Sin and evil are real, and they brought about the original fall of man, yet they will never overshadow God's almighty and all-loving deity. Evil cannot have an independent existence and has no creative ability. It may only exercise its destructive and mocking power, perverting the good. God, the Prime Mover, Creator and Sustainer of all things, brooks no competition, hence any theory of dualism or Manichaeism proves in this light invalid.[147] St. Augustine illuminates the problem of good and evil in his *City of God* and elsewhere, employing the light and dark analogy. Evil is the absence of good, as darkness is the absence of light. He says that:

> Since evil is not the positive presence of something, it cannot be the efficient cause of sin, but it is a deficient cause in the creature. Evil, being the absence of good, or the presence of a lesser good, is the result of the creature's turning away from the commands of God to a lesser good: the will of the creature. Herein is the essence of evil: it is the creature, not God, who is the creator of sin.[148]

Recalling the light and dark parallel, one can conclude that darkness has no existence on its own, nor does it wield a power of making; it is an abyss devoid of light and good, which have been rejected by man's free will.

A completely different view on the archetype of light and dark was brought forth by the 20th c. psychoanalytical theory. Carl Gustav Jung (1875–1961) devoted much space and thought to this problem, especially to the archetypal nature of the shadow, which he saw as the embodiment of the dark and suppressed side of human self.[149] He presented the notion of the shadow as one of the primary archetypes, reading its darkness as a symbol of the unconscious, and the light as a symbol of the conscious. However wicked and shameful the contents of the shadow may be, the shadow makes, according to Jung, an essential part of our self-awareness and constitutes our *alter ego*; a view that largely contradicts the

---

Ramey Watson, 'Enlarging Augustinian systems: C. S. Lewis's *The Great Divorce* and *Till We Have Faces*', [in:] *Renascence*; spring 1994, Vol. 46, Issue 3, pp. 163–178; and John Houghton, and Neal K. Keesee, 'Tolkien, King Alfred, and Boethius: Platonist Views of Evil in *The Lord of The Rings*' [in:] *Tolkien Studies*, vol. 2, 2005, pp. 131–159.

147 Crampton, *A Biblical Theodicy*, p. 41.

148 St. Augustine, *City of God*, trans. D. Marchs; Philip Schaff, ed. (Edinburgh: WM. B. Eerdmans Publishing Company, 1886, 2002), p. 47.

149 Carl Gustav Jung, *The Collected Works: Psychology and Religion: West and East*, vol. 11, R. F. C. Hull (New York: Pantheon Books, 1958).

Christian radical rejection of evil.[150] We may spot our shadows in the mirror which we find in other people when employing an unconscious mechanism of projection. We tend to project our disowned desires and denied traits on others in an attempt to disinherit them. Jung clearly states that a complete self requires wholeness, and this necessitates integration of its two extreme polarities, that is the conscious and unconscious strata of selfhood: 'everyone carries a shadow, and the less it is embodied in the individual's conscious life, the blacker and denser it is,' he asserts.[151] Jung believes that instead of struggling to escape from one's shadow man should much rather embrace and absorb it as it is, in order to recognize its darkness in all its dread, and then illuminate it and repair. Becoming aware of one's shadow, recognizing its baseness and giving it a careful trim is Jung's recipe for a wholesome self.[152] In her ruminations upon Jungian tenets, which are reflected in her works, Le Guin writes that:

> The shadow is on the other side of our psyche, the dark brother of the conscious mind. It is Cain, Caliban, Frankenstein's monster, Mr. Hyde, (…) Frodo's enemy Gollum. It is the Doppelgänger (…), the werewolf; the wolf, the bear, (…) it is the serpent, Lucifer.[153]

Employing the light and dark antinomy as a metaphor of a relationship between one's self and its alter ego, Jung himself says that:

> To confront a person with [their] shadow is to show them their own light.(…) Anyone who perceives their shadow and their light simultaneously sees themselves from two sides and thus gets in the middle.[154]

To Jung, confronting one's shadow is the path towards light and self-enlightenment, a view which contradicts the Christian philosophy that excludes any compromise between dark and light, evil and good. In the Jungian interpretation, the shadow is the path of the inner journey into one's true self, its complementary element, and a guide rather than a threat; a twin rather than a foe. It must be noted that Jungian psychotherapy is non-Christian, not to say anti-Christian, and, in a sense, antireligious as well, inasmuch as Jung considered religions as collective mythologies and imaginary illusions, and although he valued their impact on human psyche as an important source of spiritual support and did not dismiss them outright in the way Freud did (calling religion 'the universal obsessional

---

150 Jung, *The Collected Works: Good and Evil in Analytical Psychology*, vol. 10, ed. R. F. C. Hull, ed. (New York: Pantheon Books, 1959), p. 77.
151 Jung, ibid., p. 76.
152 Jung, ibid., pp. 98–102.
153 Le Guin, *Language of the Night*, pp. 53–54.
154 Jung, *The Collected Works: Good and Evil*, p. 872.

235

neurosis of humanity'), he considered religions as nothing but useful myths to be replaced by a new 'religion' of psychoanalysis.[155]

> I imagine a far finer and more comprehensive task for [psychoanalysis] than alliance with an ethical fraternity [Jung declares]. I think we must give it time to infiltrate into people from many centers, to revivify among intellectuals a feeling for symbol and myth, ever so gently to transform Christ back into the soothsaying god of the vine, which he was, and in this way absorb those ecstatic instinctual forces of Christianity for the one purpose of making the cult and the sacred myth what they once were - a drunken feast of joy where man regained the ethos and holiness of an animal.[156]

Since Jung mythologizes religion, his thought is a heresy when approached from the Christian perspective; a queer mix of blasphemy, psychology and mythology. As Thomas Szasz, an American psychiatrist, observes, 'in Jung's view religions are indispensable spiritual supports, whereas in Freud's they are illusory crutches', but it is Freud's and Jung's shared opinion that religions are to give way to psychoanalysis.[157]

After that lengthy introduction it is time to discuss the use of light and dark in high fantasy of the Inklings and of Le Guin. I would like to approach it in terms of two techniques borrowed from visual arts: chiaroscuro and sfumato.

Chiaroscuro (in Italian, *chiaro* – light, *scuro* – dark) is a bold contrast between light and dark.[158] One of the early masters of the technique was Leonardo da Vinci, yet it was not the Renaissance but the Baroque period that helped chiaroscuro gain popularity and weight. Baroque dramatic aestheticism necessitated in painting a radical contrast between a source of light and a profound darkness surrounding it. Michelangelo Merisi da Caravaggio developed a further technique called tenebrism or dramatic illumination, which is a heightened form of chiaroscuro that uses violent contrasts of light and dark (Italian *tenebroso* means

---

155 Sigmund Freud, *The Future of an Illusion*, trans. James Strachey, ed. (New York: W. W. Norton and Company, Inc. 1961), p. 43.

156 C. G. Jung as quoted by Richard Noll. *The Jung Cult: Origins of a Charismatic Movement* (Princeton: Princeton University Press, 1994), p. 188. Jung's father was a Protestant minister, but Jung's apostasy happened already in his childhood.

157 Thomas Szasz, *The Myth of Psychotherapy* (Garden City: Doubleday/Anchor Press, 1978), p. 173. Frankl's logotherapy, although partly derived from psychoanalysis, appears different in this respect from Freud's and Jung's attitude to religion, as Frankl valued religion as a source of truth, unconditional meaning and spiritual life, remained himself a life-long believer of Judaism, and greatly respected his second wife's Catholicism.

158 *The Collins Italian Dictionary*, http://www.collinsdictionary.com/dictionary/english-italian, accessed 23 April 2016.

murky).[159] Art historians associate this technique also with the Spanish painters and some works of Rembrandt, Tintoretto and Mannerists. Rudolf Wittkower explains the origins of tenebrism, saying that 'darkness in Caravaggio's paintings is something negative; darkness is where light is not, and it is for this reason that light strikes upon his figures and objects as upon solid, impenetrable forms, and does not dissolve them.'[160] In tenebrism light and dark are two separate entities which have nothing in common, which never overlap and are never equal. The above-quoted statement of Wittkower's asserting that 'darkness is where light is not' resounds of the Augustinian and Boethian philosophy of theodicy.[161]

The theodicy of absence seems to be reflected in Tolkien's approach to the question of good and evil, the two irreconcilable opposites that stand in sharp contrast, have very clear implications and unambiguous symbolism. Scott A. Davidson explains Tolkien's endorsement of Augustinian theodicy quoting the writer's statement: 'In my story [*The Lord of the Rings*] I do not deal with Absolute Evil. I do not think there is such a thing, since that is Zero.'[162] It seems, Davidson observes, that 'St. Augustine and Tolkien agree that nothing is completely and utterly evil, because such a thing could not even exist, since existence itself is good; and they both believe that whereas goodness is primary and independent, evil is secondary and dependent on goodness.'[163]

Darkness does not have an independent existence but appears where light is suppressed by man's free choice. Shadows undoubtedly belong to darkness, and testify to the corrupting power of evil gradually leading to iniquity, unless the splinter of light inherently planted in the creation overcomes the dark. Curiously enough, in his analysis of Tolkien's works, Shippey suggests that the Augustinian and Boethian theodicy of absence has actually been combined by Tolkien with a quasi-Manichaean vision, which advocates a necessary battle with evil, a powerful and almost omnipresent reality.[164] Since the latter view may seem

159 Ibid.
160 Rudolf Wittkower, *Art and Architecture in Italy, 1600–1750*, 3rd ed. (London: Penguin Books, 1973), p. 57.
161 Wittkower, ibid., p. 57.
162 Tolkien, *Letters*, p. 243.
163 Scott A. Davidson, 'Tolkien and the Nature of Evil' [in:] *The Lord of the Rings and Philosophy: One Book to Rule Them All*, Gregory Bassham and Eric Bronson, eds. (Popular Culture and Philosophy, 2003), pp. 99–109, 102.
164 Shippey, *The Road to Middle-earth* (London: HarperCollins, 2003), p. 128. Cf. Steven Runciman, *The Medieval Manichee: A Study of the Christian Dualist Heresy* (Cambridge: Cambridge University Press, 1982).

preposterous in the light of Tolkien's firm Catholic faith, which rejects Manichaeism as a heresy, Shippey justifies his observation referring to Tolkien's heroic view of the battle with evil, similar to the one rendered by King Alfred in
his Old English translation of Boethius. In the book Boethius argues that evil
is the inner weakness, a pitiable condition of the lack of good, which shows the
malefactor in a more sympathetic light than the victim. The Anglo-Saxon heroic
tradition, as well as Tolkien's traumatic experience of the First World War, made
for him that point of the Boethian theodicy hard to accept. Those two life-long
impacts seem to have proved to Tolkien that evil exists externally and may not always be pardoned. As a result, Shippey argues, Tolkienian mythos unites the two
philosophies of good and evil, making a complex and unique fusion.[165] Tolkien's
awareness of the necessary battle with evil and his conviction that evil tends to
gain the upper hand over good on earth and in mankind, the ultimate victory of
good being certain to occur, as St. John's Apocalypse foresees, only at the end of
time, is nevertheless a strictly Catholic, not Manichean, belief.[166]

Evil is the absence or suppression of good, and does not have an independent existence, Boethius and Augustine claim, and there are many instances in
Tolkien's works which echo this view. 'Nothing is evil in the beginning,' Tolkien
says in *The Lord of the Rings* through Elrond's words, and adds: 'Even Sauron
was not so.'[167] Frodo expresses another Boethian principle observing that 'the
Shadow (…) can only mock, it cannot make; not real new things of its own.'[168]
Similarly, Trolls, the creatures of evil, are 'only counterfeits, made by the Enemy
in the Great Darkness, in mockery of Ents, as Orcs were of Elves.'[169] Only good is
capable of making, for evil can merely pervert the works of creation. 'The theme
of the creator passing into the thing created is pervasive in Tolkien's work; the
"false" creations of evil beings are never more than a diminution and diffusion
of themselves, while Eru's creations are limitless, yet He is never diminished,'
recapitulates Robert Blackham.[170]

Another picture of evil originating as a perversion and eventually an absence of
good is painted in Tolkien's *The Silmarillion*. All works created by Eru Ilúvatar are
good, and it is the conceit and envy of Melkor, an Ainu, originally an immaculate

---

165   Shippey, *The Road to Middle-earth*, p. 129.
166   Cf. Chapters 19 and 20 of St. John's Revelation (Apocalypse), which describe the final
      defeat of evil.
167   Tolkien, *The Lord of the Rings*, (*LtR*), vol. I (London: Mariner Books, 2005), p. 261.
168   Ibid., vol. III, p. 190.
169   Ibid., vol. II, p. 89.
170   Robert Blackham, *The Roots of Tolkien's Middle-earth* (London: Tempus, 2006), p. 27.

divine creature, that gives rise to evil. Melkor, later called Morgoth Bauglir, is the true Dark Enemy Tyrant, whom all subsequent villains serve, including Sauron, the Lord of the Rings. In Quenya, Mor means 'dark, black or a shadow'; hence Mordor is the Land of the Shadow or the Land where the Shadows lie. Melkor causes darkness to emerge as he destroys the main sources of light created by the Valar, namely the Two Lamps: Illuin and Ormal, which illuminate Arda.

Although there are many reverberations of the Boethian theodicy in Tolkien's mythology, Shippey claims, upholding his reading of Tolkien's oeuvre, that they have been intertwined with some streaks of a quasi-Manichean weave: 'it is perhaps fair to say that while the balances are maintained, we are on the whole more conscious of evil as an objective power and of good as a subjective impulse.'[171] Mordor and 'the Shadow' are nearer and more visible than the Valar or the other powers of good. Shippey calls it 'a lack of symmetry' and links with the prevailing insecurity that overshadows the anti-quest of destroying the Ring. If the fellows of the Ring fail to complete their mission, the Shadow will devour Middle-earth, but if they accept the burden, it may destroy them equally. This double-edged sword results from Tolkien's conviction that a victory over evil can only be temporary on earth. The final destruction will only be possible at the end of the world, with the second coming of the Saviour. Being fully aware of the tremendous power of the Shadow, Gandalf says, 'the evil of Sauron cannot be wholly cured, nor made as if it had not been;' and adds, 'I am Gandalf, Gandalf the White, but Black is mightier still.'[172] This declaration sounds indeed Manichaean, however in the case of Tolkien it is just a sign of some kind of pessimism, resulting from his Christian awareness that the final victory over evil will only take place beyond the walls of this world, when time ceases to be.

Furthermore, Shippey argues that the prevalent air of doom and defeat is the tone which Tolkien had learnt from the Northern mythology, where doing what is right was not rewarded by hope of salvation or virtue.[173] Verlyn Flieger, on the other hand, explains this defeatism with reference to Tolkien's childhood trauma of losing his parents, especially mother, and his bitter experience of the death of his best friends in the trenches on the Somme.[174] Another cause of that quasi-Manichean streak in Tolkien's thought and fiction could perhaps be the historical

---

171 Shippey, *The Road to Middle-earth*, p. 139.
172 *LtR*, vol. II, p. 98.
173 Shippey, *The Road to Middle-earth*, p. 140.
174 Verlyn Flieger, *Splinter of Light: Logos and Language in Tolkien's World* (Kent: Kent State University Press 2002), p. 62. Two of Tolkien's best friends from Birmingham that had belonged to the Tea Club Barrovian Society (T. C. B. S.) died during the

context of his work – *The Lord of the Rings* was being written during and in the wake of the Second World War, in which evil had fully demonstrated its power.

Nevertheless, against that pervasive sense of defeatism Tolkien himself casts his Christian hope of the ultimate 'Eucatastrophe' ('Consolation of the Happy Ending' or a 'happy catastrophe'), completed upon the second coming of God to the earth; the return upon which evil will be ultimately destroyed, at a time unknown and unforeseeable.[175] It is with a similar stunning Eucatastrophe that Tolkien resolves many critical turns of the plot, leading towards a sudden and unexpected fortunate dénouement. All in all, 'the good side in *The Lord of the Rings* does win,' concludes Shippey, 'but its casualties include, besides Théoden and Boromir, beauty, Lothlórien, parts of Middle-earth, and even Gollum.'[176] The characters are aware of their losses all the time, and bear the burden of regret. They just have to make the best of things and must not confuse sorrow with despair.[177]

Interpreting the relationship between light and dark, good and evil, Shippey implies that the Tolkienian blended nature of evil, combining threads of contrastive philosophies, is best reflected through the Ring of Sauron.[178] On the one hand, the Ring feeds on inner weaknesses and unconscious wickedness of the Ring-bearers and on the evil of Ringwraiths, but on the other hand, it is also a token of a powerful external force which comes from the outside and must be challenged and battled. A fine example of this amalgamate may be the scene at Sammath Naur, the Cracks of Doom, when the external force of Sauron accumulated in the Ring is abetted by Frodo's inner weakness, who refutes his mission as he says, 'I will not do this deed. The Ring is mine.'[179] 'Maybe all sins need some combination of external prompting and inner weakness,' suggests Shippey.[180] 'At any rate, the narrative of *The Lord of the Rings* (…) is neither a saint's life, all about temptation, nor a complicated war game, all about tactics; it's the unique fusion of the two which allows the moral and philosophical depth of the epic.

---

war; the third, Christopher Wiseman (1893–1987), survived, and Tolkien named his third son Christopher after Wiseman.

175   Tolkien introduces and expands upon his concept of 'Eucatastrophe' in his essay 'On Fairy Stories', pp. 153–155, presented in detail in Chapter Seven of this book.

176   Shippey, *The Road to Middle-earth*, p. 143.

177   Shippey, ibid., p. 143.

178   Shippey, ibid., p. 129.

179   Shippey, p. 133, *LtR*, vol. III, p. 924.

180   Shippey, ibid., p. 133.

The Lord of the Rings would be a much lesser work if it had swerved towards either extreme,' the scholar concludes.[181]

No matter whether Shippey's interpretation is accepted or challenged, what seems indisputable is that Tolkien unambiguously associates evil with darkness and shadow, and sees no viability of a merger or compromise of light and dark. As the only true power, light will defeat darkness and forever erase all its shadows, so that there will be no more death, yet this will happen at the end of time, as Christian eschatology teaches. Light and dark, as depicted by Tolkien, appear as two uncompromising extremes, whose union is unattainable. If one may apply art terms, this resembles chiaroscuro, especially its Baroque rendition, and sometimes even tenebrism.[182] Strong contrasts between light and dark seem to leave no permanent space for mingling or mixing of the two. Tolkienian characters who are on the verge of corruption represent shadows of their former selves and they may either fall or rise, but cannot linger in between for long. This does not mean that light has no colours, because whiteness is multicoloured, as Gandalf observes quoting Saruman.[183] It can be refracted through a prism, producing amazing hues that make the dispersed miscellany of creation. In Tolkien's view man is a splintered light of God. In his poem 'Philomythus to Misomythus' (dedicated to Lewis just before the Lewis's conversion to Christianity), better known as 'Mythopoeia', Tolkien observes:

Man, Sub-creator, the refracted light
Through whom is splintered from a single White
To many hues, and endlessly combined
In living shapes that move from mind to mind.[184]

According to Tolkien, human works represent Sub-creation, which is possible solely thanks to God's love and grace, and they reflect the life-giving light of God, being a remote reflection of His divine illumination. Every human being is a splinter of this light and hence wields a creative power, a shimmer of God's light that evil cannot stand. George MacDonald, a proto-Inkling, writes that 'man is (…) a passing flame, moving unquietly amid the surrounding rest of night;

---

181 Shippey, ibid., p. 133.
182 The only book I have encountered that deals with the transposition of visual techniques in literature is Constance A. Pedoto's *Painting Literature* (University Press of America, 1993), which analyses literary epitomes of chiaroscuro, sfumato, incollato and impasto.
183 Tolkien, *The Lord of the Rings*, *The Fellowship of the Ring*, p. 158.
184 Tolkien, 'Mythopoeia', lines 61–64.

without which he yet could not be, and whereof he is in part compounded.'[185] Human life, which is a 'passing flame' splintered from God's light, looks like a path of light carved out among the shadows of darkness, and even though its light does not last long, it disrupts darkness and illuminates it briefly. Man comes from Logos, from the Word and the Light, and carries in him its splinter. St. John says: that Word 'was the true Light, which lightens every man that comes into this world' (John 1:9). As an essentially good creature, man reflects a speck of God's light and is designated to imitate the works of creation according to his or her abilities. Man must be aware of evil, though, for 'of Evil this/Alone is deadly certain: Evil is,' Tolkien points out in 'Mythopoeia.'[186]

The Tolkienian view of evil is very closely connected with the concept of a shadow. 'Shadows are the absence of light, and so don't exist in themselves,' Shippey notes, following the Boethian theodicy, yet 'they are still visible and palpable just as if they did,' he adds.[187] Shippey argues that this view is precisely Tolkienian, and tracks it down to the Old English sources, especially to the poem *Solomon and Saturn II*, a fine riddle-contest reflected in *The Hobbit*, in which there is a shadow riddle.[188] Another Old English inspiration for Tolkien was certainly *Beowulf*, in which Grendel drags people 'under shadow' (*under sceadu*).[189] The motif of being dragged *under sceadu* can be read as one of the leitmotifs of Tolkien's epic. Frodo is tormented by the shadow and drawn to it, and completes his anti-quest in the Land of the Shadow, nearly becoming a shadow of his own self, a petty wraith, were it not for Gollum's inadvertently redeeming intervention. It is so because, apart from serving as an embodiment of evil, the shadow in Tolkien's mythology also signifies the shadow of one's former self. Gollum appears as a visualisation of what Frodo might become, a miserable corrupt hobbit, and it is Gollum who stops Frodo from turning into a wraith and succumbing to the power of the Ring completely. Tolkien's depiction of the shadow is also a personification of Sauron and the symbol of Mordor, the land 'where shadows lie'. The ancient prophesy in *The Lord of the Rings* explicitly draws on this image, presaging the rise of the new king, Aragorn, who will spread light over Middle-earth:

---

185   George MacDonald, *Phantastes: A Faerie Romance for Men and Women*. 3rd ed. (Grand Rapids: Wm. Eerdmans Publishing Co., 1981), p. 97.
186   Tolkien, 'Mythopoeia', lines 79–80.
187   Shippey, *The Road to Middle-earth*, p. 133.
188   Saturn asks Solomon, 'What things were that were not?' and the answer includes the word *besceadeð*, that is shadows. (cf. Shippey, *The Road to Middle-earth*, p. 133).
189   Shippey, ibid., p. 134.

From the ashes a fire shall be woken,
A light from the shadows shall spring;
Renewed shall be blade that was broken,
The crownless again shall be king.[190]

An interesting problem that puzzles Tolkien is the question of light and dark reflected in the races of the Middle-earth. Having studied the Icelandic mythology of Snorri Sturluson (*Prose Edda* of 1230), an account of the Danish lore by
Nikolai Grundtvig of 1808–1832, and its German equivalent by Jacob Grimm
of 1835, Tolkien encountered the so-called 'elf problem' connected with a division of elves into Light-elves, Dark-elves and Black-elves.[191] Snorri draws a sign of
equality between Dark-elves, Black-elves and Dwarves, thus distinguishing them
from the light, angelic elves, yet maintaining their elvish benevolent nature. As
Shippey remarks, some critics have read this antithesis of light and black elves as
a 'dualism of spirits good and bad, between angels of light and of darkness'.[192] It
seems, though, that the association with the dark implies here a dwarfish interest
in smithcraft and mining rather than any connotation with evil. Grundtvig also
recognizes Black-elves as Dwarves, however he suggests that Dark-elves make
perhaps yet another group, which he labels 'elves of the twilight'.[193] Grimm questions Snorri's equation as a simplistic reduction and opts for an explanation closer
to Grundtvig's.[194] This problem must have inspired Tolkien, who elaborated his
own explanation. In the *Book of the Lost Tales* he seems to have accepted the notion of Black-elves meaning Dwarves, directly tackling the problem in *The Silmarillion*. Here the writer develops the distinction between the Light-elves who have
seen the Light of the Two Trees, Telperion and Laurelin, and the Wood-elves, who
appear in *The Hobbit*, and who are the elves of the twilight, loving the stars and
running in the woods by moonlight.[195]

Moreover, in *The Silmarillion*, Tolkien introduces Eöl, the Dark Elf, who lives
in deep shadow, and who befriends Dwarves and masters their craft of metal-
work, producing a black and shining metal, which he uses to make his armour.
His son, Maeglin, is called a 'Child of the Twilight' and starts a race of Elves that

---

190 *LtR*, vol. I, p. 152.
191 Shippey, 'Light-elves, Dark-elves and Others: Tolkien's Elvish Problem' [in:] *Tolkien
     Studies*, vol. I; Douglas Anderson, Michael Drout and VerlynFlieger, eds. (Morgan-
     town: West Virginia University, 2004), p. 14.
192 Shippey, 'Light-elves, Dark-elves and Others', p. 16.
193 Shippey, ibid., p. 17.
194 Shippey, ibid., p. 19.
195 Shippey, ibid., p. 19.

are Dark Elves of the twilight. In Tolkien's cosmogony, therefore, there are no black Elves as such, save for Eöl, a friend of the Dwarves, who was alone called the Dark or Black Elf. The love of twilight and starlight, attributed to Wood Elves, does not make them children of the shadow and darkness, yet reminds of their kinship with the Dwarves, Children of Ilúvatar, fond of the underground. Black and dark in this case seem to suggest affiliation of different races rather than their corrupt nature.

To recapitulate, it seems that Tolkien's vision of light and dark, that is of good and evil, follows the Boethian philosophy and also perhaps the quasi-Manichaean perspective, and in terms of painting it could correspond to a contrasting juxtaposition resembling chiaroscuro or sometimes even tenebrism. The ominous growing shadow often dominates the picture, yet it never depreciates the quality of light and never makes it off-white. Flieger seems to write about the Tolkienian chiaroscuro, without using the term, when she observes that 'the alternation between (…) light and dark is the essence both of Tolkien and of his work. The contrast and interplay of light and dark are essential elements of his fiction. The light-dark polarity operates on all levels – literal, metaphoric, [and] symbolic.'[196] Flieger concludes that:

> No careful reader of Tolkien's fiction can fail to be aware of the polarities that give it form and tension. His work is built on contrasts - between hope and despair, between good and evil, between enlightenment and ignorance – and these contrasts are embodied in the polarities of light and dark that are the creative outgrowth of his contrary moods, the 'antitheses' of his nature.[197]

The Tolkienian chiaroscuro is perhaps even sharper in C. S. Lewis's fantasy works, considering his taste for allegory and commitment to Christian apologetic writing. There is profound allegory and symbolism in his oeuvre, including fantasy fiction, in which light implies the good that subdues the dark, the iniquitous. The leonine Christ represented as Aslan in *The Chronicles of Narnia* is not an allegory, as Lewis is careful to point out, but a fantasy rendition of what Christ might be like in the Narnian world:

> If Aslan represented the immaterial Deity in the same way in which Giant Despair represents Despair [a tangible person represents an intangible quality], he would be an allegorical figure. In reality however, he is an invention giving an imaginary answer to the question, 'what might Christ become like if there really were a world like Narnia and

---

196   Flieger, *Splinter of Light*, p. 4.
197   Flieger, ibid., p. 2.

He chose to be incarnate and die and rise again in that world as He actually has done in ours?' This is not allegory at all.[198]

Aslan's golden mane, with 'hair like pure gold', and his eyes as bright 'as gold that is liquid in the furnace', as well as the warm sunlight and the silver stars of Narnia emphasize benevolence and love; Jadis the witch's unnatural morbid whiteness implies severe winter, freezing cold and death, and she is like the biblical 'whitewashed tombs, which look beautiful on the outside but on the inside are full of the bones of the dead and everything unclean' (Matthew 23:27); whereas blackness surrounding the stable of the Ape and most of the Calormenes in the final scenes of the Narnian heptalogy stands for nothingness and evil. The end of Narnia happens when Aslan makes all the stars fall and orders Time to extinguish the Narnian sun, after which total blackness and ice-cold air enwrap the dead land, and Narnia is no more:

> Then Aslan said [to the great Time-giant]: 'Now make an end.'
>
> The giant threw his horn into the sea. Then he stretched out one arm – very black it looked, and thousands of miles long – across the sky till his hand reached the Sun. He took the Sun and squeezed it in his hand as you would squeeze an orange. And instantly there was total darkness.[199]

Aslan, pure light and good, is the exact opposite of Tash, a hideous malevolent demon of darkness, upon whom Aslan inflicts a crushing defeat at the end of Narnia, Calormen and that world. Lewis's design of light and dark in his Narnia tales seems therefore to match the chiaroscuro imagery of sharp contrasts. Lewis's love of light and good resembles Tolkien's, for both Inklings view those as attributes of the Maker and as imperfect patchy splinters of His love and perfection that will be fully revealed beyond this world:

> Any patch of sunlight in a wood will show you something, [Lewis says], something which you could never get from reading books on astronomy. These pure and spontaneous pleasures are 'patches of Godlight' in the woods of our experience.[200]

Lewis's Christian apologetics, whose otherworldly reflection emerges also from his Narnian Chronicles, likewise seems to rest on the chiaroscuro antagonism,

---

198 Lewis, *Letters of C. S. Lewis*, W. H. Lewis, ed. (London: Houghton Mifflin Harcourt, 2003), p. 48.

199 Lewis, *The Chronicles of Narnia: The Last Battle* (London: HarperCollins Publishers, 2002), p. 148.

200 Lewis, *Letters to Malcolm*, p. 91.

in which light leads up a 'path of the Divine radiance to the Logos itself.'[201] That radical rejection of the dark is what Le Guin, a 'congenital non-Christian' writer exploring Jungian themes, considers an oversimplification, labelling Lewis's writings, unlike Tolkien's, whose fiction is subtler and more elusive, as 'simply Christian apologia.'[202]

It would certainly be interesting to view the use of light and dark in the works of the third most prolific Inkling, Charles Williams – a study which, none the less, is not included in this book. The reason is that Williams's fantasy novels, mingling thriller and horror stories with Christian allegories and tales of the esoteric and supernatural, do not sub-create the otherworldliness in the way Tolkien's Middle-earth or Lewis's Narnia do, and do not share their fairy nature, as his fiction belongs to a rather different, hardly definable or comparable genre, which requires a separate analysis.

Returning to the pictorial symbolism of light and dark within the scope of high fantasy, one needs to regard its use in Le Guin's fantasy tales, whose mythopoeic otherworldliness of Earthsea does in some ways resemble Tolkien's. Enchanted with the Tolkienesque mythology though she is, Le Guin has notwithstanding created hers, by 'discovering', as she says, the Earthsea world.[203] Light and dark, the self and the shadow, also make the warp and the woof of her fantasy, yet their fabric is not Christian or Platonic philosophy but much rather elements of anthropology and Taoism. To Le Guin, light and dark are two interdependent and complementary opposites, responsible for maintaining Equilibrium, like the yin-yang duality. Yin is the dark, passive and feminine element, whereas yang represents its bright, active and masculine match. They stand for night and day, death and life, and have no absolute power or superiority over each other, but instead create a perfect dichotomy, which is cyclical and mobile. They consume and support each other and may also turn into each other. This equilibrium lies at the fundaments of Earthsea. 'To light a candle is to cast a shadow', explains Master Hand of Roke.[204] In *The Left Hand of Darkness*, Le Guin writes that:

---

201   James S. Cutsinger, 'C. S. Lewis as Apologist and Mystic', 2007; lecture delivered for the Narnia Clubs of New York, December 1998 ; http://cutsinger.net/pdf/lewis_as_ apologist_ and_mystic.pdf, accessed 10 May 2015.

202   Le Guin, *The Language of the Night*, p. 55; Maya Jaggi, 'The Magician' with fragments of an interview with Le Guin', 2005.

203   Le Guin, Foreword *to The Other Wind*, p. xi.

204   Le Guin, *The Earthsea Cycle: A Wizard of Earthsea* (New York: Houghton Mifflin, 2005), p. 44.

Light is the left hand of darkness and darkness is the right hand of light.
Two are one, life and death, lying together like lovers in kemmer,
like hands joined together, like the end and the way.[205]

Similar tenets of the Taoist equilibrium reverberate throughout the Earthsea series. The 'Song of Éa', which extolls the Creation of Éa by Segoy, proclaims:

Only in silence the word, only in dark the light, only in dying life:
Bright the hawk's flight on the empty sky.[206]

A perfect example of the restored equilibrium is Ged, the protagonist of Le Guin's Earthsea hexalogy, who having fled and then chased his shadow in the end embraces it and heals the rift in himself, between his self and its shadow-self. The shadow is merely himself, his dark, suppressed side of ambition and power. Only by incorporating it can Ged become a whole person, and can come of age. Recognising the unwanted *alter ego* is a Jungian archetype of the shadow, which, when accepted and controlled, enriches the self in maturity and wisdom. Without embracing one's own shadow, Le Guin seems to argue, one lacks balance and peace. When Ged finally faces his shadow, he 'reaches out his hands and [takes] hold of his shadow, of the black self that reached out to him. Light and darkness [meet], and join and [become] one'.[207]

By doing so, 'Ged makes himself whole; a man, who, knowing his whole true self, cannot be used or possessed by any power other than himself, and whose life therefore is lived for life's sake, and never in the service of ruin, or pain, or hatred or the dark.'[208] 'Only by coming to know oneself completely and truly,' Harnsberger infers, 'does one triumph over their nature and resist the temptation of evil.'[209] This is the Equilibrium advised by Ged and his masters: Ogion, and the wizards of Roke. Ged remarks that 'in being opposite, [light and dark] yearn toward each other (…), giving birth to each other and [in turn being] forever reborn.'[210] The true light in Earthsea is the light of good which is only seen when contrasted with evil and the dark. Its tiny splinter is the 'werelight' of wizards, an illusion of light which can illuminate the dark for a while. Ged's inner

---

205   Le Guin, *The Left Hand of Darkness* (New York: Ace Books, 2000), p. 1.
206   Le Guin, *A Wizard of Earthsea*, p. 2.
207   Le Guin, *The Farthest Shore*, p. 179.
208   Jessica Harnsberger, 'Shadows and Darkness: Learning to Triumph over Human Weakness', 2004, http://www.victorianweb.org/authors/gm/harnsberger14.html, accessed 23 April 2016.
209   Harnsberger, ibid.
210   Le Guin, *The Farthest Shore*, p. 179.

light manages to overcome the darkness of the Tombs of Atuan in the Kargish land, where he saves Tenar from the evil murk of the ancient Nameless Ones, the wicked spirits that abhor light and truth. Persuaded by Ged, 'Tenar chooses to be a whole person instead of a dark half, and when she is given back her true name, the light and the dark come together to form one whole.'[211] The rejoining of the ring of Erreth-Akbe completed by Ged with Tenar's help symbolically represents this wholeness.

In *The Farthest Shore*, the third part of the hexalogy, darkness spreads over Earthsea, leaking from behind a wall of the dead, as the corrupt wizard Cob creates an artificial life for the dead in the land of the shadows. Instead of life, though, he offers them suffering and eternal death. Assisted by Arren, Ged spends all his power to close the breach and restore Equilibrium, and succeeds, sacrificing all his great gift of wizardry. As Jan Griffin points out, the twist in this book is that Cob is not altogether evil, as he wants to eliminate death, yet in so doing he profoundly disturbs the balance, which affects all races, men and dragons equally.[212] The equilibrium between life and death, light and dark, must not be broken.

Tehanu, the eponymous heroine of the next book of the cycle, turns out to be a dragoness and a woman at the same time, cruelly abused by her human parents, yet able to communicate with the dragons and displaying enormous mental power. Her name is the name of a star of Earthsea, and in her hybrid dragonish and human nature Tehanu in a way unites pure light with chastising fire, the dark past of her childhood trauma with her undisturbed being of a dragon. In *The Other Wind* she plays a crucial role in restoring the ancient peace between dragons and men and in mending the violated balance between life and death. Following Jungian psychology, Le Guin argues in her Earthsea mythology that recognition, acceptance and mastering one's shadow, which necessitates humility and meekness, guarantee the wholeness of the self. Yielding to the shadow turns a person into a 'gebbeth', a mere puppet of evil and a ghost of the true self. The shadow, like Ged's, must be tamed and subdued to make a mature self, yet its presence and contribution is vital to achieving wholeness and gaining self-knowledge and understanding. Le Guin's view seems to parallel Voland's provocative words spoken to Matthew Levi in Mikhail Bulgakov's novel *The Master and Margarita*: 'What would your good do if evil did not exist, and what would the earth look like if shadows disappeared from it?'[213] Le Guin seems to suggest that good needs evil

---

211   Jan Griffin, 'Ursula Le Guin's Magical World of Earthsea', in *The Alan Review*, vol. 23 (Blacksburg: University Libraries, Virginia Tech, 1996), p. 6.

212   Griffin, 'Ursula Le Guin's Magical World of Earthsea', p. 9.

213   Mikhail Bulgakov, *The Master and Margarita* (London: Vintage, 1996, 4ᵗʰ ed.), p. 360.

to mark its difference, just as much as light requires dark to be recognised. The Christian and Boethian desire for the ultimate eradication of the dark does not quite apply to Le Guin's world, as it appears destructive to its dichotomous Equilibrium of Earthsea.

When attempting to match a painting technique with Le Guin's high fantasy, it appears that the Taoist and Jungian thought that permeates her writings resembles sfumato. All concepts have their opposites, with which they mingle, making binaries, and immersing into one another. The smoky, misty imagery seems to be built by ranges of subtle shimmering hues, which gradually turn into others. Contrasts and rifts do not appear as drastic as in chiaroscuro, as they also comply with the overriding principle of maintaining equilibrium. *Wu wei*, or the Taoist tenet of action through inertia and patience, means refraining from abrupt actions.[214] Light in Le Guin's Earthsea needs the dark as its foil and corollary, and as a twin shadow. Here 'the dark powers of evil shall not be forgotten or disregarded but acknowledged and contained by human beings willing to fight for goodness.'[215] The clashing forces of light and dark 'must exist together, for each draws its very meaning and power from the presence of the other, like good and evil, life and death,' Harnsberger observes.[216]

Tolkien's interpretation of light and dark tends to correspond to the technique and symbolism of sharp contrasts, as in chiaroscuro, although his use of shadows, twilight and greyness (e.g., Gandalf the Grey that becomes Gandalf the White), might at times suggest elements of sfumato, different though it is from Le Guin's. Tolkien's momentary sfumato does not contradict the unbridgeable gap between good and evil, heaven and hell, and abides by it, whereas Le Guin seems to reject any such radically different and irreconcilable extremities. Lewis's imagery tends to draw on the chiaroscuro pattern only. Tolkien himself 'believe[s] that the road to fairyland is not the road to Heaven; nor even to Hell, though some have held that it may lead thither indirectly by the Devil's tithe', a statement which might appear germane to this chiaroscuro imagery interpretation, with some elements of his unique sfumato, different from Le Guin's, who does not espouse the concepts of heaven and hell at all.[217] To illustrate his point Tolkien quotes the medieval ballad *Thomas the Rhymer*, about Thomas of Erceldoune, a Scottish laird, who was

---

214 Cf. David Loy, 'Wei-wu-wei: Nondual Action', in *Philosophy East and West*, Vol. 35, 4th ed., no. 1 (January 1985), pp. 734–787.
215 Harnsberger, 'Shadows and Darkness'.
216 Harnsberger, ibid.
217 Tolkien, 'On Fairy-Stories', p. 110.

carried away by the Queen of Elfland and who returned from Elfland after seven years with a gift of prophecy:

> O see ye not yon narrow road
> So thick beset wi' thorns and briers?
> That is the path of Righteousness,
> Though after it but few inquires.
> And see ye not yon braid, braid road
> That lies across the lily leven?
> That is the path of Wickedness,
> Though some call it the Road to Heaven.
> And see ye not yon bonny road
> That winds about yon fernie brae?
> That is the road to fair Elfland,
> Where thou and I this night maun gae.'[218]

As in Christianity, the path to Heaven is narrow and thorny, while the road to Hell is broad and comfortable, but the road to Faërie looks beautiful, and leads in between, for where its perilous realm might lead to depends on the faith and reason of the man who trespasses its borders. Within the chiaroscuro contrast between Heaven and Hell there appears Faërie, a sfumato effect itself, conceived in Tolkien's momentary fashion, for it is suspended in between the two opposites, and, depending on its human use, it may turn into either extremity. If it is to be therapeutic, then its healing and benevolent nature embedded in its 'strong moral element' needs to be recognised and explored, so that the Fantasy of Faërie produces Enchantment, Consolation, Recovery and Eucatastrophe, rather than 'delusion, hallucination', 'silliness and morbidity'.[219]

The use of light and dark, essential to ekphrastic narratives of various literary genres, apart from building otherworldliness appears symbolically meaningful in fantasy, just like in myths. Does it also appear therapeutic? It would be an exaggeration to talk about some literary phototherapy (or heliotherapy) in the way in which it is used in medicine, for instance in the treatment of some psychiatric disorders such as depression, yet the writers' design of the light and dark

---

218 Tolkien, ibid., p. 110. The modern version reads: 'O do you see that narrow, narrow road,/So thick beset with thorn and briar?/That is the path of righteousness,/Though after it but few enquire./Do you see yonder broad broad road,/That lies across the lovely lawn?/That is the path of wickedness,/Though some call it the road to heaven. And do you see yon bonny bonny road,/That winds about the fern hillside?/That is the road to fair Elfland,/Where you and I this night must go.'

219 Tolkien, 'On Fairy-Stories', pp. 118, 139, and 140.

dichotomy engages the readers' imagination, senses, mind and psyche: light wins in Tolkien's and Lewis's mythos, whereas it forever maintains balance with darkness and does not remain overshadowed by evil in Le Guin's world. The interplay of light and dark, as arranged by Tolkien and Lewis, seems to suggest: 'take heart', as light overcomes darkness and awaits its final triumph at the end of time. And so it does in Lewis's Narnia, pointing towards light and joy beyond death. Le Guin, in turn, presents the coexistence of light and dark, good and evil, emphasising the necessity to fight with overwhelming darkness in order to restore a balance, but also to accept its implanted in this world as a warning, a challenge and a purifying element, which makes one discover, admit, and subdue their inner dark side: the shadow. Although, unsurprisingly, the Inklings are here at issue with Le Guin over the relationship between dark and light, good and evil, they all seem to draw on the pictorial and ekphrastic capacity of fantasy narrative achieving some kind of therapeutic aesthetics of meaning, which is addressed as a generic property of high fantasy fiction in the next chapter.

Chapter Six

Mythopathy, logotherapy and (non)sensopaedia or the psychotherapeutic properties of high fantasy ethos, as reflected in the works of the Inklings and of U. K. Le Guin

This chapter seeks to address the essence of my book, that is the psychotherapeutic properties of fantasy narrative in the works of the Inklings and of Le Guin, now focusing on the genre itself, as endorsed by the writers in question. The previously made assumptions about a therapeutic dimension of narrative as such, (concerning what could be termed as therapy through narrative), and of art (that is art therapy), as reflected in literature and made possible thanks to its pictoriality, musicality, and, generally, its interartistic ekphrastic plasticity, obviously still hold their ground, for they provide an important context for therapy. Since these qualities regard various literary genres, in this chapter, however, I intend to outline psychotherapeutic properties that pertain specifically to high fantasy literature, that is the fantasy fiction stipulated by Tolkien and advocated to an appreciable extent by C. S. Lewis and Le Guin. In so doing the previously introduced concepts of mythopathy, logotherapy and *therapia pauperum* are called upon in order to determine the psychotherapeutic potential of Faërie. The initial premise of my argument is that high fantasy genre has its own ethos, according to which the genre is value-based and moral, although not really moralizing; and hence, it enhances an unconditional meaning, or Logos, which in Faërie is bound up with language, the latter being pure and incorrupt, as in myth.[1] This status of 'fantasy ethos' puts the genre at odds with the mainstream thought of postmodernity, which defies permanent values and foundations, and shuns generic prescriptiveness, as argued in the previous chapters, especially in Chapter Three.[2]

---

1 Lewis's fantasy works might sometimes be considered to be moralizing, because of the 'hot-gospelling' quality of all his post-conversion writing, and the frequently used Christian allegorizing mode of his works.

2 I have addressed the generic marks of high fantasy also in a paper 'High fantasy fiction and the fantastic mode: against the anti-prescriptiveness of genre in contemporary literature?' [in:] *Genre in Contemporary English Studies*, Olga Glebova, ed. (Częstochowa: Jan Długosz University Press, 2014), pp. 37–65.

Situated on the borderline of the theory of music and the theory of literature, the first part of this chapter argues that the ancient theory of ethos, which refers to music, may apply to literature as well, and that fantasy genre in particular has its own ethos of a specific therapeutic effect that works through catharsis towards consolation.

The theory of ethos

In the ancient theory of music, in which music was inextricably connected with lyrics and choreography, instrumental music being at first of secondary importance, all Greek scales (later Latinized into modes) were considered to have unique properties and a particular psychological effect on the listener and the performer. They were believed to generate and foster a particular 'moral response' (in Greek *ethos*, ἦθος, means a 'disposition' or 'character'; whereas ἔθος, transcribed likewise, refers to 'a custom; or 'habit'): for instance, the Dorian mode was associated with a strong, heroic, austere and virile character; the Phrygian mode was ecstatic and emotional; the Lydian mode sounded intimate, lascivious or fearful; whereas the Mixolydian mode expressed sorrow and pain.[3] The invention and elaboration of the scales is often attributed to Pythagoras and his pupils. After the Pythagoreans, some of the most prominent ancient thinkers developed and espoused the theory of ethos, which is briefly sketched below.

In his *Republic* Plato stresses the educational values of the Dorian and Phrygian mode, and warns against the softening influence of the Lydian scale.[4]'A musical disciplinarian', Plato is preoccupied with the ethical aspects of music, viewed as a union of sound, poetry and dance, and expands on the disadvantages of instrumental music, which he considers a frivolous entertainment drawing

---

3   Martin Litchfield West, *Ancient Greek Music* (Oxford: Oxford University Press, 1992), p. 246. Ethos, (in Greek: 'disposition' or 'character') is 'the character or emotions of a speaker or writer that are expressed in the attempt to persuade an audience', as distinguished from pathos, which is 'the emotion the speaker or writer hopes to induce in the audience.' The two terms were understood in a broader sense by ancient classical authors, who used pathos when referring to the violent emotions and ethos to mean the calmer ones. Ethos was the 'natural disposition or moral character, an abiding quality, and pathos a temporary and often violent emotional state.' For Renaissance writers the distinction was a different one: ethos described character and pathos an emotional appeal; cf. 'Ethos', *The New Grove Dictionary of Music Online*, 2012, L. Macy, ed. http://www.grovemusic.com, accessed 23 April 2016. Cf. Liddell and Scott's *Greek-English Lexicon*.

4   West, ibid., p. 247.

on purely technical skill, and lacking in genuine emotion.[5] According to Plato, music conveys ethos through mimesis, that is imitation; and in order to have a benevolent influence on people it must follow the principles of 'singleness, straightforward simplicity, and universality.'[6]

Damon, a Pythagorean philosopher of Syracuse of the 5th c. BC, names and catalogues a set of modal scales, describing their notes, rhythms and qualities, and recommends or condemns different rhythms and tempi. He advocates the use of the modes that promote courage, justice and moderation, and warns against others, on account of their detrimental effect on the listeners' psyche and spirits.[7] Damon's primary tenet is that 'liberal and beautiful songs and dances create a similar soul, and the reverse kind creates a reverse kind of soul.'[8]

Another outstanding representative of the theory of ethos, Aristotle distinguishes three types of musical modes: the practical, the ethical, and the enthusiastic, arguing that the 'ethical' modes affect man's ethos 'either by endowing man with ethical stability (the Dorian mode) or by destroying it (the wistful Mixolydian mode or the Ionian one with its enervating spell).'[9] The 'practical' modes suggest in turn certain acts of will, while the 'enthusiastic' ones, especially the Phrygian mode, lead to ecstasy, and bring emotional relief.[10] Challenging at this point Plato's doctrine, Aristotle defends instrumental music as another musical source of 'psychagogic influence' on the human soul, which works 'even in the absence of a text, owing to the rhythms and melodies themselves.'[11] Moreover,

---

5   West, ibid., p. 248.
6   Edward A. Lippman, *Musical Thought in Ancient Greece* (New York: Columbia University Press, 1964), p. 62.
7   Aristotle, as quoted in *The History of Aesthetics: Aesthetics of Music*, vol. 3, W. Tatarkiewicz, J. Harrell, Cyril Barrett, D. Petsch, eds. (London: Thoemmes, 2006), p. 223.
8   Warren D. Anderson, *Ethos and Education in Greek Music* (Cambridge, MA: Harvard University Press, 1968), p. 39.
9   Ibid., p. 223.
10   Ibid., p. 224. 'Aristotle', *The New Grove Dictionary of Music Online*.
11   Anderson, *Ethos and Education in Greek Music*, p. 125. The term 'psychagogy' or 'psychagogics' comes from the Greek word Ψυχαγωγία [psixagogia], which originally meant 'leading the soul' or 'guidance of the soul'; cf. Ilsetraut Hadot, 'The Spiritual Guide', [in:] *Classical Mediterranean Spirituality: Egyptian, Greek, Roman*, A. H. Armstrong, ed. (New York: Crossroad, 1986), p. 101. In modern Greek the term also refers to 'pleasure, entertainment or recreation'; cf. http://translation.babylon.com/. In psychotherapy psychagogy means today 'a method of affecting behavior by assisting in the choice of desirable life goals', cf. http://www. thefreedictionary. com/psychagogy, accessed 23 April 2016.

unlike Plato, Aristotle acknowledges other than educational purposes of music, declaring that music is also useful for entertainment, and that, more importantly, it empowers catharsis, that is purgation of emotions, which consists in relieving an emotional state by rousing the same type of feeling by means of a specific musical scale.[12] Thus, drawing on the theory of ethos, as propounded by the Pythagoreans and Plato, Aristotle expands the uses of music and identifies among its many qualities the purifying cathartic potential of some scales, which he famously ascribes in his *Poetics* also to tragedy, whose 'ethos' draws on two feelings: pity and fear, (*eleos kai phobos*), conducive to catharsis.[13]

In the treatise *On Music* (3rd c. AD), Aristides Quintilian refers to Aristotle's division of musical modes when introducing his own nomenclature. The three types of modes devised by Aristides represent the 'diastaltic ethos' (implying grandeur, virility and heroism), 'systaltic ethos' (expressing effeminacy and amorousness), and 'hesycastic ethos'(establishing emotional stability).[14] Interestingly, there is an analogous classification of ancient literature, to which the same threefold division can be applied: the first, 'diastaltic' type of ethos, corresponds to tragedy; the second, the 'systaltic' type, refers to laments; whereas the third type, the 'hesycastic ethos', relates to hymns and paeans.[15] As suggested above, both Aristotle and Aristides Quintillian ascribe the theory of ethos to musical modes as well as to literary 'species'.

Aristotle and his followers focused mostly on the phenomenology of the effects of particular modes of music, which were soon denied by the followers of a utilitarian approach (e.g., Philodemus), who did not ascribe any psychological effect to music itself, but rather to the attitude of the listener or the musician. However, the ancient foundations of music therapy and a theory that might be called literature therapy or bibliotherapy, as laid by the supporters of the ethos theory, have survived and may still appear cogent today.

Another theory of musical aesthetics that draws on the ancient theory of ethos is the Baroque doctrine of affects, known also as the doctrine of the affections (*Affektenlehre* in German), according to which music is able to arouse a variety of specific emotions within the listener and the performer. Its major theoretician, Johann Mattheson, claims in his work of 1739 that 'joy can be elicited by large

---

12 Anderson, *Ethos and Education in Greek Music*, p. 139.
13 The concept of catharsis, barely hinted here, is discussed in more detail in Chapter Seven of this book with regard to its possible application to fantasy literature of the Inklings through Tolkien's notion of 'Eucatastrophe'.
14 *History of Aesthetics: Aesthetics of Music*, p. 224.
15 Ibid., p. 224.

intervals, and sadness by small ones; that fury may be aroused by a roughness of harmony coupled with a rapid melody; whereas obstinacy is evoked by the contrapuntal combination of highly independent (obstinate) melodies.[16] The major exponents of the doctrine of affects were Carl Philipp Emanuel Bach (1714–88), one of Johann Sebastian Bach's sons, and the composers of the Mannheim school.

Influenced by the Enlightenment tendency to organize knowledge encyclopaedically, the Baroque musicians attempted thus to delineate music into affective categories, and their belief in the emotional impact of music continued beyond the 18th c. and informed also the Romantic and Neo-Romantic movements. Contemporary music theory has also had periods of rededication to the theory of ethos and the doctrine of the affections, drawing on the recurrent and rather obvious observation that music is connected to human emotions. So is art as such, and so is literature, and any other human (sub)creative activity, one might add.

The question now is whether the theory of ethos can in anyway be applied to literature. May some literary genres evoke specific emotions? Is it possible to talk about prescriptive properties of particular genres, especially today, in times of genre hybridization, extensive mutation and fuzziness, when genre boundaries seem to be on the wane? Are there any clear-cut genres that can be delineated in terms of their psychological or psychagogic qualities? This section seeks to argue that the theory of ethos might apply to some literary genres, especially to high fantasy, an idea developed a posteriori from analyzing fantasy fiction and non-fiction on fantasy written by Tolkien, Lewis, and Le Guin, whom I consider as the classicists of the genre.

The ethos of Faërie

The central thesis of this chapter is that literature, similarly to music, has its ethical or psychagogic properties inherent to some of its 'categorised modes', that is genres, which are generically able to convey and enhance certain emotions.[17]

---

16 Gordon Epperson, 'Doctrine of the Affections' [in:] *Encyclopaedia Britannica*, http://www.britannica.com/EBchecked/topic/7687/doctrine-of-the-affections, accessed 23 April 2016.

17 The term 'mode' is used here to suggest that literary genres may correspond to musical modes (scales) in the sense that they contain some inherent affective qualities. It must be noted, though, that a 'literary mode' cannot be equated with genre, as these are different notions: the mode of literature being 'an unspecific critical term usually designating a broad but identifiable kind of literary method, mood, or manner that is not tied exclusively to a particular form or genre. Examples are the satiric mode, the

Those properties result partly from the genres' 'morphology', that is a specific lyric, narrative or dramatic form, structure, style, tone, and language, but also, perhaps more importantly, from their content and underlying thought. Thus, some literary genres, especially those of classical origin, such as elegy, lament, eclogue, epithalamion, tragedy, or comedy, as well as some literary modes, such as the pastoral, the satiric, ironic or didactic, despite their millennia-long history, evolution, and innumerable instances of texts, may still evoke specific moods that can in each case be typified and defined.

A more modern example of a genre that also seems to have its own ethos is the dystopian novel, which appears to be an instance of a deeply disturbing genre, whose impact on some readers at least may resemble shock therapy. Although likely to be violent and drastic, it may also be a form of therapy. In the context of bibliotherapy, shock therapy does not, of course, involve using drugs or electric current to induce shock, as in clinical treatment, but it does induce shock by means of its dystopian creation of an oppressive reality of terror.[18] It might help 'reboot' the system of the person's emotions and reconnect them to the world. Moreover, even though it differs radically from Faërie, for dystopia's 'arresting strangeness' is a universal nightmare, whereas Faërie's 'arresting strangeness' is a fantastic enchantment, dystopian fiction can enable the reader to view their consensus reality in a new, fresher way, perhaps with more awareness of and resistance to its implanted 'toxicity'.[19]

Implosive (or implosion) therapy, which could also be associated with the workings of the dystopian novel next to shock therapy, is, in turn, a form of exposure therapy that draws on 'intensive recollection and review of anxiety-producing situations or events in a patient's life in an attempt to develop more appropriate responses to similar situations in the future.'[20] It means that the person is flooded with (in case of the dystopian novel – vicarious) experiences of something dreadful, until becoming either able to overcome the fear or to ignore it. Implosion therapy is similar although not identical to flooding, another psychotherapeutic technique:

---

ironic, the comic, the pastoral, and the didactic.' Chris Baldick, *Dictionary of Literary Terms* (Oxford: Oxford University Press, 2008), p. 213.

18 Cf. http://www.britannica.com/EBchecked/topic/541334/shock-therapy, accessed 23 April 2016.

19 'Arresting strangeness' is one of the attributes of Faërie; cf. Tolkien, 'On Fairy-Stories', p. 139.

20 http://www.thefreedictionary.com/implosion+therapy, accessed 23 April 2016.

[Whereas] flooding deals with the actual stimulus or its image, implosion arouses a much higher anxiety, as the imagined scenes are exaggerated by the therapist who also introduces commentaries on the worst of the person's fears. So while in flooding you might be asked to picture a spider, perhaps at various distances so that you become desensitized to the image, in implosive therapy you might be asked to imagine the spider entering your mouth as you sleep, if that was an anticipated fantasy aspect of your fear.[21]

Thus, while flooding is usually done in real life, implosion works in the realm of imagination, and involves 'hypothesized cues', which 'might draw upon a wide range of factors, derived from psychodynamic or other realms', conducive to the emergence of anxiety.[22] Implosion technique seems to resemble some of the vicarious effects of reading a dystopian novel, providing that the theory of genre ethos is not impracticable, and that some parallels between the effects of bibliotherapy and psychotherapy may be drawn. An important difference, though, is that, unlike implosion and flooding therapy, dystopian fiction does not usually aim at familiarizing the person with what they fear and abhor, nor does it intend to assist the reader in overcoming that fear by making the person inure themselves to what causes it. On the contrary, the shock it gives the reader is usually meant to be an impulse to rethink and review one's position and priorities, and seek sense of their life and a particular situation. Dystopian fiction soaks the mind with horror, fear and pity, and builds up violent and negative emotions that cause tension and must find their outlet in a cathartic relief; it may help readers identify their feelings, especially fear, pity and anxiety, and their negative attitude towards the actions or attitudes that have generated them, as well as make them realize a need for overcoming those pent-up emotions. Of course, the thesis of the psychotherapeutic effect of dystopian fiction needs a thorough study, which is not provided here, the point being merely that dystopian fiction as a genre has its own ethos.

Returning to Faërie and its ethos, it is important to note that even though fantasy genre lies at the opposite extreme from dystopian fiction, if one considers their radically different psychological effect, it does not mean that fantasy literature is utopian. It is true that through its otherworldliness Faërie at first decentres the readers from their habitual perception of the world, for the secondary world appears initially to be defamiliarized; however, through the mechanisms of 'arresting strangeness', wonder, enchantment, and paradox, it eventually helps the readers to embrace the difference between the habitual perception of reality,

---

21   http://www.britannica.com/EBchecked/topic/541334/shock-therapy, accessed 23 April 2016.

22   Jerry Duvinsky, 'Exposure Therapy: Implosion', http://www.mindfulexposurebook.com/exposure-therapy-implosion/, accessed 20 April 2015.

and the reality itself, and hence to view the reality in a fresh and comprehensive way.[23] What is more, high fantasy may contain dystopian elements, such as the penultimate chapter of Tolkien's *The Lord of the Rings* – 'The Scouring of the Shire', because, as Tolkien remarks, 'creative Fantasy is founded upon the hard recognition that things are so in the world as it appears under the sun; on a recognition of fact, but not a slavery to it.'[24] He also adds that:

> If men were ever in the state in which they did not want to know or could not perceive truth (facts or evidence), then Fantasy would languish until they were cured. If they ever get into that state (it would not seem at all impossible), Fantasy will perish, and become Morbid Delusion.[25]

Fantasy is thus a piece of realism cast in a secondary world, whose 'inner consistency of reality', to use Tolkien's phrase, must be even greater than that of consensus reality, if the secondary world is to match the 'fantastic device of human language'.[26] Tolkien provides an example of that necessarily intensified logic and coherence of Faërie, (the qualities not often found elsewhere), in the following way:

> Anyone can say the green sun. Many can then imagine or picture it. But that is not enough (…) to make a Secondary World inside which the green sun will be credible, commanding Secondary belief, will probably require labour and thought, and will certainly demand a special skill, a kind of elvish craft. Few attempt such difficult tasks. But when they are attempted and in any degree accomplished, then we have a rare achievement of Art: indeed narrative art, story-making in its primary and most potent mode.[27]

It appears, therefore, that the enchantment of otherworldliness, of distance, and of remote time, which lies at the heart of Faërie, is neither dystopian nor utopian, according to Tolkien's notion of the genre; but, instead, it has a predominantly sobering and purifying potential. It helps to recover a fresh and clear vision of reality, and an understanding of it, which does not mean slavery, though. This is so because, as Tolkien notes,

> Actually fairy-stories deal largely, or (the better ones) mainly, with simple or fundamental things, untouched by Fantasy, but these simplicities are made all the more luminous by

---

23 Tolkien, 'On Fairy-Stories', p. 132.
24 Tolkien, ibid., p. 144.
25 Ibid., p. 144; quoted also in Chapter Four of this book.
26 Ibid., p. 140.
27 Tolkien, 'On Fairy-Stories', p. 140. The frequent accusations of Faërie being unrealistic and escapist are addressed also in Chapter One of this book.

their setting. For the story-maker who allows himself to be 'free with' Nature can be her lover not her slave.[28]

Otherworldliness can also reconnect the reader with the physical world, overcoming the fetishism and commodification of the object, and can help obtain a full picture of reality available only from a distance, both in time and space. Tolkien refers to that peculiar effect of fairy-stories when he observes that:

> [Fairy-] stories have now a mythical or total (unanalysable) effect, an effect quite independent of the findings of Comparative Folk-lore, and one which it cannot spoil or explain; they open a door on Other Time, and if we pass through, though only for a moment, we stand outside our own time, outside time itself, maybe.[29]

And in another place he emphasizes the power of that timeless meaning (that I call *logos*) which resides in the genre; and the essence of natural things that is to be rediscovered there: 'It was in fairy-stories that I first divined the potency of the words, and the wonder of the things, such as stone, and wood, and iron; tree and grass; house and fire; bread and wine.'[30]

The 'potency of the words' which might allow a glimpse at the essence of things and at their 'embodiment' is perhaps one of the effects of Faërie's enchantment and timelessness, and it could be argued that, when viewed from this perspective, the inner workings of Faërie reverse the mechanism of simulation, and counteract the artificiality and emptiness of postmodern hyperreality, for in Faërie the original referent of things can in each case be recovered.[31] Tolkien seems to mark this quality of the genre, calling it 'the prophylactic against the loss' and 'a means of recovery':

> If [Faërie] speaks of bread or wine or stone or tree, it appeals to the whole of these things, to their ideas; yet each hearer will give them a peculiar personal embodiment in his [or her] imagination. Should the story say 'he ate bread', (...) the hearer of the story will think of bread in general and picture it in some form of his [or her] own. If a story says 'he climbed a hill and saw a river in the valley below', (...) every hearer of the words will

---

28 Tolkien, ibid., p. 147.
29 Tolkien, ibid., p. 129. Italics are Tolkien's.
30 Tolkien, ibid., p. 147.
31 Hyperreality is the postmodern condition of not being able to distinguish reality from a simulation of reality. Jean Baudrillard refers to hyperreality as 'the generation by models of a real without origin or reality', that is a representation or a sign without the original referent, and explains it in terms of simulacra and simulation (*Simulacra and Simulation*, University of Michigan Press, 1994, p. 1). Some other philosophers who analyze the effects of hyperreality are Albert Borgmann, Daniel J. Boorstin, Neil Postman, and Umberto Eco.

have his [or her] own picture, and it will be made out of all the hills and rivers and dales he [she] has ever seen, but specially out of The Hill., The River, The Valley which were for him [or her] the first embodiment of the word.[32]

It seems that Faërie takes one back to the origin of things (and of language, too), and thus helps recover the fresh vision of the world, based on reality rather than hyperreality. The refreshing purity of Faërie counteracts the 'drabness', 'silliness', and 'delirium' of the manipulation that has come to be named postmodern hyperreality, and the workings of its simulation and simulacra, as identified by Jean Baudrillard.[33] The ethos of high fantasy genre, as Tolkien seems to point out, enables one to:

> Look at green again, and be startled anew (but not blinded) by blue and yellow and red. We should met the centaur and the dragon [there], and then perhaps suddenly behold, like the ancient shepherds, sheep, and dogs, and horses – and wolves. This recovery fairy-stories help us to make. In that sense only a taste for them may make us, or keep us, childish.[34]

The 'inherent morality' of Faërie[35]

Even though neither the Inklings nor Le Guin ever mention the words 'healing' or 'therapy' with regard to their fantasy oeuvre, they seem to be unanimously acknowledging value-based, wholesome, purifying and uplifting qualities of the genre, which I call here its generic ethos. The first fundamental property of Faërie's ethos is, as I wish to suggest, what Tolkien calls its 'strong moral character' and 'inherent morality (not to be confused with any 'allegorical *significatio*').[36]

Le Guin expands on that value-based and meaning-oriented essence of the genre, observing that 'ethics flourishes in the timeless soil of Fantasy, where ideologies wither on the vine.'[37] She also argues that the journey or the quest, which organises most 'of the great works of fantasy' fiction, 'seems to be not only a psychic one, but a moral one', for 'most great fantasies contain a very strong, striking

---

32 Tolkien, 'On Fairy-Stories', p. 146, and footnote E, p. 159.

33 Jean Baudrillard, *Simulacra and Simulation*, trans. Sheila Faria Glaser (Ann Arbor: University of Michigan Press, 1994).

34 Tolkien, ibid., p. 146.

35 This is Tolkien's phrase, as quoted before in this chapter; cf. Tolkien, 'On Fairy-Stories', p. 118.

36 Tolkien, ibid., p. 118.

37 Le Guin, 'Le Guin Introduces Le Guin', *Science Fiction Studies 3*, Spring 1974, [in:] *The Language of the Night*, p. 9.

moral dialectic, often expressed as a struggle between the Darkness and the Light.[38] The unalterable moral backbone of fantasy tales contrasts sharply with the (post)modern 'chaos [that] becomes elegant', with the 'unsettling, impermanent flicker of electronics', and with the postmodern 'commodified fantasy', which 'invents nothing, but imitates and trivialises', and which 'proceeds by depriving the old stories of their intellectual and ethical complexity, turning their action to violence, their actors to dolls, and their truth-telling to sentimental platitude.'[39] Le Guin seems to draw division between fake fantasy, (that is the commodified counterfeit of Faërie, whose only purpose is to make money), and high fantasy, a genre of its own ethos. As she argues, fake fantasy, so popular today, lacks in the 'strong moral character', identified by Tolkien as one of the landmarks of Faërie, because in the mass-produced stories that strive to imitate fantasy 'profoundly disturbing moral choices are sanitized, made cue, made safe'; and their 'heroes brandish their swords, lasers, wands, as mechanically as combine harvesters, reaping profits.'[40]

Moreover, Le Guin suggests that what Tolkien names the 'inherent morality' of high fantasy is partly due to its otherworldliness and deliberate departure from the 'consensus reality', the measures taken by fantasy writers precisely so as to show the reality from a more comprehensive perspective and in a fresh way, thus allowing its full view: 'Distancing, the pulling back from "reality" in order to see it better, is perhaps the essential gesture of [fantasy and] science fiction. It is by distancing that fantasy and science fiction achieve aesthetic joy, tragic tension, and moral cogency,' she claims.[41]

The moral character of fantasy fiction (and also science fiction) based on foundational thought, much against the mainstream philosophy of postmodernity, is what emerges from C. S. Lewis's works as well. In his book *The Abolition of Man*, Lewis refers to this moral element essential to value-based imaginative fiction as 'the *Tao*', which might mistakenly suggest its affinity to Taoism, the philosophy endorsed by Le Guin, whereas, in fact, the *Tao* is to Lewis 'the doctrine of objective value, the belief that certain attitudes are really true, and others really false, to the kind of thing the universe is and the kind of things we are.'[42] Lewis does

38 Le Guin, 'The Child and the Shadow', p. 55.

39 Le Guin, 'Foreword' to *Tales from Earthsea* (London: Orion, 2003), pp. xiii–xiv.

40 Le Guin, 'Foreword' to *Tales from Earthsea*, p. xiv. Tolkien, 'On Fairy-Stories', p. 118.

41 Le Guin, 'On Norman Spinrad's *The Iron Dream*' [in:] *Science Fiction Studies* 1, spring 1973, quoted in *The Language of the Night*, p. 9.

42 Lewis, *The Abolition of Man* (Cambridge: Cambridge University Press, 1946, 2009), p. 16.

not associate the *Tao* with any religion or particular philosophy, although he is a devout Christian, but recognizes it in all value-based systems of thought, such as 'Platonic, Aristotelian, Stoic, Christian and Oriental alike':[43]

> This thing which I have called for convenience the *Tao*, [he observes], and which others may call Natural Law or Traditional Morality or the First Principles of Practical Reason or the First Platitudes, is not one among a series of possible systems of value. It is the sole source of all value judgements.[44]

Tolkien seems to refer to the same, defining it as the 'inherent morality', which to Lewis is the essence of the *Tao*.[45] In *Mere Christianity*, based on his BBC talks (1942–1944), Lewis also draws on the concept of the *Tao*, defining it as 'the Law of Human Nature', and the same notion appears in his Narnian Chronicles, where in *The Lion, the Witch and the Wardrobe* (1950) Lewis speaks of the *Tao* in the language of myth and enchantment, calling it the 'Deep Magic from the Dawn of Time.'[46]

The *Tao* is a system that recognizes objective moral values, and belongs to foundational, anti-nihilistic thought; and it means, as Lewis views it, acceptance of objective values without questioning them, for they dwell in the *Tao* 'from time immemorial' and 'they are nowhere else'; 'the *Tao* being to the world of action what axioms are to the world of theory'.[47] 'Stepping outside the Tao', Lewis argues, is stepping 'into the void', that is into emptiness and nothingness, which resounds of the prevailing (neo)nihilistic philosophy of postmodernity that seems to focus on the void instead of a solid foundation, as discussed in Chapter Three of this book.[48] In the contemporary culture without objective values, Lewis concludes, 'Man's final conquest has proved to be the abolition of Man', a scenario similar to various dystopian predictions, in which 'Man's conquest of Nature turns out, in the moment of its consummation, to be Nature's conquest of Man.'[49] Lewis's objection

---

43 Lewis, ibid., p. 16.
44 Lewis, ibid., p. 29.
45 Tolkien, 'On Fairy-Stories', p. 118.
46 Lewis, *Mere Christianity* (London: Geoffrey Bles, 1952); *The Lion, the Witch and the Wardrobe* (London: Geoffrey Bles, 1950).
47 Lewis, *The Abolition of Man*, ibid., p. 27.
48 Lewis, ibid., pp. 39–40.
49 Lewis, ibid., p. 41. I mean here Aldous Huxley's *Brave New World* (1932), in which 'Man's conquest of Nature' has, if I understand Lewis's words correctly, resulted in 'Nature's conquest of Man', because people, living in the ethically sterile void, have turned into 'meat', as Bernard Marx repeatedly observes, into mere objects of dehumanized physical desire, which are cremated when no longer efficient and sufficiently

is that 'if man chooses to treat himself as raw material., raw material he will be: not raw material to be manipulated, as he fondly imagined, by himself, but by mere appetite, that is, mere Nature, in the person of his de-humanized Conditioners.'[50]

Lewis's concept of the *Tao*, which is to him the prerequisite of humanness and humanity, essentially based on unquestionable values, as promoted by the world's major philosophies and religions, is not, none the less, an 'ethical potpourri' consisting of the contradictions and absurdities that inevitably result from lumping together the 'traditional moralities of East and West, the Christian, the Pagan, and the Jew.'[51] Indeed, Lewis admits, 'some criticism, some removal of contradictions, even some real development, is required;' 'but there are two very different kinds of criticism', he adds: 'organic' or 'internal' criticism, which comes from within, from those who understand and respect the spirit of the *Tao*, and make the alterations benevolent; and the other type of criticism – the 'surgical' or 'external' criticism, which acts from the outside and instead of allowing development, it lessens and detracts from the wealth of the *Tao*.[52] Therefore, Lewis asserts, 'outside the Tao there is no ground for criticising either the Tao or anything else.'[53]

People who eschew the *Tao* are, according to Lewis, 'men without chests', 'half-hearted sceptics who still hope to find "real" values when they have debunked the traditional ones' (the attitude which, to Lewis, is 'the rejection of the concept of value altogether'); they are either solely cerebral or solely visceral 'geldings'.[54] Similarly, literature promoted by such men, deprived of an objective value system, represents 'a sort of ghastly simplicity', 'castrated' of its most vital element.[55] Contemporary 'Innovators' or 'Conditioners', that is 'men without

---

'pneumatic' for sex. Huxley's dystopian vision seems to illustrate Lewis's concern with a society that 'stands outside all judgements of value' and that 'cannot have any ground for preferring one of their own impulses to another except the emotional strength of that impulse', (*The Abolition of Man*, p. 40), which, in the case of the 'Brave New World' is actually also reduced to the minimum by soma, pills and an elaborate system of man-conditioning. Of course, there are definitely many more such literary instances of a society in which 'the abolition of Man' has been completed.

50 Lewis, *The Abolition of Man*, p. 44. Lewis's concept of the 'Conditioners' seems to resound of Aldous Huxley's notion of the human conditioning technology and ideology, producing the five castes (Alphas, Betas, Deltas, Gammas and Epsilons) of the Fordian 'Brave New World'.

51 Lewis, ibid., p. 30.

52 Lewis, ibid., p. 30.

53 Lewis, ibid., p. 31.

54 Lewis, ibid., pp. 19 and 33.

55 Lewis, ibid., p. 20.

chests', as Lewis calls them, the people who promote valueless (and worthless, one might add,) fiction, 'debunk traditional or (as they would say) "sentimental" values', and 'claim to be cutting away the parasitic growth of emotion, religious sanction, and inherited taboos, in order that "real" or "basic" values may emerge.'[56] Lewis claims that the 'Innovators', who shun imaginative literature, and fantasy tales in particular, follow 'an ethics based on instinct', in which they will find no foundation, nor 'the basis for a system of values':[57]

> The Innovator attacks traditional values (the *Tao*) in defence of what he [or she] at first supposes to be (in some special sense) 'rational' or 'biological' values. But (…) all the values which he[she] uses in attacking the *Tao*, and even claims tom be substituting for it, are themselves derived from the *Tao*. Only by such shreds of the *Tao* as he {she} has inherited is he [she] enabled even to attack it. The questions therefore arises what title he [she] has to select bits of it for acceptance and to reject others. For if the bits he[she] rejects have no authority, neither have those he [she] retains. If [the *Tao*] is rejected, all value is rejected. If any value is retained, it is retained.[58]

What remains once the *Tao* is negated is the 'saurian ooze', one might add borrowing the phrase from Le Guin – the ooze of mere commodification and profit-mindedness, which has starved imagination and desire to aim at truth.[59] Le Guin seems in fact also to refer to the 'Innovators' or 'Conditioners' whom Lewis discusses in detail, although she does not call them so, yet identifies them as 'the hard-working, over-thirty American males, who run this country', and whose ideology has spread globally and insidiously conquered much of the Western thought.[60] Their mind-set, Le Guin notes, rests solely on the notion of 'am immediate tangible profit', for they 'have learnt to repress their imagination, to reject it as something childish or effeminate, unprofitable, and probably sinful.'[61] Those men 'are not only anti-fantasy', Le Guin adds, 'but altogether antifiction', which results from their 'work ethic, profit-mindedness, and even sexual mores.'[62] Such people are afraid of fiction because they fear truth and values, and because they are afraid of freedom. They know that 'truth challenges, even

---

56 Lewis, ibid., p. 22.
57 Lewis, ibid., p. 27.
58 Lewis, ibid., pp. 28–29.
59 Le Guin uses 'the saurian ooze' phrase in her essay 'A Citizen of Mondath' [in:] *The Language of the Night*, pp. 15–20, 17.
60 Le Guin, 'Why Are Americans Afraid of Dragons', [in:] *The Language of the Night*, pp. 28–35, 30.
61 Le Guin, ibid., pp. 30–32.
62 Le Guin, ibid., p. 30.

threatens, all that is false, all that is phony, unnecessary, and trivial in the life they have let themselves be forced into living.'[63] Instead of value-based imaginative fiction they choose 'hopelessly sterile genres', such as 'the daily stock market report', which are dead pieces of 'fake realism' and 'total unreality', a quality that is 'a reassurance to them, rather than a defect.'[64]

The postmodern anti-*Tao* ideology of the 'Innovators', which corresponds to the anti-foundational philosophy of neonihilism, according to Lewis stands for just another 'rebellion against the *Tao*', which, as a matter of fact, is 'a rebellion of the branches against the tree: if the rebels could succeed they would find that they had destroyed themselves.'[65] This appears so, one might add, inasmuch as man is merely a 'sub-creator', to use Tolkien's term, and not 'a Maker'; and therefore, 'the human mind has no more power of inventing a new value than of imagining a new primary colour, or, indeed, of creating a new sun and a new sky for it to move in.'[66] Tolkien calls that anti-foundational culture, which Lewis associates with 'the abolition of man', 'an age of improved means to deteriorated ends', and an era of 'essential malady of such days – producing the desire to escape, not indeed from life, but from our present time and self-made misery - that we are acutely conscious both of the ugliness of our works, and of their evil.'[67] Although Lewis does not employ the term 'neo-nihilism' or 'postmodernity', he seems to refer critically to what they represent, for he uses the notion of 'post-humanity', that is 'the rule of the Conditioners over the conditioned human material', the era in which 'some knowingly and some unknowingly are labouring' [to debunk] traditional values represented by the *Tao*.[68] When the thinkers of post-humanity dissect the *Tao*, however, all value dies, and so does all knowledge, Lewis warns, because the branches of the tree cannot live once its roots are cut.[69]

As an exponent of foundational thought and the *Tao*, and, more specifically, as a Theist, and a Christian in particular, Lewis makes a disclaimer similar to the one Victor Frankl makes when presenting his philosophy of logotherapy, which, as a matter of fact, appears akin to Lewis's thought, in that the *Tao* seems to correspond to Frankl's *logos*. Lewis remarks:

63 L e Guin, ibid., p. 34.
64 Le Guin, ibid., p. 32.
65 Lewis, *The Abolition of Man*, pp. 29–30.
66 Lewis, ibid., p. 30. Tolkien, 'On Fairy-Stories', p. 139.
67 Tolkien, ibid., p. 151.
68 Lewis, *The Abolition of Man*, p. 45.
69 Lewis, ibid., p. 45.

In order to avoid misunderstanding, I may add that though I myself am a Theist, and indeed, a Christian, I am not here attempting any indirect argument for Theism. I am simply arguing that if we are to have values at all we must accept the ultimate platitudes of Practical Reason as having absolute validity: that any attempt, having become sceptical about these, to reintroduce value lower down on some supposedly more 'realistic' basis, is doomed. Whether this position implies a supernatural origin for the *Tao* is a question I am not here concerned with.

Frankl's therapy through meaning does not endorse any religion, either; just like fairy-stories and high fantasy tales, which thrive on the ethos of the *Tao*, whether Christian, as in the Inklings' works, or Oriental and Taoist, as in Le Guin's. They are all universal and timeless, as they draw on the rock foundation of moral values and unconditional meaning. 'Logotherapy is neither teaching nor preaching,' Frankl declares, its aim being to enable people to see life from new and different perspectives, to broaden their inner 'visual [or noölogical] field so that the whole spectrum of potential meaning becomes conscious and visible to [them].'[70] 'A dogmatic belief in objective [moral] value [which Frankl views as the source of unconditional meaning, that is *logos*,] is necessary to the very idea of a rule which is not tyranny or an obedience which is not slavery', Lewis observes.[71] Not only does the *Tao* (which may correspond to Frankl's *logos*) allow one to find meaning and purpose, even in the most trying life situations, but also it offers freedom and order.

Thus, assuming a correspondence between Lewis's and Frankl's thought, one could place Frankl's *logos* within the universal moral values of Lewis's *Tao*, irrespective of culture, religion and time. Myth, fairy-stories and high fantasy tales seem to recognise the importance of both: the inherent morality (or the *Tao*), and of meaning that resides in words (the *logos*; which to the Inklings was the Christian Logos – the divine element of God Himself). Just like logotherapy, fantasy genre is 'neither teaching nor preaching'; although it contains a wealth of meaning that emerges from its meaningful worlds. Le Guin, for instance, admits that she sometimes 'wrestles with the temptation to moralize', but at the same time remembers that 'to clinch a point is to close it'; so that 'to leave the reader free to decide what [the] work means, [is] the real art; [for] it makes the work inexhaustible.'[72] Again, that approach to fiction as a potential guideline towards

---

70 Frankl, *Man's Search for Meaning*, p. 114.
71 Lewis, *The Abolition of Man*, p. 46.
72 'The Magician', an interview with Ursula K. Le Guin conducted by Maya Jaggi, http://www.theguardian.com/books/2005/dec/17/booksforchildrenandteenagers.shopping, 2005, accessed 23 April 2016.

meaning rather than absurdity seems to contradict the neonihilistic void, and may be associated with the assumptions of logotherapy, which aims at helping people discover meaning of their own unique lives and experience.

Interestingly, a connection between the *Tao* and Logos, viewed as components of a similar moral structure, has been noticed and mentioned for instance by Aldous Huxley, who in the 1946 *Foreword* to a new edition of his dystopian *Brave New World* regrets not offering John the Savage another option of living with other exiles and refugees within the borders of the Reservation, so as to give him a chance to dedicate his life to 'the conscious and intelligent pursuit of sanity, of man's Final End, [and] the unitive knowledge of the immanent Tao or Logos.'[73]

As this chapter seeks to demonstrate, the meaning-oriented approach is what allows determining some affinity between the inherently moral ethos of Faërie and the essence of logotherapy, regarded as a school of thought. Viewed as another expression of value-and-meaning-oriented approach, high fantasy genre corresponds to the therapeutic effects of logotherapy, observable within the realm of bibliotherapy. How close the fantasy genre approaches *logos,* and in what way it may offer logotherapy, as well as *mythopathy* (therapy through myth) and 'sensopaedia' (a term of my coinage, explained below), is discussed further on in this chapter. Before embarking on some parallels between the ethos of Faërie, which appears therapeutic, and logotherapy, it may be worthwhile, though, to present Tolkien's and Le Guin's views suggesting that high fantasy genre can be therapeutic.

It ought to be remarked that the Inklings do not seem to endorse psychotherapy *per se,* when it deals only with man's psychosomatic dimension and disregards the realm of the spirit. If psychotherapy exists outside the value system, or Lewis's *Tao,* then it also belongs to the void and cannot counteract the process of 'the horrifying dehumanization that inevitably follows [neo]nihilism.'[74] The Inklings and Le Guin seem to try to look beyond medical science, towards the realm of the moral aspect of human dilemmas, which again appears somehow akin to the foundation of Frankl's logotherapy, a unique school of psychotherapy and philosophy that recognizes the origins of human predicament in the noölogical or spiritual dimension, possibly but not necessarily reflected also in the psychosomatic condition. Lewis regrets that it is an 'increasing modern habit of

---

73 Aldous Huxley, 'Foreword 'to the *Brave New World* (London: Grafton Books, 1988), pp. 8–9.

74 David Rozema,' Lewis's Rejection of Nihilism: The Tao and the Problem of Moral Knowledge', [in:] *In Pursuit of Truth. In Pursuit of Truth. A Journal of Christian Scholarship,* September 2007, http://www.cslewis. org/journal/lewiss-rejection-of-nihilism-the-tao-and-the-problem-of-moral-knowledge/, accessed 23 April 2016.

seeing all personal difficulties in terms of disease and cure, [like in medicine and mainstream psychotherapy], and so reducing things that are really moral or intellectual or both to the pathological element.'[75] Psychosomatically oriented psychotherapy, Frankl implies, does not apply to existential neurosis, which results from the feeling of meaninglessness and absurdity of life. Psychoanalysis, Frankl claims, misses and negates the most important aspect of humanness – the noölogical or spiritual dimension, far superior to man's biochemical machinery and reflected in man's 'will to meaning' rather than will to sex, pleasure or power.[76] Logotherapy, a profoundly humanistic thought, is the only psychotherapeutic school that addresses existential neurosis (termed by Frankl as 'noögenic neurosis'), and that contradicts dehumanisation by reconfirming traditional values and unconditional meaningfulness of existence.

In his essay 'Humanitarianism and Punishment' Lewis criticises modern psychotherapy, which to him can almost be equated with Freud's psychoanalysis, and which he deems amoral, for it rejects the spiritual dimension of man's being, violates human dignity and freedom of thought, and attempts at an Orwellian conditioning:

> (…) [D]o not let us be deceived by a name. To be taken without consent from my home and friends; to lose my liberty; to undergo all those assaults on my personality which modern psychotherapy knows how to deliver; to be re-made after some pattern of 'normality' hatched in a Viennese laboratory to which I never professed allegiance; to know that this process will never end until either my captors have succeeded or I grown wise enough to cheat them with apparent success -- who cares whether this is called Punishment or not? That it includes most of the elements for which any punishment is feared - shame, exile, bondage, and years eaten by the locust - is obvious.[77]

To Lewis, psychotherapy entails assaulting individual personalities when it reduces man to a mechanism of chemical processes separated from his or her intellectual and moral depths. Instead, Lewis emphasizes the need for counteracting the nihilistic anti-fiction and anti-fantasy culture of the 'Innovators' by means of promoting foundational, that is *Tao*-based, thought, as reflected, for instance, in meaning-based imaginative fiction, whose inherent morality and humanness

---

75 Lewis to Lofstrom, 18 February 1959, quoted in Katryn Lindskoog's 'Lewis's Correspondence on Psychotherapy, Psychoanalysis, Sermons and Humility', [in:] *The Lewis Legacy*, issue 71, winter 1997, http://www.discovery.org/a/995, accessed 23 April 2016.
76 Frankl, *Man's Search for Meaning*, p. 58.
77 Lewis, 'Humanitarianism and Punishment' [in:] *Offenders or Citizens: Readings in Rehabilitation*, pp. 116–118, Philip Priestly, Maurice Vanstone, eds. (Oxford: Willan Publishing, 2011), p. 117.

might offer some kind of remedy for the postmodern condition, and, which, as argued in this book, have psychotherapeutic properties, beyond the clinical and purely scientific measures. The other Inklings, as well as Le Guin, seem to share Lewis's point of view, striving likewise to seek the source of healing and integrity in the realm of timeless truths and morality, reflected in myth and primordial language. The Inklings were especially negative towards psychoanalysis – the 'new secular religion' of Freud, who, continuing Feuerbach's thought, considered religion as 'wish fulfillment' and a 'crutch for emotionally weak people,' and preached that 'anatomy [that is pure physicality] is destiny'.[78]

A former declared atheist and follower of Freud's secular worldview, upon embracing Christianity Lewis came to reject Freud's materialism and battled a war against Freudianism, as presented, for instance in his *The Pilgrim's Regress*, written only two years after Lewis's conversion, and discussed, for instance, in Arman Nicholi's book *The Question of God: C. S. Lewis and Sigmund Freud Debate God, Love, Sex, and the Meaning of Life*.[79] In *The Pilgrim's Regress* Lewis satirises Freud as 'Sigismund Enlightenment' (S), Mr Enlightenment's son, who conducts a 'mini psychoanalytical session' with John the Pilgrim (J), referring to the latter's desire to find an island:

S—'It may save you trouble if I tell you at once the best reason for not trying to escape: namely, that there is nowhere to escape to.
J—How do you know that there is no such place as my island?
S—Do you wish very much that there was?
J—I do.
S—Have you ever imagined anything to be true because you greatly wished for it?
John thought for a while and then he said, "Yes."
S—And your island is like an imagination – isn't it?
J—I suppose so.

---

78 Sigmund Freud, *The Future of an Illusion* (New York: Martino Fine Books, 2011), pp. 38 and 51.

79 Mark St. Germain, an American playwright, has written a play *Freud's Last Session* (2009), set back in September 1939 in London, a few weeks before Freud's death (23 September 1939), in which St. Germain imagines what a riveting intellectual debate between Freud, an old man suffering from cancer (of the jaw), and Lewis, a young and little-known Oxford professor, might have been like if the two had met. The two antagonists' brilliant discourse is punctuated by the radio news about Hitler's invasion of Poland, and the UK's and France's declaration of war on Germany (3 September 1939).

S—It's just the sort of thing you would imagine merely through wanting it – the whole thing is very suspicious.'[80]

Lewis sums up his argument against Freudianism (and also Marxism) in his essay 'Bulverism', considering these ideologies as examples of logical fallacy, that is of 'bulverism', a term of Lewis's own coinage:

> The Freudians have discovered that we exist as bundles of complexes. The Marxians have discovered that we exist as members of some economic class.... Their (our) thoughts are ideologically tainted at the source. Now this is obviously great fun; but it has not always been noticed that there is a bill to pay for it. There are two questions that people who say this kind of thing ought to be asked. The first is, Are all thoughts thus tainted at the source, or only some? The second is, Does the taint invalidate the tainted thought in the sense of making it untrue—or not?... If they say that all thoughts are thus tainted, then of course.... The Freudian and the Marxian are in the same boat with all the rest of us and cannot criticize us from the outside. They have sawn off the branch they are sitting on. If, on the other hand, they say that the taint need not invalidate their thinking, then neither need it invalidate ours. In which case, they have saved their own branch, but also saved ours along with it.[81]

As for Tolkien's disapproval of Freudianism, including Freud's approach to the fantastic, David Sandner's study the *Critical Discourses of the Fantastic, 1712–1831*, may be consulted, although it is barely mentioned here.[82] With reference to Todorov's interpretation of the fantastic (the concept which Todorov associates with 'the fantastic uncanny' and 'the fantastic marvellous'), Sandner observes that 'Tolkien's and Freud's work might, indeed, be read as two divergent outcomes of the same encounter with what Todorov names the 'fantastic'.[83] However, he also adds that 'these divergent outcomes remain necessarily contingent readings, always uncertain of themselves, hovering between the promise of the

---

80 Lewis, *The Pilgrim's Regress* (Grand Rapids, MI: Wm. B. Eerdmans Publishing Co., 1992), book II. Sigismund was Freud's birth name, which he changed into Sigmund.

81 Lewis, 'Bulverism' [in:] *God in the Dock: Essays on Theology and Ethics* (Grand Rapids, MI: Wm. B. Eerdmans Publishing Co., 1972), pp. 271–277, 272.

82 David Sandner, *Critical Discourses of the Fantastic, 1712–1831* (Farnham: Ashgate, 2011), chapter 2: 'The Interlocked Definitions; The Fantastic, The Sublime, the Uncanny', pp. 17–25. Another study that brings up the issue of Tolkien's stance towards Freudianism is, for instance, Peter Kreeft's *The Philosophy of Tolkien: The Worldview behind the Lord of the Rings* (San Francisco: Ignatius Press, 2005), pp. 99–112.

83 Tzvetan Todorov, *Introduction à la littérature fantastique* (1970), English title: *The Fantastic: A Structural Approach to a Literary Genre*, trans. Richard Howard (Ithaca, NY: Cornell University Press, 1975). Sandner, ibid., p. 24.

marvellous (Tolkien's Joy) and the danger of the loss of identity in the uncanny dissolution of reality and/or the psyche).'[84]

Their reservations about psychotherapy, and Freud's psychoanalysis in particular, do not mean, however, that the Inklings were against medicine or physicians, suffice it to mention doctor Humphrey Havard, an Inkling, Lewis's and Tolkien's doctor and friend, and Tolkien's fellow-Catholic, who regularly met the other Inklings and attended mass with Tolkien.[85] Lewis admits that if there is 'a pathological element' in one's condition, 'of course it is "proper" to make all efforts after relief.'[86] It is not medicine and healing but psychological manipulation and spiritual thwarting that the Inklings, and also Le Guin, (much as she finds Jungian psychology of the unconscious and archetypical insightful), reject. Little wonder then that they issue warnings against corrupt psychotherapy, for instance by means of the 'mad scientist' trope in dystopian fiction, whereby they expose the hazards of wicked psychotherapy and hypnosis, which consist in brainwashing. For instance, in *That Hideous Strength (A Modern Fairy-Tale for Grown-Ups)*, Lewis shows a group of wicked scientists working at the N. I. C. E. (National Institute for Co-ordinated Experiments), who attempt to use Jane Studdock's prophetic dreams for their evil purpose by means of tortures, and who relegate the meaning of emotions and spiritual desires to a mere 'chemical phenomenon'.[87] Similarly, Le Guin warns of corrupt psychotherapists and psychiatrists in her science fiction novel *The Lathe of Heaven*, where Dr William Haber represents an evil scientist and sleep researcher who manipulates his patient, George Orr, directing George's reality-becoming dreams in the way to achieve global power.[88]

This is not, therefore, that the Inklings and Le Guin disapprove of psychotherapy *per se*, but of what it was in the heyday of psychoanalysis, and what it can still be when ill-used and abused, that is when psychotherapy is developed outside objective moral values, which Lewis calls the *Tao*, and which Frankl associates with unconditional meaningfulness of existence, or *logos*. Similarly to Lewis, Tolkien sees the core of the postmodern crisis in the spiritual dimension of humanity which has been denied, rather than in its psychosomatic exteriors, and in his works he refers numerous times to healing, which regards both the bodily and the moral aspects of human condition. In *Silmarillion* Tolkien writes for instance that:

---

84 Sandner, ibid., pp. 24–25.
85 David Bratman, 'Humphrey Havard' [in:] *J. R. R. Tolkien Encyclopedia: Scholarship and Critical Assessment*, Michael D. C. Drout, ed., p. 266.
86 Lewis to Lofstrom, 18 February 1959.
87 Lewis, *That Hideous Strength*, pp. 354–355.
88 Le Guin, *The Lathe of Heaven* (New York: Simon and Schuster, 1971).

In later days he [Olórin] dearly loved the Children of Eru, and took pity on their sorrows. Those who hearkened to him arose from despair; and in their hearts the desire to heal and to renew awoke, and thoughts of fair things that had not yet been but might yet be made for the enrichment of Arda.[89]

Commenting on the theme of illness and healing in Tolkien's fairy world, Richard Scott Nokes observes that Tolkien has reversed the Old English stereotype of Elves inflicting ailment upon humans (being 'elfshot' had meant to be ill from an unknown cause): in Tolkien's fiction 'Elves are skilled healers, not the cause of illness.'[90] Most importantly, however, Tolkien ascribes the healing power not only to Elves but, generally speaking, to the very 'elvish craft' of Faërie, that is the genre itself, (the 'healing quality' which I would like to identify as yet another element of Faërie's ethos), inasmuch as in the very essence of fairy-stories Tolkien recognises and names the effect of 'Recovery', apparently akin to therapy, because the 'Recovery includes return and renewal of health', 'a re-gaining of a clear view', and 'prophylactic against loss.'[91] The loss to which Tolkien refers is probably the loss of meaning, hope and of joy; the loss of enchantment that simple natural things produce; the loss of humbleness and communion with other living things and the natural world; and the loss of a clear and fresh vision of reality – all the vital elements of the wholesomeness and inherent morality of 'high fantasy' genre.[92] The Recovery offered by Faërie, Tolkien continues, draws on 'creative fantasy', which 'may open your hoard and let all the locked things fly away like cage-birds. The gems all turn into flowers and flames, and you will be warned that all you had (or knew) was dangerous and potent, not really effectively chained, free and wild; no more yours than they were you.'[93] That 'Recovery of freshness of vision' is a virtue, Tolkien claims, for it gives freedom, independence, and true knowledge of oneself, as it releases the hidden and the locked resources, turning them into natural treasure that can be used.[94] Cutting loose from the confines is also a specific form of escape, intrinsic to Faërie and essential to the experience of freedom and responsibility, as discussed in another

---

89 Tolkien, *The Later Silmarillion: Morgoth's Ring*, Christopher Tolkien, ed. (London: HarperCollins Publishers, 1995), part 3: The Later *Quenta Silmarillion*, §10b, p. 147.
90 Richard Scott Nokes, 'Health and Medicine' [in:] *J. R. R. Tolkien Encyclopedia: Scholarship and Critical Assessment*, p. 266. There are, however, some Elves of Tolkien's that do not have benevolent nature.
91 Tolkien, 'On Fairy-Stories', p. 146.
92 Tolkien, ibid., pp. 146–147.
93 Ibid., p. 147.
94 Tolkien, ibid., p. 147.

part of this chapter. It is also a step towards one's purification and coming to terms with both universal and particular human dilemmas – a vital element of cathartic therapy presented in Chapter Seven of this book.

The therapeutic potential of high fantasy, which emerges from Tolkien's vision of the genre (although neither Tolkien nor Lewis, nor any other Inkling uses the term 'high fantasy' or 'therapy' in this context), results also from the fact that Faërie has 'three faces: the Mystical towards the Supernatural; the Magical towards Nature; and the Mirror of scorn and pity towards Man', the most important of which is the middle one: 'the Magical', the others varying in degree or even absent.[95] 'The Magical, the fairy-story, may be used as a *Mirour de l'Omme*', Tolkien explains; 'and it may [also] (but not easily) be made a vehicle of Mystery.'[96] Faërie's embedment in those three dimensions and its openness to the spiritual, moral and transcendental realm, as much as to the natural and human one, seem tantamount to the 'strong moral character' of fairy-stories and their inclination towards meaning-oriented explorations, in which man may come into contact with 'the Mystical towards the Supernatural', as well as with 'the Magical towards Nature'.[97] The feelings of 'scorn and pity towards Man', mirrored in Faërie, are, in turn, connected to the cathartic process of eucatastrophe, addressed in the next chapter.

Finally, as mentioned before, Tolkien identifies four unique attributes of Faërie: Fantasy, Recovery, Escape, and Consolation, which, as I wish to argue, are all constituents of the genre's ethos, and the sources of its therapeutic potential, even though Tolkien regretfully and half-ironically adds that 'most of them are nowadays very commonly considered to be bad for anybody.'[98]

> If written with art, the prime value of fairy-stories will simply be that value which, as literature, they share with other literary forms. But fairy-stories offer also, in a peculiar degree or mode, these things: Fantasy, Recovery, Escape, Consolation, all things of which children have, as a rule, less need than older people.[99]

Fantasy, which Tolkien considers to be imagination enriched with sub-creative art, has been discussed above in this chapter. So have Recovery and Escape. What

---

95 Tolkien, ibid., p. 124.
96 Tolkien, ibid., p. 125. The French term '*Mirour de l'Omme*' means the 'Mirror of Mankind'; it is a title of a long narrative poem of John Gower's, known also as 'Speculum Hominis' or 'Speculum Meditantis' (ca. 1376–1379).
97 Tolkien, ibid., p. 125.
98 Tolkien, ibid., p. 138.
99 Tolkien, ibid., p. 138.

is left is Consolation, which appears inextricably linked with Tolkien's concept of eucatastrophe, given special attention in the last chapter of this book.

Lewis also seems to refer to a therapeutic power of high fantasy fiction, although he does not name it so, either, when he remarks succinctly that:

> The inhibitions which I hoped my [Narnian] stories would overcome in a child's mind may exist in a grown-up's mind too, and may perhaps be overcome by the same means. Sometimes Fairy tales may say best what's to be said.[100]

Le Guin likewise notes that 'fantasy is the natural, the appropriate, language for the recounting of the spiritual journey and the struggle of good and evil in the soul.'[101] She expands on the special effect of fantasy fiction, which appears therapeutic, emphasising its benevolent impact on the unconscious, and its generic ethics of moral order, meaning, and personal growth:

> The great fantasies, myths, and tales are indeed like dreams: they speak *from* the unconscious *to* the unconscious, in the *language* of the unconscious – symbol and archetype. Though they use words, they work the way music does: they short-circuit verbal reasoning, and go straight to the thoughts that lie too deep to utter. They cannot be translated fully into the language of reason, but only a Logical Positivist, who also finds Beethoven's Ninth Symphony meaningless, would claim that they are therefore meaningless. They are profoundly meaningful, and usable – practical – in terms of ethics; of insight; of growth.[102]

Referring to Le Guin's fantasy tales, especially to her Earthsea cycle, Barbara J. Bucknall seems to point to the genre's ethics and its therapeutic power:

> These stories are ageless because they deal with problems that confront us at any age. They are about attaining maturity and self-knowledge, a theme for which we are never too old. As long as we truly live we grow, and as long as we grow there is room for greater self-knowledge and for new dimensions of [meaning and] maturity.(…) In the Earthsea [world], marvels are there from the very beginning, and at the end of each journey is the goal of greater psychological maturity. And there is magic, too, in abundance – magic that is governed by the law of the psyche.[103]

The same can probably be said about the fantasy tales of Tolkien and Lewis. Tolkien speaks of that magic as well, linking it directly with Faërie, and with a specific 'mood' (which I call here 'ethos'), and a special 'power' (which I associate with therapy): 'Faërie itself may perhaps most nearly be translated by Magic – but it is

---

100   Lewis, 'Sometimes Fairy Tales May Say Best What's To Be Said', p. 36.
101   Le Guin, 'The Child and the Shadow' [in:] *The Language of the Night*, p. 59.
102   Le Guin, ibid., p. 52.
103   Barbara J. Bucknall, *Ursula K. Le Guin* (New York: Frederick Ungar, 1984), p. 37.

magic of a peculiar mood and power, at the furthest pole from the vulgar devices of the laborious, scientific, magician.'[104] Hence, Tolkien's wizard, Gandalf, and Le Guin's mages, for instance Ogion or Ged, are not merely mages or magicians, a sort of craftsmen, but rather artists, and, as Lewis might add, 'men with chests', immersed in the *Tao*, and dedicated to the *logos*. 'It is useless to teach magic to those without the power to use it. This provides another reason for saying that the wizard is like an artist', Bucknall observes.[105]

It is true that Le Guin's interest in and endorsement of the Taoist philosophy of the East (not to be confused with Lewis's concept of the *Tao*), makes the moral character of her fantasy fiction different from that of Tolkien or Lewis, the Christian writers, yet it cannot be questioned that her fantasy fiction is equally well founded on objective values and a foundational thought of sense and order. 'The Taoist world is orderly, not chaotic, but its order is not one imposed by man or by a personal or humane deity', Le Guin explains; 'the true laws – ethical and aesthetic, as surely as scientific – are not imposed from above by any authority, but exist in things and are to be found – discovered.'[106]

It shall also be noted that Tolkien, Lewis and Le Guin trace the roots of the profound moral cogency of the fantasy genre in the nature of imagination itself.[107] So do the other Inklings, for instance Owen Barfield, who treasured Tolkien's 'On Fairy-Stories' essay and Lewis's works, especially the latter's on *The Abolition of Man*, about which Barfield said: 'There may be a piece of contemporary writing in which precision of thought, liveliness of expression and depth of meaning unite with the same felicity, but I have not come across it.'[108] Le Guin quotes Percy Bysshe Shelley's statement made in his *Defence of Poetry* (1821), where he argues that 'the great instrument of moral good is imagination.'[109] Imagination is also

104   Tolkien, 'On Fairy-Stories', p. 118.

105   Bucknall, *Ursula K. Le Guin*, p. 39.

106   Le Guin, 'Dreams must Explain Themselves' [in:] *The Language of the Night*, pp. 37–46, 39.

107   Lewis praises Tolkien's essay 'On Fairy-Stores' in his book *On Stories: and Other Essays on Literature* (London: Mariner Books, 2002).

108   Owen Barfield, quoted in 'Study Guide to The Abolition of Man', http://www.cslewis. org/resources/studyguides/Study%20Guide%20-%20The%20Abolition%20of%20 Man.pdf, accessed 23 April 2016.

109   Le Guin, Maxine Cushing Gray Award Acceptance Speech, 18 October 2006, Washington State Book Awards, Seattle; http://www.ursulakleguin.com/MCGrayFellowship-Speech.html, accessed 23 April 2016.

a powerful medium of therapy, instrumental in art therapy, music therapy and bibliotherapy.

A cornerstone of fantasy genre, imagination is employed in Faërie in a twofold way. As in any other literary genre, imagination is indispensable for the reader to enter the fictitious world, yet its frames belong to the everyday contemporary or historical reality. In fantasy literature, and high fantasy in particular, the world does not belong to the primary reality, and needs to be reimagined after the writer's creation before the reader is able to experience Faërie and its enchantment. Moreover, the process of entering the realm of Fantasy entails individual interpretation, as the reader's imagination, uninhibited by the consensus reality, creates its own image of the secondary world, unique to every individual.

To Tolkien, 'Imagination is the faculty of conceiving images' or simply 'image-making'; whereas Fantasy is to him the higher form of Imagination, heightened by the combination with sub-creative Art.'[110] Thus, what other writers tend to call Imagination, Tolkien refers to as 'Fantasy', but he also links it with moral integrity and 'the most nearly pure and most potent form of Art.'[111] Tolkien points to the inherent congruence and benevolence of Fantasy, which must not be confounded with 'Dreaming, in which there is no Art; and with mental disorders, in which there is not even control: with delusion and hallucination.'[112] He also claims that 'fantasy is a rational, not an irrational activity', which never produces 'silliness and morbidity' unless twisted and abused.[113]

Therapeutic significance of imagination and its contribution to Faërie's moral ethos appear clear not only in the light of the works of the Inklings and of Le Guin, but also in various studies of psychotherapists. In the realm of Fantasy (that is, as Tolkien sees it, artistic, sub-creative Imagination), one can return to nature and feel as its legitimate offspring, holding communion with other living things, oneself and the other, difficult thought it tends to be. 'Imagination is our way back into that space we entered so effortlessly as children when we began, not long after birth, to play,' psychotherapists say.[114] It is perhaps the neo-Romantic streak in the Inklings' thought that makes them focus so much on the importance of imagination and child-like (but not childish) openness and faith. Imagination is neither reductionist nor nihilistic; it is 'naturally open [to both material and supernatural things]; it wants to see everything and that is a large

---

110   Tolkien, 'On Fairy-Stories', pp. 138–139.
111   Tolkien, ibid., p. 139.
112   Tolkien, ibid., p. 139.
113   Tolkien, ibid., p. 139, footnote no. 2; and p. 140.
114   Ann and Barry Ulanov, *Healing Imagination* (London: Daimon Verlag, 1999), p. 15.

part of its healing power.'[115] 'For me', Lewis admits, 'reason is the natural organ of truth; but imagination is the organ of meaning. Imagination, producing new metaphors or revivifying old, is not the cause of truth, but its condition.'[116]

Psychotherapists emphasise the healing power of imagination, as applied in art, music and bibliotherapy, and its comprehensive reference to man as a union of the spirit, the psyche and the body:

> If we stretch our imagination, we find ourselves at the centre of things. This is to say, we find our Selves... we accept the possibility of living with our own being, of inspecting it, of seeing all its positive and negative qualities, and of accepting it. With our imagination stretched, we enter the healing precincts where scarred surfaces or pitted insides really are acceptable and so are the accomplishments of body and psyche and soul, whatever their size.[117]

In Faërie, imagination leads us along the path of 'arresting strangeness' through genuine enchantment to understanding and joy, which can only be achieved spiritually, not empirically or in a sensory way. Imagination lifts the mind towards the sublime and the transcendent; and this seems to be another quality of Faërie's ethos. 'Taking freedom with our imagination may kindle a divine spark within us; there under the rubble of neglect, all bits crushed by the tyranny of the prosaic, it may enable us to create the selves we are meant to be', psychotherapists note.[118]

The 'moral imagination' of Faërie

Faërie's ethos and its 'inherent morality' (Tolkien's phrase), which results from the genre's embedment in the *Tao*, (Lewis's term for objective, unquestionable values), draw on imagination, and, more precisely, on 'moral imagination', to use the phrase that, although never used by the Inklings or Le Guin, seems to inform their view on the genre. The notion of 'moral imagination' was probably first introduced by Edmund Burke in his *Reflections on the Revolution in France* (1790), where he laments the quick and radical social changes taking place in the wake of the Revolution. Reiterated in the works of the twentieth century 'imaginative conservatives' representing the 'Burke revival', such as Robert Nisbet (1913–1996), a professor of sociology, and Russell Kirk (1918–1994), a political theorist, moralist and literary critic, 'moral imagination' is, according to Jonathan Jones:

---

115   The Ulanovs, ibid., p. 27.
116   Lewis, *Mere Christianity*, p. 32.
117   The Ulanovs, *Healing Imagination*, p. 7.
118   The Ulanovs, ibid., p. 8.

A uniquely human ability to conceive of fellow humanity as moral beings and as persons, not as objects whose value rests in utility or usefulness. It is a process by which a self 'creates' metaphor from images recorded by the senses and stored in memory, which are then occupied to find and suppose moral correspondences in experience. An intuitive ability to perceive ethical truths and abiding law in the midst of chaotic experience, the moral imagination should be an aspiration to a proper ordering of the soul and, consequently, of the commonwealth.[119]

Moral imagination must not be associated with moralizing, but with a foundational thought that opposes the view of a meaningless and absurd existence and chaotic universe. 'The ordering of the soul', that is some spiritual peace and order, as Jones suggests, implies a 'configuration of the mind in communion with the divine and beyond the rational', a mind-set which Lewis came to embrace after his conversion, and which characterizes the thought of the other Inklings as well, with their interest in the divine, in the primordial poetic imagery of myth and metaphor, and in 'wisdom inaccessible by scientific method'.[120] Sadly, seldom do the modern writers who discuss moral imagination (the concept became popular in the 1980s and 1990s) refer to Lewis's *The Abolition of Man* (1943), a work mentioned above in this chapter, in which Lewis addresses the problem of *Tao*-less education, culture and literature, and the ensuing imaginative impoverishment, and stresses the importance of the essential human faculty that is tantamount to moral imagination. As Peter J. Schakel argues regarding Lewis's legacy:

> Except for salvation, imagination is the most important matter in the thought and life of C. S. Lewis. He believed the imagination was a crucial contributor to the moral life, as well as an important source of pleasure in life and a vital evangelistic tool (much of Lewis's effectiveness as an apologist lies in his ability to illuminate difficult concepts through apt analogies). Without the imagination, morality remains ethics—abstract reflections on principles that we might never put into practice. The imagination enables us to connect abstract principles to everyday life, and to relate to the injustices faced by others as we imagine what they experience and feel.[121]

In *The Abolition of Man* Lewis claims that 'the task of the modern educator is not to cut down jungles [of imagination] but to irrigate deserts [of dry intellect

119 Jonathan Jones, 'Defining Moral Imagination' [in:] *First Things: Journal of Religion and Public Life*; July 1, 2009, http://www.firstthings.com/blogs/firstthoughts/2009/07/defining-moral-imagination, accessed 23 April 2016.
120 Jones, ibid.
121 Peter J. Schakel, 'Irrigating Deserts with Moral Imagination' [in:] *Inklings of Glory*, volume 11 of *Christian Reflection: A Series in Faith and Ethics* (Waco: The Center for Christian Ethics at Baylor University, 2004), pp. 21–29, 23.

that eschews imagination]. (...) By starving the sensibility [imaginativeness] of our pupils we only make them easier prey to the propagandist when he comes. For famished nature will be avenged and a hard heart is no infallible protection against a soft head.'[122] 'Children's and adolescents' imaginations need to be fed, not starved', Schakel adds, and the same refers to adults' imagination, of course.[123] The task of 'irrigating deserts' and protecting jungles is also the task of a writer, especially a writer of 'imaginative fiction', who needs to feed the imagination of adults, not with pornography, violence and vulgarity, the common practice that Le Guin compares to 'feeding adults with plastic' (quite eagerly devoured by grown-ups), but instead with moral albeit not moralising content.[124]

As suggested before in this chapter, Le Guin's essay 'Why Are Americans Afraid of Dragons' seems in many ways to synchronize with Lewis's thought expressed in his *The Abolition of Man*, although Le Guin speaks there of American mentality of the 1970s and an American campaign to exterminate the faculty of imaginative creativity, which I associate with 'moral imagination', whereas in his essay Lewis regards England and its system of education of the 1940s. Le Guin claims that:

[What] goes very deep in the American character [is] a moral disapproval of fantasy, disapproval so intense, and often so aggressive, that I cannot help but see it as arising, fundamentally, from fear. So, why are Americans afraid of dragons? (...) It isn't only Americans who are afraid of dragons. I suspect that almost all very highly technological peoples are more or less antifantasy.[125]

Without the nurturing capacity of moral imagination, Le Guin seems to argue, man

Will most likely end up watching bloody detective thrillers on the television, or reading hack Westerns or sports stories, or going in for pornography, from *Playboy* on down. It is starved imagination, craving nourishment, that forces him to do so. But he can rationalize such entertainment by saying that it is realistic – after all sex exists, and there are criminals, and there are baseball players, and there used to be cowboys.(...) that all these genres are sterile, hopelessly sterile, is a reassurance to him, rather than a defect. If they were genuinely realistic, which is to say genuinely imagined and imaginative, he would be afraid of them.[126]

---

122 Lewis, *The Abolition of Man*, pp. 6–7.
123 Schakel, 'Irrigating Deserts with Moral Imagination', p. 26.
124 Le Guin, 'Dreams Must Explain Themselves', p. 45.
125 Le Guin, 'Why Are Americans Afraid of Dragons', p. 29.
126 Le Guin, ibid., p. 32.

Despite all efforts of postmodernity, 'the ancient hungers of the imagination are hard to deny,' says Russell Kirk, pointing to the importance of moral imagination to education and art.[127] Regarding the context of literature, Le Guin notes that discarding meaning-based fantasy fiction results from the suppression of imagination, especially of the moral imagination of fantasy world, which clashes with the deeply-ingrained Puritan mind-set, now thriving in the West as secular Puritanism or a mentality that tends to reject anything that gives spiritual joy, pleasure and delight, and reaps no profits.[128] Le Guin prioritises the importance of what is defined in this chapter as moral imagination, declaring that:

> One of the most deeply human, and humane, of these faculties is the power of imagination: so that it is our pleasant duty, as librarians, or teachers, or parents, or writers, or simply as grownups, to encourage that faculty of imagination in our children, to encourage it to grow freely, to flourish like the green bay tree, by giving it the best, absolutely the best and purest, nourishment that it can absorb. And never, under any circumstances, to squelch it, or sneer at it, or imply that it is childish, or unmanly, or untrue.(...) If you truly eradicated [moral] imagination in a child, he [or she] would grow up to be an eggplant.[129]

What is moral about that imagination embedded in fantasy is its purity and nourishment, and its natural connection to truth. Le Guin makes it clear addressing the very core of Faërie when she admits that:

> It is by such statements as, 'Once upon a time there was a dragon,' or 'In a hole in the ground there lived a hobbit' – it is by such beautiful non-facts that we fantastic human beings may arrive, in our peculiar fashion, at the truth.[130]

Le Guin also argues that 'it is above all by the imagination that we achieve perception, and compassion, and hope.'[131]

To Lewis the essential faculty identified here as moral imagination is likewise the quality which makes man a man, not merely a purely 'cerebral or visceral' creature; it is the most nurturing and rewarding human faculty that enriches the power of reason.[132] Commenting on Lewis's enhancement of imagination and reason, (or faith and reason, a quality characteristic of the Inklings), Schakel

---

127   Russell Kirk, *Decadence and Renewal in the Higher Learning: An Episodic History of American University and College since 1953* (Washington: Gateway, 1978), pp. 36–37.
128   Le Guin, 'Why Are Americans Afraid of Dragons', p. 32.
129   Le Guin, ibid., pp. 32 and 34.
130   Le Guin, 'Why Are Americans Afraid of Dragons', p. 35.
131   Le Guin, 'National Book Award acceptance speech' [in:] *The Language of the Night*, p. 48.
132   Lewis, *The Abolition of Man*, p. 10.

observes that 'the faculty of reason is important in perceiving and articulating principles of morality, but in one sense it remains subservient to imagination because until those principles are internalized by a person and connected to life situations, they do not become meaningful and affect behaviour.'[133] Lewis illustrates this point with one of his memorable practical analogies: 'I had sooner play cards against a man who was quite sceptical about ethics, but bred to believe that "a gentleman does not cheat," than against an irreproachable moral philosopher who had been brought up among sharpers.'[134]

The postmodern world, with its hyperreal virtual wonders and denial of objective values, frequently proves 'stripped of ontological and metaphysical dimension,' as it increasingly lacks the quality which is tantamount to moral imagination.[135] Because of its ethos, which draws on meaning, unconditional values and moral cogency, high fantasy fiction, as I would like to argue, is a realm that accommodates moral imagination, even though the genre is often disparagingly degraded as juvenile, escapist or unrealistic. These false accusations resulting from misunderstanding the essence of Faërie have already been dismissed, as shown through the writings of Tolkien, Lewis and Le Guin, especially in Chapter One of this book. 'Fantasy [genre] is a serious business even though it chooses, on occasion, to present itself as mere entertainment', critics say.[136] It is serious because of its commitment to human dilemmas, represented in Faërie as a triad of pain, guilt and death (a concept I borrow from Frankl's logotherapy), without denying them or providing easy but false solutions; because of the genre's engagement in man's search for meaning, whose discovery is the object of the most important of human yearnings (the tenet which I quote again after Frankl's thought); and last but not least, because of its immersion in moral imagination, which may but does not have to be connected to religion. 'The imagination is the secret and marrow of civilization. It is the very eye of faith,' says Henry Ward Beecher, a 19th century American clergyman and abolitionist campaigner.[137]

Finally, it must be noted again that the 'inherent morality' of high fantasy tales, which, as this chapter suggests, lays foundation for the genre's ethos, appears inextricably connected with Faërie's preoccupation with *logos*, understood

---

133   Schakel, 'Irrigating Deserts with Moral Imagination', p. 27.
134   Lewis, *The Abolition of Man*, p. 10.
135   Marina Warner, *Signs and Wonders: Essays on Literature and Culture* (London: Vintage, 2004), p. 453.
136   Mary Duggan and Roger Grainger, *Imagination, Identification and Catharsis in Theatre and Therapy* (London: Jessica Kingsley Publishers, 1997), p. 9.
137   Henry Ward Beecher, *Proverbs from Plymouth Pulpit*, 1887 (Ulan Press, 2012).

as both word and meaning, and by virtue of its meaning-oriented constitution is seen here as akin to Frankl's logotherapy.[138] Being another element of high fantasy ethos, *logos* testifies to the genre's natural indebtedness to myth and to primordial language, the other sources of Faërie's therapeutic properties, discussed in more detail below.

Myth, logos and Faërie - mythopathy, logotherapy and (non)sensopaedia, in high fantasy literature

Logos, as I wish to argue, contributes to the ethos of high fantasy fiction and seems to allow a connection between Faërie and the therapeutic system of logotherapy. Logos naturally implies sense, understood as 'meaning, import or signification', rather than 'gumption, physical faculties of perception', or 'a sane or practical attitude to situations', in spite or maybe on account of the postmodern (or post-human, to quote Lewis) aura of disillusionment and celebrated emptiness.[139] Meaninglessness, relativity, absurdity and the flickering quality of life deprived of commonly recognized foundations are the known symptoms of the postmodern condition, for which science may find no cure. Its language, which consistently eliminates abstract concepts, works on the carefully sanitised surface and enhances a rapid impoverishment of meaning. This is so inasmuch as 'one of the most important and effective uses of language is not the rational and informative but the emotional', Lewis remarks; the function which gets so commonly discarded by postmodern thinkers, yet which is so wholly legitimate and inherent to human nature.[140] Obviously, the purely rational and informative lingo of science, business and economy never touches upon this ground, upon this 'primary use of language', Lewis argues, or, at its best, it 'masquerades [emotions] by plain hypocrisy or self-deceit'.[141]

The artificial nature of modern language, generated by scientific, empirical, commodified discourse at the expense of its ancient imaginative and emotional (or poetic) quality, leads to manipulation, fragmentation and, as a result, falsification of reality, Lewis contends.[142] Moreover, the postmodern aversion to

---

138   The 'inherent morality' of Faërie is Tolkien's phrase, ('On Fairy-Stories', p. 118), as quoted above in this chapter.
139   *The Compact Oxford English Dictionary*, p. 992. Lewis, *The Abolition of Man*, p. 45.
140   Lewis, *Studies in Words* (Cambridge: Cambridge University Press, 1990, 2nd edition), p. 314.
141   Lewis, ibid., p. 314.
142   Lewis, *Studies in Words*, p. 314.

deeper truths, wider perspectives, wholesome entities and traditional vantage points, cannot but debilitate the grasp of logic and of complete meaning. The once rich logosphere, the domain of meaning, is turning into a desert, having been swept off and substituted by a glamorous iconosphere – a kaleidoscopic panorama of empty symbols and signs which either make no sense, or which have curtailed and compromised their once complex meaning. In such a culture of an unsettling mental transformation, when 'large simplicities get complicated, chaos becomes elegant, and what everybody knows is true turns out to be what some people used to think', Le Guin says, meaning is continually trivialised, instrumentalised, relativised and stripped of its intellectual and ethical complexity.[143] Eventually, its cleansed, flattened, ersatz dimension is made cute and safe, becoming the modern mumbo-jumbo or claptrap, associated by Lewis with 'bulverism', a form of logical fallacy.[144] What facilitates this phenomenon of starving the poetic element of logos and feeding the prosaic aspect of an icon, is, according to Lewis, the commonly committed verbicide, or an act of killing whole words or some of their meanings.

People commit verbicide because they want to 'snatch a word as a party banner to appropriate its selling quality', Lewis explains, and also because they would rather evaluate things than describe them.[145] Examples of verbicide include the word 'awfully' used for 'very'; 'tremendous' for 'great'; or 'unthinkable' for 'undesirable'.[146] Another case of language abuse is verbiage, Lewis claims, that is using a word as a kind of promise that will never be kept, for instance when the word 'significant' does not indicate what the thing it describes is significant of.[147] Furthermore, malapropism is becoming a mass phenomenon, when for a host of reasons words appear in a wrong sense, Lewis ruefully remarks, such as 'deprecate' instead of 'depreciate', or 'scarify' when 'scare' ought to be used.[148] Last but not least, double speak and newspeak have been twisting and maltreating language in various manners, as a weapon used by modern orators in a regular war waged against the clarity and honesty of sense, and the most that can be done, Lewis concludes, is not to imitate these practices of language abuse and slaughter.[149]

143 Le Guin, 'Foreword' to *The Tales from Earthsea*, p. xiv.
144 Lewis's term 'bulverism' has been discussed earlier in this chapter.
145 Lewis, *Studies in Words*, p. 315.
146 Lewis, ibid., p. 7.
147 Lewis, ibid., p. 7.
148 Lewis, ibid., p. 14.
149 Lewis, ibid., p. 132.

Indubitably, language itself is a very imperfect tool of communication, Lewis admits, because it expresses some things so inadequately that we never attempt to communicate them by words (*logoi*) if a more efficient medium is available, such as picture, movement or sound.[150] There is, however, 'a poetic element in all meaningful language', hence the scientific discourse can never be the only means of gaining knowledge, Owen Barfield, asserts.[151] In his illuminating dissertation *Poetic Diction: A Study in Meaning* (1927), Barfield argues that logical speech is tautologous and cannot add to the sum of knowledge, for it does not create new meaning and can only draw on the existing one.[152] Logic and reason may make one more precisely aware of the meaning already implicit in words (if they are used in an honest and wholesome way), but the 'meaning must first of all be there, and if it is there, it will always be found to have been deposited or imparted by the poetic activity,' Barfield claims.[153] Thus, the purpose of logical reasoning is not extending knowledge but 'engendering subjectivity', he observes.[154]

What appears essential to restoring the original wholeness and wholesomeness of language is the counterpart of science, that is art, home to the poetic logos, which rests on the creative power of imagination and feelings, and, which, when verbalised, can be called poetry. Barfield uses the term 'poetry' to name all creative writing, both verse and prose, (in Greek *poesis* means 'making, production or composition'), because language employed creatively by an artist necessarily contains the poetic element, and 'the distinction between poetry and the poetic on the one hand, and prose and the prosaic on the other, is a spiritual one, not confined to literature only.'[155] This is so insofar as the very essence of poetry (*poesis*) dwells in the metaphorical language, understood as a domain of 'making the before unapprehended relations of things,' and as a mould for shaping logos, that is the meaning of words, regardless of their arrangement, scansion and prosody.[156]

Barfield believes that 'art, the individualized poetic, is the very source and fountain-hood of all meaning,' and constitutes a prerequisite of both language and, consequently, literature.[157] This individualized poetic element represents, however, just a means rather than an end to sense. Sense can be reconstructed

---

150   Lewis, ibid., p. 133.
151   Barfield, *Poetic Diction: A Study in Meaning*, p. 31.
152   Barfield, ibid., p. 31.
153   Barfield, ibid., p. 31.
154   Barfield, ibid., p. 31.
155   Barfield, ibid., p. 32.
156   Barfield, ibid., p. 67.
157   Barfield, ibid., p. 140.

from logos by means of imagination, which rediscovers the original poetic element inherent to logos and gives life and meaning to language. This poetic element in language flows from two different sources, Barfield explains: firstly, from the nature of language itself, which in its earlier stages was all poetry, thus metaphor; and, secondly, from the individualized imagination of a poet or writer.[158] 'Only by imagination can the world be known,' Barfield observes, 'and what is needed is not only that larger and larger telescopes and more and more sensible callipers should be constructed, but that the human mind should become increasingly aware of its own creative activity.'[159] Imagination seeks for material in which to incarnate its inspiration, so it seizes on a suitable word or phrase and uses it as a metaphor, thus creating meaning.

Barfield views the rapport between language and imagination in the following way:

Language is the storehouse of imagination. It cannot continue to be itself without performing its function. But its function is to mediate transition from the unindividualized, dreaming spirit that carried the infancy of the world to the individualized human spirit, which has the future in its charge. If therefore [people] succeed in expunging from language all the substance of its past, in which it is naturally rich, and finally converting it into the species of algebra that is best adapted to the uses of indoctrination and empirical science, a long and important step forward will have been taken in the selfless cause of the liquidation of the human spirit.[160]

The liquidation of the human spirit implies ultimate chaos, degeneration of language and thought, dehumanisation, relativity and possibly inhumane technocracy of some artificial intelligence.

To Barfield, just like the other Inklings, and to Le Guin, imagination is an essential complementation to reason, for the former acts on the spur of inspiration or perception, whereby it seizes a suitable word or phrase and as a result produces a metaphor. In this way imagination creates or re-constructs meaning, Barfield contends, whereas reason is merely able to imitate, question or abolish the existing sense.[161] It is not so, nevertheless, that the poetic element should 'tyrannize the rational, but that they should coexist in proportion.'[162] Doing justice to reason, Barfield remarks that the rational element produces consciousness of the world, but only imagination and poetry, that is a creative use of language,

---

158   Barfield, ibid., p. 29.
159   Barfield, ibid., p. 29.
160   Barfield, ibid., p. 23.
161   Barfield, ibid., p. 141.
162   Barfield, ibid., p. 142.

may expand this consciousness, 'pouring into language its creative intuitions,' so that they may 'preserve its living meaning and prevent it from crystallizing into a kind of algebra.'[163] If we fall solely into the poetic principle, we become either mystics or madmen, Barfield concludes; if we choose the rational only, we turn into collectors of data and artefacts, which resembles Lewis's distinction of 'visceral or cerebral men.'[164]

As Barfield argues, the most conspicuous point of contact between meaning and poetry is metaphor, the fruit of imagination and reason, and the kernel of myth. Metaphors, which are akin to myth, relate the 'inner' experience to the 'outer' one, Barfield explains, because, as Ralph Waldo Emerson notes, 'man is an analogist,' and 'there is nothing lucky or capricious in these analogies, but that they are constant and pervade nature.'[165] At its inception language consisted of true metaphors, that is those which represented real, concrete experience, without a 'conscious hypostatization of ideas.'[166] 'As we go back in history [Barfield claims], language becomes more picturesque, until its infancy, when it is all poetry; or all spiritual facts are represented by natural symbols.'[167] Every modern language, Barfield continues, is therefore 'apparently nothing, from beginning to end, but an unconscionable tissue of dead or petrified metaphors,' – metaphors that have been dissected and denaturalized, or simply wasted in the total 'sanitation and simplification campaign.'[168] The intrinsically poetic, metaphorical and imaginative quality of original language, scarcely perceptible nowadays, points to its ancient roots, which are inseparably entangled with myth and fantasy.

Myth is the space where the Greek *logos* ('word, thought, meaning, reason, and logic at the same time) is best preserved and exemplified, for myth and language are both products of the same mysterious, 'metaphorical period,' when the inventive ingenuity of humanity is said to have burgeoned and sprouted as never before or since,' Barfield remarks, adding that 'nothing could be more damning to the "root" conception of language than the ubiquitous phenomenon of the Myth.'[169] Therefore he calls mythology 'the ghost [or shadow] of concrete meaning,' revealing natural connections between discrete phenomena in a most

---

163   Barfield, ibid., p. 60.
164   Barfield, ibid., p. 60.
165   Barfield, ibid., p. 92. Ralph Waldo Emerson, *Nature*, Chapter IV, 'Language' (London: Penguin Classics, 2003, 4th edition), p. 85.
166   Barfield, ibid., p. 201.
167   Barfield, ibid., p. 92. Emerson, *Nature*, p. 86.
168   Barfield, ibid., p. 60.
169   Barfield, ibid., p. 89.

unpretentious way.[170] If we trace words back far enough in the history of meaning, we reach the period when they all had a mythical content, and we may hear the noise of 'the footsteps of nature,' resounding in primitive language and in the finest metaphors of poets alike.[171] It is so because myths are just like metaphors, Barfield suggests, and myth, as the blueprint of all stories, dwells in the very heart of language; therefore, 'to ask what is the origin of stories is to ask what is the origin of language and the mind,' Tolkien adds.[172]

Although they do not contain facts and from the modern perspective are only a far-away echo of concrete experience, myths and Faërie are 'largely made of truth,' Tolkien argues, 'and indeed, they present aspects of it that can only be received in this [poetic, mythopoeic] mode.'[173] Myth, poetry and metaphor, 'are "lies" by necessity'; none the less, they 'have an element of truth that represents the world,' reconciling fantasy and fact, Duriez argues.[174] Myths are not 'lies breathed through silver', as Lewis once said before his conversion, but stories of universal import, combining spirit and nature, imagination and intellect, heaven and earth, thought and feeling.[175]

In his *Very Short Introduction to Myth*, Robert Segal defines myth as 'a story about something significant, which may happen in the past, the present or the future, and [which] expresses a conviction that must be held tenaciously by adherents; but whether the story is true or not is an open-ended question.'[176] Myth is the reservoir of words and senses that have not lost their edge and are uncontaminated by the subsequent rational, logical, scientific thought. They mirror the spontaneous wish to understand and interpret the world. Myth is not factual, yet according to its inner laws, it is coherent and genuine, and so are fantasy tales that spring from it. In myth and Faërie we stand outside time and space and can make sense of our immediate reality, because they 'open a door to Other time and if we pass through, though only for a moment, we stand outside our own time, outside Time itself, maybe,' Tolkien explains.[177] The realm of myth enables us to 'survey the depths of space and time and hold communion with other living

---

170 Barfield, ibid., p. 92.
171 Barfield, ibid., p. 86.
172 Tolkien, 'On Fairy-Stories,' p. 117.
173 Tolkien, ibid., p. 147.
174 Duriez, *The Gift of Friendship*, p. 59.
175 Tolkien, 'On Fairy-Stories', p. 143.
176 Robert Segal, *Myth: A Very Short Introduction* (Oxford: Oxford University Press, 2004), p. 5.
177 Tolkien, 'On Fairy Stories', p. 123; cf. Chapter One.

things,' which is possible because myths and fantasy tales 'have a greater sense and grasp of the endlessness of the World of Story than most modern "realistic" stories, already hemmed within the narrow confines of their own small time'.[178]

Fairy-stories share in the peculiarities of myths, as the former are also 'very ancient indeed', 'appear in very early records; and are found universally, wherever there is language', Tolkien notes, stressing the kinship between Faërie and mythology.[179] 'Whether we get instruction in it or not, the literary imagination of fantasy belongs to us all. All of us have been told stories, tell ourselves stories, make up tales, fables, exemplary cautionings to tell others', psychotherapists say.[180] The universality and familiarity of Faërie can hardly be challenged by any other literary genre. They appear in all cultures, nations and continents, and interact in time and space according to the principle defined by Tolkien as independent evolution or invention, inscribed into their historical and cultural background, inheritance from common ancestry, that is borrowing in time, and, last but not least, diffusion, that is borrowing in space[181] Undoubtedly, fairy tales are the first form of literature produced by ancient mankind, which is still being produced and read, and has not lost any of its relevance and import.

What is more, myths and fantasy tales present, paradoxically, a more acute sense of reality than much of what is called realistic fiction, as their intrinsic otherworldliness offers a fresher view of reality, a distance and an objective perspective, thanks to which one may take account and make sense of the actuality. Seeing the whole picture of reality and having a basis for comparison is what this otherworldliness generously grants, and its essence consists of an 'arresting strangeness' rather than an implausible daydreaming.[182] In fantasy tales the confrontation with universal human dilemmas and ordinary life becomes 'intense to a degree which a merely realistic story could hardly attain', Tolkien says.[183] 'It is one of the properties of Fairy Story thus to enlarge the scene and the actors; or rather it is one of the properties that are distilled by literary alchemy when old deep-rooted stories are rehandled by a real poet with an imagination of his [or

---

178 Tolkien, ibid., p. 119, and p. 161, note H.
179 Tolkien, ibid., p. 121.
180 Ann and Bary Ulanov, *Healing Imagination*, p. 18.
181 Tolkien, 'On Fairy Stories', p. 121.
182 Tolkien, ibid., p. 120.
183 Tolkien, 'Sir Gawain and the Green Knight' [in:] *The Monsters and the Critics*, pp. 72–108, 83.

her] own,' he adds, stressing again the poeticity of language in ancient myths and in their offspring Faërie, when they are genuine and represent a work of art.[184]

Much criticism to which Le Guin refers as an anti-fantasy, or generally, anti-fiction phobia, rests probably on the strength of a nodding acquaintance with myth and fantasy and an automatic refutation of this 'unmanly lit' and 'escapist fodder'.[185] The truth is that, because of its poetic veracity and seemingly estranged immediacy, myth 'challenges and even threatens all that is false, phoney, unnecessary and trivial,' Le Guin argues, to the effect that, to quote Tolkien, 'bread, wine, water, tree [and] stone are [again] what they used to be'.[186] There is a powerful element of magic and imagination in myth and Faërie, but 'besides elves and fays, (…), dwarfs, witches, trolls, giants, or dragons, fantasy holds the seas, the sun, the moon, the sky, and the earth, and all things that are in it: tree and bird, water and stone, wine and bread, [at their simplest and purest,] and [similarly,] ourselves, mortal men, when we are enchanted.'[187]

In this way, myth and the related tales of Faërie restore the original sense of things and the sense of words, or logos, which they guard against the modern contamination and violation, for in their mythical simplicity and uncompromising firmness of values, so often erroneously associated with a childish mind-set, they nurse the pure, wholesome, poetic logos, safe from manipulation and abuse. 'Words are signs of natural facts,' Emerson remarks, as quoted by Barfield; and it seems that there is hardly any context of language more akin to natural facts than myth.[188] Moreover, 'particular natural facts are symbols of particular spiritual facts,' and 'nature is the symbol of spirit', Emerson adds.[189] Therefore, the logos of natural facts embedded so deeply in myth bespeaks spirituality of its makers in the most natural way. Barfield seems to be writing about the same when he observes that the beginning of myth reaches the times when people's thinking was 'not merely *of* Nature but was Nature herself.'[190] Myth and Faërie are the seeds of nature that come from 'the Tree of Life', Barfield asserts, 'which is much older than the Tree of Knowledge,' and which has perhaps been discovered by Tolkien's Niggle in the secondary world.[191]

---

184 Tolkien, ibid., p. 83.
185 Le Guin, 'Why Are Americans afraid of dragons?' p. 32.
186 Le Guin, ibid., p. 35. Tolkien, 'On Fairy-Stories', p. 123.
187 Tolkien, ibid., p. 123.
188 Emerson, *Nature*, p. 90.
189 Emerson, ibid., p. 92.
190 Barfield, *Poetic Diction*, p. 147; italics are Barfield's.
191 Barfield, ibid., p. 90.

Tracing the affinity between myth and Faërie, Tolkien asserts that fairy-stories are 'derived from myth and [cannot] be sharply separated from it, and are capable in poetic hands of turning into it, that is of becoming largely significant, as a whole, accepted unanalysed.'[192] Moreover, Tolkien believes that 'there is no fundamental distinction between the higher and lower mythologies', that is between classical 'Olympian nature-myths' and modern mythopoeic (or fantasy) tales, inasmuch as 'their peoples live (if they live at all) by the same life, just as in the mortal world do kings and peasants.'[193]

Also Le Guin acknowledges the affinity between myth and fantasy fiction, its modern descendant, and emphasises their instructive force and benevolent power that result from the natural knowledge they convey. 'The use of fantasy is to give pleasure and delight, and to deepen our understanding of our world, and our fellow men, and our own feelings, and our destiny,' she admits.[194].

Elaborating on the kinship between myth and Faërie, Barfield adds that 'myths still live on a ghostly life as fables [or fairy and fantasy stories] after they have died as real meaning.'[195] Tolkien, who endorses this view, highlights the intimate connection between the original pre-logical language and more modern fairy tales that might make its sole treasury. Fairy tales and 'legends depend on the language to which they belong,' he believes, 'but a living language depends equally on the legends which it conveys by tradition.'[196]

Likewise, Lewis admits that he chose fantasy narrative in his Narnian stories because it is the 'genre best fitted for what [he] wanted to say,' which endows the imaginative and mythopoeic forms with his own religious beliefs.[197] 'Myths explain why "the lies" of the poet or fiction writers capture profound realities, which can't be captured in any other way,' Duriez notes.[198] Obviously, 'the significance of myth is not easily to be pinned by analytical reasoning,' as it escapes formulas and definitions, Tolkien remarks.[199] This is so inasmuch as myth and Faërie 'cannot be caught in a net of words,' he says, for they are 'indescribable but not imperceptible.'[200]

192 Tolkien, 'Sir Gawain and the Green Knight', p. 73.
193 Tolkien, 'On Fairy Stories', p. 123.
194 Le Guin, 'Why Are Americans afraid of dragons?' p. 33.
195 Barfield, Poetic Diction, p. 147.
196 Tolkien, The Letters of J. R. R. Tolkien, p. 231.
197 Colin Duriez, Tolkien and C. S. Lewis: The Gift of Friendship, p. 178.
198 Duriez, Tolkien and C. S. Lewis, p. 58.
199 Tolkien, 'Sir Gawain and the Green Knight', p. 73.
200 Tolkien, 'On Fairy Stories', p. 114.

Due to Faërie's particular relationship with myth, resulting from numerous generic similarities, it seems that Faërie may also mediate another form of therapy, which has been defined in this book as 'mythopathy' (therapy through myth), for it involves a return to the origins of human culture and thought, to the very sources of language and moral imagination, to the union with nature and natural things, and to the sensitivity to an unquestionable meaning and word. Why can myths be therapeutic?

Myths preserve ancient knowledge about man. They 'define aliens and enemies, and in conjuring them up they say who we are and what we want, they tell stories to impose structure and order. Like fiction, they can tell the truth even while they're making it all up,' Marina Warner notes.[201] Moreover, 'perceived as survivals from ancient oral culture (orature), long despised as suspect and even ignorant atavism, and consequently identified with women, children and primitive peoples, myth and [F]aërie rediscover a special affinity with the unfettered, self-generated fantasy, and offer the means to reinhabit the lived experience of the Other – of exiles, slaves, the disappeared.'[202] The affiliation of myth and fantasy fiction with imagination, as well as the self, which can only be meaningful in the context of otherness, seems only too evident. In the English tradition, Arthurian myth has been particularly seminal, as reflected literature, for instance, of the 20th c. in the works of Tolkien and Williams (the latter's Arthurian poetry). Also the dragon lore and Nordic mythology have largely shaped the realm of Faërie, as manifested in the fantasy worlds of Tolkien, Lewis, and to some extent Le Guin (for example in her science fiction novel *Rocannon's World*), and, for Le Guin native American mythology and Eastern lore provide other important sources of inspiration.

Drawing on timeless narratives of poetic imagination, which address both the immediate reality and the transcendent realm, mythopathy can work hand in hand with logotherapy, because logos from the depths of time and beyond time dwells in myth, and thus also in its offspring: tales of Faërie. Myth and fantasy fiction might appear nonsensical, for they are not factual and empirical, but this does not seem to be the yardstick of their truthfulness and meaningfulness. The infamous and long-abolished theorem of Max Müller stipulates that myth is the disease of language, but when inverted by Tolkien it affirms the opposite, namely that it is 'languages that are the disease of myth', as they undergo rapid corruption

---

201   Marina Warner, *Signs and Wonders: Essays on Literature and Culture*, p. 28.
202   Warner, 'Myth and Faërie: Rewritings and Recoveries', [in:] *Signs and Wonders*, pp. 444–457, 446.

and degeneration, whereas myth remains intact and universal.[203] The modern development of technology and science proves unsustainable not only in terms of its effect on the natural habitat but also on language, which, just like the environment and endangered species, is being contaminated, devastated and abused.

In the thought of the Inklings, and of Le Guin, the connection between myth (and hence also fantasy tales) and meaning appears very close, and entails the presence of what has been called here 'moral imagination'. The most concise expression of this relationship is perhaps Barfield's dictum that 'myth is the true child of Meaning begotten on imagination'.[204] For instance, the word *spiritus*, Barfield explains, in the ancient language meant 'breath, wind and divinity' at the same time, and naturally enhanced the poeticity of its use.[205] The same multidimensionality used to apply to many other ancient words and concepts. Therefore, the depth, wealth and lucidity of sense that dwells in the mythical substance of *logos* appear to counterbalance the meaninglessness, sterility and fashionable superficiality of postmodernity. Tolkien emphasises that teleogical transparency of Faërie viewing it in terms of 'moral teaching', which, although complex, is most natural and unimposing: 'There is indeed no better medium for moral teaching than a good fairy story – a real deep-rooted tale, told as a tale and not a thinly-disguised moral allegory'.[206] Because of its orientation towards meaning and unconditional values, and also its reliance on moral imagination and artistic creativity, myth, as the primary imaginative literary paradigm and parent to fairy tales, seems to correspond to the thought of logotherapy (therapy through meaning), and, as this chapter seeks to argue, also to some kind of 'sensopaedia', that is instruction in meaning, (in Greek: *paedia* – knowledge, learning,) which in myth remains complete and wholesome.[207]

Myths, and their offspring, Faërie, Barfield explains, come from the pre-logical period when there was no distinction between the subjective and the objective.[208] 'The subjective is inseparable from the rational or discursive thought operating in abstract ideas; consequently, the subjective could not have existed in the pre-logical

203   Max Müller, *The Science of Language* (London: Kessinger Publishing, 2003, 6th edition), p. 454. Tolkien, 'On Fairy Stories', p. 121.
204   Barfield, *Poetic Diction*, p. 14.
205   Barfield, ibid., p. 11.
206   Tolkien, 'Sir Gawain and the Green Knight', p. 73.
207   *Modern Greek Dictionary*, http://www.lexilogos.com/english/greek_dictionary.htm, accessed 20 July 2016.
208   Barfield, *Poetic Diction*, p. 204.

times at all.'[209] Therefore, mythical *logos* contains a genuine, unaffected, objective understanding of reality, undistorted by analytical reasoning and 'logomorphism', that is projecting the post-logical thoughts onto the pre-logical imagination.[210] 'Imagination is an organ of meaning', Lewis argues, voicing the opinion shared by the other Inklings.[211] Modern meaning, however, developed when imagination was downplayed and restrained by the rational element of cognition, Barfield adds, which occurred 'at an advanced stage of self-consciousness', of individuation and subjectivity, rather late in the history of language, and hence modern meaning leans towards the prosaic, not the poetic element.[212] Self-consciousness emerged from the rational principle, which 'shuts off the human ego from the living meaning in the outer world, and encloses that same ego in the network of its own, now abstract, thoughts', which have lost their connection with the immediate reality and concrete collective experience as perceived by an imaginative, irrational and unconscious self.[213] Self-consciousness, Barfield continues, makes indeed a *sine qua non* of 'undreaming knowledge, but it is not knowledge, it is more like its opposite, [for] once it has been achieved, logic is *functus officio*', or a redundant faculty that has already performed its role.[214]

If self-consciousness involves 'undreaming knowledge', as Barfield suggests, then myth, a product of the pre-self-conscious period, is a dream that we have not stopped dreaming, for myth is still around. It is a dream whose poetic and irrational fabric is often confused with illusion and lies, yet which has its origins in a spontaneous expression of truth, and which cannot be severed from human nature. 'We are such stuff as dreams are made on', Shakespeare says through Prospero's mouth in *The Tempest*.[215] The affinity to myth results from the essentially poetic nature of human mind and thought, when they are yet untainted by the recognition of self-consciousness and emergence of subjectivity.

Rational and scientific thinking dissects metaphors and constricts the original *logos*, as it becomes a tool of gaining power and meeting personal ends to the effect that language may lose its ability to create pure, spontaneous art, which Tolkien dubs 'elvish' – the art that is never instrumental and that thrives only 'at

209   Barfield, ibid., p. 204.
210   Barfield, ibid., p. 204.
211   Duriez, *The Gift of Friendship*, p. 178.
212   Barfield, *Poetic Diction*, p. 137.
213   Barfield, ibid., p. 143.
214   Barfield, ibid., p. 30.
215   Shakespeare, *The Tempest*, Act Four, Scene One, lines 148–149 (London: Penguin Books, 2001), p. 81.

the furthest pole from the vulgar devises of the laborious, scientific, magician.[216] Language is the disease of myth, and the excess of rational component that expunges the poetic one is the disease of language, causing its defilement and semiotic impoverishment. Perhaps this is why Caliban reproaches Miranda and Prospero, who have taught him the language, with these words:

'You taught me language, and my profit on 't
Is, I know how to curse: the red plague rid you
For learning me your language.'[217]

To a pre-logical self, modern language may thus prove useless and even harmful, as it corrupts its purity and innocence and exposes the self to the previously unknown evil. The language of a technologically advanced civilisation does not seem to convey the ideas of people untouched by civilisation, whose minds still linger in the pre-logical times. What they absorb when coming in contact with the language produced by a self-conscious self may thus be its most corrupt part. Imbued with mythical quality, the pre-logical *logos* dates to time immemorial, to the very dawn of creation. The holy scriptures of many religions cherish the sacred logos and contain a myth which they revere as true, for it signifies the divine which endows universe with sense. In the divine Logos rests the power of the Maker, whoever one may conceive Him to be. The Christian metaphor of the Book of Genesis reveals that ancient Logos, the primary living power and ultimate meaning, is God Himself, the only *spiritus movens* (St. John's Gospel, 1:1–14), and that language was the tool of Creation. Pre-Christians and non-Christians often interpret logos likewise as the source of all meaning, a power animating universe and containing all intelligible words.

A devout Catholic, Tolkien interprets the Gospels as the matrix of all fairy tales and believes that 'the Gospels contain a fairy-story, or a story of a larger kind which embraces all the essence of fairy-stories; they contain many marvels – peculiarly artistic, beautiful, and moving: "mythical" in their perfect, self-contained significance.'[218] To Tolkien and Lewis, the Christian history of Salvation and Incarnation with the eucatastrophic Resurrection is the confirmation and sanctification of the ancient myth of a dying god, which has come true.[219]

Furthermore, when examining the concept of sensopaedia in myth and in Faërie, it must be noted that *logos* is a sacrosanct issue in both. Tolkien sees

---

216   Tolkien, 'On Fairy Stories', p. 114.
217   Shakespeare, *The Tempest*, Act One, Scene Two, lines 352–66, p. 39.
218   Tolkien, 'On Fairy Stories', p. 155.
219   Duriez, *The Gift of Friendship*, p. 52.

logos as the beginning and end of all creative writing, just as St. John sees *Logos* as the beginning and end of all creation. 'I always (…) start with a name. Give me a name and it produces a story, not the other way about normally,' Tolkien declares.[220] After his conversion to Christianity, Lewis declared: 'I must admit that mind was no late-come epiphenomenon; that the whole universe was, in the last resort, mental; that our logic was participation in a cosmic Logos.'[221] Colin Duriez emphasises this mythopoeic quality of Tolkien's and Lewis's thought and their writings in the following way:

> Fiction, for Tolkien and Lewis, was the creation of meaning rather than the literal restating of truths. It reflected for them the greater creativity of God, when he originated and put together his universe and ourselves. Natural objects and people are not mere facts. Their meaning comes from their relationship to God. They have a created unity, and their fullness and meaning derive from that.[222]

Duriez calls Tolkien's seminal poem *Mythopoeia* the writer's 'beatitude to the makers of legend' and myth, who do not lie but attempt to sub-create art made of truth, following in the footsteps of 'a Maker'.[223]

Because of their divine origin, all words and languages have powerful meaning in Tolkien's and Lewis's mythologies and must not be abused, and similarly, the ancient *logos* known as the Old Speech is the origin and centre of Le Guin's world of Earthsea. Knowing the true name of a man, animal, thing or a phenomenon, gives an absolute power over them and is a treasure few people may gain, and a gift even fewer are born with. Only dragons, Le Guin's primordial creatures, who are more ancient than the human species, speak naturally the Old Speech, whereby they often express their thoughts in metaphors and sometimes in seeming contradictions, which results from the wealth of simultaneous meanings of words that are not scientifically tapered. Nothing binds dragons more than the power of the Old Speech, whose *logos* maintains the sense of existence and conditions the Equilibrium in Earthsea, that is the balance of life and death, as well as between good and evil.

The Old Speech is 'the language dragons speak, and the language Segoy [the Creator of Earthsea] spoke, and the language of lays and songs, spells, enchantments,

---

220 Duriez, ibid., p. 5.
221 Lewis, *Surprised by Joy*, pp. 208–209.
222 Duriez, *The Gift of Friendship*, p. 178.
223 Duriez, ibid., p. 179.

and invocations,' Le Guin explains.[224] 'Its words lie hidden and changed among Hardic' (common language spoken in some parts of Earthsea), some words of that ancient Speech 'have been lost over ages, and some have been hidden, and some are known only to dragons and to the Old Powers of Earth, and some are known to no living creature; and no man could learn them all. For there is no end to that language,' Le Guin remarks.[225] The Old Speech of Le Guin's Earthsea, which seems to correspond to the mythical *logos* of the original language, which was all poetry, is a magic treasury of natural knowledge and power, and the essence of wisdom and art. Ged, the Archmage and greatest of Earthsea wizards, states that:

> Knowing names is my job, [for] to weave the magic of a thing (…), one must find its true name out.(…) There is great power, and great peril, in a name. Once, at the beginning of time, when Segoy raised the isles of Earthsea from the ocean deeps, all things bore their own true names. And all doing of magic, all wizardry, hangs still upon the knowledge – the relearning, the remembering – of that true and ancient language of the Making. There are spells to learn, of course, ways to use the words; and one must know the consequences, too. But what a wizard spends his life at is finding out the names of things, and finding out how to find out the names of things.[226]

Barbara Bucknall comments on the importance of language and words to Le Guin's fantasy world in the following way: 'What [*The Wizard of Earthsea*] is really about, from start to finish, is naming and being named. Ged is to handle words in such a way that they identify the inner reality of what he is naming and, by naming, controlling.'[227]

The ability to give names and speak a verbal language appears crucial also to the otherwise mute and dumb creatures in myth and Faërie. This special ability characterises, for instance, Tolkien's Ents, Le Guin's dragons and Lewis's Talking Animals in Narnia.

In modern myths and fantasy works, engendered by ancient myths, there may reside a power of logos that has not been undermined by semantic verbicide, verbiage or malapropism. If this intact and wholesome sense can be found in the logos of myth and Faërie, then the mythopoeic works that derive from myth may perform some literary sensopaedia and a kind of artistic logotherapy, carried out by a fantasy narrative on the strength of its meaningful language and moral imagination by means of metaphors and applicability, rather than by a therapist's

---

224 Le Guin, *The Earthsea Quartet: A Wizard of Earthsea* (London: Penguin Books, 1993), pp. 50–51.

225 Le Guin, ibid., pp. 50–51.

226 Le Guin, *The Earthsea Quartet: The Tombs of Atuan*, pp. 266–267.

227 Bucknall, *Ursula K. Le Guin*, p. 39.

story that guides the patient towards a discovery of a meaning of their life and particular life situation during their conversation. 'Deeper meaning resides in the fairy tales told to me in my childhood than in the truth that is taught by life,' Friedrich Schiller says, pointing to the genre's immersion in *logos*.[228] Fantasy tales, similarly to myths and legends, seriously face all the 'whys' that every generation asks, and attempt to suggest solutions, without mockery, scorn or pretence.

The logotherapeutic nature of fantasy fiction, especially of fairy tales, emerges also from the thought of Bruno Bettelheim (1903–1990), an Austrian-born American child psychologist, who, similarly to Victor Frankl, studied in Vienna, and survived the Holocaust.[229] Although Bettelheim does not refer to logotherapy and never uses the term, the tenets of logotherapy reverberate through his famous work *The Uses of Enchantment: The Meaning and Importance of Fairy Tales*, which he begins with the following statement:

> If we hope to live not just from moment to moment, but in true consciousness of our existence, then our greatest need and most difficult achievement is to find meaning in our lives. It is well known how many have lost the will to live, and have stopped trying, [or lost their will to meaning, as Frankl would say], because such meaning has evaded them.[230]

Bettelheim also observes that 'the fairy tale could not have its psychological impact on the child were it not first and foremost a work of art,' which, in turn, sounds reminiscent of Tolkien's emphasis on the highest artistic quality of fairy-stories.[231] Although Bettelheim's interpretations of fairy tales draw on Freud's psychoanalysis, despised by the Inklings, Bettelheim's conviction of the meaningful world of spirituality offered by fairy tales, and of their 'strong moral character', as Tolkien would say, bridges his thought in a way with that of the Inklings. In fact, in his book Bettelheim actually refers to Chesterton and Lewis, and quotes them, making a point of the spiritual wealth of fairy-stories that help to discover true meaning of life: 'Literary critics such as G. K. Chesterton and C. S.

---

228   Friedrich Schiller, quoted in Peter Lahnstein's *Schillers Leben* (Frankfurt am Main: Fischer, 1984), p. 30. *The Piccolini*, III, p. 4.

229   Bettelheim's work on the causes of autism in children is largely discredited today. There are also many controversies regarding his attitude towards children in his psychotherapeutic practice, based on accusations of brutality and violence. His thought concerning the psychological importance of fairy tales appears still valid and insightful, though.

230   Bruno Bettelheim, *The Uses of Enchantment: The Meaning and Importance of Fairy Tales* (London: Penguin Books, 1991), p. 3.

231   Bettelheim, ibid., p. 12.

Lewis felt that fairy stories are "spiritual explorations" and hence "the most life-like" since they reveal "human life as seen, or felt, or divined from the inside."[232]

Bettelheim also summarises Mircea Eliade's anthropological research, which proves that fairy tales are 'models for human behaviour that (…) give meaning and value to life', as they address the universal human dilemmas and enhance psychological development of children and adults alike.[233] Similarly to Tolkien, Bettelheim contrasts fairy tales with the delusion of dreams, and points to the unique quality of fairy tales identified by Tolkien as eucatastrophe: 'the fairy tale does the opposite [to what dreams do]: it projects the relief of all pressures and not only offers ways to solve problems but promises that a "happy" solution will be found.'[234]

Presenting genuine human dilemmas, which ultimately find their resolution, and supporting the good, which is eventually rewarded, high fantasy tales endorse *logos*, because in the world of Faërie all events and situations, even if they seem insignificant or irrelevant, have meaning that is necessary to complete an existential jigsaw and arrive at a sense of life and of particular situations. The heroes and heroines of fairy stories are challenged, tested and often painfully tried, but the meaning and truth that they eventually discover appear perennial and never fail. 'We are meaning-seeking creatures,' says Irvin Yalom, a psychotherapist, reiterating Frankl's tenet, and 'meaning provides a sense of mastery: feeling helpless and confused in the face of random, unpatterned events, we seek to order them and, in so doing, gain a sense of control over them. Even more important, meaning gives birth to values and, hence, to a code of behaviour: thus the answer to 'why' questions (Why do I live?) supplies an answer to 'how' questions (How do I live?)'[235] With all the 'why' and 'how' questions fantasy realm reflects the timelessness of experiences represented by archetypal characters, situations and events. The main theme of fairy tales is that of metamorphic phenomena and of dying and becoming, of passing away, transforming and recovering. Never losing faith in the good in man and nature, and never abandoning hope, fantasy tales seem to secure the space for reflection and rumination, away from the hectic reality and its fragmented chaos. They embrace the world where hope and good do not fail, and meaning enhances ineradicable values (or Lewis's *Tao*).

---

232   Bettelheim, ibid., p. 24. Bettelheim quotes from G. K. Chesterton's *Orthodoxy* (London: Jane Lane, 1909), and from Lewis's *The Allegory of Love* (Oxford: Oxford University Press, 1936).
233   Bettelheim, ibid., p. 35.
234   Bettelheim, ibid., p. 36.
235   Irvin Yalom, *Love's Executioner and Other Tales of Psychotherapy* (London: Penguin Books, 1989), p. 12.

It is widely known that fantasy tales, especially short folk tales and fairy stories have found significant application in psychotherapy and clinical practice, when, carefully selected, they are read, told and discussed by patients and therapists. In his engrossing analysis of the role fairy tales play in psychotherapy, Erich Franzke, a psychotherapist, enumerates the following advantages of Faërie applied in therapy:

- by elevating matters to the supernatural fairy-tale level, the patient does not directly betray personal and familial information, so that feelings of loyalty and solidarity with the family are less easily hurt;
- the feeling of being left alone with one's problems is alleviated by the general character of fairy tales. Thus, also the narcisstic injury of being the only incapable, the only abnormal person alive in the world is avoided;
- a positive approach to encountering conflicts and problems is fostered;
- identification is allowed with the heroes/heroines (or even minor figures) in fairy tales, who, like the patients, have travelled an often difficult path and are unsure whether obedience or disobedience is the next proper step;
- experiences are made in the border realm, between the real and the fairy tale world;
- representative archetypes and magical beings are encountered;
- the metamorphic phenomena of dying and becoming are promoted, and the old is implemented into the forming of the new. Metamorphoses and transitions occur in the realm between the real and the fantastic, and lead to maturation, growth and individuation. Psychotherapy involves metamorphosis leading to a new development, and individual creation. It is about dying of old habits and traumas, and becoming a new revitalized person.[236]

Franzke's conclusions, supported by his psychotherapeutic practice, seem to confirm the therapeutic properties of fantasy literature, associated with what I call the ethos of Faërie and its mythopathic and logotherapeutic potential in the context of *therapia pauperum*, that is a type of self-therapy for every reader (and possibly author), but also a useful means of clinical practice. Franzke observes that:

Just reading fairy tales … can often have a positive effect on the therapeutic atmosphere. Themes such as the necessity to start out on a journey, to accept a risk, to overcome dangers, to carry burdens, and in particular, to forsake one thing, so that another may develop – in short, the themes of dying and becoming- may influence the client [and the reader]. In addition, in many tales breaking rules or conventions leads to surprising developments. In all forms of psychotherapy that serve to evoke insight and increase functional capabilities, thoughts, fantasies and later on trail step-wise action, leading

236 Erich Franzke, *Fairy Tales in Psychotherapy: The Creative use of Old and New Tales*, trans. Joseph A. Smith, (Toronto: Hagrefe and Huber Publishers, 1989), p. 121.

beyond previous boundaries are essential, for only in this manner can the client acquire and implement new ways of approaching life.[237]

It seems that myth and Faërie may adopt the role of an imaginary 'ophthalmologist', who, as Victor Frankl suggests, helps the reader broaden their 'visual field, so that the whole spectrum of meaning becomes conscious and visible to him [or her].'[238] This auxiliary function of myth and Faërie that focuses on logosphere, becomes possible due to the affinity between myth and logos. Just like Frankl's logotherapy, which helps patients seek meaning in their life, especially in confrontation with pain, suffering and death, the mythopathic and mythopoeic logotherapy and sensopaedia do not endorse any religion, but attempt to show a lost path towards the hidden sense and order through the intrinsic poeticity of language. Perhaps myth and Faërie can serve as a litmus paper, testing the wholesomeness of language and intactness of sense, for when their *logos* fails, they prove a mere commodity, a gaudy gimmick, whose otherworldly nonsense irks and irritates. An essential element of mythopoeic logotherapy seems also the inherent association of sensibility that dwells in myth, that is the long-lost union of thought and feeling, mind and emotion, which enhances the wealth and coherence of meaning, as manifested by means of the pre-logical, poetic language.

It is important to remember, none the less, that the healing power of fantasy literature, which addresses man's will to meaning (according to Frankl, the most essential human desire), cannot be mistaken for a spiritual guidance. Fantasy logotherapy may only hint at some large universal meaning of good and evil, at a sense of life, yet by no means can it perform the function of a spiritual system. It is rather a medium of transition from the rational and scientific towards the spiritual, for its language takes us far away from the contemporary *horror vacui* towards sense, which may eventually be fully found in religion. Tolkien observes that:

> Something really 'higher' is occasionally glimpsed in mythology: Divinity, the right to power (as distinct from its possession), the due of worship; in fact 'religion'. Andrew Lang said, and is by some still condemned for saying, that mythology and religion (in the strict sense of that word) are two distinct things that have become inextricably entangled, though mythology is in itself almost devoid of religious significance.[239]

Little wonder, then, that myth and Faërie laid Lewis's path from atheism to theism and then to Christianity. For Le Guin, it has been an expression of her Taoist approach to life, with its Three Jewels of compassion, moderation and humility.

---

237 Franzke, *Fairy Tales in Psychotherapy*, p. 18.
238 Frankl, *Man's Search for Meaning*, p. 115.
239 Tolkien, 'On Fairy Stories', p. 124.

To conclude, the realm of Faërie may offer a kind of *therapia pauperum*, a natural first aid remedy for a postmodern crisis of meaning; a remedy that hints at and leads towards large truths propounded by systems of moral imagination that shall be (re)discovered. Consolation, the last element of its therapeutic ethos, bound up with the cathartic notion of eucatastrophe, remains to be discussed in the next chapter of this book.

Chapter Seven
Therapy through catharsis – eucatastrophic Consolation of Faërie

In the previous chapter I have based my argument stipulating psychotherapeutic properties of fantasy literature on the Greek theory of ethos, by ascribing specific generic qualities to Faërie, as manifested in the works of the Inklings and of Le Guin. The idea of projecting the theory of ethos governing modes of music onto the ground of literature also comes from ancient Greek thought, which introduces such parallels, as mentioned in Chapter Six of this book, and reflected, for instance, in Aristotle's definition of Tragedy and Comedy, each of which appears to have its own ethos, which I understand as moral character and disposition:[1] Now, in the last chapter, I attempt to address the last but not the least of the unique qualities of fairy-stories as identified by Tolkien, that is Consolation achieved through Eucatastrophe, which, as I wish to argue, draws on the notion and effect of catharsis, and thus reaches back to Aristotle's thought. In *The Poetics*, chapter VI, Aristotle defines Tragedy as follows:

> Tragedy (…) is an imitation of a worthy or illustrious and perfect action, possessing magnitude, in pleasing language, using separately the several species of imitation in its parts, by men acting, and not through narration, through pity and fear effecting a purification from such like passions. (…) By pleasing language I mean language possessing rhythm, harmony and melody.[2]

Thus, the ethos of Tragedy seems to rest on its serious subject, action that 'possesses magnitude', matter expressed in 'pleasing language'; and, even more importantly, on an arousal of fear and pity that happens by design, and not by chance (when a noble character falls due to *hamartia*, the term translated differently across centuries, for instance as a 'mistake of fact', 'ignorance of fact', or 'moral defect'), allowing for a 'purification' or 'cleansing' (*katharsis*) of the

---

1   Greek thought views music and literature in terms of sisterly arts also with regard to catharsis. Aristoxenus says, for instance, that 'Pythagoreans used medicine to purify the body, and music to purify souls'; music having thus an effect very similar to that of tragedy; cf. Leonid Zhmud, *Pythagoras and the Early Pythagoreans*, trans. Kevin Windle and Rosh Ireland (Oxford: Oxford University Press, 2012), p. 288.
2   Aristotle, *Poetics*, Chapter VI, trans. Theodore Buckley (Amherst: Prometheus Books, 1992), pp. 10–11.

spectator's passions of pity (*eleos*) and fear (*phobos*), which happens at the end of the play and is the most distinctive feature of Tragedy.[3] 'Tragedy is an imitation not only of a complete action, but also of objects of fear and pity, and these arise most of all when events happen contrary to expectation but in consequence of one another,' Aristotle observes in chapter IX of his *Poetics*.[4]

Rooted in the logical order of universe, Tragedy is not only a work of moral magnitude and refinement, but also a work of beauty, which results from its lofty language, dignified verse, specifically prescribed rhythm, melody and harmony, as well as from its orderly structure of the plot (*mythos*) and a great internal integrity (the unities of place, time and action). That sense of all-encompassing concentration and moral transparency is rendered in some critics' translation of the term catharsis itself, which they interpret as 'intellectual clarification' rather than purification, purgation or cleansing.[5]

In a statement that refers to both drama and epic poetry, as both are based on stories, however different and differently represented, Aristotle remarks that:

> It is (...) needful that well put-together stories not begin from just anywhere at random, nor end just anywhere at random ...And beauty resides in size and order ...the oneness and wholeness of the beautiful thing being present all at once in contemplation ...in stories, just as in human organizations and in living things.[6]

The beauty of Tragedy appears unique, though, due to its cathartic effect. Thus, as Aristotle argues in chapter XXVI of his *Poetics*, Tragedy is not a literary 'species' within which some works are beautiful and others not; it is itself a species of beauty.[7]

Aristotle ascribes specific ethos to each 'species' (that is genre) of *poïesis* (that is imaginative literature) existing in his days, observing, for instance, that epic poetry, as represented by the epic poem (translated by Buckley as the epopee), 'is an attendant on Tragedy', which, despite having a different subject, matter (simple meter) and method (narrative structure), also exemplifies 'an imitation of worthy characters and actions,' but does not, for instance, enhance the unity of

---

3   Cf. T. C. W. Stinton, 'Hamartia in Aristotle and Greek Tragedy' [in:] *The Classical Quarterly New Series*, vol. 25, No. 2 (Dec., 1975) (Cambridge: Cambridge University Press, 1975), pp. 221–254.

4   Aristotle, *Poetics*, Chapter VI, trans. Joe Sachs, p. 19.

5   One of such is Leon Golden, cf. his 'Epic, Tragedy and Catharsis' [in:] *Classical Philology*, Vol. 71, No. 1 (Chicago: University of Chicago Press, 1976), pp. 77–85.

6   Aristotle, *Poetics*, Chapter VII, p. 21.

7   Cf. Joe Sachs, 'Aristotle – Poetics' [in:] *The Internet Encyclopaedia of Philosophy*, http://www.iep.utm. edu/aris-poe/, accessed 23 April 2016.

action, space and time required in Tragedy.[8] By contrast, the ethos of Comedy is, according to Aristotle, rather base, for 'Comedy is (...) an imitation indeed of bad characters, yet it does not imitate them according to every vice, [but the ridiculous only;] since the ridiculous is a portion of turpitude. For the ridiculous is a certain error, and turpitude unattended with pain, and not destructive.'[9]

Of course, these extremely cursory references to Aristotle's *Poetics* scarcely scratch the surface of his capital work, yet they serve here as a starting point for a discussion of Tolkien's eucatastrophic Consolation and its (cathartic) effect, and they set the scene for some parallels between the ethos of Tragedy, as stipulated by Aristotle, and the ethos of Faërie, as suggested by Tolkien, whose compatibility seems to result, generally speaking, from their mutual affinity to therapy, even though Tolkien does not name it so.

'Being washed in wonderment' – Tragedy, Faërie, and an ethos of catharsis[10]

As I have attempted to argue in Chapter Six, Faërie is a literary genre of its own specific ethos, and Tolkien's essay 'On Fairy-Stories' treats of this, in a sense just like Aristotle's magnificent work *The Poetics* addresses the characteristics of *poïesis* in general, and Tragedy in particular. In other respects a comparison between Aristotle's and Tolkien's work, disregarding the wealth of the former's thought, and drawn by such an ill-qualified person as myself, will obviously appear ludicrous. Worth noticing, however, could be some elements of both works, which I hope to view in terms of possible affinity, paradoxical and unlikely though it may appear, yet whose common denominator seems to be catharsis achieved by art, thanks to the therapeutic potential of both Tragedy and high fantasy fiction.

The only paper that I know which addresses this problem by analysing similarities and differences between Tolkien's concept of eucatastrophe and Aristotle's catharsis is Professor Andrzej Wicher's 'Therapeutic Categories. Some Remarks on the Relationship between Tolkien's "Eucatastrophe" and Aristotle's "Catharsis", included as the last chapter of his book *Selected Medieval and Religious Themes in*

---

8   Aristotle, *Poetics*, Chapter V, trans. Theodore Buckley, p. 10. The Greek word *poïesis* means 'making' or 'creation', and comes from the verb *poiein*, ποιεῖν, that is 'to make'; cf. *Online Etymology Dictionary*, Douglas Harper, ed. http://www.etymonline.com/, accessed 23 April 2016.

9   Aristotle, *Poetics*, Chapter V, trans. Theodore Buckley, p. 9. The parenthesis is Buckley's.

10   'Being washed in wonderment' is a phrase used by Joe Sachs in his essay 'Aristotle – Poetics', quoted also further on in this chapter.

the Works of C. S. Lewis and J. R. R. Tolkien (2013). The first issue which emerges from both works, that is Aristotle's *Poetics* and Tolkien's 'On Fairy-Stories', is, as I would like to argue, Tragedy's and Faërie's special embedment in and indebtedness to art, and their arguably highest artistic status among literary genres. Aristotle clearly regards Tragedy not only as the highest form of *poïesis*, but also as one of the highest forms of art. Regardless of his great respect for Homer, Aristotle holds Tragedy in higher esteem than epic poetry, and considers Tragedy as 'the culmination of a teleological development of art form which began with dithyrambs and phallic songs.'[11] Tolkien, in turn, considers Fantasy (the sub-creative Imagination and the key to Faërie) to be 'not a lower but a higher form of Art, indeed the most nearly pure form, and so (when achieved) the most potent.'[12] Making fairy-stories is to him 'a kind of elvish craft', and 'when in any degree accomplished', it is 'a rare achievement of Art: indeed narrative art, story-making in its primary and most potent mode.'[13]

Interestingly, in his essay 'On Fairy-Stories' Tolkien refers several times to Tragedy, acknowledging that it is 'the true form of Drama' and 'its highest function.'[14] The term 'form', recurrent in the aforementioned definitions of Tragedy and Faërie, has, as Wicher remarks, 'strong Platonic and Aristotelian associations, so that 'it makes [one] look for some kind of essence that is not identical with the things in which the presence of that essence can be detected.'[15] Unlike Aristotle, however, Tolkien does not use it in this classical sense, but, as Wicher suggests, Tolkien 'probably means that, while not all dramas are tragedies, (…) tragedy comes nearest to the deepest nature of drama in which the idea of drama finds its most perfect realisation.'[16]

Despite this distinction of Tragedy, Tolkien places its notion, understood as both: a dramatic genre, and an unhappy event that happens to the protagonist(s) and provides a sad denouement to the plot, at the opposite pole to Faërie, contrasting the tragic effect of Tragedy (or the tragic 'catastrophe'), with its antonym that marks

---

11 Jonathan Lear, 'Katharsis' [in:] *Essays on Aristotle's Poetics*, Amélie Oksenberg Rorty, ed. (Princeton: Princeton University Press, 1992), pp. 315–341, 320.

12 Tolkien, 'On Fairy-Stories', p. 139.

13 Tolkien, ibid., p. 140.

14 Tolkien, ibid., p. 153.

15 Andrzej Wicher, 'Therapeutic Categories. Some Remarks on the Relationship between Tolkien's "Eucatastrophe" and Aristotle's "Catharsis" [in:] *Selected Medieval and Religious Themes in the Works of C. S. Lewis and J. R. R. Tolkien* (Łódź: Łódzkie Towarzystwo Naukowe, 2013), p. 296.

16 Wicher, ibid., p. 296.

the end of a 'true fairy-tale', that is with the happy resolution or 'eucatastrophe', (the term crucial to therapeutic power of high fantasy genre, considered in detail further on in this chapter).[17] Faërie and Tragedy are generically and generally poles apart, Tolkien claims, because 'Drama is naturally hostile to Fantasy', that is to the sub-creative power of image-making and to the act of creating secondary (that is imaginary) worlds.[18]

Explaining that inherent hostility Tolkien argues that, because of the fact that Tragedy involves stage performance, even if it its plot contains fantastic elements (such as the witches in Shakespeare's *Macbeth*), Fantasy in drama is nipped in the bud once the play is visibly and audibly acted; so that it may only achieve 'buffoonery and mimicry', but not Fantasy, because dramatisation kills the enchantment and cripples the inexhaustible (sub)creativity of imagination.[19] As Tolkien views it, 'Drama has, of its very nature, already attempted a kind of bogus, or (...) at least substitute, magic' by coercing *the visible and audible presentation of imaginary men in a story*', which amounts to 'counterfeit[ing] the magicians' wand'.[20] If Fantasy were to dwell in tragedy, then tragedy would need to be written as a story, Tolkien believes, or perhaps a closet drama, one might add.[21] This is so, Tolkien explains, inasmuch as, 'even though it uses a similar material (words, verse, plot), [Drama is] an art fundamentally different from narrative art', and 'the characters, and even the scenes are in Drama not imagined but actually beheld'.[22] Besides, 'Drama is anthropocentric', Tolkien adds, whereas 'fairy-story and Fantasy need not be'.[23] The power of drama, unlike that of Faërie, resides mostly in its being performed and dramatised in various ways, depending on the interpretation and choice of the actors and other artists, just perhaps like the power of music, with which it was originally symbiotically merged, and which,

---

17 Tolkien, 'On Fairy-Stories', p. 153.
18 Tolkien, ibid., p. 140.
19 Tolkien, ibid., p. 140. I use here the term 'sub-creativity', of my coinage, as man's creative ability, analogically to its effect that is sub-creation. The prefix 'sub' reflects Tolkien's conviction that full creativity and creation are reserved exclusively for 'a Maker', that is God (cf. ibid., p. 144). 'We make in our measure and in our derivative mode', Tolkien claims, 'because we are made: and not only made, but made in the image and likeness of a Maker.' (ibid., p. 145).
20 Tolkien, ibid., p. 141. Italics are Tolkien's.
21 Tolkien, ibid., p. 141. It should be noted that other Inklings were fonder of drama than Tolkien. Williams, for sentence, wrote several plays, and Hugo Dyson was an expert on Shakespeare.
22 Tolkien, ibid., p. 142.
23 Tolkien, ibid., note F, p. 160.

although existing today in scores on paper, necessitates some kind of 'dramatisation' that gives life and artistic quality to it, as music requires performance, even if one is able to read music and hear it in their mind.

Of course, considering the paramount importance of theatrical performances to the culture and society of ancient Greece, and to the development of literature itself, it is impossible to imagine Greek drama not being performed. Indeed, along drama, there existed an incredible wealth of Greek myths, which had shaped the language, thought, and drama alike. It was myth that furnished material for Greek tragedy, and for the world's fairy-stories as well; therefore, an element of affinity that emerges from essential differences between the two genres is their common parentage and kinship to myth. Tolkien, in fact, calls Greek mythology, (or 'the Greek tale', as he refers to it) 'high fairy-story', and one of the timeless master patterns or perhaps an elder sisterly genre to both ancient and modern fantasy tales.[24]

Another link between Tragedy and Faërie seems to be, as I would like to suggest, their shared quality of intrinsic beauty, which Aristotle and Tolkien stress with reference to tragedy and Faërie respectively. Aristotle's remarks concerning the beauty of tragedy as a literary 'species' have been mentioned above.[25] But the beauty of tragedy lies not only in its magnificence, magnanimity, concentration and coherence; it also results from its cathartic effect. As Joe Sachs suggests, 'the closest thing (…) to the feeling at the end of a [Greek] tragedy is the one that comes with the sudden, unexpected appearance of something beautiful' – a statement that appears to correspond to Tolkien's notion of eucatastrophe, considered in detail below, and defined by Tolkien as 'a sudden "turn"', which, 'when it comes, gives us 'a piercing glimpse of joy, and heart's desire, and that for a moment passes outside the frame, rends indeed the very web of story, and lets a gleam come through.'[26] Beauty lives in the very heart of Faërie, Tolkien argues, and is one of the effects it produces on man, because 'the realm of fairy-story is wide and deep and high and filled with many things', among which there is 'beauty that is an enchantment, and an ever-present peril; both joy and sorrow as

---

24 Tolkien, 'On Fairy-Stories', note H, p. 161. The relationship between Greek tragedy and myth is discussed, for instance, by James Vincent Cunningham in his book *Woe or Wonder. The Emotional Effect of Shakespearian Tragedy* (Denver: Swallow, 1951), Chapter 2, pp. 60–98.

25 Cf. footnote 8 in this chapter.

26 Sachs, 'Aristotle - *Poetics*'. Tolkien, 'On Fairy-Stories', p. 154. Eucatastrophe is discussed in detail further on in this chapter.

sharp as swords.'[27] The 'sharpness' and 'piercing' quality of eucatastrophe seems to resemble the effect of Tragedy, that of pity and fear, which is almost unbearable. 'Great tragedies are readable and watchable because they make our hearts ache and our consciences tremble', says Brandon Emrys; 'they are just short of more than we can bear.'[28] The same could be said about great fairy stories, that is largely high fantasy: their 'fantastic or terrible adventures' lead to a climax resolved by eucatastrophe, which creates such a 'powerful and poignant effect' that is almost unbearable, 'as sharp as swords', and 'poignant as grief'.[29]

What appears concomitant with both Tragedy and Faërie is thus a cathartic effect, vaguely defined by Aristotle and differently translated into English: as 'a purification' achieved through pity and fear, by means of 'cleansing' of 'such like passions' or as a purgation': 'Tragedy through pity and fear effects a purgation of such emotions', Aristotle says (Δι'ελέου και φόβου περαίνουσα τήν των τοιούτων παθημάτων κάθαρσιν).[30] Tolkien seems to refer to the cathartic effect of fairy-stories proposing his concept of eucatastrophe, which, just like in Tragedy, where catharsis somehow sooths the tragic catastrophe, produces an effect of Consolation.[31] Consolation has two aspects in Faërie, Tolkien remarks: the first being its affinity with the Escape from Deathlessness, that is helping one come to terms with death as a natural end of human life, which in Tolkien's (Christian) thought implies a transition to another, ultimate life; the other aspect being 'the Consolation of the Happy Ending', which appears as a twin notion to Eucatastrophe.[32] Tolkien observes that he 'would [almost] venture to assert that all complete stories must have [a eucatastrophe]', because 'the eucatastrophic tale is the true form of fairy-tale, and its highest function;' just like a true tragedy, the highest form of Drama, must have a *dyscatastrophe*, that is a catastrophe (final resolution) of sorrow and failure.[33] In fact, eucatastrophe does not deny dyscatastrophe but rather entails it, and instead of making it a final resolution, it surpasses it and crosses over it towards 'the joy of deliverance'.[34]

27 Tolkien, 'On Fairy-Stories', p. 109.
28 Brandon Emrys, 'Paradox of Tragedy', http://branemrys.blogspot.com/2011/06/para-dox-of-tragedy.html, accessed 20 May 2015.
29 Tolkien, 'On Fairy-Stories', p. 109.
30 Aristotle *Poetics*, Chapter VI.
31 Aristotle, ibid., Chapter VI, quoted above in this chapter.
32 Tolkien, 'On Fairy-Stories', p. 153.
33 Tolkien, ibid., p. 153.
34 Tolkien, ibid., p. 153.

Tolkien elaborates on the notion of Eucatastrophe defining it (on the basis of its Greek etymology) as 'a sudden "turn"', which, 'when it comes, gives us 'a piercing glimpse of joy, and heart's desire, and that for a moment passes outside the frame, rends indeed the very web of story, and lets a gleam come through.'[35] This joy is, as Tolkien adds, 'a sudden glimpse of the underlying reality of truth' residing in Faërie, despite its not partaking in the consensus reality in a typical way.[36] It is a gleam of ultimate sense, of grasping a splinter of cosmic logos, which must produce joy; the joy of catching a glimpse of truth. 'It is a mark of a good fairy-story, of the higher and more complete kind, [classified in this book as high fantasy] that however wild its events, however fantastic or terrible the adventure, it can give to child or man that hears it, when the 'turn' [or Eucatastrophe] comes, a catch of the breath, a beat and lifting of the heart, near to (or indeed accompanied by) tears, as keen as that given by any form of literary art, and having a peculiar quality.'[37] It is a bitter-sweet resolution, because much as eucatastrophe 'denies (…) universal final defeat and in so far is *evangelium*, giving a fleeting glimpse of Joy, Joy beyond the walls of the world, [it is at the same time] poignant as grief,' Tolkien explains.[38]

Moreover, 'Eucatastrophe is not only a "consolation" for the sorrow of this world', Tolkien adds, 'but a satisfaction, and an answer to that question, 'Is it true?'[39] And the answer is, he argues, 'if you have built your little world well, yes: it is true in that world, and that is enough for the artist.'[40] Hence, Eucatastrophe appears as one of the prerequisites of Faërie's 'inherent consistency of reality', paradoxical and wondrous though it is.[41] Similarly, dyscatastrophe (or the tragic resolution) is one of the landmarks of Tragedy, and a yardstick of its very 'tragicness'. However, when one approaches eucatastrophe there is a greater thing behind – the Christian story, which, according to Tolkien, constitutes the master fairy-story of mankind; a fairy-story by standards of its 'many marvels – peculiarly artistic (the Art is here in the story itself rather in the telling; for the Author of the story was not the evangelists), beautiful, and moving: "mythical"

---

35 Tolkien, ibid., p. 154.
36 Tolkien, ibid., 'Epilogue', p. 155.
37 Tolkien, ibid., p. 154.
38 Tolkien, ibid., p. 153.
39 Ibid., p. 155.
40 Ibid., p. 155.
41 This phrase is used by Tolkien several times in 'On Fairy-Stories', for instance on p. 156.

in their perfect, self-contained significance.'[42] 'And among the marvels [of the Christian story] is the greatest and most complete conceivable Eucatastrophe, which entered History and the primary world', Tolkien claims, so that 'the desire and aspiration of sub-creation has been raised to the fulfillment of Creation: the Birth of Christ is the eucatastrophe of Man's history; the Resurrection is the eucatastrophe of the story of the Incarnation.'[43] In the light of this interpretation of the Christian story of redemption, the Gospels (in Greek *Evangelium* or the Good News) is the primary fairy-story: full of marvels and wonder, yet true, for it 'has entered History and primary world', and sanctified man's derivative mode of fantastic storytelling.[44] It has the quality of the marvellous but maintains its 'inner consistency of reality' and is good news precisely due to its rather unexpected eucatastrophic resolution. 'To reject [the truth of this Greatest Eucatastrophe] leads either to sadness or to wrath', Tolkien asserts, which is tantamount to leaving one either with the bitter sorrow of tragedy or with rage and displeasure, without discharging those harmful emotions, as happens in Tragedy, or transforming them into joy, as occurs in Faërie.[45]

It appears that some similarities between Aristotle's catharsis and Tolkien's eucatastrophe are hard to ignore, yet, there are obvious differences. Since this study focuses on the therapeutic potential of literature, only this aspect of the genres is considered here. As Wicher notes, even though 'both make, or attempt to make tragedy [that is its tragic catastrophe] functional, or therapeutic', Aristotelian catharsis 'proposes a therapy based on the notion of getting rid of a harmful surplus', while Tolkien's eucatastrophe 'strives to forge, as it were, the substance of tragedy into a source of joy', reflecting the Christian thought of Christ's resurrection, which was the 'Great Eucatastrophe' changing the tragedy of Christ's Passion into a joy, almost unbearable and certainly paradoxical and wondrous.[46]

These reflections on the nature of Tragedy's catharsis and Faërie's eucatastrophic Consolation reveal that in their apparent affinity lies a complex paradox. Wicher comments on this seeming inconsistency pointing out that the cathartic power of Tragedy is what attempts to 'overcome the negativity' of its tragic catastrophe (or dyscatastrophe, as Tolkien names it), which contributes to the paradoxical nature of catharsis: being a crucial property of the tragedy in Tragedy, catharsis, at the same time, 'makes tragedy somewhat less tragic, by

42 Ibid., p. 156.
43 Ibid., p. 156.
44 Ibid., p. 156.
45 Ibid., p. 156.
46 Wicher, 'Therapeutic Categories', p. 299. Tolkien, 'On Fairy-Stories', p. 156.

submitting it to the therapeutic project, the aim of which is some kind of "happy ending" [Tolkien's Eucatastrophe], that is an outcome which in itself is a denial of the spirit of tragedy.[47] Thus, as I understand it, although catharsis affirms the tragic ending of Tragedy, and, indeed, empowers it, (as without fear and pity Tragedy would not be tragic, and sorrow would not arise – Wicher argues that 'catharsis is the true form of Tragedy'), at the same time it denies and somehow 'arrests' the tragic nature of Tragedy.[48] Following this train of thought, one arrives at yet another paradox: the tragic catharsis seems akin to the 'happy catharsis' of Eucatastrophe, as both in their own ways 'overcome the negativity' of the tragic denouement.[49] This is perhaps also an aspect of the cathartic effect that Joe Sachs compares to 'being washed in wonderment.'[50] Indeed, the nature of catharsis accomplished in Tragedy and in Faërie in two different ways appears marvellous, and with regard to Tragedy by overcoming its 'tragicness' it produces what Sachs calls a 'peculiar tragic pleasure':

> [In tragedy] you have witnessed horrible things and felt painful feelings, but the mark of tragedy is that it brings you out the other side. Aristotle's use of the word catharsis is not a technical reference to purgation or purification but a beautiful metaphor for the peculiar tragic pleasure, the feeling of being washed or cleansed.[51]

'The tragic pleasure is a paradox', Sachs adds, which seems to bring natural associations with Tolkien's concept of Eucatastrophe.[52] In the context of Greek tragedy, the term 'catastrophe' means' a dénouement of a drama, especially of a classical tragedy'; while in modern usage the term 'catastrophe' can be equated with a disaster (the Greek *katastrophē* means 'overturning, a sudden turn'; from *kata* – 'down' and *strophē* '- 'turning', and *strephein* - 'to turn').[53] The element of that turning motion is present in Tolkien's description of eucatastrophe, represented as a 'sudden joyous "turn"', which 'does not deny the existence of dyscatastrophe, of sorrow and failure.'[54] Therefore, Tolkien's neologism is derived from Greek.

47 Wicher, ibid., p. 297.
48 Wicher, ibid., p. 297.
49 This phrase of 'overcoming the negativity of tragedy' is used by Andrzej Wicher, as quoted above.
50 Sachs, 'Aristotle – *Poetics*'.
51 Sachs, ibid.
52 Sachs, ibid.
53 Oxford Dictionary of English, http://www.oxforddictionaries.com/, accessed 23 April 2016.
54 Tolkien, 'On Fairy-Stories', p. 153.

When adhering to the first meaning of the term, that is of a resolution of the events in drama, Tolkien's Eucatastrophe implies a 'happy resolution' of a tragic plot, that is a 'happy end' to fairy-stories, which Tolkien names so with regard to Consolation, one of the key (therapeutic) qualities of Faërie. However, even though he draws on the Greek language (using such terms as *catastrophe, dyscatastrophe, eucatastrophe, evangelium*), he makes no explicit references to the Greek thought. Thus, were it possible to view the term 'catastrophe' also in the light of its modern connotation, that of a calamity, one would arrive at another paradox when approaching 'Eucatastrophe', and this paradox would result from the combination of the words 'good' and 'catastrophe' (disaster, calamity). A 'good disaster' seems to be a contradiction in terms, just like, for instance, Aristotle's 'tragic pleasure' or Charles Williams's 'terrifying good'.[55] What could provide a common denominator for them, though, is, next to paradox, perhaps the concept of 'wonder', as discussed below, although, again, it is hard to compare Aristotle's understanding thereof with Tolkien's.

Before considering the notion of wonder and its function in Tragedy and Faërie, however, another element linking the terms catastrophe, Eucatastrophe and catharsis, which emerges from their etymology, must be named. In his book *Catharsis: On the Art of Medicine*, mentioned in Chapter Five, Andrzej Szczeklik points to the 'ka' element, contained in the word 'catharsis', but also in the terms 'catastrophe' and 'Eucatastrophe', which I find interesting.[56] In ancient Egypt 'ka' was a term difficult to define and grasp, and practically indefinable, but it is known that it referred to some life-sustaining force, vital essence, creative power, and one of the five constituents of the human soul.[57] Before Egyptian civilisation developed, in Hindu religion 'Ka' had been a name of the father of gods, and a life-giving element pervading universe. That Hindu name of the father of gods

---

55 The problem whether 'terrifying good' is possible is considered by Pauline Anstruther, the protagonist of Williams's fantasy novel *Descent into Hell*. Williams provides an answer through another character of the novel, Peter Stanhope: 'Are our tremors to measure the Omnipotence?' (Grand Rapids, MI: William B. Eerdmans Publishing Company, 1980, p. 17). In a sense Williams's concept of the 'terrifying good' might be reminiscent of Yeats's 'terrible beauty', which is 'born' in the aftermath of the Easter Uprising of 1916, the basis for both paradoxes being perhaps catharsis.

56 Andrzej Szczeklik, *Catharsis: On the Art of Medicine*, trans. Antonia Lloyd-Jones, foreword by Czesław Miłosz (Chicago: The University of Chicago Press, 2005), p. 81. The original Polish title reads: *Katharsis. O uzdrowicielskiej mocy natury i sztuki* (Kraków, Wydawnictwo Znak, 2003).

57 *Encyclopaedia Britannica*, http://www.britannica.com/EBchecked/topic/309120/ka, accessed 20 July 2016.

means 'who?', and the first reaction to this question, as Szczeklik suggests, was that of 'an utmost wonder'.[58]

In his study of Hindu mythology, William Joseph Wilkins explains that the Hindu 'exalted the interrogative pronoun itself into a deity, and acknowledged a god, Ka? or "'Who?"'.[59] In some of their sacred scriptures, such as Taittiriya Brāhmana, Kanshītaki Brāhmana, Tāndya Brāhmana, and Satapatha Brāhmana, 'wherever interrogative verses occur, the author states that Ka is Prajāpati, or the lord of creatures'.[60] Also in the later Sanskrit literature of the Purānas, 'Ka appears as a recognized god, with a genealogy of his own'.[61]

What emerges from that pre-Greek history of the word is thus an element of essential vitality, life-sustaining force, deity and wonder, touching upon the essence of life and some cosmic logos. It is a matter of discussion, though, whether that element has been preserved in the Greek language or not, and whether it can be said to have shaped such terms as 'catharsis' and 'catastrophe'. According to Szczeklik the pre-Greek meaning of 'ka' cannot be ignored if one attempts to grasp the meaning of catharsis, and I wish to argue the same, extending it also to the terms 'catastrophe' and 'eucatastrophe'.

Focusing on the Greek etymology, Andrzej Wicher, in turn, pays attention to the 'kata' element included in the words: catastrophe and Eucatastrophe, which is their common component, together with the afore-mentioned word 'strophe' (στροφή meaning 'turning, circling'). The Greek κατά ('kata') denotes a downward movement, a 'motion from above', and as a prefix has an opposite meaning to 'ana' (Greek 'ανα'), which implies 'motion upwards'.[62] However, as Wicher points out, 'the two words do not always form logical [antonymous] pairs', for instance the word αναστροφη [anastrophe] is not exactly the opposite to καταστροφη [catastrophe], the former being translated as 'an overturning', whereas the latter as 'a turning upside down', which 'might suggest that the words which we expected to be antonyms are in fact synonyms'.[63] 'The circular motion of "στροφή" [strophe] [Wicher concludes] makes every "καταστροφη" [catastrophe], at least potentially, an "αναστροφη" [anastrophe], and the other way

58 Szczeklik, *Catharsis: On the Art of Medicine*, p. 81.
59 William Joseph Wilkins, *Hindu Mythology. Vedic and Puranic* (Whitefish, MT: Kessinger Publishing, 2010), p. 481.
60 Wilkins, ibid., p. 481.
61 Wilkins, 'Therapeutic Categories', p. 481.
62 Wicher, ibid., p. 295; cf. Henry George Liddell, and Robert Scott, *An Intermediate Greek–English Lexicon* (Oxford: Clarendon Press, 1889).
63 Wicher, ibid., p. 295.

round.'[64] This quality of being apparently antonymous, but in fact sharing in the opposite quality, is what marks eucatastrophe, as presented by Tolkien, Wicher suggests: Eucatastrophe is apparently opposite to a tragic ending, but, at the same time, it likewise overcomes the negativity of tragedy and denies its 'tragicness', to use the word mentioned above in this chapter.[65]

In his reflections concerning Tolkien's eucatastrophe, Wicher proposes an interesting term to embrace the peculiar 'eucatastrophic catharsis' of Faërie as 'a true form of eucatastrophe', namely 'anarsis'.[66] 'Etymologically speaking, anarsis is a reversal of catharsis,' inasmuch as 'flowing down' (catharsis) is opposite to 'flowing up'.[67] The anartic 'flowing up' is the opposite to the cathartic 'washing [down] in wonderment', as Sachs calls it. The implication of water flowing up is a little illogical, Wicher remarks, therefore little wonder that the word does not probably exist in Greek; yet its paradoxical nature is precisely what is needed to match Tolkien's Eucatastrophe: 'a sudden and miraculous grace; never to be counted on to recur'.[68] Although paradoxical and miraculous, eucatastrophe is purposeful and meaningful – a grace that 'denies (in the face of much evidence, if you will) universal final defeat'.[69] Eucatastrophe denies despair and nothingness, as it does not let down; it takes one up, so that one may follow the upwards direction and take heart, following the *sursum corda* (lift up the hearts) dictum, to which Tolkien indirectly refers, when he says that eucatastrophe offers the reader 'a beat and lifting of the heart'.[70]

In psychotherapy, and especially Freudian psychoanalysis, a term that is used as a reversal of catharsis (discharge of harmful passions) is cathexis, a charge of psychic energy, although the word's etymology has less to do with catharsis than anarsis (in Greek káthexis means 'a keeping', equivalent to kathek- variant stem of katéchein, which means to keep, hold on to, and equivalent to cat; cat- + échein means to have, hold; + -sis, as translation of German *Besetzung*: 'a taking possession of', which is Freud's term).[71] In short, catharsis entails a release of

---

64 Wicher, ibid., p. 295.
65 Wicher, ibid., p. 296.
66 Wicher, ibid., p. 301.
67 Wicher, ibid., p. 301.
68 Wicher, ibid., p. 301. Tolkien, 'On Fairy-Stories', p. 153.
69 Tolkien, ibid., p. 153.
70 *Sursum corda* is the opening dialogue to the Preface of the Eucharistic Prayer or Anaphora in the liturgies of the Christian Church, dating back to probably the third century. In Greek it reads "Ἄνω σχῶμεν τὰς καρδίας'). Tolkien, 'On Fairy-Stories', p. 154.
71 Cf. http://dictionary.reference.com/browse/cathectic, accessed 23 April 2016.

emotions and breaking of bonds, whereas cathexis means creating connections and concentrating psychic energy on a given person or object.

Another point of apparent affinity between Tragedy and Faërie, revolving around the concept of therapeutic catharsis, is, as signaled above, the effect of wonder. In the realm of Faërie, 'a man may, perhaps, count himself fortunate to have wandered, but its very richness and strangeness tie the tongue of a traveller who would report them', Tolkien observes.[72] Marvels, richness and 'arresting strangeness' of Faërie are its intrinsic characteristics, which result from the genre's dependence on perfect logic and congruence on the one hand, (because 'Fantasy does not blur the sharp outlines of the real world; for it depends on them); and on wonder on the other; and these are the seemingly antagonistic features that, in fact, are interrelated, as Tolkien repeatedly observes, declaring that the wonder of secondary worlds has an 'inner consistency of reality'.[73] The same qualities are, interestingly, indicated by Aristotle in his definition of Tragedy, as shown below. Hence, apart from their partaking in art and beauty, (an attribute which may refer to many other genres as well), and their connection to the concept of catharsis, (a rather unique mutual share), in spite of radical generic differences, both Tragedy and Faërie draw on a sense of 'wonder'. Aristotle admits that 'wonder and awe' (θαυμαστον or *thaumaston*) is indispensable if art is to be achieved in epics, however, in a perhaps lesser degree, wonder must also be accomplished in Tragedy, difficult though it is because of its performative nature. In fact, Aristotle appears to refer to that very 'deficiency' of Tragedy, as I would call it, that is its inevitable reduction of the sense of wonder, when he observes that:

> Wonder needs to be produced in tragedies, but in the epic there is more room for that which confounds reason, by means of which wonder comes about most of all, since in the epic one does not see the person who performs the action; the events surrounding the pursuit of Hector would seem ridiculous if they were on stage …But wonder is sweet …And Homer most of all has taught the rest of us how one ought to speak of what is untrue [that is, belongs to myth or the secondary world, as Tolkien would say]. One ought to choose likely impossibilities in preference to unconvincing possibilities …And if a poet has represented impossible things, then he has missed the mark, but that is the right thing to do if he thereby hits the mark that is the end of the poetic art itself, that is, if in that way he makes that or some other part more wondrous.[74]

---

72 Tolkien, 'On Fairy-Stories', p. 109.
73 Cf. Tolkien, ibid., pp. 144, 156, and note G, p. 160.
74 Aristotle, *Poetics*, Chapters XXIV–XXV, trans. Joe Sachs, pp. 57–59. In his translation of these fragments, Theodore Buckley translates wonder as 'the wonderful', (pp. 55–57), and Ingram Bywater as 'the marvellous' (pp. 60–61).

Another translation of this passage reads that 'the marvellous is certainly required in tragedy', and that 'the marvellous is a cause of pleasure. As is shown by the fact that we all tell a story with additions, in the belief we are doing our hearers a pleasure.'[75]

Indeed, in Chapter IX of his *Poetics* Aristotle argues that 'pity and fear arise most of all where wonder does', suggesting that they are most effective when they involve wonder; and in Chapters XXIV and XXV he observes that 'wonder is the aim of the poetic art itself, into which the aim of Tragedy in particular merges.'[76] Sachs identifies Aristotle's notion of catharsis as 'the feeling of being washed in wonderment', arguing that 'our feelings of pity and fear make us recognize what we care for and cherish', so that, paradoxically, what is lost at the end of tragedy is also, by the very same means, found, which is possible precisely to that 'marvellous' or 'wonderful' quality of Tragedy.[77] 'It is not so strange that we learn the worth of something by losing it; what is astonishing [and wonderful, however,] is what the tragedians are able to achieve by making use of that common experience: they lift it up into a state of wonder', Sachs observes.[78] Interestingly, Sachs refers here to the 'motion up' mechanism, which, as has been suggested before, could be connected to anarsis and its (Faërian) effect of wonderful hope (always encouraging to 'lift up the hearts').

A most comprehensive study of wonder in Greek and Renaissance tragedy has been provided by the American poet and literary critic James Vincent Cunningham in his book *Woe and Wonder. The Emotional Effect of Shakespearian Tragedy* (1945, 1951), in which he identifies wonder as the principal effect of both Greek and Shakespearean Tragedy, raising it to an equal status with woe (sorrow), fear, and pity, the qualities usually cited after Aristotle as the foremost characteristics of Tragedy.[79] Fear and sorrow are the 'appropriate emotions' of tragedy, Cunningham says: it is the fear of the catastrophe, and sorrow at its accomplishment'; in brief: the tragic atmosphere and anticipation of the tragic catastrophe

---

75 Aristotle, *Poetics*, chapters XXIV-XXV, trans. Ingram Bywater, ed. [in:] *Aristotle on the Art of Poetry* (Oxford: Oxford University Press, 1909, 1920), p. 42.
76 Cf. Joe Sachs, 'Aristotle – Poetics'.
77 Sachs, ibid.
78 Sachs, ibid.
79 James Vincent Cunningham, *Woe and Wonder. The Emotional Effect of Shakespearian Tragedy* (Denver: University of Denver Press, 1951), p. 42. Cunningham cites here Horatio's words from *Hamlet*, Act 5 Scene 2, where Horatio says to Fortinbras: 'What is it ye would see? If aught of woe or wonder, cease your search.'

is fearful; the catastrophe woeful.'[80] 'They are appropriate because they are the natural emotions with which men regard death in prospect and in fulfilment', he adds, and because 'they are emotions of a public and impersonal order.'[81]

Curiously, the qualities of woe and wonder proposed as twin landmarks of Tragedy, both of antiquity and of Renaissance, seem to be relevant to the essence of Faërie as well, for, according to Tolkien, in genuine fairy-stories the piercing sorrow accompanying an imminent (dys)catastrophe (tragic resolution of the plot) is unexpectedly replaced by a happy resolution, that is eucatastrophe[82]. Faërie's wonder seems to operate in manifold ways: it is the genre's Enchantment resulting from its otherworldliness and its strangeness; it is its proximity to Tragedy and to its tragic catastrophe, which fills one with fear and wonder as to the development of the plot and the protagonist's end, when complications in the plot seem to inevitably lead to a disaster; and finally, it is the wonder or the marvellous quality of an unexpected happy ending, which fills one with poignant joy. When discussing wonder in tragedy, Cunningham argues that:

> Wonder is (…) the effect of the surprising and the marvellous; it is an extremity of feeling, and hence maybe either joy or sorrow, fear or rapture.(…) Wonder is associated not only with extreme fear, but also with extreme joy, and is marked by silence and immobility. It is the shocked limit of feeling.'[83]

His words seem relevant to Faërie as well. The sorrow and joy, fear and rapture that result from wonder is what Tolkien emphasises when referring to eucatastrophe (that is a 'happy ending' to a story that has narrowly missed a tragedy, which marks a genuine fairy-story): 'it gives a fleeting glimpse of Joy, Joy beyond the walls of the world', because it is a spark of the divine joy of eternity, the joy of a meaningful suffering, the joy which is as 'poignant as grief.'[84]

Moreover, Cunningham links wonder with myths and 'marvellous stories', in other words referring to fantasy tales as to a genre parallel to Tragedy in its reliance upon wonder:

> Wonder is, first of all, the natural effect of a marvellous story, and hence of those myths which furnished the plots of ancient tragedy and epic, as well as those extraordinary

---

80 Cunningham, *Woe and Wonder*, pp. 42 and 56.
81 Cunningham, ibid., p. 42.
82 Tolkien, 'On Fairy-Stories', p. 155.
83 Cunningham, *Woe and Wonder*, pp. 89–90.
84 Tolkien, 'On Fairy-Stories', p. 153.

events which in later Hellenistic times, as earlier in Herodotus, are narrated in certain types of history and in the marvellous tale.[85]

Also Tolkien defines Fantasy, a sub-creative image-making art and a characteristic crucial to the realm of Faërie, in terms of wonder: it is 'a quality essential to fairy-story', which 'embrace[s] both the Sub-creative Art in itself and a quality of strangeness and wonder in the Expression, derived from the Image'.[86] The sub-creative creation of a secondary world that constitutes Faërie rests on strangeness and 'wonder in the Expression', which is 'derived from the Image' of some particular otherworldliness that comes from the Primary World, as based on the images master-created by 'a Maker' at the dawn of time.[87]

There is another strand of the meaning of wonder that needs to be unravelled, namely its affiliation with the words admiration and astonishment. *Admiratio* in Latin means 'wonder', and this quality appears as a landmark of tragedy in Sir Philip Sidney's *The Defense of Poesy* (1583), where he views 'poesy' (Aristotle's *poïesis)* as all imaginative literature, including lyric poetry, epic poetry, and drama, distinct from history and philosophy.[88] Sidney argues that 'high and excellent tragedy (…) openeth the greatest wounds, and showeth forth the ulcers that are covered with tissue; (…) maketh kings fear to be tyrants, and tyrants manifest their tyrannical humours;', and 'with stirring the effects of admiration and commiseration teacheth the uncertainty of this world, and upon how weak foundations gilded roofs are builded.'[89]

Wonder understood as admiration involves also astonishment (*ekplexis, thaumaston*), which is irresistible and which 'overpowers the hearer and puts him in a state of transport', as Cunningham notes.[90] In ancient thought the concept of wonder understood as admiration is connected with rhetoric and is said to result from elevated style and unusual diction, the issue discussed, for instance, in the famous treatise *On the Sublime*, ascribed to Pseudo-Longinus, where wonder is viewed as astonishment resulting from the loftiness of language and style. This stance continues well into modern times, and is commonplace in the Renaissance,

---

85 Cunningham, *Woe and Wonder*, p. 66.
86 Tolkien, 'On Fairy-Stories', p. 139.
87 Cf. Tolkien, ibid., p. 153.
88 Charlton T. Lewis, and Charles Short, *A Latin Dictionary* (Oxford: Clarendon Press, 1879), p. 58.
89 Sir Philip Sidney, 'The Defense of Poesy' [in:] *The Miscellaneous Works of Sir Philip Sidney, Knt, with a Life of the Author and Illustrative Notes by William Gray, Esq.* (Oxford: D. A. Talboys, 1829), p. 33.
90 Cunningham, *Woe and Wonder*, p. 73.

when 'wonder is the effect of theological discourse, being, of course, the highest subject-matter and hence affording by its very nature the highest eloquence,' like in Edmund Spenser's works (for instance *The Faerie Queene*), and later on, beyond the Renaissance, in Milton's (for instance *Paradise Lost*).[91]

While this aspect of wonder pertains to Tragedy, it does not refer to Faërie in the same sense, for its language and style are not meant to impress. Rather, they are hoped to be simple but transparent and pure in their meaning and wealth. I identify Faërie with high fantasy fiction not by virtue of its language, which is not 'high' in terms of rhetoric, sophistication and florid style, but 'high' due to its preoccupation with meaning, and its 'strong moral element', as Tolkien says, that is Fantasy's 'inherent morality' revealed through its subject matter and language.[92] Worth reminding is the fact that 'Faërie cannot be caught in the net of words; for it is one of its qualities to be indescribable, though not imperceptible. It has many ingredients, but analysis will not necessarily discover the secret of the whole,' as Tolkien asserts.[93] While in Faërie, one may reach the borders of language, where it mingles with other arts and co-produces the effect of wonder.

Besides, wonder in Faërie results from its intrinsically miraculous nature, which, in the works of the Inklings draws on Christian doctrine. As St. Augustine declares, 'A miracle [is] anything great and difficult or unusual that happens beyond the expectation or ability of the man who wonders at it.'[94] St. Thomas integrates the Augustinian definition of wonder with the Aristotelian, observing that 'what is wonderful to one man may not be wonderful to another, but a miracle is fully wonderful since it has a cause absolutely hidden from all, namely God.'[95] As mentioned above, to Tolkien eucatastrophe is a miraculous turn of the otherwise tragic plot, exemplified by the most miraculous of all happy endings to woe and wonder, that is first by Christ's Birth, and next, by His Resurrection.[96]

It seems that the sense and the state of wonder is what informs Faërie in multiple ways. Faërie 'works enchantment', Tolkien notes, and it is not only an enchantment of distance and of other time, and of marvellous otherworldliness, but also the enchantment of a 'mythical or total (unanalysable) effect, an effect quite independent of the findings of Comparative Folk-lore, and one which it cannot

91 Cunningham, ibid., p. 83.
92 Tolkien, 'On Fairy-Stories', p. 118.
93 Tolkien, ibid., p. 118.
94 St. Augustine, *De Utilitate Credendi* [*On the Profit of Believing*], 16. 34.
95 Cf. Cunningham, *Woe and Wonder*, p. 76. St. Thomas, *Summa Theologiae* [*Summa Theologica*], 1.105.7.
96 Tolkien, 'On Fairy-Stories', p. 156.

spoil or explain.[97] This is the enchantment of a successful sub-creation, and of belief, which does not have to be 'willingly suspended'.[98] This enchantment does not imply 'an uncritical wonder, nor indeed an uncritical tenderness', though.[99] Wonder, which Tolkien calls Enchantment, is a 'more skilled and effortless Art', a 'more potent and specially elvish craft', which produces a 'Secondary World into which both the designer and spectator can enter, to the satisfaction of their senses while they are inside; but in its purity it is artistic in desire and purpose.'[100] Interestingly, the terms Tolkien uses in this definition of Faërie's Enchantment, that is 'the designer', the 'spectator', and the 'Secondary World', might, in fact, be related to drama as well, for, in a sense, it also creates a kind of 'Secondary World' on stage, based on reality, yet designed in a different way.

When discussing the effect of wonder and the theme of 'the wonderful' as another element of kinship between Tragedy and Faërie, it is also worth noticing that Aristotle refers to fables observing that, although they provide more room for 'the wonderful' than tragedies, 'fables also should not be composed from irrational parts, [but as much as possible, indeed, they should have nothing irrational in them]', – a statement echoed in the thought of Tolkien, who, as quoted in the previous chapters, says that 'Fantasy does not destroy or even insult Reason. On the contrary. The keener and the clearer is the reason, the better fantasy will it make.'[101] The fables that Aristotle means are obviously beast fables, mostly associated with Aesop's authorship, and discussed in greater detail in Aristotle's *Rhetoric* (2:20) and other works (*Meteorology and On the Parts of Animals*), but, although Tolkien excludes them from the realm of Faërie, they come nearest to modern high fantasy genre in Aristotle's original classification.

Despite defining Drama as a genre 'naturally hostile to Fantasy', as stated above, Tolkien does speak of Drama which seems to maintain that element of 'wonder' or enchantment or 'arresting strangeness' at its highest, that is at the level reserved for Faërie only, and normally impossible to achieve in Drama[102]. This is what Tolkien names 'Faërian drama', which produces 'Fantasy with a realism and immediacy beyond the compass of any human mechanism', and which

97   Tolkien, ibid., pp. 129 and 139.
98   Tolkien, ibid., pp. 132–133.
99   Tolkien, ibid., p. 136.
100   Tolkien, ibid., p. 143.
101   Aristotle, *Poetics*, Chapter XXIV, trans. Theodore Buckley, p. 56. Tolkien, 'On Fairy-Stories', p. 144.
102   Tolkien, 'On Fairy-Stories', p. 140.

offers a bodily presence in its Secondary World.[103] Faërian drama resembles dreaming, but shall not be confounded with it, Tolkien warns; it is, however, like being in a dream, but the dream is being woven by 'some other mind'.[104] This mind performs 'elvish craft', which is beyond human capacity, and allows one to experience *directly* a Secondary World, producing a fantastic potion of Enchantment, which is only too strong for men when experienced unmediatedly rather than vicariously, Tolkien says.[105]

Vague though it appears, the concept of Faërian drama, as suggested by Tolkien, juxtaposes or perhaps rather links Faërie with Drama again; and this is what emerges from Aristotle's work as well, where he refers to myth and fables several times, while focusing on Tragedy. Those 'bilateral' comments, although perhaps accidental and incidental, might support my thesis of some kind of astonishing comparability of the two genres.

Returning to Aristotle's Tragedy and the concept of wonder, one can recapitulate after Cunningham that in Tragedy wonder is predominantly the 'effect of tragic incident and tragic style, as well as of the marvellous turn in events'; and, secondly, it is 'the result of a surprising and unexpected turn in events [*strophe*], and is thus intimately involved in the tragic catastrophe and its proper effect.'[106] It seems that the same could apply to the 'happy catastrophe' or eucatastrophe that marks Faërie, inasmuch as it is even more wondrous because if its radical and unexpected positivity. Indeed, as Cunningham notes, 'the purpose of myth (…) is pleasure and wonder'.[107] Besides, 'wonder is an effect of beauty', Cunningham adds, and beauty, as has been argued before, is one of distinguishing marks of both Tragedy and Faërie.[108] Beauty produces pleasure, and, as Cunningham claims, 'wonder and pleasure are the principal effects of art [*per se*], and consequently of tragedy and the tragic catastrophe; [as well as of Faërie and its happy catastrophe, one might add]; they are its end.'[109] Wonder and pleasure are correlative, Cunningham argues, 'for the one is the motive for inference, the other its natural accompaniment.'[110] The synergy of beauty, wonder and pleasure with the astonishment resulting from the

---

103   Tolkien, ibid., p. 142.
104   Tolkien, ibid., p. 142.
105   Tolkien, ibid., p. 142. Italics are Tolkien's.
106   Cunningham, *Woe and Wonder*, p. 66.
107   Cunningham, ibid., p. 67.
108   Cunningham, ibid., p. 67.
109   Cunningham, ibid., p. 63.
110   Cunningham, ibid., p. 63.

turn of the plot and from being 'washed in wonderment' appears therapeutic.[111] What is important, there seems to be a connection between the notions of wonder and catharsis. As Cunnigham remarks when considering the importance of wonder to the inner workings of tragedy, 'in the resolution of wonder there is a kind of catharsis, a further effect of the effect of the catastrophe.'[112] The tragic catastrophe is therefore a 'resolution of wonder', which contributes to the effect of catharsis, because 'to be struck is the effect of wonder', Cunningham notes; and to be changed and purified is what ensues, one might conclude.[113]

Exploring further different aspects of the concept of wonder, as related to catharsis and therapy, one shall add that, in a philosophical sense, wonder is also 'the primary cause of learning', which attracts man's curiosity and attention – an observation made by Plato, according to whom philosophy is grounded in wonder (*thaumazein*), and appropriated by various generations of modern philosophers.[114] Wonder is what makes one search for meaning and understanding, thus for some foundational thought, which seems to resound of seeking *logos*, or of man's search for meaning.

Another result of the fact that knowledge springs forth from wonder is that this adds to the pleasure that wonder offers *per se*. Wonder is pleasurable in itself, Aristotle observes, but it is even more pleasurable when combined with gaining knowledge, because wonder provides an occasion and motive for learning, and

---

111   This is Joe Sachs's phrase, used in his essay 'Aristotle – *Poetics*', as quoted above in this chapter.

112   Cunningham, *Woe and Wonder*, p. 95.

113   Cunningham, ibid., p. 38. Cunningham claims that three of Shakespeare's plays: *Hamlet*, *Anthony and Cleopatra*, and *Coriolanus*, as well as Shakespeare's narrative poem *The Rape of Lucrece* 'are intended explicitly to evoke the emotional effect of woe and wonder; ibid., p. 103.

114   Cunningham, ibid., p. 94. That observation of Plato comes from his works *Theaetetus*, which records a dialogue between Socrates and Theaetetus, in which Theaetetus says: 'Yes, indeed, by the gods, Socrates, I wonder exceedingly as to why (what) in the world these things are, and sometimes in looking at them I truly get dizzy'; to which Socrates replies:
(…) '[T]his experience is very much a philosopher's, that of wondering. For nothing else is the beginning (principle) of philosophy than this, and, seemingly, whoever's genealogy it was, that Iris was the offspring of Thaumas (wonder), it's not a bad one.' Cf. Plato, *Theaetetus*, trans. Seth Bernardette (Chicago: The University of Chicago Press, 1986), 155 c–d. Iris, the daughter of Thaumas, a sea god, and Electra, a cloud nymph, is the messenger of the gods and a personification of the rainbow. In Greek mythology she links the gods to humanity.

this makes an extra source of pleasure.[115] In the *Metaphysics* Aristotle reiterates Socrates's and Plato's observations concerning the birth of philosophy, noting that:

> (...) [I]t is owing to their wonder that men both now begin and at first began to philosophize.(...) And a man who is puzzled and wonders thinks himself ignorant (whence even the lover of myth is in a sense a lover of Wisdom, for the myth is composed of wonders)...[116]

As Cunningham comments on Aristotle's thought, 'wonder has an absolute value in itself', and 'in the strict mathematical sense [it] is a function of pity and fear: PF=W.'[117] However, the measure of the pity and fear that wonder provokes in the plot of a tragedy is 'the degree of surprise and the amount of the marvellous', Cunningham admits, indicating again the qualities otherwise remarkable of Faërie.

When it comes to Faërie, this last sense of wonder, referring to curiosity and a desire to understand, is perhaps what motivates the readers to explore Faërie despite its numerous perils and its 'arresting strangeness' (and 'many people dislike being 'arrested', Tolkien admits); and it is perhaps also what inspires them to desire a kind of recognition, which does not have to be tragic, whereby they may trace meaning, that is *logos*, which dwells in the genre's 'strong moral' character and its value-based uncorrupted language.[118]

It must also be noted that according to Aristotle, wonder produces knowledge by means of a mechanism of a tragic recognition, which he calls *anagnorisis* (a change from ignorance to knowledge), and which may be gained in tragedy in six different ways: through marks, tokens, artistic contrivances, memory, reasoning, and, best of all, events themselves.[119] *Anagnorisis* seems to apply to fantasy tales as well due to the common parentage of Tragedy and Faërie, rooted in myth. An example of the last type of *anagnorisis*, as introduced by Aristotle, could be perhaps Ged's tragic recognition of having lost all his wizardry power, which is the price he has to pay for mending the breach between the world of the living and the world of the dead that had been torn open by Cob, the evil wizard, as presented by Le Guin in *The Farthest Shore*. When Ged finally defeats Cob in the Dry Land, he has sacrificed all his extraordinary abilities, and as a result of

---

115   Aristotle, *Rhetoric*, 1.11 1371b 4–12.
116   Aristotle, *Metaphysics,* trans. W. D. Ross, 1.2. 082b11-19., http://classics.mit.edu/ Aristotle/metaphysics. 1.i.html, accessed 23 April 2016.
117   Cunningham, *Woe and Wonder*, p. 64.
118   Tolkien, 'On Fairy-Stories', p. 139.
119   Aristotle, *Poetics,* chapters XVI-XVIII. It is interesting that the term *anagnorisis* includes the *ana-* prefix, discussed above in juxtaposition with the *kata-* prefix.

spending his power, Ged ceases to be a wizard and the Archmage of Roke, and withdraws from public life, becoming an anonymous farmer and a goatherd on his native island of Gont.[120] His tragic recognition seems to correspond to a change from ignorance to knowledge because, although he has done with the great knowledge of wizardry, he has learnt a lesson of humility and greater wisdom, coming closer to an ultimate meaning of life.

A similar example is perhaps Tolkien's ending of Frodo's anti-quest in *The Lord of the Rings*. At the Crack of Doom, instead of destroying the Ring, Frodo unexpectedly declares to keep it and claims his ownership of this token of power. The destruction of the Ring in the fire of Mount Doom does occur, but, paradoxically, only thanks to Gollum, who, having fought with Frodo for the Ring, accidentally slips into the volcanic fissure clutching Frodo's severed finger with the Ring. Once the Ring has been destroyed, Frodo, rescued by Sam, becomes himself again, but he has learnt his lesson of humbleness and fallibility. Andrzej Wicher comments on this eucatastrophic resolution of Frodo's anti-quest, which had almost finished as a dyscatastrophe, in the following way: 'The arduous task of the Ring-bearer saps Frodo's life forces', so that 'after his triumph, which (…) was not quite his, he gradually withdraws into himself', which is perhaps the moment of his tragic recognition.[121] That radical change and gaining far greater understanding of himself and of his nature, makes Frodo change his life, 'withdraw into himself', but also withdraw from the world, so that 'eventually [he] decides to "pass over Sea" and return, together with other Ring-bearers, mainly Gandalf and Galadriel, to "West-over-Sea", or the "Undying Land", that is a version of either Christian Heaven, or the pagan Elysian Fields, which marks the end of non-human races, first of all of the Elves, and the advent of the Fourth Age, the age of "the Dominion of Men".[122]

One should also comment on another source of wonder, namely that connected with watching some shocking and ugly things, which involves 'being arrested before such a sight' and 'feels in some way perverse, [as it] has some conflict in the feeling it arouses, when we stare at the victims of a car wreck', Sachs observes.[123] Wonder resulting from contemplating the disgusting and appalling should not, however, be associated with the effect of wonder meant by Aristotle, Sachs claims, and by Tolkien, I would like to add. This is so by virtue of the fact that 'the sight of the ugly or disgusting, when it is felt as such, does not have the

---

120   Le Guin, *The Farthest Shore*, the third part of the Earthsea hexalogy.
121   Wicher, 'Therapeutic Categories', p. 300.
122   Wicher, ibid., p. 300.
123   Joe Sachs, 'Aristotle – *Poetics*'.

settled repose or willing surrender that are characteristic of wonder', Sachs remarks, arguing after Aristotle that, essentially, 'wonder is sweet'.[124]

What Tragedy and Faërie have in common by virtue of their connectedness to
the sorrow of an imminent catastrophe (realised in Tragedy as dyscatastrophe,
and narrowly avoided in Faërie thanks to eucatastrophe), is also their mutual
share in suffering, which, when inevitable, is transformed into a meaningful and
purposeful experience, and confirms an order of universe. Both genres seem to
acknowledge the Aeschylean dictum of 'learning through suffering' (*pathei mathos*, that is 'suffer and learn', or 'experience through suffering and learn'), according to which wisdom arises from personal suffering.[125] To Aeschylus, what
afflicts man can come from the gods, Nature or some supra-personal source, but
also from within man, and, regardless of its cause, may be a formative experience
by virtue of the hardship, grief and suffering involved, which enables one to enter
a path towards true knowledge, that is knowledge that makes sense of suffering
and of life, inextricably linked with suffering as it is.

In his book *Moira: Fate, Good, and Evil in Greek Thought* (1944, reprinted
1963), William Chase Greene comments on the role of the *pathei mathos* principle in the Greek Tragedy and culture, arguing that not only is it the essence of
Tragedy, but also, at least to Greek heroes and heroines, of the very challenge of
making sense of life:

> Taught by suffering: drop by drop wisdom is distilled from pain. This is the link between
> *aristeia* [a scene in an epic narrative when the hero in battle has his finest moments] and
> the tragic ethos. A Greek aristos would rather be educated by suffering than be happy his
> whole life long, because you don't get educated by happiness. No one is wised up by getting
> things the way he wants—that just consolidates the idiotism in him, makes his ego think
> the world exists for its sake, as the ego has always suspected. Suffering shows the schism
> between what we want and how the world is organized, the contraindication the world
> gives us that we've been strategizing from totally wrong precepts. Suffering is the collision
> between human delusions and real truth. Not every human being [however] has equal
> potential to learn from suffering. Some people just suffer, or just respond with alternative
> tactics.[126]

One could add that suffering, which is a tension and a 'collision between human
delusions and real truth' of life, may be transformed into wisdom only when its
negativity is overcome, that is in a process similar to catharsis, when harmful

---

124 Sachs, ibid.

125 Aeschylus uses this phrase in his tragedy *Agamemnon*.

126 William Chase Greene, *Moira: Fate, Good, and Evil in Greek Thought* (London:
     Harper Torchbooks, 1963), p. 7.

emotions of sorrow and pain are turned into joy - the joy (and wonder) that comes from gaining understanding and getting closer to the 'real truth', as Greene calls it. Tolkien seems to refer to that experience of turning suffering into a formative and positive experience as well by means of the concept of eucatastrophe, which can allow for a transition from tragic pathos to *aristeia* (some spectacular success of the struggling protagonist, such as Aslan's resurrection in Lewis's *Chronicles of Narnia*), and always produces joy, which 'is not only a "consolation" for the sorrow of this world, but a satisfaction, and an answer to that question, "Is it true?"'[127] Tolkien's understanding of what he calls Joy, which is the fruit of eucatastrophe, is that of a recognition of a larger pattern of things, of a previously-hidden or un-comprehended meaning, which 'lets a gleam [of true wisdom] come through.'[128]

Needless to say, the heroic *pathei mathos* is not the only possible response to suffering. It is in fact the most demanding and the rarest. As Greene observes, human reaction to afflictions, as represented in the ancient Greek thought,

> Rranges from brooding melancholy to stark pessimism and the cry that 'it were best never to have been born' (μὴ φῦναι [me psunai]); from kindly consolation of others, and counsels of moderation (sophrosyne) and the avoidance of risks ('the half is better than the whole'; 'excess in nothing,' μηδὲν ἄγαν [meden agan], 'live in obscurity,' λάθε βιώσας [lathe biosas], 'endure and renounce,' ἀνέχου καὶ ἀπέχου [anechou kai apechou]) to manly endurance of hardship (tlemosyne), or even to the discovery that wisdom may come through suffering (πάθει μάθος [pathei mathos]), which is a school of character.[129]

The '*pathei mathos*' principle is thus the most difficult but also the most auspicious response to personal hardship, inasmuch as it makes a necessary stage of one's search for meaning, conducive to the discovery of an unconditional *logos*.

The meaningful result of suffering, when it is accepted as a possible lesson of self-formation leading to one's greater dignity, wisdom and understanding of things, resembles the third, most demanding option of making sense of life and life situations identified by Victor Frankl in his logotherapeutic thought, whose central concept is suffering embraced in the triad of pain, death and guilt (discussed in Chapter Three of this book). What appears to correspond to the Aeschylean *pathei mathos*, and, as a matter of fact, to be directly derived from it, is Frankl's preoccupation with the 'logos of pathos', or the meaning of suffering, which he affirms both as a survivor of the Holocaust and as a psychiatrist and psychotherapist, naming it the most challenging and profoundest way of arriving

---

127   Tolkien, 'On Fairy-Stories', p. 155, as quoted above in this chapter.
128   Tolkien, ibid., p. 154.
129   Greene, *Moira: Fate, Good, and Evil in Greek Thought*, p. 8.

at a meaning of life. To Frankl, the most comprehensive way of learning is the Aeschylean learning through suffering.

Pathei mathos is also an important theme in the thought of Hans-Georg Gadamer (1900–2002), a prominent philosopher of hermeneutics who considered his work on Greek philosophy as the best part of his scholarship. Gadamer connects the '*pathei mathos*' theme with his concepts of finitude and infinitude. 'What a man has to learn through suffering is not this or that particular thing, but the knowledge of the limitations of humanity, of the absoluteness of the barrier that separates him from the divine. It is ultimately a religious insight - that kind of insight which gave birth to Greek tragedy,' he notes.[130] Suffering brings man 'face to face' with radical finitude, and, at the same time, makes him aware of the infinitude of the divine, or of *Logos*, as I would like to argue.[131] Drawing on the myth of the nature of love, as recorded by Plato in his *Symposium*, according to which human beings were first spherical and perfect, but because of their pride were punished by the gods, who cut them in half, Gadamer claims that, just like in the myth, man has ever since been just a fragment, 'a countermark, a *symbolon*, divided into two out of one.'[132] Hence, in every man, despite his finitude, there is an implication of the infinitude, or 'a concealed point to the infinite.'[133]

This reminds of Tolkien's belief that in very human being dwells a splinter of the light of a Maker, and a yearning for the perfect wholeness and perfection, and that the awareness of one's finitude is most acutely felt and understood in suffering. In his poem 'Mythopoeia', dedicated to C. S. Lewis '('Philomythus to Misomythus'), Tolkien, a Christian myth-maker, calls 'Man the refracted light/through whom [the Light of timeless *Logos*] is splintered from a single White/to many hues.' Man is a painfully limited creature, yet contains a particle of the divine infinitude. In the same poem Tolkien seems to refer to that infinite part lost by human nature (in the aftermath of original sin), and missed ever since, when he says:

The heart of Man (…) draws some wisdom from the only Wise,
and still recalls him. Though now long estranged,
Man is not wholly lost nor wholly changed.

---

130   Hans-Georg Gadamer, *Truth and Method* (London: Bloomsbury Academic, 2004), 2nd rev. ed., p. 351.

131   Cf. Donna M. Orange, *The Suffering Stranger: Hermeneutics for Everyday Clinical Practice* (London: Routledge, 2011), p. 24.

132   In Greek *symbállein* means to put together two halves of the same thing; cf. Donatella Di Cesare, *Gadamer: A Philosophical Portrait*, trans. Niall Keane (Minneapolis: Indiana University Press, 2013), p. 24.

133   Donatella Di Cesare, *Gadamer: A Philosophical Portrait*, p. 67.

Dis-graced he may be, yet is not dethroned,
and keeps the rags of lordship once he owned.

Interestingly, in the same text in which he explicates his understanding of mytho-poeia (myth-making and the sub-creative art crucial to Faërie), Tolkien seems to allude to the *pathei mathos* principle, when he remarks that 'pain is pain,/not for itself to be desired, but ill;/or else to strive or to subdue the will/alike were graceless.'[134] It appears that Tolkien reiterates the same truth, as articulated by Aeschylus: the experience of pain and suffering is not to be desired for its own sake, because that would be morbid and masochistic; it can be beneficial, though, as an opportunity to subdue one's own will and struggle with one's own limita-tions, in order to understand human limitedness and helplessness. Without the experience of pain, subduing one's own will and pride would appear a 'graceless' and ridiculous exercise in the state of shallow happiness. Suffering makes people grasp best their 'homuncular', as Tolkien calls it, nature, that is that of being poor finite miniatures and a far reflection of God's infinite image.

To Gadamer, who also perceives suffering as a meeting point between fini-tude and infinitude, an important way of showing the connection between the two realms is, in line with his hermeneutic interests, 'the way of language'.[135] Language is certainly a proof of human finitude, but, at the same time, its open-ness and yearning for other words which can express better what one means, 'evoke the absent infinitude of what still remains to be said and what lets itself be said.'[136] As Donatella Di Cesare observes analysing Gadamer's thought, 'the limit of every word is thus always the beginning of something infinitely new.'[137] Here, however, if my suggestions are valid, the apparent similarity between Tolkien's and Gadamer's understanding of suffering, and of language as a means of contacting the finitude with infinitude, ends. It ends abruptly because Gad-amer rejects any foundational thought, and Tolkien, like all Inklings, defends it, affirming the Christian, and, in particular, Catholic foundation. Di Cesare accounts for that foundation-less character of Gadamer's philosophical herme-neutics as follows:

> In this moment when hermeneutics follows the path of language, it renounces as phi-losophy any *ultimate foundation*. For wherever one insists on an ultimate foundation, language must be ignored, and wherever language is admitted, the ultimate foundation

---

134   Tolkien, 'Mythopoeia'.
135   Cf. Donatella Di Cesare, *Gadamer: A Philosophical Portrait*, p. 68.
136   Donatella Di Cesare, ibid., p. 68.
137   Di Cesare, ibid., p. 68.

must be renounced. How could the claim for an ultimate foundation, the idea of the system, the principle, the founding, the derivation, be brought into harmony with language, in which there is neither a first nor a last word – but only reciprocity? (…) Hermeneutics is 'inifinite dialogue' between the finite and the infinite, (…) and [their] reciprocal participation; (…) and its logos is being dialectically interwoven.[138]

This concept of philosophical hermeneutics has been criticised by some scholars as untenable on various grounds, and, it would certainly have been considered so by Tolkien, Lewis and the other Inklings, whose approach to language, text, and meaning, is inseparable from their recognition of the Christian *Logos*, built upon the first and the last Word, that is the beginning and end of all things, and that became flesh and entered human history:

In the beginning was the Word, and the Word was with God, and the Word was God. He was with God in the beginning. Through him all things were made; without him nothing was made that has been made. In him was life, and that life was the light of all mankind. The light shines in the darkness, and the darkness has not overcome[understood] it.[139]

Returning to the *pathei mathos* dictum, one ought to note that an encounter with the divine *Logos* through suffering (which became His experience as well through His Passion and Death), which is the very reality of human experience, is well represented in the thought and works of the Inklings. Thanks to the foundation of their thought, human finitude experienced especially in suffering does not ultimately lead to despair or absurdity, suffice it to mention Lewis's two non-fictional books addressing the issue: *The Problem of Pain* (1940) and *A Grief Observed* (1960–1961). While the former provides theoretical reflections on how to reconcile the trying experience of suffering with the Christian dogma of the just, loving and omnipotent God, the latter book puts those arguments to the test, as Lewis struggles here with the most difficult pain he has ever suffered, that is the experience of bereavement following his wife's, Joy Davidman's, death. The cathartic process of giving vent to his grief that verges on despair ultimately reconciles Lewis with the inevitability of suffering and its purifying power.

Moreover, just like in Tragedy, the meaning of suffering and learning through suffering are the key themes in Faërie. For instance, in Tolkien's *The Lord of the Rings*, Frodo suffers and his anti-quest leading him to the top of Mount Doom resembles Via Mortis. Although Frodo does not die, he suffers physically, and, above all, psychically, as he fails himself to complete the task of the Ring-bearer, and it is his painful *anagnorisis* that teaches him greater wisdom. Tolkien's beloved story of

---

138   Di Cesare, *Gadamer: A Philosophical Portrait*, p. 70. Italics are Di Cesare's.
139   St. John's Gospel, 1:1–5. New International Version.

Beren and Lúthien is full of suffering as well. When the mortal Beren dies killed by Carcharoth, the greatest werewolf, having recovered the Silmaril from the beast, Lúthien, the immortal Elf-maiden, dies of grief. She comes to Mandos, the keeper of the elvish souls, and moves him so much with her grief that Mandos grants Beren life, and Lúthien mortality. This is through sorrow and suffering that Lúthien becomes aware of true knowledge, and sacrifices her immortality for the sake of love, living with Beren the life of mortals, and then dying a mortal's death.

In Lewis's *Chronicles of Narnia* Aslan suffers tortures and dies a cruel death, only to rise even stronger and mightier, and to grant understanding of 'the deep Magic from before the dawn of time' to the Pevensie children, who vicariously experience his suffering as well. In the last part of the heptalogy, *The Last Battle*, Narnia itself dies, and so do the Pevensie siblings (except Susan), perishing in a train crash. Only then do they enter 'real England' and True Narnia with Aslan – the land beyond pain and death.

Referring again to the main theme of this part of the chapter, that is identifying some similarities and differences between Tragedy and Faërie resulting from their mutual partaking in catharsis, one may distinguish and attempt to unravel yet another strand of some potential affinity between the genres, although it operates on a different level. This is the effect of arrest, which Tolkien mentions as a peculiar mechanism of the inner workings of Faërie, consisting in its 'arresting strangeness', which may discourage some readers, for 'many people dislike being "arrested".[140] The effect of temporary arrest appears to be connected to the feeling of wonder, and conducive to a cathartic catastrophe, which finally relieves it, also in the light of Aristotle's definition of Tragedy. This seems to be so due to the 'strophic', that is turning, movement inherent to the notion of catastrophe (as observed above, the Greek word *strophe* means 'turning, circling, or a turn'), whose stage is a moment of arrest and immobility. It is precisely owing to that moment of suspension and uncertainty, I wish to suggest, that the effect of wonder is possible, during the otherwise circular motion of 'the ancient wheel of fortune'. Curiously, this interpretation finds support in James Joyce's *A Portrait of the Artist as a Young Man*, in Stephen Dedalus's definition of pity and fear, concerning Aristotle's theory; the notions which, next to catharsis, remain enigmatic in Aristotle's *Poetics* and are open to interpretations. Stephen says to his fellow-student Lynch:

> Aristotle has not defined pity and terror. I have. I say (…) Pity is the feeling which arrests the mind in the presence of whatsoever is grave and constant in human-sufferings and unites it with the human sufferer. Terror, [or fear], is the feeling which arrests the mind

---

140   Tolkien, 'On Fairy-Stories', p. 139.

in the presence of whatsoever is grave and constant in human sufferings and unites it with the secret cause.[141]

Interestingly, in both definitions Stephen uses the word 'arrest', referring to the state of the mind that is being arrested in the presence of some burden, whose gravity and constancy result from human sufferings. Pity unites the arrested mind with the human sufferer, creating an empathic bond; whereas terror or fear unites the arrested mind with the secret cause of those sufferings, the cause which can inflict suffering on that very mind as well. Better still, Stephen in fact focuses on the word 'arrest', expanding on its importance not only as a recurrent theme underlying his understanding of the two passions, but also as a key to the notion of tragedy (or tragic emotion) itself in Tragedy:

> The tragic emotion, in fact, is a face looking two ways, towards terror and towards pity, both of which are phases of it. You see I use the word *arrest*. I mean that the tragic emotion is static. Or rather the dramatic emotion is. The feelings excited by improper art are kinetic, desire or loathing. Desire urges us to possess, to go to something; loathing urges us to abandon, to go from something. These are kinetic emotions. The arts which excite them, pornographical or didactic, are therefore improper arts. The aesthetic emotion (I use the general term) is therefore static. The mind is arrested and raised above desire and loathing.[142]

To Stephen, the state of the mind being arrested is a prerequisite of art, of aesthetic emotion, and also of pure beauty, which must be independent of and superior to 'pornographic or didactic', and thus 'improper', arts. The arrest, as Joyce shows it, conditions a motion upwards, 'rais[ing] [the mind] above desire and loathing', a movement that might bring associations with anastrophe, the concept mentioned before in this chapter, as introduced by Wicher in his remarks on the nature of catharsis in Aristotle's Tragedy and Tolkien's Faërie. Thus, Joyce's observations regarding Aristotle's theory of catharsis and aesthetics seem to correspond to the effect of arrest, relevant, as I seek to argue, to both Tragedy and Faërie.

Last but not least, Wicher concentrates on the element of arrest as well when analysing 'the strophic' (turning) nature of Tolkien's idea of Eucatastrophe.[143] Tolkien's representation of Eucatastrophe seems to consist of recurrent stages of

---

141   James Joyce, *A Portrait of the Artist as a Young Man* (London: Penguin Books, 1996), p. 232.

142   Joyce, ibid., p. 232.

143   Although apparently similar, the motion should be confused with W. B. Yeats's gyres, as Yeats's concept of the spinning cones is essentially different in its apocalyptic assumptions from Tolkien's Christian message of a happy resolution and joy 'beyond the walls of this world.'

arrest, inasmuch as he describes it in terms of 'sudden' and 'miraculous' turns, which, as Wicher sees them, are tantamount to some 'jerky, irregular progress', rather than a continuous rolling movement.[144] 'This jerkiness' and 'this convulsiveness', Wicher continues, 'is guaranteed by the idea of paradox', resulting from the fact that *eucatastrophe* is a kind of joy that, [as Tolkien says], is "as poignant as grief"'.[145] It is by no means a coincidence that the word 'poignant' 'comes ultimately from Latin *pungere*, Wicher notes, 'which denotes the idea of "pricking, jabbing, poking" with some sharp pointed instrument', [as 'sharp as swords', Tolkien explains, and giving a 'piercing glimpse of joy',] and indicates a very different reality than that of a revolving wheel'.[146] 'In other words', Wicher concludes addressing the very essence of the problem of the effect of arrest:

> [Tolkien's] eucatastrophe has some mechanism that preserves it from being dissolved, or at least from becoming too quickly dissolved in the environment of the difference-denying circularity. This mechanism is based on the idea of 'two in one', *eucastastrophe* will not turn into its opposite because it already contains its opposite. It is a victory snatched from the jaws of defeat, a victory whose supreme taste is largely based on its being so closely related to defeat, or tragedy.[147]

Thus, it appears that due to its correlation to, and, indeed, participation in dyscatastrophe, which is here very narrowly avoided, or 'arrested', eucatastrophe cannot be denied cathartic properties, which perhaps makes it possible to suggest that the ethos of Faërie is also, in a sense, an ethos of catharsis. Some references to the role that catharsis plays in psychotherapy and literary theory are provided below as an extended introduction to its representation in the fantasy works of the Inklings and of Le Guin.

Finally, an affinity between Tragedy (seen in broader terms as drama) and fantasy fiction, resulting from both genres' cathartic potential, emerges also from the work of modern psychotherapists and drama therapists. Both genres draw on the 'as if' principle of construing reality, which in Faërie is the basis of its otherworldliness, and in drama it assures the lifelike quality of what is taking place on stage. In their book *Imagination, Identification and Catharsis in Theatre and Therapy* (1997), Mary Duggan and Roger Grainger observe that 'in the shared world of imagination, the "as if" principle of archetypal and atavistic psychology achieves epistemological value as a way of approaching human truths'; hence

---

144 Wicher, 'Therapeutic Categories', p. 298.
145 Wicher, ibid., p. 298.
146 Wicher, ibid., p. 298. Tolkien, 'On Fairy-Stories', pp. 109 and 154.
147 Wicher, ibid., pp. 298–299.

'the imaginative personification of archetypal images is encounter rather than escape.'[148] This encounter, which leads to catharsis in both drama and fantasy, 'makes the feelings which were previously unmanageable become manageable, that is acknowledged and lived through.'[149]

Moreover, like drama, fantasy fiction can also be viewed as a 'metaphor within a metaphor', projected in one's imagination; a metaphor in which 'play, safety and adventure take place within a specially structured framework.'[150] Both drama and fantasy tales as 'Secondary Worlds' offer an alternative to reality and provide a safe environment for the expression, experience and clarification of one's separate identity as confronted with otherness. 'Drama originates in reciprocal fantasy, in sharing our fantasies with other people, involving them in our inventions, and becoming involved in theirs,' observe drama therapists.[151]

Nevertheless, in their mutual reliance on fantasy (or, as Tolkien refers to it, 'Fantasy', the image-making imaginative faculty of creating secondary worlds), there is an important difference between drama and fantasy fiction. It can be best explained with reference to Coleridge's concept of the 'willing suspension of disbelief', as commented on by Tolkien. In his *Biographia Literaria* (1817), Coleridge suggests that theatre functions according to the principle of the 'willing suspension of disbelief': 'we should be willing to believe in another, less immediate reality than ours, communicated to us by imaginative involvement in the happenings on stage,' he writes.[152] 'That willing suspension of disbelief' is to Coleridge the *sine qua non* of theatre, its basic prerequisite and foundation. It conditions genuine ideation, that is an understanding of the hero's or heroine's actions, as well as identification, empathy, and, finally, catharsis. 'Suspension of disbelief' is also a landmark in Tolkien's interpretation of fantasy tales. Tolkien refers to Coleridge's concept, yet departs from its meaning. He believes that a fantasy world is a little 'sub-creation', a unique Secondary World created by the writer recalling the greatest act of genesis of the Primary World created by God. To Tolkien, 'fantasy is the reality which, when genuinely understood and accepted, is enchantment rather than suspended or stifled disbelief.'[153] Within its boundaries, it is therefore an authentic 'as if' reality, which does not require a

148   Mary Duggan and Roger Grainger, *Identification and Catharsis in Theatre and Therapy* (London: Jessica Kingsley Publishers, 1997), p. 22.
149   Duggan and Grainger, ibid., p. 42.
150   Duggan and Grainger, ibid., p. 47.
151   Duggan and Grainger, ibid., p. 14.
152   Samuel Taylor Coleridge, *Biographia Literaria*, Chapter XIV.
153   Tolkien, 'On Fairy Stories', p. 132.

disarmament of rational disbelief and hostility. In Tolkien's view, the imaginary world of fantasy is in a way elevated to an in-depth experience superior to a mere 'suspension of disbelief'.

These are only a few remarks concerning similarities and differences that could be traced when viewing Tragedy and high fantasy fiction from a quasi-therapeutic perspective. One point of convergence seems to be catharsis: a tragic one in the former genre, resulting from its dyscatastrophe; and a joyous one in the latter, dubbed by Tolkien a 'eucatastrophe', which brings consolation and hope, and hence which may have even more powerful therapeutic properties. Catharsis affects both the writer (or the teller) of fantasy stories, and the reader (or listener). How Aristotle's concept of catharsis has been interpreted by some prominent modern thinkers, and how they view its effect with regard to psycho-therapy and literary studies is presented below.

Some interpretations of catharsis and its implications for advances in therapeutic and literary studies

Aristotle's notion of catharsis has been a subject of an on-going debate among philosophers, critics, writers, artists, anthropologists, aestheticians, and also doctors of medicine and psychologists. It is not clear whether Aristotle understood catharsis as *katharsis peri to soma* (translated into Latin as *purgatio* and into English as purgation, referring to the body), or *katharsis peri to psyche* (in Latin *purificatio*, and in English purification, regarding psychological or spiritual processes); or, perhaps, both. The Greek word *katharsis* meant purgation, 'or the elimination of offensive humours' in the medical context; while in the religious sense the word referred to rebirth or initiation; and in the moral and spiritual contexts it meant relief of the soul and the spirit by means of purification.'[154] The wealth of these possible (polysemous) meanings centred upon an act of cleansing and relieving has generated numerous varying interpretations of catharsis, and hence confusion and inconsistency. Many readers of Aristotle's works, for instance Andrzej Szczeklik (a professor of medicine, an artist and a humanist at the same time), believe that Aristotle's catharsis probably contains both the medical

---

154 Michael Nichols, Melvin Zax, *Catharsis in Psychotherapy* (New York: Gardner Press, 1977), p. 2. I have addressed this theme in my paper 'Therapy through catharsis in fantasy literature as exemplified by the works of the Inklings (J. R. R. Tolkien and C. S. Lewis) and of U. Le Guin,' [in:] *Language and Identity in the Age of Globalization*, Z. Mazur, T. Bela, eds. (Cracow: Jagiellonian University Press, 2006), pp. 461–475.

and the orphic (mystic and ritual) elements.[155] Szczeklik argues that it might be good that there is no single, plain meaning of catharsis, and no mathematic formula defining the term, (no matter whether this apparent polysemy results from Aristotle's intended ambiguity or from the loss of a treatise in which Aristotle did explicate his understanding thereof): the wealth of possible related meanings is precisely what makes catharsis such a complex and appealing concept.

The fact is that each age understands catharsis differently and gives it certain connotations; however despite the unremitting validity of the concept there have been relatively few systematic and comprehensive studies of catharsis and of its interpretations across centuries, the most important of which are briefly sketched below.

One of the first pioneering studies of catharsis incorporated into the history of the sublime and sublimity is an 18th century's work of Samuel Monk's, followed by Eric Auerbach's study of mimesis, originating in Aristotle's understanding of imitation. At the end of the same century catharsis receives more prominent recognition in the Hegelian dialectic, interpreted within Hegel's three axes of a thesis, antithesis and synthesis as a universal and not merely aesthetic phenomenon.[156] Furthermore, at the beginning of the 20th century Ernst Cassirer (1874–1945) in his work *Sprache und Mythos* perceives catharsis as a universal phenomenon involving not only the spectator but also the reader, and inducing the state of rest and peace to people's contradictory emotions. According to Cassirer, a cathartic response begins with emotive arousal and ends with cognition and a reconciliation of emotions, so that it combines emotional excitation and intellectual understanding.[157] Cassirer distinguishes seven stages of catharsis and coins a term of ideation, which is thinking on the part of the spectator, and which ends with an understanding of what happened on the stage. This understanding can be moral, metaphysical or psychological, depending on the spectator's individual character.[158]

The next cornerstone in the studies of catharsis is the work of Jakob Bernays of 1857, in which he associates catharsis with a 'homeopathic cure' that helps 'universalize our emotions.'[159] Bernays's approach to catharsis served later on as a starting point for Freud who integrated catharsis into psychology and psychoanalysis. In 1909 Ingram Bywater, a translator of Aristotle's works, explores further the theory

---

155   Szczeklik, *Catharsis. On the Healing Power of Nature and Art*, p. 83.
156   Cf. Adnan K. Abdulla, *Catharsis in Literature* (Bloomington: Indiana UP, 1985), p. 34.
157   Ernst Cassirer, *Sprache und Mythos* [*Language and Myth*], trans. Susanne Katherina Knauth Langer (New York: Dover Publications, 1953).
158   Cf. Abdulla, *Catharsis in Literature*, p. 38.
159   Cf. Abdulla, ibid., p. 45.

of catharsis, presenting a medical application of catharsis understood as a relief of pent-up emotions and a healing therapy.[160] Next, catharsis becomes a major axis in Freud's psychoanalytical theory and practice. Freud (1856–1939) transfers 'the cathartic experience of drama' to several other forms of what he calls 'creative writing', such as epic poetry.[161]

Freud's contribution to the development of studies on catharsis is remarkable, for he moves catharsis from the realm of aesthetics to therapeutics, from a literary effect to psychology, from the audience of a tragedy to a reader and a patient in psychotherapy. What is more, Freud indicates the connection between catharsis and identification, between catharsis and self-expression in therapy. Catharsis in therapy, as introduced by Freud, is a release of energy through breaking psychological bonds; a release of disquieting, disruptive feelings in an experiential process.[162] It must be noted, however, that although very influential, Freud's interpretation of catharsis may appear reductionist, as it tends to be, in a typically Freudian fashion, 'wrapped up in sex', and promoted with 'his usual innuendo-laden gusto', without much thorough scientific study.[163] Freud's explanation of catharsis, which later on he renounced himself, draws on a hydraulic model, which, although useful, contains, as Nichols and Zax argue, 'certain non-verifiable and misleading assumptions'.[164] Freud states that when emotions are not discharged, they are stored in some inner space, accumulating tension; thus, when affect is not ventilated, pressure increases to a point when it becomes destructive, because 'affects are like water boiling in a kettle'; and 'if the kettle is not allowed to blow off steam, it will explode.'[165] Catharsis is an element of Freud's safety-valve theory of emotion, in which emotions are the subjective experience of drives: 'when action to satisfy an instinctual drive is impossible or dangerous, catharsis permits internal discharge and the reduction of tension.'[166]

---

160 Ibid., p. 46.
161 Freud, 'Creative Writers and Daydreaming' (1908), [in:] *Criticism: the Major Statements*, Charles Kaplan, ed. (New York: St. Martin's, 1991), pp. 419–428; cf. Abdulla, ibid., p. 23.
162 Cf. Abdulla, *Catharsis in Literature*, p. 66.
163 This is what Derek Lee Miller claims in his 'Catharsis: From Aristotle to Freud to an Egg Salad Sandwich' [in:] *Minnesota Playlist Magazine*, http://minnesotaplaylist.com/magazine/article/catharsis-aristotle-freud-egg-salad-sandwich, accessed 23 April 2016.
164 Nichols and Zax, *Catharsis in Psychotherapy*, p. 3.
165 Nichols and Zax, ibid., p. 4.
166 Nichols and Zax, ibid., p. 4.

According to Nichols and Zax, one problem with Freud's hydraulic model of catharsis, which draws on his 'nonverifiable or misleading assumptions', is that it interprets human psyche in terms of psychic energy contained in a closed system; another, to mention two controversies only, is that, to Freud every emotion which has not been discharged is somehow 'collected into a pool' and felt as tension, impairing other emotions and 'interfering with conflict-free rationality'.[167]

Influenced by Bernays, who advocates catharsis in medical treatment, Freud refers to catharsis as 'abreaction' or 'the expression and emotional discharge of unconscious material (as a repressed idea or emotion) by verbalization, especially in the presence of a therapist'.[168] Abreaction is a cathartic process that involves emotional release of an unconscious traumatic content, which has been relived in a less traumatic context; and 'an act of giving vent in speech and action to repressed experiences, and thereby disburdening one's self of their unconscious influences'.[169] In their joint work *Studies on Hysteria* (1895), which proposes abreaction accomplished via venting, purging, screaming, expunging, or merely verbalizing feelings as a treatment for hysterical patients, Freud and Josef Breuer argue that 'language serves as a substitute for action; by its help, an affect can be "abreacted" almost as effectively'.[170]

In his declining years, however, Freud abandoned cathartic abreaction concluding that it was an ineffective tool of psychoanalysis, the reason for this rejection lying perhaps in the essence of psychoanalysis: abreaction without a deeper understanding of feelings and without recognition of man's spirituality can be, as Bruce Wilson claims, not only ineffective, but also 'nontherapeutic (…) and dangerous'.[171] An inappropriate approach to an emotional upheaval may prove 'retraumatizing', Wilson warns, inasmuch as 'dredging up feelings without a clear understanding of what's going on is a recipe for disaster'.[172] What has to be acknowledged, though, is the fact that Freud was one of the first psychologists to use elements of catharsis in psychotherapy, and that he substantially influenced

167 Nichols and Zax, ibid., p. 5.
168 It is partly derived from Freud's German term *Abreagierung*, in which 'ab' means off, away, and *Reagierung* is reaction; cf. http://www.merriam-webster.com/dictionary/abreaction, accessed 23 April 2016.
169 Bruce Wilson, 'The Primal Mind', http://theprimalmind.com/?p=278, accessed 2 June 2014.
170 Josef Breuer, and Sigmund Freud, *Studies on Hysteria*, trans. Nicola Luckhurst (London: Penguin Classics, 2004).
171 Bruce Wilson, 'The Primal Mind'.
172 Wilson, 'The Primal Mind'.

the subsequent schools of therapy, for instance psychodynamic psychotherapy, Jungian psychology, and logotherapy as well.

As Nichols and Zax argue, the critique of catharsis provided eventually by Freud and after him by some other psychologists and psychotherapists, (for instance by Berkowitz and Bendura, who claim that 'catharsis of aggression leads to more aggression'), does not result from therapeutic inadequacy of catharsis itself, but rather from a varying and inconsistent usage of the term, lack of its operational definition, and from its clinical misapplications.[173] A widely used term, catharsis has been very vaguely defined, often identified with 'a process which relieves tension and anxiety by expressing emotions' – a definition that opens up a plethora of possible interpretations and practical applications. Freud understood catharsis as an act of recalling single instances of previously forgotten memories made by hysterical patients; Berkowitz and Bandura meant an act of children engaging directly or vicariously in destructive and hostile behaviour towards their peers; whereas Alexander Lowen (who praised catharsis as a highly effective therapeutic tool) referred to expressive physical movements.[174]

Some other influential insights into the nature of catharsis in therapy and also in literature after Freud come from Sandor Ferenczi, Abraham Arden Brill, Jacob Levy Moreno, Kenneth Burke and Northrop Frye. Sandor Ferenczi (1873–1933), a Freudian psychotherapist from Hungary, developed a concept of neocatharsis, that is 'active catharsis', applied to adults, which consists in therapists' identifying themselves with an infantile side of the patient, and transferring the course of therapy to their infantile mentality.[175] Abraham Arden Brill, a translator of many works of Freud, introduced two distinct types of catharsis: emotional and mental, which correspond to Cassirer's two stages of emotional and intellectual cleansing.[176]

That 'discharge theme' of catharsis, as Wilson names it, is evident also in the works of Pierre Janet (1859–1947), Freud's contemporary, who, instead of using the term 'abreaction', introduced the notion of 'mental liquidation' of harmful emotions.[177] Cathartic techniques provided basis also for the therapy proposed for psychotic patients by Andries Hoek (1807–1885), a Dutch physician; and later on, by psychologists and psychiatrists working with the First and the Second World

---

173 Nichols and Zax, *Catharsis in Psychotherapy*, p. 1.

174 Nichols and Zax, ibid., p. 1.

175 Sandor Ferenczi, 'The Principle of Relaxation and Neo-Catharsis' [in:] *International Journal of Psychoanalysis 11* (1930), pp. 428–443.

176 Abdulla, *Catharsis in Literature*, p. 38.

177 Pierre Janet, *Psychological Healing*, 2 vols., trans. Eden and Cedar Paul (London: Allen & Unwin, 1925).

War veterans; in the latter case, however, as Wilson observes, 'the focus shifted toward *controlling* emotions rather than finding resolution through their expression.[178] Ernst Simmel, a German medical officer during the Second World War, viewed catharsis as an opportunity for the soldiers to master their emotions intellectually rather than achieve consolation and purification through their release.[179] After 1945, Wilson notes, with the advent of postmodernity 'emotional expression in psychotherapy became more mechanized and increasingly detached from the patient's inner being.[180] A rare exception to that mainstream orientation of psychotherapy is logotherapy, which, although somehow indebted to psychoanalysis like all other schools of psychotherapy, focuses on the inner, spiritual dimension of man as a meaning-seeking individual, and when using elements of catharsis, logotherapy orientates therapy toward 'existential review, search for meaning, and the consciousness of responsibility.[181] As Pavel Somov remarks, 'recovery [in logotherapy] is not itself a goal, but a means to a goal, a means to facilitating a meaningful life,' because if recovery does not bring one closer towards discovering a sense of life and of particular life situations, sooner or later it fails.[182] 'Indeed', Somov notes, 'a person coming out of an otherwise successful [cathartic] rehabilitation may ask (…), "OK, so I got clean… Now what?!" Leaving this question unanswered seems to be an invitation to relapse,' he concludes.[183]

An interesting approach to catharsis emerges from Lev Vygotsky's reflections concerning his theory of art as propounded in the *Psychology of Art* (1925), mentioned in Chapter Four of this book. Vygotsky views catharsis as an essential element of the psychological impact of art, and one of its basic affective mechanisms. More than that, he actually defines art as a form of aesthetic and psychic catharsis ('art as a catharsis' is the title of one of the chapters in his book). Vygotsky links catharsis with a universal aesthetic response to a work of art (including a work of literature), and sees catharsis as a 'transformation of affects, and the explosive response which culminates in the discharge of emotions' generated by contradictions that result from manifold conflicts incorporated into a work of art, for instance a clash between artistic form, material and content, or

178   Cf. Wilson, 'The Primal Mind'; italics are Wilson's.
179   Wilson, ibid.
180   Wilson, ibid.
181   Pavel G. Somov, *Recovery Equation: Logotherapy, Psychodrama and Choice Awareness Training for Substance Use/Addictions Treatment* (Eau Claire, WI: PESI Publishing and Media, 2008), p. 32.
182   Somov, ibid., p. 36.
183   Somov, ibid., p. 25.

between the reader's or spectator's expectations regarding the plot or resolution of a given work of art, and authorial intent and realisation thereof.[184]

> A work of art (such as a fable, a short story, a tragedy), always includes an affective contradiction, causes conflicting feelings, and leads to the short-circuiting and destruction of these emotions. This is the true effect of a work of art. We come now to the concept of catharsis used by Aristotle as the basis for his explanation of tragedy, and repeatedly mentioned by him with regard to the other arts.[185]

Vygotsky's own definition of catharsis, which is provided in the context of his psychological approach to art, reads that:

> Aesthetic reaction as such is nothing but catharsis, that is, a complex transformation of feelings. Though little is known at present about the process of catharsis, we do know, however, that the discharge of nervous energy (which is the essence of any emotion) takes place in a direction which opposes the conventional one, and that art therefore becomes a most powerful means for important and appropriate discharges of nervous energy. The basis for this process reveals itself in the contradiction which inheres in the structure of any work of art.[186]

Interestingly, as a concomitant of artistic catharsis Vygotsky identifies the feelings opposite to pity, fear, and to a discord of conflicting ideas, namely the feelings that can perhaps be associated with joy and peace, transformed from sorrow and anxiety – an approach to catharsis that might be reminiscent of Tolkien's notion of a eucatastrophic transformation of tragic feelings into Joy – a proposition discussed in the previous part of this chapter, and, although not nominally cathartic, appearing profoundly so.

Thus, it seems that to Vygotsky catharsis is not just a discharge of negative feelings, but also a transformation of those feelings into their positive counterparts. Concluding his ruminations upon catharsis Vygotsky remarks:

> Despite the indefiniteness of its content, despite our failure to explain the meaning of this term in the Aristotelian sense, there is no other term in psychology which so completely expresses the central fact of aesthetic reaction, according to which painful and unpleasant affects are discharged and transformed into their opposites.[187]

Tolkien, in turn, when commenting on his concept of Eucatastrophe, explains:

---

184   Vygotsky, *The Psychology of Art*, p. 301.
185   Vygotsky, ibid., p. 299.
186   Vygotsky, ibid., p. 299.
187   Vygotsky, ibid., p. 299.

I coined the word 'eucatastrophe': the sudden happy turn in a story which pierces you with a joy that brings tears (which I argued it is the highest function of fairy-stories to produce). And I was there led to the view that it produces its peculiar effect because it is a sudden glimpse of Truth, your whole nature chained in material cause and effect, the chain of death, feels a sudden relief as if a major limb out of joint had suddenly snapped back. It perceives – if the story has literary 'truth' on the second plane (....) – that this is indeed how things really do work in the Great World for which our nature is made. And I concluded by saying that the Resurrection was the greatest 'eucatastrophe' possible in the greatest Fairy Story – and produces that essential emotion: Christian joy which produces tears because it is qualitatively so like sorrow, because it comes from those places where Joy and Sorrow are at one, reconciled, as selfishness and altruism are lost in Love.[188]

Of course, this juxtaposition of Vygotsky's and Tolkien's views on different aspects of catharsis in literature is only my suggestion, as, to the best of my knowledge, neither Vygotsky nor Tolkien were aware of each other's writings and thought.

A further interpretation of catharsis, which makes a cornerstone of modern psychotherapy, draws on the clinical experience of Jacob Levy Moreno (1889–1974), the inventor of the theatre of spontaneity and the creator of psychodrama. Moreno regards the Greek tragedy as a therapeutic device integral to the daily life of ancient Greeks, providing a natural channel of communication, emotional release, abreaction and purgation. Developed from the Spontaneity Theatre, Moreno's psychodrama is designed to compensate for the loss of the opportunity to exercise the atavistic tendency towards self-expression and cleansing by giving a full vent to fear, anger, pity, anxiety and other disturbing emotions. The main techniques applied in psychodrama and borrowed from ancient tragedy include role reversal, soliloquy, as well as the mirror and the double, all exercised within a therapy group. The two prerequisites to Moreno's psychodramatic therapy are creativity and spontaneity.[189]

As signalled above with regard to Freud's interpretation of catharsis, its notion understood as a medium of emotional arousal and expression has found an important application in psychotherapy, especially psychoanalysis, hypnotherapy and psychodrama. Many other therapeutic approaches, such as Primal therapy, Gestalt therapy or Re-Evaluation Counseling, also 'place extraordinary emphasis on emotional catharsis in the treatment process,' and, as the psychotherapists Nichols and Zax assert, they 'are cathartic therapies.'[190] Although neither the Inklings nor Le Guin have endorsed any school of psychotherapy, I refer here to some

---

188   Tolkien, *Letters*, no. 89.

189   Cf. Jacob Moreno, *Psychodrama* (New York: Beacon House, 1959).

190   Nichols and Zax, *Catharsis in Psychotherapy*, book jacket.

most important applications of catharsis therein with the aim of illustrating the enduring healing or at least auxiliary power of catharsis. This is not to say that cathartic therapy is a new invention, of course, for, as Nichols and Zax duly note, 'catharsis as a vehicle of behaviour change is traced back to ancient magic and religious healing rituals', and still functions likewise today.[191] In many contemporary tribal societies catharsis is still 'one of the basic functional mechanisms of magical rites through which passion are partially spent, even though not gratified'.[192]

According to Nichols and Zax, 'the Aristotelian concept of tragedy is not simply a passive intellectual exercise', although it may initially include a stage of 'arrest', as argued before in this chapter; yet ultimately it leads to a 'profound upheaval, charged with emotion generated through similarities between the tragic hero's experience and the audience's experiences.'[193] The therapeutic potential of catharsis rests in what follows the upheaval, namely in 'the shock of the emotional arousal and purgation, [which] helps to rearrange perceptions and so leads to a modification of the audience's self-concept and world view.'[194] Nichols and Zax argue that 'the powerful intellectual and affective experience of having anxiety dissolve in tears fosters personal exploration and development', and hence is an important auxiliary of psychotherapy.[195] The aim of cathartic therapy is, as the two psychotherapists argue, accomplishing an 'increased freedom of expressivity and action', and an 'ability to respond actively in ways appropriate to present not past circumstances', so that 'feelings of competence and enjoyment of living' are enhanced.[196] Nichols and Zax conclude that:

> If cathartic therapy is successful, it should lead neither to suppressing nor reflexively discharging emotions, but recognizing – in realistic proportions – the actions that they predispose. In this way, actions can be chosen and planned wisely. The outcome of cathartic therapy affects the future, not the past.[197]

Proceeding to some selected interpretations of catharsis pertaining to literary studies, from among various notable critics engaged in the on-going discussion on catharsis it is important to mention Kenneth Burke (1897–1993), an American literary theorist, who emphasizes a universal significance of catharsis, arguing

---

191   Nichols and Zax, ibid., book jacket.
192   Nichols and Zax, ibid., p. 15.
193   Nichols and Zax, ibid., p. 2.
194   Nichols and Zax, ibid., p. 2.
195   Nichols and Zax, ibid., p. 2.
196   Nichols and Zax, ibid., p. 233.
197   Nichols and Zax, ibid., p. 232.

that 'catharsis is not simply a literary term but a concept that involves the reader, the critic, the society and man's overall concern with symbols.'[198] An important novelty introduced by Burke is explaining catharsis through love, not through pity and fear, and seeking its religious connotations. Burke believes that 'tragic catharsis through pity and fear operates as a substitute for catharsis through love. One's state of identification or communion with the object of one's pity is nearly like the kind of identification or communion one feels for a loved object.'[199]

In addition, Burke employs two other notions to pinpoint the archetypal and atavistic dimension of catharsis: 'vicariousness' and 'victimage' (the process of 'scapegoating' or blaming others for one's guilt), connected to his theory of dramatism, used by Burke to analyse human relationships. Burke argues that drama is the best metaphor of life, and that the ultimate motive of man's rhetoric is to purge oneself of one's sense of guilt.[200] He calls this rhetoric 'new rhetoric', as contrasted with the 'old rhetoric', as presented by Aristotle and other ancient thinkers, whose main aim was persuasion. The main plot of human life, that is of human drama, is to Burke 'guilt redemption', which can be achieved via purgation.

Burke puts forth four theses concerning the concept of purgation or catharsis, making an important contribution to its modern understanding, and to its transcription from drama to other literary genres, including high fantasy fiction:

1. catharsis can be related not only to drama, theatre and spectators but also to a poet, the audience or to the critic;
2. catharsis has a therapeutic effect, and a vital social and aesthetic function;
3. catharsis is an action and a symbol-laden acclimatization;
4. catharsis is inseparably combined with concepts such as: uncleanliness, purgation, victimage, mortification, transcendence and communication.[201]

Burke's theory lays considerable emphasis on catharsis, which is viewed as an indispensable part of human life seen as a drama: catharsis is a therapeutic action and process, both social and aesthetic, both personal and vicarious, serving a purpose of purging one of the feeling of guilt, drawing on communication and leading beyond the ordinary toward the transcendent. That interpretation of catharsis seems to bridge its original Aristotelian quarters established in drama as

198   Quoted in Abdulla, *Catharsis in Literature*, p. 21.
199   Kenneth Burke, 'Catharsis – Second View' [in:] *Centennial Review of Arts and Sciences*, 5 (1961): pp. 107–132, 112.
200   Iain L. Mangham and M. A. Overington, *Dramatism and the theatrical metaphor. Life as theater: A dramaturgical sourcebook* (2nd ed.) (New Brunswick, NJ: Transaction Publishers, 2005), pp. 333–346.
201   Cf. Abdulla, *Catharsis in Literature*, p. 69.

a literary genre (and in music) with the new premises of catharsis in other (literary and, in general, artistic) genres, in which catharsis acts as a vicarious tool of purgation; and also it links the ancient ritualistic catharsis with the non-literary realm of contemporary social communication and psychotherapy, in which cathartic purgation conditions, as Burke seems to argue, all forms of human relationships. Burke's emphasis on the necessity of purging the sense of guilt might be reminiscent of Frankl's concept of the most trying triad of human experience: suffering, death and guilt, in which the last is often the worst of the three.[202]

Another prominent literary critic who made an important contribution to the debate concerning catharsis and its therapeutic power is the foremost Canadian literary theoretician of the past century, Northrop Frye (1912–1991). To Frye, who approaches literature as a 'central and most important extension of mythology', based on the pre-literary categories such as ritual, myth, and folk-tale', (a critical standpoint which may somehow link his theory with the neo-Romantic and mythological elements in the thought of the Inklings), catharsis is Aristotle's central concept.[203] Frye does not interpret it in terms of purification, purgation or clarification, though, but rather of 'detachment of the spectator' – a detachment 'both from the work of art itself and from the author'.[204] Extending the notion of catharsis to non-dramatic genres, especially to narrative fiction, in his *Anatomy of Criticism* (1957) Frye views catharsis as 'not the raising of an actual emotion, but the raising and casting out of an actual emotion on a wave of something else'; this 'something else' being 'exhilaration or exuberance', an experience 'as much intellectual as emotional.'[205]

It is impossible within the scope of this dissertation to do justice to the wealth of Frye's thought concerning catharsis and Aristotle's theory as such, yet viewing it very selectively from the perspective of my argument, one could observe that Frye's interpretation of catharsis might again imply the affinity between catharsis and joy (joy, as identified by Tolkien, and 'exhilaration and exuberance', as named by Frye), and perhaps a solution to the Eliotian aporia of the dissociation of sensibility, a remedy which may be produced by of the cathartic nature of art, including literature, whose affective and intellectual dimensions, when equally respected and used well, may perhaps help unite the rift between reason and feeling.

---

202   Cf. Victor Frankl, *Man's Search for Meaning*, and *The Unheard cry for Meaning*.
203   Frye, *Words with Power: Being a Second Study of 'The Bible and Literature'*, Michael Dolzani, ed. (Toronto: University of Toronto Press, 2008), p. xiii;
204   Frye, *Anatomy of Criticism* (Princeton: Princeton University Press, 1957, 2000), p. 66.
205   Frye, ibid., p. 79.

As signalled above with regard to Freud's interpretation of catharsis, its notion understood as a medium of emotional arousal and expression has found an important application in psychotherapy, especially psychoanalysis and hypnotherapy. Many therapeutic approaches, such as Primal therapy, Gestalt therapy, Re-Evaluation Counseling, and Psychodrama 'place extraordinary emphasis on emotional catharsis in the treatment process', and, as psychotherapists Michael Nichols and Melvin Zax assert, 'are cathartic therapies'.[206] This is not to say that cathartic therapy is a new invention, of course, for, as Nichols and Zax duly note, 'catharsis as a vehicle of behaviour change is traced back to ancient magic and religious healing rituals', and still functions likewise today.[207] In many contemporary tribal societies catharsis is still 'one of the basic functional mechanisms of magical rites through which passion are partially spent, even though not gratified'.[208]

According to Nichols and Zax, 'the Aristotelian concept of tragedy is not simply a passive intellectual exercise', although it may initially include a stage of 'arrest', as argued before in this chapter; yet ultimately it leads to a 'profound upheaval, charged with emotion generated through similarities between the tragic hero's experience and the audience's experiences'.[209] The therapeutic potential of catharsis rests in what follows the upheaval, namely in 'the shock of the emotional arousal and purgation, [which] helps to rearrange perceptions and so leads to a modification of the audience's self-concept and world view'.[210] Nichols and Zax argue that 'the powerful intellectual and affective experience of having anxiety dissolve in tears fosters personal exploration and development', and hence is an important auxiliary of psychotherapy.[211] The aim of cathartic therapy is, as the two psychotherapists argue, accomplishing an 'increased freedom of expressivity and action', and an 'ability to respond actively in ways appropriate to present not past circumstances', so that 'feelings of competence and enjoyment of living' are enhanced.[212] Nichols and Zax conclude that:

> If cathartic therapy is successful, it should lead neither to suppressing nor reflexively discharging emotions, but recognizing – in realistic proportions – the actions that they

206   Nichols and Zax, *Catharsis in Psychotherapy*, book jacket.
207   Ibid., book jacket.
208   Ibid., p. 15.
209   Ibid., p. 2.
210   Ibid., p. 2.
211   Ibid., p. 2.
212   Ibid., p. 233.

predispose. In this way, actions can be chosen and planned wisely. The outcome of cathartic therapy affects the future, not the past.[213]

The above rough outline of the development of scholarship on catharsis shows its
indebtedness to ancient Tragedy, yet at the same time points towards a more universal approach to catharsis, relating it also to non-dramatic writings, visual arts
and music. Moreover, according to some interpretations of catharsis, the traumas
of fear and pity are not only relived and discharged, but also transformed into
an enriching experience of joy and integrity, which produces a synergy effect of
profound purgation and consolation. Moreover, what seems to emerge from that
cursory survey is an observation that catharsis is relevant to the narrative fiction
that has a special affinity to arts (as Vygotsky sees it, a peculiar mediation of visual
images and music), and as Frye views it, the fiction that has the closest relationship with myth and folk tales; and, last but not least, that places most emphasis
on imagination. These clues, as I wish to argue, can lead to high fantasy as a genre
which, next to Tragedy, appears particularly well-suited to provide ground for a
cathartic effect.

In the following section of this chapter I provide some examples of eucatastrophic catharsis selected from the works of Tolkien, Lewis and Le Guin,
hoping to illustrate its therapeutic properties.

Therapy through catharsis in the fantasy works of the Inklings and of Le Guin

If, as this chapter seeks to argue, high fantasy fiction has a special ethos of catharsis, and more specifically, of eucatastrophe, it is time now to see how it works in
practice, that is in the works of Tolkien, Lewis and Le Guin, and whether it may
have any therapeutic potential.

Lewis draws closely on the Christian myth and employs it within transparent frames of allegory. His *Chronicles of Narnia* (1950–1956) meant for children
yet addressed as a parable to adults as well, seem to exemplify tales of catharsis
through eucatastrophe. The primary cathartic eucatastrophe of the Narnian tales
is the moment of turning from death to life of Aslan, the leonine symbol of Christ,
who defeats the evil power of the White Witch in the first part of the Chronicles, *The Magician's Nephew*. A profoundly cathartic experience is also forgiveness
granted by Aslan to the treacherous Edmund Pevensie, who has betrayed Narnia,
his siblings and Aslan, led into temptation of power (princehood) and gluttony

---

213 Ibid., p. 232.

(the Turkish Delight treat) by the White Witch. Rescued from the Witch and for-given by Aslan, in the end Edmund bitterly regrets his betrayal, and repents:[214]

> 'Now, Edmund, are you truly sorry for what you have done?' [Aslan] stressed.
> 'Yes, I'm so sorry. Could you ever forgive me, Aslan?' Edmund suddenly exclaimed, desperate for mercy.
> 'I do forgive you son – can you forgive yourself?' Aslan replied tenderly.
> Edmund looked down again, but then looked back up.
> 'If you help me,' he answered.
> 'I will.'

This first stage of Edmund's catharsis is followed by a more profound one when Aslan sacrifices his own life in exchange of Edmund's, which is claimed by the Witch, who says: 'You know that every traitor belongs to me as my lawful prey and that for every treachery I have a right to kill.'[215] The unspeakable suffering and death of Aslan on the sacrificial Stone Table, and his subsequent miraculous resurrection is a most powerful eucatastrophe not only to Edmund but also to Narnia itself, as Aslan rescues all the Talking Animals spell-bound by the Witch, and kills her, liberating Narnia from evil for a long time.

On a larger scale, the Lewisian series of the Narnian chronicles offers a large eucatastrophic and eschatological catharsis, in which the trauma of fear, pain and pity is ultimately alleviated by the invincible good, which quite unexpect-edly delivers peace, hope and bliss to the suffering and confounded. This is so with Aslan's resurrection in the first book, and with the death of Narnia in the last, which are only transitions to the pure state of joy that comes with tears, and pierces like sorrow. The ultimate victory of the good rewards the Pevensie children, 'sons of Adam and daughters of Eve', who have faithfully stood by Nar-nia, with an eschatological passage to the 'tertiary world of creation', the unspoilt realm of divine love, 'the deeper reality' that is man's true home, beyond pain and death.[216] When they enter the 'real Narnia', Digory, Jill, Lucy, Peter and Edmund, experience a peculiar mixture of poignant joy and gravity: 'as you know, there is a kind of happiness and wonder that makes you serious. It is too good to waste on jokes', Lewis says in one of the closing passages of *The Last Battle*.[217]

---

214 Lewis, *The Chronicles of Narnia: The Lion, the Witch and the Wardrobe* (London: Grafton, 2002), p. 121.
215 Lewis, ibid., p. 126.
216 Lewis, *The Chronicles of Narnia: The Last Battle* (London: Grafton, 2002), pp. 160–161.
217 Lewis, ibid., p. 160.

Tolkien's fantasy world is also woven of the profoundly therapeutic fabric, but it is not overtly religious or allegorical, in spite of being deeply rooted in the Christian, and specifically Catholic faith. A paragon of Eucatastrophe in *The Hobbit* is the unexpected arrival of eagles who at the last moment rescue Bilbo Bagggins's team encircled by a pack of the Wargs, the bloodthirsty evil wolves 'from over the edge of the Wild.'[218] Next, the leitmotif of Tolkien's Middle-earth epic is the theme of the Ring, the symbol of evil, which must return to the primordial fire in order to be destroyed. This theme appears cathartic itself, for the eradication of the Ring in the purifying fire of Mount Doom (to some extent and for some time) purges the world of evil, thus helping to discharge many difficult emotions of those who have opposed evil, mostly fear, pain and woe, which are transformed into joy. This eucatastrophic joy of a happy ending is nevertheless as poignant as grief, for it leaves things radically different and necessitates profound change: Frodo, Bilbo, Gandalf, Elrond, Galadriel, and many other Elves, 'pass over Sea into the West' and go to the 'Undying Lands', dwindling in the West as some of the last representatives of non-human races, 'the Days of the Rings' having been passed. They retreat, making way for the advent of the Fourth Age in the history of Middle-earth – the age of 'the Dominion of Men'.[219] When Merry, Sam and Pippin bid farewell to the Ring-bearers who are boarding a ship at the Grey Havens, Gandalf seems to speak of a fulfilled eucatastrophe, 'which pierces you with a joy that brings tears': 'Well, here at last, dear friends, on the shores of the Sea comes the end of our fellowship in Middle-earth. Go in peace! I will not say: do not weep; for not all tears are an evil.'[220]

The essentially Christian cathartic Eucatastrophe of the Inklings sheds light on the primary purgation and hope offered by Christ to man. Even though in *The Lord of the Rings* there are no direct references to Christian faith apart from its 'providential ordering and eschatological crisis,' and that the tale has been partly 're-paganized', its roots are embedded in the Christian myth of a struggle between good and evil, life and death, ending in a purifying victory of good.[221] In Lewis's fantasy world, the primary appeal to imagination is through allegory. His plot is only a net, whereby to catch something else, to catch a glimpse of the

---

218 Tolkien, *The Hobbit* (London: HarperCollins Publishers, 1999), p. 95.
219 Tolkien, *The Lord of the Rings: The Return of the King* (London: HarperCollins Publishers, 1995), p. 1006.
220 Tolkien, *The Return of the King*, p. 1007; *Letters:* Letter 89.
221 Gunnar Urang, 'Tolkien's Fantasy – The Phenomenology of Hope' [in:] *Shadows of Imagination: The Fantasies of C. S. Lewis, J. R. R. Tolkien and Charles Williams*, Mark R. Hillegas, ed. (Carbondale: Southern Illinois University Press, 1979), pp. 97–124, 119.

Primary Creation, of the Passion and Redemption that cross over the threshold of death and lead to joy, to a new 'deeper' reality, where one finally feels entirely at home, in the realm that Tolkien calls the 'Undying Lands'. Lewis's fantasy fiction seems to illustrate the Augustinian dictum of the human heart being anxious and restless until it is purged and rests in God.[222] What is important, in Christian thought finding rest and peace in a union with the ultimate Logos can only happen after one's profound purification, after a trying experience of anguish, which is reflected in the works of the Inklings.

As some critics remark, the cathartic eucatastrophies designed in the fantasy tales by the Inklings make their Faërie narratives 'unflaggingly optimistic' and in a way 'wish-fulfilling'.[223] Based on the palimpsest of atavistic myth, fantasy works of the Inklings disarm the readers of their quotidian inattention and disbelief, and prove paradoxically that 'unreality becomes the best road to reality,' and a path towards self-identity and meaning.[224] Emphasizing the dimension of Tolkien's fantasy that could be identified as therapeutic, Wystan Hugh Auden writes that *The Lord of the Rings* 'holds up the mirror to the only nature we know, our own'.[225] Should Victor Frankl's understanding of human nature be adopted, according to which the principal desire of human nature is 'the will to meaning' (or the will to *logos*), Tolkien's and Lewis's works might be regarded as fantasy tales holding up the mirror not only to man's myth-making, but, ultimately, existential meaning-making. The logocentric and logotherapeutic backbone of the Inklings' fantasy fiction does not lead the reader to the edge of a nihilistic abyss or an absurdist aporia, but through suffering and cathartic eucatastrophe brings good news and lifts towards a possibility of genuine joy. 'Fantasy should represent the image of truth,' Lewis says, and at times, this is 'an unfulfilled (and perhaps unfulfillable) yearning which itself is a kind of satisfaction'.[226] Tolkien's and Lewis's

---

222 St. Augustine says in his *Confessions*: 'our heart is restless till it rests in You', Lib 1, 1–2, 2.5, 5: CSEL 33, 1–5.

223 Charles Moorman, 'Now Entertain a Conjecture of a Time: The Fictive Worlds of C. S. Lewis and J. R. R. Tolkien' [in:] *Shadows of Imagination*, pp. 41–69, 50.

224 Clyde S. Kilby. 'Meaning in *The Lord of the Rings*' [in:] *Shadows of Imagination*, pp. 70–96, 81.

225 Quoted by Kilby, ibid., p. 83.

226 Quoted by Tanya Caroline Wood in her paper 'Is Tolkien a Renaissance Man? Sir Philip Sidney's *Defense of Poesy* and J. R. R. Tolkien's 'On Fairy-Stories' [in:] *J. R. R. Tolkien and His Literary Resonances: View of Middle-earth*, George Clark and Daniel Timmons, eds. (Portsmouth, NH: Greenwood Publishing Group, 2000), pp. 95–108, 190.

fantasy fiction 'seeks the indefinable,' John Timmerman adds, 'and its subject is nothing less than the human spirit.'[227]

Proceeding to the cathartic elements of high fantasy fiction as represented by Ursula K. Le Guin's works, one ought to note that her Earthsea world, deeply seated in a psychological reality, just like fantasy fiction of the Inklings responds to basic human yearnings and aims at seeking a path toward meaning, mostly through pain and sacrifice, which leads the protagonists to a cathartic cleansing of fear, pride and anxiety. Although the cathartic purgation in her Earthsea world is not Christian, it does seem eucatastrophic, for giving vent to the protagonist's burdensome emotions, it transforms them into serene joy and peace, as a tragic climax unexpectedly finds a challenging but happy resolution. One of the main characters of Le Guin's Earthsea hexalogy, Ged the Sparrowhawk, who becomes the Archmage of Earthsea, pursues quest for truth and understanding, which is profoundly cathartic: he undergoes a spiritual exercise of self-discipline (*askesis*) chasing an unnamed shadow that weaves evil magic across Earthsea, only to discover that the shadow is the other half of himself. Recognising his own weakness and fallibility, Ged accepts that shocking fact in a humble and brave act of embracing the shadow, his alter ego, releasing his harmful feelings and transforming that painful awareness into a purifying and enriching experience of wisdom and humility. He gets rid of his ambition to be the most powerful wizard, overcomes his foolhardy impatience, and consequently learns to control his natural powers and desires. This comes with a great relief and tears of poignant joy. Having made himself whole after the reunion with his shadow at the end of the world, Ged speaks to Vetch, his faithful companion, declaring: 'It is over,' [Ged] laughed. 'The wound is healed,' he said, 'I am whole, I am free.' Then he bent over and hid his face in his arms, weeping like a boy.'[228]

The other major cathartic experience of Ged is, as I wish to argue, the feat he accomplishes later on when he mends the rift between the worlds of the living and the dead, defeating the evil wizard Cob in the Dry Land. As a result, Ged spends all his wizardry power, but emerges wholly purified, stripped of his magic abilities, and freed of any aspirations to wield power and authority as the Archmage. This second cathartic climax gives Ged peace and puts his restlessness to an end, producing genuine joy, even though he almost dies and incurs a

---

227 John Timmerman, *Other Worlds: The Fantasy Genre* (Ohio: Bowling Green State University Press, 1983), p. 46.
228 Le Guin, *A Wizard of Earthsea* (London: Penguin Books, 1992), p. 165.

painful loss, or so it seems. Le Guin accounts for this profoundly cathartic experience of Ged gained in the ultimate encounter with Cob in the following way:

'Be thou made whole!' [Ged] said in a clear voice [to Cob], and with his staff he drew in lines of fire across the gate of rocks a figure: the rune Agnen, the rune of Ending, which closes roads and is drawn on coffin lids. And there was then no gap or void [leaking between the worlds of life and death] among the boulders. The door was shut. The earth of the Dry Land trembled under their feet, and across the unchanging, barren sky a long roll of thunder ran, and died away.

'By the word that will not be spoken until time's end I summoned thee. By the word that was spoken at the making of things I now release thee. Go free!' And bending over the blind man, who was crouched on his knees, Ged whispered in his ear, under the white tangled hair.

Cob stood up. (…) He spoke no word, but gazed at [Ged and Arren] with dark eyes. There was no anger in his face, no hate, no grief. Slowly he turned, and went off down the course of the Dry River, and soon was gone from sight.

There was no more light on Ged's yew-staff, nor in his face. He stood there in the darkness. When Arren [Ged's companion, whose name in the Old Speech was Lebannen] came to him he caught at the young man's arm to hold himself upright. For a moment a spasm of dry sobbing shook him. 'It is done,' he said. 'It is all gone.'

'It is done, dear lord. We must go.'

'Aye. We must go home.'

(…) Ged was like one bewildered or exhausted. (…) Even his body looked thin and burned, as if half consumed. (…) Arren made to get down for [Ged's staff], but Ged stopped him. 'Leave it. I spent all wizardry at that dry spring, Lebannen. I am no mage now.'[229]

Ged and Arren are taken away from the Dry Land by the Eldest Dragon, Kalessin, who braves the walls between life and death and takes them back to Earthsea. They arrive at Roke, the school of wizardry, where Arren dismounts Kalessin, parting with Ged.

'A little further yet, Kalessin,' Ged replied. 'I have not gone where I must go.' (…) [Ged] looked at the Masters and the young wizards [at Roke] and the boys and the townsfolk gathered on the slopes. (…) His face was quiet, and in his eyes there was something like that laughter in the eyes of Kalessin. Turning from them all he mounted up again by the dragon's foot and shoulder, and took his seat reinless between the great peaks of the wings, on the neck of the dragon. The red wings lifted with a drumming rattle, and Kalessin the Eldest sprang into the air. Fire came from the dragon's jaws, and smoke, and the

---

229   Le Guin, *The Farthest Shore* (London: Penguin Books, 1992), pp. 466–467.

sound of thunder and the storm-wind was in the beating of its wings. It circled the hill once and flew off (..) towards the mountain isle of Gont [Ged's native island].

[Master] Doorkeeper, smiling, said, '[Ged] has done with doing. He goes home.'[230]

Ged's personal Eucatastrophe is also one of the greatest Eucatastrophes in the history of Earthsea, when the balance between life and death, and light and darkness is restored; joyous peace fills human hearts, and order and power return to the race of dragons. The cathartic transformations of Ged and of Earthsea are symbolized and emphasized by the appearance of Kalessin, the Eldest and wisest dragon, who speaks the language of the Making when addressing Ged, the dragonlord, and offering help, thus sealing an important alliance between the two races. Kalessin's fiery power purges people and things anew, and his blaze seen by Earthsea islanders when he carries Ged and Arren across vast seas betokens hope.

Interestingly, the cathartic eucatastrophe of Ged, who ceases to be a mage but learns to be an ordinary man of valour without wizardry, is achieved through the power of *logos* understood as a Word of Old Speech, the true language of the Making, whose power closes the fissure between the worlds of life and death, and saves Earthsea that has been on the verge of annihilation, as it was already suffering a life- in-death agony.

> Knowing names is [a wizard's] job', Ged says. '[A wizard's] art. To weave the magic of a thing, you see, one must find its true name out. (..) There is great power, and great peril, in a name. Once, at the beginning of time, when Segoy raised the isles of Earthsea from the ocean deeps, all things bore their own true names. And all doing of magic, of wizardry, hangs still upon the knowledge – the relearning, the remembering – of that true and ancient language of the Making.[231]

Le Guin's fantasy world appears logocentric, and also logotherapeutic: centred upon timeless Logos – the unconditional meaning, being at the same time the Word of the dawn of time, in which all things that are partake.

The other protagonists of the Earthsea series – the two women: Tenar and Tehanu also undergo powerful cathartic transformations. Tenar, the heroine of the third book of the Earthsea hexalogy: *The Tombs of Atuan*, is a happy Kargish girl taken away from home as a little child, for she is the alleged reincarnation of Arha, the high priestess of the 'Nameless Ones', or the dark forces ruling the island of Atuan. She is forced to be the next Arha, or 'the eaten one', because her birthday coincides with the death of the previous Arha. Dark rituals and cruel practices including human sacrifices is what Tenar is trained to perform as the

---

230   Le Guin, ibid. p. 477.
231   Le Guin, *The Tombs of Atuan* (London: Penguin Books, 1992), p. 266.

high priestess. She almost loses her own identity and forgets her real name and true nature but then she unexpectedly meets Ged in the labyrinth of the Tombs of Atuan, which only she can freely enter. Ged finds there the lost half of the Erreth-Akbe ring, and deeply affects Tenar with his goodness and humbleness. Tenar spares his life, renouncing finally her status of the high priestess. 'You are like a lantern swathed and covered, hidden away in a dark place. Yet the light shines; they could not put out the light. They could not hide you', Ged says to her, recognising her inner strength that has endured the overwhelming evil.[232]

Tenar's conscious rejection of the evil imposed on her, which almost costs her life, is her profound purification: she repudiates the darkness in which she has almost spiritually drowned, and emerges purified. The Tombs fall and bury everything, but Tenar flees with Ged just in time, thanks to his wizardry, narrowly escaping the wrath of the malevolent spirits, as well as envy and revenge of one of the rival priestesses who intends to murder Tenar. A foreigner, stripped of her identity, childhood and past, Tenar arrives at Gont profoundly changed, but untainted by evil. Her inner light has ultimately overcome the malevolent darkness that she was forced to serve. Tenar rediscovers what it is to feel a joy of liberation, sharp as a sword and poignant as grief though it is, for she remembers what cruel orders she was forced to give when forced to act as Arha. From the high priestess she turns into an anonymous peasant woman and lives a simple life in a village, tending her husband's farm and raising their two children. That eucatastrophic experience literally saves her life at the last moment, but even more importantly, it saves her humanness and enables her to start living a new life, a real life, however simple she chooses it to be, settling among farmers and goatherds.

The most moving and dramatic catharsis in the Earthsea hexalogy is, however, probably the transformation of Therru, the protagonist of the fourth and the sixth, the last of Earthsea books. A girl raped by a group of vagabonds and left to die, half-burnt in a camp fire by her father, Therru, (whose name, given to her by Tenar, in Kargish means a 'flame') is adopted by Tenar, now a widow, who runs her late husband's farm, when they are joined by Ged, who has spent all his wizardry defeating Cob, and is no longer a mage. When the vagabonds discover that Tenar has nursed Therru back to life and taken care of her, they repeatedly attempt to seize the girl, in so doing collaborating with Aspen, a wicked wizard who hates Ged for his victory over Cob, and who puts evil spells on Ged and Tenar, for some reason fearing Therru. Crippled for life, with her half-burnt body, terrible scars on her face, one eye burnt, and the fingers of her right hand twisted

---

232   Le Guin, ibid., p. 267.

and fused in a claw, Therru has been physically mutilated, but even more painfully abused emotionally by her natural father and relatives, and, despite Ged's and Tenar's caring love towards her, she fears future, and perhaps, herself.[233] When Ged and Tenar almost die, bewitched by Aspen, who makes them hurl themselves off a cliff, Therru summons Kalessin, the Eldest dragon, who defends them and burns Aspen and his men to ashes. Therru starts to discover for herself and reveal to others her true nature: she is a double being, half-human, half-dragon, a beloved daughter of Kalessin, and at the same time the prophesied 'woman of Gont', said to become the Archmage of Roke, the one of paramount power. This moment is a eucatastrophe, for Ged's and Tenar's impending death is narrowly and miraculously avoided (no one has expected a little shy child, 'whose voice was seldom more than a whisper', to speak the Old Speech, call for the greatest of the dragons, and be immediately obeyed).[234] When Therru speaks to Kalessin, who uses her real name, Tehanu, she partly gets rid of fear and anguish, and experiences the taste of profound joy of learning about her true self, her double being: half-human, half-dragonish.

The ultimate catharsis and final Eucatastrophe, of Tehanu, and of Earthsea as well, is however completed at the end of the last book of the series, that is *The Other Wind*. Tehanu and her sister Irian, who also has a hybrid human and dragonish nature, with the help of Alder, a simple farmer, and some mages, close the deadliest wound in the balance of the Earthsea world, a conflict between dragons and men, inflicted by the greed of some evil sorcerers, who have trespassed the dragons' realm, violating 'Vedurnan' – an ancient agreement between dragons and humans, trying to steal the dragons' share of immortality.

At the moment when Tehanu fully realises her dragonish nature and her desire to join her folk of air and fire, she confesses to Tenar, whom she hates to leave:

> I think that when I die, I can breathe back the breath that made me live. I can give back to the world all that I didn't do, all that I might have been and couldn't be. All the choices I didn't make. All the things I lost and spent and waste. I can give them back to the world. To the lives that haven't been lived yet. That will be my gift back to the world that gave me the life I did live, the love I loved, the breath I breathed.[235]

The breach being healed, Tehanu turns into a dragon, a magnificent one, of a beautiful, whole and no longer disfigured body, and together with Irian and

---

233 Some critics have noticed similarities between Therru and Shireen Baratheon, a character from G. R. R. Martin's fantasy series *A Song of Ice and Fire*.
234 Le Guin, *The Other Wind* (London: Orion, 2004), p. 239.
235 Le Guin, ibid., p. 231.

Kalessin she 'flies golden on the other wind', beyond the wind of the human world, 'on the Dragons' Way', where only dragons can fly.[236] Tehanu's half-burnt and desecrated body is literally purged and made whole and golden now; but, above all, her spirit is finally liberated, as she gets rid of harmful emotions she has lived with, and enjoys peace, purity and joy. As a result of that cathartic and eucatastrophic process, which is in a sense her resurrection, Tehanu also discovers the ultimate meaning of her existence:

> [Tehanu] reached up her arms [towards Kalessin]. Fire ran along her hands, her arms, into her hair, into her face and body, flamed up into great wings above her head, and lifted her into the air, a creature all fire, blazing, beautiful. She cried out aloud, a clear, wordless cry. She flew high, headlong, fast, up into the sky where the light was growing and a white wind had erased the unmeaning stars.[237]

A child cruelly abused, tortured and forsaken by her natural family, Tehanu turns out to be the mightiest of people, the spiritual daughter of the greatest of dragons, whose unlearnt wisdom and knowledge of things exceeds all the learning of the mages. Her personal catharsis has triggered cathartic purifications of other characters of the Earthsea cycle, and, in fact, contributed to a cathartic cleansing of human nature in Earthsea.

Disregarding various possible psychoanalytic interpretations of cathartic Eucatastrophes in the fantasy works of the Inklings and of Le Guin, it seems that when experienced vicariously by readers they can have a therapeutic effect of consolation and recovery, as they turn suffering and sorrow into a meaningful experience, producing joy, even if only beyond the realm of this world, 'outside the frame', 'let[ting] a gleam of [the light of *Logos*] come through.'[238] As one critic comments on that effect, 'eucatastrophe is our astonishment, which is a sudden gratification of a deeply held yearning for the world of the spirit, for evangelium [good news], a fleeting glimpse of an answer to the question: is the fantasy story true?'[239] As I hope to have suggested, in the therapeutic and uplifting context of high fantasy ethos, it is.

---

236 Le Guin, ibid., p. 237.
237 Le Guin, *The Other Wind*, p. 238.
238 Tolkien, 'On Fairy-Stories', p. 154.
239 David Sandner, "'Joy Beyond the Walls of the World': The Secondary World-Making of J. R. R. Tolkien and C. S. Lewis' [in:] *J. R. R. Tolkien and His Literary Resonances: Views of Middle-earth*, pp. 133–145, 138.

It is the mark of a good fairy-story, of the higher or more complete kind, [Tolkien concludes], that however wild its events, however fantastic or terrible the adventures, it can give to child or man that hears it, when the [eucatastrophic] 'turn' comes, a catch of the breath, a beat and lifting of the heart, near to (or indeed accompanied by) tears, as keen as that given by any form of literary art, [but] having a peculiar [therapeutic] quality.[240]

---

240 Tolkien, 'On Fairy-Stories', pp. 153–154.

Coda

I have attempted to view modern high fantasy fiction, as established by the Inklings and by Le Guin, in terms of their assumed psychotherapeutic properties. The essential contribution of the writers to the rise of the fantastic mode in contemporary literature cannot be ignored on the strength of its purely literary merits, which I have briefly signalled in the first two chapters of this work. The bulk of this book addresses, however, the psychotherapeutic properties of fantasy literature, which I attempt to view from various angles, starting with the most general statement regarding psychotherapeutic power of narrative itself, and then proceeding to the role of art in psychotherapy, and of imaginative literature approached as its specific type, finally reaching the problem of psychotherapeutic properties residing in the genre of Faërie, as stipulated by J. R. R. Tolkien.

The axis of my thesis is a correspondence between literature and psychotherapy, which I seek by transposing the tenets of a particular school of psychotherapy and philosophy, that is Victor Frankl's logotherapy, onto the grounds of literary theory and literary studies. I seek to argue that high fantasy, in its peculiar vicarious way, conducts logotherapy, drawing on its immersion in what I call mythopathy and sensopaedia, and centred upon *logos*, understood as both word and meaning, and upon moral imagination. Fantasy, Recovery, Escape and Consolation, the qualities enumerated by Tolkien as the key characteristics of Faërie, are the marks of the genre's therapeutic potential, most effectively accomplished through the concept of eucatastrophe, which seems comparable to Aristotle's concept of catharsis, attributed predominantly to Tragedy.

It is my hope to suggest that in the wake of the profound existential crisis of postmodernity, high fantasy as rehabilitated by the Inklings and by Le Guin may offer a wholesome alternative and can function as a medium of *therapia pauperum*, steering clear of the contrary winds of the neonihilistic mainstream, and returning to a foundational thought and some unconditional meaning of life, difficult to grasp though it is.

> Blessed are the men of Noah's race that build
> their little arks, though frail and poorly filled,
> and steer through winds contrary towards a wraith,
> a rumour of a harbour guessed by faith,

says Tolkien in his 'Mythopoeia'.

As Philip and Carol Zaleski observe, the Inklings:

> Had fashioned a new narrative of hope amid the ruins of war, industrialization, cultural disintegration, skepticism, and anomie. They listened to the last enchantments of the Middle Ages, heard the horns of Elfland, and made designs on the culture that our own age is only beginning fully to appreciate.[1]

Moreover, the Zaleskis call the Inklings 'philomyths', and 'lovers of logos (the ordering power of words) and mythos (the regenerative power of story)', which seems to correspond to my thesis of a logotherapeutic and mythopathic quality of their fantasy works.[2] The connection between the ethos of Faërie, (as endorsed by the Inklings, especially by Tolkien and Lewis, and by Le Guin,) and Frankl's therapy through meaning, may find its confirmation also in another statement of the Zaleskis, who view the legacy of the Inklings as 'work of recovery', 'shot through with meaning', and conclude that 'the Inklings were, one and all, guilty of the heresy of the Happy Ending', that is the eucatastrophic denouement achieved through suffering and sacrifice.[3] What emerges from the realm of Faërie is a message which could be in turn linked with Frankl's observation that 'in some ways suffering ceases to be suffering at the moment it finds a meaning, such as the meaning of a sacrifice.'[4] Thus, 'life is never made unbearable by circumstances, but only by lack of meaning and purpose.'[5]

My last, perhaps surprising and perhaps erroneous, suggestion is that modern Faërie, as revitalized specifically by Tolkien, Lewis, and Le Guin, followed by generations of younger writers, resembles 'a tower', built by a man of 'the old stone' that used to be 'part of an older hall' and had been accumulated in a field he had inherited from his ancestors.[6] The tower has been 'pushed over', for some people, 'without troubling to climb the steps' desired to 'look for [its] hidden carvings and inscriptions, or to discover whence the man's distant forefathers had obtained their building material' or to find 'a deposit of coal under the soil.'[7] 'They said (after pushing it over): "What a muddle it is in!" And even the man's own descendants (…) were heard to murmur: 'He's such an odd fellow! Imagine his using these old stones just to build a nonsensical tower! Why did not he

---

1   The Zaleskis, *The Fellowship*, p. 4.
2   Ibid., p. 4.
3   Ibid., pp. 510–511.
4   Frankl, *Man's Search for Meaning*, p. 135.
5   Frankl, ibid., p 154.
6   Tolkien, 'Beowulf: The Monsters and the Critics' [in:] *The Monsters and the Critics and Other Essays*, p. 7.
7   Ibid., p. 8.

restore the old house? He had no sense of proportion." But from the top of that tower the man had been able to look upon the sea.'[8]

If Tolkien's allegory concerning *Beowulf* might apply to the 'perilous realm' of Faërie as well, it seems that what tends to be forgotten or missed out in literary studies of the genre and of its masterpieces is that special effect which Faërie produces when viewed from a different perspective, with its artistic and therapeutic potential acknowledged. The image of the sea and the sound of its primordial music is what, I would like to argue, stands for the genre's ability to reach beyond its very form and content, into the higher realm of genuine meaning, which Lewis calls 'the deeper magic from before the dawn of time', and which is interpreted in this book as therapeutic. Only when climbing the tower and viewing it as an entity aiming at the skies, rather than dissecting its particular building blocks, can one discover the amazing vista it offers, and a new perspective on life, on oneself, and on the world; the panorama which the Zaleskis relate to an 'ocean of myth teeming with symbol, meaning, and loveliness'.[9]

How much this vista of an ocean, of a 'larger reality', is needed today has also been emphasized by Le Guin, who in her speech at the National Book Awards of 2014, almost a month after her 85th birthday, said:

> Hard times are coming, when we'll be wanting the voices of writers who can see alternatives to how we live now, can see through our fear-stricken society and its obsessive technologies to other ways of being, and even imagine real grounds for hope. We'll need writers who can remember freedom – poets, visionaries – realists of a larger reality.[10]

I conclude this book with another citation, now of Tolkien's words from the Epilogue to his essay 'On Fairy-Stories', which, although feeling unworthy to refer to myself, I humbly borrow:

> If by grace what I say has in any respect any validity, it is, of course, only one facet of a truth incalculably rich: finite only because the capacity of Man for whom this was done is finite.[11]

---

8   Tolkien, ibid., p. 8.
9   The Zaleskis, p. 216.
10   Le Guin's speech at National Book Awards, 20 November 2014, when she received the National Book Foundation's Medal for Distinguished Contribution to American Letters; accessed 23 April 2016; https://www.theguardian.com/books/2014/nov/20/ursula-k-le-guin- national-book- awards-speech.
11   Tolkien, 'On Fairy-Stories', Epilogue, p. 155.

Selected bibliography

Primary sources

Barfield, Owen, *Poetic Diction: A Study in Meaning* (London: Wesleyan Paperback, 1984)

Havard, Robert, 'Jack at ease' [in:] *C. S. Lewis at the Breakfast Table, and Other Reminiscences*, James T. Como, ed. (London: Harcourt Publishers, 1992)

Le Guin, Ursula, *The Language of the Night. Essays on Fantasy and Science Fiction*, Susan Wood, ed. (New York: Berkley Books 1982)

– *The Earthsea Quartet: A Wizard of Earthsea, The Farthest Shores, The Tombs of Atuan, Tehanu* (London: Penguin Books, 1993)

– *The Other Wind* (London: Orion, 2004)

– *Tales from Earthsea* (London: Orion, 2003)

– *The Left Hand of Darkness* (New York: Ace Books, 1987)

Lewis, Clive Staples, *The Abolition of Man* (Cambridge: Cambridge University Press, 1946, 2009)

– 'Humanitarianism and Punishment' [in:] *Offenders or Citizens: Readings in Rehabilitation*, Philip Priestly, Maurice Vanstone, eds. (Oxford: Willan Publishing, 2011), pp. 116–118

– *Mere Christianity* (London: Geoffrey Bles, 1952); (San Francisco: Harper San Francisco, 2009)

– *The Lion, the Witch and the Wardrobe* (London: Geoffrey Bles, 1950)

– *The Chronicles of Narnia: The Last Battle* (London: Grafton, 2002)

– *God in the Dock: Essays on Theology and Ethics* (Grand Rapids, MI: Wm. B. Eerdmans Publishing Co., 1972)

– *Preface* to *George MacDonald – An Anthology. 365 Readings*, C. S. Lewis, ed. (London: HarperCollins, 2009)

– *The Magician's Nephew* (London: HarperCollins 1955, 2002)

– *Of Other Worlds. Essays and Stories*, (London: Geoffrey Bles, 1986)

– *The Pilgrim's Regress*, rev. ed. (London: Geoffrey Bles, 1933, 1946)

– *The Collected Letters of C. S. Lewis*, Walter Hooper, ed. (San Francisco: HarperCollins, 2004)

– *De description temporum*, an inaugural lecture, Cambridge University, 25 November 1954

- *Surprised by Joy: The Shape of My Early Life* (London: Harcourt, 1966)
- *That Hideous Strength* (London: Scribner, 2003)
- *Studies in Words* (Cambridge: Cambridge University Press, 1990)
- 'Undergraduate Criticism' [in:] *Broadsheet* (Cambridge) 8, no. 17, March 9, 1960
- *An Experiment in Criticism* (Cambridge, UK: Cambridge University Press, 1961, 2004)
- *Essays Presented to Charles Williams*, C. S. Lewis, ed. (London: Geoffrey Cumberlege, Oxford University Press, 1947)

Lewis, Warren Hamilton, *Brothers and Friends: The Diaries of Major Warren Hamilton Lewis*, Clyde S. Kilby, Marjorie Lamp Mead, eds. (New York: HarperCollins, 1982)

Tolkien, John Ronald Reuel, *The Monsters and the Critics and Other Essays,* including 'On Fairy-Stories' and 'Sir Gawain and the Green Knight' (London: HarperCollins Publishers, 1997)
- *The Letters of J. R. R. Tolkien*, Christopher Tolkien, Humphrey Carpenter, eds. (London: Mariner Books, 2000)
- *The Silmarillion*, Christopher Tolkien, ed. (New York: Ballantine Books, 1977, 2001)
- 'Leaf by Niggle' [in:] *Tales from the Perilous Realm* (London: HarperCollins, 2002)
- *The Lord of the Rings* (London: HarperCollins, 1996)
- *The Hobbit* (London: HarperCollins Publishers, 1999)
- *The Later Silmarillion: Morgoth's Ring*, Christopher Tolkien, ed. (London: HarperCollins Publishers, 1995)

Williams, Charles, *Outline of Romantic Theology* (Berkeley: Apocryphile Press, 2005)
- *Poetry at Present* (Oxford: Clarendon, 1930)
- *Descent into Hell* (Grand Rapids, MI: William B. Eerdmans Publishing Company, 1980)
- *War in Heaven* (Grand Rapids, Michigan: William B. Eerdmans, 1930, 1949)

Secondary sources

Abdulla, Adnan K., *Catharsis in Literature* (Bloomington: Indiana UP, 1985)

Adey, Lionel, *C. S. Lewis's 'Great War' with Owen Barfield* (London: Ink Books, 2000)

Adorno, Theodor W., *Minima Moralia. Reflections from Damaged Life* (London: Verso, 2005)

Anderson, Perry, *The Origins of Postmodernity* (London: Verso, 1998)

Anderson, Warren D., *Ethos and Education in Greek Music* (Cambridge, MA: Harvard University Press, 1968)

Aristotle, *Poetics*, trans. Theodore Buckley, (Amherst: Prometheus Books, 1992); trans. Joe Sachs (Boston: Focus Philosophical Library, Pullins Press, 2006)

Stinton, T. C. W., 'Hamartia in Aristotle and Greek Tragedy' [in:] *The Classical Quarterly New Series*, vol. 25, No. 2 (Dec., 1975), (Cambridge: Cambridge University Press, 1975)

Ashenden, Gavin, *Charles Williams: Alchemy and Integration* (Cleveland: The Kent State University Press, 2007)

Bakhtin, Mikhail, *The Dialogic Imagination: Four Essays,* trans. Caryl Emerson and Michael Holquist; Michael Holquist, ed. (Austin and London: University of Texas Press, 1981)

Bakhtin, Mikhail, *Speech Genres and Other Late Essays,* trans. Vern W. McGee (Austin: University of Texas Press, 1986)

Baudrillard, Jean, *Postmodern Fables*, trans. Georges Van Den Abbeele (Minneapolis: University of Minnesota Press, 1997)

Baudrillard, Jean, 'On Nihilism' [in:] *Simulacra and Simulation*, trans. S. F. Glaser (Ann Arbor: Michigan University Press, 1994)

Bauman, Zygmunt, *Intimations of Postmodernity* (London: Routledge, 1992)

Beecher, Henry Ward, *Proverbs from Plymouth Pulpit* (Ulan Press, 2012)

Benson, Stephen, *Literary Music: Writing Music in Contemporary Fiction* (Aldershot: Ashgate Publishing Limited, 2006)

Bettelheim, Bruno, *The Uses of Enchantment: The Meaning and Importance of Fairy Tales* (London: Vintage, 1989)

Birtchnell, John, 'Art Therapy as a Form of Psychotherapy' [in:] *Art as Therapy: An Introduction to the Use of Art as a Therapeutic Technique*, Tessa Dalley, ed. (London: Tavistock, 1984), pp. 30–45

Bloom, Harold, ed. *J. R. R. Tolkien's The Lord of the Rings* (New York: Bloom's Literary Criticism, 2008)

Bray, Suzanne, 'C. S. Lewis as an Anglican' [in:] *Persona and Paradox: Issues of Identity for C. S. Lewis, his Friends and Associates*, Suzanne Brey, William Gray, eds. (Newcastle upon Tyne: Cambridge Scholars Publishing, 2012), pp. 19–36

– 'Dorothy L. Sayers: Disciple and Interpreter of Charles Williams' [in:] *Charles Williams and His Contemporaries*, Suzanne Bray and Richard Sturch, eds. (Newcastle upon Tyne: Cambridge Scholars Publishing, 2009), pp. 96–116.

Browning, Lydia R., 'Charles Williams's Anti-Modernist *Descent into Hell*' [in:] *Mythlore*, Vol. 31, No. 1–2, 2012, pp. 5–19

Bruner, Edward, 'Ethnography as Narrative' [in:] *The Anthropology of Experience*, W. Turner and E. M. Bruner, eds. (Chicago: University of Illinois Press, 1986)

Bruner, Jerome, *Making Stories: Law, Literature, Life* (New York: Farrar, Straus and Giroux, 2002)

Bruner, Jerome, 'The Narrative Construction of Reality' [in:] *Critical Inquiry*, 18:1, pp. 1–21, 1991

Bruner, Jerome, *Acts of Meaning* (Cambridge, MA: Harvard University Press, 1990)

Bucknall, Barbara J., *Ursula K. Le Guin* (New York: Frederick Ungar, 1984)

Burke, Kenneth, 'Catharsis – Second View' [in:] *Centennial Review of Arts and Sciences*, 5 (1961), pp. 107–132

Carpenter, Humphrey, *J. R. R. Tolkien: A Biography* (London: Houghton Mifflin Company, 1979, 2000)

– *The Inklings: C. S. Lewis, J. R. R. Tolkien, Charles Williams and Their Friends. A Group of Writers Whose Literary Fantasies Still Fire the Imagination of All Those Who Seek a Truth Beyond Reality* (London: George Allen and Unwin, 1978. Later editions: HarperCollins Publishers, 1981, 2006)

Carter, Lin, *Imaginary Worlds* (London: Ballantine Books, 1973)

Cassirer, Ernst, *Sprache und Mythos* [*Language and Myth*], trans. Susanne Katherina Knauth Langer (New York: Dover Publications, 1953)

Chaika, Elaine, *Linguistics, Pragmatics and Psychotherapy* (London: Whurr Publishers, 2000)

Critchley, Simon, *Very Little...Almost Nothing: Death, Philosophy, Literature* (London: Routledge, 1997)

Cholewa-Purgał, Anna, 'Sfumato and Chiaroscuro or the Symbolic Interplay of Light and Shade in the Fantasy Works of J. R. R. Tolkien and U. K. Le Guin' [in:] PASE Papers 2007: *Studies in Culture and Literature*, vol. 2, Wojciech Kalaga, Marzena Kubisz, and Jacek Mydla, eds. (Katowice, University of Silesia Press, 2007), pp. 64–79.

– 'A few inklings on the Inklings and (post)modernism' [in:] Wielo-wymiarowość i Perspektywy Nauki za Progiem XXI w., E. Widawska, K. Kowal, eds. (Częstochowa: Jan Długosz University Press, 20120), pp. 79–94

– 'Framing ekphrasis in fantasy narrative: chiaroscuro and sfumato in the works of J. R. R. Tolkien and U. K. Le Guin' [in:] *Image, Imagery, Imagination in Contemporary English Studies*, B. Cetnarowska, O. Glebova, eds. (Częstochowa: Jan Długosz University Press, 2012), pp. 48–80

- 'High fantasy fiction and the fantastic mode: against the anti-prescriptiveness of genre in contemporary literature?' [in:] *Genre in Contemporary English Studies*, Olga Glebova, ed. (Częstochowa: Jan Długosz University Press, 2014), pp. 37–65

- 'Neo-nihilism and the Self-industry of Logotherapy' [in:] *The Self-Industry. Therapy and Fiction*, J. Szurman, A. Woźniakowska, Krzysztof Kowalczyk-Twarowski, eds. (Katowice: University of Silesia Press, 2015), pp. 205–227

Clark, George, and Daniel Timmons, eds., *J. R. R. Tolkien and His Literary Resonances: Views of Middle-earth* (Westport, CT: Greenwood Press, 2000)

Cummins, Elizabeth, *Understanding Ursula K. Le Guin* (Columbia: University of South Carolina Press, 1993)

Cunningham, James Vincent, *Woe or Wonder. The Emotional Effect of Shakespearian Tragedy* (Denver: Swallow, 1951)

Cushman, Philip, 'Why the self is empty: toward a historically-situated psychology' [in:] *American Psychologist, 45*, 1990, pp. 599–611

Davenport, John D., 'Happy Endings and Religious Hope: *The Lord of the Rings* as an Epic Fairy Tale' [in:] *The Lord of the Rings and Philosophy: One Book to Rule Them All*, Gregory Bassham, and Eric Bronson, eds. (Chicago: Open Court, 2003), pp. 204–218

Davies, Whitney, *A General Theory of Visual Culture* (Princeton: Princeton University Press, 2011)

Dēmaras, Kōnstantinos, *A History of Modern Greek Literature* (New York: SUNY Press, 1972)

Di Cesare, Donatella, *Gadamer: A Philosophical Portrait*, trans. Niall Keane, (Minneapolis: Indiana University Press, 2013)

Drout, Michael D. C., *J. R. R. Tolkien Encyclopaedia: Scholarship and Critical Assessment* (London: Routledge, 2006)

Duggan, Mary and Roger Grainger, *Imagination, Identification and Catharsis in Theatre and Therapy* (London: Jessica Kingsley Publishers, 1997)

Duriez, Colin, and David Porter, *The Inklings Handbook: The Lives, Thought and Writings of C. S. Lewis, J. R. R. Tolkien, Charles Williams, Owen Barfield, and Their Friends* (London: Azure, 2001)

Duriez, Colin, *Tolkien and C. S. Lewis: The Gift of Friendship* (London: Hiddenspring, 2003)

- *J. R. R. Tolkien: The Making of a Legend* (Oxford: Lion Hudson, 2012)

Eco, Umberto, 'Postscript' to *The name of the Rose* (London: Harvest Books, 1994)

Eliot, Thomas Stearns, *The Waste Land* (New York: Classic Books International, 2010)

Emerson, Ralph Waldo, *Nature* (London: Penguin Classics, 2003, 4th edition)

Ferenczi, Sandor, 'The Principle of Relaxation and Neo-Catharsis' [in:] *International Journal of Psychoanalysis 11* (1930), pp. 428–443

Frankl, Victor, *The Unheard Cry for Meaning* (New York: Washington Square Press, 1978, 1997)

– *Man's Search for Meaning* (*Man's Search for Meaning* (New York: Pocket Books, 1959, 1984)

– *The Will to Meaning: From Psychotherapy to Logotherapy. Foundations and Applications of Logotherapy* (Cleveland: The World Publishing Company, 1969)

– *The Doctor and the Soul* (New York: Second Vintage Books Edition, 1986)

Franzke, Erich, *Fairy Tales in Psychotherapy: The Creative use of Old and New Tales*, trans. Joseph A. Smith, (Toronto: Hagrefe and Huber Publishers, 1989)

Frederick, Candice and Sam McBride, *Women Among the Inklings: Gender, C. S. Lewis, J. R. R. Tolkien, and Charles Williams. Contribution s in Women's Studies* (Santa Barbara: Praeger, 2001)

Freud, Sigmund, 'Creative Writers and Daydreaming' (1908) [in:] *Criticism: the Major Statements*, Charles Kaplan, ed. (New York: St. Martin's, 1991), pp. 419–428

– *The Future of an Illusion* (New York: Martino Fine Books, 2011)

Friedrich, Rainer, 'The Enlightenment Gone Mad. The Dismal Discourse of Postmodernism's Grand Narratives' [in:] *Arion: Journal of Humanities and the Classics at Boston University* (Boston, MA, 2012), *Arion* 19–3, winter 2012; pp. 31–47

Fruoco, Jonathan, 'C. S. Lewis and T. S. Eliot – Questions of Identity' [in:] *Persona and Paradox: Issues of Identity for C. S. Lewis, His Friends and Associates*, Suzanne Bray, William Gray, eds. (Newcastle upon Tyne: Cambridge Scholars Publishing, 2012), pp. 81–92

Frye, Northrop, 'The Archetypes of Literature' [in:] *Criticism: the Major Statements* (New York: St. Martin's, 1991), 3rd ed., Charles Kaplan and William Anderson, eds., pp. 500–514

– *Words with Power: Being a Second Study of 'The Bible and Literature'*, Michael Dolzani, ed. (Toronto: University of Toronto Press, 2008)

– *Anatomy of Criticism* (Princeton: Princeton University Press, 1957, 2000)

Fubini, Enrico, *Historia estetyki muzycznej* [The History of Musical Aesthetic], trans. Z. Skowron, (Kraków: Wydawnictwo Musica Jagiellonica, 1997)

Gadamer, Hans-Georg, *Truth and Method* (London: Bloomsbury Academic, 2004)

Gergen, Kenneth J., *The Saturated Self. Dilemmas of Identity in Contemporary Life* (New York: Basic Books, 1991)

Gershoni, Jacob, *Psychodrama in the 21st Century: Clinical and Educational Applications* (New York: Springer, 2003)

Gilroy, Andrea, *Art Therapy: Research and Evidence-based Practice* (London: Sage Publications, 2006)

Grabowicz, George G., 'Translator's Introduction' [in:] Ingarden, *The Literary Work of Art*, pp. xlv-lxx

Green, Roger Lancelyn, and Walter Hooper, *C. S. Lewis: A Biography* (London: Collins, 1974)

Greene, William Chase, *Moira: Fate, Good, and Evil in Greek Thought* (London: Harper Torchbooks, 1963)

Gritten, Anthony, 'Literary Music: Writing Music in Contemporary Fiction' [in:] *Journal of Aesthetics and Art Criticism*, Vol. 66, 2008

Hadfield, Alice Mary, *Charles Williams: An Exploration of His Life and Work* (Oxford: Oxford University Press, 1983)

Heidegger, Martin, *Sein und Zeit* [Being and Time], (1927), trans. Joan Stambaugh (Albany: State University of New York Press, 1996)

Heffernan, James A. W., *Cultivating Picturacy: Visual Art and Verbal Interventions* (Waco, TX: Baylor University Press, 2006)

– *Museum of Words: The Poetics of Ekphrasis from Homer to* Ashbery (Chicago and London: University of Chicago Press, 1993)

Henderson, Kerryl Lynne, '"It is Love that I am Seeking"': Charles Williams and *The Silver Stair*' [in:] *Charles Williams: A Celebration*, Brian Horne, ed. (London: Gracewing, 1995), pp. 131–152

Hillegas, Mark, ed. *Shadows of the Imagination: The Fantasies of C. S. Lewis, J. R. R. Tolkien, and Charles Williams* (Carbondale: Southern Illinois University Press, 1969)

Howard, Thomas, 'What About Charles Williams?' [in:] *Touchstone*, Vol. 17, issue 10 (Chicago, 2004), pp. 30–36

Huxley, Aldous, 'Foreword to the *Brave New World*' (London: Grafton Books, 1988)

Ingarden, Roman, *The Literary Work of Art*, trans. George G. Grabowicz (Evanston: Northwestern University Press, 1973)

Jacobs, Alan, *The Narnian: The Life and Imagination of C. S. Lewis* (London: HarperCollins, 2005)

Jameson, Frederic, *Postmodernism, or The Cultural Logic of Late Capitalism* (New York: Verso, 1991)

Janet, Pierre, *Psychological Healing*, 2 vols., trans. Eden and Cedar Paul (London: Allen & Unwin, 1925)

John Paul II, *The Theology of the Body* (Boston, MA: Pauline Books and Media, 1997)

John Paul II, *Memory and Identity: Conversations at the Dawn of a Millennium* (New York: Rizzoli, 2005)

Joyce, James, *A Portrait of the Artist as a Young Man* (London: Penguin Books, 1996)

Jung, Carl, *Memories, Dreams, Reflections*; trans. by Aniela Jaffé (New York: Random House, 1965)

Kirk, Russell, *Decadence and Renewal in the Higher Learning: An Episodic History of American University and College since 1953* (Washington: Gateway, 1978)

Kivy, Peter, *The Performance of Reading: An Essay in the Philosophy of Literature* (Malden, MA: Blackwell, 2006)

Kilby, Clyde S., 'Meaning in *The Lord of the Rings*' [in:] *Shadows of Imagination, The Fantasies of C. S. Lewis, J. R. R. Tolkien and Charles Williams*, Mark Hillegas, ed. (Carbondale: Southern Illinois University Press, 1979), pp. 70–96

Knight, Gareth, *The Magical World of the Inklings* (Cheltenham: Skylight Press, 1990, 2nd ed., 2010)

Langford, David, 'Digging Up the Future: On G. K. Chesterton' [in:] *Up Through an Empty House of Stairs. Reviews and Essays 1980–2002* (Rockville: Wildside Press, 2003)

Lear, Jonathan, 'Katharsis' [in:] *Essays on Aristotle's Poetics*, Amélie Oksenberg Rorty, ed. (Princeton: Princeton University Press, 1992), pp. 315–341

Leedy, Jack J., ed. *Poetry the Healer: Mending the Troubled Mind* (New York: Vanguard, 1985)

Leuner, Hanscarl, 'Guided Affected Imagery': Abbreviation of a lecture given at the New Jersey Neuropsychiatric Institute, Princeton, N. J., May 16, 1966. Reprinted from *American Journal of Psychotherapy*, vol. XXIII, No. 1, pp. 4–22, January 1969

Litchfield West, Martin, *Ancient Greek Music* (Oxford: Oxford University Press, 1992)

Lindop, Grevel, *Charles Williams: The Third Inkling* (Oxford: Oxford University Press, 2015)

Lippman, Edward A., *Musical Thought in Ancient Greece* (New York: Columbia University Press, 1964)

Lyotard, Jean-François, 'Notes on the Return and Kapital', trans. Roger McKeon, [in:] *Semiotexte* 3.1. (1978), pp. 44–53

MacDonald, George, *The Gifts of the Child Christ and Other Stories and Fairy Tales,* Glenn Edward Sadler, ed. (Grand Rapids: Wm. B. Eerdmans Publishing Company, 1996)

Mascall, E. L., 'Charles Williams as I Knew Him' [in:] *Charles Williams: A Celebration*, Brian Horne, ed. (London: Gracewing, 1995)

MacIntyre, Alasdair, *After Virtue: A Study in Moral Theory* (London: Duckworth, 1981)

Macksey, Richard, 'Review of James Heffernan's Museum of Words' [in:] *Comparative Literature Issue*, vol. 10, no. 4, pp. 1010–1015

Mangham, Iain L., and M. A. Overington, *Dramatism and the theatrical metaphor. Life as theater: A dramaturgical sourcebook* (2nd ed.), (New Brunswick, NJ: Transaction Publishers, 2005)

Marinoff, Lou, *Plato, Not Prozac!: Applying Eternal Wisdom to Everyday Problems* (New York: HarperCollins, 1999)

McGee, Alexandra, *To Live or To Love: The Hero's Goal in the Science Fiction of Ursula K. Le Guin and C. S. Lewis* (Amazon Digital Services, 2012), kindle edition

McGee, Rosemary S., *Poetic Justice – Writing for Health and Emotional Freedom: Creating a Therapeutic Writing Programme for Chronically Ailing Poor* (Ann Arbor: ProQuest LLC, 2009)

McLeod, John, *Narrative and Psychotherapy* (London: Sage Publications, 2006)

Milbank, Alison, *Chesterton and Tolkien as Theologians. The Fantasy of the Real* (Bloomsbury T&T Clark, 2009)

Mitchell, W. J. T., *Iconology: Image, Text, Ideology* (Chicago: University of Chicago Press, 1987)

Moorcock, Michael, 'Epic Pooh' [in:] *J. R. R. Tolkien's The Lord of the Rings*, Harold Bloom, ed., pp. 3–18

Moorman, Charles, *Arthurian Triptych: Mythic Materials in Charles Williams, C. S. Lewis and T. S. Eliot* (Berkeley: University of California Press, 1960)

– 'Now Entertain a Conjecture of a Time: The Fictive Worlds of C. S. Lewis and J. R. R. Tolkien' [in:] *Shadows of Imagination*, pp. 41–69

Mortimer, Patchen, 'Tolkien and Modernism' [in:] *Tolkien Studies 2005: An Annual Scholarly Review*, Douglas A. Anderson, Michael D. C. Drout, Verlyn Flieger, eds., vol. 2, (Morgantown: West Virginia University Press, 2005), pp. 113–129

Mosley, Nicholas, *Natalie Natalia* (London: Delkey Archive Press, 1996)

Müller, Max, *The Science of Language* (London: Kessinger Publishing, 2003, 6th edition)

Nemerov, Howard, 'Foreword' to Owen Barfield's *Poetic Diction* (Middletown: Wesleyan University Press, 1978)

Newman, Barbara, 'Eliot's Affirmative Way: Julian of Norwich, Charles Williams, and Little Gidding' [in:] *Modern Philology*, Vol. 108, No. 3 (February 2011), (Chicago: University of Chicago Press), pp. 427–446

Nichols, Michael, and Melvin Zax, *Catharsis in Psychotherapy* (New York: Gardner Press, 1977)

Nicolson, Marjorie Hope, *Voyages to the Moon* (London: Macmillan, 1948, 1st ed.)

Nietzsche, Friedrich, *Will to Power*, trans. Walter Kaufmann and R. J. Hollingdale; W. Kaufmann, ed. (New York: Vintage, 1968)

– *Human. All-Too-Human: A Book for Free Spirits*, trans. Helen Zimmern (New York: Prometheus Books, 2009)

Nishitani, Keiji, *The Self-Overcoming of Nihilism*, trans. Graham Parkes with Setsuko Aihara (Albany: State University of New York Press, 1990)

O'Donoghue, Heather, *From Asgard to Valhalla: the Remarkable History of the North Myths* (London: I. B. Tauris, 2008)

Orange, Donna M., *The Suffering Stranger: Hermeneutics for Everyday Clinical Practice* (London: Routledge, 2011)

Pavlac Glyer, Diana. *The Company They Keep: C. S. Lewis and J. R. R. Tolkien as Writers in Community* (Kent: Kent State University Press, 2007)

Plimmer, Charlotte and Denis Plimmer, 'The Man Who Understands Hobbits', an interview with J. R. R. Tolkien, [in:] *Daily Telegraph Magazine*, 22 March 1968, pp. 31–35

Polkinghorne, Donald E., 'Narrative Knowing and the Self-Concept' [in:] *Journal of Narrative and Life History*, 1, 1991, pp. 135–153

Pound, Ezra, *Poetry and Prose*, 11 vols, (London: Garland, 1991)

– *The Selected Letters of Ezra Pound, 1907–1941*, D. D. Paige, ed. (New York: New Directions, 1950, 1971)

Pseudo-Longinus, 'Perihupsos' ['On the Sublime'], trans. W. Rhys Roberts (Cambridge: Cambridge University Press, 2011)

Rateliff, John D. *The History of the Hobbit* (New York: Houghton Mifflin Harcourt, 2007)

Ready, William Bernard, *Understanding Tolkien and The Lord Of The Rings* (London: Warner Paperback Library, 1973)

Reilly, Robert James, *Romantic Religion: A Study of Barfield, Lewis, Williams and Tolkien* (Athens, GA: University of Georgia Press, 1972, 2006).

Renard, Jules, *The Handy Buddhism Book* (Mumbai: Jaico Publishing House, 2005)

Ricks, Christopher, *T. S. Eliot and Prejudice* (London: Faber and Faber, 1994)

Ricoeur, Paul, *Time and Narrative* (*Temps et Récit*), trans. Kathleen McLaughlin and David Pellauer, (Chicago: University of Chicago Press, 1985)

de Rivera, Joseph, 'The Structure and Dynamics of Emotion' [in:] *Approaches to Understanding Lives. Perspectives in Personality,* Vol. 3. Part A. A. J. Stewart, J. M. Healy, Jr., and D. Ozer, eds. (London: Jessica Kinsley, 1990), pp. 191–212

Sacks, Oliver, *The Man who Mistook his Wife for a Hat* (London: Duckworth, 1985)

Sandner, David, 'Joy Beyond the Walls of the World': The Secondary World-Making of J. R. R. Tolkien and C. S. Lewis', [in:] *J. R. R. Tolkien and His Literary Resonances: Views of Middle-earth,* George Clark, Daniel Timmons, eds. (Westport, CT: Greenwood Press), pp. 133–145

– *Fantastic Literature: A Critical Reader* (Westport, Connecticut: Praeger 2004)

Sarbin, Theodore, ed. *Narrative Psychology: The Storied Nature of Human Conduct* (Santa Barbara: Praeger Publishers, 1986)

Sartre, Jean-Paul, *Nausea,* trans. Robert Baldick (London: Penguin Books, 1965)

Schakel, Peter J., 'Irrigating Deserts with Moral Imagination' [in:] *Inklings of Glory,* volume 11 of *Christian Reflection: A Series in Faith and Ethics* (Waco: The Center for Christian Ethics at Baylor University, 2004)

Segal, Robert, *Myth: A Very Short Introduction* (Oxford: Oxford University Press, 2004)

Shakespeare, William, *The Tempest* (London: Penguin Books, 2001)

Sherman, 'Cordelia, 'The Princess and the Wizard: The Fantasy Worlds of Ursula K. Le Guin and George MacDonald' [in:] *Children's Literature Association Quarterly,* Volume 12, Number 1, Spring 1987; pp. 24–28

Shippey, Tom, *J. R. R. Tolkien. Author of the Century* (London: HarperCollins Publishers 2000)

– *The Road to Middle-earth* (London: Mariner Books, 2003)

Snaevarr, Stefán, 'Don Quixote and the Narrative Self' [in:] *Philosophy Now*, Rick Lewis, ed., issue no. 60, 2007, pp. 19–27

Somov, Pavel G., *Recovery Equation: Logotherapy, Psychodrama and Choice Awareness Training for Substance Use/Addictions Treatment* (Eau Claire, WI: PESI Publishing and Media, 2008)

Sprague de Camp, Lyon, *Literary Swordsmen and Sorcerers: The Makers of Heroic Fantasy* (Sauk City: Arkham House, 1976)

Spruyt, Bart Jan, 'One of the enemy: C. S. Lewis on the very great evil of T. S. Eliot's work' [in:] *De Edmund Burke Stichting* (The Hague, 2004)

Stableford, Brian, *The A to Z Fantasy Literature*, *The A to Z Guide Series, No. 46* (Plymouth, UK: The Scarecrow Press, 2009)

Stade, George, and Karen Karbiener, eds., *The Encyclopaedia of British Writers* (London: Infobase, 2009)

Storr, Anthony, *Music and the Mind* (New York: Ballantine Books, 1992)

Swamikannu, Stanislaus, '*Fides et Ratio* and Metaphysics' [in:] *Faith and Reason Today: Fides Et Ratio in a Post-modern Era*, Varghese Manimala, ed. (Washington: Council for Research in Values & Philosophy 2008), pp. 51–63

Szczeklik, Andrzej, *Katharsis. O uzdrowicielskiej mocy natury i sztuki*, [Catharsis: On the Healing Power of Nature and Art], (Kraków: Wydawnictwo Znak, 2003)

Tatarkiewicz, W., J. Harrell, Cyril Barrett, and D. Petsch, eds., *The History of Aesthetics: Aesthetics of Music*, vol. 3, (London: Thoemmes, 2006)

Taylor, Charles, *Sources of the Self: The Making of Modern Identity* (Cambridge, Mass.: Harvard University Press, 1989)

Tennyson, Georg Bernhard, 'Owen Barfield:· First and Last Inkling' [in:] *The World and I, Owen Barfield*, April 1990, pp. 540–555

Terrell, C. Jeffrey, and William Lyddon, 'Narrative and Psychotherapy' [in:] *Journal of Constructivist Psychology*, Vol. 9, Issue 1, (London: Routledge, 1996)

Timmerman, John, *Other Worlds: The Fantasy Genre* (Ohio: Bowling Green State University Press, 1983)

Todorov, Tzvetan, *The Fantastic: A Structural Approach to a Genre* (Ithaca, New York: Cornell University Press, 1970, 1975), trans. by Richard Howard

Ulanov, Ann, and Barry Ulanov, *Healing Imagination* (London: Daimon Verlag, 1999)

Urang, Gunnar, 'Tolkien's Fantasy - The Phenomenology of Hope' [in:] *Shadows of Imagination: The Fantasies of C. S. Lewis, J. R. R. Tolkien and Charles Williams*, Mark R. Hillegas, ed. (Carbondale: Southern Illinois University Press, 1979)

Vattimo, Gianni, 'Hermeneutics and Democracy' [in:] *Philosophy and Social Criticism* 23.4 (1997), pp. 1–7

– *The End of Modernity: Nihilism and Hermeneutics in Post-Modern Culture*, trans. John R. Snyder, (Baltimore: John Hopkins University Press, 1988)

Vygotsky, Lev, *The Psychology of Art* (Cambridge, MA: The MIT Press, 1974)

Wagner, Peter, ed. *Icons – Texts – Iconotexts: Essays on Ekphrasis and Intermediary* (New York: de Gruyter, 1996)

Wain, John, *Sprightly Running: Part of an Autobiography* (New York: St. Martin's, 1962)

Warner, Marina, *Signs and Wonders: Essays on Literature and Culture* (London: Vintage, 2004)

White, William Luther, *The Image of Man in C. S. Lewis* (Eugene, OR: Wipf and Stock, 1969, 2008)

Wicher, Andrzej, *Selected Medieval and Religious Themes in the Works of C. S. Lewis and J. R. R. Tolkien* (Łódź: Łódzkie Towarzystwo Naukowe, 2013)

Williams, William Carlos, *Autobiography* (New York: New Directions, 1967)

Wilkins, William Joseph, *Hindu Mythology. Vedic and Puranic* (Whitefish, MT: Kessinger Publishing, 2010)

Wilson, Andrew Norman, *C. S. Lewis: A Biography*, (London: Collins, 1990)

Woolf, Virginia, *A Change of Perspective: Letters of Virginia Woolf*, III, 1923–1928, Nigel Nicolson, ed. (London: The Hogarth Press, 1977, 1994)

Wood, Tanya Caroline, 'Is Tolkien a Renaissance Man? Sir Philip Sidney's *Defense of Poesy* and J. R. R. Tolkien's 'On Fairy-Stories' [in:] *J. R. R. Tolkien and His Literary Resonances: View of Middle-earth*, George Clark, and Daniel Timmons, eds. (Portsmouth, NH: Greenwood Publishing Group, 2000), pp. 95–108

Woodward, Ashley, *Nihilism in Postmodernity: Lyotard, Baudrillard, Vattimo*, (Denver: The Davies Group Publishers, 2009)

Yalom, Irvin, *Love's Executioner and Other Tales of Psychotherapy* (London: Penguin Books, 1989)

Zaleski Phlilip and Carol Zaleski, *The Fellowship: The Literary Lives of the Inklings: J. R. R. Tolkien, C. S. Lewis, Owen Barfield, Charles Williams* (New York: Farrar, Straus and Giroux, 2015)

Zhmud, Leonid, *Pythagoras and the Early Pythagoreans*, trans. Kevin Windle and Rosh Ireland, (Oxford: Oxford University Press, 2012)

Reference books

Alexander, Michael, *The History of English Literature* (London: Palgrave Macmillan, 2000, 2013, 3rd edn.)

Blamires, Harry, *A Short History of English Literature* (Oxford: Oxford University Press, 1984, 2nd edn.)

The Cambridge Companion to American Novelists, Timothy Parrish, ed. (Cambridge: Cambridge University Press, 2013)

A Dictionary of Psychotherapy, Sue Walrond-Skinner, ed. (London: Routledge, 2014)

Encyclopaedia Britannica, http://www.britannica.com/, accessed 2 May 2016

The Encyclopedia of Fantasy, John Clute and John Grant, eds. (London: Orbit, 1997)

Greek Philosophical Terms: A Historical Lexicon, Francis E. Peters, ed. (New York: New York University Press, 1967)

An Intermediate Greek–English Lexicon, Henry George Liddell and Robert Scott, eds. (Oxford: Clarendon Press, 1889)

The Johns Hopkins Guide to Literary Theory and Criticism, Michael Groden, Martin Kreiswirth, eds. (Johns Hopkins University Press, 2004), 2nd edn.

Lewis, Charlton T., and Charles Short, *A Latin Dictionary* (Oxford: Clarendon Press, 1879; 1958)

The Light Verse: Qur'ānic Text and Sūfī Interpretation, trans. Gerhard Böwering, *Oriens*, vol. 36 (2001)

The New Oxford Dictionary of English, Judy Pearsall, ed. (Oxford: Oxford University Press, 1998)

Norton Anthology of American Literature, vol. E: American Literature since 1945, Nina Baym, Robert S. Levine, gen. eds. (New York: W. W. Norton and Company, 2011), 8th edn.

The Oxford Anthology of English Literature, Frank Kermode, John Hollander, gen. eds. (New York: Oxford University Press)

Oxford Dictionary of Literary Terms, Chris Baldick, ed. (Oxford: Oxford University Press, 2008)

Peck John and Martin Coyle, *A Brief History of English Literature* (London: Palgrave Macmillan, 2002, 2013)

Sanders Andrew, *The Short Oxford History of English Literature* (Oxford: Oxford University Press, 2004)

Web sites

Augustine, St., of Hippo, *Confessions*, trans. Edward Bouverie Pusey, http://www.sacred-texts.com/chr/augconf.htm, accessed 20 July 2016

Beyst, Stefan, 'W. J. T. Mitchell and the Image: The Discovery of the Imagetext,' a review of Mitchell's *Iconology: Image, Text, Ideology*, and of his *Picture Theory: Essays on Verbal and Visual Representation*, http://d-sites.net/english/mitchell.htm, July 2010; accessed 2 June 2016

Blaxland-de Lange, Simon, 'Obituary for Owen Barfield,' accessed 23 April 2016, http://davidlavery.net/barfield/barfield_resources/death.html

– 'Owen Barfield Funeral Address,' December 18, 1997, http://davidlavery.net/barfield/barfield_resources/death.html, accessed 23 April 2016

Boethius, *De Institutione Musica*, http://cmed.faculty.ku.edu/private/boethius.html, accessed 20 July 2016

Charlton, Bruce, 'Tolkien's The Notion Club Papers,' http://notionclubpapers.blogspot.com/2012/12/was-tolkien-jealous-of-charles-williams.html, accessed 20 July 2016

Docx, Edward, 'Postmodernism is dead,' *Prospect Magazine*, July 20, 2011; http://www.prospectmagazine.co.uk/magazine/postmodernism-is-dead-va-exhibition-age-of-authenticism, accessed 15 May 2014

Fisher, H. Dennis, 'C. S. Lewis, Platonism and Aslan's Country: Symbols of Heaven in *The Chronicles of Narnia*' [in:] *Inklings Forever, vol. VII, A Collection of Essays Presented at the Seventh Frances White Ewbank Colloquium on C. S. Lewis and Friends*, Taylor University, 2010, Upland, Indiana, https://library.taylor.edu/dotAsset/bc583632-9dc1-47fe-9edf-6f42bf8d64ee.pdf, accessed 20 July 2016

Harnsberger, Jessica, 'Shadows and Darkness: Learning to Triumph over Human Weakness,' 2004, Brown University, http://www.victorianweb.org/authors/gm/harnsberger14.html, accessed 20 July 2016

'Images by J. R. R. Tolkien' at Tolkien Gateway, http://tolkiengateway.net/wiki/Category:Images _by_ J. R. R._Tolkien, accessed 20 July 2016

John Paul II, *Fides et Ratio Encyclical Letter*, 1998, http://www.vatican.va/holy_father/john_paul_ii/encyclicals/documents/hf_jp-ii_enc_15101998_fides-et-ratio_en.html, accessed 23 April 2016

Jones, Jonathan, 'Defining Moral Imagination' [in:] *First Things: Journal of Religion and Public Life*; July 1, 2009, http://www.firstthings.com/blogs/firstthoughts/2009/07/defining-moral-imagination), accessed 10 May 2016

Keep, Christopher, Tim McLaughlin, Robin Parmar, 'Postmodernity and the Postmodern novel', http://www2.iath.virginia.edu/elab/hfl0256.html, accessed 23 April 2016

Le Guin, Ursula K., 'Maxine Cushing Gray Award Acceptance Speech', 18 October 2006, Washington State Book Awards, Seattle; http://www.ursulakleguin.com/MCGrayFellowship-Speech.html, accessed 1 May 2016

Le Guin, Ursula K., 'Le Guin's Hypothesis', June 18, 2012, http://bookviewcafe.com/blog/2012/06/18/le-guin-s-hypothesis/; accessed 23 April 2016

Le Guin, Ursula K., '65th National Book Awards speech', 20 November 2014, accessed 23 April 2016, https://www.theguardian.com/books/2014/nov/20/ursula-k-le-guin-national-book-awards-speech

Lindskoog, Katryn, 'Lewis's Correspondence on Psychotherapy, Psychoanalysis, Sermons and Humility' [in:] The Lewis Legacy, issue 71, winter 1997, http://www.discovery.org/a/995, accessed 10 May 2016

'The Magician', an interview with Ursula K. Le Guin conducted by Maya Jaggi, http://www.theguardian.com/books/2005/dec/17/booksforchildrenandteenagers.shopping, accessed 2 May 2016

Mitchell, W. J. T., 'Iconoscape: Method, Madness, and Montage', a part of a work in progress, delivered at the Institute of Fine Arts, New York, and accessed on 22 July 2016 at https://vimeo.com/161061426

Nolan, Simon F., 'The Philosopher Pope: Pope John Paul II and the Human Person', pp. 1–13; www.carmelites.ie/PDF/PhilosopherPope.pdf, accessed March 2, 2014

The Online Etymology Dictionary, Douglas Harper, ed. 2013. http://www. etymonline.com/

Reynolds, John Mark N., 'Narnia, Plato, and C. S. Lewis on the Hope of Heaven', March 28, 2013, http://www.patheos.com/blogs/philosophicalfragments/2013/03/28/narnia-plato-and-c-s-lewis-on-the-hope-of-heaven/, accessed 20 July 2016

Rozema, David, 'Lewis's Rejection of Nihilism: The Tao and the Problem of Moral Knowledge' [in:] In Pursuit of Truth. A Journal of Christian Scholarship, September 2007, http://www.cslewis.org/journal/lewiss-rejection-of-nihilism-the-tao-and-the-problem-of-moral-knowledge/, accessed 2 May 2016

Sachs, Joe, 'Aristotle – Poetics' [in:] The Internet Encyclopaedia of Philosophy, http://www.iep.utm. edu/aris-poe/, accessed 20 May 2016

'The 100 Best Spiritual Books of the Century: A List', accessed 20 May 2016, http://www.faith. com/library/articlesfaith/articles/f_lib_books_home_bestlist.html

Marion E. Wade Center of Wheaton College, Illinois, the US, http://www.whea-ton.edu/wadecenter, accessed 23 April 2016

http://www.suicide.org/suicide-statistics.html, accessed 23 April 2016

http://www.who.int/mental_health/prevention/suicide/suicideprevent/en/, accessed 23 April 2016